The Fiber of Democracy:

Readings in American Government and Politics

The Fiber of

Readings in

EDITED BY

CANFIELD PRESS
A Department of Harper & Row, Publishers, Inc.

emocracy

American Government and Politics

William E. Brigman

John S. Vanderoef

The Florida State University

San Francisco

Contents

Preface   ix

1   The Context of American Politics   1

*Fundamental Principles of Democracy: Bases of Agreement
and Disagreement*   2
JAMES W. PROTHRO, CHARLES M. GRIGG

Democratic Practice and Democratic Theory   14
BERNARD BERELSON

How American Politics Really Works   24
R. JOSEPH MONSEN, JR., MARK W. CANNON

How American Democracy Really Works: A Radical View   33
ARNOLD S. KAUFMAN

What's Bugging the Students   41
IRVING KRISTOL

2   The Making of the Constitution   47

The Founding Fathers: A Reform Caucus in Action   49
JOHN P. ROCHE

Madison's Essentials of a "New System"   71
JOHN S. VANDEROEF

The Nature of Our Federal Union Reconsidered   77
ALPHEUS T. MASON

3   Federalism   89

The States and the Nation   90
DANIEL J. ELAZAR

Creative Tensions   116
TERRY SANFORD

The Relationship of Federal to Local Authorities   122
DANIEL P. MOYNIHAN

4   Political Parties and the Electoral System   129

The Quest for Party Government   130
FRANK J. SORAUF

Candidate Selection   143
LEON D. EPSTEIN

The End of the Two-Party System   153
HARVEY WHEELER

5   Interest Groups   160

The Quiet Victory of the Cigarette Lobby   162
ELIZABETH BRENNER DREW

Lobbying as a Means of Protest: The NAACP as an Agent of Equality   170
GILBERT WARE

Why the Poor People's Campaign Failed   178
TOM KAHN

6   The Congress   189

Theories of Congress   190
ROGER H. DAVIDSON, DAVID M. KOVENOCK, MICHAEL K. O'LEARY

*The Folkways of the United States Senate: Conformity
to Group Norms and Legislative Effectiveness*   209
DONALD R. MATTHEWS

Inside Capitol Hill: How the House Really Works   233
LARRY L. KING

7   The Presidency   247

What Is the President's True Role?   248
SIDNEY HYMAN

Presidents of Action and Presidents of Restraint   254
ERWIN C. HARGROVE

The Three Models Reconsidered   265
JAMES MACGREGOR BURNS

The Limits and Excesses of Presidential Power   271
ARTHUR SCHLESINGER, JR.

Presidential Power   280
RICHARD E. NEUSTADT

How the President Makes a Decision   290
THEODORE C. SORENSEN

8   The Bureaucracy   301

The Bureaucracy Problem   302
JAMES Q. WILSON

J. Edgar Hoover: The Compleat Bureaucrat   308
JOSEPH KRAFT

The Bureaucracy in Pressure Politics   313
J. LEIPER FREEMAN

9   The Courts   324

*Decision-Making in a Democracy: The Supreme Court
as a National Policy-Maker*   327
ROBERT A. DAHL

5 to 4: Are the Justices Really Objective?   341
PAUL FREUND

Civil Disobedience: The Law Is Never Blind   *343*
JOSEPH L. SAX

U.S. v. O'Brien   *350*

Miranda v. Arizona   *354*

Engel et al. v. Vitale et al.   *358*

Prayer and Politics: The Impact of Engel *and* Schempp
on the Political Process   *363*
WILLIAM M. BEANEY, EDWARD N. BEISER

10   The New Politics   387

Dissent and Democracy   *389*
OSCAR HANDLIN

From Civil Rights to Black Liberation: The Unsettled 1960s   *396*
ROBERT L. ZANGRANDO

Dissent Is Not Enough   *405*
JOHN COGLEY

The Resisters Support U.S. Traditions and Interests   *407*
PAUL GOODMAN

*A Right Way to Remedy a Wrong, a Wrong Way to Secure
a Right*   *409*
SIDNEY HOOK

The Political Response Must Be Weighed   *411*
BAYARD RUSTIN

The Old Politics, the New Politics, the New, *New Politics*   *412*
IRVING KRISTOL

Notes   424

Preface

Most American government textbooks, however they may differ in approach and organization, present a relatively common core of subject matter. The purpose of the collection of readings offered here is to expand and supplement that core.

In selecting the material for this volume, we looked for readings that would both stimulate student interest and, at the same time, contribute to a deeper understanding of the workings of the American political system. The readings we chose were drawn primarily from two sources: from the work of recognized scholars whose research has added to the store of knowledge about the American political process and from the writings of men who have been active in that process. We feel that both a scholar applying research skills to a study of the Presidency and a close presidential adviser who knows the president's problems can throw light on the nature of executive decision-making. The analysis of an expert on the political party system and the observations of an experienced and astute campaign worker can both be used to sharpen the student's awareness of the political process. A political scientist's exploration of the complexities of federalism can have much greater meaning when supplemented by a former Governor's account of his own grapplings with federal-state relationships.

Thus we have drawn upon diverse types of literature in order to expose the reader to the subject matter from many different angles. A collection of readings is, of necessity, selective, but this one, we believe, will at least be representative of the various approaches to the most significant areas to be explored in a study of American government and politics.

We have tried to incorporate theory and practice, description and analysis. We hope that the selections we have chosen will not only inform but also provide the student with a basis for evaluating America's political institutions and processes in this time of change and challenge.

W.E.B.

J.S.V.

The Context of
American Politics

Political decisions are not made in a vacuum, separate and distinct from the world outside. The political system and the society are constantly interacting, and the nature of the society becomes a major factor in shaping political events.

James W. Prothro and Charles M. Grigg examine empirically the "Fundamental Principles of Democracy" to determine the degree of consensus regarding basic democratic ideas held by Americans and conclude that Carl J. Friedrich was probably correct when he asserted that democracy depends on habitual patterns of behavior rather than on conscious agreement on democratic "principles."

Bernard R. Berelson *et al.* suggest in "Democratic Practice and Democratic Theory" that the classical concept of democracy errs in overstressing the importance of the virtue and devotion of the individual citizen to the success of a democracy. By their view:

> . . . Liberal democracy is more than a political system in which individual voters and political institutions operate. For political democracy to survive, other features are required: The intensity of conflict must be limited, the rate of change must be restrained, stability in the social and economic structure must be maintained, a pluralistic social organization must exist, and a basic consensus must bind together the contending parties.

How well does the system work? Three different answers are offered in the readings. R. Joseph Monsen, Jr., and Mark W. Cannon in "How American

Democracy Really Works" give a favorable evaluation. They believe the American system of majority rule and minority rights is adequately safeguarded by the multiplicity of factions and their willingness to compromise.

Arnold S. Kaufman's "A Radical View," on the other hand, represents a growing disenchantment with current American society. To Kaufman the United States is a predominantly racist society, affluent but economically unequal and without a sense of social justice.

Students in colleges and universities, and to some extent those in the high schools as well, have been the source of many of the attempts to alter American society. Irving Kristol, in "What's Bugging the Students," suggests that "Anyone who thinks of present-day campus radicalism as a kind of over-zealous political liberalism, whose extremism derives from nothing more than youthful high spirits, is deceiving himself." The students have a profound hostility toward everything that is impersonal, manipulative, and "organized" in the American political process, he says, and continues:

> Indeed, many of these students simply dismiss American democracy as a sham, a game played by the "power structure" for its own amusement and in its own interests. *True* democracy, they insist, can only mean direct democracy, where the people's will is expressed and legislated by the people themselves rather than by elected representatives, most of whom achieve office by deceit and retain office through the substantial support offered them by the vested interests.

Does the "student revolt" portend a dramatic change in American society or is it merely, as Kristol believes, a result of boredom and a desire for "self-identity"? The students will have to answer this question themselves—the editors are both over 30!

Fundamental Principles of Democracy: Bases of Agreement and Disagreement

JAMES W. PROTHRO, CHARLES M. GRIGG

The discovery that consensus on democratic principles is restricted to a few general and vague formulations might come as a surprise to a person whose only acquaintance with democracy was through the literature of political theory;

Reprinted by permission of the authors and the publisher from James W. Prothro and Charles M. Grigg, "Fundamental Principles of Democracy: Bases of Agreement and Disagreement," *The Journal of Politics*, Vol. 22 (May 1960), pp. 281–294.

it will hardly surprise those who have lived in a democracy. Every village cynic knows that the local churchgoer who sings the creed with greatest fervor often abandons the same ideas when they are put in less lyrical form. Political scientists are certainly not so naive as to expect much greater consistency in the secular sphere. The theorists who argue the necessity of consensus on such matters as the existence or absence of multifaceted truth, true equality in the right of free speech, and dedication to an equal vote for every citizen are no doubt as aware of these human frailties as the village cynic.[1] But we tend to regard that which seems a *logically necessary* belief in the light of democratic processes as being *empirically necessary* to the existence of those processes. We assume, in a two-step translation, that what people *should* (logically) believe is what they *must* believe (this being a democracy), and that what they *must* believe is what they *do* believe.

In undertaking to discover what kind of consensus actually exists, we assumed that we would find the anticipated agreement on the basic principles of democracy when they were put in a highly abstract form, but that consensus would not be found on more concrete questions involving the application of these principles. We further assumed that regional and class-related variations would be found on the specific formulation of democratic principles. In pinning down these assumptions, we are no doubt demonstrating the obvious—but such a demonstration appears necessary if the obvious is to be incorporated into the logic of political theory. With empirical support for these two assumptions, we can put the proposition about consensus in more precise form and test the following hypothesis: *Consensus in a meaningful sense (at both the abstract and specific levels) exists among some segment(s) of the population (which can be called the "carriers of the creed").* Should our findings support this hypothesis, we could reformulate the proposition about democratic consensus with reference to a smaller group than the total population, whereupon it could be tested more fully, both in the United States and in other democracies, for further refinement.

Procedure

Our research design was based upon the major assumption that the United States is a democracy. Taking this point for granted, we prepared an interviewing schedule around the presumably basic principles of democracy and interviewed samples of voters in two American cities to elicit their attitudes toward these principles.

While the general research design was thus quite simple, the preparation of a questionnaire including the basic points on which agreement is thought to be necessary was a difficult and critical step. From the literature on consensus cited above and from general literature on democracy, however, we conclude that the principles regarded as most essential to democracy are majority rule and minority rights (or freedom to dissent). At the abstract level, then, our interviewers asked for expressions of agreement or disagreement on the following statements:

PRINCIPLE OF DEMOCRACY ITSELF
   Democracy is the best form of government.

PRINCIPLE OF MAJORITY RULE
   Public officials should be chosen by majority vote.
   Every citizen should have an equal chance to influence government policy.

PRINCIPLE OF MINORITY RIGHTS
   The minority should be free to criticize majority decisions.
   People in the minority should be free to try to win majority support for their opinions.

From these general statements, specific embodiments of the principles of democracy were derived.

PRINCIPLE OF MAJORITY RULE IN SPECIFIC TERMS
   1. In a city referendum, only people who are well informed about the problem being voted on should be allowed to vote.
   2. In a city referendum deciding on tax-supported undertakings, only taxpayers should be allowed to vote.
   3. If a Negro were legally elected mayor of this city, the white people should not allow him to take office.
   4. If a Communist were legally elected mayor of this city, the people should not allow him to take office.
   5. A professional organization like the AMA (the American Medical Association) has a right to try to increase the influence of doctors by getting them to vote as a bloc in elections.

PRINCIPLE OF MINORITY RIGHTS IN SPECIFIC TERMS
   6. If a person wanted to make a speech in this city against churches and religion, he should be allowed to speak.
   7. If a person wanted to make a speech in this city favoring government ownership of all the railroads and big industries, he should be allowed to speak.
   8. If an admitted Communist wanted to make a speech in this city favoring Communism, he should be allowed to speak.
   9. A Negro should not be allowed to run for mayor of this city.
   10. A Communist should not be allowed to run for mayor of this city.

   These specific propositions are designed to embody the principles of majority rule and minority rights in such a clear fashion that a "correct" or "democratic" response can be deducted from endorsement of the general principles. The democratic responses to statements 1 and 2 are negative, for example, since a restriction of the franchise to the well-informed or to taxpayers would violate the principle that "Every citizen should have an equal chance to influence government policy."[2] The same general principle requires an affirmative answer to the fifth statement, which applies the right of people to "influence government policy" to the election efforts of a specific professional group. The correct responses to statements 3 and 4 are negative because denial of an office to any person "legally elected" would violate the principle that "public officials should be chosen by majority vote."

Of the five statements derived from the broad principle of minority rights, 6, 7, and 8 put the right of "the minority . . . to criticize majority decisions" and "to try to win majority support for their opinions" in terms of specific minority spokesmen; agreement is therefore the correct or democratic answer. Disagreement is the correct response to statements 9 and 10, since denial of the right to seek office to members of minority ethnic or ideological groups directly violates their right "to try to win majority support for their opinions."

Since the proposition being tested asserts the existence of consensus, the interviewing sample could logically have been drawn from any group of Americans. Because we assume regional and class differences, however, we could not rely on the most available respondents, our own college students. The registered voters of two academic communities, Ann Arbor, Michigan, and Tallahassee, Florida, were selected as the sampling population, primarily because they fitted the needs of the hypothesis, and partly because of their accessibility. Although a nationwide survey was ruled out simply on the ground of costs, these atypical communities offer certain advantages for our problem. First, they do permit at least a limited regional comparison of attitudes on democratic fundamentals. Second, they skew the sample by overrepresenting the more highly educated, thus permitting detailed comparison of the highly educated with the poorly educated, a comparison that could hardly be made with samples from more typical communities.

The overrepresentation of the highly educated also served to "stack the cards" in favor of the proposition on consensus. Since our hypothesis holds that consensus is limited, we further stacked the cards against the hypothesis by choosing the sample from registered voters rather than from all residents of the two communities. Although the necessity of consensus is stated in terms of the society as a whole, a line of regression is available in the argument that it need exist only among those who take part in politics. Hence our restriction of the sample to a population of registered voters.

In each city the sample was drawn by the system of random numbers from the official lists of registered voters. The sample represents 1 percent of the registered voters from the current registration list in each of the two communities. In a few cases the addresses given were incorrect, but if the person selected could be located in the community, he was included in the sample. A few questions on a limited number of individuals were not recorded in usable form, which accounts for a slight variation in the totals in the tables presented in the paper.

Findings: The Consensus Problem

In the two communities from which our samples were drawn, consensus can be said to exist among the voters on the basic principles of democracy when they are put in abstract terms. The degree of agreement on these principles ranges from 94.7 to 98.0 percent, which appears to represent consensus in a truly meaningful sense and to support the first of our preliminary assumptions. On the generalized principles, then, we need not look for "bases of disagreement"—the agreement transcends community, educational, economic, age, sex, party, and other common bases of differences in opinion.[3] We may stop with the conclusion that opinions on these abstract principles have a cultural base.

When these broad principles are translated into more specific propositions, however, consensus breaks down completely. As Table 1-1 indicates, agreement does not reach 90 percent on any of the ten propositions, either from the two samples combined or from the communities considered separately. Indeed, respondents in both communities are closer to perfect discord than to perfect consensus on over half the statements. If we keep in mind that a 50-50 division represents a total absence of consensus, then degrees of agreement ranging from 25 to 75 percent can be understood as closer to the total absence of consensus (50 percent agreement) than to its perfect realization (100 percent agreement). Responses from voters in both communities fall in this "discord" range on six of the statements (1, 4, 5, 6, 8, and 10); voters in the southern community approach maximum discord on two additional statements (3 and 9), both of which put democratic principles in terms of Negro participation in public office. These findings strongly support the second of our preliminary assumptions, that consensus does not exist on more concrete questions involving the application of democratic principles.

Three of the statements that evoke more discord than consensus deal with the extension of democratic principles to Communists, a highly unpopular group in the United States. But it should be noted that these statements are put in terms of generally approved behaviors (speaking and seeking public office), not conspiratorial or other reprehensible activities. And the other statements on which discord exceeds consensus refer to groups (as well as activities) that are not in opposition to the American form of government: the right of all citizens to vote, the right of a professional group to maximize its voting strength, and the right to criticize churches and religion.

The extent to which consensus breaks down on the specific formulation of democratic principles is even greater than suggested by our discussion of the range of discord. To this point we have ignored the content of the opinions on these principles, which would permit an overwhelming *rejection* of a democratic principle to be accepted as consensus. Specifically, responses to statement 2 were not counted as falling in the "discord" category, but the approach

TABLE 1-1

Percentage of "Democratic" Responses to Basic Principles of Democracy Among Selected Population Groups

	TOTAL N=244	EDUCATION† High N=137	Low N=106	ANN ARBOR N=144	TALLA- HASSEE N=100	INCOME‡ High N=136	Low N=99
MAJORITY RULE							
1. Only informed vote*	49.0	61.7	34.7	56.3	38.4	56.6	40.8
2. Only taxpayers vote*	21.0	22.7	18.6	20.8	21.2	20.7	21.0
3. Bar Negro from office*	80.6	89.7	68.6	88.5	66.7	83.2	77.8
4. Bar Communist from office*	46.3	56.1	34.0	46.9	45.5	48.9	43.0
5. AMA right to bloc voting**	45.0	49.6	39.2	44.8	45.5	45.5	44.4
MINORITY RIGHTS							
6. Allow anti-religious speech**	63.0	77.4	46.5	67.4	56.6	72.8	52.1
7. Allow socialist speech**	79.4	90.2	65.7	81.3	76.8	83.8	73.7
8. Allow Communist speech**	44.0	62.9	23.5	51.4	33.3	52.2	36.7
9. Bar Negro from candidacy*	75.5	86.5	60.2	85.6	58.0	78.6	71.1
10. Bar Communist from candidacy*	41.7	48.1	30.3	44.1	38.2	44.8	34.4

*For these statements, disagreement is recorded as the "democratic" response.
**For these statements, agreement is recorded as the "democratic" response.
†"High education" means more than 12 years of schooling; "low education," 12 years or less.
‡"High income" means an annual family income of $6,000 or more; "low income," less than $6,000.

to consensus in this case lies in rejection of the democratic principle of the "majority vote" with an "equal chance" for "every citizen." But the proposition about consensus holds, of course, that the consensus is in favor of democratic principles. On four statements (2, 4, 5, and 10) a majority of the voters in Ann Arbor express "undemocratic" opinions; and on six statements (1, 2, 4, 5, 8, and 10) a majority of the voters in Tallahassee express "undemocratic" opinions.

However the reactions to our specific statements are approached, they run counter to the idea of extended consensus. On none of them is there the real consensus that we found on the abstract form of the principles; responses to over half of the statements are closer to perfect discord than perfect consensus; and the responses to about half of the statements express the "wrong" answers. Unlike the general statements, then, the specific propositions call for an appraisal of bases of agreement and disagreement.

Findings: Bases of Agreement and Disagreement

The report of findings on the consensus problem has already suggested that regional subcultures are one basis of differences in opinions on democratic principles. Table 1-1 also shows differences along educational and income lines. Not included are other possible bases of disagreement that were found to have only a negligible effect, e.g., age, sex, and party.

Community, education, and income all have an effect on opinions about democratic principles. More "correct" responses came from the midwestern than from the southern community, from those with high education than from those with less education, and from those with high income than from those with low income. The systematic nature of these differences supports the assumption that regional and class-related factors affect attitudes toward democratic principles when they are put in specific terms.

Which of these variables has the greatest effect on attitudes toward basic principles of democracy? Table 1-1 suggests that education is most important on two counts: (1) for every statement, the greatest difference in opinions is found in the high education–low education dichotomy; (2) for every statement, the grouping with the most "correct" or "democratic" responses is the high education category. Before education can be accepted as the independent variable in relation to democratic attitudes, however, the relationship must be examined for true independence. Since more Ann Arbor than Tallahassee respondents fall in the high education category, and since more high income than low income respondents have high education, the education variable might prove to be spurious—with the concealed community and income factors accounting for its apparent effect. Tables 1-2 and 1-3 show that when we control for community and income, differences between the high and low educa-

TABLE 1-2

Percentage of "Democratic" Responses to Basic Principles of Democracy by Education, with Income Controlled

STATEMENT	HIGH—LOW EDUCATION DIFFERENCES N=134 N=101	LOW INCOME			HIGH INCOME		
		High Education N=42	Low Education N=58	Difference	High Education N=92	Low Education N=43	Difference
1	27.0	67.5	22.4	45.1	59.1	51.2	7.9
2	4.1	20.0	22.0	-2.0	23.9	14.0	9.9
3	21.1	94.4	64.4	30.0	87.8	73.2	14.6
4	22.1	55.0	35.0	20.0	56.5	32.6	23.9
5	10.4	52.5	39.0	13.5	48.4	39.5	8.9
6	30.9	67.5	41.1	26.4	81.7	53.5	28.2
7	24.5	87.5	64.4	23.1	91.4	67.4	24.0
8	39.4	59.0	22.0	37.0	64.5	25.6	38.9
9	26.3	86.1	59.6	26.5	86.7	61.0	25.7
10	17.8	41.0	39.8	1.2	51.1	31.0	20.1

TABLE 1-3

Percentage of "Democratic" Responses to Basic Principles of Democracy by Education, with Community Controlled

STATEMENT	HIGH—LOW EDUCATION DIFFERENCES N=137 N=106	ANN ARBOR			TALLAHASSEE		
		High Education N=92	*Low Education* N=52	*Difference*	*High Education* N=45	*Low Education* N=54	*Difference*
1	27.0	63.7	42.3	21.4	57.1	26.5	30.6
2	4.1	24.2	15.4	8.8	19.5	22.0	-2.5
3	21.1	94.4	77.6	16.9	78.4	56.8	21.6
4	22.1	56.7	28.8	27.9	54.8	39.2	15.6
5	10.4	48.4	38.5	9.9	53.3	38.9	14.4
6	30.9	80.2	47.1	33.1	71.4	45.8	25.6
7	24.5	92.3	61.5	30.8	85.7	70.0	15.7
8	39.4	67.0	23.1	43.9	53.7	24.5	29.2
9	26.3	96.6	65.3	31.3	62.2	53.8	8.4
10	17.8	48.9	34.6	14.3	46.4	25.5	20.9

tion respondents remain. When we control for education, on the other hand, the smaller differences reported in Table 1-1 by community and income tend to disappear.[4]

Since educational differences hold up consistently when other factors are "partialled out," education may be accepted as the most consequential basis of opinions on basic democratic principles.[5] Regardless of their other group identifications, people with high education accept democratic principles more than any other grouping. While the highly educated thus come closest to qualifying as the carriers of the democratic creed, the data do not support our hypothesis; consensus in a meaningful sense (on both the abstract and the specific principles) is not found even among those with high education. On only three of the ten specific statements (3, 7, and 9) does agreement among those with high education reach 90 percent in Ann Arbor, and in Tallahassee it fails to reach 90 percent on any of the statements. On the proposition that the vote should be restricted to taxpayers in referenda deciding on tax-supported undertakings, 75.8 percent of the highly educated in Ann Arbor and 81.5 percent in Tallahassee reject the democratic principle of an equal vote for every citizen. And on five statements (1, 4, 5, 8, and 10) the highly educated in both communities are closer to perfect discord than to perfect harmony. Even when the necessity of consensus is reformulated in terms of the group most in accord with democratic principles, then, consensus cannot be said to exist.

Summary and Conclusions

The attitudes of voters in selected midwestern and southern communities offer no support for the hypothesis that democracy requires a large measure of consensus among the carriers of the creed, i.e., those most consistently in accord with democratic principles. As expected, general consensus was found on the idea of democracy itself and on the broad principles of majority rule and minority rights, but it disappeared when these principles were put in more specific form. Indeed, the voters in both communities were closer to complete discord than to complete consensus; they did not reach consensus on any of the ten specific statements incorporating the principles of majority rule and minority rights; and majorities expressed the "undemocratic" attitude on about half of the statements.

In trying to identify the carriers of the creed, the expected regional and class-related variations were found in attitudes toward democratic principles in specific form, with education having the most marked effect. While attitudes on democratic fundamentals were not found to vary appreciably according to age, sex, or party affiliation, they did vary according to education, community, and income. The greatest difference on every statement was between the high-education group and the low-education group, and the high-education group gave the most democratic response to every question, whether compared with other educational, community, or income groupings. Education, but not community or income, held up consistently as a basis of disagreement when other factors were controlled. We accordingly conclude that endorsement of democratic principles is not a function of class as such (of which income is also a criterion), but of greater acquaintance with the logical implications of the broad democratic principles. Note, for example, that the highly educated renounce in much greater degree than any other group the restriction of the vote to the well-informed, a restriction that would presumably affect them least of all.

Although high education was the primary basis of agreement on democratic principles, actual consensus was not found even among this segment of the voting population. The approach to consensus is closer among the highly educated in Ann Arbor, where greater agreement exists on the extension of democratic rights to Negroes, but in both communities the highly educated are closer to discord than consensus on half of the statements. On the basis of these findings, our hypothesis appears to be invalid.

Our failure to find a more extended consensus may, of course, be attributed to the possibility that the statements we formulated do not incorporate the particular "fundamentals" that are actually necessary to democracy.[6] When the approach to consensus is in the "undemocratic" direction—as in the question about restricting the vote to taxpayers—two possible objections to our interviewing schedule are suggested. First, perhaps the question is not a logical derivation from the basic principles with which we began. Second, perhaps the respondents are not interpreting the questions in any uniform way.

On the first point, the logical connection of the specific proposition with the general proposition is virtually self-evident. In syllogistic terms, we have: major premise—every citizen should have an equal chance to influence government policy; minor premise—non-taxpayers are citizens; conclusion— non-taxpayers should be allowed to vote in a city referendum deciding on tax-supported undertakings. Since decisions on tax-supported undertakings are clearly matters of government policy, rejection of the conclusion is inconsistent with acceptance of the major premise. As a matter of policy, perhaps the vote should be restricted—as it often is—under the circumstances indicated. We simply note that such a position is inconsistent with the unqualified major premise.

As to the second apparent difficulty, varying interpretations of the questions undoubtedly influenced the results. As our pre-test of the questionnaire indicated, the wordings finally chosen conveyed common meanings but tapped different attitudes embedded in different frames of reference. In surveys, as in real political situations, citizens are confronted with the need for making decisions about questions to which they attribute varying implications. We can infer, for example, that the respondents who repudiate free speech for Communists are responding in terms of anti-Communist rather than anti-free speech sentiments, especially since they endorse the idea of free speech in general. Conversely, those who endorse free speech for Communists are presumably reflecting a more consistent dedication to free speech rather than pro-Communist sentiments. But our concern in this study is with the opinions themselves rather than with the varying functions that a given opinion may perform for different individuals.[7] The significant fact is that the opinions (and presumably the frames of reference that produce them) vary systematically from group to group, not randomly or on a meaninglessly idiosyncratic basis.

Assuming that the United States is a democracy, we cannot say without qualification that consensus on fundamental principles is a necessary condition for the existence of democracy. Nor does it appear valid to say that, although consensus need not pervade the entire voting population, it must exist at least among the highly educated, who are the carriers of the creed. Our data are not inconsistent, of course, with the qualified proposition that consensus on fundamental principles in a highly abstract form is a necessary condition for the existence of democracy. But the implication of political theory that consensus includes more specific principles is empirically invalid. Our findings accordingly suggest that the intuitive insights and logical inferences of political theorists need to be subjected more consistently to empirical validation.

Discussions of consensus tend to overlook the functional nature of apathy for the democratic system. No one is surprised to hear that what people *say* they *believe* and what they *actually do* are not necessarily the same. We usually assume that verbal positions represent a higher level—a more "democratic" stance—than nonverbal behavior. But something close to the opposite may also be true: many people express undemocratic principles in response to questioning but are too apathetic to act on their undemocratic opinions in concrete situations. And in most cases, fortunately for the democratic system, those with the most undemocratic principles are also those who are least likely to act. A sizeable number (42.0 percent) of our southern respondents said, for example, that "a Negro should not be allowed to run for mayor of this city," but a few months before the survey a Negro actually did conduct an active campaign for that office without any efforts being made by the "white" people to obstruct his candidacy.

In this case, the behavior was more democratic than the verbal expressions. If the leadership elements—the carriers of the creed—had encouraged undemocratic action, it might have materialized (as it did in Little Rock in the school desegregation crisis). But in fact, people with basically undemocratic opinions either abstained from acting or acted in a perfectly democratic fashion. "The successful working of the system is not deliberately aimed at by those who work it," John Plamenatz says, "but is the result of their behaving as they do."[8] As J. Roland Pennock puts it, democracy can tolerate less conscious agreement on principles if people are willing to compromise and to follow set rules and procedures.[9] Loose talk of consensus as a self-evident requirement of democracy should have no place beside such insightful observations as these. Carl J. Friedrich appears to have been correct in asserting, eighteen years ago, that democracy depends on habitual patterns of behavior rather than on conscious agreement on democratic "principles."[10] His argument has been largely ignored because, like the position from which he dissented, it was advanced without the support of directly relevant research findings. Our results are offered as a step toward settling the question on empirical grounds.

Democratic Practice
and Democratic Theory

BERNARD R. BERELSON, PAUL F. LAZARSFELD,
WILLIAM N. McPHEE

If the democratic system depended solely on the qualifications of the individual voter, then it seems remarkable that democracies have survived through the centuries. After examining the detailed data on how individuals misperceive political reality or respond to irrelevant social influences, one wonders how a democracy ever solves its political problems. But when one considers the data in a broader perspective—how huge segments of the society adapt to political conditions affecting them or how the political system adjusts itself to changing conditions over long periods of time—he cannot fail to be impressed with the total result. Where the rational citizen seems to abdicate, nevertheless angels seem to tread.

The eminent judge, Learned Hand, in a delightful essay on "Democracy: Its Presumptions and Reality," comes to essentially this conclusion.

> I do not know how it is with you, but for myself I generally give up at the outset. The simplest problems which come up from day to day seem to me quite unanswerable as soon as I try to get below the surface. . . .
> My vote is one of the most unimportant acts of my life; if I were to

Reprinted from Bernard R. Berelson, Paul F. Lazarsfeld, and William N. McPhee, *Voting*, pp. 311–323. Copyright 1954 by The University of Chicago. All rights reserved. Published 1954. Composed and printed by The University of Chicago Press, Chicago, Ill.

acquaint myself with the matters on which it ought really to depend, if I were to try to get a judgment on which I was willing to risk affairs of even the smallest moment, I should be doing nothing else, and that seems a fatuous conclusion to a fatuous undertaking.

Yet he recognizes the paradox—somehow the system not only works on the most difficult and complex questions but often works with distinction. "For, abuse it as you will, it gives a bloodless measure of social forces—bloodless, have you thought of that?—a means of continuity, a principle of stability, a relief from the paralyzing terror of revolution."

Justice Hand concludes that we have "outgrown" the conditions assumed in traditional democratic theory and that "the theory has ceased to work." And yet, the system that has grown out of classic democratic theory, and, in this country, out of quite different and even elementary social conditions, does continue to work—perhaps even more vigorously and effectively than ever.

That is the paradox. *Individual voters* today seem unable to satisfy the requirements for a democratic system of government outlined by political theorists. But the *system of democracy* does meet certain requirements for a going political organization. The individual members may not meet all the standards, but the whole nevertheless survives and grows. This suggests that where the classic theory is defective is in its concentration on the *individual citizen*. What are undervalued are certain collective properties that reside in the electorate as a whole and in the political and social system in which it functions.

The political philosophy we have inherited, then, has given more consideration to the virtues of the typical citizen of the democracy than to the working of the *system* as a whole. Moreover, when it dealt with the system, it mainly considered the single constitutive institutions of the system, not those general features necessary if the institutions are to work as required. For example, the rule of law, representative government, periodic elections, the party system, and the several freedoms of discussion, press, association, and assembly have all been examined by political philosophers seeking to clarify and to justify the idea of political democracy. But liberal democracy is more than a political system in which individual voters and political institutions operate. For political democracy to survive, other features are required: the intensity of conflict must be limited, the rate of change must be restrained, stability in the social and economic structure must be maintained, a pluralistic social organization must exist, and a basic consensus must bind together the contending parties.

Such features of the system of political democracy belong neither to the constitutive institutions nor to the individual voter. It might be said that they form the atmosphere or the environment in which both operate. In any case, such features have not been carefully considered by political philosophers, and it is on these broader properties of the democratic political system that more reflection and study by political theory is called for. In the most tentative fashion let us explore the values of the political system, as they involve the electorate, in the light of the foregoing considerations.

Requirements for the System

Underlying the paradox is an assumption that the population is homogeneous socially and should be homogeneous politically: that everybody is about the same in relevant social characteristics; that if something is a political virtue (like interest in the election), then everyone should have it; that there is such a thing as "the" typical citizen on whom uniform requirements can be imposed. The tendency of classic democratic literature to work with an image of "the" voter was never justified. For, as we will attempt to illustrate here, some of the most important requirements that democratic values impose on a system require a voting population that is not homogeneous but heterogeneous in its political qualities.

The need for heterogeneity arises from the contradictory functions we expect our voting system to serve. We expect the political system to adjust itself and our affairs to changing conditions; yet we demand too that it display a high degree of stability. We expect the contending interests and parties to pursue their ends vigorously and the voters to care; yet, after the election is over, we expect reconciliation. We expect the voting outcome to serve what is best for the community; yet we do not want disinterested voting unattached to the purposes and interests of different segments of that community. We want voters to express their own free and self-determined choices; yet, for the good of the community, we would like voters to avail themselves of the best information and guidance available from the groups and leaders around them. We expect a high degree of rationality to prevail in the decision; but were all irrationality and mythology absent, and all ends pursued by the most coldly rational selection of political means, it is doubtful if the system would hold together.

In short, our electoral system calls for apparently incompatible properties—which, although they cannot all reside in each individual voter, can (and do) reside in a heterogeneous electorate. What seems to be required of the electorate as a whole is a *distribution* of qualities along important dimensions. We need some people who are active in a certain respect, others in the middle, and still others passive. The contradictory things we want from the total require that the parts be different. This can be illustrated by taking up a number of important dimensions by which an electorate might be characterized.

INVOLVEMENT AND INDIFFERENCE

How could a mass democracy work if all the people were deeply involved in politics? Lack of interest by some people is not without its benefits, too.

True, the highly interested voters vote more, and know more about the campaign, and read and listen more, and participate more; however, they are also less open to persuasion and less likely to change. Extreme interest goes with extreme partisanship and might culminate in rigid fanaticism that could destroy democratic processes if generalized throughout the community. Low affect toward the election—not caring much—underlies the resolution of many political problems; votes can be resolved into a two-party split instead of fragmented into many parties (the splinter parties of the left, for example, splinter because their advocates are *too* interested in politics). Low interest provides maneuvering room for political shifts necessary for a complex society in a period of rapid change. Compromise might be based upon sophisticated awareness of costs and returns—perhaps impossible to demand of a mass society— but it is more often induced by indifference. Some people are and should be highly interested in politics, but not everyone is or needs to be. Only the doctrinaire would deprecate the moderate indifference that facilitates compromise.

Hence, an important balance between action motivated by strong sentiments and action with little passion behind it is obtained by heterogeneity within the electorate. Balance of this sort is, in practice, met by a distribution of voters rather than by a homogeneous collection of "ideal" citizens.

STABILITY AND FLEXIBILITY

A similar dimension along which an electorate might be characterized is stability–flexibility. The need for change and adaptation is clear, and the need for stability ought equally to be (especially from observation of current democratic practice in, say, certain Latin American countries).

How is political stability achieved? There are a number of social sources of political stability: the training of the younger generation before it is old enough to care much about the matter, the natural selection that surrounds the individual voter with families and friends who reinforce his own inclinations, the tendency to adjust in favor of the majority of the group, the self-perpetuating tendency of political traditions among ethnic and class and regional strata where like-minded people find themselves socially together. Political stability is based upon social stability. Family traditions, personal associations, status-related organizational memberships, ethnic affiliations, socioeconomic strata— such ties for the individual do not change rapidly or sharply, and since his vote is so importantly a product of them, neither does it. In effect, a large part of the study of voting deals not with why votes change but rather with why they do not.

In addition, the varying conditions facing the country, the varying political appeals made to the electorate, and the varying dispositions of the voters activated by these stimuli—these, combined with the long-lasting nature of the political loyalties they instill, produce an important cohesion within the system. For example, the tendencies operating in 1948 electoral decisions not only were built up in the New Deal and Fair Deal era but also dated back to parental and grandparental loyalties, to religious and ethnic cleavages of a past era, and to moribund sectional and community conflicts. Thus, in a very real sense any particular election is a composite of various elections and various political and social events. People vote for a President on a given November day, but their choice is made not simply on the basis of what has happened in the preceding months or even four years; in 1948 some people were in effect voting on the internationalism issue of 1940, others on the Depression issues of 1932, and some, indeed, on the slavery issues of 1860.

The vote is thus a kind of "moving average" of reactions to the political past. Voters carry over to each new election remnants of issues raised in previous elections—and so there is always an overlapping of old and new decisions that give a cohesion in time to the political system. Hence the composite decision "smooths out" political change. The people vote *in* the same election, but not all of them vote *on* it.

What of flexibility? Curiously, the voters least admirable when measured against individual requirements contribute most when measured against the aggregate requirement for flexibility. For those who change political preferences most readily are those who are least interested, who are subject to conflicting social pressures, who have inconsistent beliefs and erratic voting histories. Without them—if the decision were left only to the deeply concerned, well-integrated, consistently-principled ideal citizens—the political system might easily prove too rigid to adapt to changing domestic and international conditions.

In fact, it may be that the very people who are most sensitive to changing social conditions are those most susceptible to political change. For, in either case, the people exposed to membership in overlapping strata, those whose former life-patterns are being broken up, those who are moving about socially or physically, those who are forming new families and new friendships—it is they who are open to adjustments of attitudes and tastes. They may be the least partisan and the least interested voters, but they perform a valuable function for the entire system. Here again is an instance in which an individual "inadequacy" provides a positive service for the society: the campaign can be a reaffirming force for the settled majority and a creative force for the unsettled minority. There is stability on both sides and flexibility in the middle.

PROGRESS AND CONSERVATION

Closely related to the question of stability is the question of past versus future orientation of the system. In America a progressive outlook is highly valued, but, at the same time, so is a conservative one. Here a balance between the two is easily found in the party system and in the distribution of voters themselves from extreme conservatives to extreme liberals. But a balance between the two is also achieved by a distribution of political dispositions through time. There are periods of great political agitation (i.e., campaigns) alternating with periods of political dormancy. Paradoxically, the former— the campaign period—is likely to be an instrument of conservatism, often even of historical regression.

Many contemporary campaigns (not, however, 1952) must be stabilizing forces that activated past tendencies in individuals and reasserted past patterns of group voting. In 1948, for example, the middle-class Protestants reaffirmed their traditional Republican position, the working-class Protestants reverted toward their position of the 1930s and the working-class Catholics toward their position not only of the 1930s but of a generation or more earlier. In this sense the campaign was a retreat away from new issues back toward old positions.

Political campaigns tend to make people more consistent both socially and psychologically; they vote more with their social groups and agree more with their own prior ideas on the issues. But new ideas and new alignments are in their infancy manifested by inconsistency psychologically and heterogeneity socially; they are almost by definition deviant and minority points of view. To the extent that they are inhibited by pressure or simply by knowledge of what is the proper (i.e., majority) point of view in a particular group, then the campaign period is not a time to look for the growth of important new trends.

This "regressive tendency" may appear as a reaction to intense propaganda during decisive times. The term "regressive" need not imply a reversion to less-developed, less-adaptive behavior; in fact, one might argue that the revival of a Democratic vote among workers was functional for their interests. What it refers to is simply the reactivation of prior dispositions—dispositions in politics that date back years and decades, often to a prior political era.

Its counterpart, of course, is what we believe to be an important potential for progress during the periods of relaxed tension and low-pressure political and social stimuli that are especially characteristic of America between political campaigns. The very tendency for Americans to neglect their political system most of the time—to be "campaign citizens" in the sense that many are "Sunday churchgoers"—is not without its values. Change may come best from relaxation.

Again, then, a balance (between preservation of the past and receptivity to the future) seems to be required of a democratic electorate. The heterogeneous electorate in itself provides a balance between liberalism and conservatism; and so does the sequence of political events from periods of drifting change to abrupt rallies back to the loyalties of earlier years.

CONSENSUS AND CLEAVAGE

. . . American opinion on public issues is much too complex to be designated by such simple, single-minded labels as *the* housewife opinion or *the* young people's opinion or even *the* workers' opinion. If one uses as a base the central Republican–Democratic cleavage, then one finds numerous "contradictions" within individuals, within strata and groups, and within party supporters themselves. There are many issues presented, cafeteria-style, for the voter to choose from, and there are overlaps in opinion in every direction.

Similarly there are required *social* consensus and cleavage—in effect, pluralism—in politics. Such pluralism makes for enough consensus to hold the system together and enough cleavage to make it move. Too much consensus would be deadening and restrictive of liberty; too much cleavage would be destructive of the society as a whole.

Consider the pictures of the hypothetical relationships between political preference (e.g., party support) and a social characteristic as presented in this chart:

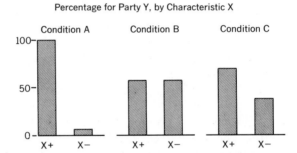

Percentage for Party Y, by Characteristic X

In Condition A there is virtual identity between the characteristic and political preference; all the people of type $X+$ vote one way, and all the people of $X-$ vote the other way. In Condition B the opposite is the case, and there is no relationship between vote and the characteristic; both parties are supported equally by people of the two types. In Condition C there is neither a complete relationship nor a complete absence; more $X+$'s than $X-$'s are partisans of a given side, but there are some members of each type in each political camp.

Now a democratic society in which Condition A was intensified would probably be in danger of its existence. The issues of politics would cut so deeply, be so keenly felt, and, especially, be so fully reinforced by other social identifications of the electorate as to threaten the basic consensus itself. This might be called "total politics"—a conception of politics, incidentally, advanced by such leading theorists of National Socialism and communism as Carl Schmitt and Lenin. This involves the mutual reinforcement of political differences and other social distinctions meaningful to the citizen. The multiplication of Condition B, on the other hand, would suggest a community in which politics was of no "real" importance to the community, in which it was not associated with special interests. Condition C is a combination of Conditions A and B—that is, a situation in which special interests are of some but not of overriding importance. It portrays neither the extremist or fanatical community like A nor the "pure" or utopian community like B. . . .

Thus again a requirement we might place on an electoral system—balance between total political war between segments of the society and total political indifference to group interests of that society—translates into varied requirements for different individuals. With respect to group or bloc voting, as with other aspects of political behavior, it is perhaps not unfortunate that "some do and some do not."

INDIVIDUALISM AND COLLECTIVISM

Lord Bryce pointed out the difficulties in a theory of democracy that assumes that each citizen must himself be capable of voting intelligently:

> Orthodox democratic theory assumes that every citizen has, or ought to have, thought out for himself certain opinions, i.e., ought to have a definite view, defensible by argument, of what the country needs, of what principles ought to be applied in governing it, of the man to whose hands the government ought to be entrusted. There are persons who talk, though certainly very few who act, as if they believed this theory, which may be compared to the theory of some ultra-Protestants that every good Christian has or ought to have . . . worked out for himself from the Bible a system of theology.

In the first place, however, the information available to the individual voter is not limited to that directly possessed by him. True, the individual casts his own personal ballot. But . . . that is perhaps the most individualized action he takes in an election. His vote is formed in the midst of his fellows in a sort of group decision—if, indeed, it may be called a decision at all—and the total information and knowledge possessed in the group's present and past generations can be made available for the group's choice. Here is where opinion-leading relationships, for example, play an active role.

Second, and probably more important, the individual voter may not have a great deal of detailed information, but he usually has picked up the crucial *general* information as part of his social learning itself. He may not know the parties' positions on the tariff, or who is for reciprocal trade treaties, or what are the differences on Asiatic policy, or how the parties split on civil rights, or how many security risks were exposed by whom. But he cannot live in an American community without knowing broadly where the parties stand. He has learned that the Republicans are more conservative and the Democrats more liberal—and he can locate his own sentiments and cast his vote accordingly. After all, he must vote for one or the other party, and, if he knows the big thing about the parties, he does not need to know all the little things. The basic role a party plays as an institution in American life is more important to his voting than a particular stand on a particular issue.

It would be unthinkable to try to maintain our present economic style of life without a complex system of delegating to others what we are not competent to do ourselves, without accepting and giving training to each other about what each is expected to do, without accepting our dependence on others in many spheres and taking responsibility for their dependence on us in some spheres. And, like it or not, to maintain our present political style of life, we may have to accept much the same interdependence with others in collective behavior. We have learned slowly in economic life that it is useful not to have everyone a butcher or a baker, any more than it is useful to have no one skilled in such activities. The same kind of division of labor—as repugnant as it may be in some respects to our individualistic tradition—is serving as well today in mass politics. There is an implicit division of political labor within the electorate.

Conclusion

In short, when we turn from requirements for "average" citizens to requirements for the survival of the total democratic system, we find it unnecessary for the individual voter to be an "average citizen" cast in the classic or any other single mold. With our increasingly complex and differentiated citizenry has grown up an equally complex political system, and it is perhaps not simply a fortunate accident that they have grown and prospered together.

But it is a dangerous act of mental complacency to assume that conditions found surviving together are, therefore, positively "functional" for each other. The apathetic segment of America probably has helped to hold the system together and cushioned the shock of disagreement, adjustment, and change. But that is not to say that we can stand apathy without limit. Similarly, there must be some limit to the degree of stability or nonadaptation that a political society can maintain and still survive in a changing world. And surely the quality and amount of conformity that is necessary and desirable can be exceeded, as it has been in times of war and in the present Communist scare, to the damage of the society itself and of the other societies with which it must survive in the world.

How can our analysis be reconciled with the classical theory of liberal political democracy? Is the theory "wrong"? Must it be discarded in favor of empirical political sociology? Must its ethical or normative content be dismissed as incompatible with the nature of modern man or of mass society? That is not our view. Rather, it seems to us that modern political theory of democracy stands in need of revision and not replacement by empirical sociology. The classical political philosophers were right in the direction of their assessment of the virtues of the citizen. But they demanded those virtues in too extreme or doctrinal a form. The voter does have some principles, he does have information and rationality, he does have interest—but he does not have them in the extreme, elaborate, comprehensive, or detailed form in which they were uniformly recommended by political philosophers. Like Justice Hand, the typical citizen has other interests in life, and it is good, even for the political system, that he pursues them. The classical requirements are more appropriate for the opinion leaders in the society, but even they do not meet them directly. Happily for the system, voters distribute themselves along a continuum:

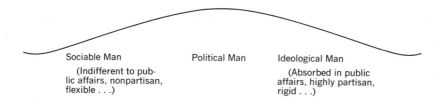

Sociable Man	Political Man	Ideological Man
(Indifferent to public affairs, nonpartisan, flexible . . .)		(Absorbed in public affairs, highly partisan, rigid . . .)

And it turns out that this distribution itself, with its internal checks and balances, can perform the functions and incorporate the same values ascribed by some theorists to each individual in the system as well as to the constitutive political institutions!

Twentieth-century political theory—both analytic and normative—will arise only from hard and long observation of the actual world of politics, closely identified with the deeper problems of practical politics. Values and the behavior they are meant to guide are not distinctly separate or separable parts of life as it is lived; and how Elmirans choose their governors is not completely unrelated to the considerations of how they are *supposed* to choose them. We disagree equally with those who believe that normative theory about the proper health of a democracy has nothing to gain from analytic studies like ours; with those who believe that the whole political tradition from Mill to Locke is irrelevant to our realistic understanding and assessment of modern democracy; or with those like Harold Laski who believe that "the decisions of men, when they come to choose their governors, are influenced by considerations which escape all scientific analysis."

We agree with Cobban: "For a century and a half the Western democracies have been living on the stock of basic political ideas that were last restated toward the end of the eighteenth century. That is a long time. . . . The gap thus formed between political facts and political ideas has steadily widened. It has taken a long time for the results to become evident; but now that we have seen what politics devoid of a contemporary moral and political theory means, it is possible that something may be done about it."

How American Democracy
Really Works

R. JOSEPH MONSEN, JR., MARK W. CANNON

Despite the recognition by such Founding Fathers as Madison that "the majority who rule . . . are the safest guardians both of the public good and private rights,"[11] he and others who framed the Constitution were also aware of the dangers of majority power being uncontrollably inflicted to the damage of minorities. In American thought there is an element which generally opposes drastic action toward minority groups. Most citizens like the idea of a government which corresponds to Teddy Roosevelt's slogan of a "square deal" for all citizens whether laborers, farmers, or professional people.

But people are motivated by their interests. What is to prevent minorities from being seriously damaged under a system of majority rule? This has been a crucial problem of American democracy. For as Thomas Nixon Carver observed in a rather extreme caricature: "There are few things more democratic than a lynching bee, where everybody is satisfied except a small and insignificant minority of one."[12] Or as former Harvard president A. Lawrence Lowell pointed out, if two highwaymen steal a wallet from a belated traveler, it would be an abuse of terms to say that in that lonely assemblage public opinion favored a redistribution of property.[13]

The idea that there is something sacred about the figure 50 percent plus one, and that this is the real source of policy-making, is a myth. Lord Bryce observed that "government was always government by the few, whether in the name of the one, the few, or the many."[14] The truthfulness of this statement is borne out by the fact that the average turnout of eligible voters in presidential elections in the last forty years has been only 53.6 percent; no president in this period has ever come close to receiving a majority of votes of the nation's citizens.[15] In a different way, this lack of political participation is even found among lobbyists themselves, 44 percent having never been active in a political party.[16] Clearly, the central tendency and characteristic of American politics is not found in the will of the majority. To dramatize this point, Robert Dahl stated that "the eight largest states with 54 percent of the voters have the same number of votes in the Senate as the eight smallest states with less than 3 percent of the voters."[17] He further found that "a majority of votes in the

Senate can be cast by Senators representing less than 15 percent of the voters."[18] As further evidence on this point, one has only to see the massive compilation of polls in *Public Opinion, 1935–1946*,[19] by Hadley Cantril and Mildred Strunk, to note that, in retrospect, the majority opinions registered on public polls frequently did not correlate with public policy outcomes. In E. E. Schattschneider's words: "It is necessary only to look at the polls . . . to realize that public opinion about specific issues does not necessarily govern the course of public policy."[20] In a 1960 study of state legislators, Wahlke, Buchanan, Eulau, and Ferguson postulated that "public interest is never more than the harmonization of . . . partial and private interests and that organized interest groups . . . play an indispensable part in defining and legislating in the public interest."[21]

"The American political system is less able to use the democratic device of majority rule than almost any other modern democracy. Nearly everyone makes obeisance to the majority, but the ideal of majority rule has not been well institutionalized, and never been fully legitimatized."[22] In fact Edward Hollett Carr has said:

> History points unmistakably to the fact that political democracy, in the forms in which it has hitherto been known, flourishes best where some of the people, but not all the people, are free and equal; and, since this conclusion is incompatible with the conditions of the new society and repugnant to the contemporary conscience, the task of saving democracy in our time is the task of reconciling it with the postulate of popular sovereignty and mass civilization.[23]

There is no particular logic in numbers that gives a majority the right to impose a decision on a minority, since intensity of feeling is not thereby measured or allowed nor is justice assured to the minority. Majority rule is not an obviously correct or true principle—particularly when it is based upon majority tyranny. Dahl contends that

> The likelihood of peaceful adjustment to a conflict is increased if there exist institutional arrangements that encourage consultation, negotiation, the exploration of beneficial solutions. Conversely, the prospects of deadlock and coercion are increased if institutional arrangements severely inhibit such activities.[24]

Majority rule, without safeguards, could lead to some rather absurd situations. For example, if 51 percent rather mildly favor the confiscation of property of the other 49 percent of the society, the logic of unrestrained majoritarianism would so dictate. Judge Learned Hand has said: "The Spirit of Liberty is the spirit which is not too sure that it is right."[25]

Dahl also found that Americans have always had voter lethargy. For example, in 1784 New Haven became a city. At that time about 250 people were excluded as voters either because they did not hold property or because they had been loyal to England. Of the 343 remaining eligible males, about one-fourth failed to take the oath, and therefore they could not vote in elections, and on the first election day only about 100 citizens of the 261 eligible cast their votes.[26] This problem is not peculiar to America alone. Aristotle wrote in the fourth century B.C.:

> Payment for attendance at the assembly was, at first, a step which they [the restored democrats, once more in control after the perturbations at the end of the Peloponnesian War] refused to take. The citizens, however, failed to attend; and the presidents of the assembly were driven to one device after another in order to induce the populace to present themselves for the purpose of ratifying measures. In these circumstances Agyrrhius began by providing an obol a day for attendance; Heraclides . . . increased it to two obols; and Agyrrhius afterward advanced it to three.[27]

It is obvious that not all men are instinctively political animals. People do not always care what happens in politics. Nor do they know much about political events or share in making decisions. It is Dahl's contention that an individual is unlikely to get involved in politics unless he believes the outcome will be relatively unsatisfactory without his involvement. The percentage of voters rises sharply in depression years such as 1873 to 1878 or in a movement such as the Populist in 1893 to 1897.[28]

It is in the light of the above-mentioned facts that the appeal of majority rule for many Americans as well as its actual operation must be examined. Thomas Jefferson declared in his first inaugural address: "The will of the majority is in all cases to prevail."[29] How did the early Democrats such as Jefferson, as well as Thomas Paine, John Taylor, and Samuel Adams, handle the problem of potential tyranny of the majority? Jefferson had no illusion that the majority would always be right. He recognized that to be rightful the majority will had to be reasonable and that the minority possessed their equal rights, "which equal law must protect and to violate would be oppression."[30] Jefferson did, however, have the optimistic view that men were capable of making reasonable decisions. There is also an emphasis upon men's being able to make judgments within a framework of the public interest.[31] As the Puritan democrat John Wise asserted, "Man is not so wedded to his own interest, but that he can make the common good the mark of his aim.[32]

The Jeffersonians also hoped to ward off majority tyranny through specific prohibitions against government's infringing on rights, particularly through the Bill of Rights.

A different view of man and the prevention of majority tyranny was taken by such Federalists as James Madison and John Adams. They believed people to be more emotional and less rational than did Jefferson.[33] Adams warned that "majoritarian democracy would lead to candidates pandering to every popular 'passion and prejudice' and exploiting every flattery, trick, bribe, feast, and threat possible.[34]

Many conservative theories of democracy have stemmed from similar views that human reason is too fallible, rare, and capricious to rely on. These theories call for traditions, religion, or "delicately contrived equilibria of the forces struggling for power,"[35] to prevent tyranny of the majority.

Along these lines the objectives of the preponderance of the participants in the Constitutional Convention were to restrain and disperse power so as to minimize the danger of majoritarian tyranny. The main substance of constitutionalism is to balance liberty and authority between the powers of government and individual rights.[36] The rule of law and the separate powers given to the three main divisions of government were to stand "as a guarantee of individual liberty against the exercise of arbitrary governmental power."[37] As Andrew Hacker says, "The rights of individuals—as distinct from groups—can only be protected if some department of the government intervenes and exercises power on their behalf."[38]

The Founding Fathers believed they could protect minorities through an ingenious constitutional system with three key devices.[39] The first was the written constitutional prohibitions upon certain government powers, such as the taking of private property without due process of law. The second was the detachment of most of the government from direct election, thereby giving them a cushion against the passing passions of popular majorities. Thus, Senators were to be elected by state legislatures. The President was to be elected by the electoral college, and judges were to be appointed by the President with confirmation of the Senate. Only the House of Representatives was subject directly to the will of the people by popular election.

The third device was a dispersion of power both vertically between the state and federal levels of government (federalism)[40] and horizontally between the executive, legislative, and judicial branches of government (separation of powers). Such functions were never "separate and distinct."[41] The design of such a checks-and-balances system was explained by Mr. Justice Brandeis: "The purpose was not to avoid friction, but, by means of the inevitable friction incident to the distribution of governmental powers among three departments, to save the people from autocracy."[42]

These structural principles of the constitutional architects have been greatly modified and diluted with the development of a complex, interdependent, technological society.

The pressures for stronger presidential leadership in a mass democracy to produce more uniform and efficient national programs of ever greater scope have ameliorated the originally conceived system of dispersed power. What possible alternatives exist to the now somewhat emaciated system of dispersion of power previously envisaged?

An alternative which has been recognized is the dispersion of power among highly organized, alert private groups with consequent checks and balances.

> In terms of society, Madison said that "the social whole would be broken into so many parts, interests, and classes of citizens." No single part or interest or class would contain a majority of citizens: if a majority were formed on any issue, it would simply consist of a transient coalition of groups. For example, there is a Protestant majority in America, and it may be inquired why its representatives do not enact legislation penalizing the Catholic minority in the country. Madison's answer was not that the Protestants were notably tolerant nor was it that they believe in religious liberty for all. The answer was that the Protestant majority is itself a coalition of Baptists, Methodists, Episcopalians, Presbyterians, and Lutherans. Each of these denominations had had its own history of persecution when it was in the minority, and therefore all of them agree to tolerate other religions—including the Catholics—for fear that they may at some future time be subjected to majority oppression.[43]

These groups are all relatively large minorities in our total society. With their growth, in the course of history, a concomitant development has occurred. That is, as these groups have increased in size, they have developed bureaucracies. A rationalized organizational structure has developed which attempts to speak for the group within the national area, thereby making the group effective even though many of its members are passive.

J. K. Galbraith has called this development "countervailing power." While Galbraith, an economist, has focused on the central issue in explaining the manner in which policy is determined in this country, the theory of countervailing power lacks complete realism and consistency. Galbraith defines countervailing power most succinctly as "the neutralization of one position of power by another.[44] He calls it the "answering bargaining power" to check the power of sellers or buyers by the organizing of those subject to such power. "Private economic power begets the countervailing power of those who are subject to it."[45] The development of strong unions, in this argument, is viewed as an inevitable and automatic development to neutralize or balance the power of the large firms. One wonders, however, whether the present structure of strong unionism would have been achieved without the changed economic ideology and power congregation that developed during the Great Depression. Galbraith summarizes his theory by saying:

> Private economic power is held in check by the countervailing power of those who are subject to it. The first begets the second. The long trend toward concentration of industrial enterprise in the hands of a few firms has brought into existence not only strong sellers . . . but also strong buyers.[46]

Government's role under this theory is to assist in the development of countervailing power. Competition then, Galbraith argues, has been replaced as the autonomous regulator of economic activity by the self-generating forces of countervailing power.

Without going into an analysis of countervailing power in more detail, perhaps it can be most succinctly evaluated in the following manner. On the positive side, countervailing power does focus upon the crucial fact that it is the major economic groups in this country who hold power and make public policy. Furthermore it spotlights the natural impulse of a dominated group to seek devices to strengthen its bargaining position.

Galbraith's groups, however, are vague; the role of politics, politicians, and ideology are undeveloped, and historically the development of countervailing power groups has not occurred inevitably and automatically in response to other power groups. Further, since the theory is stated in equilibrium terms (that is, it describes society as in balance between opposing forces), it must maintain that the power of one group will automatically be offset by its opposition. There is nothing, however, to prevent government from becoming the dominating power or to prevent collusion from occurring between various power blocs to maintain an indefinite upper hand. Galbraith did not develop the theory sufficiently to handle these and other problems. Stigler, in his review, says: "Galbraith's notion of countervailing power is a dogma, not a theory. It lacks rational development and must be accepted or rejected without reference to its unstated logical antecedents."[47]

It is interesting that the Founding Fathers (with perhaps the exception of Madison) failed to see the potential benefits of groups or factions. On the contrary, they felt that factionalism was fraught with danger and evil. Even political parties were not anticipated. The parties emerged out of the necessity of organizing power to gain control of government once the differences between the Federalists and Democrats became clear. In fact, one writer suggests that "political parties exist, not because there are two sides to every issue, but because there are two sides to every office—an inside and an outside."[48]

Actually the majoritarianists who hoped men would be rational and pursue the public good, and the conservative Federalists who believed that majorities would be created by the pursuit of economic gain and emotional causes, both had considerable insight. Both beliefs contribute to an understanding of the fact that America, with certain exceptions, has not generally had flagrant oppression by the majority or a minority, but has developed a system of minorities rule.[49] For example:

> To take some . . . recent decisions, how many people indicated their preferences in a politically relevant way when governmental leaders: decided to contract with large corporations for operating the atomic energy installations? legislated against imports of European cheese and other agricultural products? refused for the umpteenth time to approve the St. Lawrence Seaway project? passed legislation setting up the council

of economic advisors? agreed on the Pick-Slan plan for the Missouri Valley? Each of these decisions was a product of a tiny minority.[50]

The term "minorities rule" describes the situation in which "public policies are the result of opinions and interests of neither a majority nor a minority, but rather arise through compromises of the interests of various organized and vocal minorities. This model differs fundamentally from the traditional descriptions of democratic politics."[51]

Thus Madison's principal anxiety about faction, that a self-seeking majority in the lower classes would vitiate the property rights of the minority in the upper classes, has never been realized. Had Madison's apprehensions been realized, something very close to economic equality could have resulted. Yet, even though many of the traditional structural supports of freedom have been eroded, nothing approaching income equality has yet been obtained or demanded by the poorer majority. The relative position of the wealthy has not been radically lowered in modern times.

> The distribution of personal income does not shift violently from year to year. Rising total and average money income changes the relative proportions among the income size brackets: in 1945 fewer than 10% of the spending units received as much as $5,000; by 1950, 20% received as much as that or more. . . . However, while the proportion of spending units in, and personal income received by, the $5,000 and over class was increasing by more than 100% and almost 90% respectively, the share of the top 10% of the income receivers increased from 29% in 1945 to 33% in 1947 and then returned to 29% in 1950. The bottom half of the income receivers had 22%, 21%, and 23% in the corresponding years.[52]

In 1956 the top 1 percent of adults owned 26 percent of the wealth in the United States. This share of wealth was smaller, but not substantially smaller, than the 31.6 percent owned by the top 1 percent in 1922, before the impact of progressive income taxes.[53]

To illustrate the small change which has taken place in the lower income groups, the percentage of national personal income before taxes received by the poorer half of the United States was evidently 27 percent in 1910, which dropped to 23 percent by 1959.[54]

It was reported by the Federal Income Tax Bureau that those reporting an income in excess of $1 million was higher in 1962 than in any year since 1929. Thus, in spite of the considerable talk about the confiscation of wealth due to the steeply progressive income tax (and there have been a few individuals who actually paid 91 percent of a part of their income), most wealthy people avoid or minimize such high rates by income splitting with a spouse, by delaying part of their income through certain types of pension plans, by arranging to earn a high share of their income through stock options and capital gains, which are taxed at a maximum of only 25 percent, and by investing in municipal bonds which are exempt from federal taxes. Furthermore, many other taxes, such as sales and gasoline taxes, are regressive—that is, they take a higher percentage of the income of the poor than of the rich. Thus when the total tax system is analyzed, one study concludes, there is only mild progressiveness in the middle- and lower-income portions of the structure.[55] A more recent conservative tax authority concluded that the structure displayed almost no progressiveness and was actually regressive, if Social Security is included, until people earn almost $15,000 a year, and it is steeply progressive only for a small percentage of people with high incomes.[56]

In spite of the fact that the tax structure does not appear to be progressive except at the high income levels, there is still some redistribution of wealth through government, both state and local as well as national, because poor people benefit from government expenditures more in relation to their tax payments than do rich people.[57]

The point is that in spite of the ideology of labor unions, for example, in calling for elimination of tax loopholes, and for steeper inheritance taxes, they have not as yet moved our society any significant distance toward a "dead level" equality, feared by the wealthy. "The most common and durable source of factions has been the various and unequal distribution of property." Had Madison's fears been realized, it would have been easy for labor unions to form a majority coalition of the less well off and rewrite the tax laws accordingly.

Why has this not been done? To answer this question, further elaboration of the operation of minorities rule is necessary, especially as it involves Jefferson's hope that men would seek the public good.

Calhoun's desire, that a concurrent majority of all the regions in the country be required to prevent the ganging up on a minority region for legislation, was never adopted. Yet something approaching a concurrent majority among the major power groups has become a *modus operandi*. This does not mean that a minority can veto any action, as John Fischer apparently believed.[58] In the statutes enacted in the legislative arena there are real winners and losers, as seen in the Wagner Act and Taft-Hartley Act and in the inability of the bankers to "veto" Franklin D. Roosevelt's currency reforms.

What all this means is that beyond the point of moderation, a group often can veto damaging enactments. Why is this? First, the threat of truly serious damage to a group would normally produce an extraordinary intensity of political activity on the part of the minority affected. This could vastly multiply its political influence because of the widespread apathy which generally characterizes the citizenry. This apathy is illustrated by the fact that only 7 percent of the adults contributed money to a party or candidate during a four-year period.

Second, American society involves overlapping memberships. There are very few Balkanized groups such as the Arabs and the Jews in the Middle East. This American system of overlapping memberships allows a threatened minority to multiply its influence through its members' using their other affiliations to gain the sympathy of segments of other groups.

Third, in most battles there are numerous groups which do not become deeply involved but prefer to remain on the sidelines. Many members of a group can be activated if they perceive that another group's power is being fundamentally and unfairly damaged. Thus the response of business to the Wagner Act was to work toward a new coalition which later won the battles of the Taft-Hartley and Landrum-Griffin bills. Many groups which sometimes cooperate with labor did not rush to labor's defense during these struggles because they viewed the reforms as being valid in the public interest (and the reforms did not circumscribe any group but labor).

Suppose, however, that the proposals had gone much farther than these laws. For example, suppose that the proposals included a national right-to-work law and the disassembling of labor unions under the antitrust laws. Some minorities would have become activated in labor's behalf, fearing that such a blow might serve as a precedent against them. Some otherwise neutral groups on labor issues, such as the intellectuals and the bureaucracy, would likely have come to labor's rescue, because they would have felt it was not in the public interest to weaken a basic group that much. Just as Great Britain traditionally gave its support to the weaker nations in order to maintain a balance of power in Europe, many groups would give their support to labor if necessary to maintain a political balance of power. In fact, it was perhaps the widespread feeling that labor had attained excessive power that put many groups, at least tacitly, on the side of business.

Madison was correct when he contended that "factions" would use politics for economic gain. Jefferson was also correct in hoping people could take into account the public interest. As William Fulbright pointed out, citizens are not "incapable of reason."[59] This reason can attempt to calculate public interest as well as to fulfill personal interests. It is the examination of apparent public interest, particularly by groups which have little at stake and which are not tied by overriding obligations to one of the contending groups in a particular battle, which helps produce a compromise which is not excessively harsh on the losing group.[60] Similarly, in Congress the solons who do not have one-sided constituency pressures and who are not tied by obligation to fellow legislators on either side of an issue are freer to be "statesmen," giving primary weight to the public interest as they perceive it. This operation of both the early American conservative and liberal conceptions of man in the actual functioning of the system of minorities rule has been little recognized.

Even though the groups which are the legislative combatants are more highly organized and politically sophisticated now than earlier, the style of negotiation and compromise has long been fundamental to the Western political tradition. American democracy suffered a grave threat during the Civil War and the Reconstruction when these tenets were largely deserted. Desertion of this style of politics again could result in renewed civil war, strife, riots, oppression of minorities, or totalitarianism.

In developing nations, minorities of one type or another—whether they be Communist, militarist, traditionalist, or nationalist—attempt to take over by force and often refuse to negotiate a compromise with the other groups in the society. Democracy, as we know it, has no chance unless there is a general tacit agreement that disputes are to be settled by nonviolent negotiation and compromise among the interested parties. Peter Odegard has said that he would "like to see political scientists exerting more of their energies in defense of reason in politics."[61] This basic consensus or reasonable approach to the solving of community problems is not rooted in most of the older traditional societies where elites of one form or another have always ruled by force. It requires an entirely new educational process to bring about a basic unity within a society so that its decisions are reached by peaceful bargaining means between the various groups in the society rather than by the domination or force of one group (even if a majority) over the whole society.

How American Democracy Really Works: A Radical View

ARNOLD S. KAUFMAN

1. The Distribution of Wealth

The United States is economically one of the most unequal societies in the world, and the most affluent. The fifth of the nation that is poverty-stricken gives the lie to any claim that we have learned how to manage our affluence in a humanly acceptable way.

The very magnitude of our national resources makes it possible to maintain an adequate incentive system and still meet all the functional needs generated by the moral preeminence of personal self-development in the liberal scheme of things. Ironically, just when Communist nations are discovering that they must reintroduce sharper material incentives, the United States is in a position to reverse the emphasis traditionally placed on them.

Increasingly, the most important incentives are the quality of the conditions of work and the value the individual places on the products of his labor. It is clear that the main barriers to redistribution are not those that flow from the requirements of continued economic growth, but the entrenched power of moneyed elites who, either out of habit or acquisitiveness, insist on interpreting the rhetoric of American freedom in the least human way possible. These forces are often unwittingly abetted by good-hearted folk who are willing to accept the first, tiny product of massive legislative effort as sufficient because it is so beguilingly packaged by the Great Society.

For the indefinite future, the problems of redistribution are going to be complicated by the technological revolution that is in process. The long-term prospect is steady attrition in the supply of jobs. Thus, the nation is conditioned to accept as a triumph of political statesmanship a rate of unemployment that a humane society should not tolerate.

The dialectic of disorder operates with increasing ferocity in this area. Rent strikes, a rising crime rate, intensified problems of juvenile delinquency, and the growth of general contempt for formal authority are only a few of the by-products of the growing gap between the rhetoric of affluence and the reality of poverty. And these disorders are increasingly independent of the problem of race.

2. Civil Rights

The United States is still a predominantly racist society. Economically, socially, legally, politically, and perhaps most important of all, educationally, we have eliminated many legal barriers, yet have made little progress in fact. In comparison with fifteen years ago, Negroes are more segregated, receive a smaller proportion of the national income, constitute a higher proportion of the unemployed, the undereducated, and the blue-collar work force. The only area in which Negroes appear to have made massive gains during the last decade and a half is in the proportion of wartime casualties they are constrained to accept. For in the Vietnam War, over 14 percent of the combatants and 18 percent of the casualties are Negro soldiers, though only about 10 percent of the total population is Negro.[62] Thus we are confronted by the supreme moral irony; those who share least in the fruits of American freedom are, in its alleged defense, making the supreme sacrifice proportionately more of the time than those who benefit most.

The white majority and its allies within the Negro middle class are oblivious to these facts. They are all too ready to accept the tokens of political appointment, the forms of a changing legal code, the apparent moderation of more virulent racial attitudes, and the promise of presidential rhetoric for the substance of significant change. But though there may have been substantial progress for a small proportion of lucky Negroes, the great bulk of the 20 million Negroes in America have participated in this progress only to the extent that their expectations have risen without a proportionate increase in the relative extent to which those expectations are satisfied.

Twelve years after the school desegregation decision, 95 percent of southern schools are segregated. Though unemployment for all groups is down, the rate of Negro unemployment relative to whites is rising. Since 1955, in Alabama, 20 persons have been murdered in circumstances growing out of the civil rights movement, and no one has to date been convicted for any of these crimes. In Harlem the mortality rate at birth for Negroes is currently 45 per 1,000; for the total New York City population, including the Negroes of Harlem, about 25 per 1,000. In Mississippi the median income for Negroes is 32 percent of the median income for whites. These are but a few of the large number of facts that dramatize the gap between what Negroes have been promised and what they have actually received. A white majority, spoon-fed facts that largely point to progress in civil rights, is then utterly astonished by violence in Watts or Rochester.

This white majority and its Negro allies then grow impatient at the rising tempo of demonstrations, violence, and threatened violence by Negroes. The characteristic reaction of officialdom, whether in Selma or in Watts, is to club the incorrigibles into submission. In no other phase of domestic life, however, does the dialectic of disorder work with such ruthless efficiency to destroy the illusions of those "decent and respectable" Americans who stand ready to do anything—anything at all—to improve human relations—*except* seriously to contemplate the necessity of relinquishing many of their basic social and economic prerogatives.

3. Education

The Groves of Academe are increasingly the scene of guerrilla warfare. Sit-ins, teach-ins, demonstrations, filthy speech, and teachers' strikes—all are the products of the same fundamental disorders of American education. Disorderly process in our schools, a source of so much perplexity to most, is not difficult to understand from the point of view of liberalism.

For education, more than any other process, is essential to the achievement of a society in which persons carve out their destiny according to their natures and their own deliberative choices. It is in our schools that the traditions of reason should be honored and cultivated, the power of the human agent to live authentically and autonomously celebrated and encouraged. And in large measure reason is honored, autonomy is celebrated. But the prevailing rhetoric is not translated into educational policy. Quite the reverse, the actual trend of developments makes more and more difficult the achievement of promised goals. The Socratic ideal of the examined life gives way to an educational process that rewards academic imperialism, fits individuals to socially needed functional slots, and by means of paternal manipulation, adapts students for that conformity to the conventional wisdom which a society devoted to consensus and minimal disturbance of the social order requires.

But academic administrators, no more than political leaders, can escape the impact of the dialectic of disorder. Youngsters who are promised one thing, given another, and provided with enough of the intellectual and moral resources to realize that they have been defrauded will, at least occasionally, take it out on the "system." And well they should.

Disraeli's aphorism, "Any man who is not a radical in his twenties lacks a heart, while any man who remains a radical after thirty lacks a head," is, in its application to the United States, only half right. The tragedy of student radicalism is not that it exists, but that it so quickly atrophies. How could it be otherwise? Student radicals have been deprived to the same extent as their more conservative contemporaries of systematic training in the disciplines of reason and of exposure to morally serious models whose notion of "responsibility" does not preclude radical dissent. No group in higher education is more massively victimized than undergraduates—who suffer most from the inverted system of priorities that rewards organizational skills more than research, research more than graduate teaching, graduate teaching more than undergraduate teaching, the teaching of undergraduate honor students more than the teaching of those whose need for skilled and dedicated teachers is greatest.

If life in the multiversity is too often fraudulent, it at least provides the increasingly essential passport to the fulfillment of those more material aspirations that American society encourages one to have. Hence, the fact that millions are excluded from the privileges of higher education for economic reasons alone is doubly scandalous. Not only are these persons deprived of even the illusion of participating in what is promised by American rhetoric, they are also excluded from the material opportunities necessary to participate in the reality of commercial success. And even when opportunities are available, inadequate early education deprives millions of others of developing either the motivation or the necessary skills for achieving what is conventionally termed "success" in more advanced schooling.

This is not to deny that the United States is doing better than most in educating youth. But for a nation possessing our resources, today's best is at least a light-year away from being good enough. Thus, we have another American dilemma—bad educational processes, inequitably accessible, rationalized by an almost empty rhetoric of educational ideals.

4. Conditions of Work

Due primarily to industrial organization and the unprecedented period of relative prosperity this nation has enjoyed since the beginning of World War

II, the opportunity to exercise power arbitrarily has greatly diminished in our work-places. This abatement of industrial tyranny is due primarily to the creation of a system of industrial due process that, though far from being comprehensive, does protect most blue- and white-collar workers. This system of due process—and not rising wages and salaries—is trade unionism's major achievement. Ask any fairly sophisticated group of leaders from union locals, as I have done, and they will tell you that this is so.

But if due process is an achievement, and a historic agenda that remains to be completed, there is another problem that has hardly been perceived, let alone attacked. For, though the work-place is not the theater of tyrannical exercise of power in its more blatant forms (e.g., sweatshops, company stores, Pinkertons, brutal foremen, etc., are gradually disappearing), it is the place where life is lived in its most routine, uncreative, spirit-searing—in a word, dehumanized—forms.

In an article in which he brilliantly analyzes the impact of modern industrial conditions on workers, Harvey Swados suggests that until workers acquire control of production standards, the very rules of the industrial game, no matter how impartially applied, will perpetuate and aggravate this dehumanizing aspect of the work process.[63] (Shades of early Marx.) For the company's primary concern is to increase profits. When wages, fringe benefits, and the more general conditions of work are rigidly prescribed by collective bargaining agreement, the competitive pressures with which the company will normally deal will force management to do one of two things: make technological improvements that eliminate jobs or speed up the work process. The threat of the former gives them a lever by which they can achieve the latter. The imperatives of speed-up require the elimination of all those "frictional" concessions that mitigate efficiency. Moreover, the very existence of due process removes the last reservation the conscientious manager might have about authorizing a speed-up. It actually permits him to treat the worker like a machine with good conscience. For the worker has his contract and is guaranteed his day in court, should he disagree with the manager's application of its provisions. Doesn't he?

Once again the dialectic of disorder operates with a ruthless impartiality. Unless trade unions take appropriate steps, the day is coming when most strikes will be unofficial and directed not against employers, but against labor leadership itself. For, in the very nature of the case, "responsible" union leadership "must" support employers in their legitimate application of contractual provisions and therefore often assist marginal producers to survive by stretching points in their favor, both during and after negotiations. But the rhetoric of the trade union movement proclaims that the trade union leader is a worker's best friend. Confronted by the gap between that rhetoric and the dehumanized reality of the work process, there will be disorder within the industrial community. And all the decent and respectable members of the professional middle class will decry the "irresponsibility" of the "greedy" workers.

Liberalism's course is clear. It must reinterpret and apply the moral insights of older syndicalist theorists of industrial democracy, like G. D. H. Cole and John Dewey. For in the industrial community, as in the larger political community, protection of human rights requires democratic process.

5. Legal Justice

If due process is close to having been realized in that part of industry which is organized, it is far from having been achieved within the formal structures of the law. The legal rights of the poor, of the Negroes, and of those who profess unpopular political creeds are still too often violated. This comes about partly through unequal administration of existing rules, but more often through the social prejudice that influences the very construction of rules of legal process.

Almost all executions are of persons that come from deprived backgrounds. Indigents rarely get adequate legal counsel; and when they do, they often obtain that counsel after their rights have already been violated in the pretrial process. The Imbau method of interrogation, now widely used by police, is refined brainwashing. The drawing of juries and grand juries is often so contaminated by racial and social prejudice that there is little possibility of a fair trial. Standards of mitigation and criminal responsibility all favor the more socially respectable members of the community. And the severity of the sentences that American justices often hand out are an international scandal.

Conditions of penal servitude and rules of legal commitment frequently violate the most basic principles of liberalism. In the guise of *treatment*, the individual's basic right to freedom of choice, with all the fateful consequences for good and ill in his own life and in the life of society, is violated. Reform is all right when the process and aim is the development of the virtues of a free citizen, not when it masks an effort to manipulate the criminal or patient into conformity. In the guise of liberal reform, commitment to mental institutions has become a thoroughly illiberal device for getting obnoxious persons out of sight and under guard.

One is not less a manipulating tyrant if he makes his appearance as warden, psychiatrist, prison guard, hospital attendant, hospital administrator, or social worker. To no social evil is the basic thrust of liberal theory more definite and more important. For if, in the name of abstract justice, morally committed persons will not protect a person to whom family and neighbor are likely to be indifferent, who will?

It is, therefore, not enough to acknowledge real virtues in the existing system of law, or the substantial progress that has been made in the last half century. Liberals must devise means of dealing with the extremely recalcitrant problems that remain.

6. Urban and Rural Life

As antiseptic suburbs grow, and the decay of central cities is accelerated by materialism, exhaust, and rapacious landlords, the natural setting in which the dialectic of disorder can play itself out is created.

The problem of creating a decent physical environment for urban Americans has become so acute that the President [Lyndon Johnson, in 1965] has created the Department of Urban Affairs [now known as the Department of Housing and Urban Development] and has proposed a Department of Transportation [created in 1966]. But no administrative gimmick, nor any of the Administration's current proposals for remedying the situation, has any prospect of correcting the basic problem—entrenched property interests that generally have the power to kill any decent measure of reform, and in pursuit of more profits almost invariably exercise that power in ways that subordinate or ignore considerations of aesthetics, health, and morality. Urban renewal is an anodyne that generally benefits middle-income groups more than lower-income people who are displaced by the public projects. Desegregation by law seems only to hasten segregation in fact in urban school districts. And the ugliness of the central city is mitigated only by the central city businessmen's efforts to lure the shopping-center crowd back through "beautification" of their surroundings.

7. Cumulative Impact

Liberalism is concerned not only that a person have freedom to do those things he prefers, but that what he prefers result from the fullest possible exposure to the existing range of possibilities. For only then can the freedom to choose in a deliberative way be assured. Only then can we have any reasonable assurance that choice is a fulfillment, and not a waste of a person's power.

Liberals must tread a delicate line between cultural authoritarianism and cultural liberation—but in the name of the latter they must criticize the cultural marketplace that so restricts choice that what exists today comes close to being a cultural wasteland. Those who have the time and money, and know where to look, can find the cultural products they are seeking. But most ordinary Americans with relatively educated tastes find that they are discriminated against in a most egregious fashion. Here, as always, commercial criteria conflict sharply with the deliberative and aesthetic criteria that mark the difference between amusement and intensely human experience.

This is not to say that any male with a Ph.D., gonads, and a masculine ego is incapable of enjoying half-nude women and Western bravado very much. But during any given evening, during any given hour, both he and his female counterpart should like at least to have the opportunity to taste aesthetically and intellectually more venturesome fare than is available on radio and television in most places. Yet, in the final analysis, it must be admitted that the debasement of taste in this country is not the primary responsibility of those who presently control the media of mass communication. With the best will in the world, and many active in the mass media have very good will, they are constrained by conditions of the market. Defiance would take greater social and financial courage than is normally allotted to businessmen. These conditions are the cumulative product of institutional derangements described in all that has preceded. If an individual's life were rich in other respects, he would normally neither need to escape by consuming debased cultural fare, nor suffer harm or loss if he did. It is against the background of dehumanization from cradle to grave that the provision of special cultural opportunities takes on special importance.

The impact of the conditions I have described on our cultural lives is bad; their cumulative effect on the texture of the whole of American life is disastrous. The gap between rhetoric and reality is so wide, the values actually operative so unrelated to biological, intellectual, and spiritual development in its fullest sense, that an authentically human existence for most Americans is an impossibility. Perhaps most disastrous of all is that the operative criteria of public esteem, on which one's self-esteem and self-respect are so dependent, are sufficiently remote from the rhetoric of morality, intellect, and aesthetics proclaimed on ceremonial occasions that the very possibility of living a life of integrity is deeply eroded when it is not destroyed. This is the common experience of the sensitive youngsters an older generation does not permit itself to understand fully. Understanding would require these older persons to face the lies that have controlled and impoverished their own lives. An older person cannot normally be expected to admit this to himself. For error, persistently pursued, traps the human mind. The more fateful the error, the more complete the entrapment. And so human error normally enlarges itself. The parent who has guided the child mistakenly redoubles his effort to "bring the child to his senses." The President who has guided his nation mistakenly does the same. The fault must be made to lie elsewhere—for sanity's sake.

Our spiritual, educational, and political leaders celebrate "freedom"; but they too often mean "bend your knee to power and consensus." They proclaim "democracy"; but they too often mean submission to the existing structure of corporate power. They call for "honesty, truth, and morality"; but they too often practice deception, hypocrisy, and ruthless violation of the rights of others in "patriotic" pursuit of policy aims "vital to the national interest." They debase the quality of the democratic process and attribute what they do to "love of country."

Where once the basic power and prerogatives of privileged elites was maintained primarily through more naked exercise of power, reliance is increasingly placed instead on the effort to limit the mind's power rationally to understand public policy. The result is extremism on the Right, and manipulated consensus in the middle.

What can a person of the Left who values authenticity do in the light of such conditions except grow progressively alienated from our predominantly middle-class culture—and, quite incidentally, grow long fingernails and a beard?

What's Bugging the Students

IRVING KRISTOL

No one, except perhaps a few college administrators, mourns the passing of "the Silent Generation." But it must be said in its favor that at least one knew what the American university students of the 1950s were silent about, and why. They were conformists for plain, indeed obvious and traditional, conformist reasons. We may have been distressed and vexed by this conformism; we were not mystified by it; whereas we are very much mystified by the nonconformism of the students of the Sixties.

Many of the same middle-aged critics who so fervently and eloquently condemned the Silent Generation are now considerably upset and puzzled at the way students are "misbehaving" these days. One wanted the young to be idealistic, perhaps even somewhat radical, possibly even a bit militant—but not like this! It used to be said that the revolution devours its children. It now appears that these children have devoured this revolution.

What is it all about? One thing is fairly clear: the teach-ins, the sit-ins, the lay-downs, the mass picketing, and all the rest are not *merely* about Vietnam, or civil rights, or the size of classes at Berkeley, or the recognition of Red China. They are about these issues surely, and most sincerely. But there is, transparently, a passion behind the protests that refuses to be satisfied by the various topics which incite it. This passion reaches far beyond politics, as we ordinarily understand that term. Anyone who believes the turbulence will subside once we reach a settlement in Vietnam is in for a rude surprise. Similarly, anyone who thinks of present-day campus radicalism as a kind of over-zealous political liberalism, whose extremism derives from nothing more than youthful high spirits, is deceiving himself. What we are witnessing is an event *in* American politics, but not *of* it.

Indeed, one of the most striking features of the new radicalism on the campus is that it is, in one sense, so apolitical. It is a strange experience to see a radical mood in search of a radical program; it is usually very much the other way around. These young American radicals are in the historically unique position of not being able to demand *a single piece of legislation* from their government—their "platform" is literally without one legislative plank. Their passion for "freedom now" coexists with a remarkable indifference to everything the United States government is doing, or might do, in this direction.

If one read every campus leaflet published these past two years and attended every campus or off-campus demonstration, and knew only what one learned from these sources, one would hardly be aware that the Johnson Administration had enacted in the area of civil rights the most far-reaching reforms in a century of legislative history. There has been no campus meeting to celebrate the passage of the Civil Rights Act or the Voting Rights Act. There has not even been any meeting criticizing these laws for "not going far enough." It's as if nothing had happened—or, to put it more precisely, as if whatever happens in Washington has nothing to do with the world the students live and act in.

The same sort of thing is to be seen with regard to the War on Poverty, a topic upon which students will declaim passionately and with unquestionable sincerity. But it seems that their passion is so pure, their sensibility so fine, that these would be violated by a consideration of anything so vulgar as how to get more money into poor people's pockets. The recent increase in Social Security and the Medicare bill made their way through Congress without the benefit of so much as a benevolent nod from the campuses. Whenever I have mentioned this legislation in conversation, I have received an icy stare of incomprehension and disdain, as if I were some kind of political idiot who actually believed what he read in the New York *Times.*

Even in the single area where one would most expect specific and tangible proposals of reform, the organization of the multiversity, these have not made their appearance. For an entire year the students of the University of California at Berkeley have given dramatic evidence of dissatisfaction with their university experience—and does anyone know specifically what they would like, by way of improvement? The university officials certainly don't know, nor do the Regents, nor do the faculty. Some outsiders *think* they know. Berkeley is too large, they say, too anonymous; there is no possibility of a face-to-face community of scholars, young and old. This is true enough. But the Riverside branch of this same university is a small liberal arts college, with great intimacy and comfort, and for the past decade it has had much difficulty in attracting enough students. They all want to go to Berkeley, and the reason, they will explain, is: "That is where the action is."

The denunciations of the multiversity suspiciously resemble the way New Yorkers excoriate "megalopolis"—having come there in the first place, and determinedly remaining there, for no other reason than that New York *is* a megalopolis. All Americans will always insist that they adore small towns and detest great cities, but the movement of population from towns to cities remains strangely unaffected. And Berkeley, even today, has far more student applications than it can handle; one might even say, *especially* today, for I understand that the number of applications has, in fact, slightly increased.

No, the upsurge of left-wing sentiment and left-wing opinion on the American campus today is not the sort of thing progressive parents and educators had in mind ten years ago when they benevolently urged students to become "socially committed" and "more idealistic." They naively wished them to have intelligent discussions of Vietnam, not to hurl insults and epithets at Averell Harriman (as happened at Cornell), or tear up their draft cards, or laud the Viet Cong. They wished them to be urbane and tolerant about sex, not to carry placards with dirty words, or demand the sale of contraceptives in the college bookstore. They wished them to be concerned for civic and social equality for the Negro, not to denounce "white America" as a pious fraud, whose "integration" did not differ essentially from South Africa's apartheid, or express sympathy with a mindless (if occasionally eloquent) black nationalism. They wished—they wished, in short, that their children be just like them, only a wee bit bolder and more enlightened. Instead, these children are making it very clear that being just like their parents, progressive or not, is the fate they wish most desperately to avoid.

And this, I think, is the crux of the matter. The new student radicalism is so fundamentally at odds with our conventional political categories because it is, above all, an *existentialist* revolt. The term is unfortunately chic, and ambiguous, too. But in this context it has a fairly definite meaning: the students are in rebellion, not so much because things are bad for them, or for others, but because things are what they are for them and for others.

Clues to the meaning of this rebellion may be found in two phrases that now appear ever more commonly in the left-wing campus vocabulary. The first is "organized America." The second is "participatory democracy."

"Organized America" is, quite simply, America, and not, as one might think, some transient bureaucratic excrescence on the body of America. As a matter of fact, today's students are immensely skillful in coping with bureaucracies and their paper work. They fill out forms and applications with a briskness and competence that startle the middle-aged observer. (I would guess that no one over the age of forty could properly fill out a college application form unless he received guidance from some kindly youngster.) What bugs the students is not these trivia but the society they emanate from—the affluent society, welfare state and all. The liberalism (and the radicalism, too) of the 1930s and 1940s has borne its fruit, and it tastes bitter to the children, setting their teeth on edge. That is why American students, amidst reasonably general prosperity and under a liberal administration that is expanding the welfare state more aggressively and successfully than anyone had thought possible, feel more "alienated" than ever before. So many college students "go left" for the same reason that so many high school students "go delinquent." *They are bored*. They see their lives laid out neatly before them; they see themselves moving ahead sedately and more or less inexorably in their professional careers; they know that with a college degree even "failure" in their careers will represent no harsh punishment; they know "it's all laid on"—and they react against this bourgeois utopia their parents so ardently strove for.

One of the unforeseen consequences of the welfare state is that it leaves so little room for personal idealism; another is that it mutes the challenge to self-definition. All this is but another way of saying that it satisfies the anxieties of the middle-aged while stifling the creative energies of the young. Practically every college student these days understands what is meant by an "identity crisis": it is one of the cliches of the Sixties. It is not, perhaps, too much to say that mass picketing on the campus is one of the last, convulsive twitches of a slowly expiring American individualism.

American youth, however, has had one grand idealistic experience: the civil rights movement. This has been the formative experience for the activists of the 1960s; it is this movement that gave them a sense of personal power and personal purpose; and it is the civil rights movement which instructed them in the tactics of civil disobedience that are now resorted to at the drop of a hat. Unfortunately, the civil rights movement has had one great drawback: so far from being a proper "dissenting" movement, it has behind it the President, Congress, the courts, the laws of the land, and a majority of public opinion. This fact helps explain why the younger militants have constantly pushed the movement toward "extremes"—for example, demanding utter, complete, and immediate *equality of condition* for the Negro, as against mere equality of opportunity.

Such equality of condition is what "freedom now" has come to mean. And since this demand cannot be fulfilled without repealing three centuries of history, and since even Lyndon Johnson hasn't figured out a way to do this, there is some satisfaction in such a maneuver. The trouble is that the students do not know how to fulfill this demand either, and are even running out of extremist slogans; which is why so many of them are receptive to the idea of switching their attention to Vietnam, where they can be more splendidly, less ambiguously, in "the opposition."

A second theme of student radicalism today, and a polar twin to the concept of "organized America," is the idea of "participatory democracy." This is a vague notion, but a dynamic one. It expresses a profound hostility toward, and proposes an alternative to, everything that is impersonal, manipulative, "organized" in the American political process. Indeed, many of these students simply dismiss American democracy as a sham, a game played by the "power structure" for its own amusement and in its own interests. *True* democracy, they insist, can only mean direct democracy, where the people's will is expressed and legislated by the people themselves rather than by elected representatives, most of whom achieve office by deceit and retain office through the substantial support offered them by the vested interests.

One is reminded by this of nothing so much as the Russian Narodniki ("populists," our textbooks call them) of the end of the nineteenth century. They, too, were largely middle-class students who selflessly turned their backs on the careers the Czarist bureaucracy offered them. They, too, "returned to the people," leaving the fleshpots of Petrograd for the villages of the interior, much as our students leave comfortable homes in New York or Chicago for southern ghettos and slums. And they, too, were hostile to the nascent liberal institutions of their day, seeing political salvation only in a transformed and redeemed people rather than in improvements in any kind of system of representative government. It is also interesting to recall that, though they were as individuals the gentlest and most humane of their time, they nevertheless believed in the justice and efficacy of terrorism against the status quo and assassination against its spokesmen.

The analogy is, of course, very superficial: the United States today is not Czarist Russia of yesterday. But it is nevertheless illuminating, because it helps reveal the inner logic of the idea of "participatory democracy," a logic which proceeds from the most exemplary democratic premises to the most illiberal conclusions. Though few students these days learn it in their social studies course, the Founding Fathers of the American republic were exceedingly familiar with the idea of "participatory democracy"; as a matter of fact, this was what the word "democracy" usually meant prior to 1789. They rejected "participatory democracy" (they called it "direct democracy") in favor of "representative government" for two reasons. First, they didn't see how it could work in so large and complex a nation, as against a small city-state. Second, and more important, they thought it inconsistent with the idea of free government—that is, a government that respected the liberties of the individual. For participatory democracy requires that all people be fit to govern; and this in turn requires that all people *be made* fit to govern, by rigid and uniform educational training, constant public indoctrination, close supervision of private morals and beliefs, and so forth. No legislator can be as free as a private citizen, and to make all the people legislators is willy-nilly to abolish the category of private citizen altogether.

This, of course, is exactly what the Communists do, after their own fashion. They claim to exemplify a truer, more "direct," more "participatory," more "popular" democracy than is to be found in the representative institutions of the bourgeois West. The claim has a certain plausibility, in that regimes established by mass movements and mass revolutions certainly "involve the people" more than does any merely elected government. The semblance of "involvement" is perpetuated, as we know, through the mass organizations of the Communist state, and the fact that it is done under compulsion, and becomes more of a farce with every passing Communist year, is one of the inner contradictions both of the Communist system and of the myth of direct democracy itself.

These contradictions our left-wing students are not entirely unaware of. Though many of them are, to one degree or another, either pro-Communist or belligerently "neutralist," theirs is a very qualified and unconventional version of this attitude; which is why conventional anti-Communist propaganda tends to pass them by. They are, for instance, extraordinarily uninterested in the Soviet Union, and they become ever less interested to the degree that the Soviet Union liberalizes its regime—that is to say, to the extent that the Soviet Union becomes merely another "organized" system of rule.

What they seek is a pure and self-perpetuating popular revolution, not a "planned economy" or anything like that. And this is why they are so attracted to Castro's Cuba and Mao's China, countries where the popular revolution has not yet become "bourgeoisified." As for mass terror in Cuba and China— well, this actually may be taken as a kind of testimony to the ardor and authenticity of the regime's revolutionary fervor. Our radical students, like other radical students before them, find it possible to be genuinely heartsick at the injustices and brutalities of American society, while blandly approving of injustice and brutality committed elsewhere in the name of "the revolution."

Like other radical student generations before them, they are going to discover one day that their revolution, too, has been betrayed, that "organized society" is what revolutions establish as well as destroy. One hopes they will not be made too miserable by their disillusionment. One also hopes, it must be added, that they won't make *us* too miserable before that day arrives.

The Making of the Constitution

It would probably have astonished the framers of the Constitution if they had been told that the document they were drafting in the summer of 1787 would continue as the basic framework of government for their descendents in an age of communications satellites and moon landings. And yet, with comparatively little formal change, the Constitution has endured to govern Americans two hundred years after its birth.

Such longevity might not have pleased Thomas Jefferson, who once argued that the Constitution ought to be rewritten each generation to prevent the dead from governing the living. The Constitution has come closer to fulfilling John Marshall's hope that it endure for ages to come. And yet, the Constitution's survival ultimately might not have displeased Jefferson, if he could have appreciated the extent to which it has become a "living" Constitution, quite capable of being interpreted and amended to accommodate the forces of change in twentieth-century America. In this regard the Founding Fathers built perhaps better than they knew.

John P. Roche's article on the Founding Fathers offers a provocative interpretation of the differences which emerged during the Constitutional Convention, and yet it does not minimize the degree of consensus which underlay the delegates' deliberations—a consensus without which the final compromises would not have been possible.

Professor Roche clearly points out James Madison's "quest for a unitary central government" which has eluded many scholars of the Constitutional Convention. In "Madison's Essentials of a 'New System,' " John S. Vanderoef makes use of Madison's pre-Convention correspondence to substantiate Roche's contention. As subsequently incorporated in the Virginia Plan put forth at the Convention by Edmund Randolph, Madison's proposals were designed to eliminate as completely as possible the basis of government upon which the Articles of Confederation rested, that is, state sovereignty. Madison hoped to achieve a restructuring of government through the implementation of three major changes: (1) establishment of representation on the basis of population rather than on state equality, (2) constitutional incorporation of a national veto power over state legislation, and (3) ratification of the Constitution by the people, confirming the populace, and not the state governments, as the legitimate source of authority and the ultimate location of sovereignty.

The Constitution created a new system of government, a federal system which was a "compromise" between the consolidated one-nation government envisioned by the Virginia Plan and the perpetuation of the state sovereignty of the Articles of Confederation embodied in the New Jersey Plan. Alpheus T. Mason, in his scholarly "The Nature of Our Federal Union Reconsidered," asks the question, "Did not the Founding Fathers, with noble motives and good intentions, plant in the Constitution itself a time bomb that, after 1860, burst the nation asunder in civil war?" The "time bomb," according to Mason, was the doctrine that the Constitution was not founded upon the people but upon a compact among the states—a claim used to justify secession and ultimately civil war. Was this "time bomb" inherent in the Constitution itself or was it the result of an "ambiguity" that "lay not so much in the Constitution" as in its exegesis, particularly by James Madison in *The Federalist*? Mason's article is a major contribution toward an understanding of the differences leading to the tragedy of a Civil War which threatened the very existence of the government of "We, the People."

The Founding Fathers:
A Reform Caucus in Action

JOHN P. ROCHE

Over the last century and a half, the work of the Constitutional Convention and the motives of the Founding Fathers have been analyzed under a number of different ideological auspices. To one generation of historians, the hand of God was moving in the assembly; under a later dispensation, the dialectic (at various levels of philosophical sophistication) replaced the Deity: "relationships of production" moved into the niche previously reserved for Love of Country. Thus in counterpoint to the Zeitgeist, the Framers have undergone miraculous metamorphoses: at one time acclaimed as liberals and bold social engineers, today they appear in the guise of sound Burkean conservatives, men who in our time would subscribe to *Fortune*, look to Walter Lippmann for political theory, and chuckle patronizingly at the antics of Barry Goldwater. The implicit assumption is that if James Madison were among us, he would be President of the Ford Foundation, while Alexander Hamilton would chair the Committee for Economic Development.

The "Fathers" have thus been admitted to our best circles; the revolutionary ferocity which confiscated all Tory property in reach and populated New Brunswick with outlaws has been converted by the "Miltown School" of American historians into a benign dedication to "consensus" and "prescriptive rights." The Daughters of the American Revolution have, through the ministrations of Professors Boorstin, Hartz, and Rossiter, at last found ancestors worthy of their descendants. It is not my purpose here to argue that the "Fathers" were, in fact, radical revolutionaries; that proposition has been brilliantly demonstrated by Robert R. Palmer in his *Age of the Democratic Revolution*. My concern is with the further position that not only were they revolutionaries, but also they were democrats. Indeed, in my view, there is one fundamental truth about the Founding Fathers that *every* generation of Zeitgeisters has done its best to obscure: they were first and foremost superb democratic politicians. I suspect that in a contemporary setting, James Madison would be Speaker of the House of Representatives and Hamilton would be the *eminence grise* dominating (*pace* Theodore Sorenson or Sherman Adams) the Executive Office of the President. They were, with their colleagues, *political*

Reprinted by permission of the author and the publisher from John P. Roche, "The Founding Fathers: A Reform Caucus In Action," *The American Political Science Review*, Vol. LV, No. 4 (December 1961), pp. 799–816.

men—not metaphysicians, disembodied conservatives or Agents of History—and as recent research into the nature of American politics in the 1780s confirms,[1] they were committed (perhaps willy-nilly) to working within the democratic framework, within a universe of public approval. Charles Beard *and* the filiopietists to the contrary notwithstanding, the Philadelphia Convention was not a College of Cardinals or a council of Platonic guardians working within a manipulative, pre-democratic framework; it was a *nationalist* reform caucus which had to operate with great delicacy and skill in a political cosmos full of enemies to achieve the one definitive goal—popular approbation.

Perhaps the time has come, to borrow Walton Hamilton's fine phrase, to raise the Framers from immortality to mortality, to give them credit for their magnificent demonstration of the art of democratic politics. The point must be reemphasized; they *made* history and did it within the limits of consensus. There was nothing inevitable about the future in 1787; the *Zeitgeist*, that fine Hegelian technique of begging causal questions, could only be discerned in retrospect. What they did was to hammer out a pragmatic compromise which would both bolster the "National interest" and be acceptable to the people. What inspiration they got came from their collective experience as professional politicians in a democratic society. As John Dickinson put it to his fellow delegates on August 13, "Experience must be our guide. Reason may mislead us."

In this context, let us examine the problems they confronted and the solutions they evolved. The Convention has been described picturesquely as a counter-revolutionary junta and the Constitution as a *coup d'etat*,[2] but this has been accomplished by withdrawing the whole history of the movement for constitutional reform from its true context. No doubt the goals of the constitutional elite were "subversive" to the existing political order, but it is overlooked that their subversion could only have succeeded if the people of the United States endorsed it by regularized procedures. Indubitably they were "plotting" to establish a much stronger central government than existed under the Articles, but only in the sense in which one could argue equally well that John F. Kennedy was, from 1956 to 1960, "plotting" to become President. In short, on the fundamental *procedural* level, the Constitutionalists had to work according to the prevailing rules of the game. Whether they liked it or not is a topic for spiritualists—and is irrelevant: one may be quite certain that had Washington agreed to play the De Gaulle (as the Cincinnati once urged), Hamilton would willingly have held his horse, but such fertile speculation in no way alters the actual context in which events took place.

I

When the Constitutionalists went forth to subvert the Confederation, they utilized the mechanisms of political legitimacy. And the roadblocks which confronted them were formidable. At the same time, they were endowed with certain potent political assets. The history of the United States from 1786 to 1790 was largely one of a masterful employment of political expertise by the Constitutionalists as against bumbling, erratic behavior by the opponents of reform. Effectively, the Constitutionalists had to induce the states, by democratic techniques of coercion, to emasculate themselves. To be specific, if New York had refused to join the new Union, the project was doomed; yet before New York was safely in, the reluctant state legislature had *sua sponte* to take the following steps: (1) agree to send delegates to the Philadelphia Convention; (2) provide maintenance for these delegates (these were distinct stages: New Hampshire was early in naming delegates, but did not provide for their maintenance until July); (3) set up the special *ad hoc* convention to decide on ratification; and (4) concede to the decision of the *ad hoc* convention that New York should participate. New York admittedly was a tricky state, with a strong interest in a *status quo* which permitted her to exploit New Jersey and Connecticut, but the same legal hurdles existed in every state. And at the risk of becoming boring, it must be reiterated that the *only* weapon in the Constitutionalist arsenal was an effective mobilization of public opinion.

The group which undertook this struggle was an interesting amalgam of a few dedicated nationalists with the self-interested spokesmen of various parochial bailiwicks. The Georgians, for example, wanted a strong central authority to provide military protection for their huge, underpopulated state against the Creek Confederacy; Jerseymen and Connecticuters wanted to escape from economic bondage to New York; the Virginians hoped to establish a system which would give that great state its rightful place in the councils of the republic. The dominant figures in the politics of these states therefore cooperated in the call for the Convention.[3] In other states, the thrust towards national reform was taken up by opposition groups who added the "national interest" to their weapons system; in Pennsylvania, for instance, the group fighting to revise the Constitution of 1776 came out four square behind the Constitutionalists, and in New York, Hamilton and the Schuyler *ambiance* took the same tack against George Clinton.[4] There was, of course, a large element of personality in the affair: there is reason to suspect that Patrick Henry's opposition to the Convention and the Constitution was founded on his conviction that Jefferson was behind both, and a close study of local politics elsewhere would surely reveal that others supported the Constitution for the simple (and politically quite sufficient) reason that the "wrong" people were against it.

To say this is not to suggest that the Constitution rested on a foundation of impure or base motives. It is rather to argue that in politics there are no immaculate conceptions, and that in the drive for a stronger general government, motives of all sorts played a part. Few men in the history of mankind have espoused a view of the "common good" or "public interest" that militated against their private status; even Plato with all his reverence for disembodied reason managed to put philosophers on top of the pile. Thus it is not surprising that a number of diversified private interests joined to push the nationalist public interest; what would have been surprising was the absence of such a pragmatic united front. And the fact remains that, however motivated, these men did demonstrate a willingness to compromise their parochial interests in behalf of an ideal which took shape before their eyes and under their ministrations.

As Stanley Elkins and Eric McKitrick have suggested in a perceptive essay,[5] what distinguished the leaders of the Constitutionalist caucus from their enemies was a "Continental" approach to political, economic, and military issues. To the extent that they shared an institutional base of operations, it was the Continental Congress (thirty-nine of the delegates to the Federal Convention had served in Congress[6]), and this was hardly a locale which inspired respect for the state governments. Robert de Jouvenal observed French politics half a century ago and noted that a revolutionary Deputy had more in common with a nonrevolutionary Deputy than he had with the revolutionary non-Deputy;[7] similarly one can surmise that membership in the Congress under the Articles of Confederation worked to establish a continental frame of reference, that a Congressman from Pennsylvania and one from South Carolina would share a universe of discourse which provided them with a conceptual common denominator vis-à-vis their respective state legislatures. This was particularly true with respect to external affairs: the average state legislator was probably about as concerned with foreign policy then as he is today, but Congressmen were constantly forced to take the broad view of American prestige, were compelled to listen to the reports of Secretary John Jay and to the dispatches and pleas from their frustrated envoys in Britain, France, and Spain.[8] From considerations such as these, a "Continental" ideology developed which seems to have demanded a revision of our domestic institutions primarily on the ground that only by invigorating our general government could we assume our rightful place in the international arena. Indeed, an argument with great force—particularly since Washington was its incarnation—urged that our very survival in the Hobbesian jungle of world politics depended upon a reordering and strengthening of our national sovereignty.[9]

Note that I am not endorsing the "Critical Period" thesis; on the contrary, Merrill Jensen seems to me quite sound in his view that for most Americans, engaged as they were in self-sustaining agriculture, the "Critical Period" was not particularly critical.[10] In fact, the great achievement of the Constitutionalists was their ultimate success in convincing the elected representatives of a majority of the white male population that change was imperative. A small group of political leaders with a Continental vision and essentially a consciousness of the United States' *international* impotence, provided the matrix of the movement. To their standard other leaders rallied with their own parallel ambitions. Their great assets were: (1) the presence in their caucus of the one authentic American "father figure," George Washington, whose prestige was enormous;[11]

(2) the energy and talent of their leadership (in which one must include the towering intellectuals of the time, John Adams and Thomas Jefferson, despite their absence abroad), and their communications "network," which was far superior to anything on the opposition side;[12] (3) the preemptive skill which made "their" issue The Issue and kept the locally oriented opposition permanently on the defensive; and (4) the subjective consideration that these men were spokesmen of a new and compelling credo: *American* nationalism, that ill-defined but nonetheless potent sense of collective purpose that emerged from the American Revolution.

Despite great institutional handicaps, the Constitutionalists managed in the mid-1780s to mount an offensive which gained momentum as years went by. Their greatest problem was lethargy, and paradoxically, the number of barriers in their path may have proved an advantage in the long run. Beginning with the initial battle to get the Constitutional Convention called and delegates appointed, they could never relax, never let up the pressure. In practical terms, this meant that the local "organizations" created by the Constitutionalists were perpetually in movement building up their cadres for the next fight. (The word "organization" has to be used with great caution: a political organization in the United States—as in contemporary England[13]—generally consisted of a magnate and his following, or a coalition of magnates. This did not necessarily mean that it was "undemocratic" or "aristocratic," in the Aristotelian sense of the word: while a few magnates such as the Livingstons could draft their followings, most exercised their leadership without coercion on the basis of popular endorsement. The absence of organized opposition did not imply the impossibility of competition any more than low public participation in elections necessarily indicated an undemocratic suffrage.)

The Constitutionalists got the jump on the "opposition" (a collective noun: "oppositions" would be more correct) at the outset with the demand for a Convention. Their opponents were caught in an old political trap: They were not being asked to approve any specific program of reform, but only to endorse a meeting to discuss and recommend needed reforms. If they took a hard line at the first stage, they were put in the position of glorifying the *status quo* and of denying the need for *any* changes. Moreover, the Constitutionalists could go to the people with a persuasive argument for "fair play"—"How can you condemn reform before you know precisely what is involved?" Since the state legislatures obviously would have the final say on any proposals that might emerge from the Convention, the Constitutionalists were merely reasonable men asking for a chance. Besides, since they did not make any concrete proposals at that stage, they were in a position to capitalize on every sort of generalized discontent with the Confederation.

Perhaps because of their poor intelligence system, perhaps because of overconfidence generated by the failure of all previous efforts to alter the Articles,[14] the opposition awoke too late to the dangers that confronted them in 1787.

Not only did the Constitutionalists manage to get every state but Rhode Island (where politics was enlivened by a party system reminiscent of the "Blues" and the "Greens" in the Byzantine Empire)[15] to appoint delegates to Philadelphia, but when the results were in, it appeared that they dominated the delegations. Given the apathy of the opposition, this was a natural phenomenon: in an ideologically nonpolarized political atmosphere those who get appointed to a special committee are likely to be the men who supported the movement for its creation. Even George Clinton, who seems to have been the first opposition leader to awake to the possibility of trouble, could not prevent the New York legislature from appointing Alexander Hamilton—though he did have the foresight to send two of his henchmen to dominate the delegation. Incidentally, much has been made of the fact that the delegates to Philadelphia were not elected by the people; some have adduced this fact as evidence of the "undemocratic" character of the gathering. But put in the context of the time, this argument is wholly specious: the central government under the Articles was considered a creature of the component states and in all the states but Rhode Island, Connecticut, and New Hampshire, members of the national Congress were chosen by the state legislatures. This was not a consequence of elitism or fear of the mob; it was a logical extension of states' rights doctrine to guarantee that the national institution did not end-run the state legislatures and make direct contact with the people.[16]

II

With delegations safely named, the focus shifted to Philadelphia. While waiting for a quorum to assemble, James Madison got busy and drafted the so-called Randolph or Virginia Plan with the aid of the Virginia delegation. This was a political master-stroke. Its consequence was that once business got underway, the framework of discussion was established on Madison's terms. There was no interminable argument over agenda; instead the delegates took the Virginia Resolutions—"just for purposes of discussion"—as their point of departure. And along with Madison's proposals, many of which were buried in the course of the summer, went his major premise: a new start on a Constitution rather than piecemeal amendment. This was not necessarily revolutionary—a little exegesis could demonstrate that a new Constitution might be formulated as "amendments" to the Articles of Confederation—but Madison's proposal that this "lump sum" amendment go into effect after approval by nine states (the Articles required unanimous state approval for any amendment) was thoroughly subversive.[17]

Standard treatments of the Convention divide the delegates into "nationalists" and "states' righters" with various improvised shadings ("moderate nationalists," etc.), but these are *a posteriori* categories which obfuscate more than they clarify. What is striking to one who analyzes the Convention as a case study in democratic politics is the lack of clear-cut ideological divisions in the Convention. Indeed, I submit that the evidence—Madison's *Notes*, the correspondence of the delegates, and debates on ratification—indicates that this was a remarkably homogeneous body on the ideological level. Yates and Lansing, Clinton's two chaperones for Hamilton, left in disgust on July 10. (Is there anything more tedious than sitting through endless disputes on matters one deems fundamentally misconceived? It takes an iron will to spend a hot summer as an ideological *agent provocateur*.) Luther Martin, Maryland's bibulous narcissist, left on September 4 in a huff when he discovered that others did not share his self-esteem; others went home for personal reasons. But the hard core of delegates accepted a grinding regimen throughout the attrition of a Philadelphia summer precisely because they shared the Constitutionalist goal.

Basic differences of opinion emerged, of course, but these were not ideological; they were *structural*. If the so-called "states' rights" group had not accepted the fundamental purposes of the Convention, they could simply have pulled out and by doing so have aborted the whole enterprise. Instead of bolting, they returned day after day to argue and to compromise. An interesting symbol of this basic homogeneity was the initial agreement on secrecy: these professional politicians did not want to become prisoners of publicity; they wanted to retain that freedom of maneuver which is only possible when men are not forced to take public stands in the preliminary stages of negotiation.[18] There was no legal means of binding the tongues of the delegates: at any stage in the game a delegate with basic principled objections to the emerging project could have taken the stump (as Luther Martin did after his exit) and denounced the convention to the skies. Yet Madison did not even inform Thomas Jefferson in Paris of the course of the deliberations[19] and available correspondence indicates that the delegates generally observed the injunction. Secrecy is certainly uncharacteristic of any assembly marked by strong ideological polarization. This was noted at the time: the *New York Daily Advertiser*, August 14, 1787, commented that the ". . . profound secrecy hitherto observed by the Convention [we consider] a happy omen, as it demonstrates that the spirit of party on any great and essential point cannot have arisen to any height."[20]

Commentators on the Constitution who have read *The Federalist* in lieu of reading the actual debates have credited the Fathers with the invention of a sublime concept called "Federalism."[21] Unfortunately *The Federalist* is probative evidence for only one proposition: that Hamilton and Madison were inspired propagandists with a genius for retrospective symmetry. Federalism, as the theory is generally defined, was an improvisation which was later promoted into a political theory. Experts on "federalism" should take to heart the advice of David Hume, who warned in his *Of the Rise and Progress of the Arts and Sciences* that ". . . there is no subject in which we must proceed with more caution than in [history], lest we assign causes which never existed and reduce what is merely contingent to stable and universal principles." In any event, the final balance in the Constitution between the states and the nation must have come as a great disappointment to Madison, while Hamilton's unitary views are too well known to need elucidation.

It is indeed astonishing how those who have glibly designated James Madison the "father" of Federalism have overlooked the solid body of fact which indicates that he shared Hamilton's quest for a unitary central government. To be specific, they have avoided examining the clear import of the Madison-Virginia Plan,[22] and have disregarded Madison's dogged inch-by-inch retreat from the bastions of centralization. The Virginia Plan envisioned a unitary national government effectively freed from and dominant over the states. The lower house of the national legislature was to be elected directly by the people of the states with membership proportional to population. The upper house was to be selected by the lower and the two chambers would elect the executive and choose the judges. The national government would be thus cut completely loose from the states.[23]

The structure of the general government was freed from state control in a truly radical fashion, but the scope of the authority of the national sovereign as Madison initially formulated it was breathtaking—it was a formulation worthy of the Sage of Malmesbury himself. The national legislature was to be empowered to disallow the acts of state legislatures,[24] and the central government was vested, in addition to the powers of the nation under the Articles of Confederation, with plenary authority wherever ". . . the separate States are incompetent or in which the harmony of the United States may be interrupted by the exercise of individual legislation."[25] Finally, just to lock the door against state intrusion, the national Congress was to be given the power to use military force on recalcitrant states.[26] This was Madison's "model" of an ideal national government, though it later received little publicity in *The Federalist*.

The interesting thing was the reaction of the Convention to this militant program for a strong autonomous central government. Some delegates were startled, some obviously leery of so comprehensive a project of reform,[27] but nobody set off any fireworks and nobody walked out. Moreover, in the two weeks that followed, the Virginia Plan received substantial endorsement *en principe;* the initial temper of the gathering can be deduced from the approval "without debate or dissent," on May 31, of the Sixth Resolution which granted Congress the authority to disallow state legislation ". . . contravening *in its opinion* the Articles of Union." Indeed, an amendment was included to bar states from contravening national treaties.[28]

The Virginia Plan may therefore be considered, in ideological terms, as the delegates' Utopia, but as the discussions continued and became more specific, many of those present began to have second thoughts. After all, they were not residents of Utopia or guardians in Plato's Republic who could simply impose a philosophical ideal on subordinate strata of the population. They were practical politicians in a democratic society, and no matter what their private dreams might be, they had to take home an acceptable package and defend it—and their own political futures—against predictable attack. On June 14 the breaking point between dream and reality took place. Apparently realizing that under the Virginia Plan, Massachusetts, Virginia, and Pennsylvania could virtually dominate the national government—and probably appreciating that to sell this program to "the folks back home" would be impossible—the delegates from the small states dug in their heels and demanded time for a consideration of alternatives. One gets a graphic sense of the inner politics from John Dickinson's reproach to Madison: "You see the consequences of pushing things too far. Some of the members from the small States wish for two branches in the General Legislature and are friends to a good National Government; but we would sooner submit to a foreign power than . . . be deprived of an equality of suffrage in both branches of the Legislature, and thereby be thrown under the domination of the large States."[29]

The bare outline of the *Journal* entry for Tuesday, June 14, is suggestive to anyone with extensive experience in deliberative bodies. "It was moved by Mr. Patterson [*sic,* Paterson's name was one of those consistently misspelled by Madison and everybody else] seconded by Mr. Randolph that the further consideration of the report from the Committee of the whole House [endorsing the Virginia Plan] be postponed til tomorrow, and before the question for postponement was taken. It was moved by Mr. Randolph seconded by Mr. Patterson that the House adjourn."[30] The House adjourned by obvious pre-arrangement of the two principals: since the preceding Saturday when Brearley and Paterson of New Jersey had announced their fundamental discontent with the representational features of the Virginia Plan, the informal pressure had certainly been building up to slow down the steamroller. Doubtless there were extended arguments at the Indian Queen between Madison and Paterson, the latter insisting that events were moving rapidly towards a probably disastrous conclusion, towards a political suicide pact. Now the process of accommodation was put into action smoothly—and wisely, given the character and strength of the doubters. Madison had the votes, but this was one of those situations where the enforcement of mechanical majoritarianism could easily have destroyed the objectives of the majority: the Constitutionalists were in quest of a qualitative as well as a quantitative consensus. This was hardly from deference to local Quaker custom; it was a political imperative if they were to attain ratification.

III

According to the standard script, at this point the "states' rights" group intervened in force behind the New Jersey Plan, which has been characteristically portrayed as a reversion to the *status quo* under the Articles of Confederation with but minor modifications. A careful examination of the evidence indicates that only in a marginal sense is this an accurate description. It is true that the New Jersey Plan put the states back into the institutional picture, but one could argue that to do so was a recognition of political reality rather than an affirmation of states' rights. A serious case can be made that the advocates of the New Jersey Plan, far from being ideological addicts of states' rights, intended to substitute for the Virginia Plan a system which would both retain strong national power and have a chance of adoption in the states. The leading spokesman for the project asserted quite clearly that his views were based more on counsels of expediency than on principle; said Paterson on June 16: "I came here not to speak my own sentiments, but the sentiments of those who sent me. Our object is not such a Governmt. as may be best in itself, but such a one as our Constituents have authorized us to prepare, and as they will approve."[31] This is Madison's version; in Yates' transcription, there is a crucial sentence following the remarks above: "I believe that a little practical virtue is to be preferred to the finest theoretical principles, which cannot be carried into effect."[32] In his preliminary speech on June 9, Paterson had stated ". . . to the public mind we must accommodate ourselves,"[33] and in his notes for this and his later efforts as well, the emphasis is the same. The *structure* of government under the Articles should be retained:

> 2. Because it accords with the Sentiments of the People
>   [Proof:] 1. Coms. [Commissions from state legislatures defining the jurisdiction of the delegates]
>   2. News-papers—Political Barometer. Jersey never would have sent Delegates under the first [Virginia] Plan—
> Not here to sport Opinions of my own. Wt. [What] can be done. A little practicable Virtue preferrable to Theory.[34]

This was a defense of political acumen, not of states' rights. In fact, Paterson's notes of his speech can easily be construed as an argument for attaining the substantive objectives of the Virginia Plan by a sound political route, i.e., pouring the new wine in the old bottles. With a shrewd eye, Paterson queried:

> Will the Operation and Force of the [central] Govt. depend upon the mode of Representn.—No—it will depend upon the Quantum of Power lodged in the leg. ex. and judy. Departments—Give [the existing] Congress the same Powers that you intend to give the two Branches [under the Virginia Plan], and I apprehend they will act with as much Propriety and more Energy . . . [35]

In other words, the advocates of the New Jersey Plan concentrated their fire on what they held to be the *political liabilities* of the Virginia Plan—which were matters of institutional structure—rather than on the proposed scope of national authority. Indeed, the Supremacy Clause of the Constitution first saw the light of day in Paterson's Sixth Resolution; the New Jersey Plan contemplated the use of military force to secure compliance with national law; and finally Paterson made clear his view that under either the Virginia or the New Jersey systems, the general government would ". . . act on individuals and not on states."[36] From the states' rights viewpoint, this was heresy: the fundament of that doctrine was the proposition that any central government had as its constituents the states, not the people, and could only reach the people through the agency of the state government.

Paterson then reopened the agenda of the Convention, but he did so within a distinctly nationalist framework. Paterson's position was one of favoring a strong central government in principle, but opposing one which in fact *put the big states in the saddle.* (The Virginia Plan, for all its abstract merits, did very well by Virginia.) As evidence for this speculation, there is a curious and intriguing proposal among Paterson's preliminary drafts of the New Jersey Plan:

> Whereas it is necessary in Order to form the People of the U. S. of America in to a Nation, that the States should be consolidated, by which means all the Citizens thereof will become equally intitled to and will equally participate in the same Privileges and Rights . . . it is therefore resolved, that all the Lands contained within the Limits of each state individually, and of the U. S. generally be considered as constituting one Body or Mass, and be divided into thirteen or more integral parts.
>
> Resolved, That such Divisions or integral Parts shall be styled Districts.[37]

This makes it sound as though Paterson was prepared to accept a strong unified central government along the lines of the Virginia Plan if the existing states were eliminated. He may have gotten the idea from his New Jersey colleague Judge David Brearley, who on June 9 had commented that the only remedy to the dilemma over representation was ". . . that a map of the U. S. be spread out, that all the existing boundaries be erased, and that a new partition of the whole be made into 13 equal parts."[38] According to Yates, Brearley added at this point, ". . . then a government on the present [Virginia Plan] system will be just."[39]

This proposition was never pushed—it was patently unrealistic—but one can appreciate its purpose: it would have separated the men from the boys in the large-state delegations. How attached would the Virginians have been to their reform principles if Virginia were to disappear as a component geographical unit (the largest) for representational purposes? Up to this point, the Virginians had been in the happy position of supporting high ideals with that inner confidence born of knowledge that the "public interest" they endorsed would nourish their private interest. Worse, they had shown little willingness to compromise. Now the delegates from the small states announced that they were unprepared to be offered up as sacrificial victims to a "national

interest" which reflected Virginia's parochial ambition. Caustic Charles Pinckney was not far off when he remarked sardonically that ". . . the whole [con-
flict] comes to this": "Give N. Jersey an equal vote, and she will dismiss her
scruples, and concur in the Natil. system."[40] What he rather unfairly did not
add was that the Jersey delegates were not free agents who could adhere to
their private convictions; they had to take back, sponsor and risk their reputations on the reforms approved by the Convention—and in New Jersey, not
in Virginia.

Paterson spoke on Saturday, and one can surmise that over the weekend
there was a good deal of consultation, argument, and caucusing among the
delegates. One member at least prepared a full length address: on Monday
Alexander Hamilton, previously mute, rose and delivered a six-hour oration.[41]
It was a remarkably apolitical speech; the gist of his position was that *both*
the Virginia and New Jersey Plans were inadequately centralist, and he detailed a reform program which was reminiscent of the Protectorate under the
Cromwellian *Instrument of Government* of 1653. It has been suggested that
Hamilton did this in the best political tradition to emphasize the moderate
character of the Virginia Plan,[42] to give the cautious delegates something *really*
to worry about; but this interpretation seems somehow too clever. Particularly
since the sentiments Hamilton expressed happened to be completely consistent
with those he privately—and sometimes publicly—expressed throughout his
life. He wanted, to take a striking phrase from a letter to George Washington,
a "strong well mounted government";[43] in essence, the Hamilton Plan contemplated an elected life monarch, virtually free of public control, on the
Hobbesian ground that only in this fashion could strength and stability be
achieved. The other alternatives, he argued, would put policy-making at the
mercy of the passions of the mob; only if the sovereign was beyond the reach
of selfish influence would it be possible to have government in the interests
of the whole community.[44]

From all accounts, this was a masterful and compelling speech, but (aside
from furnishing John Lansing and Luther Martin with ammunition for later
use against the Constitution) it made little impact. Hamilton was simply transmitting on a different wave-length from the rest of the delegates; the latter
adjourned after his great effort, admired his rhetoric, and then returned to
business.[45] It was rather as if they had taken a day off to attend the opera.
Hamilton, never a particularly patient man or much of a negotiator, stayed
for another ten days and then left, in considerable disgust, for New York.[46]
Although he came back to Philadelphia sporadically and attended the last two
weeks of the Convention, Hamilton played no part in the laborious task of
hammering out the Constitution. His day came later when he led the New
York Constitutionalists into the savage imbroglio over ratification—an arena
in which his unmatched talent for dirty political in-fighting may well have
won the day. For instance, in the New York Ratifying Convention, Lansing

threw back into Hamilton's teeth the sentiments the latter had expressed in his June 18 oration in the Convention. However, having since retreated to the fine defensive positions immortalized in *The Federalist,* the Colonel flatly denied that he had ever been an enemy of the states, or had believed that conflict between states and nation was inexorable! As Madison's authoritative *Notes* did not appear until 1840, and there had been no press coverage, there was no way to verify his assertions, so in the words of the reporter, ". . . a warm personal altercation between [Lansing and Hamilton] engrossed the remainder of the day [June 28, 1788]."[47]

IV

On Tuesday morning, June 19, the vacation was over. James Madison led off with a long, carefully reasoned speech analyzing the New Jersey Plan which, while intellectually vigorous in its criticisms, was quite conciliatory in mood. "The great difficulty," he observed, "lies in the affair of Representation; and if this could be adjusted, all others would be surmountable."[48] (As events were to demonstrate, this diagnosis was correct.) When he finished, a vote was taken on whether to continue with the Virginia Plan as the nucleus for a new constitution: seven states voted "Yes"; New York, New Jersey, and Delaware voted "No"; and Maryland, whose position often depended on which delegates happened to be on the floor, divided.[49] Paterson, it seems, lost decisively; yet in a fundamental sense he and his allies had achieved their purpose: from that day onward, it could never be forgotten that the state governments loomed ominously in the background and that no verbal incantations could exorcise their power. Moreover, nobody bolted the convention: Paterson and his colleagues took their defeat in stride and set to work to modify the Virginia Plan, particularly with respect to its provisions on representation in the national legislature. Indeed, they won an immediate rhetorical bonus; when Oliver Ellsworth of Connecticut rose to move that the word "national" be expunged from the Third Virginia Resolution ("Resolved that a *national* Government ought to be established consisting of a *supreme* Legislative, Executive and Judiciary"[50]), Randolph agreed and the motion passed unanimously.[51] The process of compromise had begun.

For the next two weeks, the delegates circled around the problem of legislative representation. The Connecticut delegation appears to have evolved a possible compromise quite early in the debates, but the Virginians and particularly Madison (unaware that he would later be acclaimed as the prophet of "federalism") fought obdurately against providing for equal representation of states in the second chamber. There was a good deal of acrimony and at one point Benjamin Franklin—of all people—proposed the institution of a daily prayer; practical politicians in the gathering, however, were meditating more on the merits of a good committee than on the utility of Divine inter-vention. On July 2, the ice began to break when through a number of for-tuitous events[52]—and one that seems deliberate[53]—the majority against equal-ity of representation was converted into a dead tie. The Convention had reached the stage where it was "ripe" for a solution (presumably all the therapeutic speeches had been made), and the South Carolinians proposed a committee. Madison and James Wilson wanted none of it, but with only Pennsylvania dissenting, the body voted to establish a working party on the problem of representation.

The members of this committee, one from each state, were elected by the delegates—and a very interesting committee it was. Despite the fact that the Virginia Plan had held majority support up to that date, neither Madison nor Randolph was selected (Mason was the Virginian) and Baldwin of Georgia, whose shift in position had resulted in the tie, was chosen. From the com-position, it was clear that this was not to be a "fighting" committee: the emphasis in membership was on what might be described as "second-level political entrepreneurs." On the basis of the discussions up to that time, only Luther Martin of Maryland could be described as a "bitter-ender." Admittedly, some divination enters into this sort of analysis, but one does get a sense of the mood of the delegates from these choices—including the interesting selec-tion of Benjamin Franklin, despite his age and intellectual wobbliness, over the brilliant and incisive Wilson or the sharp, polemical Gouverneur Morris, to represent Pennsylvania. His passion for conciliation was more valuable at this juncture than Wilson's logical genius, or Morris' acerbic wit.

There is a common rumor that the Framers divided their time between philosophical discussions of government and reading the classics in political theory. Perhaps this is as good a time as any to note that their concerns were highly practical, that they spent little time canvassing abstractions. A number of them had some acquaintance with the history of political theory (probably gained from reading John Adams' monumental compilation *A Defense of the Constitutions of Government,*[54] the first volume of which appeared in 1786), and it was a poor rhetorician indeed who could not cite Locke, Montesquieu, or Harrington *in support* of a desired goal. Yet up to this point in the de-liberations, no one had expounded a defense of states' rights or the "separation of powers" on anything resembling a theoretical basis. It should be reiterated that the Madison model had no room either for the states or for the "separa-tion of powers": effectively *all* governmental power was vested in the national legislature. The merits of Montesquieu did not turn up until *The Federalist;* and although a perverse argument could be made that Madison's ideal was truly in the tradition of John Locke's *Second Treatise of Government,*[55] the Locke whom the American rebels treated as an honorary president was a pluralistic defender of vested rights,[56] not of parliamentary supremacy.

It would be tedious to continue a blow-by-blow analysis of the work of the delegates; the critical fight was over representation of the states and once the Connecticut Compromise was adopted on July 17, the Convention was over the hump. Madison, James Wilson, and Gouverneur Morris of New York (who was there representing Pennsylvania!) fought the compromise all the way in a last-ditch effort to get a unitary state with parliamentary supremacy. But their allies deserted them and they demonstrated after their defeat the essentially opportunist character of their objections—using "opportunist" here is a nonpejorative sense, to indicate a willingness to swallow their objections and get on with the business. Moreover, once the compromise had carried (by five states to four, with one state divided), its advocates threw themselves vigorously into the job of strengthening the general government's substantive powers—as might have been predicted, indeed, from Paterson's early statements. It nourishes an increased respect for Madison's devotion to the art of politics, to realize that this dogged fighter could sit down six months later and prepare essays for *The Federalist* in contradiction to his basic convictions about the true course the Convention should have taken.

V

Two tricky issues will serve to illustrate the later process of accommodation: The first was the institutional position of the Executive. Madison argued for an executive chosen by the National Legislature and on May 29 this had been adopted with a provision that after his seven-year term was concluded, the chief magistrate should not be eligible for reelection. In late July this was reopened and for a week the matter was argued from several different points of view. A good deal of desultory speechmaking ensued, but the gist of the problem was the opposition from two sources to election by the legislature. One group felt that the states should have a hand in the process; another small but influential circle urged direct election by the people. There were a number of proposals: election by the people, election by state Governors, by electors chosen by state legislatures, by the National Legislature (James Wilson, perhaps ironically, proposed at one point that an Electoral College be chosen by lot from the National Legislature!), and there was some resemblance to three-dimensional chess in the dispute because of the presence of two other variables, length of tenure and reeligibility. Finally, after opening, reopening, and re-reopening the debate, the thorny problem was consigned to a committee for resolution.

The Brearley Committee on Postponed Matters was a superb aggregation of talent and its compromise on the Executive was a masterpiece of political improvisation. (The Electoral College, its creation, however, had little in its favor as an *institution*—as the delegates well appreciated.) The point of departure for all discussion about the Presidency in the Convention was that in immediate terms, the problem was nonexistent; in other words, everybody present knew that under any system devised, George Washington would be President. Thus they were dealing in the future tense and to a body of working politicians the merits of the Brearley proposal were obvious: everybody got a piece of cake. (Or to put it more academically, each viewpoint could leave the Convention and argue to its constituents that it had *really* won the day.) First, the state legislatures had the right to determine the mode of selection of the electors; second, the small states received a bonus in the Electoral College in the form of a guaranteed minimum of three votes while the big states got acceptance of the principle of proportional power; third, if the state legislatures agreed (as six did in the first presidential election), the people could be involved directly in the choice of electors; and finally, if no candidate received a majority in the College, the right of decision passed to the National Legislature with each state exercising equal strength. (In the Brearley recommendation, the election went to the Senate, but a motion from the floor substituted the House; this was accepted on the ground that the Senate already had enough authority over the executive in its treaty and appointment powers.)

This compromise was almost too good to be true, and the Framers snapped it up with little debate or controversy. No one seemed to think well of the College as an *institution;* indeed, what evidence there is suggests that there was an assumption that once Washington had finished his tenure as President, the electors would cease to produce majorities and the Chief Executive would usually be chosen in the House. George Mason observed casually that the selection would be made in the House nineteen times in twenty and no one seriously disputed this point. The vital aspect of the Electoral College was that it got the Convention over the hurdle and protected everybody's interests. The future was left to cope with the problem of what to do with this Rube Goldberg mechanism.

In short, the Framers did not in their wisdom endow the United States with a College of Cardinals—the Electoral College was neither an exercise in applied Platonism nor an experiment in indirect government based on elitist distrust of the masses. It was merely a jerry-rigged improvisation which has subsequently been endowed with a high theoretical content. When an elector from Oklahoma in 1960 refused to cast his vote for Nixon (naming Byrd and Goldwater instead) on the ground that the Founding Fathers intended him to exercise his great independent wisdom, he was indulging in historical fantasy. If one were to indulge in counter-fantasy, he would be tempted to suggest that the Fathers would be startled to find the College still in operation—and perhaps even dismayed at their descendants' lack of judgment or inventiveness.[57]

The second issue on which some substantial practical bargaining took place was slavery. The morality of slavery was, by design, not at issue,[58] but in its other concrete aspects, slavery colored the arguments over taxation, commerce, and representation. The "Three-Fifths Compromise," that three-fifths of the slaves would be counted both for representation and for purposes of direct taxation (which was drawn from the past—it was a formula of Madison's utilized by Congress in 1783 to establish the basis of state contributions to the Confederation treasury) had allayed some northern fears about southern overrepresentation (no one then foresaw the trivial role that direct taxation would play in later federal financial policy), but doubts still remained. The Southerners, on the other hand, were afraid that congressional control over commerce would lead to the exclusion of slaves or to their excessive taxation as imports. Moreover, the Southerners were disturbed over "navigation acts," i.e., tariffs, or special legislation providing, for example, that exports be carried only in American ships; as a section depending upon exports, they wanted protection from the potential voracity of their commercial brethren of the eastern states. To achieve this end, Mason and others urged that the Constitution include a proviso that navigation and commercial laws should require a two-thirds vote in Congress.

These problems came to a head in late August and, as usual, were handed to a committee in the hope that, in Gouverneur Morris' words, ". . . these things may form a bargain among the Northern and Southern states."[59] The Committee reported its measures of reconciliation on August 25, and on August 29 the package was wrapped up and delivered. What occurred can best be described in George Mason's dour version (he anticipated Calhoun in his conviction that permitting navigation acts to pass by majority vote would put the South in economic bondage to the North—it was mainly on this ground that he refused to sign the Constitution):

> The Constitution as agreed to till a fortnight before the Convention rose was such a one as he would have set his hand and heart to. . . . [Until that time] The 3 New England States were constantly with us in all questions . . . so that it was these three States with the 5 Southern ones against Pennsylvania, Jersey and Delaware. With respect to the importation of slaves, [decision-making] was left to Congress. This disturbed the two Southernmost States who knew that Congress would immediately suppress the importation of slaves. Those two States therefore struck up a bargain with the three New England States. If they would join to admit slaves for some years, the two Southern-most States would join in changing the clause which required the ⅔ of the Legislature in any vote [on navigation acts]. It was done.[60]

On the floor of the Convention there was a virtual love feast on this happy occasion. Charles Pinckney of South Carolina attempted to overturn the committee's decision, when the compromise was reported to the Convention, by insisting that the South needed protection from the imperialism of the northern states. But his southern colleagues were not prepared to rock the boat and

General C. C. Pinckney arose to spread oil on the suddenly ruffled waters; he admitted that:

> It was in the true interest of the S[outhern] States to have no regulation of commerce; but considering the loss brought on the commerce of the Eastern States by the Revolution, their liberal conduct towards the views of South Carolina [on the regulation of the slave trade] and the interests the weak Southn. States had in being united with the strong Eastern states, he thought it proper that no fetters should be imposed on the power of making commercial regulations; *and that his constituents, though preju-diced against the Eastern States, would be reconciled to this liberality.* He had himself prejudices agst the Eastern States before he came here, but would acknowledge that he had found them as liberal and candid as any men whatever. (Italics added)[61]

Pierce Butler took the same tack, essentially arguing that he was not too happy about the possible consequences, but that a deal was a deal.[62] Many southern leaders were later—in the wake of the "Tariff of Abominations"—to rue this day of reconciliation; Calhoun's *Disquisition on Government* was little more than an extension of the argument in the Convention against per-mitting a congressional majority to enact navigation acts.[63]

VI

Drawing on their vast collective political experience, utilizing every weapon in the politician's arsenal, looking constantly over their shoulders at their con-stituents, the delegates put together a Constitution. It was a makeshift affair; some sticky issues (for example, the qualification of voters) they ducked en-tirely; others they mastered with that ancient instrument of political sagacity, studied ambiguity (for example, citizenship), and some they just overlooked. In this last category, I suspect, fell the matter of the power of the federal courts to determine the constitutionality of acts of Congress. When the judicial article was formulated (Article III of the Constitution), deliberations were still in the stage where the legislature was endowed with broad power under the Randolph formulation, authority which by its own terms was scarcely amen-able to judicial review. In essence, courts could hardly determine when ". . . the separate States are incompetent or . . . the harmony of the United States may be interrupted"; the National Legislature, as critics pointed out, was free to define its own jurisdiction. Later the definition of legislative au-thority was changed into the form we know, a series of stipulated powers, *but the delegates never seriously reexamined the jurisdiction of the judiciary under this new limited formulation.*[64] All arguments on the intention of the Framers in this matter are thus deductive and *a posteriori,* though some obviously make more sense than others.[65]

The Framers were busy and distinguished men, anxious to get back to their families, their positions, and their constituents, not members of the French Academy devoting a lifetime to a dictionary. They were trying to do an important job, and do it in such a fashion that their handiwork would be acceptable to very diverse constituencies. No one was rhapsodic about the final document, but it was a beginning, a move in the right direction, and one they had reason to believe the people would endorse. In addition, since they had modified the impossible amendment provisions of the Articles (the requirement of unanimity which could always be frustrated by "Rogues Island") to one demanding approval by only three-quarters of the states, they seemed confident that gaps in the fabric which experience would reveal could be rewoven without undue difficulty.

So with a neat phrase introduced by Benjamin Franklin (but devised by Gouverneur Morris)[66] which made their decision sound unanimous, and an inspired benediction by the Old Doctor urging doubters to doubt their own infallibility, the Constitution was accepted and signed. Curiously, Edmund Randolph, who had played so vital a role throughout, refused to sign, as did his fellow Virginian George Mason and Elbridge Gerry of Massachusetts. Randolph's behavior was eccentric, to say the least—his excuses for refusing his signature have a factitious ring even at this late date; the best explanation seems to be that he was afraid that the Constitution would prove to be a liability in Virginia politics, where Patrick Henry was burning up the countryside with impassioned denunciations. Presumably, Randolph wanted to check the temper of the populace before he risked his reputation, and perhaps his job, in a fight with both Henry and Richard Henry Lee.[67] Events lend some justification to this speculation: after much temporizing and use of the conditional subjunctive tense, Randolph endorsed ratification in Virginia and ended up getting the best of both worlds.

Madison, despite his reservations about the Constitution, was the campaign manager in ratification. His first task was to get the Congress in New York to light its own funeral pyre by approving the "amendments" to the Articles and sending them on to the state legislatures. Above all, momentum had to be maintained. The anti-Constitutionalists, now thoroughly alarmed and no novices in politics, realized that their best tactic was attrition rather than direct opposition. Thus they settled on a position expressing qualified approval but calling for a second Convention to remedy various defects (the one with the most demagogic appeal was the lack of a Bill of Rights). Madison knew that to accede to this demand would be equivalent to losing the battle, nor would he agree to conditional approval (despite wavering even by Hamilton). This was an all-or-nothing proposition: national salvation or national impotence with no intermediate positions possible. Unable to get congressional approval, he settled for second best: a unanimous resolution of Congress transmitting the Constitution to the states for whatever action they saw fit to take. The opponents then moved from New York and the Congress, where they had attempted to attach amendments and conditions, to the states for the final battle.[68]

At first the campaign for ratification went beautifully: within eight months after the delegates set their names to the document, eight states had ratified. Only in Massachusetts had the result been close (187–168). Theoretically, a ratification by one more state convention would set the new government in motion, but in fact until Virginia and New York acceded to the new Union, the latter was a fiction. New Hampshire was the next to ratify; Rhode Island was involved in its characteristic political convulsions (the legislature there sent the Constitution out to the towns for decision by popular vote and it got lost among a series of local issues);[69] North Carolina's convention did not meet until July and then postponed a final decision. This is hardly the place for an extensive analysis of the conventions of New York and Virginia. Suffice it to say that the Constitutionalists clearly outmaneuvered their opponents, forced them into impossible political positions, and won both states narrowly. The Virginia Convention could serve as a classic study in effective floor management: Patrick Henry had to be contained, and a reading of the debates discloses a standard two-stage technique. Henry would give a four- or five-hour speech denouncing some section of the Constitution on every conceivable ground (the federal district, he averred at one point, would become a haven for convicts escaping from state authority!);[70] when Henry subsided, "Mr. Lee of Westmoreland" would rise and literally pole-axe him with sardonic invective (when Henry complained about the militia power, "Lighthorse Harry" really punched below the belt: observing that while the former Governor had been sitting in Richmond during the Revolution, *he* had been out in the trenches with the troops and thus felt better qualified to discuss military affairs).[71] Then the gentlemanly Constitutionalists (Madison, Pendleton, and Marshall) would pick up the matters at issue and examine them in the light of reason.

Indeed, modern Americans who tend to think of James Madison as a rather dessicated character should spend some time with this transcript. Probably Madison put on his most spectacular demonstration of nimble rhetoric in what might be called "The Battle of the Absent Authorities." Patrick Henry in the course of one of his harangues alleged that Jefferson was known to be opposed to Virginia's approving the Constitution. This was clever: Henry hated Jefferson, but was prepared to use any weapon that came to hand. Madison's riposte was superb: First, he said that with all due respect to the great reputation of Jefferson, he was not in the country and therefore could not formulate an adequate judgment; second, no one should utilize the reputation of an outsider—the Virginia Convention was there to think for itself; third, if there were to be recourse to outsiders, the opinions of George Washington should certainly be taken into consideration; and finally, he knew from privileged personal communications from Jefferson that in fact the latter *strongly favored* the Constitution.[72] To devise an assault route into this rhetorical fortress was literally impossible.

VII

The fight was over; all that remained now was to establish the new frame of government in the spirit of its framers. And who were better qualified for this task than the Framers themselves? Thus victory for the Constitution meant simultaneous victory for the Constitutionalists; the anti-Constitutionalists either capitulated or vanished into limbo—soon Patrick Henry would be offered a seat on the Supreme Court[73] and Luther Martin would be known as the Federalist "bull-dog."[74] And irony of ironies, Alexander Hamilton and James Madison would shortly accumulate a reputation as the formulators of what is often alleged to be our political theory, the concept of "federalism." Also, on the other side of the ledger, the arguments would soon appear over what the Framers "really meant"; while these disputes have assumed the proportions of a big scholarly business in the last century, they began almost before the ink on the Constitution was dry. One of the best early ones featured Hamilton versus Madison on the scope of presidential power, and other Framers characteristically assumed positions in this and other disputes on the basis of their political convictions.

Probably our greatest difficulty is that we know so much more about what the Framers *should have meant* than they themselves did. We are intimately acquainted with the problems that their Constitution should have been designed to master; in short, we have read the mystery story backwards. If we are to get the right "feel" for their time and their circumstances, we must, in Maitland's phrase, ". . . think ourselves back into a twilight." Obviously, no one can pretend completely to escape from the solipsistic web of his own environment, but if the effort is made, it is possible to appreciate the past roughly on its own terms. The first step in this process is to abandon the academic premise that because we can ask a question, there must be an answer.

Thus we can ask what the Framers meant when they gave Congress the power to regulate interstate and foreign commerce, and we emerge, reluctantly perhaps, with the reply that (Professor Crosskey to the contrary notwithstanding)[75] they may not have known what they meant, that there may not have been any semantic consensus. The Convention was not a seminar in analytic philosophy or linguistic analysis. Commerce was *commerce*—and if different interpretations of the word arose, later generations could worry about the problem of definition. The delegates were in a hurry to get a new government established; when definitional arguments arose, they characteristically took refuge in ambiguity. If different men voted for the same proposition for varying reasons, that was politics (and still is); if later generations were unsettled by this lack of precision, that would be their problem.

There was a good deal of definitional pluralism with respect to the problems the delegates did discuss, but when we move to the question of extrapolated intentions, we enter the realm of spiritualism. When men in our time, for instance, launch into elaborate talmudic exegesis to demonstrate that federal aid to parochial schools is (or is not) in accord with the intentions of the men who established the Republic and endorsed the Bill of Rights, they are engaging in historical Extra-Sensory Perception. (If one were to join this E. S. P. contingent for a minute, he might suggest that the hard-boiled politicians who wrote the Constitution and Bill of Rights would chuckle scornfully at such an invocation of authority: obviously a politician would chart his course on the intentions of the living, not of the dead, and count the number of Catholics in his constituency.)

The Constitution, then, was not an apotheosis of "constitutionalism," a triumph of architectonic genius; it was a patchwork sewn together under the pressure of both time and events by a group of extremely talented democratic politicians. They refused to attempt the establishment of a strong, centralized sovereignty on the principle of legislative supremacy for the excellent reason that the people would not accept it. They risked their political fortunes by opposing the established doctrines of state sovereignty because they were convinced that the existing system was leading to national impotence and probably foreign domination. For two years, they worked to get a convention established. For over three months, in what must have seemed to the faithful participants an endless process of give-and-take, they reasoned, cajoled, threatened, and bargained amongst themselves. The result was a Constitution which the people, in fact, by democratic processes, did accept, and a new and far better national government was established.

Beginning with the inspired propaganda of Hamilton, Madison, and Jay, the ideological buildup got under way. *The Federalist* had little impact on the ratification of the Constitution, except perhaps in New York, but this volume had enormous influence on the image of the Constitution in the minds of future generations, particularly on historians and political scientists who have an innate fondness for theoretical symmetry. Yet, while the shades of Locke and Montesquieu *may* have been hovering in the background, and the delegates *may* have been unconscious instruments of a transcendent *telos*, the careful observer of the day-to-day work of the Convention finds no over-arching principles. The "separation of powers" to him seems to be a by-product of suspicion, and "federalism" he views as a *pis aller*, as the farthest point the delegates felt they could go in the destruction of state power without themselves inviting repudiation.

To conclude, the Constitution was neither a victory for abstract theory nor a great practical success. Well over half a million men had to die on the battlefields of the Civil War before certain constitutional principles could be defined —a baleful consideration which is somehow overlooked in our customary tributes to the farsighted genius of the Framers and to the supposed American talent for "constitutionalism." The Constitution was, however, a vivid demonstration of effective democratic political action, and of the forging of a national elite which literally persuaded its countrymen to hoist themselves by their own boot straps. American proconsuls would be wise not to translate the Constitution into Japanese, or Swahili, or treat it as a work of semi-Divine origin; but when students of comparative politics examine the process of nation-building in countries newly freed from colonial rule, they may find the American experience instructive as a classic example of the potentialities of a democratic elite.

Madison's Essentials of a "New System"

JOHN S. VANDEROEF

It has become commonplace to point out that the Virginia Plan, submitted to the Constitutional Convention by Edmund Randolph, was predominantly the work of James Madison. The plan's essential components were foreshadowed in Madison's correspondence written from New York in the months immediately preceding the Convention. A sampling of this correspondence reveals ideas which correlate strongly with the main provisions of the Virginia Plan and with Madison's arguments in its behalf on the floor of the Convention.

The most concise statement of Madison's overall position may be found in a letter to Edmund Randolph of April 8, 1787, in which he writes:

> I hold it for a fundamental point that an individual independence of the States is utterly irreconcilable with the idea of an aggregate sovereignty. I think, at the same time, that a consolidation of the States into one simple republic is not less unattainable than it would be inexpedient. Let it be tried, then, whether any middle ground can be taken, which will at once support a due supremacy of the national authority and leave in force the local authorities so far as they can be subordinately useful.[76]

While disclaiming any intention to advocate the consolidation of the states into a unitary government, Madison's prescription for a "middle way" certainly seems to shift the locus of power of the governmental system of the Confederation. The "local authorities" (states) would be retained in force "so far as they can be subordinately useful" under a "due supremacy of the national authority."

John S. Vanderoef, "Madison's Essentials of a 'New System,'" adapted from a Ph.D. dissertation, Princeton University, copyrighted by the author.

How was this design to be effected? Madison communicated his thoughts in almost identical fashion to Thomas Jefferson, George Washington, and Edmund Randolph. In a letter to Randolph, dated April 1, 1787, Madison wrote:

> The first step to be taken is, I think, a change in the principle of representation. According to the present form of the Union, an equality of suffrage, if not just towards the larger members of it, is at least safe to them, as the liberty they exercise of rejecting or executing the acts of Congress is uncontrollable by the nominal sovereignty of Congress. Under a system which would operate without the intervention of the States, the case would be materially altered. A vote from Delaware would have the same effect as one from Massachusetts or Virginia.[77]

To Thomas Jefferson, Madison, in a letter of March 19, also urged the necessity to

> . . . change the principle of Representation in the federal system. Whilst the execution of the acts of Congress depend on the several Legislatures, the equality of votes does not destroy the inequality of importance and influence in the States. But in case of such an augmentation of the federal power as will render it efficient without the intervention of the Legislatures, a vote in the general Councils from Delaware would be of equal value with one from Massachusetts or Virginia. This change, therefore, is just. I think also, it will be practicable. A majority of the States conceive that they will be gainers by it. It is recommended to the Eastern States by the actual superiority of their populousness, and to the Southern by their expected superiority; and if a majority of the larger States concur, the fewer and smaller States must finally bend to them. This point being gained, many of the objections now urged in the leading States against renunciations of power will vanish.[78]

As revealed in these letters, Madison's primary concern was to achieve "an augmentation of the federal power as will render it efficient without the intervention of the Legislatures" of the states.

A second principal requirement was deemed essential to fortify national supremacy. It consisted of no less than a veto by the national government over acts of state legislatures. Madison wrote Jefferson:

> I think myself that it will be expedient . . . over and above the positive power of regulating trade and sundry other matters in which uniformity is proper, to arm the federal head with a negative *in all cases whatsoever* on the local Legislatures. Without this defensive power, experience and reflection have satisfied me that, however ample the federal powers may be made, or however clearly their boundaries may be delineated on paper, they will be easily and continually baffled by the Legislative sovereignties of the States. The effects of this provision would be not only to guard the national rights and interests against invasion, but also to restrain the

States from thwarting and molesting each other; and even from oppressing the minority within themselves by paper money and other unrighteous measures which favor the interest of the majority. In order to render the exercise of such a negative prerogative convenient, an emanation of it must be vested in some set of men within the several States, so far as to enable them to give a temporary sanction to laws of immediate necessity.[79]

This last sentence illustrates the degree of national supremacy envisioned by Madison; it would extend even to representatives of national authority situated in the states, armed with a reviewing power over acts of state legislatures.

Three weeks later Madison urged the same necessity for a national veto upon Randolph. He repeated his advocacy of arming the national government "with a positive and complete authority in all cases where uniform measures are necessary, as in trade, &c., &c."[80] He added:

Let it [the national government] have a negative in all cases whatsoever, on the Legislative acts of the States, as the King of Great Britain heretofore had. This I conceive to be essential and the least possible abridgment of the State sovereignties. Without such a defensive power, every positive power that can be given on paper will be unavailing. It will also give internal stability to the States.[81]

George Washington also received Madison's recommendation in this regard. While expressed in almost identical language, the correspondence to Washington also elaborated on the reasons which necessitated such a national veto power. As Madison put it:

Without this defensive power, every positive power that can be given on paper will be evaded & defeated. The States will continue to invade the National Jurisdiction, to violate treaties and the law of nations & to harass each other with rival and spiteful measures dictated by mistaken views of interest. Another happy effect of this prerogative would be its controul on the internal vicissitudes of State policy, and the aggressions of interested majorities on the rights of minorities and of individuals.[82]

To Madison, a national negative would provide the essential element heretofore lacking in all republican governments, that is, a disinterested arbiter reconciling the parochial and clashing interests of component members of the governmental system. He explains to Washington:

The great desideratum which has not yet been found for Republican Governments seems to be some disinterested & dispassionate umpire in disputes between different passions & interests in the State. The majority who alone have the right of decision, have frequently an interest, real or supposed, in abusing it. In Monarchies the sovereign is more neutral to the interests and views of different parties; but, unfortunely [*sic*] he too often forms interests of his own repugnant to those of the whole. Might not the national prerogative here suggested be found sufficiently disinterested for the decision of local questions of policy, whilst it would itself be sufficiently restrained from the pursuit of interests adverse to those of the whole Society. There has not been any moment since the peace at which the representatives of the Union would have given an assent to paper money or any other measure of a kindred nature.[83]

Madison also expressed to Washington the desirability of inserting an article "expressly guarantying [sic] the tranquility of the States against internal as well as external dangers."[84] And he repeated his plea, forcefully detailed during the years of the Confederation Congress, for a national power of coercion binding upon the states. He hoped that the provision for a national veto would produce that result. As he explained to Washington:

The right of coercion should be expressly declared. With the resources of Commerce in hand, the National administration might always find means of exerting it either by sea or land; But the difficulty & awkwardness of operating by force on the collective will of a State, render it particularly desirable that the necessity of it might be precluded. Perhaps the negative on the laws might create such a mutuality of dependence between the General and particular authorities, as to answer this purpose or perhaps some defined objects of taxation might be submitted along with commerce, to the general authority.[85]

The third major element in the reconstruction of the political system was one that went to the heart of the nature of the Union. The Articles of Confederation had been ratified by the authority of the legislatures of the states. Madison wrote to Jefferson:

I think myself that it will be expedient, in the first place, to lay the foundation of the new system in such a ratification by the people themselves of the several States as will render it clearly paramount to their Legislative authorities.[86]

To Randolph, Madison urged the same necessity. "To give the new system its proper energy," he wrote, "it will be desirable to have it ratified by the authority of the people, and not merely by that of the Legislatures."[87]

Thus can be seen the three primary alterations of the political system Madison deemed essential: first, a change in the principle of representation currently based on state equality; second, a national negative on state legislation; third, ratification of the "new system" by the people instead of by state legislatures. Only through the implementation of these three fundamental changes in the political system did he feel that the government could be made adequate to meet the needs of the times and the American people.

State sovereignty, Madison insisted, must be replaced by a national government founded on the people as the source of power. The three changes advocated by Madison were designed to bring this about. The base of power of the

Confederation, resting upon state sovereignty, must be supplanted. A "new system" must be erected. Indeed, a striking element in this pre-Convention correspondence of Madison is the recurrent use of the phrase "the new system." Even in the letter to Randolph in which he agreed with the desirability of retaining "as much as possible of the old Confederation," he added, "though I doubt whether it may not be best to work the valuable articles into the new system, instead of engrafting the latter on the former."[88] However it was to be accomplished, there is little doubt that Madison intended to replace "the old Confederation" with a substantively "new system." The concept of national supremacy founded on popular ratification was the goal he sought.

Madison was, in fact, explicit in using the term "national supremacy." His primary concern was the structure and powers of the national legislature, but he did not overlook the role of the national judiciary in this regard either. In his April 8 letter to Randolph, he wrote:

> Let this national supremacy be extended also to the Judiciary department. If the Judges in the last resort depend on the States, and are bound by their oaths to them and not to the Union, the intention of the law and the interests of the nation may be defeated by the obsequiousness of the tribunals to the policy or prejudices of the States. It seems at least essential that an appeal should lie to some national tribunals in all cases which concern foreigners, or inhabitants of other States. The admiralty jurisdiction may be fully submitted to the National Government.[89]

The Madison of the Constitutional Convention was the advocate of the "new system," presented in the Virginia Plan, embodying those principles which would effectively recast the basis and scope of power of the "old Confederation." Winning on some points and losing on others in the Convention, the Madison of *The Federalist* and of the Virginia ratifying convention became the advocate of the Connecticut Compromise effected by the Convention. The compromise did not meet his highest hopes; it did not comprise all the elements of the "new system" he considered most conducive to the preservation of free government. At best it gave hope of arresting the plunge into anarchy that he dreaded.

Writing to Jefferson from Philadelphia on September 6, less than two weeks before the Convention completed its work, Madison gave a thumbnail sketch of the structure and powers of the proposed government, then added gloomily:

> These are the outlines. The extent of them may perhaps surprize [*sic*] you. I hazard an opinion nevertheless that the plan should it be adopted will neither effectually answer its national object nor prevent the local mischiefs which every where excite disgusts against the state governments.[90]

This rather grim appraisal of the Convention's labors, however, would not lead Madison to abandon his advocacy of the Constitution. He continued:

The public however is certainly in the dark with regard to it [the plan of the Convention]. The Convention is equally in the dark as to the reception which may be given to it on its publication. . . . My own idea is that the public mind will now or in a very little time receive any thing that promises stability to the public Councils and security to private rights, and that no regard ought to be had to local prejudices or temporary considerations. If the present moment be lost it is hard to say what may be our fate.[91]

Madison had succeeded in his advocacy of popular ratification and popular election combined with proportional representation and voting in the first branch of the legislature. He suffered defeat in the extension of the latter principle to the second branch and in his advocacy of a veto on state laws. Where he succeeded, the principle of a national government founded upon and acting directly upon the people was incorporated into the Constitution. Where he failed, the "political capacity" of the states, the legacy of the Confederation, had been preserved in the "new system."

This failure undoubtedly accounted for Madison's pessimistic evaluation of the new government and his description of the new government, in a post-Convention letter to Jefferson, as "a feudal system of republics." Yet, in this letter his opening remarks summarized the consensus of the delegates on general principles. "It was generally agreed," he wrote,

that the objects of the Union could not be secured by any system founded on the principle of a confederation of Sovereign States. A *voluntary* observance of the federal law by all the members could never be hoped for. A *compulsive* one could evidently never be reduced to practice, and if it could, involved equal calamities to the innocent & the guilty, the necessity of a military force both obnoxious & dangerous, and in general a scene resembling much more a civil war than the administration of a regular Government.

Hence was embraced the alternative of a Government which instead of operating on the States, should operate without their intervention on the individuals composing them; and hence the change in the principle and proportion of representation.[92]

The work of the Convention was a compromise. But, and this is an essential point, it was a compromise within a framework of a consensus. This consensus consisted, in Madison's own words, of a general agreement by the delegates "that the objects of the Union could not be secured by any system founded on the principle of a confederation of Sovereign States." Madison did not achieve his goal of removing from the states all elements of their "sovereignty" and "political capacity." But it seems undeniable that Madison succeeded more than he failed—and succeeded more than he realized.

Madison was not the "Father of the Constitution" in the sense of working for the "Grand Compromise" which broke the deadlock between the large and small states over the issue of state equality and which thus opened the way to the successful outcome of the Convention's efforts. But the title is not a complete misnomer, for the fact remains that Madison was instrumental in bringing about that essential degree of abridgment of state sovereignty which enabled the "new system" to be founded upon and directly acting upon the people.

The federal system was not the invention of Madison. In a real sense it was not the invention of anyone. It *emerged* from the debates, decisions, and compromises of the delegates. But a federal system is not a confederal one. To the degree it gives power and authority to the national government founded on the people, Madison was, in large part, the architect. True, the states, through their power base in the Senate, the Electoral College, and the amending process, retained their "political capacity" in the "new system." But their relative power and position *vis-à-vis* the national government in the political system has been, and will be, subject to change. The Founding Fathers provided a new general framework of government in which evolutionary change in nation-state relations was made possible. Under the system of the Confederation, change was most difficult—if not impossible. It was primarily due to Madison's efforts and successes in the Convention that the "new system" was empowered with this potential to meet the demands of succeeding generations of the American people. With the Convention's actions the groundwork for a strong national system had been laid, and Madison played a leading role in its construction.

The Nature of Our Federal Union Reconsidered

ALPHEUS THOMAS MASON

The thinking of any age, including our own, tends to be pervaded by the illusory notion that human beings are at some final crossroads or other, that men must choose and choose quickly between extreme alternatives. Thereafter, the ceaseless struggle which had heretofore racked mankind presumably ends, and society sinks at last into the normalcy of peace. Even the politically astute James Madison sometimes spoke in apocalyptic terms. The Philadelphia Con-

Reprinted with permission from the *Political Science Quarterly*, Vol. LXV (December 1950), pp. 502–522.

vention, as he saw it in 1787, was deciding "forever the fate of Republican Government. . . ."[93] "The two extremes before us," he said, "are a perfect separation and a perfect incorporation of the 13 States. In the first case they would be independent nations subject to no law, but the law of nations. In the last, they would be mere counties of one entire republic, subject to one common law."[94] Subsequent proceedings proved that the possibilities were far less narrow, various compromises being achieved, even on the most controversial issues. Yet these remarkable successes did not preclude future controversy or bring national repose. The Constitution provided only the basis on which the nation could resume the march of history—a workable makeshift perhaps to avoid "civil war," as Hamilton suggested, ". . . dismemberment of the Union and monarchies in different portions of it."

For their achievement, the Founding Fathers have not always been applauded. They have, on occasion, been accused of writing into the Constitution itself an irreconcilable ambiguity. In the struggle over ratification, strategic considerations drove the contestants to minimize or to exaggerate, thus making the evidence as to the Constitution's meaning less than clear-cut. To allay the fears of opponents, advocates of ratification, especially Madison, said things which, in later years, proved embarrassing to him and misleading to scholars. Certain of the Constitution's enemies turned alarmist, portraying the proposed national charter in the most extreme terms. That is why substantial support for the revolutionary changes wrought by the Philadelphia Convention comes especially from those vigorously opposing ratification—Samuel Adams, Patrick Henry, Richard Henry Lee, Luther Martin, among others.

The upshot was that the Constitution, a "bundle of compromises," as someone has described it, was neither altogether satisfactory, nor crystal clear to its enemies or its supporters. To friends of union and energetic government, like Hamilton, it was bitterly disappointing; to defenders of the "sovereign" states, it made for a "consolidated system," one "consolidated government" calculated to be as obnoxious as that the colonists had thrown off in 1776.[95] Jefferson's position is distinguishable from that of both Federalists and Antifederalists. Particular provisions of the document impressed him less than the Constitution's demonstration of reason as the solvent of varying interests and divergent points of view. "I am captivated," he wrote James Madison, December 20, 1787, "by the compromise of the opposite claims of the great and little States, of the last to equal, and the former to proportional influence."[96]

But was not the accommodation of interests Jefferson saw, or thought he saw, reflected in the Constitution more apparent than real? Did not both sides make concessions, and yet couch what had been surrendered in language so equivocal as to disguise the Constitution's true import? Obviously the Constitution did not draw the boundary line between the general government and the states, nor indicate the source from which its powers were derived, so distinctly clear as to escape sharp diversities of opinion, protracted controversy, and finally civil war. Did not the Founding Fathers, with noble motives and good intentions, plant in the Constitution itself a time bomb that, after 1860, burst the nation asunder in civil war?

Examination of this question proceeds on the generally accepted view that slavery was the occasion, not the cause, of the Civil War. Basically that conflict arose out of irreconcilable differences as to the nature of the Union.[97] Any number of issues besides slavery might easily have provoked the holocaust— tariffs, regulation of interstate commerce, national taxing power, and so on. Indeed, dispute over certain of these matters had carried the nation more than once to the very brink of open conflict.[98] Before the slavery issue matured to the explosive stage, Lincoln himself set this tragic aspect of the war in clear perspective: "I would save the Union. . . . If I could save the Union without freeing any slave, I would do it; and if I could save it by freeing all the slaves, I would do it. . . ."[99] This is but another way of saying that at bottom the war grew out of bitter differences as to the nature of the organism the Founding Fathers had brought into being during the years 1787 to 1789.

Was the Constitution, as John Taylor, John C. Calhoun, and others fiercely maintained, a compact of states, or was it rooted in what Hamilton called "that pure, original fountain of all legitimate authority"—"*The Consent of The People*"?[100] One answer to these questions may be found in dry-as-dust documents; the other is written in blood. The first answer is deeply embedded in the vast record accumulated during the framing and ratification of the Constitution. When prolonged debate and bitter controversy failed to yield a conclusive verdict, the contestants carried this baffling poser of political theory to the battlefield to be settled by the arbitrament of the sword. Let us first consider the contemporary record.

If there be any single proposition to which Americans, since 1776, have been dedicated, it is this: that the people have a right to change their government, "laying its foundations on such principles, and organizing its powers in such form, as to them should seem most likely to effect their Safety and Happiness." The Declaration of Independence averred that the people alone were the rightful source of legitimate authority. The opening sentence of that document speaks of the "one people" dissolving the "political bands which have connected them with another." By that act one people of thirteen united states "assumed among the Powers of the earth, the separate and equal station to which the Laws of Nature and Nature's God entitled them."[101] "Civil liberty," Benjamin Hichborn declared, March 5, 1777, is "not a government by laws, made agreeable to charters, bills of rights or compacts." It is a "power existing in the people at large," the power "to alter or annihilate both the mode and essence of any former government," "for any cause or for no cause at all, but their own sovereign pleasure."[102]

James Wilson called this (and many others agreed with him) "the leading principle in politics and that which pervades the American constitutions." Never before put into practice, this theory—that "Supreme power resides in the people"—so clearly expounded in the writings of "the great Locke," had been working itself in the minds of men for many ages. In 1776, Americans declared themselves free and independent states, by authority of the whole people. "The distinctions between Virginians, Pennsylvanians, New Yorkers, and New Englanders are no more," Patrick Henry had told the First Continental Congress in 1774. "I am not a Virginian, but an American. . . . All distinctions are thrown down. All America is thrown into one mass."[103] "It is only in our united Character as an Empire," George Washington wrote Governor William Livingston, June 12, 1783, "that our Independence is acknowledged, that our power can be regarded, or our Credit supported, among foreign Nations."[104] Lincoln echoed Washington (as did a host of nationalist orators during the intervening years) in his first inaugural address, proclaiming that "The Union is much older than the Constitution."[105]

Under this nationalist theory, the Articles of Confederation were but a step, as inconsistent as they were important,[106] toward union. This was "an experiment of inestimable value, even by its failure," John Quincy Adams remarked in 1836. "It taught our fathers the lesson, that they had more, infinitely more to do than merely to achieve their Independence by War. That they must form their social compact upon principles never before attempted upon earth."[107] To deal effectively with the national exigencies following Yorktown it had been as necessary in 1787 as in 1776 "to go," as James Wilson said on the floor of the Philadelphia Convention, "to the original powers of Society"[108]—the people. The Convention, in short, was a revolutionary body, acting in accordance with the proposition that "all authority is derived from the people."[109] The Declaration of Independence and the Constitution are thus "parts of one consistent whole."[110] Each rests fundamentally on the natural right of a people to dislodge or alter their government and to reinstitute such new forms as they see fit.

But to assert this doctrine against a tyrannical mother country was one thing; to ground new institutions of government in such a high-toned principle was something else. In his address of 1787 to the people of the United States, Dr. Benjamin Rush observed:

> There is nothing more common than to confound the terms of the *American Revolution* with those of the *late American War*. The American War is over: but this is far from being the case with the American revolution. On the contrary, nothing but the first act of the great drama is closed. It remains yet to establish and perfect our new forms of government; and to prepare the principles, morals, and manners of our citizens for these forms of government, after they are established and brought to perfection. . . . Patriots of 1774, 1775, 1776—heroes of 1778, 1779, 1780! come forward! your country demands your services!—Philosophers and friends to

mankind, come forward! your country demands your studies and speculations!
THE REVOLUTION IS NOT OVER![111]

Before 1787 Dr. Rush's theory—that the American colonies constituted "one people" and the continuing nature of the revolution initiated in 1776—was widely recognized and accepted. This notion, "in itself so simple," John Quincy Adams wrote in 1836, "addressed itself at once so forcibly to the reason, to the imagination, and to the benevolent feelings of all, that it can scarcely be supposed to have escaped the mind of any reflecting man from Maine to Georgia." And yet, when this elemental doctrine was projected and acted upon in the Philadelphia Convention, it stirred "State Sovereignties, corporate feudal baronies, tenacious of their own liberty, impatient of a superior and jealous, and disdainful of a paramount Sovereign, even in the whole democracy of the nation."[112] The people, that is to say, could exert themselves negatively and unitedly against the tyrannous oppression of Great Britain, but when that same ultimate authority moved constructively in the face of well-nigh insurmountable internal complexities, vested interests and political prejudice were profoundly aroused.

It was generally recognized that, to achieve the energy necessary for an effective national government, extensive restrictions would have to be imposed upon the corporate action of states, passionately claiming to be indepedent and sovereign. It was also recognized that such "binding ligaments," as John Quincy Adams said, could be properly imposed by "no earthly power other than the People themselves."[113] "Federal liberty is to States," James Wilson observed in the Philadelphia Convention, "what civil liberty is to private individuals. And States are not more unwilling to purchase it, by the necessary concession of their political sovereignty, than the savage is to purchase civil liberty by the surrender of the personal sovereignty which he enjoys in a State of nature."[114]

What, then, was the nature of the change effected by the Constitution? Did it merely continue and guarantee, as Luther Martin insisted at the Philadelphia Convention, the relationship of "sovereign," "independent" states existing under the Articles of Confederation;[115] or did it, as James Wilson and others maintained, by deriving authority from the people, preclude (at least in theory) any possibility of thereafter interposing the states against national authority?[116] The answer to these questions falls into two parts. There is, on the one hand, the reply of advocates of ratification, like James Wilson and Alexander Hamilton; and, on the other, the view of opponents of the Constitution, such as Richard Henry Lee and Samuel Adams.

Under the Randolph Plan the government established was to be "paramount to the state constitutions." "Can an individual retain his equality," James Wilson argued on the floor of the Pennsylvania ratifying convention, "when he becomes a member of civil government? He cannot. . . . As little can a sovereign state," Wilson reasoned, "when it becomes a member of the federal government."[117]. Hamilton was equally emphatic. The Constitution of 1787 was intended to scotch forever that "gross heresy . . . that a *party* to a *compact* has a right to revoke that *compact*."[118] Emanating from "We the People of the United States," the Constitution transformed a "League of Friendship," a "loose alliance," into a government. In providing for national authority, acting on individuals rather than on states, the Constitution of 1787 substituted a government of law for one whose only instrument had been prayerful requisition or force. "This . . . is not a government founded upon compact," James Wilson told the Pennsylvania ratifying convention. "It is founded upon the power of the people. . . . The power both of the general government, and the state governments, under this system, are acknowledged to be so many emanations of power from the people."[119]

Ironically enough, impressive support for this nationalistic theory came from the Constitution's most rabid opponents. "It is, in its very *introduction, declared* to be a compact between the people of the United States as individuals," Luther Martin complained, "and it is to be ratified by the *people* at large, in their capacity *as individuals.*" All this, Martin explained, "would be quite right and proper, if there were *no State governments*, if *all the people* of this continent were in a *state of nature*, and we were forming one *national government* for *them* as *individuals.*"[120] "The Constitution is an ordinance," Richard Henry Lee protested, "not of the people of New Hampshire," and so on, but of "the people of America."[121] "What right had they to say, *We the people* . . . instead of, *We the states*?", Patrick Henry inquired in the Virginia ratifying convention. "The question turns, sir, on that poor little thing—the expression, We, the People, instead of the States of America. . . . Here is a resolution as radical as that which separated us from Great Britain."[122]

Responding December 3, 1787, to Richard Henry Lee, who had sent him a copy of the "new Constitution," Samuel Adams voiced similar sentiments and opposed ratification for the same reason:

> I am not able to conceive why the Wisdom of the Convention led them to give the Preference to the former [national government] before the latter [sovereign states]. If the several states in the Union are to become one entire Nation, under one Legislature, the Powers of which shall extend to every Subject of Legislation, and its Laws be supreme and control the whole, the Idea of Sovereignty in these States must be lost.[123]

"Whether the Constitution be good or bad," George Mason said, going to the heart of the matter, "it is a national government, and no longer a confederation."[124]

The Constitution was intended, its friends insisted (and on this basic point its enemies agreed), to remedy the congenital defect that had plagued the central government under the Articles of Confederation—that "it never had a ratification by the People." Hamilton argued emphatically that by "extending to the individuals" it would slay the "political monster"—*"imperium in imperio."*[125]

How, in the face of historical evidence so abundantly conclusive; how, in a debate where the participants were agreed as to the revolutionary character of the Constitution of 1787, could the doctrine that our fundamental law was a mere compact between sovereign states—the doctrine boldly asserted by Jefferson in the Kentucky Resolutions of 1798, by Madison in the Virginia Resolutions of 1799—the doctrine acted upon by the slave states—receive any credibility at all? How could our "leading principle in politics . . . that the supreme power resides in the people," the doctrine so universally accepted in 1787, be converted into the self-stultifying notion that the Constitution was a compact of independent, sovereign entities? How could states' rights advocates, John C. Calhoun in particular, claim for entities called states a prerogative that belongs, under our theory of government, only to people or populations? How, in short, could the highest political capacity of the people be transmuted into the capacity of corporate bodies—the states? Investigation of these questions leads ultimately to James Madison. In the divisive effort culminating in civil war, all major participants on the side of disunion derived essential support from him.

The position of Madison on the nature of the Constitution and of the Union, also as to the scope of the powers granted the national government, stands in bold contrast to the clear-cut views of the Constitution's major supporters as well as of its radical opponents. In *Federalist* No. 39, Madison maintained:

> The Constitution is to be founded on the assent and ratification of the people of America, given by deputies elected for the special purpose. . . . This assent and ratification is to be given by the people, not as individuals composing one entire nation, but as composing the distinct and independent States to which they respectively belong. It is to be the assent and ratification of the several States, derived from the supreme authority in each State—the authority of the people themselves. The act, therefore, establishing the Constitution, will not be a *national*, but a *federal act*. . . . Each State, in ratifying the Constitution, is considered as a sovereign body, independent of all others, and only to be bound by its own voluntary act. In this relation, then, the new Constitution will, if established, be a *federal*, and not a *national* Constitution.[126]

Madison labored the point; for him the distinction was fundamental. Yet Hamilton passed it over lightly in Essay 9 as "a distinction, more subtle than accurate. . . ."

For Madison the task of the Convention was not to abolish the Articles of Confederation but "to reduce" them. He spells out his meaning in *Federalist* No. 40: "The truth is, that the great principles of the Constitution proposed by the Convention may be considered less as absolutely new, than as the expansion of principles which are found in the articles of Confederation." The Father of the Constitution elaborated his thought further in *Federalist* No. 45, dealing specifically with the nature and scope of national power: "The change which it [the Constitution] proposes consists much less in the addition of NEW POWERS to the Union than in the invigoration of its ORIGINAL POWERS." The powers of the new government, he said, "are few and defined."

The sharpness of the contrast between Madison and his collaborator, Hamilton, grew out of basic disagreement as to the source from which the powers of the national government emanated. For Hamilton the Articles of Confederation, being fatally defective, must be destroyed, liquidated, not merely "reduced." "The evils we experience do not proceed," he wrote, in *Federalist* No. 15, "from minute or partial imperfections, but from fundamental errors in the structure of the building, which cannot be amended otherwise than by an alteration in the first principles and main pillars of the fabric." The capital infirmity of the existing system was congenital—"it never had ratification by the People." To avoid the "gross heresy" that a "party to a compact has a right to revoke that compact, the fabric of American empire ought to rest on the solid basis of *The Consent of The People*." In Essay 15 he had portrayed the Constitution as the proper corrective of "the great and radical vice"— "legislation for states . . . as contradistinguished from the individuals of which they consist." There follows his classic expression of nationalistic doctrine:

> If we are unwilling to be placed in this perilous situation; if we still will adhere to the design of a national government, or, which is the same thing, of a superintending power, under the direction of a common council, we must resolve to incorporate into our plan those ingredients which may be considered as forming the characteristic difference between a league and a government; we must extend the authority of the Union to the persons of the citizens—the only proper objects of government.

"The great bulk of the citizens of America are with reason convinced," Hamilton observed in *Federalist* No. 84, "that Union is the basis of their political happiness."[127] "We have neither troops, nor treasury, nor government," he had remarked in *Federalist* No. 15. Having thus "reached almost the last stage of national humiliation," should we permit, he inquired, "that sacred knot which binds the people of America together to be severed or dissolved by ambition or by avarice, by jealousy, or by misrepresentation?"

It followed, in consequence, that the powers granted the national government by the proposed Constitution had to be new and "undefined"—indeed, undefinable in view of the great interests committed to the care of the national government. Far from possessing, as Madison asserted, only "a few and defined powers," the national government possessed "all the power which a free people *ought to delegate to any government*."[128]

Nor was the vigor of the new government to be applied so exclusively, as Madison suggested, in the field of foreign relations. Hamilton conceived of the "Union," and of the central government, as an essential force in domestic affairs as well—especially as a "barrier against domestic faction and insurrection."[129] "A government ought to contain in itself every power requisite to the full accomplishment of the objects committed to its care . . . free from every other control but a regard to the public good and to the sense of the People."[130] It would be, Hamilton argued, "both unwise and dangerous to deny the federal government an unconfined authority, as to all those objects which are intrusted to its management."[131]

"Let us at last break the fatal charm," Hamilton pleaded dramatically in *Federalist* No. 15, "which has too long seduced us from the paths of felicity and prosperity." "Let us not attempt," he reiterated in *Federalist* No. 23, "to reconcile contradictions, but firmly embrace a rational alternative." Hamilton's exhortations might well have been addressed to his *Federalist* collaborator, Madison.

Someone has characterized the personality of the *Federalist* as "split."[132] It would perhaps be closer to the mark to call it schizophrenic. The major authors not only disagreed on basic issues but, at certain points, Madison was in disagreement with himself, embracing the Hamiltonian theory that the Constitution emanates from the people, as well as his collaborator's theory of the broad and "unconfined" scope of national authority.[133] For the most part, however, Madison saw the Constitution as resting precisely on those flimsy foundations Hamilton cited as incurably defective.

These equivocal views of the Father of the Constitution, expressed in a series of essays designed to win ratification, provided the leaders of nullification and secession with exactly the formula, the destructive ammunition, they used in their abortive attempt to blow up the Union. Nor is this all. Madison's theory that the Constitution emanates from and was ratified by "the people . . . comprising the distinct and independent states" is the more extraordinary because of its novelty. In 1787, "People of the States" and "People of the United States" were not antagonistic conceptions, as Madison's interpretation in *Federalist* No. 39 implies. The polar concepts familiar to the men of that day—"States" and "People," "Governments" and "People"—had been inherited from John Locke. The term "State" usually meant, as Dr. Johnson said in the Philadelphia Convention, "districts of people forming one Political Society." "Governments" were universally regarded as properly the creations of people, and the term "People" meant an aggregation of individuals endowed with the natural right to determine their form of government.[134] The state and federal governments were, as Madison said in *Federalist* No. 46, but "different agencies and trustees of the people." A "constitution" represented a fresh manifestation of the inexhaustible, inalienable right of people to govern themselves.[135] In this sense the Philadelphia Convention of 1787 had assembled "to raise," as John Quincy Adams observed in 1839, "the marble palace of the people to stand the test of time."

In the years after 1798, Madison's explosively novel theory became the stock in trade of Antifederalist leadership; it was the central idea on which nullificationists and secessionists built their ill-fated case. Madison himself employed it in the Virginia Resolutions, declaring that the powers of the federal government are derived from

> the compact to which the States are parties . . . and that, in case of a deliberate, palpable, and dangerous exercise of other powers not granted by the said compact, the States who are parties thereto, have the right and are in duty bound to interpose for arresting the progress of the evil, and for maintaining within their respective limits the authorities, rights, and liberties appertaining to them.[136]

The year before, Jefferson had asserted in his Kentucky Resolutions that the Constitution was a compact of states, and that, "as in all other cases of compact among parties having no common judge, each party has an equal right to judge for itself, as well of infractions as of measures of redress."[137]

John Taylor of Caroline County, Virginia, gleefully appropriated Madison's theory in his vehement attack on Hamilton's and Marshall's nationalistic views of the Constitution and of the Union. Taylor's intellectual gymnastics, however, were mixed with legerdemain. Opponents of the Constitution, as we have seen, vigorously attacked it, primarily because its provisions made, as they said, for a "consolidated government." After 1820, Taylor, drawing heavily from Madison's numbers of the *Federalist*,[138] held that the Convention had rejected the idea of "consolidation" and of national supremacy, and John Marshall, notwithstanding this decisive repudiation, had achieved the forbidden end by judicial interpretation![139] In other words, a secessionist position, otherwise difficult, if not impossible, to maintain, was made comparatively easy by James Madison, whose numbers of the *Federalist* supplied John Taylor with the authoritative ammunition he leveled against Hamilton's and Marshall's doctrines of national supremacy.

It was not, however, until 1861 that the slave states cut loose. Then, enlisting Madison's authority, they held that the Constitution emanated from the sovereign states, that they therefore had the right to interpose their judgment against any acts of the national government deemed by them unauthorized, and that they might therefore secede from the Union.[140] It was on this theory, entangled with ethics and economics, that the South went on to Harper's Ferry, Shiloh, and Appomatox.

One need not accuse the Father of the Constitution of instigating the Civil War—he died in 1836—but one may venture the suggestion that his numbers of the *Federalist* papers planted the verbal bomb that, after 1861, flared tragically. The ambiguity lay not so much in the Constitution as in what he said about it. One may reach this conclusion, and still be "captivated," as Jefferson was, "by the compromise [or semblance of it] of the opposite claims of the great and little states." It may be that this was an occasion that called for the sort of equivocation in which Madison so freely indulged. It may be that his equivocal views were rooted in far more wisdom than the comparatively greater forthrightness of his collaborator, Hamilton; for, without Madison's concessions to rampant state loyalties, there may not have been any Constitution of 1787. One may recall that Hamilton himself in 1780 shied off from his own suggestion that the Congress under the Articles of Confederation, in order to cope with the crisis, might assert and exercise discretionary power —power adequate to deal with national exigencies. This course then seemed "too bold an expedient."[141] That is why he advocated calling a convention as the safer course.

Nevertheless the grim verdict at Appomatox repudiated Madison as conclusively as the record of 1787–1789. A theory of the Union which reason had proved powerless to resolve was finally established by resort to force. Washington had suggested war as a possibility when he (according to Gouverneur Morris' recollections) told the Convention: "It is too probable that no plan we propose will be adopted. Perhaps another dreadful conflict is to be sustained. . . ." And yet, even after the first shots were fired on Sumter and secession was a fact, Lincoln still searched for a theory of the Union that would go deeper than the great constitutional debates then rife. He finally hit upon an idea suggested in 1774, ironically enough, by Patrick Henry, that the

> Union is perpetual . . . much older than the Constitution. It was formed, in fact, by the Articles of Association in 1774, . . . matured and continued by the Declaration of Independence in 1776. It was further matured by the Articles of Confederation in 1778. And finally, in 1787, one of the declared objectives for ordaining and establishing the Constitution was "to form a more perfect union."[142]

These successive efforts proved to be in vain, but eight years after Lincoln made his pronouncement, the United States Supreme Court adopted his reasoning, almost his very words. Chief Justice Chase, holding that Texas had failed in its attempt to secede, said:

> Union of the states never was a purely artificial and arbitrary relation. It began among the colonies . . . and received definite form, and character, and sanction from the Articles of Confederation. By these the Union was solemnly declared to be "perpetual" . . . the Constitution was ordained "to form a more perfect union." It is difficult to convey the idea of indissoluble unity more clearly than by these words.

And so, through Washington, Hamilton, Marshall, and Lincoln, this, the organic view of the Union conceived of as rooted in the consent of the people, had steadily advanced. Repeatedly tested by pen, and, finally, by musket, the

Union was at last seen, not as "a purely artificial and arbitrary relation," but as fused, in Chief Justice Chase's words, "out of common origin, mutual sympathies, kindred principles, similar interest, and geographical relations."[143] Justice Holmes, himself a soldier in Lincoln's army, reinforced this nationalist theory of the Union in a Supreme Court opinion in 1919:

> When we are dealing with words that are also a constituent act, like the Constitution of the United States, we must realize that they [the Framers] have called into life a being the development of which could not have been foreseen completely by the most gifted of its begetters. It was enough for them to realize or to hope, that they had created an organism; it has taken a century and cost their successors much sweat and blood to prove that they created a nation.[144]

After Sumter, reason could no longer serve as the instrument for achieving the ends of nationalist statesmanship.[145] Thus, union, like the Constitution itself, had to be "extorted from the grinding necessities of a reluctant nation."[146]

Federalism

The rapid expansion of national government since the 1930s has tended to obscure the equally rapid growth of state and local governments in the United States. Critics of the central government's increasing powers have bemoaned the eclipse of the states and predicted their eventual demotion to the status of administrative units of the federal government.

While it cannot be denied that the relative status of the two levels of government has altered, in the two centuries since the nation's birth, it is also true that the states are still a viable part of the American governmental system. At the present time, in fact, state and local expenditures are increasing more rapidly than the expenditures of the national government and may exceed them in a few years. The states, standing in the center of the American federal structure, are, as Daniel J. Elazar asserts in "The States and the Nation," the "keystones of the American governmental arch."

The states, and federalism, derive their importance not from their formal constitutional status but from their political roles. Elazar addresses himself to two questions: "What kinds of issues are raised in American politics because the states (and their cities) exist as they do?" and, "How are issues developed and resolved in the American political system because of the existence of the states (and their cities) in their present form?"

Terry Sanford, former governor of North Carolina, takes a more optimistic view about the value of federalism and the role of the states. In "Creative

Tensions" he examines some of the major problems confronting state governments today and, while admitting that the problems are great, he pleads for a rejuvenation of the states, stressing their value as laboratories in which to experiment with different remedies for society's ills.

The crisis in state government that Sanford describes was created largely by the growth of a national urban society. Partly because of malapportionment favoring rural interests in their legislatures, the states have been extremely reluctant to deal with the problems of urban areas. As a result, the federal government has been moving to help the cities directly. Potentially, a close working relationship between the cities and the federal government could undermine the position of the states. Daniel P. Moynihan, however, examining "The Relationship of Federal to Local Authorities" as it is likely to develop up to the year 2000, suggests that, despite its weaknesses, the structure of the system is likely to continue much the same. The article anticipates that the increasing use of federal fiscal power will help to evolve a multi-tiered system of bureaucracies and governmental units and that more special-purpose local governments will develop.

The readings in this section are intended to illustrate the present federal-state balance and to outline probable future developments. Federalism is more, however, than the legal and political balance between the central government and the states. The federal structure affects the operation of all our agencies of politics and government. The student can find articles in the following sections that show the effect of federalism on the operation of the political party system, interest groups, the courts, and so on.

The States and the Nation

DANIEL J. ELAZAR

The states, standing as they do in the center of the American federal structure —between the powerful federal government and the burgeoning metropolitan communities—are the keystones of the American governmental arch. This was the case when the Constitution was adopted in 1789 and remains true despite the great changes that have taken place in the intervening years. One student of contemporary American government has said, "As far as domestic

From "The States and the Nation" by Daniel J. Elazer in *Politics in the American States,* edited by Herbert Jacob and Kenneth N. Vines, pp. 449–476 (478, note 28). Copyright © 1965 by Little, Brown and Company (Inc.). Reprinted by permission of the editors and the publisher.

civilian public affairs are concerned, the state and local governments are yet dominant in our governmental life, with every prospect that they will continue to be so."[1] This assertion runs counter to most contemporary perceptions of American government which place the federal government at the center of everything. If it were based upon an analysis of the formalistic constitutional place of the states alone, there would be great difficulty in substantiating it. It is the political position of the states within the federal Union, protected by formal constitutional guarantees but transcending formal limits, that gives them their central role. Unlike the more or less visible constitutional status of the states, their political position is generally of low visibility, not only to the public at large, but often even to those people involved in the day-to-day operations of government. This . . . [exploration will examine] the way in which the states function as political keystones, serving (or not serving) their municipal subdivisions and supporting (or not supporting) the over-all structure of national government.

The States as Autonomous Political Systems

Federalism—national unification without elimination of subnational political systems—is a very familiar aspect of American government. The American federal system is different from a unitary political system where the central authority can centralize as well as decentralize.[2] In a unitary system, a power allowed the local authorities at one time may be taken away by the central government at another. In the United States, there are constitutional limits imposed on either course of action. No matter how much the federal government may expand, it cannot take away the rights of the states to act in most areas of domestic concern.[3] American federalism is also different from a confederation of essentially separate political systems where the center is continually weak. In the United States, the federal government is indeed powerful.

It has been rightly said that without the states there could be no such political body as the United States. It is as much a concern of the United States Constitution to preserve the states and their political systems, as it is to preserve the Union and the national political system. To put the matter more formally, "The Constitution, in all of its provisions, looks to an indestructible Union, composed of indestructible States."[4] This means that political issues in the United States must be considered with two questions in mind, viz.: *What kinds of issues are raised in American politics because the states (and their cities) exist as they do?* and, *How are issues developed and resolved in the American political system because of the existence of the states (and their cities) in their present form?*

The relationship of the states to the federal system is not a mere "structural" question—it is essentially a "political" question. This is particularly evident in a matter like the civil rights issue. Despite constant reaffirmations by the federal courts in the past two decades that Negro rights are protected under the United States Constitution and despite presidential willingness to intervene with force in places where certain states have allowed these rights to be publicly suppressed by force, the entire question of Negro rights remains greatly dependent on the willingness of the states to aid in their maintenance, or at least to comply with national policy in this matter.

Accordingly, the immediate problems of overcoming discrimination in the United States are linked to the enduring problems of the federal-state relationship. Discussion of these problems as political issues revolves around such issues as the limits of federal jurisdiction under the Constitution, "states' rights" as a means of promoting or hindering the protection of individual rights, and the proper role of the United States Supreme Court. Progress in overcoming discrimination is measured state by state and pressure to make progress is applied on the same basis.

The Negro rights problem, in many respects, represents the hardest possible case for demonstrating the noncentralizing influence of federalism and the role of the states as civil societies. Here is a problem in which the moral issue is paramount. Even if the Constitution did not offer the guarantee it does, there would be great pressure on the federal government and the states to secure full rights of citizenship for Negroes. Moreover, less than one-fifth of the states are resisting national demands on this issue, coming into direct conflict not only with the national government but with a large majority of their sister states as well.

However, with explicit constitutional guarantees, *plus* court rulings, *plus* federal executive and legislative actions in the past decade to enforce those guarantees, *plus* the legislative and executive action of some thirty-five states to extend civil rights beyond existing federal law, we might expect the minority of recalcitrant southern states to succumb to the overwhelming influence and power of the nation as a whole. Indeed, if southern resistance were only a matter of localities directly opposing the concentrated might of a central government, overt resistance would undoubtedly have been overcome some time ago by directly limiting the power of the local governments to act in areas which involved discrimination. A central legislature representing a majority of four-to-one could have ordered local compliance directly under the threat of ordering the appropriate central administrative agencies to assume direct control of such functions as education, welfare, and the management of elections. It was in this way that the northern and western states eliminated legal discrimination.[5]

Federalism, as it functions in the United States, changes not only the terms in which the issue is considered but also the manner of its resolution. Under the American federal system, the actual implementation of constitutional provisions, be they "separate but equal" or "equal and not separate," lies primarily with the states. Although the national Constitution may set the standard (and the national Supreme Court may set the guidelines), the state governments are left to apply those guidelines within their own boundaries in a manner consonant with their respective political systems. Only in those cases where it has been clearly demonstrated that the states cannot or will not implement the Constitution as interpreted does it become possible for the federal authorities to intervene. Even then their power to intervene is limited and in no case can intervention be more than temporary.

School integration, the first target of recent efforts to desegregate the southern states, is a particularly revealing case. Though federal efforts have led to some school desegregation in all of the segregationist states since 1954, ten years after the Supreme Court's school desegregation decision of that year only 9 percent of the school children in the border states and less than 1 percent in the states of the Deep South were attending integrated schools.

Table 3-1 shows that there is no simple relationship between the extent of federal pressure and the degree of school desegregation achieved in any particular state. The clearest relationship is an inverse one—the more open pressure, the less desegregation. This is not a cause and effect association, but is symptomatic of the power of the states to maintain previously established positions even in the face of federal power. It is clear that desegregation has gone farther in those states whose leadership decided to comply with the Supreme Court ruling without additional federal pressure. Furthermore, regardless of the kind of federal pressure applied, state governments often have been able to restore segregated conditions after the federal intervention has spent itself or, in any case, have been able to confine integration to a token level. Indeed, those states which have chosen nominal compliance from the first generally have been able to maintain their own "timetables," slow as they may be.

Politics and the Constitutional System

National Intervention and State Autonomy. Considering the continuous involvement of the states and the federal government with similar public concerns, we can ask two important questions: What are some of the ways in which the constitutional and political systems operate to bring order out of the uncertainty that comes from dealing with nationwide concerns in an interlocking system of states and national governments? How do those ways serve to strengthen the viability of the states as political systems?

One thing is clear: Interests unable to gain satisfaction at one level of government can turn to another in an effort to better their fortunes. We know how states when their citizens stand together, as in the desegregation issue, can function even in opposition to national demands. We have also noted that few issues confronting the American people have so great an impact on the states as to unite their people in a common front. In most cases, people unable to gain the ends they seek from their state governments directly will turn to

TABLE 3-1

Federal Pressure and School Desegregation in Southern States

	PERCENTAGE OF NEGROES ATTENDING DESEGREGATED SCHOOLS		
State	June 1963	December 1963	May 1964

1. States complying with Supreme Court rulings with state and local public support; federal pressure confined to occasional court rulings:

Delaware	55.9	55.4	56.5
Kentucky	54.1	54.8	54.4
Maryland	45.1	48.3	47.8
Missouri	38.8	42.1	42.1
Oklahoma	23.6	28.1	28.0
West Virginia	61.4	87.9	58.2

2. States reluctantly complying with federal court rulings as issued to avoid showdown; federal pressure confined to regular court rulings and spot intervention by the Justice Department, usually in cooperation with state authorities:

Florida	.67	1.53	1.53
Georgia	.01	.05	.05
North Carolina*	.26	.54	.54
South Carolina	.00	.004	.004
Tennessee*	1.10	2.71	2.72
Texas*	2.30	4.29	5.52

3. States attempting massive resistance but abandoning it for reluctant compliance; federal pressure has involved the use of troops or marshals or heavy legal pressure:

Arkansas†	.21	.97	.33
Louisiana†	.04	.60	.60
Virginia	.53	1.57	1.63

4. States resisting desegregation massively through agencies of state and local government; federal pressure involves regular use of troops and/or U.S. marshals.

Alabama	.000	.004	.007
Mississippi	.000	.000	.000

*Violent local resistance to state's decision to comply reduced by state intervention.
†State compliance modified by state-sanctioned local resistance.
SOURCE: *Southern School News*, June 1964.

outside assistance from whatever source available. This sometimes means an appeal to local government but more frequently means turning to the federal government. If the issue and the hour are right, this appeal will be answered, often redounding upon the states with great force to alter the internal balance of political forces within them.

This situation is most likely to occur when substantial majorities within most states advocate or accept the necessity for a particular program or course of action which their state governments will not adopt or cannot adopt alone. Where there are popular majorities in most of the states and the state governments do not act, it usually means they cannot. The state governments, no matter how willing, are simply unable to cope with certain problems without federal assistance, and in these cases when federal assistance comes it almost invariably acts to strengthen the states.[6] Regulation of interstate commerce is a case in point. The state governments, no matter how willing, could not regulate the great interstate railroads alone, nor could they deal with the great interstate industrial combines. Federal intervention in both cases actually strengthened the abilities of the states to deal with the problems generated by these enterprises within their boundaries. On a different level, most states would have never been able to finance the great water resource projects undertaken within their limits even if they were the principal beneficiaries; federal "intervention" helped to construct them. Or, in yet another kind of problem, until the federal government made it advantageous for all the states to adopt unemployment compensation programs, those which wished to do so were handicapped by threats of major employers to move elsewhere.

There are times, however, when minorities within the states turn to the federal government for assistance. Minority appeals "outward" occur most frequently in states divided between dominant and minority political subcultures, but also happen in any state divided into two or more camps on matters of policy. The possibility for this kind of appeal makes it difficult for the states to maintain autonomous *politics* unaffected by national currents in their "domestic" decisions even as they maintain reasonably autonomous *political systems*. The autonomy of their political systems may allow the states to bend in the face of blows from the outside and to recover more or less intact after their initial impact (a phenomenon not to be minimized), but it does not necessarily enable them to prevent outside blows in the first place.

The example of the public welfare reformers is, perhaps, classic in this respect. During the first decades of the twentieth century, reform groups working within the states sought to enlarge drastically the public welfare programs of the states and their local subdivisions in order to cope with the dislocations incident to an industrial society. After some initial successes in the regulatory field, they were generally rebuffed in their efforts to secure positive programs partly because their proposed programs were expensive and state legislatures did not wish to raise taxes and partly because the interests generally dominant in the states (and in the nation as a whole) opposed such programs. After repeated failures, the reformers began to intensify their efforts to gain federal assistance for their programs without abandoning their efforts at the state level. With the coming of the Great Depression, they were given a tremendous boost by the change in economic conditions and their programs were enacted into law. A system of federal grants to the states was introduced to stimulate the creation of five basic welfare programs in every state under minimal national standards. Given this federal assistance, the welfare reformers were able to gain control over their programs in most of the states, excluding only those states in which (a) the political organizations were too strong, and (b) where there were really no significant indigenous groups of welfare reformers ready to take over. Federal grants replaced "bread and coal basket politics" and a major instrument of party organization and, at least temporarily, weakened traditional political machines, opening the way for reform groups to act on a number of fronts. Federal merit system requirements broke the back of state patronage in welfare departments, opening the door for professional welfare workers to assume basic responsibility for the operation of even general relief programs. The increased funds available to each state opened the door to greater administrative complexity in political systems long noted for resistance to bureaucracy. These and other changes meant that state politics had to be readjusted so that the state political systems could assimilate the new demands placed upon them.[7]

Today urban reformers interested in reconstructing America's cities are following much the same course of action, turning to Washington for aid unobtainable from most of the states in the hope that through Washington they will become powerful in their respective state capitals as well. The reaction of even the ostensibly conservative big city press to the recent court decisions on reapportionment reveals their hope in this regard. These decisions are not only supported but are endorsed on the grounds that more equitable urban representation in the state legislatures will prevent further "drift" of power toward Washington.

While many of the urban reformers may not care whether the federal government seeks to involve the states in federally-aided programs or not, the existence of the Constitution demands state participation. At the very least, the states must pass enabling legislation before any of their cities can participate in federal-aid programs or take federal funds. In most cases, the federal legislation is so drawn—by men who respect the Constitution—as to either require state participation or at least give the states the option to participate or not. Thus, the impetus for political change which is no respecter of institutions is brought to heel by the Constitution, to the great benefit of the states as political systems.[8]

The Constitutional Place of the States. The constitutional place of the states in the federal system is determined by four sets of material: the provisions in the federal and state constitutions that either limit or guarantee the powers of the states *vis-à-vis* the federal government; the provisions in those constitutions which give the states a role in the composition of the national government; the subsequent interpretations of both sets of provisions by the courts (particularly by the United States Supreme Court); and the unwritten constitutional traditions which have evolved informally and have only later been formally recognized.

The precise federal constitutional provisions outlining the general position of the states must always be taken into consideration by those who govern even if they are to be transcended through politics. Table 3-2 shows the specific limitations and guarantees of state powers. These limitations and guarantees fall into four basic categories—a general concern with the integrity of the states as well as their subordination to the Union; some brief provisions insuring the states a role in the common defense; a delineation of the role of the states in the management of commerce and raising of revenues; and a description of state responsibilities in the administration of justice. Table 3-3 outlines the role that must be played by the states if the federal government is to function and clarifies the constitutional limits of that role.

The state constitutions are generally silent about federal-state relations. Where they speak at all, it is essentially to ratify the requirements of the federal Constitution by making them applicable to specific local situations. Most state constitutions formally delineate their inviolable borders. In the constitutions of the public land states (created under the tutelage of the federal government after the adoption of the United States Constitution) provisions governing the commitment of federal land grants for specific public purposes serve as a formal acknowledgement of the federal-state partnership which had become important as early as 1802 when Ohio, the first state of this group, adopted its first constitution.[9] The constitutions of the reconstructed southern states were required to include specific acknowledgements of federal supremacy and ad- jurations of the "right" of secession.

The Political Process and Intergovernmental Collaboration. American fed- eralism is delineated, maintained, and made functional only partly by constitu- tional devices. While the role of such devices should not be minimized, the way in which the institutions and purposes of federalism are maintained through the political process is more important.

The party system has become the organizing principle around which national and state politics (and federalism itself) have been able to develop. American political parties rarely centralize power at all. Characteristically they do the reverse, serving as a canopy under which special and local interests are repre- sented with little regard for anything that can be called a party program. More- over, party operations produce through Congress the basic division of functions between the federal government, on the one hand, and state and local govern- ments, on the other. The operation of parties transforms the Supreme Court's well-known permissiveness with respect to the expansion of national powers into legislation that characteristically provides important roles for state and local governments.[10]

The major effect of the expansion of the role of politics as a means of modi- fying the Constitution has been to increase the level of intergovernmental col- laboration. It has provided means for interests to make demands on the federal government successfully while, at the same time, insuring that the federal re- sponse be guided by a solicitude for the position of the states. This solicitude has meant that federal action usually reinforces the actions of the states and, at the very least, provides for their participation in some way.

TABLE 3-2

Federal Constitutional Provisions Specifically Limiting or Guaranteeing State Powers

GUARANTEES	LIMITS
A. State Integrity and Sovereignty	
No division or consolidation of states without state legislative consent (IV–2)*	States cannot enter into treaties, alliances, or confederations (I–10)
Republican form of government (IV–2)	No separate coinage (I–10)
Protection against invasion (IV–2)	No grants of titles of nobility (I–10)
Protection against domestic violence on application of proper state authorities (IV–2)	No interstate or foreign compacts without congressional consent (I–10)
Powers not delegated to the U.S. by the Constitution, nor prohibited by it to the states, are reserved to the states (Amendment X)	U.S. Constitution, all laws and treaties made under it to be supreme law of the land, binding on every state (VI)
	Slavery forbidden (Amendment XIII)
States cannot be sued by citizens of another state or a foreign nation (Amendment XI)	All state legislative, executive, and judicial officers, and state representatives in Congress to be bound by U.S. Constitution (VI)
	No abridgment of privileges and immunities of U.S. citizens (Amendment XIV)
	Reduction of representation in U.S. House of Representatives for denial of franchise to citizens (Amendment XIV)
	No payment of debts incurred in aid of insurrection or rebellion against U.S. or for emancipation of slaves (Amendment XIV)
	No abridgment of right to vote on account of race, color, or previous condition of servitude (Amendment XV)
	Popular election of Senators (Amendment XVII)
	No abridgment of right to vote on account of sex (Amendment XIX)
	No poll taxes in federal elections (Amendment XXIV)

*Numbers in parentheses refer to the Article and Section of the Constitution containing the provision.

TABLE 3-2 (*continued*)

GUARANTEES	LIMITS

B. Military Affairs and Defense

Power to maintain militia and appoint militia officers (I–8, Amendment II)	No letters of marque and reprisal (I-10)
	No maintenance of standing military forces in peacetime without Congress's consent (I–10)
	No engaging in war without Congress's consent, except to repel invasion (I–10)

C. Commerce and Taxation

Equal apportionment of federal direct taxes (I–2, 9)	No levying of duties on vessels of sister states (I–9)
No federal export duties (I–9)	No legal tender other than gold or silver (I–10)
No preferential treatment for ports of one state (I–9)	No impairment of obligations of contracts (I–10)
Reciprocal full faith and credit among states for public acts, records, and judicial proceedings (IV–1)	No levying of import or export duties without consent of Congress except reasonable inspection fees (I–10)
Reciprocal privileges and immunities for citizens of the several states (IV–2)	No tonnage duties without Congress's consent (I–10)
Intoxicating liquor may not be imported into states where its sale or use is prohibited (Amendment XXI–2)	

D. Administration of Justice

Federal criminal trials to be held in state where crime was committed (III–2)†	No bills of attainder (I–10)
Extradition for crimes (IV–2)	No ex post facto laws (I–10)
Federal criminal juries to be chosen from states and district in which crime was committed (Amendment VI)†	U.S. Supreme Court has original jurisdiction over all cases in which a state shall be a party (III–2)
Federal judicial power to extend to controversies between two or more states, a state or citizens of another state when state is plaintiff, and between foreign nation or its citizens with original jurisdiction vested in the Supreme Court (III–2)	Judges in every state bounded by U.S. Constitution and all laws and treaties made under it, notwithstanding the constitutions or laws of any state (VI)
	No denial of life, liberty, or property without due process of law (Amendment XIV)
	No denial of equal protection of state laws to persons within its limits (Amendment XIV)

†This provision insures the integrity of the state's common law in federal cases.

TABLE 3-3

Federal Constitutional Provisions Specifically Giving the States a Role in the Composition of the National Government

GUARANTEES	LIMITS
A. National Legislature	
Members of House of Representatives chosen by people of several states based on those qualified to vote for most numerous house of state legislature (I–2)	Representatives must be 25 years old and citizens of the U.S. for 7 years (I–2)
	Senators must be 30 years old and citizens of the U.S. for 9 years (I–3)
Representatives must be inhabitants of states from which they are elected at time of election (I–2)	
	Congress may make or alter regulations as to the times, places, and manner of holding elections for Senators and Representatives (I–4)
Representatives to be apportioned among the states according to population every ten years (I–2)	
	Each House shall be the judge of the elections, returns, and qualifications of its own members, punish its members for disorderly behavior and expel a member by two-thirds vote (I–5)
State executive has authority to fill vacancies (I–2)	
Each state shall have at least one Representative (I–2)	
	Basis for apportionment of representation in House of Representatives may be reduced proportionate to state deprivation of the right to vote of otherwise qualified citizens (Amendment XIV–2)
Senate shall be composed of two Senators from each state (I–3) chosen by the people qualified to vote for the most numerous house of the state legislature (Amendment XVII) with vacancies to be filled as prescribed by state legislation (Amendment XVII)	
	States cannot be represented by persons who have taken an oath to support Constitution and since engaged in insurrection, without express consent of two-thirds of Congress (Amendment XIV–3)
Senators must be inhabitants of the states from which they are chosen at time of election (I–3)	
Times, places, and manner of holding elections for Senators and Representatives shall be prescribed for each state by its legislature (I–4)	
No state to be deprived of equal representation in the Senate without its consent (V)	

TABLE 3-3 (*continued*)

GUARANTEES	LIMITS

B. National Executive

To be selected by the electors of the several states with each state allotted a number of electors equal to the total number of its Senators and Representatives (II–1)

Congress may determine the time of choosing electors and a uniform day on which they shall cast their votes (II–1)

Each state to have one vote if presidential election is decided in House of Representatives (II–1)

Approval of presidential appointees by the Senate as Congress shall prescribe (II–2)

C. Amendment of Constitution

Amendments must be ratified by three-fourths of the states (V)

Amendments must be proposed by two-thirds of the states (V)

D. Voting Rights

Cannot be denied or abridged on grounds of race, color, or previous condition of servitude (Amendment XV–1)

Cannot be denied or abridged on account of sex (Amendment XIX–1)

No poll tax may be levied as requirement to vote in federal elections (Amendment XXIV)

E. Foreign Affairs

Treaties must be ratified by two-thirds of Senate (II–2)

Treaties binding on states as supreme law of the land (VI)

Appointment of foreign service officers subjected to Senate confirmation (II–2)

F. Military Affairs and Defense

Power to appoint the officers of and train the militia when not in federal service reserved to the states (I–8)

Congress may provide for organizing, arming, and disciplining the militia when it is not in federal service and for governing it when it is (I–8)

Such collaboration, long dominant in American federalism, has been progressively expanded to include virtually every governmental function. From public welfare to public recreation, from national defense to local police protection, the system of sharing has become so pervasive that it is often difficult for the uninformed bystander to tell just who is doing what under which hat.[11] The federal-state mixture of responsibility and activity in serving the nation's "great constituencies"—Agriculture, Business, and Labor—illustrates this situation clearly, as indicated in Table 3-4.

This system of sharing or partnership has become tripartite over the years, with the localities carving out a role for themselves as a third level of government. Because they are protected by the same political diffusion of power that protects the position of the states *vis-à-vis* the federal government, local communities have been able to use their political power to secure a measure of autonomy not formally theirs under constitutional law. This has given them a measure of control over all government activities within their limits regardless of the level of government formally responsible for them.[12]

The Partnership System in Action. The Constitution itself requires federal-state cooperation in some areas (administration of elections, for example) and makes cooperation in other areas possible by giving both governments broad concurrent powers. Since 1790, the courts, Congress, and custom have virtually eliminated all possible restrictions on joint federal-state action, even while generally reaffirming the necessity for institutional dualism. Where concurrent jurisdiction was clearly constitutional it has been sustained, and where the issue was in doubt concurrent powers have been extended.[13]

This trend has often been viewed as a simple expansion of federal power at the expense of the states. In reality, it has meant an expansion of the realm of activities of both federal and state governments to generate an increase in the velocity of government (that is, the amount of governmental activity in relation to the total activity of society) in the nation as a whole. Thus, the acts of Congress have tended to neutralize centralizing Supreme Court decisions by providing the states with a firm share in virtually all federal domestic programs, including several in which the federal government is apparently given the right to claim exclusive jurisdiction in the words of the Constitution itself. For example, the improvement of navigable waters is a federal responsibility involving the federal government, the states, and their local subdivisions in cooperative projects. By the same token, policing the waters, originally a state and local responsibility, has come to involve the United States Coast Guard as well.

In some cases, Congress has even "overruled" the Court and turned functions given it by judicial interpretation over to the states. Ownership of the off-shore oil lands, regulation of the insurance business, and preemptive powers in the field of labor legislation are cases in point. In all three cases, the Supreme Court ruled that federal authority was preeminent, and in all three Congress ceded that authority in all or in part back to the states.[14]

Part of the reason for the development of this kind of sharing as a means to maintain the position of the states and their localities lies in the very real supremacy of the federal government in matters of taxing and spending. Though the power to tax and spend is constitutionally concurrent, the federal

TABLE 3-4

The Mixture of Federal-State Activity in Serving the Great Constituencies

I. BUSINESS

A. Establishing Favorable Conditions

1. Protection of private property rights
2. Establishment of organizational forms for business and enterprise
   States have primary responsibility; federal government has limited role

3. Establishing rules of bankruptcy and business reorganization
   Shared responsibility

4. Granting of patent rights
5. Maintaining a monetary system
   Federal responsibility

B. Direct Aids

1. Tariffs
2. Price supports
   Federal aid

3. Industrial subsidies
4. Data gathering and economic studies
5. Money or credit lending
   Shared aid (federal share generally larger)

C. Regulation

1. Maintenance of competition
2. Transportation regulation
3. Atomic energy regulation
4. Regulating banking, bank credit, bank deposits
5. Protecting investors
   Shared: federal role largest

6. Licensing of ordinary business
   State responsibility

7. Utility regulation
   Shared

8. Regulation of communications
   Federal responsibility; states have minor role

II. LABOR

A. Protection against Exploitation

1. Limiting child labor
2. Protecting women workers
3. Limiting hours of work
4. Establishing minimum wages
   Shared responsibility with federal share larger

5. Preventing racial and religious discrimination
6. Protecting migratory labor
   Primarily state responsibility with federal share growing

7. Compensation for injuries on-the-job
   State responsibility supported by federal action

TABLE 3-4 (*continued*)

II. LABOR (*continued*)

B. Protection of Right to Organize and Bargain Collectively

1. Protecting right to organize	
2. Protecting right to strike	Shared responsibility; federal share larger
3. Providing mechanisms for settling labor-management disputes	

C. Assistance in Finding and Keeping Jobs

1. Providing employment offices	Shared responsibility; states have primary role, federal government in supporting role
2. Stimulating employment opportunities	
3. Assisting in manpower retraining	
4. Providing unemployment compensation	

III. AGRICULTURE

A. Increasing Productivity

1. Managing research	Shared; states have primary role with federal support
2. Diffusing knowledge	
3. Providing technical assistance	
4. Developing field projects	Shared equally

B. Maintaining Commodity Prices

1. Insuring parity and supporting prices	
2. Regulating production	Largely federal with state support
3. Acquiring and storing surpluses	

C. Regulating Quality of Produce

1. Sanitary inspection	
2. Health inspection	Shared
3. Grading and quality inspection	

D. Developing Agricultural Markets

1. Securing tariff concessions	Federal responsibility
2. Disposing of the stored agricultural surplus	Primarily federal
3. Promoting produce use	Primarily state
4. Opening new markets	Shared

---

government has been, over the years, clearly in a better position to use its share of the power. Rather than resist this trend, the states and localities have developed means to capitalize on it in a manner calculated to maximize their ability to control the expenditure of funds passing through their hands, no matter what their source. The states have actually used such funds to extend their control over their own local subdivisions.

Political pressures generated in the states and localities to gain federal financial assistance for governmental services, coupled with an increasing interest in those services on the part of federal officials (particularly professionals in the various functional fields), have led to the development of an elaborate system of federal transfers of payments to the states and localities for a wide variety of activities. Since the early nineteenth century, it has been clear that Congress may use its taxing (and other revenue-raising) powers to support federal-state cooperative programs, attaching such conditions to its grants as it deems proper and providing for the revocation of such grants as it deems necessary. In the years since the establishment of the Republic, a highly institutionalized system of federal-state cooperation has developed which has really become part of the nation's constitutional tradition. Under this cooperative system, the federal government, the states, and the localities share the burden for the great domestic programs by making the larger governments primarily responsible for raising revenue and setting standards and the smaller ones primarily responsible for administration of the programs.

If the federal system had been predicated on a clean separation of functions as well as structure (i.e., dual federalism), then centralization would probably have been inevitable as it became necessary for the federal government to intervene in problems that, by their very nature, transcended state lines. In actuality, federal intervention can be supplementary and stimulatory rather than preemptive because of the possibilities for intergovernmental collaboration. When and where federal action was considered necessary, it could be used to stimulate state action as well, and federal-state cooperation could be so structured as to vest the greatest amount of operating responsibility in the local community.

Since federal involvement in any given program rarely came after substantial state involvement, there are few cases of federal expansion at the expense of ongoing state operations. On the contrary, federal involvement has usually stimulated a great expansion of state activity in the same field and an over-all enlargement of the scope of the state governmental operations. Such expansion has meant not only greater state expenditure of funds but also an increase in the number and quality of the personnel involved in carrying out the state's operations. This, in turn, has led to an increase in the states' ability to make policy for the internal operation of cooperative programs and to make their policy decisions "stick" even in the face of federal opposition.

Take the great federal-state welfare programs which were considered to be such radical attempts at centralization in the 1930s. We commonly think of those grant programs as Federal (meaning national out-of-Washington) programs. Yet in reality they are federal (meaning shared-by-Washington-and-the-states) programs with the emphasis for shaping them increasingly placed on the states. While Washington sets certain basic standards for each welfare program, it is actually the province of the states not only to administer those programs which their legislatures have authorized but also to determine a major share of the policy they will follow. Within certain limits, the states determine the size of welfare payments and the eligibility for different forms of assistance while Congress guarantees to match the state expenditures according to a pre-set formula (approximately but not exactly fifty-fifty, depending on the program) no matter how large they may be. Indeed, if Congress has not appropriated enough money to cover the federal share, it must, by law, make the necessary deficiency appropriations. The federal administrators oversee the transfer of funds and audit their use but do little to interfere with the operations of state welfare programs.[15]

It is misleading, however, to think of the shared aspects of these programs as reflective of a residual state-local obstructionism based on existing political alignments powerful enough to defeat the upwardly-striving federal administrators. Unfortunately, the more spectacular examples of the power of the states within the cooperative framework tend to reflect obstructionism (or something akin to it). The Negro rights problem is clearly a case in point, and even the Illinois welfare case has such overtones. In the less-publicized problems of highway construction, public health, conservation, and the like, and in the routines of day-to-day collaboration common to every program, there is generally little conflict between levels of government as such. When such conflict does erupt, the power of the states and localities is as frequently used to advance projects commonly considered to be in the public interest against what might be called federal "obscurantism." Governor Rockefeller has related one good example of this aspect of the federal-state relationship involving New York. His state wished to acquire certain surplus military lands for park purposes. Private developers who wished to acquire the lands for subdivision put pressure on the federal General Services Administration which put a high price tag on the land, primarily to gain greater return for the federal treasury. The state officials, who felt that the lands should be made available to New York at reduced cost since a public purpose was involved saw to it that the lands were zoned (a power reserved to the states and their subdivisions) in such a way as to prevent their subdivision. The subdividers then had no further use for the property, withdrew their bids, and the G.S.A. had to allow the state to take possession, under the law.[16]

In some cases, the states use their powers to advance clearly national interests. During the late 1950s when the testing of nuclear weapons in the atmosphere was raising levels of radiation to new peaks to the dismay of many scientists and medical experts, the federal Atomic Energy Commission repeatedly ignored any efforts on the part of the public to ascertain the exact amounts of radioactive fallout and contamination reaching the American people. At that point, several of the states on their own initiative—through their own legislation and the activities of their own public health departments —began collecting samples of the atmosphere, the soil, and their local crops, tested these, and made their findings public. The states not only reported their findings but, in some cases, began to take steps to control potential sources of public contamination.

The states could do this despite Atomic Energy Commission recalcitrance and even in the face of A.E.C. opposition because they had independent agencies with independent sources of power. Though these agencies used federal funds for some of their activities, in the last analysis they remained beholden to their states. And even though their officials undoubtedly saw eye to eye with their federal counterparts on most matters, they could take public issue with a federal agency with impunity when they felt it necessary to do so.

Sharing Revenues. Though the most characteristic element in the partnership system is the cash grant-in-aid (federal-state, state-local, or federal-local), the system actually operates through several devices, among them:

1. Grants-in-aid (both cash and land grants);
2. Shared revenues (examples: timber and mineral royalties, shared license fees);
3. Direct payments to individuals (examples: federal payments for agricultural programs and veterans' pensions, state higher education scholarships, local general assistance aid);
4. Payments to states and localities for discharging federal responsibilities (example: housing federal prisoners);
5. Services-in-aid (the provision of technical assistance through lending or assigning personnel by one level of government to another);
6. Grants and contracts awarded on similar terms to public and private applicants (example: federal research grants to universities);
7. Grants-in-kind (surplus commodities, obsolete military equipment, etc.).

Each of these devices has a long history extending back at least into the nineteenth century, and each has been sanctioned through different modes of constitutional interpretation. Furthermore, each has its own "politics," a variation on the over-all theme of the partnership.

Perhaps the most outstanding characteristic of the federal grants and shared revenues in the context of internal state politics is that the political struggle over the use and distribution of the money is essentially an intrastate matter. In practically all the major programs channeled through the states, the federal funds are so mixed with state funds after their transfer that the local beneficiaries have no idea whose money they are receiving. Their efforts to obtain funds are essentially directed toward the state house, not toward the national Capitol.[17].

There are three exceptions to this rule. Occasionally the localities must struggle with the state legislature to gain state participation in a federal program that might benefit them or state authorization for them to participate if it is a direct federal-local program (as in the case of urban renewal). Such conflicts are particularly frequent in states that are in transition from a rural orientation to dominance by larger cities. The rural interests, endeavoring to hang on to a passing era, tend to resist virtually all the demands of the state's burgeoning cities. Such was the case in Iowa until 1961. The rural-oriented legislature refused to allow the state's cities to participate in federal-aid urban renewal programs until that year.[18]

A second exception occurs in some of the smaller federal-state programs where the amount of federal funds allocated to each state is too little to satisfy local demands. Local communities then enter into competition at the state level to gain a share of the allocated funds for their own projects. While this competition is also intrastate in character, it is initiated for specific federally-aided projects known to the localities. In certain situations, the localities are even able to call upon federal personnel stationed within them to assist them in advancing their claims.[19]

Finally, in recent years the "pilot project" has become a new way for local communities to get additional federal aid. In many of these cases, the localities must compete with other local communities in Washington for special grants. In most of these cases, they are supported by legislative and administrative representatives of their states, but the burden of the struggle still remains on their shoulders.

The greatest impact of federal spending within the United States comes not from transfers of payments but from defense-related expenditures and direct payments to private individuals, primarily farmers and veterans. The latter, including government grants to institutions for civilian research, average out to approximately one-third of the total amount transferred to the states through federal grants each year. Defense contracts represent the great bulk of the direct federal expenditures within the states. In fiscal 1962 alone, new contracts worth $27,800,400,000 were awarded, approximately four times the total amount distributed through federal grants that same year.[20]

When the state-by-state distribution of federal defense contract expenditures is considered, it is apparent that the old adage, "Them that has, gets," applies. Those states "tooled up" for defense production are repeatedly favored. This is not just a matter of objective efficiency. Part of the "having" is having well-developed methods for influencing the allocation of contracts. Local industries seeking contracts and local communities seeking defense installations work closely in hand with state congressional delegations and state and local political officials lobbying in Washington. In some cases, states and the larger cities have established "Washington offices," virtually embassies, to work with their congressional delegations. Massachusetts has been particularly active in this regard for two decades, its Washington office having been opened in 1941. The gains registered by that state since 1961 were not simply a matter of having a Kennedy in the White House, but represented the fruition of hard work by the state's "man in Washington" beginning in 1956 when Governor Foster Furcolo reorganized the office and formalized its relationships with the Massachusetts congressional delegation.[21]

In fact, states in different sections of the country are favored differently by different kinds of federal aid. To cite some examples: southern and smaller western states are favored with a higher per capita return of federal grant funds as part of the ostensibly equalizing aspects of federal grants-in-aid programs. Southern states have been favored with military installations since the Spanish-American War; their Congressmen and chambers of commerce have become specially adept at securing and maintaining such installations. The states of the Southwest and Far West have been particularly successful in gaining military contracts which have led to the creation of whole new industries which, in turn, have enabled those states to maintain or enlarge their "boom" conditions. They have been particularly successful in acquiring a virtual monopoly over the nation's aerospace programs, offering climate as an inducement to those interested in year-round testing operations and year-round "outdoor living." The New England states have had a measure of success in attracting federal funds for research and development by capitalizing on their already excellent research and educational facilities and by developing channels of influence in Washington.

The two kinds of federal transfers of payments serve to divide the political struggle over funds into two parts—the intrastate struggle for funds to be used for public services and the interstate struggle for federal defense expeditures. It appears that there is little interstate struggle for the public service dollar. By now Washington has the formula system down pat, and all that must be done is to arrive at an agreement on what kind of formula to use when new programs are inaugurated or old ones revised. Since it has become clear that the margin of allowable gain within the formula structure is limited and the representatives of the states generally recognize the virtues of some measure of redistribution of wealth through federal grants, Congress spends relatively little effort in fighting over it.

By the same token, there is little intrastate conflict over defense funds. This is not only because defense funds represent direct federal expenditures which do not pass through state hands. There is a gentleman's agreement in most states that, while localities are free to submit their own bids up to a point, once the federal authorities have indicated any preferences the entire state will concentrate its efforts on behalf of the favored community.

The federal government also provides some direct aid to localities. Contrary to the general impression, the federal government has been supplying direct aid to local communities since the early nineteenth century, then as now primarily in the field of internal improvements.[22] In recent years, however, great metropolitan centers have emerged which face problems of urban reconstruction of unprecedented magnitude. These great cities are politically able to make their influence felt in Washington and are organizationally strong enough to handle the complexities of administering cooperative programs. They have been active in securing the right to develop direct city-federal relationships in certain aspects of the airport construction, urban renewal, and housing fields. Even in these cases, the states retain the right to involve themselves in the relationship if they choose to do so.

Protecting State Integrity. The constitutional document binding the federal government and the states clearly provides for federal supremacy and gives the federal authorities the power to maintain that supremacy. At the same time, the constitutional traditions which have grown up around the document have tempered its use by inducing a policy of federal self-restraint and providing political means for the maintenance of that policy.

The states are best able to protect themselves and to induce federal self-restraint when the problems which confront them are handled through regular political channels and are least able to do so when the problems are not, constitutional guarantees notwithstanding. For example, the United States Supreme Court has recently taken upon itself, as the ultimate arbiter of the basis of legislative representation, the drawing of electoral districts for choosing of state and national legislators. The Court has seen fit to do this despite clear constitutional provisions granting Congress the power to regulate congressional elections and a history of congressional legislation in the field, as well as the not quite so clear reservation that the states apportion their own legislatures. The consequences of the Court's entrance into the political thicket of apportionment are not yet clear. What is clear is that in this case, as in so many others, accepted prerogatives of the states are being challenged by the one institution that is least subject to control through the normal channels of politics.[23] Perhaps the influence of the political process will lead to a smoothing out of the "either-or" decision of the Court.[24] Perhaps the states will resort to amendment of the Constitution to protect themselves. Perhaps the Court's intervention here will lead to a greater change in the relations between the states and their local subdivisions than in the relationship between the states and Washington.

Even with the entrance of the Supreme Court into the apportionment question and the increasing concern of all three branches of the federal government with protecting the rights of Negroes to vote in the southern states, voting in all elections—federal, state, and local—remains a state-regulated activity. This provides the states with a *de facto* bulwark against overassertion of federal authority subject only to the explicit restrictions placed on it by the Fifteenth, Nineteenth, and Twenty-Fourth Amendments, and the relatively few acts of Congress and Court decisions enforcing these Amendments. Congress actually exercised more control over federal elections a century ago than it does today. In any case, the total number, times, and places of elections are set by the states, as are the age and residence requirements for voters.[25]

The representation of the states in Congress provides another very important way for them to maintain their integrity and internal autonomy—through a highly institutionalized system of congressional interference into executive actions. In order to understand this system, it is necessary to look briefly at the growth of administrative rule-making powers.

The discretionary rule-making power of federal administrative agencies has been substantially increased to the point where their rule-making activities have nearly as much effect on state-federal relations as formal legislation and judicial interpretation. The sheer mass of federal business has made this necessary. Congress can, at best, set forth the general guidelines for the implementation of federal-state programs, the awarding of contracts, or the administration of federal programs that touch upon the individual directly (such as the major agricultural and veterans' programs). Once these guidelines are established, however, federal administrators must make the specific rules and then apply them. The individual states, in turn, have found that they must have some means of recourse to influence the way in which those rules will affect them, short of trying to alter the general legislation.

The representatives of the states have found such a recourse in the institutionalization of "interference" (the term is used in a neutral sense). The tradition of such interference is well developed, dating back to the beginning of the Republic. There are two kinds of interference. Best known is the formal system of legislative oversight with its tradition of insuring a place on key committees for representatives of states and even localities most seriously affected by the actions of those committees. This has given the states an important line of access to national policy-making through the powers of the committees to review proposed legislation and investigate on-going programs and through the powers of committee members to demand consideration for their constituents and constituencies as the price for supporting the administration. Considering the important role of the committees, this institution has indeed become a crucial one in the perpetuation of the noncentralized traditions of American federalism.[26]

The states and localities not only possess virtual representation on committees, their interests are also represented by their Congressmen acting singly. Very early in the history of the Republic, Congressmen and their constituents interpreted the right of petition as the right to interfere in administrative affairs on behalf of their constituents—private or public—establishing the right of congressional interference as part of the nation's unwritten constitution. With the increasing bureaucracy of the federal executive branch, this interference, or "case-work" as it has come to be called, has only the barest connection with the original constitutional right of petition. It is basically a political device rooted in the power of local groups and the desire of Congressmen to build up credit with potential supporters. Considering only its effects on the relations between the states and localities and the federal government, it is a most useful device for gaining administrative consideration for state and local needs *after* legislation has been enacted and at the point where administrative discretion in statutory interpretation becomes important.[27] Congressional staffs, which have grown in size primarily because of this responsibility, handle their case-work with great care, knowing that their Congressman's performance in that area is likely to influence more voters than his actions on national issues. Administrative agencies also go to great lengths to serve congressional interests and, by indirection, the interests of the individuals, groups, states, and localities the Congressmen represent because they know that future congressional support is often dependent on this kind of service. While the great majority of the cases which lead to congressional interference do not involve other governments, they are nonetheless important to the maintenance of the position of the states and localities. Because the states are political systems, the actions and requests of ostensibly private parties are often highly meaningful for the maintenance of state and local authority or for the development of state and local public policy. For example, a request by a chamber of commerce for the expansion of a local military installation, or a private manufacturer's petition to state and local leaders—if not governments—to promote the development of their "little" economies. Although this form of subnational governmental influence is as yet barely recognized, it is an important adjunct to the maintenance of the position of the states.

The extent to which any state takes advantage of congressional interference does not appear to follow any recognizable pattern. In one sense, every Congressman is so involved in case-work that the differences among the states are marginal. In another sense, some states organize more actively than others to handle state problems in Washington. The congressional delegations of several states meet together regularly (often once a week) to plan ways and means to serve the interests of their states. While this kind of cooperation is easier in one-party states and is most prevalent among the southern delegations whose members are past masters in serving their states through interference, states with very competitive two-party systems—such as California, Massachusetts, and Colorado—also unite in Washington without regard for party lines in matters of state interest. For many states, internal political fights stop at the state line and are replaced by a "bipartisan foreign policy" *vis-à-vis* Washington.

Even when there is cooperation between partisans, many northern and western states are hampered in their efforts to gain access to Washington because the very competitiveness of their internal politics leads to a high turnover in their congressional delegations. One constant in the measurement of influence on Capitol Hill is seniority. All other things being equal, the greater a representative's seniority, the greater his ability to serve his state and his constituents. Those states which rarely reelect men long enough to enable them to acquire seniority are invariably handicapped in their efforts.

Perhaps paradoxically, administrative rule-making often has a decentralizing effect that extends the powers of the states even beyond those allowed by con-

gressional legislation and interference. The decisions of the professional administrators in the federal service who are charged with overseeing specific programs are shaped by many factors, including the personalities of the men
involved, the character of their commitment to the program they are administering, and the influence of the professional "guild" to which they belong. This
latter factor is of prime importance since many of the ostensibly "Federal"
rules are really "federal" in origin—shaped by the associations of professionals
serving the states and localities, as well as the federal government whose
responsibility it is to implement the very same programs. Frequently, the
"Federal" standards governing the construction of interstate highways are
products of the American Association of State Highway Officials working in
cooperation with the Bureau of Public Roads. Similarly, the National Education Association and the American Association of State Universities have
major roles in shaping the rules for implementing the National Defense Education Act. The same situation prevails in most of the major cooperative programs.

When the professional qualifications of the state and local personnel involved in a given program are established, their federal counterparts are apt
to regard their views as equally valid and respectable and to give them great
leeway in managing even the federal funds granted for their programs. If the
federal administrators are also sympathetic to the idea of noncentralized government, they are more likely to minimize use of the powers they are entitled to
exercise. When federal and state administrators are in general agreement as to
the "right" way to implement particular programs, the states are most likely
to be given a free hand. But even when federal administrators "go by the
book," their state counterparts are frequently able to avoid further investigation by submitting the requisite formal documents applying for funds and
accounting for their use in the approved manner and thus "buy" freedom from
real supervision. As a general rule, the better established a program is, the
less likely it is that federal administrators will exercise the supervisory powers
legally theirs.[28]

Guarantees of State "Republicanism." While the political process has been
put to hard use to find ways to guarantee state political integrity against the
pressures of centralization, virtually nothing has been added to the constitutional guarantees that allow federal authority to be used to maintain representative government within the states. Congress has the exclusive authority to decide
whether or not a state has "a republican form of government" by accepting or
refusing to seat the state's elected representatives. It is clear that Congress will
rarely exercise its powers in this regard. Though not couched in these terms,
the recent federal Supreme Court decisions in the realm of reapportionment
may possibly be viewed as an effort to establish criteria for "republicanism" and
to enforce them through federal intervention.

The greatest opportunity for federal action to give these guarantees meaning came a century ago during the Civil War; yet no significant reliance was placed upon them at that time, either to restore the Union or to reconstruct the seceding states. The various cases of federal military intervention within the states have rarely, if ever, been justified under any of those guarantees. In the one or two cases when states have apparently abandoned representative government in spirit, they have retained the forms of republicanism, and no effort has been made to invoke federal power or even to exclude the states' representatives from Congress.

In reality then, such guarantees as exist stem from outside the written Constitution, having their source in the nationwide party system and the penetration of national political concerns into the states. While these may appear to be imperfect, short-range guarantees, in the long run they have proven quite effective in breaking or at least lessening the grip of autocracies and oligarchies which, from time to time, have assumed power in various states to frustrate the spirit of republicanism. The universality of political concerns in the United States and the use of the party system to develop nationwide responses to those concerns has meant that the internal political systems of every state have at least had to assimilate certain nationally approved devices for meeting those concerns. The grant programs, for example, have been adopted by every state, from welfare-conscious New York to oligarchical Virginia to racist Mississippi to middle-class-oriented Minnesota. In the process, a level of "republicanism" is introduced into each of those states.

The one major addition to the written Constitution which has had profound effects on the position of the states in the Union is the package of Civil War Amendments—Thirteenth, Fourteenth, and Fifteenth. That package formally ratified the supremacy of the national government along the lines set forth in Federalist political theory as embraced by the Yankee North.[29] It provided the constitutional basis for the expanded federal supervision of state actions in the field of civil and political rights of recent decades.

Even these three wartime Amendments, passed in a period of national crisis with the express purpose of asserting federal supremacy, were ultimately cut down to size through the political process. As Reconstruction ended, the restoration of southern representation in Congress and the emergence of the "Solid South" made it possible for the ex-Confederates virtually to eliminate congressional or executive action to enforce many of the provisions of these Amendments. Faced with the potentialities for federal action inherent in the War Amendments, the Southerners devised ways to keep these potentials from being translated into action. Control over the choice of presidential candidates by the Democratic Party through the two-thirds rule, the development of the seniority system in Congress, and the use of the filibuster in the Senate gave the southern states what John C. Calhoun had advocated a generation earlier—the right to demand concurrent majority decisions in all matters affecting their vital interests (particularly the race issue) and the power to exercise a veto under the concurrent majority system. They maintained this right for nearly a century.

While the Southerners were able to frustrate use of these Amendments for the protection of individual liberties, from the 1880s to the 1930s the Fourteenth Amendment was used to restrict state power to regulate private corporations. Today, this means of limiting the power of the states has been substantially overruled and the states again have wide latitude in the use of their regulatory powers. Instead, the Amendments have been used by the Supreme Court to extend its role as arbiter of the standards of fundamental liberty and criminal justice over state as well as federal law enforcement agencies.[30]

Though the first impression left by the recent use of these Amendments is that they have increased federal dominion over the states, the Court has in fact acted less to extend federal governmental authority than to establish its own position as an umpire interested in raising the standards of justice applicable at all levels of government. Even so, in virtually every case, the Court's decisions have come only after three-fifths of the states have individually adopted positions, and in no important case except those involving reapportionment have less than half of the states been on the same side as the court. This unwritten (and perhaps unconscious) "three-fifths rule" can be seen to be operative in the whole range of desegregation cases, in the Court's decision to disallow the use of illegally obtained evidence in state courts, in the recently established requirement that counsel be provided in all criminal cases, and in the prohibition of mandatory prayers and Bible reading in the schools.

Paradoxically, the three Civil War Amendments have had a dual effect. They have formally clarified federal supremacy in the written Constitution and have provided the Court with the means to make that supremacy "stick" in areas previously immune from federal intervention. Yet they also have become the catalysts for the introduction of a modified version of the concurrent majority system into the unwritten constitution for use by both Congress and the Court.

Conclusions

Politically speaking, the present system of federal-state relations appears to be maintaining itself despite its many public critics who denounce particular cooperative actions such as infringements upon "states rights" and "local self-government" and who oppose giving the states a share in federal programs on the grounds that the states are "centers of reaction." The system is popular because it provides most of the competing interests in this country—even those groups who rail against it—with enough satisfactions to convince them that it works. And it provides those satisfactions because it is amenable to political influence in the deepest sense.[31]

Perhaps there was a time when it may have been possible to generalize casually about specific interests being satisfied by different levels of government and to establish a precarious balance between the federal government, the states, and the localities by virtue of these different sources of satisfaction. There appear to have been grounds to support this view a generation ago. Today, it is no longer true about any significant interest. Every interest now tries to develop ties with every level of government and will utilize those ties to varying degrees depending upon the specific issue confronting it. This is no doubt a natural concomitant of the growing complexity of the cooperative system and the increasing involvement of all levels of government in handling the same programs.

In the last analysis, the states remain viable entities in a federal system that has every tendency toward centralization, present in all strong governments. States remain viable because they exist with political systems of their own. They maintain that existence because the American political tradition and the Constitution which embodies it give the states an important place in the over-all fabric of American civil society. The tradition and the Constitution remain viable because neither Capitol Hill nor the fifty statehouses have been able to serve all the variegated interests that compete on the American scene equally well without one another. The American people are known to appreciate the tradition and the Constitution. Most important, they seem to appreciate the partnership, too, and have learned to use all its elements to satisfy their claims on government.

Creative Tensions

TERRY SANFORD

The states are indecisive.
The states are antiquated.
The states are timid and ineffective.
The states are not willing to face their problems.
The states are not responsive.
The states are not interested in cities.

These half-dozen charges are true about all of the states some of the time and some of the states all of the time. On the other hand, at points in history, most of these charges have been applicable to both the national and local governments.

Admitting, for the sake of improvement, that there is validity to the charges, what can be done? If nothing much can be done, then indeed the states will soon be finished. And the federal system, the great compromise that brought together a wide and diverse land, will have collapsed.

Of course, something would evolve to replace the present system. It would surely be some form of unitary government. It would be a *national* government as distinguished from a *federal* government. On the face of it, as it now appears to be forming, it does not look bad. In fact, it looks more efficient. The regional offices of a completely national government would have dividing lines which make "sense." The lines of administrative authority could be drawn with more clarity. The bottlenecks, which some contend states are, would be broken. Policies and programs could be carried out with dispatch. No state could stubbornly slow down or stop a program that Congress had started.

We would have a clean-cut, efficient, neat governmental structure, capable of solving its problems, serving its people, and functioning without the confusion, muddle, and clutter of overlapping, competing levels of government that indeed were born out of compromise.

But this structure might not be what it seems. Although it might be shocking to admit, we should not try to have a neat government. Part of the genius of the American system of government is that it has been a bit untidy. More than we may realize, this has given us a flexibility, has permitted change, and has made innovation possible. If a proposal did not work in one place, it could be tried out in another. If an idea is turned down at one point, there is always another point where it might find acceptance. If something cannot be started or stopped in a state legislature, the advocates of doing something or stopping something can try city hall or their congressman. Neither the states nor Washington is the only port of entry for ideas, the single route to action, or the one blockade to mistakes.

The President rarely has his unrestrained way with the Congress. The troubles of John F. Kennedy, after his narrow victory in 1960, are much more typical than the legislative successes of Lyndon B. Johnson. It is far easier in Congress to beat something than to get it passed. Kennedy's problems were dramatized in a book by James MacGregor Burns, in which he pointed out that congressional deadlock was a common characteristic in American history, spotted as it has been with spurts of furious legislative activity.[32]

English politics rarely countenance disloyalty to the party line. The member of parliament follows his prime minister or his leader of the loyal opposition. The English fail to appreciate the flexibility of our situation where a vote on any substantive matter is seldom without dissenters and line crossing from both sides of the aisle. Our broadly based parties have differences within their ranks, and the coalition shifts from vote to vote and subject to subject. Our freewheeling system, for all its apparent disorganization, is much more democratic and more creative than the English.

When some naturalists wanted forestry practices controlled but some insisted that control would destroy nature's balance in the wilderness, our untidy response was to have both. The U.S. Forest Service follows the first alternative, the U.S. Park Service the other, and the future has been better served.

Thus we can rejoice in a competitive, combative, contentious system that brawls its way to resolution and is provided with many openings for a fair hearing as well as ample safeguards against precipitate action. Some states permit liquor bottles on the table, some allow only mixed drinks, others insist that the bottle be under the table, and still others allow neither bottle nor glass. Not neat, but apparently it satisfies a lot more people than the uniform national approach once tried. When some states were enacting laws against closed-shop clauses in union contracts, others were either declining to do so or repealing such laws already on the books. There are strong arguments being made that this contract provision should be dealt with by one national law; there are also arguments being made against a single approach. Ours is a government with alternatives.

If the nation had a single divorce law, it would be much more restrictive than that of the most lenient state and more lenient than that of the most puritanical state. Who is wise enough to formulate for one and all the proper grounds for divorce in a nation as large and varied as this one? Twenty-three states this year considered changes in their abortion laws. That changes in a subject so delicate can even be discussed without a nationwide controversy over a federal law is a tribute to our diverse structure and a credit to the system. The very fact that in the enactment of such legislation some states may seem too lax to others is of value to society. The states are the outriders who test the limitations and restrictiveness of our accepted doctrines.

Capital punishment is another debated subject in which the cause of justice is well served by the options the states offer. If some contend that doing away with the death penalty will result in more murders, this opinion doesn't lead to an endless argument. Some state can try it. Michael V. DiSalle, a former governor of Ohio, makes the point that

> In the capital punishment states, a law enforcement officer's chance of being shot down in the performance of his duty is 1.3 per 100,000. In the abolitionist states, the rate is 1.2.[33]

At the present time, thirteen states have abolished the death penalty altogether. Some states have not abolished it by statute, but have done so in practice. Vermont, which has executed two men in twenty-eight years, abolished capital punishment except for repeaters and killers of policemen and prison guards. New York passed a limited bill, retaining it only for killers of policemen and prison guards. Tennessee developed its own technique. When the abolition of capital punishment failed in the Tennessee senate by one vote after overwhelmingly passing in the house, the governor commuted the sentences of everyone on death row.

The states test whether the opinions by which we live our lives and run our governments are myths or facts. This is federalism at its best—always probing, always testing, always seeking a better way. The states allow experimentation, change, and local leadership, especially in controversial subjects involving deep societal values in which feelings run high and attitudes vary all across the nation.

Neat conformity in government is found only in dictatorships. This price is too great. The fact that we have somehow understood this all along, that we have permitted and indeed encouraged a certain amount of flexibility and local adjustment, has given added vitality to our development, and has brought many benefits over the past two hundred years.

The tension in our system stimulates competition, and the colliding loyalties encourage improvement. New ideas can surface close to home where local leadership can put them into practice with the confidence of the people. To smooth out this creative tension, then, is to waste resources. In every section of the country there are talented people who are devoted to their states and care about their cities. They are not apathetic, not selfishly protective, and they want to do what must be done.

No one locus of government has a monopoly on brains and creativity. Men with these traits follow leadership whenever leaders want to do the job. Mayor John Lindsay in New York City has assembled a first-rate group of men to pick up the reins of the toughest city anywhere. When Richard Hughes began to lead New Jersey and make its people conscious that they lived in a state, good men were attracted to his call. And in the national government, John Gardner took over a depressed and confused department and made of it the most creative place to work in Washington.

The challenge to the leadership on every level is to harness the bureaucracy to its goals. The governors and mayors share the goals of Washington's top leadership. They want to do all they can to improve education, help the poor, and find better jobs and opportunities for their people. Dismissing their suggestions, excluding their views, or disregarding their potential service undercuts the achievement of all the goals.

It is often the fashion to refer to state lines as obsolete, and therefore to treat state officials as provincial leaders of outmoded territories. But would neat and "sensible" state boundaries add anything useful to our system? Long before the New Deal, even in the nineteenth century, some political scientists were advocating regional governments to replace the illogical lines of the states. Admittedly the lines were not originally drawn with an awareness of developments to come in communications, transportation, and living patterns. But is the solution today to sit down together the best brains and computers for the purpose of redrawing them with calculated accuracy? Who has that wisdom and vision, even in tandem with computers?

Nobody can really believe that state lines will be redrawn. The Constitution stands in the way of that. Instead, new lines will come, if they do, as the invention of the technocrats after the atrophy and neglect of the present states. Then in disregard of the states and the old lines, the new administrative units of the national government could be shaped with some purpose in mind. The New York harbor would be neatly wrapped into one subdivision by some of New Jersey, Connecticut, and New York State. Newark and Atlantic City would not be together; neither, for that matter, would Los Angeles and San Francisco. Each subdivision would be designed to carry out the national objectives.

No such fantasy will be started deliberately on a draftsman's board. But it might develop if the states and the cities, giving up self-reliance, lean too much upon national aid, complaining only that they must go to too many different regional headquarters to get what is coming to them and to find out what to do. If this fantasy did come true, it would probably start with the consolidation of all regional offices, according to logical lines, but as compromised out by the various agencies that already had field offices. For a while state boundaries would be generally followed in the groupings. Later it would make more sense, be more workable, to draw the lines according to terrain and population groupings.

The whole thing would turn out to be easier to teach in school. The lines dividing the country neatly into sixteen national administrative subdivisions or units (NATS) could be flashed on the wall-high television screen. Hawaii might cause some difficulty, but it could be tucked in a corner with an arrow indicating that it belonged to the Los Angeles NAT.

It would all seem so orderly and efficient. The governors and state legislatures would not have anything substantial to do. Many critical political scientists would write that it was good that congressmen still had to come from districts drawn within the old state lines. This, they would contend, had almost eliminated logrolling. The U.S. senators would be almost irrelevant, not that the administrative personnel would not pay attention to them. They would have to; they would still vote the appropriations. But since they came from states, they would not have much meaning as far as the administrators of the NATS were concerned. Since the unit boundaries would have to be drawn with population as well as distances in mind, it would have turned out that four of the NATS had only one senator, one had nine, and the New York NAT didn't have any. But this kind of drift could only follow an abandonment of self-reliance by the states and cities.

The ultimate aim of our political structure is not orderliness and efficiency, and it is not simply to break bottlenecks or avoid blockage by state action. The chief need of the federal system is not compactness and straight lines of authority. Instead, the citizens of the United States need diversified political strengths.

Diversity, such as we have in our country, necessitates a federal system. Diverse political strength develops varied answers to assorted problems. It establishes the tensions for improvement. The power centers of the states protect our liberty from the possible tyranny of the national government, just as the power of the national government protects each citizen from the tyranny of the states.

The states are not merely subdivisions for administrative purposes. They may frequently act in that capacity, but they are more. They are, fundamentally, political units within a federal system, wherein both the parts and the whole rest on constitutional bases. No administrative subdivision could attain such a position.

Can we afford to let our present governmental relationships change substantially? We are moving into the era of joint responsibilities, the marble cake and the matrix, the partnership for seeking and solving problems, and the shared taxes. But can we allow one part of our federalism to become feeble, to lose position as a political force? The Articles of Confederation provided no power for the Congress, no way for it to withstand the political power of the individual state, no way for it to act for all the states combined into one nation. Consequently, the new nation was falling apart. The adoption of the U.S. Constitution eliminated that weakness. It created the power and authority needed for the states to act in unison. Now the question is, do we go to the other extreme?

The question can be posed very simply. Do we want a single national government, or a federal government which combines a national government with governments of the several states? The answer depends on our willingness to look for the faults and find the cures for the illnesses of state government. It is not possible to detail the disabilities of each state; some have one, and some have others, and some have too many to count. There is medicine to cure the illness and to put the states back on their feet. There remains the difficulty, however, of whether the people, the voters, want to take it.

The Relationship of Federal to Local Authorities

DANIEL P. MOYNIHAN

The past is never so clear as the future, save possibly with respect to the structure of American government. Over the years, this structure has retained a measure of complexity and contradiction of such variety that the features of the system most protested by one generation often become the qualities most valued by the next. A reemphasis of this sort appears to be in the offing. The great transformation now abroad in American society is the emergence of an educated middle-class electorate. These are certain to be notably active citizens, and it is no less certain that the complexities of the American governmental structure will both generate problems that call forth such energies and provide a bewildering array of outlets for them. No doubt the "inefficiencies" of federalism will continue to be deplored and efforts made to simplify the system, but it is most unlikely that such efforts will succeed. Thirty-five years is a short time in the history of American government; the near future is almost sure to be much like the distant past. Prolonged war, economic malaise, and racial stalemate will make for a more centrally directed system; peace, growth, and assimilation will make for a more related and permissive one. But the structure of the system is likely to continue to be much the same.

A number of large developments appear to be converging in a compatible, if not always harmonious, manner. Each of these is likely to add stability to the federal system, and none appears to generate disequilibrium.

First, there is the nationalization of public policy that has accompanied the achievement of a genuinely national society. If there is still a goodly supply of local problems, there are fewer and fewer specifically local "subjects." It has been agreed, as it were, that the most important national issues will be resolved in national terms and at the national level. This process is not complete with respect to the issues of race or education, but here, too, the transformation seems well under way. In this sense we have centralized decision-making within a federal structure and thereby greatly reduced pressures to change the latter in order to achieve the former.

The necessity for concentrating decision-making at the national level will be enhanced if current trends in racial concentration persist. Between 1960 and

Reprinted by permission from *Daedalus*, Journal of the American Academy of Arts and Sciences, Boston, Mass., Vol. 96, No. 3, 1967.

1966, the number of children under age fourteen in metropolitan areas increased by 3.3 million. Nonwhite children accounted for one third of the gain. The average annual rate of increase of nonwhite children (2.4 percent) was three times the rate for white children. Ninety-five percent of the nonwhite increase was in central cities, where the proportion of all children who are nonwhite rose from 23 percent in 1960 to 29 percent in 1966. Over-all recent increases have been rapid, and are likely to continue in the near term. According to one estimate, by 1970 Negroes will constitute 40 percent or more of the population in fourteen of the nation's major cities, including Washington, D.C., Richmond, Gary, Baltimore, Detroit, Newark, St. Louis, New Orleans, and Trenton.[34] In southern communities accustomed to taking collective measures to prevent Negro accession to power, there may be movements toward metropolitan governments in order to maintain Negroes in a minority voting status; but, in general, continued and possibly heightened racial tension is likely to inhibit greatly the development of true metropolitan governments. *A fortiori* the resolution of conflict between central cities and suburbs (which will increasingly take on "urban" qualities of their own) will have to occur at the federal level, save for the few states with sufficient political and fiscal resources to handle such matters at the level of state government.

Second, there is the rise of the federal fisc as the primary source of discretionary public expenditure. State and local revenues will continue to be committed, and overcommitted, to established programs. By contrast, federal revenues now grow at a considerable rate, and the growth is already being forecast in five-year periods. The need to expend the surplus in order to avoid fiscal drag has created within the Executive Office of the President a systematic search for new federal spending programs.

In July, 1965, for example, the Chairman of the Council of Economic Advisers testified before the Joint Economic Committee that "Federal revenues at full employment in 1970 would be expected to approach $170 billion, a rise of nearly $50 billion over the indicated revenues of 1965 and nearly $45 billion over full-employment revenues of this year [1965]." Shortly thereafter the administration began a process of military escalation that developed into a major land war in Asia. Nearly two years later this war is proceeding at, if anything, an accelerating pace, but has brought on neither a tax increase nor any considerable inflation. A cessation or decline in hostilities will only serve to emphasize the extraordinary fiscal resources of the federal government and lead to great and cogent demands that these resources be used for domestic programs.

Third, the tradition of decentralization and the fact of federalism is greatly inducive to the grant-in-aid as the principal form of federal expenditure on domestic programs. These have been increasing in both amount and variety. Between 1954 and 1964, federal grants to state and local governments rose 235 percent from $3 billion to $10 billion. This was twice the rate of increase

(118 percent) of federal grants to individuals. The variety of these problems has predictably become a problem in its own right. Thus in December, 1966, the Secretary of Housing and Urban Development reported to the Chairman of the Subcommittee on Executive Reorganization of the Senate Committee on Government Operations that there were then in existence 238 federal programs having an impact on urban areas. This maze of programs will produce periodic efforts to collapse activities into larger, more general categories, but the process is most likely to be one of alternating proliferation and consolidation, and the grant-in-aid will persist.

Fourth, the diffusion of the middle-class ideal of participation in public decision-making will add a considerable and, in a sense, unanticipated utility to the complexity of the American government structure, which requires such great citizen participation in order to operate. The 1400 governments Robert C. Wood discovered in the New York metropolitan area may prove none too many if the demand for committee work is to be met. This is not to say that government will become more efficient as the "quality" of the electorate improves and the proportion of persons taking an active part in public affairs increases. The opposite might well be the case: The more persons involved in making a decision, the more difficult it becomes to reach one. Participatory democracy is likely to be anything but a *fête d'amour*. Still, the federal system provides a singularly rich range of opportunities for participation and is apt to be valued for just that reason. Moreover, to the extent that the many small units of government in the present system reflect genuine interests, the skill and energy with which those interests are sure to be defended by a middle-class electorate are such as to suggest further that there will be a minimum of consolidation.

Six Themes for the Last Third of the Twentieth Century

I. WEDDING CAKE FEDERALISM

Morton Grodzins' image of "marble cake federalism" describing the mixing up of functions among the theoretically separate layers of governments may become less useful as federal fiscal power shapes more and more government activities. What seems to be evolving is a multi-tiered system of bureaucracies and governmental units surmounted by the person of the President (and increasingly the person of the First Lady as well). At every level, federal funds will provide much of the cake and most of the icing.

Both employment and expenditure have been increasing much faster at the state and local levels than at the federal level. Between 1952 and 1962, the expenditures of the federal government rose by 25 percent; those of state and local government by 128 percent. In 1946, state and local expenditures constituted 44 percent of government outgo. In 1962, this proportion had increased to 63 percent. But where in 1940 local government tax revenues were 5.51 percent of the national income, by 1963 they had declined to 4.64 percent. These patterns are reflected in the numbers of public employees at the different levels of government.

Government Employment, 1964

Federal*	1,434,000
State	1,873,000
Local, excluding education	2,645,000
Local, education	3,018,000

*Excludes those employed in national defense and international relations.

II. NEW VARIETIES OF GOVERNMENT

Because multi-purpose metropolitan government is not likely to emerge, special-purpose governments are likely to multiply. Some of these will be created directly by the federal government, as in the case of the elected county committees that administer the farm program, and the elected community-action boards that share in the administration of the poverty program. Significantly, much of the rationale of the poverty program elections has been that it is *good* for people to participate in government—not just a right but a remedy. Just as significantly, the lines of authority and communication within the federal system are more and more likely to assume a triangular form in which each government has direct relations with the other two clusters of public activity.

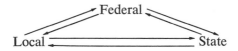

III. METROPOLITANISM IN EDUCATION

In the course of the first two-thirds of the twentieth century the most numerous and in some ways most important changes in government structure have occurred within school systems that have been steadily consolidating from quite small districts into rather large ones. Even so, at present there are some 34,678 school districts in the nation, approximately eleven times the number of counties. Despite a growing interest in "decentralization" of direction within the very large urban districts, there are still gains to be had from further mergers, and these are likely to continue. In the event that no significant measure of integration occurs in housing in the near future, there are certain to be growing demands to bring an end to the racial isolation of Negroes in public schools by establishing metropolitan school districts that encompass both the central-city Negro areas and the white suburbs. Inasmuch as education is manifestly a public function, pressures to bring about accommodations of this sort are likely to be considerably more effective than the often hapless assaults of individuals and small groups on the private-housing market.

IV. NATIONAL SOCIAL ACCOUNTS

In the middle third of the twentieth century the most powerful development in government was the emergence of a political economy capable of comprehending, predicting, and directing economic events. If this development is as yet by no means complete, its influence is already pervasive. Moreover, it provides the basis—in the form of discretionary government income—for the exploitation of what will probably be the most powerful development of the last third of the century: the emergence of a social science coupled with and based upon a system of social accounting that will give government an enlarged capacity to comprehend, predict, and direct social events. Again, it will be imperfect, but serviceable. In one political climate this may take the form of controlling society. In another it may produce a governmental system more effectively responsive to the wishes of the electorate than any society in history. More information about society will produce more information to do things for or to it. The technique of simulating social processes is likely to produce increasingly sophisticated forms of social innovation, evolving from the now widely employed "demonstration project" technique toward full-scale, controlled social experiments. At present, the social sciences are extremely rudimentary, and the likelihood of a major breakthrough is small. Indeed, the major discovery of the next generation may be that such developments are impossible. But it is certainly probable that sheer lack of information will have less influence on events in the future than it has had in the past, and that will make a difference in outcomes.

V. THE QUEST FOR COMMUNITY

A sustained concern for the conditions under which individuals from different racial, ethnic, and class groups can establish meaningful and peaceable relationships is predictable. This concern must arise from the already begun effort to enable Negro Americans to enter the larger American society, to offset the effects of "alienation in the city, trivialization in the suburbs," and the general ecological scatteration described by Scott Greer. Programs that promote a sense of community (beautification, conservation, preservation, and so forth) are likely to be given conscious priority. This effort will further encourage the multiplication of governmental forms and activities.

VI. THE REDISCOVERY OF THE MARKET

As government tries to do more, it will find it accomplishes less. This amounts to the discovery that administrative ability is not a free good, and in the absence of it the best-intentioned programs can turn out to be calamities. This proposition has been formulated by James Q. Wilson: "There are inherent limits to what can be accomplished by large, hierarchical organizations." The limitations imposed on bureaucratic performance in the United States are notable: that it expend money efficiently, but take the utmost precautions to see that not a penny is stolen; that it be responsive to special circumstances, but rigorously consistent in its actions, and so forth. Moreover, as "easy" problems are disposed of, the more marginal, intractable ones come into prominence, and the return on government effort manifestly diminishes. All this is likely to lead to what Charles E. Lindblom has termed the "rediscovery of the market" as a means of accomplishing social objectives. The logic of events is very much on the side of Lindblom's assertion: "That the market mechanism can be serviceable to planned and unplanned economies alike, to public and private enterprise alike, to collective and individual choice alike, is a discovery the significance of which may soon dwarf what we have seen of its consequences so far."[35]

In the future social problems are likely to be approached more often by means of an *income* strategy than by a *services* strategy, as defined by Lee Rainwater. Thus the concept of giving the poor the money with which to purchase what they need—be it proper housing or medical care—in the market is apt to be considered far more seriously in the future than in the immediate past, which has been much influenced by ideals of professionalization in public services. In a similar vein, more and more services that have been thought to be located necessarily in the public sector will probably be contracted out to private enterprises—particularly in areas where results are more important than processes. J. Herbert Holloman foresees the development of "the public market" for just such purposes—for example, "a profit-making organization running a chain of junior colleges under contracts with the communities in which they are located."

Business organizations, which are characteristically oriented to results rather than process, are in a position to offer to contract for a wider range of such activities on a performance basis: payment to be made on delivery of the desired result, be it clean streets, fair housing, or ninth-grade achievement in mathematics on the part of ninth-grade students. In general, whatever makes for diversity in American government in the decades ahead is very likely to be given a try.

Envoi

These notes were originally written in February, 1966, at a time when the continuity of American government seemed almost a fact of nature. Now, in the early summer of 1967, one learns that the approval of only two state legislatures is required in order for a national constitutional convention to be convened. The initiative behind this extraordinary move, which has taken the nation quite unawares, is nominally to undo the changes in state legislatures mandated by the Supreme Court's "one-man, one-vote" decision. Thus, in a sense, it is simply the most dramatic recent evidence of the resistance of the American government structure to change. But the possibility that a convention will meet and will go on to draft profoundly important innovations is altogether real. Nothing is fixed.

Political Parties
and the Electoral System

Robert Kennedy, Hubert Humphrey, Eugene McCarthy, George McGovern, George Wallace, Richard Nixon, Nelson Rockefeller, Ronald Reagan—these are the names which dominated the headlines in Election Year 1968. All belonged to men involved in the familiar quadrennial scramble for the Presidency of the United States.

But however familiar the process and the institutions involved, 1968 witnessed something more than the traditional political contest of personalities. Old Politics clashed against New, the "majority party" managed to transform itself into a minority, and the *system* itself became the subject of widespread criticism. The professional party organizations, the national party conventions and their composition, the delegate selection process—all were bitterly denounced as "unrepresentative" and failing to reflect and give expression to the will of the electorate.

Much of the criticism came, as might be expected, from supporters of presidential aspirants whose power bases were weakest within the party and convention structure. But whatever the source, this criticism did result, as far as the losing Democratic Party was concerned, in reform efforts designed to widen participation and open up leadership selection to all levels of the party organization.

For students of American government the events of 1968 highlight the significance of the process which serves as the recruitment agency for political leaders from mayor to President. The roles and functions of political parties, conventions, primaries, and the electoral system itself are the focus of the readings in this section.

That American political parties perform many functions anyone who has read an American government textbook knows. Should "governing" be one of these functions? Frank J. Sorauf, in "The Quest for Party Government," explores this question and in the process reveals much about the nature and structure of the American party system.

The method by which political parties select their candidates is central to understanding the role the parties play and the functions they perform. In most European countries the party chooses the candidate; in the United States, apart from the presidential nominating conventions, the direct primary performs this role. In his article, "Candidate Selection," Leon D. Epstein examines the significance of this voter—as opposed to party—control over the nomination process. Harvey Wheeler, writing after the 1968 nominating conventions, presents a provocative and controversial critique of the nomination process and forecasts the emergence of a new electoral coalition and a New Politics which will spell "The End of the Two-Party System."

The Quest
for Party Government

FRANK J. SORAUF

The political parties are everywhere in American legislatures and executives, and even in American judiciaries. All American executives, almost all American legislatures, and about half of the American judiciaries are selected in processes that weigh the party affiliation and loyalty of the office-seeker heavily. Moreover, the appearances of party power are more than plentiful in the party leaders and whips of legislatures and the clearly partisan cast of many executive appointments. Even the elemental struggle between "government" and "opposition," "ins" and "outs," largely follows political party lines in the American system, just as if the parties controlled cohesive government and opposition parties in office. And yet, despite the trappings and portents of

From *Party Politics in America* by Frank J. Sorauf, pp. 372–379, 390–395. Copyright © 1968 by Little, Brown and Company (Inc.). Reprinted by permission of the publisher.

power, the American major parties do not govern in the sense of mobilizing cohesive groups of office-holders behind programs and ideologies to which the parties, and their guiding organizations and activists, have committed themselves.

The discontent with this inability of the American parties to "govern" is an old one within academic political science.[1] But the dissatisfactions are with more than the American parties; they extend to the entire American political system and its fragmented centers of authority, its tendency to blur political alternatives and differences, and its built-in barriers to strong and vigorous governmental initiatives. The critics, many of them admirers of the cohesive parties and the ease of mobilizing party majorities in the British political parties, long hoped that by joining electoral majorities and office-holders to party programs they could surmount the diffusion of power in the American polity. They found an official professional and academic platform by the late 1940s in a committee of the American Political Science Association; and the 1950 report of the committee, *Toward a More Responsible Two-Party System*,[2] gave the controversy its major recent stimulus. While the ensuing academic controversy has slowly simmered down, it is by no means quiescent today.

While the controversy over "party responsibility" and "party government" has embroiled academic political science for the past twenty years, a similar and parallel concern has agitated much of the American political world. From the ideologically oriented activists in both parties have come wails of dissatisfaction with the issuelessness of American politics and the tendency of the major parties to take similar centrist positions in support of the status quo. They complain, much as did Lord Bryce some seventy years ago, that the American parties are as Tweedle-dee and Tweedle-dum. In recent years the greater concern has been within the Republican Party's conservative wing; its leaders have inveighed against the "me-too-ism" of the party's liberals and moderates, and in working for the nomination of Barry Goldwater in 1964 they pleaded for "a choice, not an echo." Others have attempted to get at the fundamental inhibition to an ideological politics, the presence in each party of differing ideological positions, by advocating a gradual realignment of partisan loyalties to produce sharply differing, frankly "liberal" and "conservative" parties.

At first blush it may seem that the somewhat hermetic controversy over party "responsibility" has not a great deal to do with the development of a distinct and different ideological personality for the parties. One would not in any event ordinarily expect such a conjunction of academic debate and popular political controversy. But the two questions are to some extent the same one. The scholarly schools favoring party government and/or responsibility have come to realize that the conditions necessary for the achievement of responsibility—party-led enactment of a party program by party office-holders—can be achieved only with the development (at least to a limited extent) of ideological political parties. And the political activists who seek ideological clarity and ideological alternatives in American parties want those ideological parties to govern, to carry their ideological imperatives into public policy. Ideological clarification is probably a necessary condition for party government, and conversely party government or responsibility is certainly the implicit role of the ideological party.

The Logic of the Responsible Party

Despite the nomenclature, the doctrines of party government and party responsibility are only secondarily concerned with political parties. They are fundamentally doctrines of democratic government—or, more precisely, doctrines advocating one particular variety of American democracy. Much of the debate over them has in fact been a debate over the kind of democracy we are to have. The whole movement for party government has sprung from a discontent over what some scholars and citizens have seen as the ills of American democracy. Part of the blame for those ills they have laid at the feet of the major American parties, and a good many of their hopes for remedying the ills rest on the possibility of reconstituting and revitalizing the parties. The parties are to be the instruments or mechanisms—perhaps even the "panaceas" —for curing the maladies of American democracy.

The proponents of party government[3] begin with a belief in strong, positive government as a very necessary force for the solution of problems in the American society and economy. And like so many of the advocates of positive government in the context of the American separation of powers, many of them see a need for strong presidential and executive leadership if the whole complex governmental apparatus is to move forward with some vigor and semblance of unity. Yet, they know all too well that the institutions and traditions of American government diffuse, disperse, and divide governmental power in ways that prevent the generation of aggressive and responsive governmental programs. Theirs is the old complaint that American political institutions, suited perhaps for the minimal, gingerly governing of the eighteenth and nineteenth centuries, are far less adapted to the present century's need for positive government action. And, clearly, decentralized political parties, each of them divided by a vast diversity of interests and points of view, only accentuate the problem of diffusion.

A second thread of argument also runs through the political diagnoses of the proponents of party government. It is their concern for the miniscule political power of the individual in a mass, popular democracy. Contemporary government becomes large, complex, and remote, and the individual, beset with his own personal concerns, finds it hard to have the time, attention, and political knowledge for an active role in the political system. He is often bewildered, alienated, and politically ineffective. He finds it especially difficult even to know and judge what his elected representatives have been doing in public office. And into the political void resulting from his ineffectiveness and ignorance rush well-organized and well-financed minorities—local elites, interest groups, party bosses, or *ad hoc* alliances. Consequently, so the argument goes, important decisions are frequently made by public officials and organized minorities without the participation or even the *post hoc* judgment of the great majority of individual citizens. The individual, for his part, drifts from one meaningless decision to another; he does not know for what the candidate stands when he first elects him, and he has no standards or information for judging his performance in office when he comes up for reelection.[4]

This sense of alarm about the American democracy, to be sure, is by no means limited to the proponents of party government. Theirs is an analysis which countless other scholars, journalists, and public figures would in varying ways subscribe to. It is a more-or-less "standard" critique from those quarters of American life committed to the "liberal" confidence in the usefulness of a broad governmental role and to the "liberal" belief in the rationality and desirability of citizen involvement in a popular democracy.[5] What sets the school of party government apart is its reliance on the organizing and consolidating powers of the competitive political party. A reconstituted (and "responsible") pair of political parties will, it is hoped, bring together masses of voters behind meaningful party programs and candidates loyal to them and then hold the elected candidates to the obligation of carrying those programs into public policy. The responsible political party thus bridges the gulf between the politically disoriented individual and the distant, complex institutions of government. At the same time it assists, through the force of loyalties to the same party program, in mobilizing fragmented executives and legislatures for unified programs of action.

In essence these are proposals for the re-invigorating and animating of popular democratic institutions through the prime organizing role of the political party. Why the political party for so crucial a role?

> As mobilizers of majorities the parties have claims on the loyalties of the American people superior to the claims of any other forms of political organization. They have extended the area of popular participation in public affairs enormously and have given elections a meaning and importance never before thought possible. . . . Moreover, party government is good democratic doctrine because the parties are the special form of political organization adapted to the mobilization of majorities. How else can the majority get organized? If democracy means anything at all it means that the majority has the right to organize for the purpose of taking over the government.[6]

Only the parties, their supporters believe, are big, stable, extensive, and visible enough to carry this representational burden. As the only completely "political" of the political organizations—and the only one with a public or "semi-public" character—the competitive political party alone has the capacity for developing the essential qualities of "responsibility."

The call for "responsible" political parties, therefore, is a call for political parties with new capacities and new goals. Specifically, the responsible political party must:

1. Evolve and enunciate a reasonably explicit statement of party programs and principles.
2. Nominate (despite the difficulties of controlling the direct primaries) candidates loyal to the party program.
3. Conduct its electoral campaigns in such a way that voters will grasp the programmatic differences between the parties and make the voting decision at least substantially on that basis.
4. Guarantee that public office-holders elected under the party label will carry the party program into public policy—and thus enable the party to take "responsibility" for their actions in office. This much seems necessary if the party is to "govern" and be responsible to the majorities which chose it to govern. The entire argument rests on the replacement of individual or group responsibility for governmental decisions with the placement of responsibility on the cohesive political party.

"Cohesion" is, indeed, the key to the responsible political party. It must be cohesive enough to enunciate a program which will distinguish it from its competitor. It must also recruit and elect a group of legislators and executives cohesive enough to unite in support of proposals carrying the party's pledges into public policy. Cohesion of that sort within the party as an organization and the party in office also presupposes clearly the development of a cohesive party electorate. And very clearly that pervasive cohesion can be built in only one way—through the development of an ideological politics with ideologically cohesive and ideologically differentiated political parties. It is precisely at this point that the scholarly advocates of party responsibility begin to seek the same goals as the nonacademic advocates of party realignment (i.e., ideological realignment) and parties that prefer a "forthright stand" to "me-too-ism."

In fact, a strong case can be made that the infusion of some ideological concerns into an essentially nonideological American politics is also the prime objective of the school of party government. As the report of the committee of the American Political Science Association argues in its very first paragraph:

> While in an election the party alternative necessarily takes the form of a choice between candidates, putting a particular candidate into office is not an end in itself. The concern of the parties with candidates, elections, and appointments is misunderstood if it is assumed that parties can afford to bring forth aspirants for office without regard to the views of those so selected. Actually, the party struggle is concerned with the direction of public affairs. Party nominations are no more than a means to this end. In short, party politics inevitably involves public policy in one way or another.[7]

The development of a concern for the policy views of candidates and the making of policy is, in other words, a necessary condition for the responsible party. Ideological politics—or at least a more substantial emphasis on policy issues in American politics—is thus both a crucial means and an important end for the advocates of party responsibility. For the whole idea of party government is inherently policy- and issue-oriented. It is concerned with capturing and using public office for predetermined goals and purposes—and not merely for the thrill of winning, the division of patronage and spoils, or the reward of the office itself. The winning of public office becomes no more than a necessary means to policy ends.

There still remains, however, a sizable platoon of American political scientists and political leaders who are, despite the persuasiveness of the advocates of party government, greatly unconvinced.[8] The journals of American political science were, in fact, dotted with rejoinders and exception-taking for several years after the publication of the report of the Committee on Political Parties in 1950. Their collective case against party government and responsibility divides into two related but independent arguments: the *undesirability* of party government and its *impossibility* (or at least its improbability). While the two points are related, both logically and polemically, no logic dictates that one must make both points if he ventures one.

On the grounds of undesirability the skeptics argue across a number of fundamental issues of political philosophy. They fear that an embrace of party government will stimulate a more ideological, politically "hyperthyroid" politics of intense, dogmatic commitment—one in which the softenings and majority-building of compromise will be more difficult. They fear, too, that by making the political party the prime avenue of political representation the advocates of party government will destroy the present richness and multiplicity of representational mechanisms in the American democracy. Interest groups and other nonparty political organizations, they feel, are necessary means of political representation in a large and heterogeneous polity; to channel the representation of such a diversity of interests into the party system would "overload" its political and representational capacity. Furthermore, the skeptics are concerned lest party government destroy the deliberative quality of American legislatures, for legislators would cease to be "free," independent men and would become the mandated, committed representatives of a fixed party position. In short, they fear what European critics often call "partyocracy"—the domination of politics and legislatures by a number of doctrinaire, unyielding political parties, none of them strong enough to govern and none willing to let others govern.

On the related grounds of realism (i.e., the questions of possibility and probability) the critics of responsible parties have argued that:

> The American voter remains insufficiently involved in ideology to be coaxed easily into viewing politics and electoral choices in programmatic terms.
>
> The complexity of American society, and the diversity of interests it

generates, is too great to be expressed in the simple set of alternatives a two-party system can frame. Consequently, there is some fear that a more ideological politics would break the bounds of the two-party system and encourage the development of splinter parties.

The parties themselves are too diffuse and decentralized—too lacking in central disciplinary authority—to ever take a single, national ideological position and then enforce it on their assorted partisans and holders of public office.

The institutions of American government stand in the way at a number of crucial points. For example, the direct primary makes it difficult for the parties to choose nominees loyal to their programs, and the separation of powers (and bicameralism) often prevents the control of all executive and legislative authority by a single party.

At every point, in other words, the model of the responsible, governing political party appears to the critics to demand too much of the American voters, the major parties, and the institutions of American government. These points are not, of course, lost on the proponents of party government. They, too, recognize at least some of the practical difficulties in implementing their reforms. So, this aspect of the argument reduces in part to the question of whether the parties and the voters are being prepared for, or can be prepared for, government by "responsible" political parties.

If the major American parties are to meet the demands and roles of party government, they must find some source of unity and cohesion with which to overcome their egregious diffusion and disunity. The problem is really one of uniting the party organization, the party in the electorate, and the party in office in active and "responsible" support of a party program—and this despite their different political goals, their different political traditions and interests, and their different levels of attention, information, and activity. Three sources of the cohesion or unity necessary for governing parties appear possible within the range of democratic parties.

1. That cohesion may be promoted by *constitutional imperatives*. The parliamentary system demands that the majority party maintain cohesion in the legislature—and to a lesser extent in the electorate and party organization— if it is to stay in office.[9] No such constitutional stimulus to party cohesion is at work on the American parties.

2. It may also be promoted by *organizational discipline*. A strong party organization may impose its discipline and cohesion on balky partisans in office if it can control renomination to office.[10] The American direct primary, however, makes that a questionable option. Alternatively, powerful party leaders or executives may enforce it through the manipulation of rewards they control (patronage, preference, access to authority, etc.). But the value of these rewards is shrinking, and popular political ethics in the United States no longer easily accepts an enforced line-toeing. Although the available rewards and a

tolerant political culture permit this kind of discipline in some American states and localities, it is an impossibility in many others.

3. Finally, the cohesion may be produced "naturally" by an all-pervasive, intraparty *agreement on ideology or program*. All three components of the party may reach some consensus on a basic party ideology or program—or at least on a "silent ideology" of interest. The activists and identifiers of the party then achieve a cohesion arising from common goals, and their relatively high cohesion is to a considerable extent a result of internalized and self-enforced commitment to those goals. Distasteful external constraints and restraints are thus less necessary.

Because it seems that only the third, the ideological, avenue to party government is a likely one for contemporary American parties, the issue of party government becomes one of ideological—or "more ideological"—politics and parties. For, if cohesion is the necessary condition for responsible, governing parties, a pervasive ideological commitment appears to be the necessary condition for cohesion. Organizational discipline may supplement and buttress it, but it does not appear to be a viable independent alternative to it. . . .

Party Responsibility, American Style

The model of "the responsible political party" is an ideal type. One does not look for it in reality, for no political system yet has developed the cohesion, discipline, and unity that its pure form would demand. Even in Great Britain, home of the hopes of the American reformers, practice falls considerably short of the model. Party cohesion in the British parliament, while it is significantly greater than in the American Congress, is by no means perfect. British cabinets and parliamentary parties, in fact, have long insisted that constitutional traditions forbade them to be bound by party decision or commitment. Even within the Labour Party, traditionally committed to the binding discipline of party decisions, a series of Labour prime ministers have made it clear that while a Labour government would consult with the party's national executive, it could not be bound by it. Even in Britain, then, the model of the responsible party serves only to measure the distance of reality from the ideal.

American practice has fallen even further from the model. To be sure, one finds in some state legislatures a high order of party discipline behind and in opposition to the program of the majority and/or the governor. The programs or principles, however, spring not so much from a party organization or the decision of the electorate—there are rarely "mandate" elections—as from the initiative of the governor or the party's legislative leadership. What responsibility there is to the voters for their program is maintained *post hoc* at subsequent elections as the voters reward or punish their programmatic stewardship.[11] Under the best circumstances a sophisticated voter may be able to identify a past policy or decision with a party, but such a "quasi-responsibility" diverges from the model in one major way: there is little role in it for the party organization, since the legislative party or the executive originates the program and enforces discipline behind it through devices such as gubernatorial patronage or the perquisites of legislative leadership. It is a responsibility resting not on the overt decisions of party activists and organizations but on the homogeneity of interests of the voters, party leaders, and constituencies supporting each of the two legislative and executive parties. It is the "responsibility," or its approximation, which springs from the cohesion of a "silent ideology" of interest.

Occasionally under the stress of crisis or catastrophe, American politics approach even more closely the model of party responsibility. A strong case can certainly be made that at the presidential election of 1936, the Democrats and Republicans were identified with sharply differing solutions to the nation's economic woes. If their positions were not truly ideological, they were at least determinedly programmatic. The burdens of the Depression may also have focused voter attention on the hopes and remedies of policy to an unusual degree. Much of the campaign oratory centered around the Roosevelt program for social and economic change and his opponents' charges that he proposed a radical departure for the American polity and economy. The combination of programmatic rhetoric and identification, plus voter attention, may well have produced something close to a "mandate" election and a mandated congressional contingent of Democrats. If the supposition about the presidential election of 1936 is correct, it suggests the explanation that the kind of ideological or programmatic concern necessary for "pure" party responsibility has been a product of crisis conditions that have prevailed only for short periods of time in recent American experience. The necessary ideological concerns and attention are not ordinary expressions of American politics as usual; they are rather the product of occasional, heightened, extra-political crisis.

These sporadic expressions of a "party responsibility, American style," have not, however, satisfied the reformers. The quasi-responsibility of a silent ideology has prevailed only unevenly among the American states; vast regions (such as the South) have traditionally maintained an issueless politics incapable even of this degree of party government. And the occasions of nationwide party responsibility have been sporadic and crisis-spawned. About the future of party responsibility in the United States, then, two questions remain. Are the political changes afoot in the American political system and within the parties inexorably bringing the conditions for a greater degree of party responsibility? And are there positive steps which anxious men can take to insure or speed the advent of government by responsible parties?

As for the first question—the possibility that the coming of ideology is leading to greater party government—it is true that a burgeoning group of ideological activists, a more sophisticated electorate, a slowly centralizing pair of party organizations, and even the development of nationally recognized issue differences between the parties may promise a trend to greater responsibility. But several sobering notes of caution ought to be mentioned:

> The American institution of the direct primary (and its undermining of party control of nominations) combined with the decentralizing effect of federalism and the separation of powers continues to work against party responsibility even in the presence of ideology. It permits the non-ideological candidate to become a representative of and spokesman for a party program. It also permits the ideological candidate and officeholder to defend to the political death a program or ideology at odds with that of his party or his President or governor. He can be ideological and yet "irresponsible."

> Much of the increasing ideological or programmatic commitment has not followed the single, unidimensional pattern necessary if ideology (or issue) is to provide the cohesion or unity essential for party government. If the divisions along SES [socio-economic status] lines do not coincide with those on Negro rights and civil liberties, or those on foreign policy, the resulting cross-cutting (multidimensional) ideologies divide much more than they unify. Then, for example, hawk-dove differences on Vietnam cut across, rather than reinforce, liberal-conservative lines on the welfare state. Only if multiple patterns of issue or ideological differences coincide do they offer the basis for two unified, cohesive programmatic parties.[12]

> Ideology has thus far not been fully translated into party organizational strength. Especially, there are few signs of an important centralization of authority within the parties; the national committees remain essentially hostages to the traditional decentralization of the parties. The ideologists of state and local party organizations may turn increasingly to like-thinking candidates, but without some centralizing, arbitrating party authority, any significant measure of party government at the national level remains unlikely.

And thus, while the spread of ideology or issue orentation may be a necessary condition for government by responsible parties, it is anything but a sufficient one in and of itself. Especially in the context of fragmenting political institutions—most especially the institutions of federalism and the separation of powers—the growth of ideology may very well work to defeat the goal of party responsibility.

If the advent of ideology will not automatically (or willy-nilly) bring the party to a greater governing role, will the more conscious and overt proposals of the reformers? The breadth of the problem of converting the American major parties into prototypic responsible parties can be gauged by examining the scope of the reformers' proposals. The Committee on Political Parties of the APSA, for example, proposed:[13]

1. *A massive shoring up of the national parties and their organizations.*

The Committee recommends that the national conventions meet at least biennially and exercise greater control over the national committee. Above all it suggests a national Party Council of some fifty members who would draft a platform for the national convention, interpret and apply it to issues between conventions, make "recommendations . . . in respect to congressional candidates," make recommendations about "conspicuous departures from general party decisions by state or local party organizations," provide a forum for "the discussion of presidential candidacies," and coordinate relations among national, state, and local party organizations.

2. *A perfecting of the instruments of ideology.* The Committee in essence proposes that the platform mean something and that it bind the party officeholders and organizations. The platform ought to deal at least partially with the party's "permanent or long-range philosophy," and it ought also to be carefully prepared and systematically interpreted. Needless to say, "the party programs should be considered generally binding" on both officeholders and state and local parties.

3. *An asserting of party control over the congressional party.* To achieve such a protean task the Committee recommends both a consolidation of the present congressional party organizations into a single-party leadership group and the elimination of those practices (such as the seniority system and the traditional power of the House Rules Committee) which work against party discipline and ultimately against party responsibility.

4. *A remodeling of the American parties into membership, participatory parties.* The Committee's hope is perhaps best expressed in its words:

> The development of a more program-conscious party membership may attract into party activity many who formerly stayed away, including public-spirited citizens with great experience and knowledge. It will thus be a factor in giving the parties a greater measure of intellectual leadership.
>
> With increased unity within the party it is likely that party membership will be given a more explicit basis. Those who claim the right to participate in framing the party's program and selecting its candidates may be very willing to support its national program by the payment of regular dues. Once machinery is established which gives the party member and his representatives a share in framing the party's objectives, once there are safeguards against internal dictation by a few in positions of influence, members and representatives will feel readier to assume an obligation to support the program.

The Committee's report ranges beyond these general points. It tackles other basic inhibitors of party responsibility: the direct primary ("the closed primary deserves preference . . ."), the Electoral College (it "fosters the blight of one-party monopoly"), political finance, and barriers to full and meaningful adult suffrage (e.g., the long ballot). In short, it becomes clear that to achieve the goal of government by responsible parties the Committee would undertake—and probably would *have* to undertake—a wholesale reconstruction not only of the American parties, but of the American electorate and political environment as well.

Some of the other proponents of party responsibility have, however, been more modest in their goals. One of the most persistent and consistent, James MacGregor Burns,[14] touches many of the same themes as the APSA Committee. There is the same emphasis on the building of grass roots, membership parties, the buttressing of the national party (the presidential party), the reconstructing of a vigorous congressional party, the same recognition of the need for change in the parties' political environment (e.g., the present restrictions on adult suffrage and the status quo in political finance). The reforms Burns suggests are, however, less drastic and sweeping—and, therefore, more "realistic"—but their direction and their pinpointing of the causes of the present lack of responsibility are not greatly different. Perhaps Burns' greater moderatism springs in part from his recognition of an essentially "Madisonian" political culture which has not tolerated any instrument—party or other—of national majoritarian political power. And in whatever form the proposals may appear, the argument for more responsible parties is exactly an argument for the parties as instruments for the more effective mobilization of national majorities.

The agenda of reform is, in conclusion, a very long one, and its measures touch the fundamentals of American political life. Even the basic American political institutions work against the development of more responsible parties —work, in other words, against a sweeping reorientation of the role of the parties in the American democracy. So also does a political culture suspicious of majoritarian political power marshalled behind programs of action, and so do the low levels of political knowledge and concern of the American electorate. Nor is there in the American political system a constitutional stimulus to disciplined, governing parties. American parties do not have to govern to maintain public office as they would have to in a parliamentary system. In fact, American institutions and traditions have always implicitly rejected the notion of "extra-constitutional" control of political power (as through a party responsible to an alert electorate) in favor of the intrainstitutional controls of divided and opposing authority (e.g., the internal "checks and balances").

For the immediate future it seems likely, barring the special conditions of crisis, that the American parties will continue only a modest governing role—a *post hoc* responsibility for carrying out programs that generally promote the interests of the party's activists and loyal electorate. Neither the American parties nor the voters can meet the demands which the classic model of party responsibility imposes on them. But binding the various sectors of the party together—despite all that divides them—is an inarticulate ideology, a commitment to a set of issue positions which sets the activists, candidates, and voters of one party apart from those of the other. In a loose, often distressingly imprecise sense, the two parties are distinct groups of "like-minded" men. Out of that tentative and limited agreement on issues comes enough cohesion to produce a modest, if variable, degree of responsibility. The American approximation of party government does indeed fall far short of the model of party responsibility and the hopes of the reformers, but the role of the political party in organizing government and the debate on public issues cannot be ignored.

If a concern with political ideologies continues to spread within the American electorate, and especially if it motivates a new activism within the party organizations, we may well see a greater degree of responsibility within the American parties—but with an important difference. It may well be contained within and relevant to only an ideological minority. Party responsibility, even under the most receptive conditions, is very likely only "responsibility" to an involved, alert, informed minority. It is one pattern of relationship the political party develops with one segment of the electorate. To the nonideological segment the party continues to make appeals on other than ideological grounds: on a mixture of traditions, interests, and personalities. Even in the classic ideological, responsible party systems, one suspects, ideological debate and discourse dull the political nerve ends of the majority who would rather be involved with a dynamic political personality or a "gut" issue. The danger for parties caught in such a conflict or mixture of appeals—as the parties of Europe have been for at least a generation—is that they either alienate the ideological minority by compromise or bore the majority by dogma.

In any event, the entire issue of party responsibility and government is chiefly one of the entire role of the political party in the political system. Any attempt to change or reform the American parties to assume a new governing responsibility—to monopolize the avenue of political representation, in other words—is at once a question of how political organizations develop patterns of structure and activity and of how one goes about changing them. . . .

Candidate Selection

LEON D. EPSTEIN

What is called candidate selection in Europe is called nomination in the United States. American parties are said to nominate candidates whether they do so in conventions or in primary elections. In the comparative context, however, it is better to adhere to the general and European usage even when discussing American practices. That way the process by which parties label candidates, of principal concern here, can be distinguished from the process by which an individual obtains a place on the ballot with or without a party label. The latter can be dismissed in a few words by saying that it involves individual "nomination" in the sense of meeting legal requirements for a certain number of signatures on a petition, and that in the United States this kind of nomination is necessary for filing both as a candidate in a primary and as an independent nonparty candidate in a general election. A similar legal requirement exists in Britain for candidates whether or not they are selected by the organized parties. I shall limit the term "nomination," then, as do the British, to the simple process of meeting this legal requirement. Thus "party nomination" in ordinary American usage becomes "candidate selection" in the present terminology.

The safest point that can be made about American practices of candidate selection is that they vary greatly at governmental levels (national, state, and local), among states, by parties, and between urban and rural areas. This is not merely because legal regulations differ, especially from state to state, but also because the social bases for political activity differ within the United States.

The best known variation is the formal legal one between the convention and the primary method. Although primaries are required for all state and local offices in all but five states, there is also the notable exception of presidential candidate selection by national party conventions. Still, there can be little doubt that the primary has become the standard form, and it is advisable not to make a major point of the variation resulting from the persistence of the convention. In addition to the fact that it *is* the exception, the convention method is not so radically different from the primary method as are both of these American methods from the European. Even the convention is regulated by law in a way that candidate selection in other nations is not. This is clear for the national

Reprinted by permission of the publisher from Leon D. Epstein, *Political Parties in Western Democracies* (New York: Frederick A. Praeger, Inc., 1967), pp. 203–215.

party conventions, whose delegates are chosen either in primaries or in state and district conventions according to state-prescribed procedures. But the surviving candidate selection by state conventions is also regulated by statute. So, for that matter, were the old conventions in states that subsequently adopted the primary. The long-established American practice had been to prescribe by law the manner of electing delegates to a convention whose selection of candidates conferred the party label appearing on the subsequent election ballot. And the tendency has been to give party voters a role in the election of convention delegates.

Thus, even before the adoption of the primary early in the twentieth century, it was possible for ordinary Republican or Democratic voters to participate in their party's selection at least to the extent of choosing the delegates who did the selecting, even though they held no formal party membership. This is not to say that large numbers of voters ever participated in this way, but the provision of the opportunity to do so is similar to the much more ample provision of the primary method. The basic similarity is apparent in the term "direct," originally and often still used to modify the word "primary." Adopting the "direct primary" meant that voters, previously given only an indirect voice in candidate selections, would now be given direct legal control. The change was considerable, but compared to practices in other democratic nations, it was only a more extreme version of the American tendency to treat parties as public rather than private organizations and to define their "membership" in an open and broad sense.

Blurring the primary-versus-convention distinction in this way is not to retreat from the generalization that American methods of candidate selection vary greatly. It only means that a particular variation is not overwhelmingly important in our comparative context. Neither is the familiar distinction between open and closed primaries. Again, one method, that of the primary open to voters without regard even to registration by party, is simply a more extreme manifestation of the general American tendency to legal openness of candidate selection. How open any of these legal provisions have actually made American candidate selection can be questioned. Here, in fact, there is a substantial variation within the United States. In some places, even with long-established primaries, candidates are selected by a handful of party leaders or even by a party boss. They still have to win the primaries in order to secure the formal party label for the subsequent general election, but they are virtually assured of victory because of the strength of organization support from the leaders who did the prior selecting. Chicago's Democratic Party is the most frequently cited case of this effective organizational control of the selection process, but there are many others. It may still be usual in many large cities. Another related but newer kind of organizational control arises in those few areas where membership parties exist. They may endorse candidates running in primaries and then lend their organizational support, which, while more ideological and less patronage-oriented than the old machine's, can similarly help the endorsed candidates. If regularly effective, this practice could convert American candidate selection to the European model. In practice, membership organizations would do the selecting, provided that their candidates customarily won the primaries, and consequently nothing would be left of the distinctive American method except the *de jure* existence of the primary to confirm the *de facto* choice of an organized party.

The United States is now a long way from this. Not only are membership organizations present in relatively few jurisdictions, but they do not always effectively control their party primaries when they are present. In both California and Wisconsin, where dues-paying organizations are most fully developed, there have been striking and important primary failures by endorsed candidates.[15] It is not clear that the formal endorsement possible in these states is any more effective than informal leadership support for particular candidates. Machine-style support, often formal as well as informal, may be assumed to be more effective, but its importance is likely to diminish as the old-style machines themselves decline in importance.

The fact is that there are large areas of American politics in which candidate selection is not controlled by any regular party process. Especially below the national and state levels, even in many urban places, there is no effective organizational control. Rather, party candidatures are simply assumed by individuals and groups able to win primary elections. In winning, they are likely to seek at least the informal help of those identified as party leaders or workers, but in much the same way as they seek the help of others outside party ranks. There may be no "party" to approve or disapprove of candidatures. As V. O. Key has said of state organizations: "Often party is in a sense fiction. No finger can be put on any group or clique that has both the power and the inclination to exercise leadership in party affairs or to speak authoritatively for it in any way."[16] Candidate selection can then become more individualistic, but it may also become more directly influenced by organized interest groups. On the assumption that some kind of organization has advantages over none, then in the absence of a meaningful party organization another organized group would be likely to assume local control.[17] It is widely believed that this has happened in the United States, but the subject has not been recently explored.

In other respects as well, the knowledge of organizational activity in American candidate selection tends to be spotty. There have been a few intensive studies of legislative candidate selection in particular states. The results show a variation from strong party organizational control in Pennsylvania, where old-style machines have been maintained in many places, to considerably less control in Wisconsin and Oregon. Even in Pennsylvania, however, party control was greater in urban than in rural counties. This suggests, as the author of the study indicates, that the political party does not, on its own, set the political style so much as its style is determined by the environment.[18] Not only is the rural environment less hospitable to organizational control of candidate selection; it may be that the entire American environment is less hospitable than other national environments. The United States does not seem to be substituting new-style boss control. The resistance to membership organizations on this score is impressive. Party voters have occasionally rejected candidates endorsed by these organizations; and elected officials themselves have often been notably unenthusiastic about having their candidatures subject to the power of ideologically-minded groups. One important California Democrat has pointedly argued that his party's membership organization, the California Democratic Council, should stick to its issue-agitation and not endorse candidates.[19] The assumption is that issue-oriented partisans would prefer candidates of their own persuasion and that these [organization-endorsed] candidates would be less appealing to the party's voters.

This is as close as anyone comes to justifying the absence of European-style membership controls of candidate selection. In most American constituencies, there are no membership organizations even to raise the question. In their absence, however, many American party reformers have wished that they existed in order to fill what they regard as a vacuum in political responsibility. The possible ideological zeal of organized partisans has seemed a virtue to reformers who want parties to take clear-cut stands on issues. Especially advantageous has been the likelihood that these partisans would select their own kind as candidates. This would strike a direct blow at the opportunism of individuals who, on their own, are able to secure the party label in primary elections.

The openness of American candidate selection has not been the only target for criticism. The decentralization of the selection process has been complained about just as much. No basis exists for doubting the fact of decentralization. No national party agency controls state or congressional candidacies. And often no state party agency controls the various local candidacies. Decentralization in this respect, as Key has said, is undoubtedly a prime characteristic of American parties.[20] What is less sure is whether the characteristic is peculiarly American, or whether it is not in large measure also true of parties in other nations. . . . What needs to be stressed here is that American party reformers have been impressed with the disadvantages of decentralization. Specifically, they have thought that nationally cohesive parties were impeded by the selection of congressional candidates according to state or local considerations. This meant that the reformers have been as dissatisfied with local organizational control, by old-fashioned city machines, as by any direct control by primary voters. The machines, oriented to local patronage if not local issues, were just as much nonnational interest groups as any other constituent interest group influencing candidate selection through a convention or primary. The preferred alternative was national control. As the leading critic, Schattschneider, wrote with emphasis: "It is necessary for national party leaders *to win power within the party before it is possible to get power within the government.*"[21] It is true that he also wanted parties rather than other groups to control the road to office, but what he meant were national parties. Therefore, Schattschneider would have had to change American candidate selection in two important ways. He would have made it the function of an organized party, or at least of its recognized leaders, and he would have centralized this organized party—that is, nationalized it for congressional candidate selection.

Specifically it is congressional candidacies that have been the main focus of attention for those who would centralize the process. Their concern, beginning especially with Democrats in the late 1930s, has been senators and representatives who refused to cast their congressional votes along lines set by their national parties and particularly by their presidential leader. An apparent remedy is to have a national party rather than a state or local party (in convention or primary) select congressional candidates. Or for those concerned for comparable legislative party cohesion at the state level, the remedy is to have a state party rather than a local party do the selecting of candidates.

Just how this remedy would operate, particularly for congressional candidates, has never been clear. No one has seriously proposed that a national party convention or a national party headquarters select congressional candidates. Since the candidates would still have to be elected in their constituencies, it has to be assumed that there be a constituency basis for their selection. But that basis could not be a local party organized around local concerns. Nor could it be an unorganized primary electorate. Neither method would insure candidacies suited to national party purposes. Therefore, there would have to be a new type of constituency organization, probably of dues-paying members, that would be branches of a national party organization. Its members would be oriented to national issues. They would have joined the party because of those issues. And their concern would be to select candidates similarly disposed. The national party headquarters would exercise some degree of control, perhaps through a veto power, over the candidates selected by its branches.

One need only sketch out so centralized a system to see how radically different it is from existing American methods, which are neither centralized nor strictly party in character. Congressional districts provide the strongest cases in point. They do not even coincide with what there is of organized party structure in the United States. Rather, as one scholar has remarked, congressional districts are in a "relatively autonomous" position with respect to the main lines of attention and communication in the party structure.[22] State and county units provide the more usual focus, and these units seldom coincide with the geographic boundaries of congressional constituencies. It is not surprising that a congressman's relations with his district organization are especially unimportant. There is not much organization for him to relate to. Thus, party has been found to rank low as a decision-making pressure on a congressman after his election and to have been relatively unimportant in his original selection as a candidate and in his election campaign.[23]

In analyzing American methods, it is reasonable to put greater emphasis on the general weakness of party control than on its decentralization. The latter may be what party reformers have primarily complained about, but it seems to derive from the general weakness. Decentralization could not be eliminated without a form of stronger party control of candidate selection. This is not to claim that stronger parties would automatically mean centralization. We have had strong local parties that may have worked against centralization. But other forms of strong parties, even at the local level, might make for centralization. At any rate, there is no way for parties to centralize control if they are not organized so as to exercise control at some level. In the United States, there is now relatively little control to centralize.

For this reason, it is hard to accept federalism as a cause for the main characteristics of American candidate selection practices.[24] It is true that, in the federal system, state parties are stronger in most respects than national parties, but many state parties do not appear to control the selection of candidates for congressional or state legislative offices. Nor do local units of state parties regularly exercise this control. The looseness, the individualism, and the interest-group influences characterizing American candidate selection are state as well as national phenomena. They cannot be attributed to federalism.

Much more likely to be mentioned as a cause for the absence of organizational control is the direct primary. In fact, the primary has been blamed for the weakness of American parties generally in the twentieth century. The argument has been powerfully and persuasively advanced in the significant work of V. O. Key. He believed that the adoption of the direct primary, in the decades just after 1900, opened the road to disruptive forces that gradually fractionalized parties, facilitating the growth of cliques and personal attachments.[25] "The new channels to power," Key wrote, "placed a premium on individualistic politics rather than on the collaborative politics of party."[26] The result, he thought, was the disintegration of statewide party hierarchies under the impact of the influences given free play by the primary. The organizational leaders could not survive the successes of nonorganizational individual candidates in primary elections.[27] There is no point in being a leader, indeed one is not really a leader at all, if one cannot control the selection of candidates.

The argument is cogent, but it is weakened by certain exceptions that Key and everyone else would grant. Not all state organizations have disintegrated to this extent. Some, despite the direct primary, have managed to maintain themselves and their control of candidacies over long periods of time. Eventually they too may be decisively weakened, but the delay has been so substantial that the direct primary could not be readily blamed as the prime cause. This suggests a slightly different explanation and a slightly different role for the direct primary. Less a cause than a symptom, the primary may have been adopted as an expression of an organizational weakness and individualism that was coming to be widely accepted in American candidate selection. Party organizations must already have been losing what strength they had, if so apparently disruptive a method as the direct primary could have been adopted. They opposed its adoption, but usually without success. In the few states where organizations did succeed, at least to the extent of limiting the primary's scope, they were subsequently able to maintain themselves more effectively. But these were states where the parties were especially strong to begin with. And, it is fair to say, these were states where strong parties were more acceptable. On the other hand, in most of the United States what was wanted were weak organizations. Adopting the primary was a way of institutionalizing this desire. Having a primary that opens candidate selection to nonorganizational factors is surely associated with weak parties. And it probably helps to foster such weakness. Still, this is not the same as saying that the primary is a principal cause for the weakness.

By treating the primary as more symptomatic than causal, I do not intend to treat it as less significant. On the contrary, I take the primary to be the most significant manifestation of the nonorganizational style of American candidate selection. It gives expression to that style even if it is not basically responsible for it. "Nonorganizational" here means nonparty, or perhaps even antiparty, organization. Americans have not wanted to leave the selection of their party candidates entirely in the hands of organized partisans. The direct primary became the favored means for trying to give the power of selection to large numbers of voters. It is true that in this attempt, beginning at the turn of the twentieth century, Americans were reacting against old-style political machines and not against European-style membership parties. Specifically, it was the supposed corrupt manipulation of these machines at party conventions that prompted many reformers. But it says something important about the United States that the reformers sought to substitute the direct primary for machine-controlled conventions rather than to substitute a new kind of party organization. Candidate selection was to be turned over to the voters of a party and not to any party membership, however reformed.

This is to return to the primary's particular purpose, in accord with the American popular democratic tradition, of giving voters a meaningful choice in areas where general election victory for the candidates of one party or the other was almost a foregone conclusion. Constituencies dominated by a single party are by no means uniquely American. Rather, as described earlier, they characterize large portions of most democratic nations. Especially when constituencies are as small as are those for the British parliament, the number of safe seats is likely to be very high. Larger European multi-member districts, with election by proportional representation, provide a basis for contest since a given party, even if always the leading party in a multi-member district, would not be expected to win all of the seats when as many as four or five were at stake. But in the single-member district system, one has to expect party strength to be so distributed that there will be many virtually predetermined election results. This has been true in the United States not only for congressional and most state legislative districts, but for entire states over long periods of time. Significantly, it was especially true around 1900 when the direct primary started. Southern states were constantly Democratic, and many northern states, particularly in the upper Midwest, were regularly Republican. These were the very states where the direct primary got its start.

The primary, however, has not regularly substituted clear bifactional intraparty politics for the absent interparty competition. There is even a question about how much electoral competition of any kind occurs in a primary. The evidence varies. Our study, focusing on congressional primaries in one-party districts, found numerous contests but few close ones. Of 965 safe-district primaries, only 214 were decided by margins closer than two to one.[28] Although the author's point is that primaries were thus not a competitive alternative, it might also be argued that they provided more competition than there would otherwise have been, at least in the 214 instances. A more substantial case, however, can be made on the basis of a few studies of primary competition in state legislative districts. V. O. Key found many primary contests where the majority-party candidate was almost sure to win the general election. Urbanism tended to increase primary competition and incumbency to decrease it. But chiefly, he concluded, the incidence of competition was a function of the given party's likely electoral success.[29] Naturally, the absence of competition in a primary of a party whose chances are hopeless does not adversely affect the argument for the efficacy of the primary. All that is required to establish its efficacy is that there be competition in the winning party's primary.

Key's findings are confirmed by other subsequent studies in Wisconsin and Pennsylvania. The Wisconsin data show that while legislative primaries were not generally contested, they tended to be contested much more in the majority party. Moreover, for the two Wisconsin election years studied most intensively, three-quarters of the contested primaries were decided by margins of less than two to one.[30] Pennsylvania findings are similar, even to the point of showing the same curious dropping off in primary competition in districts where party majority became unusually safe.[31] Thus it is in safe but not the safest districts where primary competition most often occurs.

Critics might grant that primaries provide electoral choice in districts where the general elections provide virtually none, and still remain opposed to primaries. This involves more than their standard argument that primaries fail to provide the kind of meaningful choice that party competition provides for voters who need labels in order to distinguish intelligibly between candidates. That argument is not worth much if there is no likelihood of interparty competition in a given district. But critics of the primary also believe that its existence, particularly *because* it provides a kind of competition, serves to deter the development of interparty competition. When an opposition to majority-party incumbents or to majority-party leadership can appeal to voters through a primary election, what incentive is there to build an alternative party?[32] Certainly, the strictly local incentive would seem to be absent, although not the larger national or state concerns. Of course, the relation of the locality to the larger concerns, especially national ones, would have originally produced the one-party dominance, whether we contemplate the Democratic Party in the southern Black Belt, the Republican Party in rural New England, the Democratic Party in industrial working-class areas, or the Republican Party in wealthy suburbs. As long as the relationship making for one-party dominance persists or is thought to persist, it is unlikely that there will be much local incentive for building an alternative party, even if no primary existed. The alternative party would represent what the locality opposed in state or national politics.

Further damage can be done to the argument of those who blame the primary for the absence of interparty competition. Not only is it likely, as indicated above, that one-party dominance rests on a deeper political basis than that provided by the primary, but it is possible to show that when that basis changes, the primary does not prevent the emergence of two-party competition. Thus, the upper Great Lakes states, long Republican bastions, became two-party competitive by the 1950s. Even in Wisconsin, where the primary was especially well established in its open form, the Democratic Party succeeded in replacing an intra-Republican faction as the competitive alternative (after a period of third-party effort). At most, therefore, the existence of the primary slowed the process of shifting from intraparty to interparty competition. But more impressive is the fact that states became two-party states when their sociopolitical basis came to resemble that of the national parties sufficiently to support both parties. In other words, the primary, while surely a distinctive method of candidate selection, is not easily identified as a cause for perpetuating one-party politics. The United States, it may be stressed again, is not distinctive in having large areas of one-party dominance.

One other aspect of the primary as a distinctive American method needs to be explored. This is its relation to the social bases for recruitment of political leaders. Plainly, the primary is an especially open selection method in the social as in the political sense. An aspirant for candidacy can appeal directly to the voters. In principle and to some extent in practice, he is not dependent on an establishment leadership to make him the party candidate. He can get the voters to do that themselves. Or at least he can try. We cannot be sure that "new men," defined as new by class or ethnic origin, would be more likely to be selected in a primary than by another method, but the primary does clearly open the door. An idea of its significance in comparative terms may be understood by imagining the possibility of new men like Keir Hardie and Ramsay MacDonald, standing in a British Liberal Party primary, instead of having their candidacies rejected by local Liberal caucuses. With a primary, they could not have been so easily kept from Liberal candidatures by an oligarchical leadership. They might not have won the primaries, but they would have had an open electoral chance. Curiously, Hardie actually requested a wider poll of the local party that rejected him.[33] It is at least possible that the Liberal Party, if it had adopted a more open selection method, would have been able to absorb the rising working-class leadership that eventually built the Labour party. But at the time Hardie and MacDonald sought Liberal candidatures, before 1900, the primary was not yet well established even in the United States.

It would be stretching the point, however, to suggest that the adoption of the primary in the United States, just after 1900, was a factor in precluding the rise of an American socialist working-class party.[34] We have no evidence that primaries caused the rise of working-class leaders. On the contrary, as the American data . . . show, no large or increasing number of political leaders with working-class backgrounds emerged in American politics in the twentieth century. The primary may have facilitated the rise of those with political ambitions, but that says little since the numbers were not at all like those in European socialist parties.

The effect of the primary in Britain or other nations is hard to discuss not only because the primary was never adopted outside the United States, but also because the very idea of the primary implies an openness about party organization and so about candidate selection that is peculiarly American. This openness, it may be argued, is legalistic. In practice, American candidate selection may often be decisively influenced by insiders. Nevertheless, the law prescribing open selection methods reflects an antipathy to oligarchy that is impressive even if not always successfully institutionalized. Oligarchy in candidate selection, accepted as natural for parties in other nations, remains disapproved in American politics.

The End of the Two-Party System

HARVEY WHEELER

Every mass medium revolution in history has been accompanied by a political revolution. Television, which has already had profound effects on American politics, is not only making the two-party system irrelevant, it is also producing a new political coalition and new systems of campaign communications.

In major respects, the electoral process is a communications system, a medium permitting the organization and transmission of messages to masses of people. The political party as a mass medium was brought to its maturation during the Civil War through the growing influence of the newspaper as a newly significant mass medium. This was the time of the first press lords. Recall William Lloyd Garrison and the effect that he and other abolitionists were able to mobilize. It is hardly too much to say that the Republican Party—itself a major political innovation—was the offspring of the modern mass-circulation newspaper, to which it has remained tied throughout its history.

The innovation of the Republican Party made possible the modern two-party system. Like many other communication networks, this vast system can be analyzed in terms of information theory, for it makes "yes-no" options result in a decision.

The radio epoch of Franklin Delano Roosevelt was the next communication revolution. The FDR coalition reigned supreme in American politics until the Eisenhower campaigns. It was composed of the traditional Democratic South, inland farmers, labor, certain (then) inarticulate ethnic minorities, and the urban Catholics, especially the Irish, who had gotten control of the boss-machine systems of the cities. The boss-machine system was itself an important innovation. It was a new form of the party as a "container": an organizational counterpart of the ancient Coliseum. Never before FDR had the party system been welded into a national machine. The foundation for this was only made possible by radio; for recall that American newspapers always remained as local and particularistic as Tammany Hall and similar machines had been. We still marvel at the way in which FDR was able to go over the heads of an obstructionist Congress and a hostile press and invade the living room of the average voter through his famous Fireside Chats.

The Roosevelt campaign communication system was based upon state and local machines which needed a professional "boss" such as Jim Farley, just as today a national TV campaign communications system needs professional "Madison Avenue" support. It was directly related to the federal system. In fact, the new national party organizations *were* federal organizations. The classic definition of the political party is "a loose confederation of state and local bosses." Roosevelt's so called nationalization of the party system was really its "federalization," and its federal structure remained a distinctive feature of the post-Roosevelt two-party system.

The major voting groups comprising the FDR coalition were in a state of relative economic and social depression. They were relatively immobile, socially and geographically. They harkened back to the traditional nineteenth-century themes and impulses of grass-roots, participational democracy. Not one of these features holds true for the politics of the present day.

The Republicans were the first to exploit the political potentials of television campaign communications. Dewey's gubernatorial campaign in New York, which featured a direct question-and-answer format, is widely hailed as the first successful exploitation of this novel mass medium. On the national level, of course, the Eisenhower election of 1952 was the first true TV campaign, and it possessed in embryo nearly all the features we have since come to regard as characteristic of contemporary mass medium politics.

Eisenhower was himself a newcomer to party politics; something inconceivable before TV. He was heavily financed. He employed expensive and sophisticated mass media experts. "Madison Avenue" techniques were devised to project a predesigned "image." A new kind of electoral coalition was formed, composed largely of urban, white-collar people dissociated from the grass-roots traditions of the agrarian past. His campaign cut across traditional party lines to orient itself about the personality of the candidate rather than the machine or the party. The new coalition of voter groups was socially and geographically mobile. The new politics required image manipulators rather than ballot box stuffers. The new organizations were *ad hoc* affairs created overnight by national cadres of advance men. The presidential primary overshadowed the party convention. This was to be the wave of the future. Television truly nationalized campaign communications and undermined the federal structure of the old machines. Party politics gave way to personality politics.

Then came the Kennedys. John burst onto the political scene using vast sums of money, clever exploitation of television, cadres of advance men, personality-projection technique, and the launching pad of presidential primaries. When Kennedy was in West Virginia, it was like a "High Noon" showdown between new and old. Later, the Kennedy-Nixon debates revealed the passage of an important milestone in American political history.

The politics of personality requires distinguishing oneself as a dynamic person—which in turn means polarizing the TV audience into those violently pro and con. Ronald Reagan, Eugene McCarthy, and the two Kennedys were only politically possible by virtue of this New Politics. The Kennedys may have died at the hand of their own creation.

What of the others—the remaining old-timers? Curiously enough, they are the ones left in control today: Johnson, Humphrey, and Nixon. Johnson is the first decisive victim of the obsolescence of the old party system. Yet we are left with Nixon and Humphrey, who are both television force-outs. Politics is often regarded as the choosing of the lesser of two evils. If that is the case today, the choice of our voters (this month) [this article was originally published in November 1968—*Ed.*] will almost certainly be made on the basis of which one of these candidates is *less* repugnant on television.

There is another anachronistic aspect to this year's election: Both candidates are archaic party phenomena; both have acquired their nominations through the exploitation of party machinery that has lost its relevance to our political problems and our vital social forces. That is, the traditional two-party system is no longer an effective medium of mass communications. Yet, through a series of tragedies and accidents, it is the medium that has presented us with our presidential choices. This is an ominous prospect, for one of the historic lessons of politics is that communication between the political regime and the people must be effective and mutual.

What are the specific signs that the party system is no longer serving this function well? First, consider again the FDR coalition and its chief components: the South, farmers, labor, the Irish Catholic-led urban machines. They are no longer disadvantaged. Small farmers are disappearing rapidly in the face of an enclosure movement that is converting farms into agricultural factories. Labor has joined the middle class, become conservative, moved to suburbia, and, in addition, has experienced a relative decline in numbers, compared to the other elements of the population. Catholics no longer see themselves as a disadvantaged minority group; they have become proper middle-class suburbanites, and as they have done so, they have divided themselves between the two parties.

It is said that a majority of priests voted against the election of John Kennedy. This is important because the old federalized party machinery, controlled by its predominantly Irish Catholic leadership, was a key element in weaving the various components of the FDR coalition into an effective communications medium. The traditional machine bosses have now ceased to perform this function with effectiveness. This was revealed in different ways by the 1968 primaries in Indiana and New York, two states that represented typical bastions of traditional party control.

The Indiana Primary sounded the death knell of the traditional party system as a communications medium and cast grave doubts on the validity of anything that would later come out of the national conventions. In Indiana, if anywhere, the old way remained vital—reliably erosion-proof against the New

Politics of personalized candidates. Organization of the Indiana party system followed the classical textbook pattern. It was a model of "democratic centralism" with the network of officials following clear lines of authority, from the State Central Committee through the districts and then to the county level, resting finally on the foundation of the whole thing, the precinct chairmen— who in turn competed among themselves in the ingenuity and intensity with which they carried formal principles of organization right down to the level of neighborhood and block. This meant that a constant and furiously contested struggle was perpetually under way for the machine allegiance of the voter. Any machine official whose interest or industry waned was subject to displacement by organization upstarts who coveted his office.

This structure is important for two reasons: First, Indiana was one of the few places in which the ideal party organization actually existed. (In California, for example, political newcomers who try to "find" the party organization are often astounded by the fruitlessness of their quest. A party system doesn't exist in California in the textbook—or Indiana—sense.) Second, Indiana reveals the extent to which the classic party was, at its height, a true mass medium of communications. Both factors highlight the significance of the Indiana Primary. The traditional textbook party, which still imagined itself to have the vitality and monopoly of the political process it had enjoyed in the past, was soundly defeated by the New Politics. It actually came in a poor third against makeshift cadres of "aliens" who worked the precincts and inundated the voters with television appeals based on the personalities of their circuit-riding stars from Washington.

Indiana's Democratic governor, Roger Branigan, staked his campaign on one issue: the defense of Indiana's traditional machine system against the New Politics. How could he possibly have lost? Not only was he playing the game according to the time-tested rules of politics, he also had the newspapers solidly behind him. All this made the primary a direct test of the New Politics against the Old. The Old, in solid control of its characteristic communications system of party and papers, fell victim to the New.

The next case is New York. There, Robert Kennedy had previously invaded the traditional party bastions as an obvious outlander to run for the Senate. He was explicitly and validly tagged as a carpetbagger by the old-timers. Moreover, he had the gall to joke publicly about the charge. He then overwhelmed the traditional party organization. Following his victory he was criticized—and the charge was repeated the day of his death—for failing to reorganize the state party machinery along traditional lines.

But it is possible that Senator Kennedy was wiser than the old-timers. Upon election as Senator he paid little or no attention to traditional New York State machine politics. Whether or not this was calculated wisdom or lassitude will have to await the memoirs. But we do know now that Kennedy was "right" in the sense that the Old Politics was already dead and not worth his cultivating. This was confirmed in New York by the primary that occurred after his death. A pro-McCarthy challenger, albeit a relative of an old-line O'Dwyer, overwhelmingly defeated the "machine." New York politics, like Indiana politics, had fallen prey to new forces.

What do we make of these two instances? Bastions of traditional machine politics defeated in direct confrontation with the new? For one thing, our earlier conclusion is underscored: The national conventions are politically irrelevant; they were displayed on TV as relics of the past like the machines on view at a rally of "Model T" owners. The traditional parties no longer serve as mass media of communications. Yet these political relics have determined the choices to be presented to the voters in November. The result cannot be valid. Nor would it have changed things if the conventions had "pragmatically" rejected the two front-runners to opt for those who had earlier demonstrated the superior vitality of the New over the Old Politics. For even if the traditional machines, in convention assembled, had done the "right thing," they would have done it for the wrong reason—from canny estimates of electability rather than from the results of their own organic foundations and deliberative processes.

Finally, there has occurred an erosion of the distinction between the "inside" and the "outside" of politics. This is what we are witnessing an America today in relation to the war issue, as well as in Russia *vis-à-vis* Czechoslovakia. It has brought about another type of "New" Politics. This refers not to the New Politics of the mass media, nor to that of the streets, but to a New Politics that is forming itself around the reversal of the traditional relationships between external warfare and domestic tranquility. It can be put in the hackneyed terms of Clausewitz's dictum about war as the continuation of politics by other means. What has happened in our time is that internal politics has come to be strongly influenced, and in some cases determined, by the shape of external politics. This means that the boundary line between the two has become eroded. Politics, in the internal sense, has almost become the continuation of external warfare by other means. One result is that the internal political systems of the leading nations of the world have become militarized.

This means that we must reinterpret the so-called pacifism of the Eisenhower Administration. It is true that President Eisenhower was a man of peace. But even more important was that his pacifism was primarily the result of his attempt to return to the conditions of a past when domestic affairs could be somewhat insulated from international relations, and foreign policy could be made as a result of domestic forces—rather than the other way around. Eisenhower valiantly—and in general, successfully—attempted to manage foreign affairs and defense policy so that the traditional economics, traditional politics, and traditional ways of American life could play themselves out as before. But his administration was the watershed, and immediately after it was over, each succeeding President foundered in each major political crisis on his inability to insulate internal domestic politics from foreign affairs in the old way. Kennedy and Johnson became victims of the revolution that cemented external warfare and external politics into determinants of internal politics. This aspect of the New Politics is also demonstrating the obsolescence of the national convention system. The conventions of the established parties, by their nature, reflect only local domestic forces. In short, we are confronted with the fact that the traditional party system is as obsolete as the magneto. It cannot abandon its parochial foundations and it cannot forsake its inner logic, which is to nominate those candidates best calculated to preserve the power of the party apparatus, rather than respond to the three-fold lessons of the New Politics.

What of the future? A new system of campaign communications has replaced the old, and there is a new electoral coalition to go along with it. The evidence indicates that sometime prior to his death, Robert Kennedy had perceived its chief components. The envisioned Kennedy coalition was to be composed of: (1) residual elements of the Democratic faithful; (2) the poor, the ethnic minorities, and the Negroes; (3) the functionaries of the newer service trades, largely white-collar workers; (4) the young; and (5) the intellectuals. The latter two are especially significant. From a bare statistical point of view, young adults make up a newly significant segment of the population. From a political point of view, they are of even more significance. Moreover, if the present movement to lower the voting age to eighteen bears fruit, it will bring a permanent alteration in the matrix of electoral forces.

Even more interesting is the group called intellectuals. This refers not merely to college professors, but to all those who can be said to earn their living from brain work. This includes, in addition to the entire teaching profession, those employed in all the phases of research, development, planning, systems engineering, technology, etc. It includes the entire cadre of cybernation-spawned workers who promise to expand rapidly in the next few years. It includes most of those in the arts, the entertainment industry, the mass media, and advertising. Intellectuals comprise the fastest-growing segment of our population. It is even possible—statistics are ambiguous—that they already make up the largest single occupational group in our population.

Note that the members of this potential coalition have several special characteristics. They are either politically or economically deprived—many are both. They are highly mobile, geographically and socially. They are megapolitans, natives of the super-cities. Consequently they have no spiritual ties with smalltown or farm traditions and no nostalgia for "grass-roots" democracy of fond Progressive-Populist recollection. They are post-federalist in the sense that they possess very little state chauvinism; the day of the Virginian, the Hoosier, the New Englander, and, yes, even the Texan, is over for these people. They are children of the Welfare State and have but a literary acquaintance with the private enterprise system. They recognize the erosion in the traditional distinction between foreign and domestic affairs. They are world-oriented, and foreign affairs—especially wars—are as significant to them as are domestic affairs. Their political foe is not the robber-baron, but the business-military-bureaucratic Welfare State Establishment. They regard the Protestant ethic as a relic of history, and if they are not completely unchurched, they are so religiously revolutionary as to pass for the same thing in the eyes of their elders.

The new coalition has hardly anything in common with the old. Like the old, it will produce its own characteristic campaign communications system. Some of its features are already apparent: (1) flying cadres of media experts will replace local bosses; (2) personality politics will replace party politics; (3) party federalism based on state territories will give way to a new electoral federalism based on associations; (4) the two-party system will give way to a nonparty electoral system; (5) the politics of sectional interests will be supplanted by the politics of an urban society; (6) domestic issues will make room for world issues; and finally, (7) the old agrarian traditions of grass-roots participational democracy will be supplanted by new forms of democracy resting upon urban participatory, community-building political action. In this latter movement the three strands of the New Politics will come together and coalesce the new electoral coalition into a true political movement.

Interest Groups

The formal structure of government in the United States would by itself be inadequate to represent the many shades of opinion and the varying interests of the American people. The President is the spokesman for the entire nation, the senators each represent a state, and a congressman stands for over 400,000 constituents. Obviously, the degree of representation must be inexact and every decision-maker must weigh differing, and often competing, interests. Most citizens limit their political activity to the ballot box, but for those who feel strongly about public policy, and for those whose immediate interests are vitally affected by government decisions, the formal act of voting is only the first step toward achieving the political objective. To achieve their ends they need power, and since one man is not likely to have a significant amount of power by himself, these individuals form interest groups.

Interest groups can be categorized as being either society-oriented or government-oriented. Admittedly, most groups try to influence both the public and the decision-makers, but there is a difference in emphasis. Groups which have faith in the existing political process tend to concentrate on incremental change by "encouraging" decision-makers to exercise discretion in their favor. The NAACP is recognized as a classic example of this type of pressure group. Its techniques and achievements are treated by Gilbert Ware in "Lobbying as a Means of Protest: The NAACP as an Agent of Equality."

Elizabeth B. Drew describes the machinations of a less public-spirited pressure group in "The Quiet Victory of the Cigarette Lobby." The article contends that the cigarette lobby actually won a victory when Congress voted to require that all cigarettes carry a health warning. The tobacco people had lobbied for the passage of the "health-hazard" labeling bill because the warning was not really expected to curb cigarette smoking and the law which required the warning protected the industry by prohibiting the Federal Trade Commission or the states from taking any further action against cigarettes.

As might be expected, lobbying tactics have been found ineffective by groups with limited access to the Establishment. In recent years many of these groups, primarily those dominated by Negroes and students, have turned to "direct confrontation" as a means of making their voices heard. Direct confrontation is aimed at both decision-makers and the general public. The tactic is designed to force society to recognize and deal with a problem. Boycotts, protest marches, and sit-ins are standard ploys.

How effective are such tactics? Tom Kahn evaluates one of the most publicized confrontations in "Why the Poor People's Campaign Failed" and suggests that in present-day American society, which is confused and divided, the paramount need is for alternatives which will increase rather than decrease cohesion of democratic liberal-radical forces. He maintains that urban guerilla warfare will not long be tolerated in America and that continued resort to direct action will result in repression and a turn to the Right.

The tactics of the SDS can be observed readily via the news media, but the operations of the Radical Right are less well known. Alan Westin's classic article, "The John Birch Society: Fundamentalism on the Right" is included to shed some light on the pressures employed by a right-wing extremist group.

The Quiet Victory of the Cigarette Lobby

ELIZABETH BRENNER DREW

At the Public Health Service's annual Christmas party last year, some of the agency's employees entertained their colleagues by singing their own version of "On Top of Old Smoky":

> On top of Old Smoking
>   A year has gone by
> But the smoke we're deploring
>   Still gets in our eye.

They were lamenting the fact that a full year had passed since the Report of the Surgeon General on Smoking and Health warned that "cigarette smoking is a health hazard of sufficient importance in the United States to warrant appropriate remedial action," and that still no such action had been taken. This summer Congress passed a bill requiring that cigarette packages carry the warning "Caution: Cigarette Smoking May Be Hazardous to Your Health," but the same song can be sung at the next Christmas party, and the next one, and the next one.

To hear its sponsors tell it, the new legislation "is a forthright, historic step towards the responsible protection of the health of this nation's citizens" (Senator Warren G. Magnuson, Democrat, of Washington), one that "constitutes a legislative approach in which we can take some degree of pride" (Representative Oren Harris, Democrat, of Arkansas). In fact, however, the bill is not, as its sponsors suggested, an example of congressional initiative to protect public health; it is an unabashed act to protect private industry from government regulation. Behind the facade of a requirement for printing a warning on cigarette packages (which is not expected to deter smoking much), Congress tied the hands of the Federal Trade Commission by forbidding it to proceed with its own plans to apply much more stringent regulations. Had it not been for Congress, the FTC, which is charged with preventing unfair and deceptive trade practices, would have required a warning both on cigarette packages *and in cigarette advertising.* The effect of the advertising regulation is what the cigarette industry most feared; Congress obliged by forbidding it for at least four years.

Reprinted from Elizabeth Brenner Drew, "The Quiet Victory of the Cigarette Lobby," *The Atlantic Monthly,* Vol. 216, No. 3 (1965), pp. 76–80. Copyright © 1969 The Atlantic Monthly Company, Boston, Mass. Reprinted with permission.

In another remarkable provision, the law prohibits state and local governments from taking any action on cigarette labeling or advertising. It is one thing for Congress to prohibit the states from enacting legislation which overlaps and is inconsistent with its own requirements, as in the case of the labeling, but it is a far different thing for Congress to refuse to act, and to prohibit the states from acting, as in the case of cigarette advertising.

The tobacco industry's success at winning from Congress what it wanted while still providing the lawmakers with an opportunity to appear to be all in favor of health was a brilliant stroke. The industry brought it off because the tobacco lobby employed unusually skilled and well-organized strategy; because it hired some of the best legal brains and best-connected people in Washington to help with the fight; because it successfully grafted onto its built-in congressional strength from tobacco-producing states a sufficient number of congressmen to whom the issue was not one of health, or even of the tobacco industry, but one of curbing the powers of regulatory agencies, such as the FTC; and because it succeeded in throwing a heavy smoke screen around the health issue. And finally, it was the industry's good fortune that President Johnson remained aloof from the battle.

The Report of the Surgeon General's Special Advisory Committee on Smoking and Health was instigated at the behest of private health organizations, such as the American Cancer Society, which sought a definitive government position on the accumulating studies pointing to a connection between smoking and disease. The panel of ten scientists established in 1962 to make the study had the approval of the health groups and the tobacco industry, for all parties had been allowed to veto any proposed member. The cigarette industry, it was widely assumed, had been boxed in.

After fourteen months, the panel's report was printed under the security regulations usually reserved for top-secret reports to the National Security Council, and on a Saturday (the stock market was closed) early in January, 1964, it was handed out to reporters locked in the State Department auditorium until the stipulated hour for the report's release. The Surgeon General's panel unanimously found that smoking was related to lung cancer, chronic bronchitis, emphysema, cardiovascular diseases, and cancer of the larynx.

Among those who were ready and waiting for the report was the Federal Trade Commission, which had rejected past requests for action, pending a definitive answer to the health question. Within days after the report was released, the commission announced hearings on proposed new trade regulations for the cigarette industry.

Also ready for the Surgeon General's report was the tobacco industry. Sometime in late 1963, the distinguished Washington law firm of Arnold, Fortas & Porter turned up as counsel to the Philip Morris Company. The Fortas in the firm's title is Abe Fortas, personal counsel and confidant to President Johnson—and later his first choice for the Supreme Court. Faced with the probability that the FTC would move against the companies, the industry formed a committee of lawyers from Arnold, Fortas & Porter and other top Washington firms, one representative of each of the "bix six" tobacco companies—R. J. Reynolds, American Tobacco, Brown & Williamson, Liggett & Myers, P. Lorillard, and Philip Morris—and one of the industry's defense lawyers for personal injury suits alleging that smoking had induced cancer. This committee met almost daily, from the time of formation in early 1964 through completion of congressional action on the labeling bill this year. It covered every contingency for the companies: it planned the industry argument in the FTC hearings, it planned a court test of the FTC ruling if that became necessary, and it deeply involved itself in the maneuvering in Congress. Once the issue came before Congress, the lawyers' committee wrote testimony, drafted bills and amendments, served as central casting for witnesses most likely to sell the industry's point of view, and fed to friendly congressmen statements and questions to be asked of witnesses. In gossip-prone Washington, there inevitably was speculation on whether Fortas' involvement had anything to do with the conspicuous absence of any mention of the smoking issue in President Johnson's message to Congress making various proposals in the field of public health. It is more likely, of course, that this omission was due to understandable reluctance on the part of the President to take on a bruising fight that would pit him against many members of his own party. Anyway, according to people in the Capitol, when the time came for key votes on the Hill, Fortas was busy on the telephone.

While the lawyers' committee was providing the legal brainwork for the industry, the political expertise and the overt lobbying were supplied by Earle C. Clements, former Democratic representative and senator from Kentucky, former Senate Majority Whip and lieutenant to then-Majority Leader Lyndon B. Johnson, and former director of the Senate Democratic campaign committee, which dispenses vitally needed election funds. In 1964, Clements registered as a lobbyist for the big six. A more ideal man could hardly have been found, for not only did Clements have excellent political connections; he was well liked, he was a gentleman, and he was a shrewd master of legislative infighting. Clements is believed to be the one who sold the tobacco companies on the core of their strategy, a strategy which seems now the obvious one because it worked, but which was not so obvious at the time: go to Congress and accept the package label (the least alarming and most inconspicuous one possible) in exchange for protection against advertising requirements and state regulation. The industry would then give the impression of a sweet reasonableness, whereas a rigid position might bring more severe consequences. The label might even be a boon of sorts, providing a new defense in future personal injury cases brought by cigarette smokers.

Before the FTC ruling appeared, the industry had to decide whether to fight it in the courts or to seek relief from Congress. Guessing—correctly—

that Congress was a surer thing (and a court test could always come later anyway), that is where the industry went. Clements is credited with persuading Oren Harris, chairman of the House Interstate and Foreign Commerce Committee, to hold hearings in mid-1964 on the question of cigarette regulations, even before the FTC announced its decision later that June.

As the hearings ambled into the late summer and time for going home to get reelected neared, the committee asked the FTC to delay the effect of the rulings, since Congress would not have time to act by the end of the session. The labeling ruling was to have gone into effect on January 1, 1965, and the advertising ruling six months later. The FTC complied with the committee's request, pushing the effective date for both regulations back to July 1. Thus the stage was set for this year's fight.

The normally fiercely competitive tobacco companies had long since learned to practice brotherhood when their economic interests were at stake. In 1954 in the face of major studies suggesting a link between smoking and disease, tobacco manufacturers, growers, and warehousemen, under the guidance of Hill & Knowlton, a major public relations house, established the Tobacco Industry Research Council (since renamed the Council for Tobacco Research—U.S.A.). This group has handed out over $7 million in research funds, a good bit of which has produced studies showing other causes of cancer and heart disease besides smoking. In 1958 the tobacco manufacturers established another organization, the Tobacco Institute. The institute ordinarily speaks for the industry and regularly issues a bulletin called "Reports on Tobacco and Health Research," which shows a remarkable facility for ferreting out research indicating causes of lung and heart disease other than smoking. Some examples from one issue: "Miners' Lung Cancers Triple Average"; "Rare Fungus Infection Mimics Lung Cancer" ("well nigh impossible to differentiate clinically"), and so on. Another issue duly reported evidence that charcoaled beef was conducive to cancer. Just after the Surgeon General's Report came out, it was announced that the six major companies were giving $10 million to the American Medical Association for research into smoking and health.

The industry's togetherness, as well as its careful preparation for the battle against regulation, was also apparent when it was announced with much ado in the spring of 1964 that the industry would embark on "self-regulation" in cigarette advertising, to cut the appeal of the ads to children and to stop saying or implying that smoking is good for the health. No longer would cigarette ads be placed in college newspapers or comic books; no longer would there be testimonials by noted athletes (but athletic programs were still sponsored); the virile young men and sweet young things who light up on television ads would have to be twenty-five; and there would be no advertising on programs "primarily" aimed at children. The regulations were drawn up by the same lawyers' committee that was preparing for the fight in Congress.

The exact strength of the tobacco industry itself in Congress—that is, the number of members in each chamber from areas heavily dependent on tobacco growing, distributing, and processing—is difficult to gauge and largely irrelevant. The tobacco people claim that some twenty-one states and 700,000 farm families are involved in the industry, undoubtedly counting states and farms where tobacco growing is of minimal importance. Whatever the claims of the companies, the figures on the place of the tobacco industry in the American economy are impressive: In 1963, Americans spent over $7 billion on cigarettes, buying 510 billion of them, or 4350 for each person over eighteen (as compared with 3500 in 1950). Each year the federal, state, and local governments take in at least $3 billion in taxes on the sales of cigarettes alone. And tobacco companies currently spend over $250 million on advertising.

On an issue of such importance to some of its members, the entire southern congressional bloc will tend to stay together. In addition, because federal regulatory power over a large industry was at stake, a healthy percentage of the Republican members were natural allies for the Southerners on this issue. The fact that a requirement of a warning in cigarette ads might curtail cigarette advertising and therefore cause a considerable loss of revenue for the broadcasting industry influenced still more members. The National Association of Broadcasters submitted statements firmly opposing any advertising regulation ("a substantial expansion of the role now played by government could seriously impair the effectiveness of industry self-regulation by undermining incentive"), and the broadcasters are understood to have been doing their own contacting while the bill to overturn the FTC was moving through Congress. Congressmen are particularly sensitive to the viewpoint of local station-owners, and they were aware of where the broadcasters stood.

Whatever there was of the other side was simply no match for this array of forces. Within the executive branch, the Public Health Service had to go it alone. The PHS did its best, however, to rally around itself what friends it had. Shortly after the Surgeon General's Report came out, the PHS, the Cancer Society, the American Heart Association, the National Tuberculosis Association, the American Public Health Association (comprising public health workers across the country), and a number of other private health groups formed an unusual federal-private body called the National Interagency Council on Smoking and Health. The AMA was not among the health-oriented groups which joined up. What testimony there was on the side of putting the FTC regulations into effect was better presented because of the council, and, more important, the council informed state health societies and doctors about what Congress was actually doing and stirred up a number of letters and telegrams to congressmen, urging them to hold fast for the advertising rule.

These efforts had some effect on the waverers. But the PHS was hurting from lack of true friends in Congress, an institution that has developed over the years a curious bifocal view of health issues. The lawmakers enthusiastically vote hundreds of millions of dollars—more, usually, than is requested—for health research, for when it is simply a matter of research, what congressman is against health? However, when the health officials go to Capitol Hill with proposals to put research findings into effect—to curb air pollution or discourage smoking—they are the skunks at the lawn party. For on these issues there are large economic interests at stake.

The tobacco strategists correctly deduced that the focal point for the fight to overturn the FTC would be the Senate Commerce Committee. The full Senate and the full House could be expected to follow the lead of the committee reporting out the bill, for both committees preside over legislation which affects a wide range of commercial interests and therefore have considerable leverage in their respective chambers. ("Everybody and his dog has business before those committees at some point," says one Hill aide.) The House Interstate and Foreign Commerce Committee, heavily laced with Southerners and conservatives, would be no problem; it could be expected to report out a bill requiring the label but forbidding, permanently, the FTC to require health warnings in cigarette ads. This would put the industry in the strongest possible position for bargaining with the Senate.

The Senate committee was not such a sure thing. The six Republicans were reliable enough, for this was clearly a crucial issue for Senator Thruston B. Morton of Kentucky, second-ranking GOP member of the committee, former chairman of the Republican National Committee, and current chairman of the fund-dispensing Senate Republican campaign committee. On the Democratic side, however, the only member whose political life required defense of the tobacco industry was Ross Bass of Tennessee, a freshman. Early in the hearings, Senator Vance Hartke of Indiana, another Democratic committee member, emerged as a tireless cross-examiner of those who opposed the industry's point of view. When questioned about Senator Hartke's seeming devotion to a cause of minimal importance to his own state, his aides took pains to explain that his interest did not stem from his long-time friendship with Clements, as some believed, or from the fact that Clements' campaign committee had given Hartke vitally needed election funds. Hartke himself said that he had come to the hearings thinking that there "must be some connection" between smoking and health, but came away "completely astonished" to find that the connection had not been proved. This gave the industry eight sure votes, and there were others on tap. What it wanted, however, was for the bill that went to the floor to have the support of Chairman Magnuson and of as many committee members as possible.

The industry's task was more difficult than it might have been if Senator Maurine B. Neuberger, Democrat, of Oregon, had not won a seat on the Commerce Committee when Congress opened in 1965. Mrs. Neuberger had long called for closer federal regulation of cigarette merchandising. Now she had an opportunity to challenge the witnesses who appeared before the committee and to proselytize her colleagues. To offset the attempts to undercut the FTC rulings, Mrs. Neuberger introduced legislation giving congressional sanction to what the FTC was trying to do. But in this she stood virtually alone.

The industry's presentation at the Senate hearings was masterful. Bowman Gray, chairman of the board of R. J. Reynolds, appeared for the industry, which carefully did not bombard the committee with too many tiresome witnesses, and the tone of his testimony was more in sorrow than in anger. Mr. Gray pointed out that the tobacco companies were "profoundly conscious" of the health questions and were zealously researching the problem; that "many distinguished scientists . . . are of the opinion that it has not been established that smoking causes lung cancer or any other disease"; that "millions of persons throughout the world derive pleasure and enjoyment from smoking" (as if someone were proposing to abolish the right to smoke); and that the central purpose of advertising was to compete among products, not to induce people to smoke. Mr. Gray said that the industry was naturally opposed to warnings both on labels and in advertisements, but his testimony was interlarded with the "howevers" and "ifs" that signaled the industry position: If a label is required, have Congress require it, and spell out its terms, rather than leave this to the dangerous FTC or the health-conscious Health, Education and Welfare Department, parent agency of the PHS. And if Congress requires the warning label, it should not interfere with "the right to advertise—an essential commercial right": "I am confident that the Congress will reject this extreme proposal."

Throughout the hearings, the industry, with the help of friendly senators, carefully built a record designed to show that medical opinion was split over the Surgeon General's Report—despite the fact that no medical group has ever denied its validity and only a small minority had dissented—that whatever Mrs. Neuberger or the FTC wanted to do was "extremist," and would wreak havoc in a basic American industry as old as Jamestown; and it made very effective use of the "excess" argument. According to this argument, excessive smoking may be dangerous, but so is excessive drinking, or overeating, or driving too fast. Would Congress want to put warnings of possible death on liquor, food, and automobiles? Where would it all end? This line of reasoning ignored the fact that the Surgeon General's report was not talking only about excessive smoking, and in fact stated that no safe level of smoking could be established. But the technique worked very well.

The committee quickly disposed of Mrs. Neuberger's, and the FTC's, approach on a 12–2 vote and settled down to the real issue, which was how long to suspend the effect of the FTC's ruling on advertising. Chairman Magnuson and a number of the committee's members were opposed to suspending it permanently, as the House had done, for this, too, was "extremist," and unseemly, for the rule-making authority of the regulatory agencies is supposedly independent of Congress. Where there is conflict, the issue is supposed to be decided in the courts. Moreover, although the permanent suspension may have been something devoutly to be wished by the cigarette industry, it was not something realistically to be expected. After some see-saw voting, Morton, Bass, and Hartke agreed with Magnuson to vote out a bill to require a label on packages by the following January and to suspend the advertising for three years after that. In the committee's report to the Senate, only Mrs. Neuberger objected to the suspension.

The united front of the committee and canny confusing of the issue undermined Mrs. Neuberger's attempt in the full Senate to reduce the time of suspension. As the time for the voting approached, a number of senators honestly believed that all they were about to do was to join the Commerce Committee in taking the heroic step of warning the public about the health dangers in smoking. Despite last-minute efforts by Mrs. Neuberger, Senator Robert F. Kennedy, their aides, and David Cohen, a lobbyist for the Americans for Democratic Action, to explain what else was involved, her amendment was defeated 29 to 49. The Senate then went on record to pass the bill by a vote of 72 to 5.

Meanwhile, the House committee had behaved predictably, voting out a bill to require a label on the side of the package and to bar the FTC permanently from requiring a warning in ads. The only surprise was that Mr. Harris and his colleagues felt compelled to indulge in a blatant breach of congressional etiquette to get the bill passed. One quiet Tuesday afternoon, with no prior notice, with only a few members on the House floor, and with the bill's principal opponent, Representative John E. Moss of California, out of town (but with the tobacco strategists in the gallery), the bill was called up. Moss, the sole member of the Harris committee to dissent in the committee's report and one of the Democratic Party's House whips, had had an understanding with the House leadership, or so he thought, that the bill would not be brought up until Thursday, two days later. Moss was flying back from Europe while the bill was being debated and arrived at Dulles Airport a half hour after the House passed the bill by a voice (unrecorded) vote.

Though some were surprised at the speed with which the House conferees acquiesced in the Senate's shorter ban on the FTC requirement for the warning in cigarette advertising, it was the logical thing to do for a number of reasons, among them columnist Drew Pearson. Mr. Pearson had begun to sniff out what was going on in the cigarette fight, and on the day that the House-Senate conferees first sat down to work out their differences, his column in the morning Washington *Post* was headlined, "Steamroller Goes Through House." This was not the sort of image that the tobacco companies were seeking. In addition, the companies knew that even a permanent ban would not be all-protective in the event more and more research showed direct links between smoking and disease, and if the public became sufficiently aroused. Also, Senator Magnuson was standing firm for the Senate's terms.

The best strategy at this point, then, was to accept the Senate bill—with two exceptions—and to go away quietly. The first exception was that the House conferees would not accept the Senate's provision that the label be on the front of the package (though there is reason to wonder how many know what is printed on the front *or* the side of cigarette packages other than the brand name). After some haggling, the Senate and House conferees decided to require that the warning "appear in conspicuous and legible type," but not to require that it be placed anywhere in particular, just that the place be "conspicuous." The second request—and this, too, was granted—was that the ban on the FTC action should expire on July 1, 1969, rather than on January 1. This way, there will once again be time for Congress, with another presidential election year just behind it, to go to bat for the cigarette industry and filter the "harmful elements" out of any new proposals.

Lobbying as a Means of Protest: The NAACP as an Agent of Equality

GILBERT WARE

Since its inception more than fifty years ago, the National Association for the Advancement of Colored People (NAACP) has sought justice for the Negro in America. Although its most spectacular activity has occurred in the courts, the true measure of its efforts is not to be found exclusively in the favorable decisions secured. For the NAACP has never viewed legal redress as a panacea for that ubiquitous societal malady, inequality—social, economic, political; nor has it functioned on the premise that the courts are the sole instruments of equality in our society. Commentators on these turbulent times often display a lack of perspective for the Negro revolt by ignoring or deemphasizing the non-judicial aspects of the NAACP's historic protest. This paper is an effort to provide that perspective.[1]

With the eradication of racial injustice in all public aspects of American life as its goal, the NAACP has sought to influence the formulation and execution of policy in all governmental arenas. Its goal, strategy, and tactics have been geared to the basic tenets of American democracy: the equality of men, the

Reprinted with permission of the author and the publisher from Gilbert Ware, "Lobbying as a Means of Protest: The NAACP as an Agent of Equality," *Journal of Negro Education,* Vol. XXXIII (Spring 1964), pp. 103–110.

right to petition government for redress of grievances, and so forth. Like other interest groups, the NAACP has prevailed upon leaders in government, political parties, and other groups, as well as the general public. In its constant effort to sway members of Congress, the NAACP has relied upon the normal group techniques: lobbying face-to-face before congressional committees and individual congressmen and their staffs; "backstopping" friendly legislators by drafting bills; and building up grass-roots support for the group's cause.[2]

NAACP Opposes Lynching

Early in the NAACP's history, its leaders were horrified by the frequency of tragedies such as that reported on January 27, 1921, in the Memphis (Tenn.) Press:

> More than 500 persons stood by and looked on while the Negro was slowly burning to a crisp. With the Negro chained to a log, members of the mob placed a small pile of leaves around his feet. Gasoline was then poured on the leaves, and the carrying out of the death sentence was under way.[3]

Under the leadership of its executive secretary, James Weldon Johnson, the NAACP launched a drive for federal antilynching laws. The notion of a legislator's overlapping memberships making him a point of access for a group[4] held true in that Johnson first approached Senator Arthur Capper, president of the NAACP branch in Topeka, Kansas. But Capper, knowing that an antilynching bill would have a better chance of survival if someone else sponsored it, referred Johnson to Senator Charles Curtis (R., Kan.). Curtis' offer to introduce a bill providing for an investigation of lynching fell short of the NAACP's goal. At Johnson's request, Representative L. C. Dyer (R., Mo.) presented H. R. 13. Defending the measure before the Senate Judiciary Committee (after Senator William E. Borah's subcommittee had filed an adverse report on it), Johnson said that it was aimed at the murder and anarchy which had gone beyond state control. But filibusterers assured the demise of H. R. 13 by making its withdrawal the condition for allowing other matters to be taken up.[5]

Civil rights leaders continued to press for antilynching legislation. In 1932 the NAACP's Legal Committee, assisted by Karl Llewellyn of the Columbia Law School, drafted bills which were sponsored by Senator Robert F. Wagner of New York and Edward P. Costigan of Colorado and by Representative Thomas F. Ford of California.[6] Although Johnson obtained pledges of support from fifty senators, and the Judiciary Committee made a favorable report, the Senate refused to act on such measures.[7] Three years later NAACP officials beseeched President Roosevelt to make the desired legislation a "must;" the House passed an antilynching bill; the Senate declined to concur. The hopes of civil rights champions soared in 1940 with a sympathetic report by the Senate

Judiciary Committee on a bill, but plummeted with Majority Leader Alben Barkley's assertion that it was "impractical" to make "a futile effort" to bring the bill to a vote.[8]

NAACP Versus Judge Parker

Success in the political arena depends largely on status. This applies to the courts, for judges are not insensitive to the social status of litigants. In the words of two scholars of judicial behavior:

> The symbol of the courts in this country is a blindfolded goddess of justice; and the words etched over the Supreme Court building, "Equal Justice Under Law," embody an ideal of American life. Motivated by this ideal, judges will often go to great lengths to protect people who have neither status, nor wealth, nor votes.[9]

Interest groups know this. Hence their efforts to influence the selection of judges, to support those who sympathize with their clientele, and to oppose those who do not.

It is in this light that the NAACP's opposition to Judge John J. Parker of North Carolina is to be viewed. President Hoover nominated Parker to fill the vacancy on the United States Supreme Court which was created by the death of Justice Edward T. Sanford in 1930. NAACP leaders knew little about Parker's record as a justice on the United States Circuit Court, but they did know that he approved the poll tax, literacy test, and grandfather clause provisions of his state constitution. While campaigning as the GOP gubernatorial candidate in 1920, Parker had said: "The participation of the Negro in politics is a source of evil and danger to both races and is not desired by the wise men of either race or by the Republican Party of North Carolina." The NAACP resolved to prevent the addition of Parker's views to those of a tribunal which, in its opinion, was already more concerned with property rights than with human rights.[10]

Parker refused to respond to an inquiry about the accuracy of the report which attributed the remarks to him. President Hoover denied the NAACP's request for the withdrawal of Parker's name. This ignited the NAACP protest: mass meetings were held, wires were sent to senators, visits were made to their offices—all in an attempt to block Parker's confirmation.[11] Far from idle, Parker's supporters denied that he had made the controversial statements. But NAACP lobbyists distributed to senators photostatic copies of the newspaper report of the remarks. Parker's allies made a point of urging southern senators not to yield to pressure from a group which represented Negroes. To counter this appeal, the NAACP equated a vote for Parker with aid to Hoover in rewarding North Carolina for having gone Republican in the 1928 elections in which Parker had been instrumental. To avoid the boomerang effect of lobbying the Southerners,[12] the NAACP relied on its senatorial allies to press this argument. The outcome was a vote (41 to 39) against Parker.[13]

FEPC

Subsequently, the issue of discrimination in employment reached crisis proportions. Typical of the attitude of management in the early forties was that of the president of North American Aviation Company. "While we are in complete sympathy with the Negro, it is against company policy to hire them as aircraft workers or mechanics . . . regardless of their training. . . . There will be some jobs as janitors for Negroes," he said.[14]

That this fell far short of the Negro's demands was made clear by A. Philip Randolph, president of the Brotherhood of Sleeping Car Porters. Embittered, Randolph proposed a March on Washington to protest discrimination in defense industries and in the military services. "Such a pilgrimage of 10,000 Negroes would wake up and shock official Washington as it has never been shocked before," he declared "Why? The answer is clear. Nobody expects 10,000 Negroes to get together and march anywhere for anything at any time."[15] In cooperation with the NAACP's Walter White and other civil rights leaders, Randolph made plans for the march.

The plans were cancelled after President Roosevelt agreed to prohibit discriminatory practices in industries which held government contracts as well as in vocational training for jobs in those industries. Issued on June 25, 1941, Executive Order 8802 contained the prohibition; it met another demand of civil rights groups by establishing a Fair Employment Practices Committee (FEPC) to guard against job discrimination. Roosevelt later incurred the wrath of Randolph and White when he transferred the committee to the War Manpower Commission under Paul V. McNutt. They accused the President of having reneged on a promise to retain personal control over the committee, and lamented the transfer which required it to obtain funds from a hostile Congress.

McNutt, in January, 1943, alienated Randolph and White by postponing hearings on unfair practices in railroad employment. At Randolph's instigation, a Save FEPC Conference convened in Washington in February to object to the postponement. In May the President appointed a second committee and gave it independent status in the Office of Production Management. The railroad hearings were held, but neither the railroad management nor the unions agreed to put an end to job discrimination. And in 1946 Congress refused to appropriate funds for the committee.[16] White wrote: "Thus ended the career of the agency which, more than any other, established the right of minority Americans to work at their skills and thereby increase their faith in the democratic process."[17]

With this defeat, dissension mounted within the ranks of FEPC enthusiasts.

At the time, the leading organization was the National Council for a Permanent FEPC. Conceived at the Save FEPC Conference, the Council had been created seven months later in September, 1943, to spearhead the drive for federal FEPC legislation. Although the NAACP contributed funds to the council and both White and Roy Wilkins (who was to become executive secretary of the NAACP after White's death in 1955) supported it, tension existed between the organizations. Randolph closed the council's executive committee membership to key civil rights organizations, including the NAACP; it was not until 1946 that political considerations led to an expansion of the membership. By then NAACP leaders had lost confidence in the council, but the personification of FEPC in Randolph prevented a bold bid for leadership.[18]

The council, like the March on Washington Movement before it, was of course the NAACP's competitor as well as its ally. Before FEPC became an issue, the NAACP had been the champion of the cause. As early as 1934 it had reported its "militant opposition" to unfair job practices. The decision of a joint congressional committee in 1935 to order an investigation of the Tennessee Valley Authority's abuse of Negro employees had been based in part on the testimony of the NAACP's Legal Counsel, Charles H. Houston. In the same year the NAACP had opposed a social security bill which failed to cover agricultural, casual labor, and domestic workers.[19]

Perhaps, then, a desire to regain leadership in the fight accounts largely for the severance of its ties with the National Council. The break occurred in 1946, but four years passed before the NAACP presented a direct challenge to Randolph by sponsoring a National Emergency Civil Rights Mobilization in the national capital. The pressure of the Mobilization was insufficient to break the Dixiecrat-conservative Republican coalition which blocked FEPC legislation.[20] Nevertheless the NAACP regained the initiative in the continuing quest for equality in employment.

The Right to Vote

Some observers hold that this and other goals could be reached if the Negro were armed with the ballot; others who appreciate the significance of the ballot see it as something less than a remedy for all ills. The campaign to secure Negro voting rights has been a relentless one. It has also been arduous, for America has spawned a multitude of Vardamans. To quote Senator Vardaman of Mississippi:

> I am opposed to Negro voting. It matters not what his advertised mental and moral qualifications may be. I am just as much opposed to Booker Washington as a voter, with all his Anglo-Saxon reinforcements, as I am to the . . . typical little coon, Andy Dotson, who blacks my shoes every morning. Neither is fit to perform the supreme function of citizenship.[21]

Among the bigots' weapons to prevent such performance have been violence and intimidation, literacy tests and understanding clauses, white primaries and grandfather clauses, and, of immediate concern, poll taxes.

One perceptive student of southern politics has contended that the poll tax is but one, and perhaps not the most important, disenfranchisement device.[22] Other analysts concur, adding that a surge in Negro voting in the South is unlikely to develop as long as the one-party political system exists there.[23] Such erudition has not deterred civil rights groups from seeking federal antipoll-tax legislation.[24] Walter White, for example, also saw the poll tax as but one hindrance to Negro voting. He insisted, however, that to remove any impediment is to take a step in the right direction. "We approach nearer to the goal for which we strive—a community of free men in which all are of equal stature," is the way he put it. Continuing his testimony before a Senate subcommittee during hearings on Senator Claude Pepper's antipoll-tax bill in 1942, White added:

> Passage of the . . . bill will materially affect the dangerously low morale among 13,000,000 American citizens who constitute a tenth of our population, who are disheartened, bitter, bewildered, and discouraged because the color of their skin shuts them out from that dynamic participation in the prosecution of the war against the Axis which they so passionately wish to contribute to.[25]

The Senate Judiciary Committee recommended passage of the bill, but a filibuster prevented a vote on it.

Nor did the Senate act in 1943 when the House passed a similar measure.[26] Several years later, the Senate turned a deaf ear to the NAACP's argument that the most important democratic principle, the right to vote, should not be curbed by a poll tax.[27] Filibustering senators killed the bill after President *pro tem* Arthur H. Vandenburg (R., Mich.) ruled cloture inapplicable to motions to consider.[28] The legislation sought still is not in sight.

The Filibuster

The filibuster has been, and still is, the *bête noire* of civil rights advocates, who would agree with Woodrow Wilson that: "The Senate of the United States is the only legislative body in the world which cannot act when its majority is ready for action." Why? Like Wilson, they would answer: "A little group of wilful men, representing no opinion but their own, have rendered the great government of the United States helpless and contemptible."[29] The Senate's refusal to adopt an efficacious cloture rule, Walter White once said, satisfied "every member of the bigot fringe of our own country and dictators everywhere else in the world."[30]

One obstacle to such adoption has been the Senate's approval of the contention that its rules carry over from one Congress to the next. Civil rights leaders argue, however, that the Senate, like the House, is free to adopt rules at the opening of each Congress. Moreover, the Senate has rejected the "continuous body" argument to act on treaties, nominations, and other matters. These leaders assert that new senators should share in the making of rules which will govern the Senate. If the Senate were to function under general parliamentary law at the opening of Congress, civil rights champions would have a chance to obtain a vote on a motion to adopt new rules. For they would have an opportunity (a) to seek the adoption of rules of procedure, (b) to move to adopt new rules, and (c) to move the previous question to close debate on that motion.[31]

No clean victory has been scored over King Filibuster. At the time of the Vandenburg ruling, filibusters were nominally addressing themselves to the question of amending the Journal but were in fact blocking an FEPC bill.[32] When Vice President Barkley reversed the ruling in 1949, the Senate overrode him. Senators accepted a proposal of their colleague, Kenneth S. Wherry of Nebraska, to curtail debate on motions to amend the Journal or to consider bills. For their concession to this, the southerners exacted a high price: an increase in the number of votes required for cloture from two-thirds of the senators voting to two-thirds of the Senate membership, and exemption from cloture motions to change the rules—including motions to revise Rule 22, the cloture rule, itself.[33]

On the face of it, the southerners suffered a setback in the 85th Congress when the Senate, at the suggestion of the then Majority Leader Lyndon B. Johnson of Texas, reversed itself on the concession. The requirement for cloture changed back to two-thirds of the senators present and voting, and cloture was made applicable to motions to change the rules. The rub of the matter, however, was that the rules would continue from one Congress to the next. Lamenting this proposal, the NAACP declared: "The adoption of the Johnson resolution more firmly entrenched the filibuster as an excuse for obstruction or watering down civil rights."[34]

The essence of all this is that it is unlikely that King Filibuster's reign will end soon. The Senate still has its share of "wilful men."

Conclusions

One reason for the dissatisfaction of angry young men and other critics with the NAACP's methodology is that they are uninformed about—or choose to ignore—its approach outside as well as inside the courts. They fail to grasp the essence of pressure group politics: the inevitability of bargaining and compromise, the relativity of success and defeat, the intrinsic functions of the group.

A pressure group's effectiveness is not to be measured solely by the enactment of measures which it supports or the defeat of those which it opposes. If these were the sole criteria of success, the NAACP's campaign for federal civil rights legislation, with the exception of those in 1957 and 1960, would be branded complete failures. But while falling short of announced goals, NAACP leaders express the thesis that the campaigns have contributed to the enhancement of civil rights. James Weldon Johnson believed that the Dyer antilynching bill "served to awaken the people of the southern states to the necessity of taking steps themselves to wipe out the crime [lynching]."[35] Roy Wilkins said in 1949 that the very existence of the NAACP could be justified if it had done nothing more than arouse the public opinion which had led to the sharp decline in lynching.[36] This thesis of NAACP officials is beyond proof, perhaps, but is congruous with the pattern of pressure-group politics.

Inherent in this pattern is group performance of watchdog and catalytic functions: gathering and disseminating information; drafting and securing support for bills; alerting its members, clientele, and allies to danger and spurring them to action. But the basic functions are integrative and disjunctive.[37] A political system which values public opinion must provide for the mobilization of that force. Generally, this is the concern of political parties whose expertise is such that it tends to distort beyond recognition the very perspectives and goals which are to be mobilized. To a lesser extent, pressure groups also mold and guide political opinions, countering the tendency toward unwholesome uniformity. This disjunctive function of pressure groups is as necessary as the integrative function, for "it . . . [prevents] the alienation of groups from systems which persistently distort their goals; in that sense [pressure groups] are an indispensable element of stability in such systems."

The NAACP makes no claim to exclusive representation of the Negro and others who toil on his behalf (and thus on that of the nation itself). Yet in quarters where his progress is to be determined, it is considered the preeminent agent of equality. It is no disparagement of other groups whose goals are compatible with its own to suggest that the NAACP is so regarded. From the civil rights perspective, however, none equals the NAACP as the historic integrative and disjunctive vehicle which has promoted simultaneously the maintenance of our political system and the cause of justice.

Why the Poor People's Campaign Failed

TOM KAHN

It was only a few years ago that Michael Harrington wrote, in *The Other America*, that a chief characteristic of the poor was their invisibility. The white middle class had designed its neighborhoods and traffic arteries to bypass the slums: the combined forces of urban renewal and the private housing market operated to push the poor, especially Negroes, out of view and into more densely packed ghettos. Thus there grew up a physical and cultural barrier which, it was agreed, had to be penetrated if the nation's conscience was to be awakened.

Between the publication of *The Other America* and the appearance of Resurrection City in Washington this year, a great deal happened, and it is doubtful that the poor can any longer be described as invisible in the old sense. To be sure, they have not been integrated into the economic mainstream, there is still little daily contact with the affluent majority (except in laboratory settings), and there has certainly been no basic shift in power relations. But if the poor still do not exist for us as real individuals, their collective condition has nevertheless been thrust actively into the political arena. Every schoolboy knows that there are poor people in America, that a disproportionate number of them are black, that they live in deteriorating slums and ghettos, and that there is among them a growing militance and indignation; he knows as well that there is an urban crisis in this country which is characterized by high unemployment in the slums, disorder in the schools, crime, violence, and dope in the streets. And he also knows, if he is at all alert, that there is evident today a measure of organized effort in behalf of the poor that, while still meager and ineffective, goes beyond what might have been predicted a short time ago.

Now it seems appropriate to question the notion, implicit in so much meliorist thinking, that the recognition of a problem is its solution. The affluent majority, once shown the face of poverty, can react in alternative ways. After all, to make a not irrelevant comparison, peace in Vietnam is the stated (and probably genuine) goal both of those who advocate unilateral U.S. withdrawal and of those who call for a military victory. Similarly, all are agreed that poverty in America must be eliminated, but while one approach to the problem is to work for guaranteed jobs and income, another is to conclude from recent events that the poor are their own worst enemy, and that they must be repressed into respect for law and order as a precondition for receiving any advances that the future might hold. There is, in short, nothing in the faces of the poor themselves that will necessarily inspire the sympathy or supportive political action of the majority; poverty can just as easily inspire fear and revulsion.

These thoughts have been occasioned by the Poor People's Campaign of 1968, a project which has been attacked more widely, and with more contempt, than any "radical" action in years—with the *possible* exception of the incredible New Politics Convention in Chicago last year. It is precisely for this reason that one hesitates to discuss the Poor People's Campaign seriously —which necessarily means critically. Nonetheless, the discussion must take place, for the campaign embodied ideas and techniques that have been evolving over the past five years, that therefore speak directly to our political and social experience in those years, and that, finally, are likely to manifest themselves again and again in the crucial months ahead. The discussion properly begins with some notes on the history of the Poor People's Campaign, and in particular on the role played in the campaign by Bayard Rustin. For if the Poor People's Campaign failed to produce its desired impact—and most agree that it did—then the reasons for that failure, as well as its ultimate significance, must be traced in large measure to the debate which took place last April and May between Rustin and the campaign leadership.

II

Late in 1967, when Dr. Martin Luther King first put forth the notion of a Spring Protest in Washington, he and the Southern Christian Leadership Conference had already experienced several disappointments in their effort to transplant their southern-born movement to the northern ghettos. They had so far been unable to duplicate in the big cities of the North the relatively swift and dramatic victories they had won in the South. For one thing, the highflown, basically optimistic rhetoric of the Southern Baptist minister failed to penetrate the bitter alienation and social breakdown of the big ghettos. Then, too, the opposition was politically much more sophisticated, often showing a deceptively amiable countenance; the Daley machine in Chicago was a far different animal from Bull Connor. Above all, the changes being sought were socioeconomic in nature, and hence far less easily attainable through traditional nonviolent, direct-action methods than had been, say, the desegregation of public accommodations, a relatively straightforward political goal.

SCLC was not the only civil rights organization confronted by these problems, but in some ways it was the one least suited to adjust to them. The Congress of Racial Equality, originally dominated by white pacifist-radicals, was going through a series of internal upheavals, and engaged in turning toward various versions of black nationalism in search of a base in the black community. The National Urban League, long regarded as the most conservative of the civil rights groups, had fashioned a more militant image under the leadership of Whitney Young, while maintaining its ties with enlightened big business. The NAACP, with some 450,000 members (the great majority of them black), was continuing to shoulder the legal burden but turning its attention increasingly to economic issues. (Perhaps because it is made up of some 1600 chapters throughout the country, the NAACP can vary its strategic emphases in a functional way at the local level, without requiring sudden alterations at the national level.)

Unlike these organizations, SCLC existed as the extension of one man, Dr. King. It had, and has, no membership, no regularly functioning groups (as opposed to projects) in local communities. Consequently, when SCLC workers entered a community, they often appeared as "outsiders," and were unable to attract an enduring following loyal to SCLC. The "membership" of SCLC, like that of SNCC, is its staff, now reported at 125 full-time workers. But whereas an organization like SNCC could throw out its founding leadership and, with the election of a Stokely Carmichael or an H. Rap Brown, transform the organization from top to bottom, SCLC obviously could not.

In short, the structure of SCLC and the towering figure of its leader precluded it from making the changes undertaken by other civil rights groups. (I leave aside here any evaluation of these changes.) But the pressures and frustrations that were building up in the entire movement were felt in SCLC as well. The Chicago project of 1966 had clearly failed, and the mass media, searching out "authentic" voices of the violent ghetto, were increasingly spotlighting young black militants. Inevitably, some of the SCLC staff became restive, worried that they were losing touch with the new currents and fearful that their own inspirational gifts were becoming obsolete. (As anyone knows who has known Southern Baptist ministers, each and every member of the SCLC leadership believes that his role is divinely inspired and divinely to inspire.) The presence of Dr. King served to prevent these frustrations and internal conflicts from erupting into public view. But there is evidence that the declining morale of the SCLC staff was in the back of his mind as he made plans for the Poor People's Campaign of 1968.

From the beginning, the plans were not very clear, and a debate on tactics took place among the members of King's "think tank"—an informal group outside of the SCLC structure that met irregularly at King's request. One member of the group was Bayard Rustin, the leading tactician of the civil rights movement and now executive director of the A. Philip Randolph Institute, whose relationship with King dated back to the Montgomery Bus Protest in the mid-1950s.

In a detailed three-page memorandum to King dated January 29, 1968,

Rustin outlined a series of suggestions for the strategy and tactics of the Spring Protest (as it was then called). He proposed that the project center on economic questions, and that the aims be stated in two parts, the first encompassing long-range demands "not necessarily expected to be obtained now, such as guaranteed income for those who cannot work and public works at decent wages . . . for those who can," and the second dealing with immediate demands for "jobs, housing, welfare, and passage of a strong civil rights bill."

In urging a list of specific, "realizable" demands, Rustin argued that

> . . . failure to achieve some major victories in the nation's capital at this time will, I believe, increase frustration nationally. These demands should be broad enough to insure some of them being won soon. . . .
>
> I do not believe it is possible to attract sufficient numbers to the nation's capital unless, far in advance, the strategy and tactics have fully been made clear to all concerned. We are not now in the period we were in in 1963, at the time of Selma, Birmingham, and the March on Washington, when there was absolute clarity in everyone's mind as to objectives. . . . Not only do I feel it is essential that those being called into Washington know precisely what they are being called into, but I believe it is important that those in Government should have a very clear picture of aims, strategy, and tactics.

Thus the issue of specific as opposed to general demands—an issue that was later to flare into public controversy—was raised by Rustin as early as January of this year. In the same memorandum, Rustin argued against the use of disruptive tactics in Washington:

> Given the mood in Congress, given the increasing backlash across the nation, given the fact that this is an election year, and given the high visibility of a protest movement in the nation's capital, I feel that any effort to disrupt transportation, government buildings, etc., can only lead, in this atmosphere, to further backlash and repression.
>
> Such tactics will, I believe, fail to attract persons dedicated to non-violence but, on the other hand, attract elements that cannot be controlled, and who on the contrary will converge on the project with a variety of objectives in mind other than those of civil rights. . . .
>
> I believe you should address a series of mass meetings across the country outlining clearly your plan, in order to set the tone for the Washington demonstration in advance so that certain elements would have no excuse for converging on Washington without clarity. I sincerely believe that unless this is done, many individuals could become severe problems once they are in Washington.

These excerpts effectively refute the charge, subsequently made, that Rustin had pooh-poohed the whole idea of the project. In fact, his memo recommended a number of concrete and positive tactical steps that King might take to safeguard the project from the dangers Rustin foresaw. For he did have deep reservations about the project and candidly told King so. "There is in my mind," he wrote, "a very real question . . . whether SCLC can maintain control and discipline over [the Spring Protest] even if the methods used are limited to constitutional and nonviolent tactics."

Two months later, Martin Luther King was assassinated. Rustin, shattered by grief, flew immediately to Memphis to organize the march begun by King on behalf of the sanitation workers. He brought the young militants, who had disrupted the earlier King march, into positions of responsibility as marshals; the resulting demonstration was a massive, inspiring tribute to the slain leader. Returning home to New York three sleepless days later, Rustin experienced one of those grotesque assaults by which certain publicists of the New Left earn their daily bread—a *Village Voice* article by Jack Newfield denouncing him for opposing King's Poor People's Campaign.[38]

While in Memphis, Rustin had told Rev. Ralph David Abernathy, King's successor, that he would be available for consultation on the logistics of the Poor People's Campaign. In the ensuing weeks the Campaign hit snag after snag. There were delays in getting contingents out of the South, and the first groups to arrive in Washington found arrangements incomplete at Resurrection City. In mid-May, harassed and frazzled, Abernathy telephoned Rustin and implored him to take over responsibility for the one-day Mobilization in support of the Poor People's Campaign, then scheduled for May 30. Rustin resisted, on the grounds that there was opposition to him in the SCLC staff and that his entry might stir internal bickering which Abernathy could ill afford so soon after succeeding King. (In a meeting of the "think tank" two years earlier, Rustin had incurred the wrath of some SCLC staffers by arguing against King's going into Chicago.) Abernathy was not to be dissuaded, however. He pledged that Rustin, as national coordinator, would have full authority over the Mobilization, and said he would see to it that the SCLC staff cooperated. Finally, Rustin agreed to meet with Abernathy and his key aides in Washington on May 19.

Rustin, accompanied by his assistant, Norman Hill, went to the meeting with a set of fourteen points which were his precondition for accepting Abernathy's request. He stipulated, among other things, that he have full authority for the Mobilization, including selection of staff and marshals; that the Mobilization be postponed to mid-June; that there be no disruption of government functions on the day of the Mobilization; that participation in the Mobilization be based on adherence to democracy, integration, and the strategy of nonviolence; and that "in addition to stating the broad objectives of the Poor People's Campaign for guaranteed jobs and income, the one-day Mobilization will project specific concrete demands. It will be made clear that these demands do not represent the full programs of the SCLC."

The fourteen points were agreed to, and on May 24 Rustin and Abernathy held a press conference to announce Rustin's appointment as national co-ordinator and the postponement of the Mobilization to June 19. In Aber-nathy's presence Rustin reiterated that "the Mobilization will not content itself with defining general social goals. It will make specific demands which can, and must be, immediately translated into law by congressional action and executive order."

What Rustin had in mind became clear nine days later when he issued, under his and Abernathy's names, the official Mobilization "Call." The "Call" covered the general long-range goals of the Poor People's Campaign under an "Economic Bill of Rights" that would guarantee full employment, decent wages, and an adequate income for the unemployed. It went on to list specific "attainable" demands to be made to the Congress and the President—e.g., creation of one million public service jobs; adoption of the Housing and Urban Development Act; repeal of punitive welfare restrictions; collective bargain-ing rights for farm workers; more funds for antipoverty programs; expanded food distribution; etc.

There was an immediate favorable reaction on Capitol Hill, as the "Call" gave congressional liberals some concrete legislative goals to work for. It was clear that the Poor People would not be allowed to remain in Washington indefinitely; the liberals were hoping that if the Campaign could achieve some victories, a graceful withdrawal could be effected. Publication of the "Call," along with news of Rustin's appointment, also brought in support from unions, church groups, and liberal organizations, which had earlier been uneasy over the prospect of confusion and possible violence in Washington.

The fears entertained by these groups were not entirely groundless. On the day before the Abernathy-Rustin press conference, eighteen Campaigners were arrested in an unscheduled demonstration at the office of Wilbur Mills, chair-man of the House Ways and Means Committee, an indication that SCLC was having trouble controlling the Campaign. It was also having trouble with its own staff. On the day the "Call" was issued, Rev. Hosea Williams, an Aber-nathy lieutenant, proclaimed at a rally: "The picnic is over. . . . The police want to use those billies. Well, we're going to give them a chance."

While Rustin's New York office was preparing newspaper ads, printing in-struction manuals, and getting endorsements and bus commitments from na-tional organizations, the Washington situation continued to deteriorate. Two days after the issuance of the "Call," Hosea Williams called a press conference and denounced the document as "a bunch of jazz and foolishness." He said it was "unauthorized" and asserted, furthermore, that Rustin was merely a "pub-lic-relations man" for the Mobilization. On the same day, one hundred demon-strators confronted Attorney General Ramsey Clark at the Department of Justice. In words similar to those used by Hosea Williams at the rally on June 2, one of the demonstrators shouted: "Mr. Ramsey Clark, you better tell the police to get their guns ready because we're ready. For every one of us you kill in Resurrection City, ten cities are going to burn, 'cause we ain't got nothing to lose."

The next day, in response to Williams's statements, Rustin released the full text of the fourteen-point agreement to the press and insisted that the "Call" had been cleared with Rev. Abernathy and the executive vice president of SCLC, Rev. Andrew Young. Meanwhile, the press reported Abernathy as saying, "I did not authorize and neither did I issue" the "Call."[39] Apparently forgetting one of the fourteen points he had agreed to, Abernathy added, "I do not think it is comprehensive enough to cover the demands of the Poor People's Campaign. I go along with some of his [Rustin's] ideas, but I think it's got to be broader." Abernathy made no comment on Hosea Williams's charge that Rustin had no authority over the Mobilization.

Rustin's phones were flooded with calls from people whose participation in the Mobilization had been predicated on the assumption that he would be in charge. Some groups indicated they would suspend activity until some clarification were offered. Federal authorities refused to give final approval to the line of march until it became certain that Rustin or someone else had authority to sign contracts. Meanwhile, Rustin had been trying for three days to reach Abernathy by phone, by telegram, and through intermediaries—without success. Then, on June 6, Rustin announced he was suspending his role in the Mobilization pending word from Abernathy affirming the fourteen points and Rustin's authority. (During this time, it was learned, Abernathy was tied up in all-night staff meetings at which a principal topic was the firing of Rustin—reportedly a move demanded by representatives of CORE and some peace groups.)

Finally, the next morning, Abernathy called Rustin and offered to convene a press conference to reaffirm Rustin's full authority as national coordinator. Rustin proposed that the press conference be preceded by a meeting which would include Hosea Williams and several other SCLC staff members who were known to be hostile to Rustin's role. Unless they were a party to the agreement, Rustin felt, there would be no way of putting a stop to their sniping. Abernathy argued that Rustin's proposal would weaken his position as the leader of SCLC, and he reiterated that he could keep his staff in line. Rustin replied that he thought Abernathy would be ill-advised to risk internal conflict by trying to discipline his staff and that in any case he, Rustin, did not want to be a cause of factionalism within SCLC. This impasse having been reached, Rustin told Abernathy that he was resigning, but that he would be available, behind the scenes, to help in any way Abernathy wanted. (In the following days, Rustin turned over all of the Mobilization bus lists and files to Sterling Tucker—Washington director of the Urban League, whom Abernathy had appointed as Rustin's successor—and sent $4000 he had raised to SCLC for the sound system in Washington.)

The Monday following his resignation, Rustin attended a meeting of liberal organizations, which had originally been convened to discuss Mobilization plans for June 19. He explained his reasons for resigning, but declined to participate in the ensuing discussion about what these groups should now do.

III

It is not easy to evaluate a demonstration like the June 19 Mobilization. Indeed, the value of any large demonstration is not to be measured solely by its immediate results. Also important is its effect on the participants—on their morale and on their willingness to work harder once they have returned home. Reactions, whether friendly or hostile, can take a while to register.

Yet it must be said that there is so far little evidence that the Mobilization made an impact. Although a turnout of fifty thousand people—the official estimate—is not to be sneered at, it is not momentous in these days of giant rallies. Inevitable comparisons have been made with the March on Washington of 1963, which drew nearly a quarter of a million people. It is true that the Mobilization had much less time in which to prepare, but it also enjoyed more initial support than did the 1963 March. Whereas the Kennedy administration had tried to get the March called off, the Johnson administration was favorably disposed to the Mobilization, albeit for its own reasons (it hoped that the June 19 rally would afford the residents of Resurrection City an opportunity to withdraw with dignity). Nor did the 1963 March have the open support of an organized bloc of liberal congressmen like the one which worked with SCLC. Finally, the constituent organizations of the civil rights movement had, since 1963, become more experienced in the techniques of mobilizing their members for rallies and demonstrations.

The point here is not that the Mobilization was inferior to the 1963 March but that it did not live up to its own potential. A number of organizations that had planned to send large delegations finally dispatched only token representation. Nor was there a large turnout from Washington itself, where the majority of the population is black.

On Capitol Hill, the impact of the Poor People's Campaign was hardly productive of beneficial results. Perhaps nothing could have moved the 90th Congress to act—not even the assassination of Robert F. Kennedy had induced it to pass adequate gun-control laws—and certainly many of the congressmen who harangued against the Campaign needed no excuse to oppose aid to the poor. Nevertheless, the fact remains that if the Campaign were to win substantial victories, it would have had to serve as a massive lever of support for the liberal faction in Congress. This, in effect, was the role of the 1963 March in winning passage of the 1963 Civil Rights Act. But the Campaign actually served the opposite purpose. It not only became an embarrassment to congressional liberals but, in the view of many Washington observers, it diverted attention away from the crucial battle over appropriations—including appropriations for poverty programs—that was then being waged in Congress. Instead of calling the nation's attention to this debate, the Poor People's Campaign succeeded in focusing attention mainly on itself and on the residents of Resurrection City. And that was the most damaging effect of all.

"Resurrection City itself," said *Newsweek,* "conceived as a model of communal living, had fallen into a true-to-life squalor—an ill-housed, ill-fed, self-segregated, absentee-run slum afflicted with low morale, deepening restiveness, and free-floating violence." A poignant account, printed in the New York *Post* on June 20, came from Alvin Jackson, who resigned as chief security marshal for the Mobilization:

> There is rape, robbery, and cuttings every day, and there is nothing we can do about it even if we catch the guys who did it. . . . There are about 20 guns in Resurrection City. There are lead pipes, knives, and Molotov cocktails in there. . . . The reason they leave is that men are getting tired of coming home from a day's picketing to find their belongings stolen or their wife raped.

Not even the most cynical observer can deny that one of the greatest resources of the civil rights movement has been its moral capital, its "soul power." Resurrection City was dubbed the "City of Hope." Rev. Andrew Bevel of SCLC had described the Poor People's Campaign as "political group psychiatry." In his words, "Sometimes in psychiatry the patients get mad and run away. This time we are not going to let the patients get mad and run away. We're going to make them well, man. We're also educators, and when people are educated and get rid of their emotional problems, they will hear us" (New York *Times,* May 19).

A month later, as if in reply to Bevel, the *Wall Street Journal* could say:

> . . . as the reports of rape and robbery at Resurrection City began to seep out, not only were the public's fears of violence confirmed but an even stronger emotion came into play. After all, the Campaigners were people who were condemning American society, in toto or in part, as "racist" and "sick." And what values were they offering as substitutes? Not equality and justice, but robbery and rebellion against all authority by any means.

It is easy for sophisticated liberals and radicals to dismiss this as self-righteous moralizing from the ruling class. And it must be said, in this connection, that nothing that occurred in Resurrection City was as contemptible as the outcry of those right-wing congressmen who demanded that this transplanted microcosmic slum be torn down, but who are perfectly content to let the nation's real slums—of whose misery and pathology Resurrection City was but a symbol—remain intact. But then again, I have seen the contrary argument advanced—that precisely the most progressive development of the last five years has been that the "real" Negro has come to the surface, with all his scars and hostilities painfully visible. According to this argument, which I have had repeated occasion to hear, the Poor People's Campaign was "more real" and "more true" than the 1963 March because it forced white America to see the conditions of ghetto life, not an idealized image of cheerful black-and-white togetherness.

There is a sense in which this argument rings true, for it speaks to a certain naive, idealized integrationist view of the Negro which is dangerous because it is so easily bruised by an acquaintance with reality; and once bruised, it can rapidly turn into its ugly opposite. But if we are to proceed with this style of reasoning, it is appropriate to scrutinize another stereotype which is equally dangerous—that of the heroic slum proletariat.

Too many radical intellectuals have transferred to the lumpenproletariat the sentimental image of the proletariat that was fashionable in this country in the 1930s. Today's lumpenproletariat, like yesterday's worker, is viewed by these thinkers as an inherently progressive social force. In my own view, the proletariat had, and has, many more "progressive" virtues than does the lumpenproletariat—that is, if the word "progressive" is shorn of its romantic foolishness. The working class, as Daniel P. Moynihan has pointed out, possesses an often overlooked social cohesiveness, a class identity, a culture and a moral system based largely on its more stable economic role. The lumpenproletariat lacks these qualities because it is not quite a class at all but a collection of subgroups divided by ethnic, racial, linguistic, and geographical factors.[40]

In any case, and more to the point, I am not sure that classes are progressive—or reactionary—in and of themselves, but only in relation to their social roles. If we leave aside life-style preferences for the moment, the working class may be said to be progressive in that it seeks, with varying degrees of success, to democratize the distribution of social wealth. Or, if you prefer, the bourgeoisie can be considered progressive in that it has revolutionized technology. (Needless to say, each of these classes can have—indeed, does have—reactionary features as well.) The standard is the transformative effect on society itself.

Now, the lumpenproletariat can be progressive to the extent that, by pressing its own demands for a larger piece of the action, it succeeds in reducing or abolishing poverty and inequality in society as a whole. Yet because it is a subclass, internally fragmented and extremely marginal to the political process, the lumpenproletariat is the least capable of playing an independent role. It must choose from among the directions laid before society by other social forces. In terms of political action, this means some kind of coalition.

There is, to be sure, one superficially "independent" role that the lumpenproletariat can play—a nihilistic battle against society itself that involves massive rioting, burning, looting, killing. But behavior of this kind can only redound to the advantage of other forces. In the United States, where urban guerrilla warfare will not be endured, the response will be repression and a turn to the Right. Such a turn to the Right, toward the forces of reaction, is already obvious.

Thus, it is not enough to "tell it like it is," to rub the noses of the affluent in the pathology of the slum. It is especially not enough when society as a whole is confused and divided, when liberal forces are disoriented, the backlash is growing in severity, and when extremism at both ends of the spectrum takes on profoundly anti-civil-libertarian, almost fascist, features. At such a time the paramount need is for clear programmatic alternatives and for tactics that will maximize the size and cohesion of the democratic liberal-radical forces. Measured by the extent of that need, the Poor People's Campaign, whatever its other achievements, was a failure.

The Congress

It is commonly observed of twentieth-century politics that the executive has achieved primacy over the legislative—that generally the President is "chief legislator" and Congress reacts to his plans and programs rather than initiates policy on its own. Although this assessment is largely accurate, it risks distorting the role and power of Congress. Compared to the legislature of any other democracy, the United States Congress is probably more powerful vis-à-vis the executive. If Congress does not "lead" in an executive sense, it can still have a major impact on public policy, through its cooperation with or opposition to presidential leadership.

The readings in this chapter are concerned with three areas: (1) theories of congressional functions, (2) the legislative process, and (3) legislative behavior.

In the first selection, which provides background for examining the legislative process, Davidson, Kovenock, and O'Leary describe three reasonably distinct theories of Congress and list reforms needed to bring Congress into better alignment with the ideal models.

The next two articles are concerned with aspects of legislative effectiveness and behavior. In "The Folkways of the United States Senate," Matthews shows how conformity to congressional mores is necessary for legislative effectiveness. In King's "Inside Capitol Hill: How the House Really Works," the author, a former congressional administrative assistant, examines the House of Representatives from the perspective of an insider.

The thread, explicit or implicit, which runs through this section is that Congress must make fundamental changes in its law-making and representative functions if the legislative process is to be dynamic and responsive. Whether it can remains to be seen. The blueprint for an effective and responsible legislature is not hard to draw; the difficulties lie in converting the design into reality.

Theories of Congress

ROGER H. DAVIDSON, DAVID M. KOVENOCK,
MICHAEL K. O'LEARY

The Congress that emerged from the Philadelphia Convention of 1787 was the outgrowth of a prolonged institutional struggle, which affected both sides of the Atlantic and which produced a rather explicit theory of legislative functions. Though scholars often correctly observe that the Founding Fathers were pragmatic politicians who were loath to bind succeeding generations to excessively rigid formulations, they tend to neglect the fact that the pragmatism of the Framers was conditioned by an accepted body of political thought—a set of explicit beliefs about the nature of man and his institutions that were assumed to be valid. The Framers were not always able to see what they had done, but a serious study of their debates and commentaries indicates that they were intensely aware of what it was they *intended* to do.

Nothing less should be asked of contemporary students of legislative institutions. The advice which Harold D. Smith, then director of the Budget Bureau, gave to the LaFollette-Monroney Committee in 1945 is so relevant that it deserves repeating:

> This is a different sort of world from that which existed when the Constitutional Convention devised the framework of our government. Yet we still lack a penetrating and practical restatement of the role of representa-

From *Congress in Crisis: Politics and Congressional Reform* by Roger H. Davidson, David M. Kovenock, and Michael K. O'Leary. © 1966 by Wadsworth Publishing Company, Inc., Belmont, California. Reprinted by permission of the publisher.

tive assemblies in light of the changing problems under which they operate. . . . Your own talents and the keenest minds you can command
could very well be devoted to rethinking the functions of the Congress
under present conditions. A sound reformulation of the role of the representative body is basic to all the work of your committee.[1]

This was and is sound intellectual procedure, quite apart from the question of
whether the constitutional formula demands radical revision. More important,
Smith's injunction has not always been heeded by the proponents of congressional reform, including the LaFollette-Monroney Committee itself.

In recent years, a number of students have devoted explicit attention to the
functions that the contemporary Congress performs in the political system.[2]
Sometimes their conclusions have led them to propose or to evaluate remedial
steps that would alter the roles of Congress or would assist it in performing its
present roles more effectively. But it is fair to conclude that, by and large,
students of Congress have not been sufficiently attentive to the theory of Congress. Ralph K. Huitt observed that "there is no 'model' of a proper legislature
to which men of good intention can repair."[3]

What should be included in a theory of the legislature? Such a theory would
begin with a series of factual generalizations specifying those functions that the
legislature does in fact perform in a political system. Within this framework,
specific traditions and practices may be accounted for and their consequences
(intended or not) for the system may be spelled out. The analyst who chooses
not to lay down his tools at this point would then set forth his view of an ideal
legislature in an ideal system. He would specify the points of disharmony between this ideal world and the real world. Finally, he would propose specific
innovations that would bring the ideal world into being.

Hopefully, the theorist would be attentive to the probable and the unintended
consequences of these innovations. More attention to objectives and possible
consequences would make the proposal of reforms more meaningful than it
has been in the past.[4]

Implicit in most of the recent writing on congressional reform are concepts
that can be categorized into reasonably distinct theories of the proper functions of a legislative body. These theories are three in number: the "literary"
theory, based primarily on a literal reading of the Constitution; the "executive-
force" theory, which stresses policy leadership emanating from the President
and the bureaucracy; and the "party-government" theory, which emphasizes
the legislature's responsibility to the national party constituency. In terms of
the weight given Congress in relation to the executive, the literary theory comes
closest to legislative supremacy, the executive-force theory stands at the opposite pole, and the party-government theory stands somewhere in between. The
overall weight that each theory gives to Congress is less important, however,
than the kinds of functions which each assigns to Congress and to the other
branches of government.

The Literary Theory

The literary theory is essentially a restatement of the constitutional formulation of blended and coordinate powers—the "institutionalized mutual responsibility of coequals."[5] Adherence to this position need not imply a naive belief that nothing fundamental in the congressional environment has changed since 1789; it does imply, however, that the constitutional delineation of functions is still valid and that the relative weight assigned to the three branches by the Constitution is essentially correct. Proponents of this point of view maintain that Congress should exercise *at least* its present level of power within the political system.

REVERSING THE FLOW OF EVENTS

Advocates of the literary theory are most commonly obsessed with what they interpret as a severe, and perhaps fatal, erosion of congressional prerogatives. James Burnham, whose book *Congress and the American Tradition* is a fascinating and incisive polemic, sounded the theme when he declared:

> What the American government system now needs is . . . a very considerably strengthened Congress: strengthened in the political sense of gaining (regaining, in historical fact) increased relative weight within the political equilibrium. On this assumption . . . the performance of Congress will be judged much less than stellar.[6]

The decline and fall of Congress, according to this theory, can be attributed to three developments. Most fundamental of these developments is the advent of the sprawling welfare state, which makes the executive branch the source of many governmental services now largely beyond legislative control. Secondly, the compelling public image of the strong President and the academic and journalistic criticisms of legislative institutions reduce public support for Congress. Finally, Congress itself abets its declining influence by "failing to fight back stoutly and intelligently" and by dissipating its resistance to encroachments in "verbal complaints and rhetorical grumblings, which fizzle out in petty amendments of administration projects. Congress has been shadowboxing, not fighting."[7] This theme is often heard from legislators themselves and is reminiscent of former Congressman Dewey Short's (R-Mo.) indictment of the House of Representatives as "that supine, subservient, soporific, supercilious, pusillanimous body of nitwits." Many literary-theory advocates insist that these trends toward executive empire building and judicial activism could be reversed if Congressmen would only "stiffen their spines" against unconstitutional intrusions upon their legislative powers.

At least one literary theorist does not share this pessimism over legislative decline. In fact, argues Willmoore Kendall, Congress wins more frequently than is generally supposed in its tug-of-war with the executive. For one thing, many congressional victories are hidden from public view: President Franklin D. Roosevelt obtained the highly publicized Tennessee Valley Authority, for example, but what ever happened to proposals for a spate of TVAs in other river basins? Second, no one can ever know how many proposals the executive refrains from making because of expected congressional resistance—"the ten thousand . . . drastic proposals cooking away in ten thousand bureaucratic heads in Washington that the attackers [of tradition] do not dare even to embody in a bill, do not dare even to mention, because the proposals would not stand a Chinaman's chance." Thus, Kendall enjoins the supporters of Congress to keep up their courage "if they are going to keep on winning."[8]

THE "REPUBLICAN FORCE"

Advocates of the literary theory predictably perceive that their values and interests are disadvantaged by the policies of the executive and the judiciary, and they look upon revitalization of Congress as the means of reweighting the balance in their favor. This pro-Congress contingent is a not inconsiderable group, which looks to Capitol Hill for the reversal of the long-term trends of centralism and paternalism. This "republican force," as Alfred de Grazia has termed it, has gathered many recruits during the past generation: economic conservatives, who are hostile to post-New Deal social-welfare legislation; advocates of "states' rights," who find local autonomy threatened on every front by the courts and the executive; fundamentalists, who are confused and dismayed by modernism and secularism; and "the rural folk"—rural and small-town interests who feel themselves being plowed under by the alien trends of urbanism. All of these groups demand that Congress be preserved as a check upon the hostile powers entrenched elsewhere in the governmental system.

Although the contemporary Supreme Court is consistently criticized for usurping the legislative function, the President and his executive establishment are seen as the greatest enemies of the republican virtues. As the president of the Americans for Constitutional Action told the Joint Committee on the Organization of the Congress in June 1965:

> The President is the head of the party. He exercises vast powers in spending the money appropriated by Congress. He represents the father image in the paternalistic order of government. He represents the dominant political philosophy. All the resources of the political party and of socialist-oriented intellectuals are committed to the increase of his powers and to the destruction of the constitutional restraints.[9]

Such critics insist that supporters of a strong presidency identify Congress as the "obstacle course" to their goals. "As Congress is the bulwark of that [constitutional] system, the goal of the socialist planners is to be won by rendering Congress ineffectual."[10]

Representatives and Senators have reasons quite apart from ideology for resisting the attrition of their powers and their influence. Many express the understandable frustration of men in high public office who find that their actual influence is not what they expected it would be. Thus, Senator Abraham Ribicoff (D-Conn.), certainly no friend of the policy positions of most literary theorists, complained bitterly in 1964 that Congress has "surrendered its rightful leadership in the law-making process to the White House." The legislative branch, he wrote, "now merely filters legislative proposals from the President. . . . These days no one expects Congress to devise important bills. Instead, the legislative views of the President dominate the press, the public, and Congress itself."[11] This frustration is not uncommon among legislators, regardless of their political affiliation.

TENETS OF THE THEORY

According to the advocates of the literary theory, Congress must assert its right to exercise "all legislative powers." Policies should be initiated by Congress at least as often as by the executive, for "the primary business of the legislature in a democratic republic is to answer the big questions of policy."[12] Executive officials would be consulted on technical aspects of policy-making, but they should be prohibited from lobbying or pressuring. When the executive, by necessity, initiates legislative proposals, it should do so in an advisory capacity, fully respectful of congressional supremacy in lawmaking. The ultimate authority of elected laymen to set priorities on complicated and technical matters is an indispensible feature of democratic government.

For the defender of the literary theory, the legislator's legitimacy as the ultimate policy-maker rests on his near-monopoly of the channels of communication to the sovereign electorate. Since the President also is elected by and responsible to the electorate, this monopoly is not total. But the President is the only elected official in the executive branch; his constituency is diffuse, his mandate imprecise. Congressmen, on the other hand, are specific and precise representatives, who "necessarily and properly reflect the attitudes and needs of their individual districts."[13] The legislative process, therefore, is not a simple "yes" or "no" vote on policy alternatives but a complex combinatorial process through which numerous and shifting minority claims are acknowledged. One contemporary scholar has defended the particularity of congressional representation in the following manner:

> Congress has the strength of the free enterprise system; it multiplies the decision-makers, the points of access to influence and power, and the creative moving agents. It is hard to believe that a small group of leaders could do better. What would be gained in orderliness might well be lost in vitality and in sensitiveness to the pressures for change. Moreover, Congress resembles the social system it serves; it reflects the diversity of the country. There is much to be said for a system in which almost every

interest can find some spokesman, in which every cause can strike a blow, however feeble, in its own behalf.[14]

More often than not, in a government modeled on the literary theory, no legislative decision can be reached on momentous political conflicts: on intensely felt issues at least, a government that acts before a "concurrent majority" can be found or constructed is tyrannical.[15] Thorough exploration of the consensus of the society is the high function of the elected policy maker and the essence of the "legislative way of life." Neither speed, efficiency, nor "passing a lot of laws" are valid indicators of congressional effectiveness in performing these delicate deliberative tasks. From a conservative vantage point, in fact, the refusal to pass laws is often a blessing.

All advocates of the literary theory view executive power with suspicion, but they differ on the extent to which they think the executive should be cut down. The theory requires merely a semblance of balance among the branches of government; and constitutional history provides ample precedents for a strong and autonomous executive, as well as an activist Congress. However, one version of the literary theory—which we call the "Whig" variant—would enthrone Congress as *the* dominant institution in the political system. This variant of the theory would reduce Presidents to weaklings, even in foreign and military affairs.[16] The degree to which one wishes to pare down executive power is presumably related to the depth of one's dissatisfaction with contemporary political trends.

On this much the literary theory is clear: what Congress proposes, the executive should dispose. The executive branch should engage in the detailed implementation of laws that are as specific and detailed as possible, leaving bureaucrats little leeway for interpretation. Curiously, one advocate of the literary theory, Burnham, takes an opposite view. The bureaucracy, which conducts the day-to-day operations of government, will always be able to circumvent detailed provisos laid down by Congress. Thus he reasons:

> . . . the only way to control the chief officials of the colossal managerial-bureaucratic state is to give an unambiguous main policy directive, to define clear limits, and then to insist on strict public accountability for satisfactory performance. . . .
> If the reins are kept too tight, the horse will get the bit in its teeth. They must normally be loose, if the curbing is to be effective. If Congress tries to watch each million, the billions will get away.[17]

In any event, Congress must exercise extensive supervision (usually termed "oversight") of the administration of laws, intervening vigorously and often to ensure compliance. And, if necessary, remedial legislation should be passed.

The courts, in this view, should similarly be prevented from usurping legislative functions. The jurists should recognize that a wide variety of "political questions" are the proper sphere of only the elected decision makers. In the opinion of the "constitutionalists," the judicial "lawmaking" that most impinges upon legislative autonomy is the apportionment ruling.[18] They argue, first, that electoral laws are by nature political questions which should be determined by the elected bodies themselves. Secondly, the Court's newly enunciated "one man, one vote" criterion will clearly dilute the influence of the rural minority, thus rendering the collective congressional constituency more nearly like that of the President. This melding of constituencies, in the judgment of constitutionalists, will reduce the healthy dichotomy of the two branches of government. And in political terms, it will submerge those constituencies that have traditionally been championed by Congress but not by the executive.[19]

The other major area of judicial impingement upon Congress is the Court's review of alleged violations of civil liberties that result from legislative investigations.[20] While others might argue that the Court's involvement in such questions has been marginal and discontinuous, the constitutionalist interprets such forays as a trespass upon Congress' control over its own rules and procedures.

REFORM PROPOSITIONS

While there may be differences of opinion on precise means-ends relationships, the following list of reform propositions would probably be approved by most advocates of the literary theory:

A. Constituencies and the electoral system:
   1. Rather than rigid adherence to the "one man, one vote" principle, legislative apportionment should recognize the validity of the other criteria of representation—geographic interests, for example, or political subdivisions—in order to ensure that the greatest possible diversity of interests is embodied in Congress.
   2. Congress itself—probably in concert with state and local authorities—should exercise authority over whatever electoral devices are employed.
   3. The electorate should be educated on congressional government through the initiation of public relations campaigns and the provision of more time for legislators in their districts.
B. Political parties:
   1. Innovations that would centralize the party under noncongressional control (for example, through national party councils) should be resisted.
   2. Diversified, rather than "responsible," party structure should be encouraged to stress the party function of building a national consensus.[21]
C. The Presidency:

1. The 22nd Amendment, which limits the President to two terms, should be maintained.
2. The presidential discretion in implementing policies and in withholding information from Congress should be limited.
3. Presidential messages should be answered by formal speeches from congressional leaders, both majority and minority.
4. The proposal that plans initiated by the President become effective unless vetoed by Congress should be opposed.

D. Congressional procedures:
   1. Staffs for individual legislators and committees should be moderately increased, with maximum staff assistance for minority members— perhaps even in reverse ratio to the size of the minority representation in Congress.
   2. Attempts to centralize congressional leadership should be resisted in order to maximize the deliberative and even obstructionist tendencies of the individual legislators.[22]
   3. Moderate dilatory devices, such as the Senate filibuster and a strong House Rules Committee, should be sanctioned.
   4. Legislators should continue to help constituents in dealing with the executive bureaucracy (so-called "casework").
   5. Congressional oversight of the executive should be facilitated through increased use of the General Accounting Office, of budgetary controls, of special investigative subcommittees, and of detailed committee review of legislation, appointments, and appropriations.
   6. Congress should resist formal ties to the executive through joint legislative-executive councils and should avoid dependence upon executive agencies for such commodities as travel or research facilities.

The Executive-Force Theory

In a sense, the executive-force theory reverses the formulation of the literary theory: the executive initiates and implements; the legislature modifies and ratifies.

WHICH WAY IS HISTORY GOING?

The rationales for the executive-force theory illustrate the ambiguities of historical interpretation. Advocates of this theory either (a) concur with the constitutionalists' thesis that the balance of power has shifted radically toward the executive branch but propose that reforms should be instituted to ensure this new executive hegemony or (b) disagree entirely with that assessment and hold that legislative intimidation of executives is now more extreme than ever before. In either case, the conclusion is that the executive establishment ought to be granted wide latitude for decision making and substantial insulation from legislative obstruction.

Adherents of the first rationale—the shift of the balance of power toward the executive—cite historical precedents to show that presidential ascendancy is a fulfillment of original constitutional principles. Indeed, they hold that the ponderous counterbalances devised by the Founding Fathers are viable only when supplemented by an initiator-ratifier relationship between the White House and Capitol Hill.

The architects of the Presidency at the Constitutional Convention—Alexander Hamilton, James Wilson, and Gouverneur Morris—were advocates of strong and vigorous executive responsibility. Hamilton praised "energy" as the outstanding feature of good government and declared that all men of good sense must agree on the necessity of an energetic executive.[23] Federalist political theory showed a decided preference for the executive partly because of its distrust of the people. As Leonard White has characterized the Federalist position, "Decisions on programs thought out by [well-educated and cultivated] national leaders might be subject to the vote of popular assemblies, but the latter . . . had neither the capacity, nor the unity, to work out the plans themselves."[24]

The precedents established by the strong Presidents lend historical weight to this argument. Referring to Thomas Jefferson's active intervention in legislation, Congressman Richard Bolling explains that the early House of Representatives was "the organ of ratification of the decisions presented to it by those members . . . who . . . sat as agents of the President and his advisors."[25] The demands of a national emergency—prompt, concerted action and clarity of policy—have repeatedly strengthened the executive branch. Looking back on the remarkable performance of the first New Deal Congress, Franklin Roosevelt observed: "The letter of the Constitution wisely declared a separation, but the impulse of common purpose declares a union."[26]

The present age of permanent semi-crisis has reinforced this historical tendency because every contemporary President is required to be strong. The pull of executive leadership is thus seen as inevitable and irreversible. "The cause of the opponents of a strong President," Rossiter writes with finality, "is ill-starred because they cannot win a war against American history. The strong Presidency is the product of events that cannot be undone and of forces that continue to roll."[27]

The theory of the President-as-Chief-Legislator would appear to be an abstraction of things as they are. But some critics, not so sanguine about the course of recent events, still see the cards stacked in favor of the legislature; they believe the legislative branch more meddlesome than ever. Columnist Walter Lippmann, often called Washington's "philosopher-in-residence," paints a bleak picture of executives cowering before the rampant power of legislatures. When the New Frontier program ran into legislative deadlock in 1963, he questioned, "What kind of legislative body is it that will not or cannot legislate?" And writing on the Fourth of July that year, he voiced his fears for the future of representative government:

> I find myself thinking how rarely free governments have been overthrown by foreign tyrants, except temporarily in time of war, but how often free governments have fallen because of their own weakness and incapacity. To one thinking such thoughts there is nothing reassuring about the present Congress.[28]

In Lippmann's opinion, "derangement" of powers has occurred at the governmental level because representative assemblies, supported by mass opinion, have acquired "the monopoly of effective powers." The "enfeebled" executive can no longer act decisively or rationally to solve complex public problems.[29]

A somewhat less cataclysmic interpretation of the "deadlock of democracy" is given by James M. Burns in his highly publicized critique of the Madisonian system of mutual distrust and irresponsibility. Entrenched on Capitol Hill by gerrymandered districts and the seniority system, legislators from stagnant, one-party regions are able to thwart liberal, urban majorities that represent the "presidential wings" of the two parties.[30]

From their vantage point at the western reaches of Pennsylvania Avenue, Presidents themselves are fervent believers in the power of Congress to frustrate their programs. In his television report of December 1962, President Kennedy admitted with a note of irony that "the fact is . . . that the Congress looks more powerful sitting here than it did when I was there in the Congress."[31]

THE PRESIDENT'S CONSTITUENCY

The legitimacy of executive dominance rests on a concept of representation quite at variance with the Madison-Calhoun pluralism of the literacy theorists. As the only official elected by the whole population, the President is considered the embodiment of the nation. Legislators represent partial and minority interests; the President represents the "general will" of the community. Burns has given a more precise definition of this dichotomy:

> The Madisonian system finds its tension in the competition among struggling groups, multi-party factions, and mutually checking branches of government. The Jeffersonian system, a more hierarchical arrangement, finds its tension in the relation of leader and led, with the leader usually pressing his troops, like an army commander, and the troops usually restraining, but sometimes outrunning, their leader.[32]

Thus, Theodore Roosevelt saw the President as a "steward of the people"; and, some years before his own elevation to the office, Woodrow Wilson sensed its representative potentialities. "His is the only national voice in affairs," he declared in his 1907 Columbia University lectures. "He is the representative of no constituency, but of the whole people."[33]

The electoral rationale for executive dominance has obvious consequences. Because of the pivotal power of large urban states in presidential elections and the importance of urban centers within each state under the winner-take-all electoral-college system, contemporary Presidents have become attuned to the forces of urbanism, minority rights, and the social-welfare state. And because of his unique role as the "nation's sole organ in foreign affairs," the modern President must consider his foreign "constituencies." In contrast, the congressional power system places leadership in the hands of "those members . . . least aware of the problems of industrial society and least equipped to deal with them."[34] The reaction, localism, and delay of Congress acts as a brake on the progressive nationalism of the executive. Congress must be reconstituted if it is to participate in the policies of the President and his partisans "to save ourselves from nuclear destruction, help the world feed its children and protect their lands from totalitarian Communism, put our people to work and make our cities habitable, and realize the fact as well as the name of equality."[35]

TENETS OF THE THEORY

The executive-force theory seeks to mitigate Congress' "historic role of obstructionism."[36] First, Congress must recognize that "the executive is the active power in the state, the asking and the proposing power."[37] As a prominent liberal Democratic Congressman explains, "it is the natural thing for the executive branch to take the initiative, to make proposals, and to present us with programs."[38] Congress is "the consenting power, the petitioning, the approving and the criticizing, the accepting and the refusing power."[39] Second, Congress cannot administer or "manage and meddle" in administrative provinces. As Joseph P. Harris has cautioned:

> It is not the function of the legislature to participate in executive decisions or share responsibility with executive officers, for which it is ill equipped, but rather to check on the administration in order to hold the officers in charge accountable for their decisions and for management and results.[40]

The executive-dominance theory thus emphasizes oversight as in the 1946 Legislative Reorganization Act's injunction that congressional committees exercise "continuous watchfulness" over executive agencies within their jurisdiction. To prevent this watchfulness from degenerating into meddling, however, executive theorists usually specify that congressional review be in terms of generalized policy considerations rather than details.[41]

Executive theorists point out, however, that congressional policy initiation need not be wholly foreclosed. If the President fails to act, or if there are gaps at the fringes of public policy, Congress can and must serve as a "seedbed for the breeding and maturing of new legislative ideas."[42] Senator J. William Fulbright's (D-Ark.) view of the congressional partnership in foreign policy is a notable example of this congressional role. He reasons that although Congress is poorly equipped to participate in "short-term policies and . . . day-to-day operations," it can cooperate effectively in debating "longer-range, more basic questions" and in initiating ideas "on the periphery."[43] Fulbright's own record of initiating policy alternatives demonstrates that this role need not be a niggardly one.

REFORM PROPOSITIONS

With the usual caveat on the complexity of means-ends relationships in mind, an observer may expect proponents of the executive-force theory to advocate the following reforms of Congress:

A. Parties and the electoral system:
  1. Reapportionment on the basis of population should be strongly supported on the assumption that elements of the presidential constituency (for example, urban and suburban areas) would thereby be strengthened in Congress.
  2. National party councils to develop and implement a truly national party program should be strengthened; campaign finances should be centralized in the hands of the national committees.
  3. Four-year terms that would coincide with the presidential terms should be enacted for Representatives. (Similar four-year terms for Senators would probably be desirable.)
B. The Presidency:
  1. The 22nd Amendment should be repealed.
  2. Funds for the executive branch should be appropriated on a long-term basis—two years or more.
  3. The President should be granted an "item veto"—that is, part of a measure could be vetoed without nullifying the entire bill.
C. Congressional rules and procedures:
  1. Congress should be required to act on all executive proposals within a specified period of time (for example, six months).
  2. Strong centralized congressional parties should be created.
  3. The seniority system for selecting committee leaders should be discontinued, and elections by majority and minority caucuses should be substituted.
  4. Individual Congressmen and Senators should be relieved of constituent "casework," and an Office of Administrative Counsel, under the general control of Congress, should be created to perform this service.
  5. Congress should grant relatively broad mandates to executive agencies and should cease such harassing tactics as one-year authorizations or required committee clearances for certain executive actions.

Party-Government Theory

Party government is the logical extension, and perhaps the end result, of the executive-force theory; but its roots and emphases are sufficiently distinct to warrant separate treatment. Actually, it is not a theory about Congress at all, but rather a proposal to reconstruct the American party system, so that a party would formulate a clear-cut and specific policy (platform) that would be responsibly effectuated when that party enjoyed a national majority. "The party system that is needed must be democratic, responsible, and effective," according to the academic manifesto of party government—the 1950 report of the American Political Science Association's Committee on Political Parties.[44] The basic malady of the American Congress is not myopic legislators or even archaic legislative rules and procedures, but rather the "parochialism of American life and the electoral system that fosters it." Thus, meaningful congressional reorganization can come about only through profound changes in the American party system.[45]

"AN ALMOST IDEAL FORM"

The empirical foundation of party-government theory is the familiar observation that American parties are unwieldy coalitions of parochial interests.[46] The party that is elected to power is incapable of organizing its members in the legislative and executive branches into a coherent, energetic, and effective government. The disorganization and parochialism of the parties debilitates the American political system. First, it renders impossible the "orderly, relevant, and effective politics" necessary in an era of urgent national and international problems.[47] Second, it perverts the concepts of the party platform and the public will. Frequently, a party, once in power, fails to effectuate even those programs which were delineated as electoral issues.

The Jeffersonian notion of popular majorities organized in national blocs or parties is the base of the party-government system. Such a system would have a tidiness unknown to the incoherent parties to which Americans are accustomed. A constant inspiration for many party-government theorists is the British party system, which Woodrow Wilson openly admired and which Burns calls "an almost ideal form of representative government."[48]

Coherent, democratic, and responsible parties would necessarily reflect themselves in strengthened party organizations on Capitol Hill. As the APSA Committee stated:

> A general structure of congressional party organization already exists. It should be tightened up. The party leadership in both houses already has certain functions with respect to the handling of relations with the President and the shaping of the committee structure . . . [and] other functions with respect to the legislative schedule. [These functions] should be strengthened.

If such action were taken, it would not mean that every issue would become a party issue. It would not eliminate the need for or the possibility of nonpartisan and bipartisan policies. But it would result in a more responsible approach to party programs and a more orderly handling of *all* congressional activities.[49]

Such powers as committee appointment and legislative scheduling should therefore be centralized in the elective party leadership. According to Representative Bolling, "there is every reason to justify the right of the majority to have its major proposals voted on by the whole House without undue delay. . . ."[50]

The authors of the APSA Committee's report were not optimistic about the prospects of "engineering consent" for such revisions. "It cannot be expected," they wrote, "that all congressional leaders will be sympathetic to the concept of party responsibility."[51] However, the committee hoped that nationally oriented Congressmen and Senators would take the lead in publicizing the cause of strong party organization. This hope is being partially realized in the writings of Senator Clark, Representative Bolling, and others of the "national" wings of both political parties who have worked to strengthen the party caucus and the elective leadership. . . .

REFORM PROPOSITIONS

Advocates of the party-government theory follow the executive-force theory in many respects but place particular emphasis on the following proposals:[52]

1. Control of congressional nominations and elections should be centralized—with national party clearance for candidates.
2. Congressional party leaders should be chosen after wide consultation among the entire "national" party, including the President.
3. Meaningful party policy committees should be created in each house; these committees should be responsible for legislative scheduling and for committee appointments conditioned on party loyalty.
4. Both houses should schedule frequent party caucuses, whose decisions would bind members to vote the party line on important issues.
5. Committee assignments and chairmanships should be recommended by the party policy committee, ratified by the caucus, and subject to periodic review. Ratios of party membership on committees should favor the majority party.
6. Staff assistance should be provided both majority and minority committee members.
7. The House Rules Committee should be an arm of the elective leadership in scheduling measures for floor debate.
8. The present Senate filibuster rule should be altered to allow cloture of debate by a majority vote.

Conclusion: The Parliamentary Crisis

Divergent theories of the congressional function are the outgrowth of a complex, contentious society marked by numerous and often conflicting demands upon the institutions of government. Those citizens who urge upon the federal government an interventionist, problem-solving role will conceive of a legislature far differently than will those who see the government's role as a passive consensus-building one. The rules of the political game, as defined by the structure of institutions, cannot be divorced from the stakes for which the game is played. Moreover, these differing stakes are related to divergent intellectual interpretations of the role of institutions in a democratic polity. The theories of Congress should not be characterized merely as rationalizations for one's substantive positions; yet the two levels of debate are closely related. The struggle being waged over the character of Congress is indeed a part of the "war over America's future."

When the three theories are compared, a composite picture of the American Congress emerges—a picture with important convergences and deep differences. In this . . . discussion, formal "powers" of the legislature were consciously played down, in favor of the broader and more fundamental concept of "function"—those things of major consequence that an institution (in this case, Congress) does for the political system as a whole. Table 6-1 presents a rough comparison of the functions specified for Congress by the three theories discussed . . . and the following paragraph defines these functions as they have emerged from the discussion.

Lawmaking is the traditional task of deliberating, often at a technical level, the actual content of policies. *Representation* is the process of articulating the demands or interests of geographic, economic, religious, ethnic, and professional constituencies. The legislator may accomplish this through actual contact (residence in a district, membership in a pressure group) or through "virtual" means ("taking into account" a viewpoint, perhaps by anticipating

TABLE 6-1

Three Theories of Congressional Functions

	LITERARY THEORY	EXECUTIVE-FORCE THEORY	PARTY-GOVERNMENT THEORY
Primary functions	Lawmaking Representation Consensus building Oversight	Legitimizing Oversight Representation	Policy clarification Representation
Secondary functions	Policy clarification Legitimizing	Consensus building Policy clarification Lawmaking	Lawmaking Legitimizing Consensus building

constituent response). *Consensus building* is the traditional bargaining function through which these various constituency demands are combined (or aggregated) in such a way that no significant constituency is severely or permanently disadvantaged. *Legitimizing* is the ratification of a measure or policy in such a way that it seems appropriate, acceptable, and authoritative. The legislature promotes *policy clarification* by providing a public platform where issues may be identified and publicized. *Legislative oversight* is the review of the implementation of policy in order to either alter the fundamental policy or introduce equity into the application of laws. Other functions—for example, *constituent service* and *recruitment of political leadership*—might also be explored, but are omitted here because they are not fundamental to the current debate over Congress.

The functions that theorists choose to emphasize have a profound impact upon the nature of the "model" Congress, not to mention the relationship of Congress with other elements in the political system. The most ambitious mandate is offered by the literary theory, which would involve the legislature at almost every step in the policy-making process—from initial conception to detailed review of implementation. In addition, this theory views the legislature as the prime representational and consensus-building institution in the political system. The executive-force theory, on the other hand, sees the legislature as ancillary to the executive establishment, which by the nature of things must assume the lead in both policy initiation and implementation. Like the board of directors of a corporation, Congress would have certain review powers but few operating powers; the legislature would find itself in most cases ratifying decisions of the executive "managers." According to the party-government conception, Congress (as well as the executive) would be set in motion by a strong and lucid party structure, serving chiefly as a forum for the staged confrontation of party ideologies.

No matter how far-reaching the consequences of accepting one theory over another, the differences in the concepts of the normative functions of Congress are differences of emphasis. Few observers would deny that Congress should, at one time or another, perform all the roles that have been discussed. Even the most dedicated advocate of executive dominance, for example, would undoubtedly concede that certain occasions may demand legislative initiative in policy-making. Most theories of congressional functioning therefore admit to what might be called the "multi-functionality" of the institution. The priority assigned to these various functions then becomes the all-important question.

The implications of this chapter should by now be apparent. The present "parliamentary crisis" is primarily an absence of consensus on the priorities of the traditional functions of the legislature. The Constitution left the ultimate resolution of this conflict to the workings of history upon the precarious balance of powers. The changed environment of the twentieth century has intensified the question, even throwing into doubt the viability of legislative institutions.

And the architects of legislative reconstruction cannot agree on the blueprints to be followed. The lack of consensus on congressional goals is suggested even by the nuances of wording: who could be mistaken concerning the philosophic distance between Burns' Congress of "anti-deadlock" and Burnham's Congress of "tradition"?

This lack of consensus constitutes a fundamental breach in the interlocking conditions for a rational-comprehensive approach to innovations in congressional structures and procedures. Lacking a substantial agreement on the expectations of congressional performance, observers will hardly concur on the specific shortcomings of Congress . . . much less the remedies to alleviate these shortcomings. . . .

Congressional Theories of Congress

Perhaps the simplest way to compare the views of Congressmen with those of outside observers is to determine the acceptability, within Congress, of our three models of the congressional function. As with outsiders, acceptance by Congressmen of the literary, executive-force, or party-government theories would normally be related to evaluations of current practices and of suggestions for change. To gauge the support for the tenets of the three alternative concepts, we asked members of the House four types of questions: (1) to describe the job of the Congressman as it ought to be performed; (2) to outline the functions which the Congress (and particularly the House) ought to play in the governmental system; (3) to list and discuss the problems they faced and the problems faced by the House as a whole in trying to meet the expectations that they had expressed in their first and second answers; and (4) to react to a list of statements concerning the work of Congress and Congressmen by indicating the extent to which they agreed or disagreed with each of the statements.

The Constitution serves as a powerful symbolic basis for action in the minds of many Congressmen and provides a strong argument for the literary theory as their frame of reference. In fact, when asked to describe the proper functions of Congress, more than one-third of our respondents specified—with little or no elaboration—that Congress ought to "follow the Constitution" or "carry out our constitutional function—to legislate." Better than half (55 percent) of the respondents agreed with this brief statement of the literary position: "Congress and the executive should be equal partners in the making of public policy." But it was also clear that many thought one branch should be somewhat "more equal" than the others. Fully two-thirds of the members interviewed assented to what has been termed the "Whig" variant of the literary theory: "Congress should play the major role in the making of public policy."

With so many members associating themselves in one way or another with the literary model of an active Congress, the popularity of the executive-force theory was predictably low. Nearly 70 percent of our sample disagreed with the proposition that "The executive should play the major role in the making of public policy."

The wide acceptance of the "Whiggish" variant of the literary model is further demonstrated when each member's responses to the three alternative models are combined and his overall attitude is characterized, as in Table 6-2. A majority of the Representatives espoused the "congressional supremacist" variant of the literary theory. On the other hand, a substantial group (17 percent) in the House indicated no clear preference among the competing models.

Further clarification of congressional views of the alternative theories of Congress resulted from our respondents' discussions of their major problems. It became clear that House members considered even the limited operation of the executive-force model as a major barrier to the proper performance of their perceived roles. About one half of the Representatives interviewed mentioned some form of executive branch "encroachment" as a complicating factor in their legislative work. Further, problems stemming from the contemporary operation of the separation of powers—principally conflict with the executive branch—were the second most frequently mentioned type of problem interfering with the proper functioning of the individual member and of the House as an institution.

Since executive-force theory advocates are often among the most publicly visible members of the House, outsiders underestimate the extent to which the theory is rejected within Congress. The advocates of executive initiative are inveterate speechmakers and prolific writers. Because of their frequent public expressions, their point of view appears more widely held among members than it actually is. And some Congressmen claim that executive-oriented members are better able to have their views reported and circulated in the public media, since editors themselves tend to share their position.

Our survey data clearly confirm, however, that Representatives embrace

TABLE 6-2

Acceptance of Alternative Models of Congress by Members of the House

MODEL OR VARIANT	NUMBER OF MEMBERS	PERCENT OF MEMBERS
"Pure Whig"	27	31
"Literary-Whig"	22	25
"Pure Literary"	8	9
"Literary-Executive Force"	9	10
"Pure Executive Force"	5	6
"Mixed"	15	17
No Data	1	1
	87	99

the idea of an active role for Congress and desire to strive for at least an equal status with the executive. Even a John McCormack or a Carl Albert in the House and a Mike Mansfield or a Mike Monroney in the Senate—all staunch fighters for a Democratic administration on most issues—will oppose the President and his advisors upon occasion in order to uphold their personal or institutional prerogatives. The same was true of Republican legislators during Eisenhower's tenure in the White House. The great majority of Congressmen, however "liberal" and/or nationally oriented, apparently take seriously the notion that the Constitution is not really a document of separate powers, that, rather, it is an invitation—given with much forethought—for Congress and the President to struggle for the sharing of power. Few legislators recoil from this struggle.

An earlier discussion indicated that often only a fine line distinguishes the executive-force from the party-government theory. Political analysts talk in the same breath about strong parties and strong presidential leadership of parties. Many of the trends in American politics which point toward executive supremacy in government policy-making also imply a stronger role for the President as chief of his party.

Many Congressmen, however, see a real and significant difference between strong parties *per se* and executive-branch domination of those parties (and therefore of Congress). The preference for a stronger Congress *and* stronger parties, for example, could be seen in the replies of many of the Congressmen—although the great majority of members could scarcely be classified as ardent advocates of thoroughgoing party government. Widespread pro-party sentiment was evidenced in reactions to the more modest party-oriented propositions. For example, two-thirds of our sample disagreed with the statement, "Under our form of government every individual should take an interest in government directly, not through a political party." And there was an even stronger reaction against the idea of reducing the role of parties in elections. The proposition that "The best interests of the people would be better served if Congressmen were elected without party labels" was rejected (often with obvious horror) by 86 percent of the respondents.

When more demanding criteria for the party-government model were employed, the number of advocates dropped off considerably. On the question of whether "the two parties should take clear-cut, opposing stands on more of the important and controversial issues," the members interviewed were split almost evenly (51 percent opposed the statement); and on the question of voting with one's party leadership at the cost of some district support, the party advocates fell to 38 percent.

But it does seem apparent that many members of the House would be sympathetic to a somewhat strengthened congressional party system. A substantial minority (45 percent) of our respondents gave a pro-party government response to at least three of the four propositions mentioned.[53]

. . . Congressional preference for the literary theory over the executive-force theory is easily explained in terms of institutional loyalty. Not so easily explained is the substantial minority of Representatives who combine the rejection of executive dominance with the advocacy of at least a modicum of strong party organization.

This desire for a stronger congressional party system cannot be explained as merely a device to elevate the legislature and to frustrate the executive. After all, congressional obstacles to the President's legislative program are frequently erected by small groups of strategically situated Congressmen operating independently of party leadership. We suggest that a commitment to active legislative parties does not necessarily imply the negativism that is often ascribed to congressional opponents of the executive-force theory. On the contrary, it may simply reflect the feeling that strong congressional parties with collective responsibility are essential for maintaining a political dialogue among the branches of the national government. Congressional party advocates hold that this dialogue is lacking when the President calls all the shots in public policy—just as when a "do-nothing" Congress opposes a President's programs without suggesting alternatives of its own.

The Folkways of the United States Senate: Conformity to Group Norms and Legislative Effectiveness

DONALD R. MATTHEWS

The Senate of the United States, we are told, is a "club." The image, while hopelessly imprecise and occasionally quite misleading, does have at least one advantage: it underscores the fact that there are unwritten but generally accepted and informally enforced norms of conduct in the chamber. These folkways influence the behavior of senators to a degree and in directions not yet fully understood. "There is great pressure for conformity in the Senate," one member (mercifully varying the simile) has recently said. "It's just like living

Reprinted by permission of the author and the publisher from Donald R. Matthews, "The Folkways of the United States Senate: Conformity to Group Norms and Legislative Effectiveness," *The American Political Science Review*, Vol. LIII, No. 4 (December 1959), pp. 1064–1089.

in a small town." And, as in small-town life, so too in the Senate there are occasional careers to be made out of deliberate nonconformity, sometimes only skin-deep, but sometimes quite thorough-going.

Political scientists know this in a general way. But, judging from the dearth of literature on the subject, they have deemed legislative folkways either unworthy of their attention or beyond their analytic powers.[54] Journalists and legislators—close observers and participants—are acutely aware of their importance, and have written about the Senate's folkways. While some of their efforts have shown real insight,[55] most such writings merely reaffirm the existence of the norms without telling us what they are about. Thus, most of the basic questions about the folkways of the Senate, and other legislative bodies, remain unanswered. What, specifically, do the unwritten rules say? Why do they exist? In what ways do they influence the behavior of senators? How, concretely, are they enforced? What kinds of senators obey the folkways? Which ones do not, and why? What are the political consequences of the folkways?

These are difficult questions for an outsider to analyze. Only those who have served in the Senate—and perhaps not even all of them—are likely to grasp the folkways in all their complexity. Yet, if we are ever to understand the behavior of legislators, a beginning must be made in the systematic analysis of the subject. This article, based on several months of close personal observation and interviewing of senators, congressional staff members, lobbyists and Capitol Hill journalists, is such an attempt.[56]

I. Apprenticeship

The first rule of Senate behavior—and the one most widely recognized off the Hill—is that new members are expected to serve an unobtrusive apprenticeship.

The freshman senator's subordinate status is impressed upon him in many ways. He receives the committee assignments the other senators do not want. The same is true of his office suite and his seat in the chamber. In committee rooms he is assigned to the end of the table. He is expected to do more than his share of the thankless and boring tasks of the Senate, such as presiding over the floor debate or serving on his party's Calendar Committee. According to the folkways of the Senate, the freshman is to accept such treatment as a matter of course.

Moreover, the new senator is expected to keep his mouth shut, not to take the lead in floor fights, to listen and to learn. "Like children," one freshman said in the Capitol Hill cliché, "we should be seen and not heard." Just how long this often painful silence must be maintained is not clear, but it is certainly wiser for a freshman to postpone his maiden efforts on the floor too long than to appear overly aggressive. Ideally perhaps, he should wait until pushed reluctantly to the fore.

> I attended the floor debates and voted for a year without giving a single speech [a senior senator said with pride]. Finally, one day, a matter came up with which I had considerable experience in the House. My part in it had gotten some publicity. _____ leaned over to me and said, "_____, are you going to speak on this?" I said, "No." "You know a great deal about this," he replied, "I think you should speak." I answered that I had not prepared a speech and that I would rather not speak on the bill. "Look," he said, "I'm going to get the floor and ask you a question about this bill. Then you will *have* to speak!" And that's how I made my first speech in the Senate.

Freshmen are also expected to show respect for their elders ("You may think you are smarter than the older fellows, but after a time you find that this is not true") and to seek their advice ("Keep on asking for advice, boy," the committee chairman told me. "That's the way to get ahead around here"). And they are encouraged to concentrate on developing an acquaintanceship in the Senate. ("Young senators should make a point of getting to know the other senators. This isn't very hard: there are only 95 of them. And if the other senators know and like you, it increases your effectiveness.")

The freshman who does not accept his lot as a temporary but very real second-class senator is met with thinly veiled hostility. For instance, one old-timer tells this story:

> When I came to the Senate, I sat next to Senator Borah. A few months later, he had a birthday. A number of the older men got up and made brief, laudatory speeches about it. Borah was pleased. Then a freshman senator—one who had only been in the chamber three or four months—got to his feet and started on a similar eulogy. He was an excellent speaker. But between each of his laudatory references to Borah, Borah loudly whispered, "That son-of-a-bitch, that son-of-a-bitch." He didn't dislike the speaker, personally. He just didn't feel that he should speak so soon.

Even so, the veterans in the Senate remark, rather wistfully, that the practice of serving an apprenticeship is on the way out. And, to some extent, they are undoubtedly correct. The practice seems to have begun before the popular election of senators and the exigencies of the popularly elected official have placed it under considerable strain. As one very senior senator (whose service extends back almost to the days before popular election) ruefully explained: "A new senator today represents millions of people. He feels that he has to *do* something to make a record from the start."

But this judgment is also colored by the tendency in any group for the old-timers to feel that the younger generation is going to hell in a handbasket. To the present-day freshman in the Senate, the period of apprenticeship is very real and very confining. "It reminds me a little of Hell Week in college," one of them remarked. Indeed, the nostalgic talk of the older senators about the unhappy lot of the freshman in the good old days is one way the senior senators keep the younger men in their place. One freshman Democrat, for example, after completing a floor speech found himself sitting next to Senator George, then dean of the Senate. Thinking that he should make polite conversation, the freshman asked the Georgia patriarch what major changes had taken place in the Senate during his long service. Senator George replied, "Freshmen didn't use to talk so much."

II. Legislative Work

> There are two kinds of Congressmen—show horses and work horses. If you want to get your name in the paper, be a show horse. If you want to gain the respect of your colleagues, keep quiet and be a work horse.[57]

Senator Carl Hayden of Arizona remembers being told this when he first came to the Congress many years ago. It is still true.

The great bulk of the Senate's work is highly detailed, dull and politically unrewarding. According to the folkways of the Senate, it is to these tasks that a senator *ought* to devote a major share of his time, energy and thought. Those who follow this rule are the senators most respected by their colleagues. Those who do not carry their share of the legislative burden or who appear to subordinate this responsibility to a quest for publicity and personal advancement are held in disdain.

This results in an, at first, puzzling disparity between the prestige of senators inside and outside the Senate. Some of the men most highly respected by their peers are quite unknown except on the Hill and in their own states; others whose names are household words are thought to be second-raters and slackers.[58] The words used to describe those senators who seem to slight their legislative duties are harsh—"grandstanders," "demagogues," "headline hunters," "publicity-seekers," "messiahs." They are said to do nothing but "play to the galleries," to suffer from "laziness" and "verbal diarrhea" and "not to be team players." It is even occasionally hinted that they are mentally or emotionally deranged.

But this does not mean that all publicity is undesirable. It takes publicity to get, and stay, elected. And this publicity, so long as it does not interfere with the performance of legislative duties, is considered necessary and desirable. Nor is there any objection to publicity which flows from a senator's position or performance. But the Senate folkways do prescribe that a senator place first priority upon being a *legislator*. Everything else, including his understandable desire for personal and political publicity, must be secondary to this aspect of his job.

III. Specialization

According to the folkways of the Senate, a senator should not try to know something about every bill that comes before the chamber or try to be active on a wide variety of measures. Rather, he ought to specialize, to focus his energies and attention on the relatively few matters that come before his committees or that directly and immediately affect this state. "When you come to the Senate," one administrative assistant said, "you have to decide which street corner you are going to fight on."

In part, at least, senators *ought* to specialize because they *must*: "Thousands of bills come before the Senate each Congress. If some senator knows the fine details of more than half a dozen of them, I've never heard of him." Even Robert A. Taft, who won much of his legislative reputation by his phenomenal mastery of the details of bills on the floor, could not escape the rule, and generally let foreign affairs alone. And even when a senator restricts his attention to his committee work, the job is more than one man can do.

> I belong to 12 or 13 committees and subcommittees [one vigorous, young senator says]. It's physically impossible to give them all the attention I should. So I have picked out 2 or 3 subcommittees in which I am especially interested and have concentrated on them. I believe that this is the usual practice around here.

The relatively few senators who have refused to specialize agree. One of these, a relatively young man of awesome energy, says:

> I'll be perfectly frank with you. Being active on as wide a range of issues as I have been is a man-killing job. In a few years, I suspect that I will be active on many fewer issues. I came down here a young man and I'm gradually petering out.

But the limits of human endurance are not the only reason why a senator should specialize. By restricting his attention to matters concerning his committee work and his home state, the senator is concentrating on the two things he should know best: "a senator should not make a speech unless he has something to say." Only through specialization can he know more about a subject than his colleagues and thus make a positive contribution to the operation of the chamber.

Moreover, speaking too much tends to decrease a senator's legislative impact. "Look at _____," one of them said. "He came in here with his mouth open and hasn't closed it yet. After a while, people stop listening." Furthermore, a senator who is too active outside of his specialty may destroy his influence within his area of special competence.

> When _____, one of my best friends in the Senate, came here he was known as an expert on _____, and they used to listen to him as such.

But then he began talking on many other different issues as well. He was somehow driven to express himself on many different issues. As a result, he lost some of his effectiveness on _____ matters as well as on the other issues to which he addressed himself.

Thus, almost all the senators are agreed that:

> The really effective senators are those who speak only on the subjects they have been dealing with at close quarters, not those who are on their feet on almost every subject all the time.[59]

Why this pressure for specialization? Why does this folkway exist? Two chief reasons may be suggested. The formal rules of the Senate provide for what amounts to unlimited debate. Even with the folkways limiting the activity of freshmen, discouraging "playing the galleries," and encouraging specialization, the Senate moves with glacial speed. If many more senators took full advantage of their opportunities for debate and discussion, the tempo of action would be further slowed. The specialization folkway helps make it possible for the Senate to stop talking and act.

Moreover, modern legislation is complex and technical. It comes before the Senate in crushing quantity. The committee system and specialization—in a word, a division of labor within the chamber—increase expertise and decrease the average senator's work load to something approaching manageable proportions. When a senator refuses to "go along" with specialization, he not only challenges the existing power structure, but also decreases the expert attention which legislative measures receive.

IV. Courtesy

The Senate exists to solve problems, to grapple with conflicts. Sooner or later, the hot, emotion-laden issues of our time come before it. Moreover, senators as a group are ambitious and egocentric men, chosen through an electoral battle in which a talent for invective, righteous indignation, "mud-slinging" and "engaging in personalities" are often assets. Under these circumstances, one might reasonably expect a great deal of manifest personal conflict and competition in the Senate. Such conflict does exist, but its sharp edges are blunted by the felt need—expressed in the Senate folkways—for courtesy.

A cardinal rule of Senate behavior is that political disagreements should not influence personal feelings. This is not an easy task; for as one senator said, "It's hard not to call a man a liar when you know that he is one."

Fortunately, a number of the chamber's formal rules and conventions make it possible for the senator to approximate this ideal—at least so far as overt behavior is concerned. The selection of committee members and chairmen on the basis of their seniority neatly by-passes a potential cause of grave dissension in the Senate.[60] The rules prohibit the questioning of a colleague's motives or the criticism of another state. All remarks made on the floor are, technically, addressed to the presiding officer: "Mr. President, . . ." serves as a psychological barrier between antagonists. Senators are expected to address each other not by name but by title—Earle C. Clements does not disagree with Irving M. Ives but rather the Senior Senator from Kentucky disagrees with the Senior Senator from New York.

Sometimes the senators' efforts to achieve verbal impersonality become ludicrous in their stilted formality:

> Mr. JOHNSON of Texas. The Senator from Texas does not have any objection, and the Senator from Texas wishes the Senator from California to know that the Senator from Texas knew the Senator from California did not criticize him . . .[61]

Few opportunities to praise a colleague publicly are missed in the Senate. Senators habitually refer to each other as "The distinguished Senator from _____" or "The able Senator from _____." Birthdays, anniversaries, re-election or retirement from the Senate, and the approach of adjournment are seized as opportunities for swapping praises. Sometimes, on these occasions, the sentiment is as thick as Senate bean soup. The following recent example was uttered on the Senate floor and duly printed in the *Record*:

> Mr. JOHNSON of Texas. Mr. President, if the Senate will indulge me, I should like the attention of members of both sides of the aisle for a bipartisan announcement of considerable importance. It involves the minority leader, the distinguished Senator from California (Mr. KNOW-LAND).
>
> For many years, I have been closely associated with the Senator from California. Like every member of this chamber—on either side of the aisle—I have found him to be able, patriotic, courteous, and thoughtful.
>
> But I wonder how many of my colleagues know that he is also a five-time winner in the contest for the proudest granddaddy in the Senate?
>
> His fifth victory was chalked up last Monday when Harold W. Jewett II discovered America. Anybody who has found buttons lying on the floor in front of the minority leader's desk in the past few days can know now that they popped right off BILL KNOWLAND's shirt.[62]

This kind of behavior—avoiding personal attacks on colleagues, striving for impersonality by divorcing the self from the office, "buttering-up" the opposition by extending unsolicited compliments—is thought by the senators to pay off in legislative results.[63] Personal attacks, unnecessary unpleasantness, pursuing a line of thought or action that might embarrass a colleague needlessly, are all thought to be self-defeating—"after all, your enemies on one issue may be your friends on the next." Similar considerations also suggest the undesirability of excessive partisanship.

> I want to be able to pick up votes from the other side of the aisle [one

> Republican said]. I hope that a majority of the Republicans will vote for anything I sponsor. But always some of them are going to have special problems that impel them to vote against the party.

They also suggest, despite partisan differences, that one senator should hesitate to campaign against another.

> The fellows who go around the country demagoguing and calling their fellow senators names are likely to be ineffective senators. It's just human nature that the other senators will not cooperate with them unless they have to.

In private, senators are frequently cynical about this courtesy. They say that "it doesn't mean a thing," that it is "every man for himself in the Senate," that some of their colleagues "no more should be senators than I should be Pope," that it is "just custom." Senator Barkley's advice to the freshman senator—if you think a colleague stupid, refer to him as "the able, learned and distinguished senator," but if you *know* he is stupid, refer to him as "the *very* able, learned, and distinguished senator"—is often quoted.[64] But despite its blatant hypocrisy, the practice persists. And after serving in the Senate for a period of years most senators grow to appreciate it.

> I well remember [one Republican says] that early in my service I gave a burlesque touch to this formal courtesy. A little later Senator Alben Barkley, then Democratic floor leader, came over and gently suggested that the longer I stayed in the Senate, the more I would appreciate Senatorial Courtesy. Senator Barkley was correct in his prediction.[65]

Another senator explained:

> You quickly discover that political self-preservation dictates at least a semblance of friendship. And then before you know it, you really *are* friends. It is rather like the friendships that might develop within a band of outlaws. You all hang together or you all hang separately.

Courtesy, far from being a meaningless custom as some senators seem to think it is, permits competitors to cooperate. The chaos which ensues when the folkway is ignored testifies to its vital function.

V. Reciprocity

Every senator, at one time or another, is in a position to help out a colleague. The folkways of the Senate hold that a senator ought to provide his assistance —and that he be repaid in kind.

> A man gets elected to the Senate on some kind of platform. He has made some promises or pledges that he will get this or that thing done. Then he gets down here and finds that nobody else gives a damn about his

projects. What can he do? He either must back down on his promises or begin log-rolling. At first, I was pretty cynical when I found this was necessary. But then I realized that this was the kind of compromise necessary to govern a nation like this.

The most important aspect of this pattern of reciprocity is, no doubt, the trading of votes. Occasionally, this is exhibited for all to see. The following exchange, for example, took place during a 1956 debate on acreage allotments for burley tobacco:

> Mr. LANGER [North Dakota]. We do not raise any tobacco in North Dakota, but we are interested in the tobacco situation in Kentucky, and I hope the Senator will support us in securing assistance for the wheat growers in our state.
> Mr. CLEMENTS [Kentucky]. I think the Senator will find that my support will be 100 per cent.
> Mr. BARKLEY [Kentucky]. Mr. President, will my colleague from Kentucky yield?
> Mr. CLEMENTS. I yield.
> Mr. BARKLEY. The colloquy just had confirms and justifies the Woodrow Wilsonian doctrine of open covenants openly arrived at. (Laughter).[66]

Usually, however, this kind of bargain is either made by implication or in private. Senator Douglas of Illinois, who tried unsuccessfully to combat the system, has analyzed the way in which a public works appropriation bill is passed:

> . . . This bill is built up out of a whole system of mutual accommodations in which the favors are widely distributed, with the implicit promise that no one will kick over the applecart; that if Senators do not object to the bill as a whole, they will "get theirs." It is a process, if I may use an inelegant expression, of mutual backscratching and mutual logrolling.
> Any member who tries to buck the system is only confronted with an impossible amount of work in trying to ascertain the relative merits of a given project; and any member who does ascertain them, and who feels convinced that he is correct, is unable to get an individual project turned down because the Senators from the State in which the project is located, and thus is benefiting, naturally will oppose any objection to the project; and the other members of the Senate will feel that they must support the Senators in question, because if they do not do so, similar appropriations for their own states at some time likely will be called into question.[67]

Of course, *all* bills are not passed as the result of such implicit or explicit "deals."

On the other hand, this kind of bargaining (or "logrolling" or "backscratching" or "trading off"—phrases with pejorative connotations indicating the public's attitude toward these practices) is not confined to the trading of votes.

Indeed, it is no exaggeration to say that reciprocity is a way of life in the Senate

> My boss [one highly experienced administrative assistant says] will—if it doesn't mean anything to him—do a favor for any other senator. It doesn't matter *who* he is. It's not a matter of friendship, it's just a matter of I won't be an S.O.B. if you won't be one.

This implicit bargain explains much of the behavior of senators. Each of them has vast power under the chamber's rules. A single senator, for example, can slow the Senate almost to a halt by systematically objecting to all unanimous consent requests. A few, by exercising their right to filibuster, can block the passage of all bills. Or a single senator could sneak almost any piece of legislation through the chamber by acting when floor attendance is sparse and by taking advantage of the looseness of the chamber rules. But while these and other similar powers always exist as a potential threat, the amazing thing to the outside observer is that they are rarely utilized. The spirit of reciprocity results in much, if not most, of the senators' actual power not being exercised. For if a senator *does* push his formal powers to the limit, he has broken the implicit bargain and can expect, not cooperation from his colleagues, but only retaliation in kind.

> A man in the Senate has just as much power as he has the sense to use. For this very reason he has to be careful to use it properly or else he will incur the wrath of his colleagues.

To play this game properly and effectively requires tolerance and an understanding of the often unique problems and divergent views of other senators.

> No man [one highly placed staff assistant says] can really be successful in the Senate until he has adopted a *national* point of view. Learning what the other senators' problems are and working within this framework to pass legislation gives him this outlook. If he assumes that everyone thinks and feels the same way he and his constituents do, he will be an ineffective legislator.

It demands, too, an ability to calculate how much "credit" a senator builds up with a colleague by doing him a favor or "going along." For if a senator expects too little in return, he has sold himself and his constituents short. If he expects too much, he will soon find that to ask the impossible is fruitless and that "there are some things a senator just can't do in return for help from you." Finally, this mode of procedure requires that a senator live up to his end of the bargain—no matter how implicit the bargain may have been. "You don't *have* to make these commitments," one senator said, "and if you keep your mouth shut you are often better off; but if you *do* make them, you had better live up to them."

These are subtle skills. Some men do not have them in sufficient quantity to be successful at this sort of bargaining. A few take the view that these practices are immoral and refuse, with some display of righteous indignation, to play the game that way. But this, according to the Senate folkways, is the way a senator *ought* to behave.

VI. Institutional Patriotism

Most institutions demand an emotional investment from their members. The Senate is no exception. Senators are expected to *believe* that they belong to the greatest legislative and deliberative body in the world. They are expected to be a bit suspicious of the President and the bureaucrats and just a little disdainful of the House. They are expected to revere the Senate's personnel, organization and folkways and to champion them to the outside world.

And most of them do, whether out of conviction or for the good of the order. "The most remarkable group that I have ever met anywhere," "the most able and intelligent body of men that it . . . [has] been my fortune to meet," "the best men in political life today,": thus do senators typically describe their colleagues.[68] The Senate as an institution is usually described in similar superlatives.[69]

A senator whose emotional commitment to Senate ways appears to be less than total is suspect. One who brings the Senate as an institution or senators as a class into public disrepute invites his own destruction as an effective legislator. One who seems to be using the Senate for the purposes of self-advertisement and advancement obviously does not belong. Senators are, as a group, fiercely protective of and highly patriotic about the Senate.

This, after all, is not a great deal different from the school spirit of P.S. 34, or the morale of a military outfit, or the "fight" of a football team. But, as we shall see, its political consequences are substantial. For some senators are in a better position than others to develop this emotional attachment.

VII. Influences on Conformity

We have seen that normative rules of conduct—called here folkways—exist in the Senate. Moreover, we have seen that they perform important functions.[70] They provide motivation for the performance of legislative duties that, perhaps, would not otherwise be performed. They discourage long-windedness in a chamber of one hundred highly verbal men, dependent upon publicity, and unrestrained by any formal limitations on debate. They encourage the development of expertise and division of labor and discourage those who would challenge it. They soften the inevitable personal conflict of a legislative body so that adversaries and competitors can meet (at the very least) in an atmosphere of antagonistic cooperation or (at best) in an atmosphere of friendship and mutual respect. They encourage senators to become "compromisers" and "bargainers" and to use their substantial powers with caution and restraint. Without these folkways the Senate could hardly operate in anything like its present form.

Yet they are not universally accepted or adhered to: indeed, there is some covert hostility toward them. If most senators do observe them, why don't all? This we shall try to explain in the following pages.

PREVIOUS TRAINING AND EXPERIENCE

Senators often express pride in the fact that their chamber is "democratic."

> No matter [one senior senator says] what you were before—a rich man or a poor man, a man with a good reputation or an unknown—you've got to prove yourself *in the Senate*. It's what you do when you arrive and not what you've done before that determines the amount of respect you get from your colleagues.

Or as another has expressed it, everyone "must begin at the foot of the class and spell up."[71] But it is a great deal harder for some men than others to start at the foot of the class.

A former governor who becomes a senator is often accustomed to a higher salary, more power and perquisites, a grander office, a larger staff, and more publicity than the freshman senator enjoys. He is likely to find the pace of legislative life slow and be frustrated by the necessity of cooperating with 99 equals (most of them at first far more equal than he). To move from the governorship of one of the larger states to the role of apprentice senator is, in the short run, a demotion. The result for the one-time governors is a frequent feeling of disillusionment, depression and discouragement.

> I moved from one world to another [a former governor now in the Senate says]. Back home everything revolved, or seemed to revolve, around the Governor. I had a part in practically everything that happened. There was administration. There was policy making. But down here there was just a seat at the end of the table.[72]

At the same time, the other senators complain that the former governors ". . . are the hardest group to handle; they come down here expecting to be big shots," and that they often are unwilling to realize that "they are just one of the boys." Some governors, they feel, never make the adjustment; a larger number make it slowly and painfully.

It is possible to subject this hypothesis to a rough empirical test. Crude indices of conformity can be obtained by counting the number of speeches senators make and by determining the extent to which the bills they introduce are on similar or disparate subjects.[73] These measures of the ex-governors' floor activity and legislative specialization were calculated and are compared to those of men elected from other offices in Tables 6-3 and 6-4.[74]

TABLE 6-3

Senator's Last Public Office and Frequency of Floor Speaking
(83d and 84th Congresses)

LAST PUBLIC OFFICE	FREQUENCY OF FLOOR SPEAKING			TOTAL	
	High %	*Medium* %	*Low* %	%	N
Governor	10	35	55	100	(20)
U. S. Representative	0	52	48	100	(23)
State legislator	0	33	67	100	(6)
State executive	17	17	67	100	(6)
Local official	50	50	0	100	(6)
Judge	0	60	40	100	(5)
Federal executive	33	22	45	100	(9)
None	0	50	50	100	(4)

NOTE: The two floor leaders, Johnson (D., Texas) and Knowland (R., Calif.), have been omitted from this and all subsequent tables on frequency of floor speaking. A high level of floor activity is an inevitable consequence of their positions and is not considered a breach of the folkways.

In giving floor speeches during the 83d and 84th Congresses, the ex-governors were more vocal than the former congressmen, state legislators, ex-judges and men with no office-holding experience. The former local government officials and federal executives, on the other hand, gave even more floor speeches than the erstwhile governors. In legislative specialization, only the ex-judges appear to have had a narrower range of legislative interests than the governors. Indeed, of the other senators, only the former congressmen and state legislators came even close to matching them in this respect. Thus, if our indices of conformity are reliable, the governors *as a group* seem to "go along" with the Senate folkways fairly well.

TABLE 6-4

Senator's Last Public Office and Index of Specialization (83d and 84th Congresses)

LAST PUBLIC OFFICE	INDEX OF SPECIALIZATION			TOTAL	
	High %	*Medium* %	*Low* %	%	N
Governor	35	15	50	100	(20)
U. S. Representative	8	46	46	100	(24)
State legislator	28	43	28	100	(7)
State executive	0	33	67	100	(6)
Local official	0	50	50	100	(6)
Judge	40	40	20	100	(5)
Federal executive	0	44	56	100	(9)
None	0	25	75	100	(4)

But it is the governors from the larger states, coming to the Senate with national reputations, who seem to find their initial experiences in the chamber especially trying. Moreover, their record for conformity to the folkways is bad. While they do tend to specialize quite highly, they are extremely active on the floor—even when compared to other senators from similar states (Table 6-5).

There is another peculiar feature about the former governors in the Senate: those with low seniority conform to the folkways more closely than those with high seniority. In Table 6-6, we can see that the higher the seniority of the ex-governors the more active they were in floor debate while just the opposite is true among the former representatives. Both the ex-governors and ex-representatives become more specialized as seniority increases, yet the former congressmen with high seniority specialize considerably more than the high seniority governors. While the numbers involved are too small to warrant generalization the same pattern is suggested for the former local officials and federal executives: those with high seniority conform less than the junior men. The one-time judges and state legislators, on the other hand, seem to follow the pattern of congressmen: the senior men conform more than the youngsters.

Among the present crop of senators at any rate, prolonged exposure to the folkways seems to have resulted in a high degree of conformity among the former congressmen, state legislators and judges but *not* among former governors, federal executives and local government officials.[75]

The amateur politicians—distinguished business and professional men who entered politics relatively late in life and became senators with little political experience—face many of the same problems as the former governors, compounded by their relative ignorance of political ways. One must learn to be a senator and the amateurs have a great deal to learn. As can be seen in Table 6-7, they are more likely to ignore the folkways regarding floor activity and legislative specialization than are the professionals. Moreover, the amateurs usually must learn how to be legislators in less time than those who follow other career lines to the Senate: they are the oldest group of freshmen in age. A

TABLE 6-5

Frequency of Floor Speaking of Big-State Senators, by Last Public Office
(83d and 84th Congresses)

	FREQUENCY OF FLOOR SPEAKING		
LAST PUBLIC OFFICE	*High+Medium* %	*Low* %	TOTAL % N
Governor	50	50	100 (6)
U. S. Representative	20	80	100 (6)
All other	38	62	100 (8)

NOTE: "Big state" is defined as one with more than 4,000,000 population in 1950. See note to Table 6-3.

TABLE 6-6

Last Public Office, Frequency of Floor Speaking, and Index of Specialization of Senators, by Seniority Level (84th Congress)

LAST PUBLIC OFFICE	SENIORITY	% LOW, FLOOR SPEAKING	% HIGH, INDEX OF SPECIALIZATION	N
Governor	High	78	45	(9)
	Medium	88	25	(8)
	Low	100	20	(5)
U. S. Representative	High	100	67	(6)
	Medium	88	22	(9)
	Low	94	0	(17)
State legislator	High	66	100	(3)
	Medium	50	0	(2)
	Low	50	0	(2)
State executive	High	100	0	(1)
	Medium	50	0	(2)
	Low	100	0	(4)
Local official	High	0	0	(1)
	Medium	0	0	(2)
	Low	25	0	(4)
Judge	High	100	50	(2)
	Medium	0	33	(3)
	Low	100	0	(1)
Federal executive	High	25	0	(4)
	Medium	0	0	(2)
	Low	100	33	(3)
None	High	0	0	(1)
	Medium	0	0	(1)
	Low	100	0	(2)

NOTE: See note to Table 6-3.

relatively young man can afford to be patient, to devote two or four or six years to learning the ropes and climbing the seniority ladder. A sixty-year-old man, with sufficient vigor to win election to the Senate and a distinguished career back of him, is not so likely to take the long view. At any rate, a larger proportion of the men elected to the Senate relatively late in life tend to "talk too much" than is the case for the others (Table 6-8). Thus we find a curious situation in the Senate. The greater a man's pre-Senate accomplishments (either in or out of politics) and the greater his age at election, the less likely he is to conform. For these reasons, a sort of reverse snobbism is quite widespread in the Senate. As one old-timer said, "We are skeptical of men who

TABLE 6-7

Percentage of Senator's Pre-Senate Adult Life in Public Office, Frequency of Floor Speaking, and Index of Specialization (83d and 84th Congresses)

% OF PRE-SENATE ADULT YEARS IN PUBLIC OFFICE	FREQUENCY OF FLOOR SPEAKING			
	High	*Medium*	*Low*	TOTAL
	%	%	%	% N
Under 40	21	37	42	100 (38)
40–60	0	48	52	100 (21)
Over 60	5	35	60	100 (20)

	INDEX OF SPECIALIZATION			
	High	*Medium*	*Low*	TOTAL
Under 40	10	31	59	100 (39)
40–60	10	43	48	100 (21)
Over 60	33	38	29	100 (21)

NOTE: See note to Table 6-3.

come to the Senate with big reputations." From the standpoint of protecting the Senate folkways, this skepticism is justified.

POLITICAL AMBITIONS

Higher political ambitions—and for senators this means a desire to become either President or Vice-President—can also lead to nonconformity.

First of all, strong and exalted ambitions are likely to lead to restiveness during the period of apprenticeship. A national following is seldom made by "being seen and not heard" or through faithful service on the District of Columbia Committee. In order to overcome this initial handicap, the highly

TABLE 6-8

Age at First Election/Appointment to the Senate and Frequency of Floor Speaking (83d and 84th Congresses)

AGE AT FIRST ELECTION / APPOINTMENT	FREQUENCY OF FLOOR SPEAKING			
	High	*Medium*	*Low*	TOTAL
	%	%	%	% N
30–39	8	54	38	100 (13)
40–49	4	46	50	100 (28)
50–59	17	33	50	100 (30)
Over 60	25	25	50	100 (8)

NOTE: See note to Table 6-3.

ambitious freshman may resort to extreme and unsettling tactics as, for example, Senator Kefauver is thought by his colleagues to have done in his crime investigations, and Senator McCarthy certainly did in his "crusade" against Communism. His legislatve duties are likely to be neglected in the ceaseless quest for publicity and personal advancement. His ears are likely to be ". . . attuned to noises outside the workaday drone of the Senate chamber." [76] And since the senator with higher ambitions is almost invariably shooting for the Presidency, he is likely to be attuned to the voices of somewhat different groups than are most senators. Close presidential elections are won and lost in the doubtful states containing large metropolitan populations. Popularity in these areas is generally a prerequisite for nomination and election to the Presidency. Yet these very groups are the ones under-represented in the Senate, the ones most often at odds with its present power structure. Thus, to the extent that ambitious senators *anticipate* the wants of possible future constituents, they find themselves challenging the Senate *status quo*.

In Table 6-9 we see that of the most obvious presidential aspirants during the 83d and 84th Congresses all save Symington gave more floor speeches than the average Senator and all pursued a wider range of legislative interests.

It should be immediately admitted, however, that the list of presidential aspirants used here is based entirely upon common report—latent presidential ambitions smolder in the breasts of senators not included. Moreover, the list includes both floor leaders, and the folkways regarding floor speaking and specialization are necessarily and greatly relaxed for the incumbents of these specialized positions. Finally, an occasional senator is able to be both a serious presidential candidate and a highly regarded and effective senator—Senators Taft, Johnson and Knowland are the most conspicious examples within recent years. Yet Taft was never nominated, at least in part because he was a "Senate man." Knowland seems to have found the conflict between the expectations of his Senate colleagues and his presidential ambitions too much to bear. Senator Johnson's presidential chances appear to be low [*Ed. note:* Recall this was

TABLE 6-9

Frequency of Speechmaking and Index of Specialization of Active Presidential Aspirants in the Senate (83d and 84th Congresses)

ACTIVE PRESIDENTIAL ASPIRANTS	NO. OF SPEECHES	INDEX OF SPECIALIZATION
Humphrey (D., Minn.)	1528	.32
Johnson (D., Tex.)	1203	.41
Kefauver (D., Tenn.)	446	.49
J. F. Kennedy (D., Mass.)	359	.47
Knowland (R., Calif.)	1317	.37
Symington (D., Mo.)	248	.43
Median for all senators	272	.52

written in 1959] for somewhat the same reasons as Taft's. As a general rule, it seems that a man who entirely adheres to the Senate folkways has little chance of becoming President of the United States.

CONSTITUENCY PROBLEMS

A third factor which encourages nonconformity to Senate folkways is a competitive two-party, or a large and complex, constituency.

The political insecurity of a senator from this kind of state is likely to result in a shortened time perspective, an eagerness to build a record quickly, an impatience with the slowness of the seniority system. The approved attitude for the new senator was voiced by a freshman:

> I want to be a *Senator.* I want to gain the respect of my colleagues so that I can represent my state better. I want to establish a reputation as a hard-working committee member who does his homework, who has integrity and good judgment, rather than to get my name in the paper every morning. This is taking the long view. It takes time to establish this kind of a reputation in the Senate. It's rather like starting a law practice in a new and small town, as I did in _____, _____. You can't rush it.

A senator whose seat is in grave danger is much more likely to try to "rush it" than one who can count on reelection unless he makes a major blunder.

Table 6-10 seems to support this line of reasoning. The senators from two-party states are a little more likely to be frequent floor speakers than those from modified one-party constituencies. Both are considerably more vocal than

TABLE 6-10

Type of Party System in Senator's State and His Frequency of Floor Speaking and Index of Specialization

TYPE OF PARTY SYSTEM	FREQUENCY OF FLOOR SPEAKING			
	High %	*Medium* %	*Low* %	TOTAL % N
Two-party	16	35	49	100 (43)
Modified one-party	11	39	50	100 (18)
One-party	0	50	50	100 (18)

	INDEX OF SPECIALIZATION			
	High	*Medium*	*Low*	TOTAL
Two-party	16	41	43	100 (44)
Modified one-party	6	33	61	100 (18)
One-party	26	26	47	100 (19)

NOTE: See note to Table 6-3 and footnote 76.

those from pure one-party states.[77] The picture of legislative specialization is a little different. One-party state senators seem to be the most specialized; those from modified one-party states, least specialized; while the senators from two-party areas fall in between.

The size and complexity of a senator's state also influence the likelihood of his conforming to Senate norms. A senator from a large state has a far greater burden of "casework" to process, errands to run, mail to answer, and speeches to give back home, than the man from a small state; and he has to do this without a proportionately larger staff. He is not likely to have as much time for legislating as a senator from Nevada, Wyoming or Delaware. The large states also tend to be the politically complex states—shot through with sectional, religious, economic and ethnic conflicts. As a result, a senator from one of these states is subject to greater cross-pressures than a man representing a homogeneous state with only one or two real issues, as, for example, has been the case for the southern states. His constituents also expect him to be active on more issues than the man from the smaller and simpler state, and so he will be oftener tempted to challenge the specialization folkway. And generally he is forced to grapple with those problems without the benefit of substantial seniority, which men from closely contested, large and complex states seldom achieve.

Table 6-11 appears to reinforce this speculation: the larger in size and the more urban a senator's state, the more likely he is to be hyper-active on the Senate floor. Table 6-12 presents the relationships between the same two variables and legislative specialization. Urban state senators seem to specialize less than these from rural states. The size of a senator's state, however, does not seem to have any effect on the range of his legislative interests.

TABLE 6-11

Size and Complexity of Senator's Constituency and Frequency of Floor Speaking
(83d and 84th Congresses)

% URBAN, STATE POP. (1950)	FREQUENCY OF FLOOR SPEAKING			
	High %	*Medium* %	*Low* %	TOTAL % N
Over 80	38	12	50	100 (8)
60–79	13	33	54	100 (24)
40–59	6	48	46	100 (33)
Under 40	7	43	50	100 (14)
SIZE OF STATE POP. (1950)				
Over 4,000,000	40	13	47	100 (15)
2–4,000,000	6	54	40	100 (35)
Less than 2,000,000	10	35	55	100 (31)

NOTE: See note to Table 6-3.

TABLE 6-12

Size and Complexity of Senator's Constituency and Index of Specialization
(83d and 84th Congresses)

	INDEX OF SPECIALIZATION			
% URBAN, STATE POP. (1950)	*High*	*Medium*	*Low*	TOTAL
	%	%	%	% N
Over 80	11	33	55	100 (9)
60–79	8	32	60	100 (25)
40–59	15	42	42	100 (33)
Under 40	36	29	36	100 (14)
SIZE OF STATE POP. (1950)				
Over 4,000,000	13	33	53	100 (15)
2–4,000,000	17	40	43	100 (35)
Less than 2,000,000	16	32	52	100 (31)

POLITICAL IDEOLOGY

Senators are, of necessity, tolerant of differences of opinion. A senator's political views make less difference to his acceptance or lack of it by his colleagues than is generally realized. Yet a senator's stance on political issues *does* make it easier (or harder) for him to conform to the folkways and thus, indirectly, influences his prestige and effectiveness in the chamber.

The folkways of the Senate, as we have already seen, buttress the *status quo* in the chamber. And the distribution of power within the chamber results in generally conservative policies. Thus the liberals are more likely to challenge Senate norms than the conservatives. "A reformer's life is perhaps not easy anywhere," one close observer of the Senate has remarked. "In the Senate it can be both bitter and fruitless. . . ."[78]

A man elected to the Senate as a "liberal" or "progressive" or "reformer" is under considerable pressure to produce legislative results in a hurry. The people who voted for him are not likely to be happy with small favors—dams built, rivers dredged, roads financed—but want major national legislative policy changed. Yet as a freshman or a junior senator, and many never become anything else, the liberal is in no position to do this alone. If he gives in to the pressure for conformity coming from the folkways, he must postpone the achievement of his liberal objectives. If he presses for these objectives regardless of his junior position, he will become tabbed as a nonconformist, lose popularity with his colleagues and, in most cases, his legislative effectiveness as well.

The conservative does not face this problem. He has committed himself to fewer changes in basic policies: he finds the strategic positions in the Senate occupied by like-minded senators regardless of which party organizes it. He is able to identify more strongly with the folkways of the chamber and side more easily with the Congress in its running feud with a generally more liberal President. Nor is he, as is the liberal, so dependent on the support of broad, often unorganized groups which can be reached only through the mass media. At any rate, the liberals seem to talk considerably more and to specialize less than senators of different political persuasion (Table 6-13).[79] Conservatives can afford to be quiet and patient. Reformers—by definition—find it difficult to be either.

VIII. Conformity and "Effectiveness"

All this would be very "interesting" but not particularly important to serious students of politics if the Senate folkways did not influence the distribution of power within the chamber.

But the senators believe, rightly or wrongly, that without the respect and confidence of their colleagues they can have little influence *in the Senate.* "You can't be effective," they said over and over again, "unless you are respected—on both sides of the aisle." And the safest way to obtain this respect is to conform to the folkways, to become a "real Senate man." Those who do not, run a serious risk. "In the Senate, if you don't conform, you don't get many favors for your state. You are never told that, but you soon learn."

In order to test this hypothesis, a crude index of "Legislative Effectiveness" was constructed for the 83d and 84th Congresses by calculating the proportion of all public bills and resolutions introduced by each senator that were passed

TABLE 6-13

Senators' Political Ideology and Conformity to Senate Folkways (84th Congress)

| POLITICAL IDEOLOGY ON DOMESTIC ISSUES | FREQUENCY OF FLOOR SPEAKING | | | |
	High %	*Medium* %	*Low* %	TOTAL % N
Liberal	12	23	65	100 (34)
Moderate	0	0	100	100 (19)
Conservative	0	8	92	100 (37)

| | INDEX OF SPECIALIZATION | | | |
	High	*Medium*	*Low*	TOTAL
Liberal	20	31	49	100 (35)
Moderate	21	37	42	100 (19)
Conservative	24	42	34	100 (38)

NOTE: See note to Table 6-3 and footnote 78.

by the Senate.[80] While such an index does not pretend to measure the overall power or influence of a senator, it does seem to reflect his efficiency as a legislator, narrowly defined. And, to the extent that the concept as used on Capitol Hill has any distinct meaning, "effectiveness" seems to mean the ability to get one's bill passed.

The "effectiveness" of the conforming and nonconforming senators is presented in Table 6-14. The less a senator talks on the Senate floor, and the narrower a senator's area of legislative interest and activity, the greater is his "effectiveness." Moreover, the types of senators who, as we have already seen, tend not to conform have considerably less impact on the chamber's legislative output than the conformists (Table 6-15). Conformity to the Senate folkways does, therefore, seem to "pay off" in concrete legislative results.

IX. Summary and Conclusion

There are unwritten rules of behavior, which we have called folkways, in the Senate. These rules are *normative*, that is, they define how a senator ought to behave. Nonconformity is met with moral condemnation, while senators who conform to the folkways are rewarded with high esteem by their colleagues. And partly because of this fact, the conformists tend to be the most influential and effective members of the Senate.

These folkways, we have suggested, are highly functional to the Senate social system since they provide motivation for the performance of vital duties and essential modes of behavior which, otherwise, would go unrewarded. They discourage frequent and lengthy speechmaking in a chamber without any other effective limitation on debate, encourage the development of expertise and a

TABLE 6-14

Senator's Level of Floor Speaking Activity, Index of Specialization, and Legislative Effectiveness (83d and 84th Congresses)

LEVEL OF FLOOR SPEAKING	INDEX OF LEGISLATIVE EFFECTIVENESS			
	High %	*Medium* %	*Low* %	TOTAL % N
High	0	33	67	100 (9)
Medium	3	68	29	100 (31)
Low	15	59	26	100 (39)
INDEX OF SPECIALIZATION				
High	23	69	8	100 (13)
Medium	10	62	28	100 (29)
Low	8	51	41	100 (39)

NOTE: See note to Table 6-3.

TABLE 6-15

Some Factors Associated with the "Legislative Effectiveness" of Senators
(83d and 84th Congresses)

	INDEX OF LEGISLATIVE EFFECTIVENESS			
	High %	*Medium* %	*Low* %	TOTAL % N
Last Public Office				
Governor	10	70	20	100 (20)
U. S. Representative	13	62	25	100 (24)
State legislator	29	43	29	100 (7)
State executive	0	67	33	100 (6)
Local official	0	67	33	100 (6)
Judge	20	20	60	100 (5)
Federal executive	11	44	44	100 (9)
None	0	50	50	100 (4)
Pre-Senate Adult Years in Public Office				
Under 40	8	51	41	100 (39)
40–60	5	67	29	100 (21)
Over 60	24	62	14	100 (21)
Age at First Entrance to Senate				
30–39	14	64	21	100 (14)
40–49	17	48	35	100 (29)
50–59	7	63	30	100 (30)
Over 60	0	63	37	100 (8)
Political Ambitions*				
Presidential Aspirants	0	33	67	100 (6)
Others	10	62	28	100 (73)
Party System in Senator's State				
Two-party	7	59	34	100 (44)
Modified one-party	6	67	28	100 (18)
One-party	26	47	26	100 (19)
% Urban, Senator's State Pop. (1950)				
Over 80	11	67	22	100 (9)
60–79	8	44	48	100 (25)
40–59	12	67	21	100 (33)
Less than 40	14	57	29	100 (14)
Size of Senator's State Pop. (1950)				
4,000,000 plus	13	64	33	100 (15)
2–4,000,000	6	60	34	100 (35)
Less than 2,000,000	16	58	26	100 (31)
Ideology				
Liberal	3	32	65	100 (31)
Moderate	60	0	40	100 (10)
Conservative	31	40	29	100 (45)

*Senators Johnson and Knowland omitted.

division of labor in a group of overworked laymen facing unbelievably complex problems, soften the inevitable personal conflicts of a problem-solving body, encourage bargaining and the cautious use of awesome formal powers. Without these folkways, the Senate could hardly operate with its present organization and rules.

Nonetheless, the folkways are no more perfectly obeyed than the traffic laws. Abstractly stated, the reasons for nonconformity seem to be three:

1. Men become senators at different stages in life after varying kinds of careers. The ease and frequency with which they conform is affected by these differences in their recruitment. Senators elected relatively early in life with considerable political experience seem to conform most readily and often. Not all professional politicians find the adjustment equally easy, however. Former legislators and judges seem to adjust most easily while governors from the larger states and federal executives often find the Senate a psychological demotion, their administrative skills irrelevant, their perceptions of the political process at odds with Senate realities. Amateur politicians, men who have entered politics relatively late in life after distinguished business and professional careers, have the hardest time of all.

2. The senators differ, too, in the level of their political aspirations. Most of them think of Senate service as the climax to their political lives. A minority, however, have their eyes firmly focused on an even bigger prize, the Presidency. Not only does this weaken their identification with the chamber and its ways: it also causes them to identify with a national constituency demanding modes of behavior which are sometimes subversive to the folkways.

3. All senators belong to, or identify with, many other groups in addition to the Senate, and the expectations and demands of these other groups sometimes conflict with the folkways. The most powerful of these groups is undoubtedly the senator's constituents—both present and potential. But the ability of a senator's constituents to employ their ultimate sanction varies considerably. For example, incumbent senators are rarely defeated in one-party states. Men from this kind of state need be less responsive to their constituents and thus are able to conform to the folkways more often and thoroughly than men from competitive two-party areas. Moreover, some senators are far less likely than others to be caught in the middle of cross-pressures from constituency and legislative peers. The Senate is organized in a way that greatly exaggerates the power of rural, conservative interests. The folkways justify and buttress the *status quo* in the chamber. Thus rural conservatives are less often caught in the squeeze of conflicting constituency-folkway demands than are the liberal senators from urban states. When confronted with such a conflict situation, a senator must choose between conforming to the folkways and thus appearing to "sell out," or gaining popularity back home at the expense of goodwill, esteem and effectiveness in the Senate—a course which diminishes his long-run ability to achieve what his constituents demand. For this reason, conflicts between the

immediate demands of constituents and peers are by no means automatically resolved in favor of constituents.

It would be a mistake to assume that the folkways of the Senate are unchangeable. Their origins are obscure, but sparse evidence scattered throughout senatorial memoirs suggests that they have changed little since the late eighteenth or early nineteenth century.[81] Certainly the chamber's small membership and gradual turnover is conducive to the transmission of such rules virtually unchanged from one generation to the next. Yet the trend in American politics seems to be toward more competitive two-party politics; a greater political role for the mass media of communications and those skilled in their use; larger, more urban constituencies. All these are factors which presently encourage departure from the norms of Senate behavior. Thus nonconformity to the folkways may increase in the future, if the folkways remain unchanged. Moreover, the major forces which presently push senators toward nonconformity tend to converge upon a relatively small group of senators. This is a far more unstable situation than the random distribution of such influences —and hence of nonconforming behavior—among the entire membership of the Senate.

Inside Capitol Hill:
How the House Really Works

LARRY L. KING

Out in the great American hinterland at this very moment [October 1968— before the elections] are many hundreds of able and sincere men making countless promises impossible to keep. These are neophyte candidates for Congress, and on November 5th some will be winners. It is for these we weep.

In two-year cycles a human herd descends on Washington armed with mandates they usually assume to be more demanding than others do. Some lucky few may be virgin United States Senators who—because they represent entire states in a body lately restored as the spawning ground of Presidents—may

Reprinted by permission of the author, Larry L. King, contributing editor, *Harper's Magazine,* from "Inside Capitol Hill: How the House Really Works," *Harper's Magazine,* Vol. 237 (October 1968), pp. 58–71.

reasonably expect their names and faces to be discovered outside their native precincts. Their oratorical vapors may soon mingle with those of Senator Everett McKinley Dirksen, or they might be summoned to the White House for grander purposes than receiving one of six dozen pens used to sign a new canal-barge bill into law. The majority of newcomers, however, will carry their dreams into the U.S. House of Representatives—where, statistically, each is an odds-on bet to attain immediate oblivion.

Though congressional powers have eroded with the advent of strong Presidents, the House collectively wields vast powers in establishing our tax rates, voting our pensions, dams, or post offices, drafting our sons, declaring our holier wars (if not those in Korea or Vietnam), protecting our voting rights, or giving away our oil-rich offshore tidelands to the favored coastal states. It may decide the amount of cotton or tobacco we may plant, how truthfully we shall package our commercial products, the amount of time we should allot in Leavenworth for marijuana smoked in careless circumstances, or what minimum wages we shall be paid. For good or ill it can influence almost all of our freedoms or our functions.

Individually, however, all save a corporal's guard of the 435 House members are without major influence, except in the narrow areas of their specializations as dictated by committee assignments. Thus for many Congressmen the House with its worship of seniority, jealously kept jurisdictions, and indifference to new blood is not a happy home.

"Possibly the members from his own state know him and receive him into full fellowship," Woodrow Wilson wrote of the freshman Congressman in the 1880s, "but no one else knows him, except as an adherent of this or that party, or as a newcomer from this or that state. He finds his station insignificant and his identity indistinct." Wilson need not have limited his comments to rank newcomers. In 1964 a 67-year-old freshman from California, one Everett Burkhalter, gave his reasons for declining to seek reelection: "I could see I wasn't going to get anyplace. Nobody listens to what you have to say until you've been here ten or twelve years. These old men have got everything so tied down that you can't do anything."

House Speaker John McCormack (Massachusetts) is 77; Minority Whip Les Arends (Illinois) no longer lists his age in biographical sketches, but will never greet 70 again; Majority Leader Carl Albert (Oklahoma) is a mere sapling of 60. Of the twenty-one chairmen of standing—or permanent—House committees in the 90th Congress, only three were below age 60, eleven were over 65, and seven were past 70. Many represent rural constituencies in an increasingly urbanized America: Texans chair five of the twenty-one standing committees, and they hail from the cultural centers of Anson, College Station, Waco, Lubbock, and Texarkana. South Carolina claims two chairmanships; Mississippi, Louisiana, and Arkansas one each. The Old Confederacy thus controls ten standing House committees.

Our great cities, increasingly rotted and restive, are stepchildren here. New York City, Chicago, San Francisco, and Baltimore claim only one chairman each, and none have jurisdictions especially tuned to urban problems. Los Angeles, Philadelphia, Houston, and Detroit have no chairmanships. Washington, D.C. doesn't even have a plain-vanilla Congressman: the nation's capital and the most predominantly Negro city in the country—its black population is estimated at 67 percent—must look to an aging South Carolinian, who chairs the District of Columbia Committee, for the token representation it gets.

While in theory the highest responsibility resides in the House Speaker, more and more power has accrued to crusty old committee chairmen dating from the moment the House stomped on dictatorial Speaker Joe Cannon almost sixty years ago. Only a stern and vigorous Speaker is able to deal effectively with the experienced old swordsmen who head the committees; Speaker McCormack may no longer fit that description. Congressmen trooping into the Speaker's chamber to push their legislation are increasingly treated to McCormack's discourses on his lifelong fight against "Godless Communism" or to rambling reminiscences of his triumphs as a middle-aged New Dealer. In his last years Speaker Rayburn—old, ill, unfairly burdened—lost much of his crusader's zeal; he would never consent, however, to pass the crown. Those stubborn few ruling the House committees consider themselves omnipotent, granting or withholding favor in the style of whimsical despots or prohibiting action on bills for which the public, the President, or large segments of Congress itself may be crying.

Perhaps a dozen committee chairmen truly count in the grand scheme. Others, because of their own lassitudes and deficiencies, or the limited scope of their committees, have a distinctly minor influence. The minority party generally can claim about ten senior "Outs" whose counsel is honored by the majority party "Ins." Possibly three to a half-dozen young-to-middling House members are junior consultants to their betters; their special stations may be credited to powerful sponsors, lucky breaks, unusual talents or—above all— cooperative conduct. The remaining Representatives are on the fringe, able to dictate a National Historic Site now and then or to nominate a local postmaster. These are judged worthy of special attention only when a particularly bloody partisan war looms and their votes are, temporarily, disproportionately valued.

"The Longer I'm Here . . ."

On reaching Washington the freshman Congressman is certain to suffer cultural shock. In the weeks since his election he will have become a minor sage. He may have departed his district to strobe lights and music, while happy cadres screamed their pride. A few ambitious favor-seekers, an awed old crony or two, and some unprincipled born-politicians (more likely a preacher or down-at-heels relative) will have proclaimed Destiny's varied and high future uses of him. Then, suddenly, he is the New Boy in town, ignored or scorned. In a city where prestige and power are the paramount coin of trade, he is a nobody.

Except for instances where entrenched political machines are so powerful as to pick and rule Congressmen as effortlessly as they do their county auditors, House members are free to operate their individual offices with great autonomy. It is expected of them, however, to uncomplainingly play their assigned internal bit-roles in what amounts—always structurally, often in attitudes, and despite Emerson's description of Congress as "a standing insurrection"—to a giant corporation. Even the most powerful muscles in the corporate body are tolerant of other members in a personal or political sense. One may junket, juice, philander, or cavort to excess with lobbyists without risking even a mild House rebuke—so long as proper form is observed. Despite his well-known transgressions, Representative Adam Clayton Powell angered his colleagues only after he claimed, "I haven't done anything more than other Congressmen"; when he added that "nor, by the grace of God, do I intend to do anything *less*," he was stripped of seniority, his committee chairmanship, and ultimately his House seat.

Congressmen may forgive a colleague from Dixie (or, lately, from Chicago's backlashing Polish wards or other uneasy white Yankee precincts) his intemperate inferences that the Negro was somehow created inferior by God or Darwin: survival is, after all, the Genesis rule of politics and every Congressman has a special constituency to make happy, be it bigots, powerful ward captains, or usurious bankers. Everyone is free to discover his own menaces. Speaker Rayburn's advice to Congressmen fearful of the grassroots consequences on a given vote, should they follow a difficult partisan line or unexpected tremors of conscience, was unvaried: "When in doubt, vote your district."

Any Congressman who is openly critical of his colleagues or of the parent body, or who shows impatience with accepted rituals or otherwise impinges on the mighty, risks deep trouble. "The way to get along," another bit of choice Rayburnism ran, "is to go along." The corporation tolerates only minimal deviations from protocol, abhors internal dissent, and considers "idealism" a handy word for stump speeches though a word seldom fit to muddy the eternal dialogue of pragmatic old-pro pols.

One night a few years ago a young, bright House nonentity from the Midwest complained to me as we departed Capitol Hill, "This damned place is a plenary of Rotarians. The House acts, thinks, and reacts in terms of some stodgy old Philadelphia club. It's overpolite and phony and nothing much gets done. Nobody listens to my speeches. New ideas scare these old-timers to death."

That was some fifteen years ago; my friend was a raw freshman. A term or so later he ran to fill an unexpired Senate term, but lost. He returned to his House seat burned by campaign debts, disconsolate; in his private chambers he spoke of quitting Congress for the ministry or teaching. For two or three years he growled his old frustrations: "I just don't amount to a damn. I'm not doing anybody any good. I'm stymied." One day he ceased to complain; in due course he was seen near the stations of power. Today he is among the ruling elite: welcome at the White House, a regular at the table where Speaker McCormack receives his most loyal minions over morning coffee, a confidant of Hubert Humphrey. Perhaps people listen to his speeches now, though his speeches no longer frighten old men. Indeed, he recently likened permitting "the people" to nominate their presidential candidates to permitting "fans in the stands" to name the captain of the football team rather than his being chosen "by the coach and the teammates who know him." Not all our Che Guevaras die in battle.

The standard quip of House seniors—"The longer I'm here the more I appreciate the many virtues of the seniority system"—covers up many midnight bargains, each evacuating an old dream or jettisoning certain burdensome ideals. Congressmen like to say they become more effective with time's passage. In the sense that they learn the procedural shortcuts this is true: the experienced House member is better able to exploit parliamentary loopholes, to emerge uncut from gentlemanly backbitings or from safaris into Washington's mysterious and thorny undergrowths, to cozy up to powerful despots without gagging when ambition demands or convenience recommends, or to horse-trade without—to call on Faulkner—buying too many spotted horses. Congressmen often become more "effective" only at the price of their youthful visions if not their larger capacities. "The institution itself allows for precious little ingenuity," ex-Congressman Charles Weltner of Georgia has noted. "But outcry over the seniority system is nothing new, and almost everybody is for reform—except those who have the effective power of reform. So the system clanks along, depressing eager spirits, diverting bright minds, and discouraging apt members." What results is too many drones and chairwarmers: men willing to swap intellectual potential for a rather shallow cleverness, or cocktail-party sophistication, or profuse exercises in rationalization; these they too often mistake for accumulated wisdom or seizures of statesmanship, especially as time works its dry rot in the conventional congressional mind. Some few House members remain capable of natural growth, flourishing intellectually because of their Washington experiences and despite the stifling House atmosphere. Most of these attempt to move on, to the Senate or to Governors' mansions or lately as the mayors of our giant cities. If political circumstances prohibit their leaving the House, these restless and creative few must overcome many a high-placed suspicion before their cautious elders welcome them to participation.

Sent to the Back of the Bus

A myth Congressmen promote in the interest of the corporate image is that these House elders are benevolent old daddies to new members, freely giving advice and encouragement. The truth is that only Congressmen of low or middling seniority (perhaps remembering the degradations and hazings of their own freshman years) offer generous help to fledglings; older and more powerful members are often stingy in their affections to the point of actively resenting newcomers who speak without being spoken to or who sit uninvited in certain select corners of the House cafeteria. Each new lawmaker discovers the internal generation gap. Former Representative Jerry Voorhis of California wrote of his 1937 freshman observations, "Like New York, Keokuk, and Centerville, Congress has its select circle. It consists of a number of highly prepossessing members, who have considerable influence and who are well aware of that fact. Practically always they are members of long service. A few of them seem to make a point of failing to note the presence of newer members or those not belonging to the select influence group." Dr. Ernest S. Griffith, for many years an official in the Library of Congress, observes, "Seniority is a spirit pervading the total behavior [of Congress]. This is especially true between new members and older ones. The latter want the former to seek their advice and have their own ways of clipping the wings of upstarts."[82]

A few years ago a Texas freshman took on an old congressional head in what the neophyte presumed to be proper debate; he won his minor point. Two years later the Texan, at the behest of her relatives in his district, introduced a bill to admit a young Chinese woman to the United States outside the regular immigrant quota system. He appeared in behalf of that bill before a committee chaired by his elderly adversary. To show her appreciation of the Congressman's efforts, the young Chinese woman—a teacher and artist—had painted from photographs his likeness in oils. By way of stressing the woman's talents, the Texan took his oil painting to the committee. The sour old chairman jumped at the opportunity to bait and humiliate the young Congressman. "Do you introduce bills for anyone who happens to paint a purty picture of you?" he demanded. "Do you think just because somebody paints purty pictures they'll be good citizens? How about that Diego Rivera fellah? Wasn't *he* a Communist?" The chairman also wondered whether he had visited China to pose for his purty picture. Properly avenged, the old chairman bottled the bill up in committee.

Another freshman, assigned to the House Interior and Insular Affairs Committee, objected when senior members decreed to hold only perfunctory hearings on the Hawaiian Statehood Bill on the grounds of "last year's extensive testimony"; *he* had not heard any testimony, the new Congressman insisted. The chairman, showing a grace rarely known to his breed, agreed to more meaningful hearings. He was unusually serene while testimony droned on—though other seniors snarled at the troublesome freshman, cold-shouldered him, or pointedly boycotted hearings until "repetitious matters" could be disposed of. Years later, when he could laugh without pain, the former greenhorn would confess, "I finally *begged* the chairman to abort those hearings. I apologized profusely and regularly to my offended seniors. I bowed in their presence and brought them cigars. And one day no more than six years later one of them nodded to me in the hall."

Rare is the freshman who receives a major committee assignment even though he slavishly imitates protocol by going to the "dean" of his home-state delegation to beg that presumably powerful old bird's assistance. Letters are sent to those chairmen of committees one most avidly craves. The Speaker is notified of one's more arrogant ambitions in servile terms, as is the Congressman designated as one's "geographic representative" to his party's Committee-on-Committees. After such desperate offensives the luckier freshmen may land at the foot of their third or fourth committee-of-choice.

The three most powerful House committees are Rules, Ways and Means, and Appropriations. Vacancies are especially infrequent on Rules or on Ways and Means. Because House leaders consider these units vital to House continuity and to their own control, assignments are made with unusual care, and pains are taken to select "stable" Congressmen considered good bets for re-election as well as instinctively cooperative. When prized vacancies do occur, there are always men of at least middling seniority eager to quit lesser assignment for more prestigious ones; short-timers are shoved to the back of the bus.

Since assignment to the Big Three Committees points the way toward genuine power, the brilliant-but-erratic, the loner, the gray-flannel revolutionary, or the born insurgent need not apply.[83]

The late Speaker Rayburn, a Texan, was dedicated to preserving the 27½ percent oil-depletion allowance—possibly the most obvious (and surely one of the more odious) tax loophole available to favored industries, corporations, and foundations. Rayburn required nominees to the tax-writing Ways and Means Committee to give personal assurances that they saw unusual merit in oil's merry boondoggle. No Congressman who believes that churches should pay taxes on their properties (even though untaxed church holdings are now worth billions) is likely to receive Ways and Means clearance from Speaker McCormack—a devout Catholic known behind his powerful back as "The Gentleman from Vatican City." Ways and Means is chaired by Representative Wilbur Mills of Arkansas, a strong oil champion, and is heavily weighted with Congressmen from such oil-producing states as California, Louisiana, Florida, Texas, and Montana; its makeup is consistently more conservative than the prevailing House attitude. Since in the case of Democrats this unit also functions as the Committee-on-Committees and as such dictates committee assignments, untaxed oil tycoons and affluent clergymen may relax. (Republicans hand out committee assignments through a special unit comprised of one member from each state having GOP Congressmen. As ever, seniors dominate.)

The House may appear to the untrained eye to have as many chiefs as Indians. Vast numbers of subcommittee chairmen, specializing in road building or foreign trade or exotic agricultural crops, may in their fields be judged major czars. Get them outside their specialties, however, and many are without superior leadership skills or opportunities. Most subchairmen exist only as creatures of full-committee chairmen who may predetermine their actions by stacking key subcommittees with cronies sure to remain loyal to the larger office; the full chairman also controls all jurisdictions, travels, and budgets. "The committee member who has served twenty years is not just 5 percent more powerful than the member who has served nineteen years," Representative Morris K. Udall of Arizona, one of the finest and most intelligent men in the House, notes. "If he is chairman he is 1,000 percent more powerful."

All power is, of course, relative: the chairman of the Merchant Marine and Fisheries Committee may be a demigod in the eyes of fishing-boat captains, mackerel canners, or coastal resort mayors everywhere, but he makes only a small ripple in the deeper Washington waters. The chairman of the House Un-American Activities Committee may terrify the sensitive and arouse the superpatriots, but he could absent himself from Capitol Hill for an entire two-year term without visibly slowing the democratic processes. Junior members of such lesser units are little more influential than their hometown fire chiefs.

Perhaps the *real* power rests nowhere on Capitol Hill, but in the congressional districts themselves. On the surface this seems the ideal of a grassroots democracy. I fear the opposite. Most Congressmen are elected only with the active assistance of two or three giant economic forces in their districts. The money interests are helpful far beyond the dollar: they may influence their employees' voting habits (especially in areas where unions are weak or absent and a monolithic favored industry dominates); they or their chosen men usually are the local social and political leaders. Each congressional district has its own internal Establishment—usually a combine of industrialists, financiers, businessmen, newspaper publishers, television owners, corporate lawyers, powerful ministers or priests. When the Congressman returns home these are the people he sees at civic-club luncheons and country clubs; these are the people whose lobbyists entertain him in Washington—and then report back to their superiors whether the Congressman deserves to prosper. Lawmakers may only infrequently be telephoned their voting orders, but they *are* made aware of powerful opinions dominating their districts. An NBC newsman, himself once an administrative assistant in the House, recently remarked that legislators know almost without exception how they'll vote on many key issues without troubling to learn the specific contents of the bills. "They have been conditioned by their grassroots experiences," he said. "If someone troubled to analyze the internal Establishment in every congressional district, I think he could predict with total accuracy how any major roll call would divide—and do it well in advance."

The more a Congressman prospers by close identification with such consensus constituencies, the more he is tempted to imitate them in the name of "leadership." Congressmen from swing or marginal districts with varied partisan, economic, and ethnic values are much less likely to become extremist zealots, more prone to objective evaluations of issues, more likely to grow with new experience. The terrible irony is that these members with capacities for growth are often defeated, while the safe-district parrots who rise through seniority take their prejudices along.

The Blessings of Debate, Ltd.

It is perhaps an overall blessing for the republic that the House, unlike the Senate, does not enjoy unlimited debate. The late Senator Carter Glass of Virginia, whose total service in both bodies exceeded thirty years, once said he had never seen a single vote changed nor a mind visibly swayed by oratory in either chamber. Forget Jimmy Stewart striking such oratorical sparks on his third day in Washington that old stone faces of the House and Senate are moved to tears, cheers, and patriotic actions; I doubt that even Ronald Reagan could do it.

Each bill may be debated in the House for exactly that length of time dictated by the Rules Committee; on many major bills this is one hour, to be equally divided between the pros and cons. Each has a floor leader who controls the time, parceling it out in five-, three-, and one-minute lots; he generally reserves the most generous portion for himself. Newcomers or others deemed unworthy may be denied the opportunity to speak at all. Ex-Representative Weltner recalls trying to amend a House bill so as to permit 18-year-olds to vote: "By the time all committee members had spoken, and time had been allotted, I had less than one minute to convince my colleagues of the validity of my position. Under the circumstances, the cause was hopeless and discretion demanded that the amendment be withheld for another day—which never came."

As he sits in his rear pew watching the action, an inexperienced Congressman might wonder whether he has wandered into a schoolboy's study hall while the teacher is visiting the WC, or he may ponder the words of Augustus Foster, Secretary of the British Legation, who wrote on viewing the House in the early nineteenth century: "This undoubtedly is a miserable place, but the elect of all the states are assembled in it, and really such a gang to have the affairs of an empire wanting little of the size of Russia entrusted to them, makes one shudder." Members lounge while signing mail, reading newspapers, or eying the visitors' galleries for familiar faces or pretty ones. Some sit with their knees propped against seats in front of them, chatting or laughing; others lean on the rail at the rear of the chamber to smoke or swap jokes. Congressmen wander in and out aimlessly; attendance is generally sparse. When a half-dozen Congressmen announced this July [1968] that on a given date and hour they would urge the House not to adjourn without fully debating Vietnam, only twenty-odd Congressmen appeared—most of them to argue that in this busy election year Congressmen had no time to study war. Proceedings may be interrupted by several Congressmen who—largely as delaying tactics—"suggest the absence of a quorum"; each quorum call consumes at least thirty minutes (or 217.5 Congressman-hours) and two minutes after its conclusion one couldn't find a quorum with bloodhounds. The only advantage from these wasteful quorums lies with the unimaginative chair-warmers who faithfully answer so as to advertise on the stump their "100 percent voting-attendance" records—which means nothing, but may impress the homefolks.

The back-bench member during the 90th Congress may have wondered if he—and the nation—were victims of some gigantic practical joke. The three most pressing issues—Vietnam, racial injustices, the prospect of an indecisive presidential election that could be thrown into the House for compromised settlement—were not acted on at all. As for planning toward that vague but certain day when mankind has all but bred himself off the planet, perhaps the House will get around to that after the rights of those fun-loving sportsmen in the National Rifle Association have again been assured. "Congress attacks problems piecemeal," a young Tennessee member complained last year. "You build a highway thinking only of traffic. There's no concern with displaced homes or air pollution or conservation of soil, trees, or wildlife—though all are interrelated."

When the House last year voted down money to eradicate rodents in our slums, Congressmen made bad jokes: "This foolishness should be ended *rat-cheer* (right here)." On the same day our television screens gave us the return from London of James Earl Ray *and* a Los Angeles hearing for Sirhan Sirhan, the House was constrained to reject a gun-registration bill. While ghettos burned the House reacted by mangling anti-poverty, cities, and "safe-streets" bills. It refused to enact pending civil-rights bills while making it unlawful for citizens to demonstrate on Capitol Hill. More House members urged the forcible eviction of the improvident wretches of Resurrection City than received them to hear their complaints. In the same session in which the House found it necessary to expel one member because of his odious conduct—and the proud Senate censured one of its own—legislators were either unable or unwilling to write a meaningful Code of Conduct by which its members might both be adequately measured and trusted. As it approved billions for our costliest war in one chaotic, undemocratic, and underdeveloped state, the House slashed foreign-aid funds to an all-time low and may have risked future Vietnams.

Why the Closing Rush?

An American Political Science Association study reveals that the House devotes only half its time to legislative matters. My own observation in a decade on Capitol Hill was that most House members so invest less than one-third of their available hours. Nor did one often hear them discussing great issues in their recreations. They did, however, painstakingly quiz each other about the trends in mail from constituents and they freely exchanged tips on how best to exploit politically the advantages of incumbency.

Congressional offices produce floodtides of mail calculated to do little more than promote reelection. Weekly newsletters go out to thousands of individuals chosen because of their personal stations or influences or simply because some nameless office clerk lifted every fourth name off voter-registration lists. Such mailings are sent under the free franking privilege; while they carry excellent political clout, they are almost entirely self-serving. The same holds for TV and radio scripts offered for airings back home as "a public service."

In almost every House office men and women search and clip home-district newspapers so their Congressmen can congratulate Golden Wedding celebrants, bake-off contest winners, or insurance salesmen recently welcomed to the Million Dollar Club. Weepy condolences go out to grieving widows. New mothers are furnished infant-care booklets often accompanied by poems printed on blue or pink paper. Thousands of high school graduates, tomorrow's voters as well as the children of today's, receive special scrolls signed by their men in Washington. Congressional Christmas cards lists may exceed 50,000 in some offices, and staff members must begin addressing Yuletide envelopes on July 5th.

"Polling your people with questionnaires is a greater gimmick than mailing out free flower seed," a worldly old member advised me when I first arrived on Capitol Hill. "Everyone is flattered to be asked his opinion on great issues. You get credit for putting 'democracy' into action; you advertise yourself. By releasing the compiled results to newspapers you can live off the publicity for weeks. You can use your poll to justify questionable votes later, or even to beg off a dangerous commitment when the House leadership is twisting your arm. And the beautiful thing is you can mail your poll out *free!*"

Though many Congressmen despair of having more than fifteen minutes each day to consider questions of war or peace, the politician willing to concede obvious political advantages is rarer than the swimming stone. To hope seriously that Congress will vote reforms curtailing the use of free mailing privileges or require more worthy preparations by its members, is merely an exercise in futility. Those Congressmen shunted outside the House ruling circle, their dreams of world reform fading as they grow jaded in their nation's service, tend to spend increasing hours and energy in mundane busywork pursuits. Regrettably, it is these newcomers or undistinguished time-servers who should be acquainting themselves with the strengths and weaknesses of the House so that in days of future influence they will not endlessly repeat their elders' mistakes.

Though our legislators convene in earliest January, few bills reach the voting stages until April or later. The House is slow in its awakenings. Committees meet erratically and for no more than two hours; House sessions may be gaveled to order and adjourned within minutes; the legislative "weekend" begins on Thursday night and extends to Tuesday morning. Invariably, business stacks up and schedules collapse; by late summer or early fall it is necessary to launch grinding catch-up campaigns. Efficiency and tempers are impaired in those final hectic weeks, and good bills fall victim to hurried considerations while more malodorous proposals slip by in the closing rush. Some years ago Congress "reformed" itself so as to require adjournment by June 30th except in time of national emergency. Every year since, Congress has routinely declared just such "national emergencies" and has gone its usual way.

Even the most powerful of House members feel certain frustrations, for Congress is no longer the only power game in town. Its influences have been weakened by a historic reversal of the original legislative and executive roles, under which Congress hammered out much of the national policy and programs while placid Presidents largely accepted their acts or exercised their powers only to veto. Now, however, the President proposes virtually all legislative programs; Congress has been reduced to vetoing, mitigating, or emasculating. "The only really important law originated, shaped, and passed by Congress since the Second World War is the Taft-Hartley Act," Stewart Alsop has written, "and there may never be another."

There are other faults to disenchant the student of textbook civics or well-intended young legislators: the carelessness with which financial matters are transacted (a secretive "Swiss Bank" in the House where members may hide their more embarrassing contributions, hypocritical election laws requiring the filing of fraudulent reports); 40 percent of committee meetings held behind closed doors in "executive session" (encouraging chicanery or sheltering cowardice); the speeches Congressmen pass off as their own though they have been ghosted by biased lobbyists grinding their private axes.

In the mid-1950s then-Representative Eugene McCarthy of Minnesota formed a loose unit of some youngish liberals, ultimately known as "McCarthy's Mavericks," to give men of like minds a rallying point against the predominant House attitudes. Successes were few and minor but from this, in 1959, evolved the Democratic Study Group, whose membership reached a high of 180 following the Democratic landslide of 1964. DSG has its own elected officers, an executive committee, a whip system to rally votes, a full-time staff, and internal fund-raisers. It is strong on research, holds helpful seminars to enlighten and encourage confused Congressmen, and has actually known brief triumphs of legislation or in House internal matters.

Yet, DSG is only infrequently a significant force. Because of divisions within its own councils it has formulated no Vietnam policy, no gun-control guidelines, and as a unit it avoids the periodic fights over whether the House Un-American Activities Committee is worthy of new life and appropriations. It took no stand on the cigarette-labeling bill, staying silent even as crass lobbying by the tobacco industry virtually dictated the labeling limits. It split on whether Mississippi's all-white delegation should be seated at the 1964 Democratic National Convention at the expense of the integrated Freedom Democratic party delegation. This inability to vote consistently or work as a cohesive unit is noted in the higher citadels of power. In day-to-day struggles DSG is no match for the House with its outmoded rules, its indifferent leadership, or its crazed kings. The shoddy performance of the 90th Congress offers ample evidence.

The Measure of an Institution

Defenders of Congress contend that good and hard-working men are in it, that some of its wisest and best are among its elders, that it has approved many progressive programs or improved them, that it has in times of crisis performed its duty so that all ended well; that if, say, one in six Congressmen loosely use their offices then five are blameless.

Yet a lawmaking body is most fairly measured not merely by what it has done but by what it had opportunities to do, not by its atypical performances (the "first hundred days" New Deal Congress, and what Lyndon Johnson more than thirty years later would call "the amazing 89th"), but on all the bleak and insufficient sessions in between. It should be judged as much for those national crises it has allowed to ferment or has left unattended as by those it has served.

Nor can its atypically outstanding members alone atone for the sins of their numerous if less-talented colleagues. Nor can the five mythically "blameless" men be forgiven their omissions in permitting the sixth to repeatedly sully the offices of all. Nor do infrequent little ripples of reform excuse a stubborn clinging to archaic traditions which at once bind, stunt, or handicap the Congress by preventing its best work and encouraging the conspiracy of silence enforced against its more noble voices. It is that wide gulf between what Congress *is* against what it *could* be that is our national shame. "The parliament of the world's greatest democracy," Congressman Udall says, "is not a democratic institution."

I am reminded of a time when a single car thrummed along a flat roadbed at eighty miles per hour while lizards and jackrabbits bounded away in fright, and two men—a Congressman and his associate—monitored the President's grim speech by car radio. The men were riding the campaign trail in an isolated and windswept corner of the country and they were tired and discouraged, for the day's half-dozen campaign rallies had not been good ones. The Congressman knew he was in trouble that election year: the polls hinted at it, and now his constituents were affirming it by cool eyes and limp handshakes.

Then John F. Kennedy's voice came into the speeding car, filling it, metallic and yet strangely measured, and the President of the United States demanded the Soviet Union's removal of its missiles from Cuba. It was a tough speech, a chilling one, hinting of clearly unmentionable consequences. Any man hearing it might reasonably have experienced fear, not only for himself or for his nation but for all of mankind: the Russian or the Cuban or the Afghan. He may have been forgiven a sudden recognition of his own personal insignificance, or an urgent wish to reach a telephone to call someone he loved. And these were the rather conventional reactions of the Congressman's companion.

Until, suddenly, the Congressman let out a joyous whoop of the kind usually reserved to those who have won big at love or cards or war. "I've got him *now*," the Congressman cried in ecstasy: President Kennedy's popularity would skyrocket as the nation united in its common danger, his get-tough policy would be overwhelmingly popular in the Congressman's hawkish and extremist district; the Congressman would, therefore, rush to identify with the Kennedy position "and blow my opponent's little ass right out of the water."

The wind blew while the car hummed on and the Congressman talked in glee, and his associate sat staring down the flat stretch of lonesome road thinking of how not so many years before—before he had had his glimpses of political muscle, before he had learned the duplicities of the House and its self-serving ways, before winning had come to mean everything because winning begat seniority and seniority begat power—the Congressman might first have thought of other and more innocent asses blown out of larger and bloodier waters.

The Presidency

To a marked degree American public policy is shaped by the character of the President and what he does or does not do. The concepts by which Presidents and their administrators are evaluated are power, influence, leadership, and decision-making. The readings that follow all share these terms at the same time they emphasize different approaches to the study of the Presidency.

The authors of the first three readings construct models of the Presidency and identify Presidents who typify each. Hyman defines and analyzes three different concepts of the Presidency, as represented by Presidents Buchanan, Lincoln, and Cleveland. Hargrove identifies two basic types, the Presidents of Action (the two Roosevelts and Wilson) and the Presidents of Restraint (Taft, Hoover, and Eisenhower), and focuses on individual "personalities and skills as they have helped or hindered presidential leadership." Burns examines the Presidency from the standpoint of three models—Hamiltonian, Madisonian, and Jeffersonian—as typified in this century by Theodore Roosevelt, Taft, and Wilson, in order to try to understand the nature of the Presidency and the importance of the role perceptions that individual Presidents bring to the office.

Turning his attention to events of recent years, Schlesinger argues that the impact of Lyndon Johnson's Presidency has "compelled American historians and political scientists to begin to question their traditional and rather uncriti-

cal acceptance of the virtues of a strong Presidency." The experience of the
Vietnam war, he believes, forced scholars to face a disturbing question:

> Had they promoted the cult of the strong Presidency simply because, up
> to 1965, strong Presidents had mostly been doing things which historians
> and political scientists mostly wanted done? The spectacle of a strong
> President doing things they mostly did not want done suddenly stimulated
> many of us to take a fresh look at the old problem of presidential power.

How powerful is the American President? What are the limitations on presidential power? These questions are the focus of the article by Neustadt, whose
study views the presidential prerogative as the power of persuasion rather than
of command. Sorensen, former special counsel to the late President Kennedy,
analyzes the forces that shape presidential decisions. While denying that there
is any systematic formula of presidential decision-making, Sorensen insists
that:

> The fundamental nature of the White House makes it inevitable that vital
> decisions, either many or few, will be made there, either by the President
> or with his consent, and that the same basic forces and factors will re-
> peatedly shape those decisions.

What Is the President's True Role?

SIDNEY HYMAN

President Eisenhower has often used the front-page pulpit of the White House
press conference to speak about his concept of the Presidency. Yet, at his most
recent press conferences, what he had to say on this heard in connection with
the school desegregation controversy aroused special interest.

On August 20 [1958] he was asked whether he personally favored the principle of school desegregation set forth in the Supreme Court's decisions. Mr.
Eisenhower refused to answer. He explained that he had a President's duty to
support and enforce the rulings of the Court; it was enough that everyone understood that he meant to do just that. But he felt it was unwise to talk about
the merits of the desegregation decisions. To do so would "weaken public
opinion." Moreover, "the mere fact" that he "could disagree very violently with

Reprinted from Sidney Hyman, "What Is the President's True Role?", *The New York
Times Magazine*, September 7, 1958, pp. 17, 108–109. © 1958 by The New York Times
Company. Reprinted by permission.

a decision, and would so express" himself, would make it "much more difficult to carry out" his enforcement duties.

At the August 27 press conference Mr. Eisenhower went on to hint ambiguously that he felt the actual process of school desegregation might go a bit slower. But, once again, he stood on his earlier injunction not to speak for or against the principle of desegregation in the Court's rulings. "I would never give an opinion about my conviction about the Supreme Court decisions," the President said, "because such a statement would have to indicate either approval or disapproval, and I was never going to do it about any of their decisions."

Leaving all other things out of account, those who defend the President's position do so on two tactical grounds:

First, if he gave his personal views on the merits of desegregation, he would create a distracting precedent by which he would be expected to give his personal views on Court decisions in all other matters.

Second, in whichever way he spoke about the principle of desegregation, one or another section of the country would feel that he had personally affronted them. He was right, therefore, in trying to rally the North and the South around a neutralist standard—the standard of obedience to the laws of the Union, whatever the laws may be.

The President's critics, on the other hand, say that, by limiting his role to that of a policeman on the beat when a great national controversy rages, he is so many degrees removed from the critical political needs of the hour as to border on the airy-fairy.

If, in fact, he disagrees with the position of the Court, they say, his duty is to say so by submitting draft legislation to correct the desegregation decisions he disagrees with. On the other hand, if he agrees with the Court, he ought to say so in the kind of bold and majestic terms that can win stronger popular support for what he means to enforce. But to be wooden about it all, to assert that his role is limited to a coercive nightstick in the matter—if the school controversy should again call for coercion—is to abdicate the Presidency's true place in American life.

Against the background of this controversy, it becomes all the more relevant to ask: What, in fact, is Mr. Eisenhower's concept of the Presidency? How does his concept show itself in concrete cases? Is it similar to, or does it differ from, the concepts other Presidents have had of the job? Is it a concept that is suited to mid-twentieth-century American life?

To begin with other Presidents first: if all Presidents before 1953 were placed in a mirrored hall, three fairly distinct images, representing three fairly distinct concepts that Presidents have had about the place they hold, would repeat themselves on all sides.

Identified by their clearest exemplars, one is the Buchanan concept. It repeats itself in Presidents like the two Harrisons, Fillmore, Pierce, Grant, Garfield, Arthur, Taft, Harding, Coolidge and Hoover. The second is the Lincoln concept. It repeats itself in Presidents like Jefferson, Jackson, Polk, Wilson, the two Roosevelts and Truman. And the third is the Cleveland concept. More a mode of action than of conviction, it repeats itself in Presidents like the two Adamses, Van Buren, Johnson and Hayes.

Taken in order, the Buchanan concept rejects the idea of a President as the political leader of the nation. He is rather, as President Grant expressed it, "a purely administrative officer." This means that the main function of the President is to be efficient, honest, decorous, pious, and that he should get 100 cents out of every dollar spent. He should not have any vibrant two-way connections with the argumentative political earth of the nation. He should not engage in personalities. He should not make his own political consciousness— if he has any at all—the source of a national political consciousness. He should never make any great demands on the people. As a model of self-abnegation, he should diminish his own size in the eyes of the people.

The very last thing he should do is to view his presidential oath of office as a reserve source of power that could rally the nation when all other organs of government stall in a crisis. Buchanan, for example, offered the legal opinion in January, 1860, that he had no power to use force against the seceding Southerners. All he or anyone else in the government could do was to "conciliate them." Come what may, in any movement of his parts, the Buchanan concept limits the President to a tight legal circuit involving the Congress and the Court.

Nor within that tight legal circuit should he be the main source of energy, leading the Congress from above. The political initiative rests always with the Congress. It remains for the President merely to administer the objects and situations defined for him by the Congress. In this general view of things, then, a good President is one who best integrates himself with the congressional group.

The Lincoln concept of the Presidency begins where the Buchanan concept ends. Political instead of legalistic in emphasis, it is highly articulate, highly argumentative, and it has a keen taste for political battle. Its view of man is nonangelic. It accepts conflict as a natural aspect of life itself. And since it does, it looks upon partisan politics as a creative instrument that can define and, to some extent at least, resolve things in dispute.

Since it is bent on change and innovation, it tries at times to race ahead and, by the measures taken, to produce, instead of await, an event. From this cause, it seems to be supercharged with willfulness. It communicates a will to decide, a will to force the proof that the decision was correct and a will to assume primary responsibility for what was decided. "Send the problem over to me," Roosevelt often used to say to his aides. "My shoulders are big enough to carry it." And Truman said much the same thing with the well-known sign on his desk reading: "The buck stops here."

From all these causes, the Lincoln concept makes the President himself something more than an administrative officer or a civil service reformer or a chief of state or a comptroller of the currency. It makes the President the nation's first legislator, the inventor, as well as the executor of policy, the source as well as the summation of the nation's political consciousness. In every major crisis, it places the President in the most exposed position of the firing line, like a patriot king leading troops in battle.

"Those who accept great charges," said Jefferson in a reference to his own conduct as President, "have a duty to risk themselves on great occasions, when the safety of the nation or some of its very high interests are at stake." And Lincoln repeated after him: "I felt that measures, otherwise unconstitutional, might become lawful by becoming indispensable to the preservation of the Constitution through the preservation of the nation."

The Lincolnian concept, finally, does not raise the President over the Congress or the Court. It accepts the constitutional proposition that each of these must be strong in its own right to do its own work. Each has a duty to preserve its own integrity against invasion by another. None can surrender its organic powers and duties even by a voluntary act.

The Cleveland concept of the Presidency shuttles between the other two. Now it seems to say the presidential office is chiefly an administrative one; now it seems to say that it is also a political one. Now it talks of leading a march toward brave new horizons; now it draws back from the adventure. Now it seems prepared to follow the lead of the Congress; now it seems disposed to tell the Congress to mind its own business, and to keep its nose out of executive business.

Yet, if there is any distinctive trait about Clevelandism, it is the fact that in this concept of the Presidency the essential presidential function lies in defensive directions. It lies in the legal (or political) veto, in disengagement, in the negation of what others have put into motion, or in the use of only enough executive energy to maintain an existing kinetic equilibrium. It was Cleveland, for example, who informed the Congress that, if it declared war on Spain, he could not be counted on to run the war. It was John Adams, almost a century earlier, who said virtually the same thing to his own Federalist Party when it demanded a full-scale war against France.

And now for the Eisenhower concept of the Presidency.

In part, at least, it had been spelled out for him by the Republican Party in the twenty years preceding his nomination and election as President in 1952. During those twenty years, when the White House was in the hands of two Democratic Presidents who had embraced the Lincoln concept of the Presidency, the Republicans had only the congressional forum where they could bid for the rule of the national mind. So, from that forum, they popularized the idea that everything that had gone wrong in the passing years could be laid at the door of the White House. There executive usurpations of power—and, worse still, a philanthropic tolerance of crime, corruption and Communist treason—were a daily routine.

The way to salvation, then, lay in scaling down the authority of the White House in American life. It lay in ending all further "executive usurpations of power." It lay in restoring our constitutional balance through a return to the Congress of the rightful powers denied it by a lawless executive. Let these reforms be made, and the nation might return to a golden age where all men could be like gods, and all women like woodland nymphs.

Yet the stridency with which this was said served only to intensify the growing national weariness with strife, and a growing national impatience with the whole order of politics and politicians. The hour seemed to demand a man who was wholly divorced from partisan strife, who stood above politics, who stood for the transcendent spirit of the nation as a single whole, and thus could unite the parts that were sorely divided.

The man was found in General Eisenhower. But the price he had to pay in order to win the Republican nomination was to accept the theory about the Presidency which the party had developed in the previous twenty years. Except that it was attached to the image of the D-Day commander, the incisive man of action, it was, in essence, the Buchanan theory. Throughout the 1952 presidential campaign, for example, General Eisenhower talked about the need to end "executive usurpations of power" and "to restore the Congress to its rightful place in the government." As part of the same minimizing view of the President's role of political leadership, he promised to bring in "the best business brains" to help run the government, since the running of the government by the Presidency was primarily a problem in administration, like running a big corporation.

Still, the Buchanan theory of the Presidency which General Eisenhower brought into the White House, and clung to for a long while, was not altogether something imposed on him by his party. By its inoffensiveness it seemed, rather, to be a logical corollary to the President's highly idealistic outlook on man himself. Watching and listening to Mr. Eisenhower at close range, one gained the sense that his thought process might have gone something like this:

All men are by nature good. Government alone corrupts them. Therefore, to the extent that government can be reduced in importance, the natural goodness of men will assert itself in social cooperation, voluntarily given. However irreconcilable rival interests may seem to be, once their representative men sit down and talk things over without the intervention of government, natural goodness will resolve all difficulties.

His own presidential function, then, was to be "the President of all the people." He should be a compassionate shaft of light within whose arc all men would want to live up to the better angels of their nature.

He voiced some of this in the summer of 1953 when he dedicated the Theodore Roosevelt home at Oyster Bay as a national shrine. He had recently come under criticism because of what seemed to be his overly tolerant willingness to allow the committees of the Congress to usurp, or at least nullify, presidential functions. As in his current relationship to the Court, he had even denied himself the right to comment on the work of congressional investigation committees. Added to this, he was under criticism for failing to take command of the Republican Party, to knock a few heads together, and thus get congressional support for his program. The ceremony at Oyster Bay seemed a suitable occasion to explain himself.

The President said that he had been studying the life of T. R., and felt it was altogether wrong to think of him as a man who mounted a horse and rode up Pennsylvania Avenue into the halls of Congress to demand that it do what he wanted. The truth was, said Mr. Eisenhower, that T. R. "used every form of polite advance, including many breakfasts." What Mr. Eisenhower failed to read, however, was the passage of his life story where Theodore Roosevelt wrote that he had "tried to get along with the Congress," found it was impossible, and so "appealed over the heads of the Congress to the people, who are the masters of both the Congress and the President."

With the passing of time, President Eisenhower seemed to find that he could not do any part of the work of the modern Presidency if he tied himself to the limitations inherent in the Buchanan concept. But what if he acted out the Lincoln concept? From a Republican standpoint, he would be guilty of the evils seen in his two Democratic predecessors. But if it was not to be Buchananism or Lincolnism, what remained?

The solution seemed to lie in acting out the Cleveland concept. And that, apparently, is where the Eisenhower concept of the Presidency has found its gravitational center. The Presidency does not lead. It vetoes and stops bad things other men start. It absolves itself from any duty to march well in advance of events and, by the measures taken, forestall evils.

It remains to be said that all three presidential concepts—Buchanan, Lincoln and Cleveland—are "constitutional." Divorced from all else, no one is inherently better or worse than any other. What makes them better or worse is their relevancy to the needs of the time.

If there ever was a time when the Buchanan or Cleveland concept was sufficient unto the hour, the hour has long since been left behind by the reovlutionary sweeps of history. At home and abroad, long-familiar landmarks are vanishing overnight. Old proportions are giving way to a reshuffling of what promises to be new proportions between minorities and majorities. Old lines of discrimination between justice and injustice, liberty and oppression, suddenly seem to be as indistinct as lines drawn in water. Somewhere, somehow, in the oceanic churnings, new lines will be drawn.

In such times, it would seem that the only truly relevant concept of the Presidency that can encompass and then transfigure the changes of the hour into creative, durable forms is a Lincolnian concept of the Presidency. For such a concept, above all other things previously said about it, makes the President himself the source and the master engineer of all revolutions of consent. And, on the assumption that the dominant aspect of mid-twentieth-century life is the multitude of revolutions of consent going on simultaneously around the world, the American President, of all our national officers, is the only one we have who is structurally situated to help bring about a spirit of consent to new things that will be rooted in a new habit of the heart lived lucidly, instead of depending always on force for its sanctions.

Presidents of Action and Presidents of Restraint

ERWIN C. HARGROVE

This . . . is a study of the men who have shaped the modern Presidency. The focus is on their personalities and skills as they have helped or hindered presidential leadership. Presidents of Action are compared to Presidents of Restraint in terms of the personal drives, skills, and values they have brought to the office, and conclusions are drawn about the consequences of each type of "political personality" and style of leadership for the office.

The three Presidents of Action who have most shaped the presidential office are the two Roosevelts and Wilson. Each, in his own way, greatly amplified presidential power. Each was a political artist whose deepest needs and talents were served by a political career. Presidents Truman, Kennedy, and Johnson are considered briefly as Presidents of this tradition.

The Presidents of Restraint—Taft, Hoover, and Eisenhower—went to the White House from careers as nonpolitical technicians. They did not put a high value on personal or presidential power, and in the course of their careers they did not develop political skills. Their values were hostile to strong presidential leadership, to the manipulation of others, to popular emotion, and to politics in general.

American political culture contains two important and conflicting views of the Presidency. The Whig theory, seen in the Presidents of Restraint, is almost an anti-theory, for it preaches that the incumbent should deliberately exercise restraint on his power and influence. It was shaped out of a fear of a strong, popular Presidency. This tradition does not value political skill in the President but rather stresses rectitude and dignity.

The irony is that such a view of the Presidency impedes an effective discharge of presidential tasks. A sense of power and the willingness to search for it and use it with political skill are essential today.

The other tradition calls for strong presidential leadership, for the Presidency to be the agency of popular reform. However, within this tradition, the Presidents of Action who reflect it must continually do battle with those in Congress and the public who hold to the opposing model of presidential leadership. The Presidents of Action often cause counterreactions that may eventually throw up Presidents of Restraint.

This lack of congruence between the political culture and the central political office exists in none of the other English-speaking democracies. It is in part a function of the dual nature of the presidential office which is that of both a national symbol and a partisan leader. It also reflects differing views of the importance of government action. Progressives favor presidential leadership and conservatives are skeptical of it.

Almost all students of the modern Presidency agree that the President today must be strong and skillful in his leadership of public opinion, of Congress, and of the bureaucracy beneath him. Skill has two components: a sensitivity to power relationships and the ability to act to maximize personal, that is, presidential, power in each of these areas. The President has relatively little formal power to win compliance for his policies from publics, Congress, or administrators. He must find informal ways to persuade them to support him and this requires political skill.

A set of explicit norms for the conduct of each of these presidential roles runs throughout this book. The Presidents are compared and judged in terms of the capacity their political personalities and, therefore, their skills give them to play these roles.

It is assumed that the President must lead and educate public opinion. It is his chief source of power in Washington in his dealings with other holders of power. He needs technical skill, for example, speaking ability, a sense of timing, and empathy for public moods. But, more than this, he needs the ability and will to fit his policy leadership to an over-all strategy of leadership of public opinion. He must put events and policies in context and must gradually prepare the public for new departures. He must not continually lay his reputation on the line without success, but he must try to lead if he wants to be effective. If the President did not articulate the needs of the nation our democracy would be poorer.

All Presidents are now expected to be legislative leaders. Congress requires such leadership in order to be effective in its operation because it is not organized to lead. However, the internal organization and processes of Congress and the perspectives of its members, which are so different from those of the White House, present real obstacles to presidential legislative leadership. He can use his messages, his budget, bills drafted in the executive branch, the veto power, and open appeal to the people as levers against Congress. He can also use patronage, the pork barrel, personal persuasion, accommodation and compromise, and the extraction of agreement out of collective bargaining. He must never cease to press for action and yet he cannot seem to dominate for fear of injuring congressional pride. It is a job for a man who delights in the political process.

The President has difficulty in controlling the federal executive because of its size, variety, and complexity and the fact that much of it is independent of him in law and in fact because of long-established ties with Congress. He cannot simply issue commands and expect compliance within his own branch. He cannot count on receiving the information he needs from official channels. Officials beneath him are always tempted to go into business for themselves and to tell him only what they want him to know. In addition, they are not likely to see what he needs to know. The President must ensure that the essential decisions of state remain in his hands and he must also ensure that he receives the information necessary for such decisions, as well as seeing that the decisions are implemented once they are made. Thus, he needs as many sources of information as possible, including unofficial channels. And he must so organize his administration that the major decisions come to him and he can make his presence felt throughout bureaucracy as a galvanizing force. There is no one form of organization that will do all these things, but the test of presidential skill in administration is his sensitivity and response to these inherent problems.

It is contended here that the first requisite for doing these tasks well is a sense of personal—and thus, presidential—power. This sense of power is a function of "political personality," which is an amalgam of the drives, values, and traits of the leader. It is our premise that the skills of leadership are rooted in political personality.

The model of political personality used in this study contains four variables: needs, mental traits, values, and the ego, or unifying agent, which joins the first three factors into a recognizable personality. In practice these variables so interlace that they cannot be separated and this is the value of the concept of "ego integration." We avoid the error of reducing our explanations of behavior to any one factor. The personality acts as a unity.[1]

We do not see "needs." They are constructs inferred from observation of behavior. A leader who continually seeks attention in private and public life is said to have a need for attention that his dramatizing behavior serves. Needs and mental qualities, of course, fuse together, but our use of the latter term is a common-sense one. Does a man's mind seem to have been logical and rigorous or illogical, impressionistic, and empathetic? Did he feel at home in flux or seek ordered relationships? It is obvious that mental traits may reflect needs or may have been instrumental in the development of some needs over others. This is a chicken-egg question. Certainly, mental traits serve needs and from the combination abilities develop. It is postulated that leaders seek to gratify their needs in the playing of political roles. They find some roles more congenial than others and shape roles to fit their predispositions of need, mentality, and ability.

The category of political values, or ideology, has two components: beliefs about policy and beliefs about proper behavior of the leader. Ideology is often congruent with needs and abilities. It cannot be reduced to a projection of personality needs. In the process of personal development, needs and mental traits shape abilities and all of these blend with a congenial set of values, which in turn help shape needs and mental traits. The edges of each factor are softened so that all can live together in varying degrees of comfort. The ego is the component of personality that organizes and directs these forces and mediates between them and the world. We shall assume in this study that political acts are most often a compound of several levels of political personality. It is interesting that these levels seem to reinforce each other as factors in motivation.

The choices that go into political artistry are rooted in stable predispositions, and in this sense they are intuitive as much as they are calculated. The situation helps shape the strategy and tactics of leadership but the skill in strategy or tactics is likely to be summoned forth from the reservoir of the unconscious. Most people who are quite good at something do not know why it is so. They work hard to refine their talent but the talent originally existed. Neustadt contends that the choices that go into the pursuit of presidential "power" are a function of "perception," that is, whether or not the President is sensitive to power relationships, both potential and actual.[2] Perception is a function of personality. Some people are more sensitive to power relationships than others because of the differences in their unconscious adaptive mechanisms, implicit values, mental qualities, goals, and so forth. . . .

The Presidents of Action

The two Roosevelts and Wilson shaped the modern Presidency and we shall look at the institutional contributions of each in detail. Our theme here is the qualities they had in common that made them political "masters." Their political skill was the primary factor in their policy achievements and their impact on the Presidency. They developed a tradition of skill and a set of ground rules for presidential effectiveness that have greatly influenced succeeding Presidents of Action. In fact, they influenced each other. Wilson took his ideas of strong presidential leadership, in part, from the example of Theodore Roosevelt in office. Franklin Roosevelt admired and copied both "Uncle Ted" and Wilson, whom he served. What characteristics of political personality did they have in common?

1. They were driven by the need for personal power and this was the initial reason for their choice of a political career. In each man the quality of the need to influence and direct others was different but this kind of drive is essential to great political skill.

2. Their needs seems to have stimulated them to develop their abilities to influence others. In their youth and early careers they gradually shaped themselves into effective leaders in response, not to their policy ideals, but to their inner imperatives, that is, the needs for power and attention.

The developing relationships between needs, natural abilities, and skills of leadership are charted in each chapter. An example of this interaction would be Theodore Roosevelt's dramatizing ability. A need for attention seemed to be at the root of this skill, and out of that need acting and self-dramatizing talents were developed. Perhaps the talents stimulated the need. This is not important. What is important is that this private skill was eventually used for political goals. Roosevelt served his own need for attention while he served his goals for achievement. We can see in each of these men that beneath the threshold of public action there was a second level of private need, that is, to influence others, that was always pushing, reinforcing, and guiding their public actions. The private need increased their public effectiveness. These private needs cannot be explained by their public roles. They antedated these roles and reinforced them.

3. Mental traits, another component of political personality, also contributed to political skill. In each case, qualities of mind and of temperament fitted together, for example, Franklin Roosevelt was empathetic and intuitive in his human relations and flexible and an empiricist in his mode of thinking. As we shall see, this congruence was important for the performance of presidential roles. Needs and drives and intellectual qualities gave these men a sensitivity to power relationships.

4. Values gave them a sense of purpose in the Presidency that increased their effectiveness as leaders. Technical skill alone would not have been enough to account for their policy achievements. They came to office in periods of American history when there was need for national innovation and a redefinition of national goals. All were equal to the task. The fact that they were all "cultural outsiders" to American business civilization may help to explain their role as reformers. The two Roosevelts were aristocrats with roots in a preindustrial way of life. Wilson, a Southerner by birth and upbringing, and an academic by profession, was also an outsider in his era. Each man, therefore, found one variety or another of progressivism congenial because of its criticism of the values and practices of a business civilization. However, they had "conservative" roots as well. They were not radicals but rather reformers who

were well equipped to be brokers between the past and future. They were also "marginal men" who lived and worked in several American worlds without being fully committed to any particular world. This gave them a perspective for the role of broker leaders.

5. Each man was favored by the times in which he became President. This was less true of Theodore Roosevelt than the other two, and his achievements were correspondingly less. But, in all three instances, skills of leadership were most effective when supported by favorable situations.

6. Their strengths were also their weaknesses. The same intense drives that sent them into political life and accounted for their skill and success were also their undoing at times. Theodore Roosevelt kept restraint on his ruder impulses while in the White House because he loved and gloried in the job. Out of office, at a relatively young age, he was unhappy and frustrated because his talents had no outlet. His subsequent bid to return to power smashed his own party and ruined his political career. Woodrow Wilson built many of his successes on his moral rigidity and refusal to compromise. But, in the fight for Senate approval of the League of Nations, his rigidity defeated him. Franklin Roosevelt's self-confidence was a source of national strength in time of crisis, but in the fight to pack the Supreme Court it betrayed him. There was a tragic flaw in the character of each of these men that was bound up with their talent. However, their darker qualities were not harmful to democratic institutions. When these drives got out of control they were self-defeating. The man and his policies suffered but American institutions were not harmed. The most important restraints on the drive for power, in each case, were not institutional but personal. They could not have succeeded as democratic leaders without self-control and conscience and belief in democracy as a way of life.

7. The unique contribution of each man to the institution of the Presidency was a consequence of his political personality. They shaped presidential roles in ways that were congenial to them. . . .

The Presidents of Restraint

Taft, Hoover, and Eisenhower had much in common. They were eminently non-political Presidents.

1. None had a drive for personal power like that seen in the Presidents of Action. Nor did they have self-dramatizing impulses. They shared a desire for order, harmony, and self-restraint.

2. Their needs stimulated them to develop abilities but they were not political abilities. Taft became a good judge, Hoover a fine engineer, and Eisenhower an able military leader. In each case, they emphasized technical skills in their pre-presidential work and did not spend years developing the skills of moving others by speaking, bargaining, and manipulating as did the Presidents

of Action. Hoover and Eisenhower did develop considerable ability to make larger organizations work smoothly but this was solely administrative ability in Hoover's case and diplomatic skill in Eisenhower's case. Their philosophies of personal behavior made the manipulation of others by political skill distasteful to them.

3. Each exhibited mental qualities of order, logic, and regularity. They were good with tangible matters but poor at perceiving intangibles. They were strong in structured situations, when they could exercise some control over alternatives, but weak in unstructured situations. They did not enjoy the fast-moving political process. They had little tactical skill and lacked the ability to conceive and carry out complex strategies of leadership. Because of their mental traits and character structures they could not ride many horses at once.

4. Their values complemented this style of leadership. Their conservatism often made them skeptical of the need for government action. Their Whig theory of the Presidency undermined their effectiveness in behalf of the ends they did seek. They put great emphasis on personal rectitude and the wrongness of trying to influence others by any means other than reasonable argument. Because they were technical men they overestimated the power of reason in the political process and underestimated the facts of power and conflicts of interest and values. They did not value political craftsmanship.

They were political "outsiders" unlike the Presidents of Action, but they were cultural "insiders" in the sense that they were not marginal men. Each had a stable social identity rooted in the Middle Western boyhood they experienced. They grew up in simple homogeneous environments and were trained in maxims of "Americanism," which they never really lost. This was especially true of Hoover, who lived abroad for some years, and of Eisenhower, who lived within a military world. Cut off from American life in many ways, each held to the simple maxims of his youth. This was the political culture they reflected in their values and character traits. Their view of the Presidency had its roots here.

5. Taft and Hoover did not serve in times favorable to their goals or styles of leadership. Eisenhower was luckier in this regard. Taft ran up against the Progressive movement and Hoover against a depression. In both cases, their conservative values and style of leadership were not what was felt to be needed in the White House. This must be taken into account when we judge their skills of leadership. Situations did not favor the exercise of the skills they did possess. Eisenhower benefitted by and helped to create the era of political good feeling in the 1950s. He saw it as one of his greatest accomplishments that he had helped to unify the nation after the harsh political warfare of the last Truman years. This was the kind of skill he valued. In this sense he was a successful President by his own lights.

6. None of these men made important contributions to the powers or opera-

tion of the Presidency. Given their Whig theory, we would not expect them to have done so. In different ways, and for varying reasons, each was reluctant to play all presidential roles to the hilt. Just as they resisted the tide of the progressive movement in its many forms, so did they resist the trend toward greater presidential power, which was carried along by the Presidents of Action. . . .

The Two Styles Compared

1. LEADERSHIP OF PUBLIC OPINION

The Presidents of Action were skillful in this role. The two Roosevelts developed dramatizing skills in initial response to the need for attention. These skills were first developed in private life and then used in politics. They had great intuitive sensitivity as to how to get and keep the attention of others in the playing of political roles. Certainly the way in which they led public opinion reflected this sensitivity. This need was the root of their great empathy for the thoughts and moods of others, which was a staple in their political style. Wilson did not seem to have the need for self-advertisement and his political style reflected this fact. His technical skill at leading public opinion was rooted in his drive for power over the minds of men and he developed oratorical skill in response to this imperative. But his was not a dramatizing style.

Skill in leading public opinion in all three men was also a function of their larger sense of political leadership. Their conception of the Presidency and their sense of purpose in their programs were also important factors. Needs for attention and power were likewise a part of this larger set of motivations.

The Presidents of Restraint did not have the technical skills that we value in leading public opinion because none had the needs that stimulate such skills. If anything, their personalities would not permit self-dramatization. None of their pre-presidential training encouraged them to develop such skills. Their values also were a handicap. They deprecated drama, emotion in politics, and tricks and manipulations.

Eisenhower is a possible exception to this. He was personable and popular and liked to show himself to crowds. This reflected his general liking for people and his desire to be liked. But he seems to have underestimated his ability to move people in large numbers and to have felt uncomfortable as a popular hero. His needs did not drive him to dramatize himself.

However, more important for him as well as for Taft and Hoover is the fact that none of them had very well-developed strategic ideas about how to lead public opinion. Their conception of the Presidency, their distrust of many techniques of leadership, and their resistance to popular reform suggests that this kind of President finds it most congenial to be a symbolic leader above the political strife. The hard tasks of political leadership would seem to be more congenial to those leaders who are initially propelled to win public acceptance of themselves as persons. In them this search becomes part of the fight to win acceptance for policy. In both cases, the larger conception of leadership complements needs.

2. LEGISLATIVE LEADERSHIP

The Presidents of Action possessed technical skill in leading Congress. This skill was initially rooted in their needs for personal power. Over the years, and especially in their early careers, they developed abilities that served this need. This emotional imperative can be seen as a consistent undercurrent in their legislative leadership. It was an extra incentive.

The need for power had a different quality in each case. The two Roosevelts were perhaps not so driven as Wilson and therefore they could enjoy the process of leading for its own sake without having to feel that they must win every fight. They were capable of greater flexibility than Wilson. In this sense they were more fitted for the demands of presidential legislative leadership. Wilson's inner demands were too rigid at times. He could lead Congress effectively only in certain kinds of situations. This suggests that the need for personal power, although necessary to skill, can be so intense that it becomes self-defeating. It may be that the kind of personality seen in modern dictators such as Hitler cannot rise to the top in stable democracies. Their demands for power are too intense.

The strategic skill of the Presidents of Action was rooted in the drive for personal power, but also in their conceptions of presidential leadership, their sense of purpose, and their experience in developing strategies by which to lead others. Needs supplied the technical skill but not the larger sense of strategy and purpose. Their values reinforced their skills. They saw themselves as midwives of history. The fact that other men accepted this as true helps to explain their success but the certainty itself was a factor in their sense of efficacy and thus in their skill.

The Presidents of Restraint were not driven by the need for personal power and therefore lacked the skills that follow from such a need. Not driven by the need for personal power and coming from technical professions, they emphasized reason, appeals to unity, and morality as the means of persuasion and they downgraded manipulative leadership.

Of course their lack of a larger sense of legislative strategy was due to their conception of the Presidency, their deference to Congress, and their desire to be Presidents above the political struggle. They also put less emphasis on dominating Congress because they wanted less government action than the Presidents of Action. Taft and Eisenhower lacked a sure sense of legislative purpose, which weakened their ability to lead. Hoover's sense of purpose was so rigid as to be disabling. It is interesting that the self-defeating qualities in the leadership styles of both Hoover and Wilson seem to have been rooted in similar traits of political personality, their compulsive stubbornness, mental rigidity, and moralism.

3. ADMINISTRATIVE LEADERSHIP

The drive for personal power of the Presidents of Action informed their sense of presidential power. As in legislative leadership, the two Roosevelts loved process for its own sake more than Wilson, who was more a prisoner of his need to dominate than they. This was a handicap to him in controlling bureaucracy.

Each of them saw administration as a political dimension, and saw that their control was by no means automatic. Thus, while their need for power gave them a sensitivity to presidential power, their conception of the Presidency as the center of decision was the dominant and guiding factor in their style of administration.

It is not clear that there was any relationship between their policy ideals and programs and their style of administration.

The lack of need for power in the Presidents of Restraint seems to have dulled their sense of presidential power. Hoover might seem an exception to this since he was so determined to dominate his administration. But he did not so much want power over persons as authority over organization and mastery of problems. He saw associates and subordinates as means to these ends.

As we have seen in the performance of every role, for both types, the sensitivity to and need for personal power was only one part of a larger conception of administrative leadership. Conceptions of the Presidency, a dislike of conflict, a technical background, and qualities of intellect all caused these Presidents to fail to see the political dimension of administration.

As with the Presidents of Action, there does not seem to have been any relationship between their policies and programs and their administrative style.

Real consequences follow from the administrative styles of each type of President. The two Roosevelts kept superb control over bureaucracy by treating it as a political area in which the problems of presidential power were essentially the same as those in other areas. This strategy not only made for control but it also pushed information up to the Chief Executive and gave him channels by which to implement policy. Taft and Eisenhower did not keep sufficient control over bureaucracy and thus tended to deny themselves needed information and have difficulty implementing policies once they were made. Wilson and Hoover were similar in their type of administration, which was "close to the vest," and both suffered from their unwillingness to delegate authority. This common style was perhaps rooted in their common rigidity of mind and ideology. Wilson was perhaps a less effective administrator than Hoover because of his drive for power. It was almost too intense to be useful.

4. AN IDEAL TYPE OF PRESIDENT?

The two Roosevelts came closest to having the kinds of political personalities that can best perform presidential roles by the criteria that have been advanced. They needed attention and power and these needs shaped their skills of leadership. However, these needs were not so intense as to be self-defeating. They had flexible, empirical minds, which permitted them to be adaptable and resourceful in finding solutions to problems. They seldom strayed too far in their thinking from what the traffic would bear but they were always pushing to go a little beyond that point. Their conceptions of the presidential office, as a place for political leadership, informed and guided all their efforts. They were "political men" whose image of the Presidency was of themselves in the White House. These men are rare but they are essential to effective presidential leadership.

We can expect certain consequences for the conduct of the office from such men. They will try to lead the nation in new directions, to educate the public. They will try to dominate Congress, with varying degrees of success, depending upon general political conditions. They will increase bureaucratic vitality and innovation by their catalytic style of administration. In sum, they will serve the principal purpose that a President of Action can serve, of being a catalyst to the national life. . . .

The Future

. . . Theodore Roosevelt began the creation of the modern Presidency and Wilson and Franklin Roosevelt completed the task. The Presidents of Restraint resisted many of these trends and added little to the institution itself. It has been suggested that Presidents in this tradition, and particularly conservative Presidents, are not at home in the White House because the office has become the agency of popular reform, and the catalyst to government action.

Does this mean that all modern Presidents should be Democrats, that is, Presidents of Action? I would hope not. The Republican Party must develop greater respect for political skill in the Presidency. There is a great need for a definition of skillful presidential leadership in terms of conservative values. Of course, the Republican Party could make itself over in the liberal image of the Democrats but this seems unlikely. A moderate ideology will have to be developed by leaders who can bring clear skills to the Presidency, not just the anti-skills of the three Presidents of Restraint.

However, for this to happen, the American public will have to be disabused of the notion that a politician in the White House is something of a scandal. We need expert politicians in the Presidency more than ever. It is only through politics that a democratic nation can be governed.

The Three Models Reconsidered

JAMES MacGREGOR BURNS

At the close of the eighteenth century the Washington-Hamilton administration had been followed by a Madisonian type of President in John Adams and a Jeffersonian type in Thomas Jefferson. Doubtless by pure chance the same sequence occurred at the start of the twentieth century in Theodore Roosevelt, William Howard Taft, and Woodrow Wilson. This sequence under more recent political conditions makes possible a closer view of the three types of Presidency in action. Happily for our purposes, these three men had more coherent and articulate theories of presidential power and its limitations than any other Presidents in this century.

The Madisonian Model

The *Madisonian* model, in this century, has embraced these concepts:

1. *Checks and Balances.* Each branch of the federal government possesses some kind of veto power over the two other branches. At a minimum each branch must protect its own independence arising from its unique constitutional powers and bolstered by its special constituency and method of recruitment. Even the so-called weak Presidents of the latter nineteenth century made gallant, and eventually successful, efforts to protect their powers as Chief Executives, notably their appointive powers. The widest power and the broadest duty of the President, Taft once observed, was the constitutional provision that "he shall take care that the laws be faithfully executed."[3]

2. *Minority Rights.* The chief purpose of checks and balances is the protection of minority rights. Because, as Madison noted so brilliantly in the 51st Federalist Paper, ambition must be made to counteract ambition and the "interest of the man must be connected with the constitutional rights of the place,"

each major constituency in the nation—each major interest or region or ideology—had its "own" branch or sector of government that would protect its interests. Note, however, that this was the expression of minority rights *against* federal power; this theory did not grapple with the question of the achievement of minority rights *through* government.

3. *Anti-Majoritarianism*. By the same token, the Madisonian formula quite deliberately aimed at thwarting popular majorities from getting control of government and turning it toward their own ends—usually seen as "tyrannical" or "despotic" ends. The great fear was that a majority would get control of all the branches of government, for the accumulation of powers in the same hands— even hands as numerous as majority control would imply—was considered the "very definition of tyranny." So various barricades were erected against majority rule through the mechanisms of automatic stabilizing devices, such as the presidential veto and (implicitly) judicial review, powered by separate and mutually conflicting sources of political energy in the various constituencies supporting the House, Senate, and President.

4. *Prudent, Limited Government*. The major inarticulate premise of the Madisonians was a belief in deliberate, circumscribed government, at the national level especially. They feared rash governmental action; they feared above all that government might succumb to the mob. They did not propose that government be deadlocked indefinitely—after all, they saw the need *to be governed*—but they preferred that government wait until such a popular consensus was built up in favor of some action that all the separate interests and constituencies would have been brought into agreement.

The Madisonian model required that each branch of government observe constitutional limitations and proprieties. Nobody has expressed this point of view better than Taft in a passage from his *Our Chief Magistrate and His Powers* that was clearly designed as an answer to Theodore Roosevelt's Stewardship theory: "The true view of the Executive functions is, as I conceive it," said Taft, "that the President can exercise no power which cannot be fairly and reasonably traced to some specific grant of power or justly implied and included within such express grant as proper and necessary to its exercise. Such specific grant must be either in the Federal Constitution or in an act of Congress passed in pursuance thereof. There is no undefined residuum of power which he can exercise because it seems to him to be in the public interest. . . . The grants of Executive power are necessarily in general terms in order not to embarrass the Executive within the field of action plainly marked for him, but his jurisdiction must be justified and vindicated by affirmative constitutional or statutory provision, or it does not exist. There have not been wanting, however, eminent men in high public office holding a different view and who have insisted upon the necessity for an undefined residuum of Executive power in the public interest. . . ."[4]

The Jeffersonian Model

The *Jeffersonian* model embraces somewhat antithetical concepts:[5]

1. *Unified Political System.* A united group of political leaders and government officials overcome the checks and balances (while leaving the constitutional provisions intact) through party control of the machinery of government. This party control depends on the existence of a coherent and disciplined party that won office at the last election on a meaningful and principled party platform and hence can claim a popular mandate. The leaders act as a team—usually through some such body as a cabinet.

2. *Collegial Leadership.* The party leader becomes President and governs through his party. His main responsibility in policy and programs is to the party and majority that elected him. He is a "team man" in office as well as out of office: that is, he governs with at least the passive consent of his fellow party leaders, who have some independent power. While the President as party leader can operate within fairly wide limits, ultimately he is governed by party purpose and limited, as well as supported, by the other national party leaders. In practice his leadership cuts across all sectors of government and politics, except perhaps the judiciary, but in style he may be much more the undramatic corporate leader, like Baldwin, Attlee, or Macmillan in Britain, than the heroic type.

3. *Majority Rule.* Government can act on the basis of a mandate endorsed by a majority of the voters, who have judged the competing platforms and candidates. Once granted power on this basis, the party leaders can govern subject to only two basic limitations: free criticism protected by the Bill of Rights and other constitutional safeguards; and free elections within a limited span of time. Otherwise the leaders can override traditional institutional and political restraints on action, even to the point of changing machinery (such as congressional procedure or administrative organization). According to theorists believing in majority rule, majoritarianism would not be tyrannical or despotic because any candidate who must win the support of the majority of people in a pluralistic and socially stable nation must hew to the center of the political spectrum, and so many of the various interests of the nation would be represented in any majority, that minority rights would be protected. The system, moreover, can positively protect minorities who wish to defend or expand their rights through government, rather than against government. While majority rule could operate on behalf of a laissez-faire majority, the thrust of the doctrine is toward a more energetic and productive government.

4. *Minority Opposition.* The Jeffersonian model assumes that the opposition party will maintain a vigorous and vocal opposition to the party in power. The opposition party can declare certain issues, such as "bipartisan" foreign policy, outside the arena of party rivalry, but this is the right of the opposi-

tion, not the government. The opposition party is compelled to criticize the government responsibly, and with some moderation, however, because as the alternative party it is always on the brink of gaining office and governing and hence would imperil its own tenure in office if it had made reckless and vainglorious promises.

The Hamiltonian Model

The *Hamiltonian* model is much harder to define than either of the above models, because at its core there lies a large element of opportunism and expediency. Indeed, this kind of Presidency can be and has been justified on the ground that it is flexible and resourceful enough to meet a variety of political situations. At its most limited, the Hamiltonian model could be described simply as Madisonianism plus a vigorous and versatile President; at the other extreme a Hamiltonian might use party machinery and serve as national party leader, at least for a time, in much the same style as a Jeffersonian. Still, key elements can be found in it:

1. *Heroic Leadership.* The President must be more than administrative chief or party leader. He must exert great leadership in behalf of the whole nation. He must not be unduly restricted by his party; when necessary (as he sees necessity) he can ignore it or even desert it. In practice he both uses party and "rises above" it. Heroic Presidents have some of the qualities of the hero in modern setting: they cut an impressive figure on the hustings and before the television camera; they have style; they speak movingly and even passionately; they seem to establish a direct connection with the mass public. And they are invested by the press and the people with even magical qualities: they are physically inexhaustible, it is said; thcy can read with lightning speed; they have total recall; and so on.

2. *Personal Organization.* The President depends less—and is committed less—to the party as a whole than to his personal organization built up over the years. This personal organization is far more centralized, disciplined, and efficient than the general party organization. It is bound directly to the leader by ties of intense personal loyalty and hope of reward. Its relation to the regular party is ambiguous and changeable; the personal organization is ascendant during the presidential campaign, especially in the convention fight for the nomination, but cannot control the vast and diffused regular party that has its roots in scores of state and local organizations. Both Hamilton and Theodore Roosevelt maintained personal organizations; under Lincoln the Republican Party was transmuted into the Union Party, which served as a vehicle for mobilizing support for Lincoln and the war effort.

3. *Expedient Use of Power.* It is in this respect that the Hamiltonian model differs most sharply from the Jeffersonian. A President with the backing of a

strong party enjoys a relatively assured basis of power; he may still have to marshal influence, but the building of the party and the success of the party in winning executive and congressional office at the preceding election provides the President with a reservoir of power than he can draw on from day to day. The Hamiltonian President has no such reservoir; he must employ every weapon that he has—his own reputation, his prestige, his patronage power, his political friendships—to achieve the results he wants. He must constantly fill, draw on, and replenish his own store of political credits. He depends more on personal influence than on party influence. He deals with opposition party leaders, as Theodore Roosevelt did with Senator Benjamin R. "Pitchfork Ben" Tillman in winning railroad legislation, to muster support for his policies. Because he is not obligated to a great political party, he can "rise above" party when he wishes and pose as leader of all the nation. Although the power arrangements within which he operates are somewhat institutionalized, he has far more leverage in manipulating personal and presidential power than if he were the responsible leader of a unified and disciplined party.

4. *Disorganized Opposition.* The freedom of the President from party obligation and control gives him a latitude of political tactics and governmental decision making that in turn complicates the role of the opposition party leadership. The "out" party needs a clear target to shoot at, but it sees only a constantly moving one. The President may even make off with some of the opposition's leadership, as in 1940, when Franklin Roosevelt enlisted Henry Stimson and Frank Knox to his cause on the eve of the Republican nominating convention. By flirting with the opposition the President can seem to lift certain issues above partisanship. The opposition party is tempted to become opportunistic too, to attack the President from opposite and conflicting positions, but in doing so it loses face as a party cohesive and clear-minded enough to govern.

Woodrow Wilson and Franklin D. Roosevelt are tangible examples of the latter two presidential models. Brought up in the belief that the best politics was a mighty forensic battle between two organized and principled parties over meaningful differences in platform and policy, Wilson acted as a strong party leader both as Governor of New Jersey in 1911–1912 and in his early years as President. Despite the grave weaknesses in the national Democracy of 1913, he used his party expertly to marshal opinion behind his program, and to put it through Congress. He worked closely with party and committee leaders; used the caucus to unify the congressional party behind his proposals for tariff reduction and a federal reserve system; and borrowed the influence of his fellow partisan and Secretary of State, William Jennings Bryan, to push his program through. He acted, in his own term, as "the responsible leader of the party in power." But Wilson knew that party leadership meant more than cleaving to the dead center of the party; it must be a leadership that moved with changing circumstances and popular attitudes. In 1916, with the Progressive Party of 1912 crumbling, and with much of the old Democratic Party agenda enacted or irrelevant, Wilson reoriented his party toward urban needs and claims. In that year, Link says, Wilson became "almost a new political creature, and under his leadership a Democratic Congress enacted the most sweeping and significant progressive legislation in the history of the country up to that time."[6] He led his party to victory in 1916, tried (and failed) to win a Democratic congressional majority in 1918, and made the League of Nations fight mainly a party struggle.

Contrast the political leadership of Franklin D. Roosevelt, a liberal Democrat who also had to reorient his party toward urban economic needs, internationalism, and war. Taking office during economic crisis, he assumed the role of nonpartisan leader as he urged the nation to attack depression as though it were a foreign foe. As the election of 1936 neared, he assumed the posture of party leader and conducted, at least in the final stages, one of the most militant party campaigns the nation had seen. In 1938 he took his party leadership so seriously that he tried to purge conservative members of Congress from the party. As the European crisis grew he reverted to his nonpartisan role, which he adhered to through much of the war. He had to fight the campaign of 1944 as a Democrat, however, and in the last year of his life he was apparently contemplating the possibilities of party realignment that would shift liberal Republicans into the Democratic Party and bring about "two real parties—one liberal and the other conservative."[7]

Roosevelt was a Hamiltonian in more than his party leadership. He was the gay, ebullient President who overcame economic and military crisis. He seemed to have magical personal and political gifts. He was flexible, resourceful, versatile, manipulative—even Machiavellian—in his employment of power. He developed and managed a highly personal political organization. He disorganized the opposition. And he had a clear and self-conscious desire to govern in the tradition of Hamilton, Lincoln, and Roosevelt—though often for Jeffersonian and Wilsonian goals.

But Franklin Roosevelt more than any other President exemplifies the central problem of this [article]. He made the Presidency essentially his personal instrument and he used it brilliantly to experiment, innovate, and establish important reforms. But he failed during his first two terms to realize the main goal for which he had been elected—overcoming depression. He greatly enhanced the power and reach of the presidential office, but failed to develop a political base that could have provided sustained and dependable support for long-run programs. Partly for reasons outside his control, he was unable in the end to bring into productive relation his ultimate goals, his instrumental ends, and his means; on the other hand, by his dextrous employment of presidential power he helped set the stage for the more purposeful action to come.

The Limits and Excesses
of Presidential Power

ARTHUR SCHLESINGER, JR.

The Presidency of Lyndon B. Johnson had its impact, of course, on the nation and on the world. It has also had a marked impact on thinking about the American Presidency itself. For it compelled American historians and political scientists to begin to question their traditional and rather uncritical acceptance of the virtues of a strong Presidency. After all, so far as the theory of presidential power is concerned, Lyndon Johnson's leadership in connection with the war in Vietnam was an exemplary case of presidential activism. It represented a splendid rejection of theory that the Presidency was an office of limited and enumerated powers—the Whig theory of the Presidency or, as Theodore Roosevelt liked to call it, the Buchanan-Taft theory. It represented a bold use of the spacious powers than strong Presidents such as TR, Woodrow Wilson, and Franklin Roosevelt had perceived in the Presidency and added to it.

Yet, many historians and political scientists—this writer included—who had previously been what Professor Edward S. Corwin had presciently termed in 1951 "high-flying prerogative men," found themselves deeply troubled fifteen years later by the way in which President Johnson was applying the thesis of a strong Presidency to Vietnam. Invoking honored doctrine, he sent half a million American fighting men halfway around the world to enter a war that seemed to bear no overpowering relation to the vital interests of the United States. Moreover, he did so without giving either Congress or the electorate any clear sense that they had been consulted about the decisions which had deepened the commitment and escalated the war. (To do President Johnson justice, probably a majority of both were in favor of escalation until 1968. To do Congress and the electorate justice, they might not have been had they received an accurate picture of what was going on in Vietnam.)

Moreover, the executive appeared to be swallowing up vital powers of decision as a matter not only of practice but of principle. When a former Attorney General, later an Under Secretary of State, told the Senate Foreign Relations

Reprinted from *Crisis of Confidence*. Copyright © 1967, 1968, 1969 by Arthur M. Schlesinger, Jr. Reprinted by permission of the publisher, Houghton Mifflin Company. Published as an article in *Saturday Review*, May 3, 1969.

Committee that the declaration of war, expressly reserved in the Constitution for Congress, had become "outmoded in the international arena," and that the SEATO agreement and the Gulf of Tonkin Resolution were together the "functional equivalent" of a declaration of war, the committee formally concluded that "the intent of the framers of the Constitution with respect to the exercise of the war power has been virtually nullified." President Johnson himself carried the supposed usurpation even further when he said at Omaha on June 30, 1966, "There are many, many who can recommend, advise, and sometimes a few of them consent. But there is only one that has been chosen by the American people to decide." Everett M. Dirksen added a senatorial— and Republican—blessing: "It is a rather interesting thing," he told the Senate on October 3, 1967, "I have run down many legal cases before the Supreme Court, [and] I have found as yet no delimitation on the powers of the Commander-in-Chief under the Constitution."

The Vietnam experience thus provided an unexpected demonstration that a strong Presidency might have its drawbacks. It consequently forced scholars to face a disturbing question: Had they promoted the cult of the strong Presidency simply because, up to 1965, strong Presidents had mostly been doing things which historians and political scientists had mostly wanted done? The spectacle of a strong President doing things they mostly did not want done suddenly stimulated many of us to take a fresh look at the old problem of presidential power.

Then Senator Eugene McCarthy in the 1968 campaign gave powerful expression to this rising doubt about the virtues of a strong Presidency. "The New Politics," he said, "requires a different conception of the Presidency." He declared his opposition to "the sort of presidential power which extends itself in a personal way into every institution of government." He asked: "Has the integrity of Congress, of the Cabinet, and of the military been impinged upon by undue extension of the executive power?" The powers of the Presidency, he argued, should be decentralized. As against the idea of a strong Presidency on the Jackson-FDR model, Senator McCarthy offered instead a revival of the Whig theory of a passive Presidency, though he proposed to adapt this theory to progressive purposes. "This is a good country," he once said, "if the President will just let it be." The next President, he said, "should understand that this country does not so much need leadership. . . . He must be prepared to be a kind of channel." The President's duty is to "liberate individuals so that they may determine their own lives." In a variety of ways McCarthy made clear his fear of strong presidential leadership and his faith in greater independence among the units of the national government and greater initiative in the localities. He was the first liberal this century to run *against* the Presidency.

This was one of his major differences with Robert F. Kennedy. Kennedy retained the more traditional liberal belief in a strong Presidency. He saw affirmative presidential leadership as an indispensable means of welding disparate groups together into a common cause. He knew that Franklin Roosevelt, for example, had forged his coalition and held it together through precisely the sort of presidential leadership McCarthy condemned. Roosevelt had been able to persuade the working classes of the 1930s to go along with him on issues outside their daily concern—such as foreign policy, civil liberties, and equal rights—not because they had more enlightened views on such issues than their counterparts have today, but because they had a confidence in Roosevelt founded in his leadership on the issues that *were* part of their daily concern and because, for this and other reasons, they trusted and loved him. I think that Kennedy supposed that today's white, low-income groups were similarly composed of decent, if confused, people, and that they could be similarly reclaimed for political rationality.

Kennedy saw a strong Presidency as essential not just to unite the country but to enable the country to meet its problems. Certainly President Johnson had abused his power in foreign affairs. But a general cutback in presidential power, Kennedy feared, would only increase the nation's impotence in the face of deep and angry national division. He believed that as a country we were heading into perilous times, that the ties which had precariously bound Americans together were under almost intolerable strain, and that reducing presidential authority could be a disastrous error when only a strong President could rally us to meet our most difficult and urgent internal issue: racial justice. The President, in Kennedy's view, had to be the active protector of the alienated groups, the tribune of the disinherited and the dispossessed; he had to be the active champion both of racial justice and of civil peace (and he could only be the second if he had demonstrated that he was the first); and, if any President renounced these obligations, the country might well break up.

McCarthy and Kennedy thus might agree that the Vietnam war revealed a dangerous concentration of power over war and peace in the hands of the man in the White House. But they disagreed in the conclusions they drew from this situation. McCarthy concluded that the situation demanded a general limitation of the Presidency, with all functions questioned and all powers reduced. Kennedy advocated a selective approach to the question of presidential power. He feared that if the American people recoiled indiscriminately against abuses of presidential authority in foreign affairs, they ran the risk of inviting a new period of weak Presidents—as in the dreary years from Taylor through Buchanan—at a time when only a strong President could serve as the center of action and purpose to hold the country together.

The problem of the future of the Presidency therefore resolves itself, in one of its aspects, into the question whether, if presidential power is excessive, it is unitary and must be diminished across the board, or whether presidential powers are separable—whether the President has too much power in foreign policy but conceivably not enough in domestic policy.

The argument is persuasive, it seems to me, that the problem of the American

Presidency in domestic affairs is not that he has too much power but that he has too little. He does not have in internal matters, for example, the same constitutional authority he has in foreign policy. The Supreme Court in the Curtiss-Wright case spoke of "the very delicate, plenary, and exclusive power of the President as the sole organ of the federal government in the field of international relations," adding that this power is "in origin and essential character different from that over internal affairs." Nor can a President in domestic affairs so easily shield and enhance his authority by wrapping the flag around himself, invoking patriotism, and national unity, and claiming life-and-death crisis.

He is therefore much more at the mercy of Congress. From 1938 to 1968 a series of strong Democratic Presidents sought congressional approval for social programs which, had they been enacted, might have greatly alleviated some of the tensions presently convulsing our national community. But in these thirty years a coalition, predominantly rural, of Republicans and southern Democrats in the House of Representatives blocked or whittled down most of the presidential proposals—except for a period of two years, 1965–1967, when, as a result of the Goldwater fiasco, enough northern Democrats were elected to create a short-lived but effective liberal majority in the House. Where a parliamentary prime minister can be reasonably sure that anything he suggests will become law in short order, the President of the United States cannot even be sure that *his* proposals will get to the floor of Congress for debate and vote. And no executive in any other democratic state has so little control over national economic policy as the American President.

In recent years, a second factor has arisen to limit presidential power: the growth of the executive bureaucracy. The expansion of governmental functions under the New Deal produced the modern bureaucracy—a development which the conservatives of the time, with their customary wisdom, regarded with consternation. The New Deal bureaucrats, in the demonology of the right, were the forerunners of radical revolution. Of course, as any sensible person should have expected, the government bureaucracy has turned out to be a conservatizing rather than a liberalizing force, at least against innovating Presidents. Its basic loyalty is to the established way of doing things, and, with age and size, it has acquired an independence which enables it to ignore or circumvent presidential initiative.

The rise of the modern bureaucracy has divided the executive branch between the presidential government and the permanent government. In this complex relationship, the presidential government has preferences and policies backed by a presumed mandate from the electorate. But the permanent government has preferences and policies of its own. It has vested interests of its own in programs; it has alliances of its own with congressional committees, lobbies, and the press; it has its own particular, and not seldom powerful, constituencies. Also, it is around longer. We now have, in consequence, four branches of government. An activist President may have quite as much trouble with the federal bureaucracy as with the legislative or judicial branches.

A third limitation on the Presidency in domestic affairs is the fact that nearly every President who has enlarged the power of the White House has provoked a reaction toward a more restricted idea of the Presidency, even if the reaction never quite cuts presidential power back to its earlier level. Thus Jackson and Polk were followed by a parade of weak Presidents. When Lincoln expanded presidential power, Congress took out its frustrations by impeaching his successor and establishing a generation of congressional government. Theodore Roosevelt begot Taft; Wilson begot Harding; Franklin Roosevelt and Truman begot Eisenhower. FDR, in addition, was posthumously punished by the Twenty-Second Amendment for the offense of having been elected President four times.

All these considerations make the President notably weaker in dealing with internal than with international problems. If this is so, the next question is whether it is possible to think up devices that would strengthen his hand in domestic matters and restrain his hand in foreign matters.

A number of such devices have been proposed. There would seem no convincing reason why, for example, the President and the congressional leadership should not agree that all significant presidential proposals would go to the floor for debate and vote. This would not be a guarantee of enactment, but it would be a guarantee that proposals deemed vital to the nation by the President could no longer be filed away in committee and denied consideration by the whole. Such an arrangement, incidentally, would spare the Senate the perennial row over Rule XXII [cloture]. Similarly, there would seem to be no convincing reason why the President should not have the right of item veto; even the Confederate Constitution gave Jefferson Davis authority to "approve any appropriation and disapprove any other appropriation in the same bill." There would seem to be no reason why the President should not have the authority to adjust tax rates within a specified range in order to deal with economic fluctuations, or that he should not have greater discretion in reorganizing the executive branch or in moving funds from one program to another.

Congress resists such proposals out of conditioned institutional reflexes. It has the visceral fear that structural reform will transfer further power to the executive. Yet, the era of what Wilson called "congressional government" did not fade away at the end of the nineteenth century because of structural reform. It faded away for the simple reason that through so much of the twentieth century, Presidents have seemed right and Congress wrong on issues. The people, anxious to have necessary things done, welcomed Presidents who saw the necessity of doing these things—even if the Roosevelts and Wilson thereby increased the power of the Presidency at the expense of the power of Congress. So long as Congress falls behind Presidents in the perception of the needs of the nation, so long it may expect to lose ground in the war of attrition. And the only way that Congress will reclaim lost powers is by being right on issues when the executive is wrong—as the Senate Foreign Relations Committee proved in the case of Vietnam.

The best hope for Congress lies, not in withholding from the President powers which would benefit the nation, but in modernizing itself and thereby enabling it to compete with the Presidency on judgments of policy. The place to begin, of course, would be the seniority system. Contrary to congressional impression, this system was not handed down at Mount Sinai. Many state legislatures get along very well indeed without it. Its effect in Washington is to give disproportionate influence to men born in another century and shaped by small town or rural experience—hardly men qualified to deal with the problems of young people or of black people in an urban and industrial society.

Structural revisions of this sort would help both the President and the Congress to deal more intelligently with the accumulating troubles of our national community. Are there countervailing structural revisions on the international side which would prevent the President from running away with all initiative and decision in the conduct of foreign policy? This is the area which creates the real problem of presidential power. For, as Richard Neustadt has pointed out, acts in domestic policy are generally reversible; they are subject to revision and recall through democratic processes. But acts in foreign policy are often irreversible. President Kennedy used to say that domestic policy can only defeat us; foreign policy can kill us. Moreover, the nuclear age makes this quality of irreversibility more fateful than ever before. And foreign policy decisions very often are made in emergency contexts, real, imagined, or contrived, and this fact encourages the flow of power to the White House. Is it possible through structural reform to secure for Congress, and the people, an authoritative and continuing voice in the basic decisions of war and peace?

The Senate Foreign Relations Committee thought hard about this question and came up, in 1967, with Senate Resolution 187. This resolution declared it as "the sense of the Senate" that American armed forces could not be committed to hostilities on foreign territory for any purpose other than to repel an attack on the United States or to protect American citizens or property without "affirmative action by Congress specifically intended to give rise to such commitment." This or comparable resolutions must surely pass two tests: They must offer a plausible hope that (1) they will not tie the hands of the executive in a case of genuine national emergency; and (2) they will effectively prevent a step-by-step movement from marginal to major involvement.

These questions must be considered in specific situations; the answer, one fears, is that SR 187 would probably have prevented President Roosevelt from taking his actions in 1941 in defense of American security, but that it would not have prevented President Johnson from pursuing his course of gradual military escalation in Vietnam. The reason for this is that Roosevelt would have found it difficult to put together a congressional majority for his North Atlantic policy, while, as the Gulf of Tonkin example showed, Johnson would have encountered little difficulty in getting congressional endorsement for his Vietnam policy before 1968.

This year, the committee came up with a broader resolution declaring it the sense of the Senate that "a national commitment by the United States to a foreign power necessarily and exclusively results from affirmative action taken by the executive and legislative branches of the United States Government through means of a treaty, convention, or other legislative instrumentality specifically designed to give effect to such a commitment." On the face of it, this resolution would outlaw executive agreements. The executive agreement, of course, has been an indispensable device of foreign policy since at least the Rush-Bagot agreement of 1817 limiting naval forces on the Great Lakes; the Supreme Court, in decision after decision, has endowed the executive agreement with the same legal force as a treaty. If the principle behind the resolution had prevailed in 1940, Franklin Roosevelt could not have transferred the overage destroyers to Great Britain without seeking congressional approval. He most probably could not have obtained that approval; in any case, the debate would have been angry and protracted, leading to a filibuster as bitter as the one by which the "little group of willful men" blocked Wilson's policy of arming merchant vessels in 1917, and the subsequent history of the world might have been very different.

These examples suggest, I believe, the futility of trying to solve substantive problems by structural means. The probable result of efforts to limit presidential power through institutional contrivance would be to introduce dangerous rigidities into our system of national decision which would stop Presidents from doing good as well as from doing harm, and which would ultimately cause more trouble than benefit.

The solution to the problem of excessive presidential power in foreign affairs lies, I would conclude, in the political and educational realm. The fundamental strength of the Congress in this area springs from its capacity to raise issues and thereby to shape national opinion—a proposition demonstrated in the revolt against the Vietnam policy in 1967–1968. Next to the events in Vietnam themselves, the interpretation of these events provided by the dissident Senators under the leadership of Senator Fulbright and the Foreign Relations Committee and transmitted to the electorate was probably the major factor in turning the balance of opinion against the escalation policy.

In particular, Congress is well placed to assail the myth with which every foreign office seeks to silence critics: that only those who see the top secret cables know enough to make intelligent judgments on questions of foreign policy. As one who has had the opportunity to read such cables at various times in my life, I can testify that 95 percent of the information essential for intelligent judgment is available to any careful reader of The New York *Times*.

Indeed, the American government would have had a much wiser Vietnam policy had it relied more on the *Times;* the estimate of the situation supplied by newspapermen was consistently more accurate than that supplied by the succession of ambassadors and generals in their coded dispatches. Secrecy in diplomatic communication is mostly required to protect negotiating strategies, techniques of intelligence collection, details of weaponry, and gossip about personalities. One does not require full knowledge on such points to assess a political situation. The myth of inside information has always been used to prevent democratic control of foreign policy; if Congress derides that myth, it may embolden others to doubt the infallibility of Presidents and Secretaries of State.

But the responsibility rests even more heavily on the President than on the Congress. A President must, above all, be a man who acts not just because he is sure about the wisdom of a course of action, but because he is responsive to the democratic process. It is not enough for policies to be sound. In all but the most extreme cases, that soundness must be accompanied by explanation and tested by acceptance. The President must act on the principle of self-limitation and live within the discipline of consent. He must understand the legitimacy of challenges to his own authority and wisdom. He must cherish an inner skepticism about the anointment of office, and a constant awareness of what Whitman called "the never-ending audacity of elected persons." He must be especially skeptical about the unique value of information that arrives through official channels, and about self-serving bureaucratic versions of anything. He must be sensitive to the diversity of concern and conviction in a nation; he must be sensitive in advance to the verdict of history; he must always pay "a decent respect to the opinions of mankind."

No structural solutions can guarantee the choice of such Presidents, or can guarantee that, once chosen as open and modest men, they will remain so amid the intoxications of the office. Yet, surely the whole point of democracy is that it is not an automatic system. It involves risks, because risks are the means of growth. Rather than renounce the idea of an affirmative Presidency or surround the President with hampering restrictions, it would seem better to continue to regard presidential leadership as the central instrument of American democracy, and to exercise scrupulous care in the choice of Presidents.

Certainly, it is hard to see how we can unite our tormented nation and bring the alienated groups at last into the national community without a strong Presidency. "The President," James K. Polk said, "represents in the executive department the whole people of the United States, as each member of the legislative department represents portions of them." No one else represents the whole people, and the answer to the crisis of alienation surely does not lie in the weakening of the center and the dispersion of authority to local groups. This would only turn the country over to the strongest interests in each locality—i.e., to the neighborhood bullies—and speed the decomposition of American society. If the President does not serve as the representative of the unrepresented, it is hard to see where the excluded groups will find a connection with American society. One sees no other way of restoring the moral energy of American politics, and of incorporating the grave forebodings and desperate urgencies of our time into the democratic process.

The answer lies in national leadership—but not in national leadership which gulps up all authority in the conviction of its own infallibility. If we are to develop a genuine sense of national community, it will begin to come only when national leadership gives local groups a full and active sense of participation and initiative within a framework of national purpose. And it will come finally only through the direct commitment of individual Americans—the commitment which will transform the public agonies of America into personal responsibilities.

We must understand the limits as well as the utilities of politics. The American schism today is bitter and angry; the crisis of self-confidence goes very deep. That schism and that crisis will not be resolved by pious exhortation, nor even by beneficial legislation and wise leadership. It will be resolved only by reaching across the barriers in our land which separate some of us from others of us, only by men and women acting in the end not as members of groups but as individuals fulfilling themselves through human relations with other individuals. The volunteers of our time—the young men and women in the Peace Corps and VISTA and civil rights and community action, the tutors in the slums and ghettos, the visitors in the hospitals and asylums, all those who sacrifice their own convenience to help the outcasts of our society achieve strength and dignity—point the way to our salvation. The mission of democracy, said Whitman, is "to train communities, through all their grades, beginning with individuals and ending there again, to rule themselves." And no one should be discouraged by the fear that his own contribution cannot make a difference. Robert F. Kennedy warned in memorable language against "the danger of futility," against "the belief that there is nothing one man or one woman can do against the enormous array of the world's ills—against misery and ignorance, injustice and violence. . . . Few will have the greatness to bend history itself, but each of us can work to change a small portion of events, and in the total of all those acts will be written the history of this generation."

Presidential Power

RICHARD E. NEUSTADT

In form all Presidents are leaders, nowadays. In fact this guarantees no more than that they will be clerks. Everybody now expects the man inside the White House to do something about everything. Laws and customs now reflect acceptance of him as the Great Initiator, an acceptance quite as widespread at the Capitol as at his end of Pennsylvania Avenue. But such acceptance does not signify that all the rest of government is at his feet. It merely signifies that other men have found it practically impossible to do *their* jobs without assurance of initiatives from him. Service for themselves, not power for the President, has brought them to accept his leadership in form. They find his actions useful in their business. The transformation of his routine obligations testifies to their dependence on an active White House. A President, these days, is an invaluable clerk. His services are in demand all over Washington. His influence, however, is a very different matter. Laws and customs tell us little about leadership in fact.

Why have our Presidents been honored with this clerkship? The answer is that no one else's services suffice. Our Constitution, our traditions, and our politics provide no better source for the initiatives a President can take. Executive officials need decisions, and political protection, and a referee for fights. Where are these to come from but the White House? Congressmen need an agenda from outside, something with high status to respond to or react against. What provides it better than the program of the President? Party politicians need a record to defend in the next national campaign. How can it be made except by "their" administration? Private persons with a public axe to grind may need a helping hand or they may need a grinding stone. In either case who gives more satisfaction than a President? And outside the United States, in every country where our policies and postures influence home politics, there will be people needing just the "right" thing said and done or just the "wrong" thing stopped *in Washington*. What symbolizes Washington more nearly than the White House?

A modern President is bound to face demands for aid and service from five more or less distinguishable sources: from executive officialdom, from Congress, from his partisans, from citizens at large, and from abroad. The

Reprinted by permission of the publisher from Richard E. Neustadt, *Presidential Power* (New York: John Wiley & Sons, Inc., 1964), pp. 19–21, 49–53.

Presidency's clerkship is expressive of these pressures. In effect they are constituency pressures and each President has five sets of constituents. The five are not distinguished by their membership; membership is obviously an overlapping matter. And taken one by one they do not match the man's electorate; one of them, indeed, is outside his electorate. They are distinguished, rather, by their different claims upon him. Initiatives are what they want, for five distinctive reasons. Since government and politics have offered no alternative, our laws and customs turn those wants into his obligations.

Why, then, is the President not guaranteed an influence commensurate with services performed? Constituent relations are relations of dependence. Everyone with any share in governing this country will belong to one (or two, or three) of his "constituencies." Since everyone depends on him why is he not assured of everyone's support? The answer is that no one else sits where he sits, or sees quite as he sees; no one else feels the full weight of his obligations. Those obligations are a tribute to his unique place in our political system. But just because it is unique they fall on him alone. *The same conditions that promote his leadership in form preclude a guarantee of leadership in fact.* No man or group at either end of Pennsylvania Avenue shares his peculiar status in our government and politics. That is why his services are in demand. By the same token, though, the obligations of all other men are different from his own. His Cabinet officers have departmental duties and constituents. His legislative leaders head *congressional* parties, one in either House. His national party organization stands apart from his official family. His political allies in the states need not face Washington, or one another. The private groups that seek him out are not compelled to govern. And friends abroad are not compelled to run in our elections. Lacking his position and prerogatives, these men cannot regard his obligations as their own. They have their jobs to do; none is the same as his. As they perceive their duty they may find it right to follow him, in fact, or they may not. Whether they will feel obliged *on their responsibility* to do what he wants done remains an open question. . . .

The limits on command suggest the structure of our government. The Constitutional Convention of 1787 is supposed to have created a government of "separated powers." It did nothing of the sort. Rather, it created a government of separated institutions *sharing* powers.[8] "I am part of the legislative process," Eisenhower often said in 1959 as a reminder of his veto.[9] Congress, the dispenser of authority and funds, is no less part of the administrative process. Federalism adds another set of separated institutions. The Bill of Rights adds others. Many public purposes can only be achieved by voluntary acts of private institutions; the press, for one, in Douglass Cater's phrase, is a "fourth branch of government."[10] And with the coming of alliances abroad, the separate institutions of a London, or a Bonn, share in the making of American public policy.

What the Constitution separates our political parties do not combine. The parties are themselves composed of separated organizations sharing public authority. The authority consists of nominating powers. Our national parties are confederations of state and local party institutions, with a headquarters that represents the White House, more or less, if the party has a President in office. These confederacies manage presidential nominations. All other public offices depend upon electorates confined within the states.[11] All other nominations are controlled within the states. The President and Congressmen who bear one party's label are divided by dependence upon different sets of voters. The differences are sharpest at the stage of nomination. The White House has too small a share in nominating Congressmen, and Congress has too little weight in nominating Presidents, for party to erase their constitutional separation. Party links are stronger than is frequently supposed, but nominating processes assure the separation.[12]

The separateness of institutions and the sharing of authority prescribe the terms on which a President persuades. When one man shares authority with another, but does not gain or lose his job upon the other's whim, his willingness to act upon the urging of the other turns on whether he conceives the action right for him. The essence of a President's persuasive task is to convince such men that what the White House wants of them is what they ought to do for their sake and on their authority.

Persuasive power, thus defined, amounts to more than charm or reasoned argument. These have their uses for a President, but these are not the whole of his resources. For the men he would induce to do what he wants done on their own responsibility will need or fear some acts by him on his responsibility. If they share his authority, he has some share in theirs. Presidential "powers" may be inconclusive when a President commands, but always remain relevant as he persuades. The status and authority inherent in his office reinforce his logic and his charm.

Status adds something to persuasiveness; authority adds still more. When Truman urged wage changes on his Secretary of Commerce while the latter was administering the steel mills, he and Secretary Sawyer were not just two men reasoning with one another. Had they been so, Sawyer probably would never have agreed to act. Truman's status gave him special claims to Sawyer's loyalty, or at least attention. In Walter Bagehot's charming phrase "no man can *argue* on his knees." Although there is no kneeling in this country, few men—and exceedingly few Cabinet officers—are immune to the impulse to say "yes" to the President of the United States. It grows harder to say "no" when they are seated in his oval office at the White House, or in his study on the second floor, where almost tangibly he partakes of the aura of his physical surroundings. In Sawyer's case, moreover, the President possessed formal authority to intervene in many matters of concern to the Secretary of Commerce. These matters ranged from jurisdictional disputes among the defense agencies to legislation pending before Congress and, ultimately, to the tenure of the Secretary, himself. There is nothing in the record to suggest that Truman voiced specific threats when they negotiated over wage increases. But given his *formal* powers and their relevance to Sawyer's other interests, it is safe to assume that Truman's very advocacy of wage action conveyed an implicit threat.

A President's authority and status give him great advantages in dealing with the men he would persuade. Each "power" is a vantage point for him in the degree that other men have use for his authority. From the veto to appointments, from publicity to budgeting, and so down a long list, the White House now controls the most encompassing array of vantage points in the American political system. With hardly an exception, the men who share in governing this country are aware that at some time, in some degree, the doing of *their* jobs, the furthering of *their* ambitions, may depend upon the President of the United States. Their need for presidential action, or their fear of it, is bound to be recurrent if not actually continuous. Their need or fear is his advantage.

A President's advantages are greater than mere listing of his "powers" might suggest. The men with whom he deals must deal with him until the last day of his term. Because they have continuing relationships with him, his future, while it lasts, supports his present influence. Even though there is no need or fear of him today, what he could do tomorrow may supply today's advantage. Continuing relationships may convert any "power," any aspect of his status, into vantage points in almost any case. When he induces other men to do what he wants done, a President can trade on their dependence now *and* later.

The President's advantages are checked by the advantages of others. Continuing relationships will pull in both directions. These are relationships of mutual dependence. A President depends upon the men he would persuade; he has to reckon with his need or fear of them. They too will possess status, or authority, or both, else they would be of little use to him. Their vantage points confront his own; their power tempers his.

Persuasion is a two-way street. Sawyer, it will be recalled, did not respond at once to Truman's plan for wage increases at the steel mills. On the contrary, the Secretary hesitated and delayed and only acquiesced when he was satisfied that publicly he would not bear the onus of decision. Sawyer had some points of vantage all his own from which to resist presidential pressure. If he had to reckon with coercive implications in the President's "situations of strength," so had Truman to be mindful of the implications underlying Sawyer's place as a department head, as steel administrator, and as a Cabinet spokesman for business. Loyalty is reciprocal. Having taken on a dirty job in the steel crisis, Sawyer had strong claims to loyal support. Besides, he had authority to do some things that the White House could ill afford. Emulating Wilson, he might have resigned in a huff (the removal power also works two ways). Or emulating Ellis Arnall, he might have declined to sign necessary orders. Or, he might have let it be known publicly that he deplored what he was told to do and protested its doing. By following any of these courses Sawyer almost surely would have strengthened the position of management, weakened the position of the White House, and embittered the union. But the whole purpose of a wage increase was to enhance White House persuasiveness in urging settlement upon union and companies alike. Although Sawyer's status and authority did not give him the power to prevent an increase outright, they gave him capability to undermine its purpose. If his authority over wage rates had been vested by a statute, not by revocable presidential order, his power of prevention might have been complete. So Harold Ickes demonstrated in the famous case of helium sales to Germany before the Second World War.[13]

The power to persuade is the power to bargain. Status and authority yield bargaining advantages. But in a government of "separated institutions sharing powers," they yield them to all sides. With the array of vantage points at his disposal, a President may be far more persuasive than his logic or his charm could make him. But outcomes are not guaranteed by his advantages. There remain the counter pressures those whom he would influence can bring to bear on him from vantage points at their disposal. Command has limited utility; persuasion becomes give-and-take. It is well that the White House holds the vantage points it does. In such a business any President may need them all—and more. . . .

This view of power as akin to bargaining is one we commonly accept in the sphere of congressional relations. Every textbook states and every legislative session demonstrates that save in times like the extraordinary Hundred Days of 1933—times virtually ruled out by definition at mid-century—a President will often be unable to obtain congressional action on his terms or even to halt action he opposes. The reverse is equally accepted: Congress often is frustrated by the President. Their formal powers are so intertwined that neither will accomplish very much, for very long, without the acquiescence of the other. By the same token, though, what one demands the other can resist. The stage is set for that great game, much like collective bargaining, in which each seeks to profit from the other's needs and fears. It is a game played catch-as-catch-can, case by case. And everybody knows the game, observers and participants alike.

The concept of real power as a give-and-take is equally familiar when applied to presidential influence outside the formal structure of the federal government. The Little Rock affair may be extreme, but Eisenhower's dealings with the Governor—and with the citizens—become a case in point. Less extreme but no less pertinent is the steel seizure case with respect to union leaders, and to workers, and to company executives as well. When he deals with such people a President draws bargaining advantage from his status or authority. By virtue of their public places or their private rights they have some capability to reply in kind.

In spheres of party politics the same thing follows, necessarily, from the confederal nature of our party organizations. Even in the case of national nominations a President's advantages are checked by those of others. In 1944 it is by no means clear that Roosevelt got his first choice as his running mate. In 1948 Truman, then the President, faced serious revolts against his nomination. In 1952 his intervention from the White House helped assure the choice of Adlai Stevenson, but it is far from clear that Truman could have done as much for any other candidate acceptable to him.[14] In 1956 when Eisenhower was President, the record leaves obscure just who backed Harold Stassen's effort to block Richard Nixon's renomination as Vice President. But evidently everything did not go quite as Eisenhower wanted, whatever his intentions may have been.[15] The outcomes in these instances bear all the marks of limits on command and of power checked by power that characterize congressional relations. Both in and out of politics these checks and limits seem to be quite widely understood.

Influence becomes still more a matter of give-and-take when Presidents attempt to deal with allied governments. A classic illustration is the long unhappy wrangle over Suez policy in 1956. In dealing with the British and the French before their military intervention, Eisenhower had his share of bargaining advantages but no effective power of command. His allies had their share of counter pressures, and they finally tried the most extreme of all: action despite him. His pressure then was instrumental in reversing them. But had the British government been on safe ground *at home,* Eisenhower's wishes might have made as little difference after intervention as before. Behind the decorum of diplomacy—which was not very decorous in the Suez affair— relationships among allies are not unlike relationships among state delegations at a national convention. Power is persuasion and persuasion becomes bargaining. The concept is familiar to everyone who watches foreign policy.

In only one sphere is the concept unfamiliar: the sphere of executive relations. Perhaps because of civics textbooks and teaching in our schools, Americans instinctively resist the view that power in this sphere resembles power in all others. Even Washington reporters, White House aides, and congressmen are not immune to the illusion that administrative agencies comprise a single structure, "the" Executive Branch, where presidential word is law, or ought to be. Yet . . . when a President seeks something from executive officials his persuasiveness is subject to the same sorts of limitations as in the case of congressmen, or governors, or national committeemen, or private citizens, or foreign governments. There are no generic differences, no differences in kind and only sometimes in degree. The incidents preceding the dismissal of MacArthur and the incidents surrounding seizure of the steel mills make it plain that here as elsewhere influence derives from bargaining advantages; power is a give-and-take.

Like our governmental structure as a whole, the executive establishment consists of separated institutions sharing powers. The President heads one of these; Cabinet officers, agency administrators, and military commanders head others. Below the departmental level, virtually independent bureau chiefs head many more. Under mid-century conditions, federal operations spill across dividing lines on organization charts; almost every policy entangles many agencies; almost every program calls for interagency collaboration. Everything somehow involves the President. But operating agencies owe their existence least of all to one another—and only in some part to him. Each has a separate statutory base; each has its statutes to administer; each deals with a different set of subcommittees at the Capitol. Each has its own peculiar set of clients, friends, and enemies outside the formal government. Each has a different set of specialized careerists inside its own bailiwick. Our Constitution gives the President the "take-care" clause and the appointive power. Our statutes give him central budgeting and a degree of personnel control. All agency administrators are responsible to him. But they *also* are responsible to Congress, to their clients, to their staffs, and to themselves. In short, they have five masters. Only after all of those do they owe any loyalty to each other.

"The members of the Cabinet," Charles G. Dawes used to remark, "are a President's natural enemies." Dawes had been Harding's Budget Director, Coolidge's Vice President, and Hoover's ambassador to London; he also had been General Pershing's chief assistant for supply in the First World War. The words are highly colored, but Dawes knew whereof he spoke. The men who have to serve so many masters cannot help but be somewhat the "enemy" of any one of them. By the same token, any master wanting service is in some degree the "enemy" of such a servant. A President is likely to want loyal support but not to relish trouble on his doorstep. Yet the more his Cabinet members cleave to him, the more they may need help from him in fending off the wrath of rival masters. Help, though, is synonymous with trouble. Many a Cabinet officer, with loyalty ill-rewarded by his lights and help withheld, has come to view the White House as innately hostile to department heads. Dawes's dictum can be turned around.

A senior presidential aide remarked to me in Eisenhower's time: "If some of these Cabinet members would just take time out to stop and ask themselves 'What would I want if I were President?', they wouldn't give him all the trouble he's been having." But even if they asked themselves the question, such officials often could not act upon the answer. Their personal attachment to the President is all too often overwhelmed by duty to their other masters.

Executive officials are not equally advantaged in their dealings with a President. Nor are the same officials equally advantaged all the time. Not every officeholder can resist like a MacArthur, or like Arnall, Sawyer, Wilson, in a rough descending order of effective counter pressure. The vantage points conferred upon officials by their own authority and status vary enormously. The variance is heightened by particulars of time and circumstance. In mid-

October, 1950, Truman, at a press conference, remarked of the man he had considered firing in August and would fire the next April for intolerable insubordination:

> Let me tell you something that will be good for your souls. It's a pity that you . . . can't understand the ideas of two intellectually honest men when they meet. General MacArthur . . . is a member of the government of the United States. He is loyal to that government. He is loyal to the President. He is loyal to the President in his foreign policy. . . . There is no disagreement between General MacArthur and myself. . . .[16]

MacArthur's status in and out of government was never higher than when Truman spoke those words. The words, once spoken, added to the General's credibility thereafter when he sought to use the press in his campaign against the President. And what had happened between August and October? Near-victory had happened, together with that premature conference on *post*-war plans, the meeting at Wake Island.

If the bargaining advantages of a MacArthur fluctuate with changing circumstances, this is bound to be so with subordinates who have at their disposal fewer "powers," lesser status, to fall back on. And when officials have no "powers" in their own right, or depend upon the President for status, their counter pressure may be limited indeed. White House aides, who fit both categories, are among the most responsive men of all, and for good reason. As a Director of the Budget once remarked to me, "Thank God I'm here and not across the street. If the President doesn't call me, I've got plenty I can do right here and plenty coming up to me, by rights, to justify my calling him. But those poor fellows over there, if the boss doesn't call them, doesn't ask them to do something, what *can* they do but sit?" Authority and status so conditional are frail reliances in resisting a President's own wants. Within the White House precincts, lifted eyebrows may suffice to set an aide in motion; command, coercion, even charm aside. But even in the White House a President does not monopolize effective power. Even there persuasion is akin to bargaining. A former Roosevelt aide once wrote of Cabinet officers:

> Half of a President's suggestions, which theoretically carry the weight of orders, can be safety forgotten by a Cabinet member. And if the President asks about a suggestion a second time, he can be told that it is being investigated. If he asks a third time, a wise Cabinet officer will give him at least part of what he suggests. But only occasionally, except about the most important matters, do Presidents ever get around to asking three times.[17]

The rule applies to staff as well as to the Cabinet, and certainly has been applied *by* staff in Truman's time and Eisenhower's.

Some aides will have more vantage points than a selective memory. Sherman Adams, for example, as The Assistant to the President under Eisenhower, scarcely deserved the appellation "White House aide" in the meaning of the term before his time or as applied to other members of the Eisenhower entourage. Although Adams was by no means "chief of staff" in any sense so sweeping—or so simple—as press commentaries often took for granted, he apparently became no more dependent on the President than Eisenhower on him. "I need him," said the President when Adams turned out to have been re-markably imprudent in the Goldfine case, and delegated to him even the deci-sion on his own departure.[18] This instance is extreme, but the tendency it illus-trates is common enough. Any aide who demonstrates to others that he has the President's consistent confidence and a consistent part in presidential business will acquire so much business on his own account that he becomes in some sense independent of his chief. Nothing in the Constitution keeps a well-placed aide from converting status into power of his own, usable in some degree even against the President—an outcome not unknown in Truman's regime or, by all accounts, in Eisenhower's.

The more an officeholder's status and his "powers" stem from sources in-dependent of the President, the stronger will be his potential pressure *on* the President. Department heads in general have more bargaining power than do most members of the White House staff; but bureau chiefs may have still more, and specialists at upper levels of established career services may have almost unlimited reserves of the enormous power which consists of sitting still. As Franklin Roosevelt once remarked:

> The Treasury is so large and far-flung and ingrained in its practices that I find it is almost impossible to get the action and results I want— even with Henry [Morgenthau] there. But the Treasury is not to be com-pared with the State Department. You should go through the experience of trying to get any changes in the thinking, policy, and action of the career diplomats and then you'd know what a real problem was. But the Treasury and the State Department put together are nothing compared with the Na-a-vy. The admirals are really something to cope with—and I should know. To change anything in the Na-a-vy is like punching a feather bed. You punch it with your right and you punch it with your left until you are finally exhausted, and then you find the damn bed just as it was before you started punching.[19]

In the right circumstances, of course, a President can have his way with any of these people. . . . But . . . between a President and his "subordinates," no less than others on whom he depends, real power is reciprocal and varies markedly with organization, subject matter, personality, and situation. The mere fact that persuasion is directed at executive officials signifies no necessary easing of his way. Any new congressman of the administration's party, espe-cially if narrowly elected, may turn out more amenable (though less useful) to the President than any seasoned bureau chief "downtown." *The probabilities of power do not derive from the literary theory of the Constitution.*

When Truman dismissed MacArthur, the latter lost three posts: the American command in the Far East, the Allied command for the occupation of Japan, and the United Nations command in Korea. He also lost his status as the senior officer on active duty in the United States armed forces. So long as he held those positions and that status, though, he had a duty to his troops, to his profession, to himself (the last is hard for any man to disentangle from the rest). As a public figure and a focus for men's hopes he had a duty to constituents at home, and in Korea and Japan. He owed a duty also to those other constituents, the UN governments contributing to his field forces. As a patriot he had a duty to his country. As an accountable official and an expert guide he stood at the call of Congress. As a military officer he had, besides, a duty to the President, his constitutional commander. Some of these duties may have manifested themselves in terms more tangible or more direct than others. But it would be nonsense to argue that the last *negated* all the rest, however much it might be claimed to override them. And it makes no more sense to think that anybody but MacArthur was effectively empowered to decide how he, himself, would reconcile the competing demands his duties made upon him.

Similar observations could be made about [other] executive officials. [Truman's] Price Director Arnall . . . refused in advance to sign a major price increase for steel if Mobilization Director Wilson or the White House should concede one before management had settled with the union. When Arnall did this, he took his stand, in substance, on his oath of office. He would do what he had sworn to do in *his* best judgment, so long as he was there to do it. This posture may have been assumed for purposes of bargaining and might have been abandoned had his challenge been accepted by the President. But no one could be sure and no one, certainly, could question Arnall's right to make the judgment for himself. As head of an agency and as a politician, with a program to defend and a future to advance, *he* had to decide what he had to do on matters that, from his perspective, were exceedingly important. Neither in policy nor in personal terms, nor in terms of agency survival, were the issues of a sort to be considered secondary by an Arnall, however much they might have seemed so to a Wilson (or a Truman). Nor were the merits likely to appear the same to a price stabilizer and to men with broader duties. Reasonable men, it is so often said, *ought* to be able to agree on the requirements of given situations. But when the outlook varies with the placement of each man, and the response required in his place is for each to decide, their reasoning may lead to disagreement quite as well—and quite as reasonably. Vanity, or vice, may weaken reason, to be sure, but it is idle to assign these as the cause of Arnall's threat or MacArthur's defiance. Secretary Sawyer's hesitations, cited earlier, are in the same category. One need not denigrate such men to explain their conduct. For the responsibilities they felt, the "facts" they saw, simply were not the same as those of their superiors; yet they, not the superiors, had to decide what they would do.

Outside the executive branch the situation is the same, except that loyalty to the President may often matter *less*. There is no need to spell out the comparison with governors of Arkansas, steel company executives, trade union leaders, and the like. And when one comes to congressmen who can do nothing for themselves (or their constituents) save as they are elected, term by term, in districts and through party structures *differing* from those on which a President depends, the case is very clear. An able Eisenhower aide with long congressional experience remarked to me in 1958: "The people on the Hill don't do what they might *like* to do, they do what they think they *have* to do in their own interest as *they* see it . . . ." This states the case precisely.

The essence of a President's persuasive task with Congressmen and everybody else, *is to induce them to believe that what he wants of them is what their own appraisal of their own responsibilities requires them to do in their interest, not his.* Because men may differ in their views on public policy, because differences in outlook stem from differences in duty—duty to one's office, one's constituents, oneself—that task is bound to be more like collective bargaining than like a reasoned argument among philosopher kings. Overtly or implicitly, hard bargaining has characterized all illustrations offered up to now. This is the reason why: persuasion deals in the coin of self-interest with men who have some freedom to reject what they find counterfeit.

How the President Makes a Decision

THEODORE C. SORENSEN

How does a President make up his mind? I refer not to psychoanalysis, but to the forces that shape his decisions. How does a President choose, for example, in a moment of crisis, between the olive branch of peace and the arrows of war? His alternatives, of course, are rarely that clear-cut—but, if not, why not? What limits the President's choice? What forces, what factors, what influences are blended in that final act of decision?

Obviously each President has his own style and his own standard for making decisions. These may differ from day to day or from topic to topic, using one blend for foreign affairs, for example, and another for domestic. The man affects the office as the office affects the man.

Reprinted by permission of the publisher from Theodore C. Sorensen, *Decision-Making in the White House* (New York: Columbia University Press, 1963). This article originally appeared in *Saturday Review*, July 27, 1963, pp. 12–15, 49.

Nor is decision-making something he neatly sets aside for certain times or occasions. On the contrary, the President's entire existence is a continuous process of decision—including decisions not to decide and decisions not to take action—decisions on what to say, whom to see, what to sign, whom to name, and what to do, as Commander-in-Chief and diplomatic chief, as legislative leader and political leader, as a moral leader and a free world leader, and in taking care that the laws are faithfully executed. Every policy announced is the sum of many decisions, each made in a different mold and manner.

I do not suggest, therefore, that there is any systematic formula of decision-making in the White House, any precise mixture of ingredients for one President to pass on to the next or even to use himself on successive occasions. I have no absolute tests to offer by which White House decisions can be judged, no new theories or concepts or terminology to describe this daily process. Indeed, the very frequency of the process increases the difficulty of subjecting it to logical analysis, of summarizing or synthesizing it in terms of some formal doctrine.

But I am convinced that whether a President is strong or weak, whether he initiates or avoids decisions, whether he consults with his Cabinet or his Kitchen Cabinet, his brain trust or the "meat trust," the fundamental nature of the White House makes it inevitable that vital decisions, either many or few, will be made there, either by the President or with his consent, and that the same basic forces and factors will repeatedly shape those decisions.

The analysis that follows, therefore, is concerned, not with the influence of a President's decisions, but with *what influences them*. It is my thesis that, however the institutions and the apparatus may be organized, these same basic influences are ever present—not by chance but by the nature of the office.

A President may ignore these forces or factors—he may even be unaware of them—but he cannot escape them. He may choose to decide in solitude, but he does not decide in a vacuum. As a painter mixes his colors, or a chef prepares his sauce, so he must mix these ingredients—omitting some if he wishes, or preferring others he likes, but mixing them nevertheless, in his own style and to his own taste, until the final product is fashioned.

Having participated briefly in this process, I offer my own observations of it. If some of my conclusions seem obvious, I include them only because of the dangers inherent in omitting what seems to be obvious.

In describing what forces might influence a President's decisions, I should first state with candor that these forces in the past have generally defied all description. The memoirs of some former Cabinet members would have us believe that they handed ready-made decisions to their President for his approval; yet their associates complain in *their* memoirs that the same Chief Executive was too proud to hear, much less to heed, good advice. My colleague Arthur Schlesinger, Jr., describes in fascinating fashion the maneuvers that preceded a decision by Franklin Delano Roosevelt, but then he adds: "Once the opportunity for decision came safely into his orbit, the actual process of deciding was involved and inscrutable." And Rexford Tugwell declared that Roosevelt "allowed no one to discover the governing principle" of his decisions.

President Truman wrote that "no one can know all the processes and stages of [a President's] thinking in making important decisions. Even those closest to him . . . never know all the reasons why he does certain things and why he comes to certain conclusions."

President Kennedy's analysis is still some years away from publication. [Ed. note: Recall this article was written in 1963.] Thus far he has referred simply to "the multiplicity of factors" that are involved in White House decisions.

But let us not be deterred in our quest by the characterization of this process as inscrutable or indescribable.

To begin with, White House decision-making is not a science but an art. It requires, not calculation, but judgment. There is no unit of measure that can weigh the substantive consequences of a decision against the political consequences, or judge the precise portions of public opinion and congressional pressure, or balance domestic against foreign, short-range against long-range, or private against public considerations.

Elaborate guides to decision-making in private business or even in public administration are of little help in the White House. For the breadth and scope of presidential decisions cannot be matched in any large corporation or Cabinet department, or even in the halls of Congress. For the President alone is ultimately accountable for the lives of more than 2,500,000 American servicemen, for the deeds of 2,500,000 federal employees, and he alone is ultimately held accountable to 190,000,000 citizens, to more than forty foreign allies, and, in a very real sense—as custodian of the nuclear trigger—to all men and to all mankind.

His decisions do not differ merely in degree from the decisions of others. No one else faces so many complex issues where the solutions are so remote, so dependent on the undependable, and so filled with potential disaster. No one but the President, as Woodrow Wilson said, bears such multiple responsibilities in so many different and conflicting areas. No one else knows in advance that his decisions will be subject to such scrutiny, to such calumny, or to what my friend Professor Neustadt calls such irreversibility.

In an age when not only this nation but also its chief adversary possess the capacity to inflict unacceptable disaster on another power in a matter of minutes, it is foolish to compare the role of the current President with that of any other man, including even his thirty-three predecessors.

What comes to the White House for decision? That, too, is a necessary part of the setting, but again there is no certain pattern. President Eisenhower rightly told President Kennedy: "There are no easy matters that will come to you as President. If they are easy, they will be settled at a lower level."

Some decisions are based on the requirements of a President's calendar. He must, for example, send up a budget and presumably a legislative program at the start of each year, and these mean countless decisions. Some come to him by law, including bills to be signed or vetoed, nominations to be sent to the Senate, requests for a pardon or parole, and the review of certain quasi-judicial decisions.

But for the rest there are no set criteria. President Kennedy chooses to reach out and select key issues, to initiate deliberations, to anticipate crisis. Other Presidents may prefer to decide only what cannot be decided below or only what others present.

In the White House, as elsewhere, "the squeaky wheel gets the grease." Whenever a controversy looms large in the press or the Congress or the public mind, however small it may be in true perspective, it either lands on the President's desk or confronts him at a news conference. (The advisability of corporal punishment in the District of Columbia schools, for example, is not a major issue of state, but the predominance of that issue in the Washington press prior to one news conference caused President Kennedy to examine his own thoughts on the matter, and possibly his own youth.)

More important, when a President's own prestige is involved—or his own powers, posture, or reelection—or when an issue is too important for anyone else's word to be accepted, or too sensitive, or too unprecedented, or too likely to result in damage beyond repair—then a presidential decision is usually essential.

If I were to name the one quality that characterizes most issues likely to be brought to the President, I would say it was conflict—conflict between departments, between the views of various advisers, between the Administration and Congress, between the United States and another nation, or between groups within the country.

Presidents may even encourage such clashes within the government—by deliberately overlapping authority or inviting dissent, as Franklin D. Roosevelt did to make certain he heard the alternatives.

But conflict rarely needs a stimulus. The claims of domestic and foreign policy sooner or later collide. Congressional checks and balances are written into law. Public and political needs will often be incompatible. Compelling policies or interest groups are sometimes equally deserving. And the heat that is generated by all of this friction will naturally rise to the top—to the presidential office.

Just as conflict will bring issues to the President, so a lack of conflict may sometimes keep them from him even when he should be involved. For example: Had there been some disagreement between White House and State Department officials on the contents of a press statement on nuclear warheads in Canada, it would have been brought to the President's attention before it exploded in the headlines. To cite another case: Proposed regulations on expense accounts, having been approved by everyone in Internal Revenue, were not presented to the President until they had been bitterly protested in public.

Of course, a President can so design his office and so delegate his authority as to keep certain or even most decisions away from him, but even then the decisions of others may require his intervention if he is to fulfil his constitutional obligation.

Some major issues do not regularly come before the President simply because they are low on his list of priorities, and he chooses to rely on his appointed authorities.

On the other hand, a President's personal interests may draw to him decisions normally left for others. Roosevelt, for example, took a hand in deciding postage stamp designs. I have seen President Kennedy engrossed in a list of famous Indian chiefs, deciding on an appropriate name for a nuclear submarine. (Inasmuch as most of the chiefs had earned their fame by defying the armed might of the United States, it was not an easy decision. In fact, when he finally decided on Chief Red Cloud, the Navy protested that this name had undesirable foreign policy implications.)

Time rules out many decisions. A President should not try to decide too few issues—but neither can he decide too many. Above all, he should decide what it is he need *not* decide at a given time. During the October, 1962, Cuban crisis, the President charged his Cabinet and staff to avoid the presentation of those issues that could be safely delayed or settled among themselves. The postponement of some of these decisions, of course, required a more hurried handling in later weeks to meet budget or other deadlines, and this was not without difficulty, as the case of the Skybolt missile illustrates. There were other factors here in addition to the shortness of time, however, and surely no nonfeasance can be charged respecting the postponement of this issue by the Pentagon when war and peace were at stake.

Finally, what are the component steps in White House decision-making? In ideal and mechanical terms, White House decision-making sounds easy, if somewhat elaborate. It is simply the interaction of desire and fact— simply a determination of what the national interest requires in a given situation. But unfortunately it is neither mechanical nor easy; nor, it should be added, is the amount of care and thought devoted to a particular decision necessarily proportionate to the formality and regularity of the decision-making process.

For the ideal case is the exception. Each step cannot be taken in order. The facts may be in doubt or dispute. Several policies, all good, may conflict. Several means, all bad, may be all that are open. Value judgments may differ. Stated goals may be imprecise. There may be many interpretations of what is right, what is possible, and what is in the national interest. A President's decision may vary according to how the question is formulated and even according to who presents it. All his available choices may be difficult mixtures of both good and evil.

For every course he examines, there will always be some opposition in the country, in the Congress, and even among his advisers. There will always be one adviser to say, after the fashion of certain columnists and commentators, that "on the one hand" consider this but "on the other hand" think of that. Idealists on his staff will rule out expediency. Realists will disregard morality. Some will counsel speed; others will counsel delay—yet even delay will constitute a decision.

As each President nears a final answer, he realizes that this choice is only the beginning. For each new decision sets a precedent, begetting new decisions, foreclosing others, and causing reactions that require counteraction. Roosevelt, according to Frances Perkins, "rarely got himself sewed tight to a program from which there was no turning back." And President Kennedy, aware of the enormous hazards in the confrontation with the Soviets over Cuba in October, 1962, made certain that his first move did not close out either all his options or all of theirs.

But too often a President finds that events or the decisions of others have limited his freedom of maneuver—that, as he makes a choice, that door closes behind him. And he knows that, once that door is closed, it may never open again—and he may then find himself in a one-way tunnel, or in a baffling maze, or descending a slippery slope. He cannot count on turning back—yet he cannot see his way ahead. He knows that if he is to act, some eggs must be broken to make the omelet, as the old saying goes. But he also knows that an omelet cannot lay any more eggs.

But no President is free to go as far or as fast as his advisers, his politics, and his perspective may direct him. His decisions—and their advice—are set within at least five ever-present limitations. He is free to choose only (1) within the limits of permissibility; (2) within the limits of available resources; (3) within the limits of available time; (4) within the limits of previous commitments; and (5) within the limits of available information.

LIMITS OF PERMISSIBILITY

In a government of laws, a President is not free to ignore the Constitution he is sworn to uphold, the statutes he is obliged to enforce, the decisions of our courts, and the rights of citizens and states. And to this body of law, as the world grows smaller, must be added international law, which cannot be dismissed as quickly as some claim.

For example: had the Organization of American States failed, in October, 1962, to provide the necessary two-thirds vote authorizing a Cuban quarantine, the Soviets and possibly others might have been emboldened to challenge the legality of our action, creating confusion and irresolution in the

Western camp and giving rise to all kinds of cargo insurance and admiralty questions that this nation would not enjoy untangling.

Permissibility as a limit to decision-making, however, is not a matter of law alone. A decision in foreign affairs almost always depends on its acceptance by other nations, and, as President Kennedy once ruefully remarked, the leaders of every nation seem to believe that the United States can change the minds and course of all nations but their own. A decision in domestic affairs (and often in foreign affairs, as in the case of Yugoslav trade) may depend on its being accepted, or its not being reversed, by the Congress —for the President under our system is not empowered to remake the nation in his own image.

Surprisingly enough, a President's decision in either domestic or foreign affairs may also depend upon its acceptance within the executive branch itself —on the President's ability to gain acceptance for his point of view over dissent, inertia, incompetence, or impotence among his own appointees and policy officials as well as the permanent bureaucracy. Few outsiders understand this; they view the executive branch as a monolith, where the President's every word is a command and all lines of authority run to him. But in truth there are checks and balances within the departments and agencies, and I can recall more than one occasion when it was necessary for the President to convince his own appointees before they could undertake to convince the Congress, the Soviets, or some other party.

Nor is it enough that a decision be acceptable. It must also be workable. It must be enforceable. It must be possible. The President is not omnipotent. Choices within his control may be altered by events beyond his control. Revolutions, assassinations, elections, and disasters daily change the face of the globe. A decision to maintain a nuclear test moratorium may be shattered by a Soviet resumption. A decision to use only federal marshals to protect a Negro student in Mississippi may be reversed by the violence of a mob. A decision to lower the deficit by withholding taxes on dividends may be rejected by the Congress.

In the minds of the public and the press, as Philip Jessup has said, "impossibility is sometimes confused with incompetence or indecision." In summer of 1962, for example, the pressures on the President to request a quick tax cut before the election were very large. His delay was attributed by some to indecision. Yet in the absence of economic evidence sufficiently alarming to overcome key Congressional objections—evidence which was never forthcoming—such a request would have been only an exercise in futility, and possibly a harmful one at that.

There is no clear standard of feasibility. It may depend on the President's prestige at the moment of decision. It can be affected by an unexpected turn of events—such as occurred when the thalidomide tragedy increased the acceptability of drug reform. What *is* clear is that a President's authority is not as great as his responsibility—and that what is desirable is always limited by the possible or permissible.

LIMITS OF AVAILABLE RESOURCES

Every gain incurs a cost—and the most efficient decision, therefore, is theoretically the one that produces the greatest margin of gain over cost.

A President's resources are limited not only in terms of money but also in terms of manpower, time, credibility, patronage. If he allocates a billion dollars of his budget to education, it cannot be used for public works. If large numbers of scientists are recruited for a moon-shot, they are not available for other needs.

Only a limited number of commodities can be reserved from meaningful trade negotiations. Only a limited number of times can key members of Congress or leaders of the alliance be approached with special requests. Only a limited number of televised appeals can be made to the nation without the danger of diminishing returns. Any President, in short, must continually be engaged in setting priorities and measuring costs.

LIMITS OF AVAILABLE TIME

There is a time to act and a time to wait. By not acting too soon, the President may find that the problem dissolves or resolves itself, that the facts are different from what he thought, or that the state of the nation has changed. By not waiting too long, he may make the most of the mood of the moment, or retain the element of surprise.

Franklin D. Roosevelt was reputed to be a master of political timing. Mrs. Roosevelt spoke of his "enormous patience," his ability to "wait for exactly the right moment to act." "Though he enjoyed giving the impression of snap decisions," writes Schlesinger, he "actually made few," and had, in fact, a "weakness for postponement"—waiting until the situation had crystallized, until conflicts between competing forces were resolved, until public opinion was united.

Postponement often can be a weakness. Secrecy in government is sometimes necessary, but it is rarely permanent; and the topics of decisions long postponed are likely to be revealed before the decision is taken. The desire for more argument or more facts is always pressing, but overly prolonged fact-finding and debate may produce answers to questions which no longer exist. In the White House, the future rapidly becomes the past, and delay is itself a decision.

Yet most presidential decisions are too far-reaching and too irrevocable to be taken in haste, when the facts are uncertain, when the choices are unclear, or when the long-range consequences are not as discernible as the immediate reactions and results. President Kennedy has said, with respect to the Cuban crisis: "If we had to act in the first twenty-four hours, I don't think . . . we would have chosen as prudently as we finally did."

Some observers have argued that the President should have been told of that ominous missile discovery the night the first evidence came in. Yet there was no action to be taken that night of a retaliatory or investigative nature, or any reason to believe that his options would be different in the morning, when the actual presentation could be made. The departure of dinner guests to sudden midnight meetings at the White House might have served only to spread the alarm, and untroubled presidential sleep—an all too rare and therefore carefully guarded commodity—was a better preparation for the days ahead than a fruitless night of discussion could have been.

As the exhaustive and exhausting deliberations of that long October week went forward, however, the limits of time did become more pressing. For all of us knew that, once the missile sites under construction became operational, and capable of responding to any apparent threat or command with a nuclear volley, the President's options would be drastically changed. And all of us knew that, once the Soviets learned of our information and planning, our prospects for surprise and initiative would be greatly lessened. The President, therefore, could not wait for unanimity among all his advisers or for a special congressional session. The lonely decision was his—and he made it in good time.

LIMITS OF PREVIOUS COMMITMENTS

These include commitments or principles of the nation or party, commitments or precedents of an earlier President, commitments or decisions of a subordinate official, and the statements of the President himself. Of all these, party platforms and campaign promises are often the least confining, for they are usually worded by both parties with sufficient art to permit some elasticity, if not evasion.

The clearest limitations of all are those imposed by a President's own decisions. He need not make a fetish of consistency but he must avoid confusion or the appearance of deception. He will in most cases, therefore, adopt his own policies as precedents and consider his own statements as binding, whether they were contained in an informal answer to a press conference question or in a formal document of state. If the President solemnly promises to submit a balanced budget—or to reduce the outflow of gold—or to curb civilian appropriations—the country, the Congress, and the executive branch will all assume that such pledges were not lightly made and must not be lightly taken; and the weight of those words will narrow many subsequent presidential choices.

To refer once again to this nation's response to the presence of Soviet missiles in Cuba, this decision was not wholly developed during the seven days preceding its announcement. President Kennedy, on the morning of the first of those seven days, sent for copies of all his earlier statements on Cuba—on the presence of offensive, as distinguished from defensive, weapons—on threats to our vital interests—and on our armed intervention on that island. These earlier decisions made it unlikely that he would respond to the October crisis by doing nothing and unlikely that his first step would be an invasion.

Here, too, the nation's basic commitment to tradition and principle was involved. An air strike on military installations in Cuba, without any advance warning, was rejected as a "Pearl Harbor in reverse"—and no one could devise a form of advance warning (other than the quarantine itself, which was a type of warning) that would not leave this nation vulnerable to either endless discussion and delay (while work on the missiles went forward) or to a harsh indictment in the opinion and history of the world.

Similarly, in the summer of 1961, our diplomatic and military responses to each aggravation in West Berlin were kept consistent with general allied policy in the area. And the fiscal questions this crisis posed are an example of two prior commitments in conflict. A tax cut at that time, while it might have strengthened the economy at a crucial moment, could not be included in an emergency program for increasing burdens and effort; while a tax increase, though it might have helped pay for rising defense costs, would have been incompatible with the President's pledge on the nation's economic recovery. "The special train," Dr. Jessup has said, "must run on the same tracks which carry the regularly scheduled traffic."

LIMITS OF AVAILABLE INFORMATION

Implicit in these limits is the President's need to make certain that as much information as possible is available. Reliance solely on official channels has never proven to be wise. For there will always be subordinates who are willing to tell a President only what they want him to hear, or, what is even worse, only what they think he wants to hear.

President Kennedy, for example, although he is careful to rely primarily on the responsible officers involved when a final decision is to be made, seeks independent information from a variety of unofficial sources: newspapers, magazines, books, radio, television, visitors, friends, politicians, pollsters, the spokesmen for private organizations, and a sampling of mail.

Add any or all of these to the tides of official memoranda, reports, cables, intelligence briefings, analyses, and other government documents, and the occupant of the White House risks drowning in paper. There is a temptation, consequently, to exclude unpleasant information, yet rational decisions require an understanding of opposed positions. There is a temptation to require more screening of information, with only the most salient facts filtering through on one-page memoranda. But while a President cannot permit himself to be submerged in detail, he cannot afford to know so little as to shut out perspective and new inspiration. What information he actually considers and retains may well be the key to what he decides, and those in turn may depend on his confidence in the sources and on the manner in which the facts are presented. He is certain to regard some officials and periodicals with more respect than others.

The primary problem of presidential information, however, is usually not an abundance of reliable data but a shortage, especially in foreign affairs.

In these last two years, for example, the President has had to judge whether this nation's resumption of nuclear tests would increase or diminish the prospects for a test ban treaty, whether our quarantine around the island of Cuba would lead to Soviet submarine warfare, to a Berlin blockade, or to Soviet ships turning back.

Domestic decisions also involve uncertainty: whether a presidential appeal for a health insurance program would diminish or stiffen the opposition, whether presidential criticism of a union or industry which is threatening industrial peace or price stability would bring a reconsideration or merely an angry rebuff. These are the kinds of facts a President would like to know but cannot know on the domestic scene, where one miscalculation can endanger his entire program. The gaps in presidential information are even greater on the world scene—and there one miscalculation can endanger the nation, or even life as we know it on this planet.

Yet decisions must be made. Despite gaps in his information, despite the strictures of his previous pledges, and all other limitations, the President must nevertheless make decisions every day on courses for the nation that may decide its success or survival.

Few Presidents, therefore, I am certain, could survive unless they had the capacity to say, as Franklin D. Roosevelt reportedly said to a friend: "At night, when I lay my head on my pillow . . . and I think of the things that have come before me during the day, and the decisions I have made, I say to myself —well, I have done the best I could—and I turn over and go to sleep."

President Harding, on the other hand, was one of those who did not survive; and he is reported to have burst out to a friend: "I listen to one side and they seem right, and then . . . I talk to the other side and they seem just as right, and there I am where I started. . . . God, what a job!"

What a job it is, indeed. The President may seek advice from the Congress, from the Cabinet, or from his personal advisers. He may seek the views of the press, the parties, and the public. But however numerous his counsellors, in that final moment of truth there can be no "multitudes, multitudes" in the "valley of decision." There can be only one lonely man—the President of the United States.

The Bureaucracy

Although for most Americans bureaucracy is their most frequent contact with the workings of government, the majority know little or nothing about its structure or operation. Its best image is as a collection of nonpartisan civil servants faithfully applying the law indiscriminately to all. Its worst is as a gordian knot of red tape.

This chapter is concerned with the bureaucracy in its political role. The assumption of the readings that follow is that the bureaucracy is not merely a passive agent uniformly enforcing the law but an active participant in the political system.

In "The Bureaucracy Problem," Wilson suggests that there are really three difficulties with the bureaucracy: securing accountability, ensuring equity, and maintaining efficiency. None of these problems, he argues, can be handled adequately unless the objectives of a bureaucracy are clearly defined, for otherwise the discretion that the bureaucracy possesses will allow it to thwart the plans of the policy-making branches of government.

In "J. Edgar Hoover: The Compleat Bureaucrat," Kraft shows the FBI chief in his native habitat—"the vast, sprawling apparatus of the federal bureaucracy with its untidy lines to the seats of political power in the White House and the Congress"—in order to illustrate how a bureaucratic "pro" is able to maintain his and his agency's power.

The "political" character of bureaucracy is well illustrated in Freeman's "The Bureaucracy in Pressure Politics." The author argues that bureaucracies are pressure groups and their autonomy allows them not only to promote their own interests but also to become champions of the interests they "represent."

The Bureaucracy Problem

JAMES Q. WILSON

The federal bureaucracy, whose growth and problems were once only the concern of the Right, has now become a major concern of the Left, the Center, and almost all points in between. Conservatives once feared that a powerful bureaucracy would work a social revolution. The Left now fears that this same bureaucracy is working a conservative reaction. And the Center fears that the bureaucracy isn't working at all.

Increasing federal power has always been seen by conservatives in terms of increasing *bureaucratic* power. If greater federal power merely meant, say, greater uniformity in government regulations—standardized trucking regulations, for example, or uniform professional licensing practices—a substantial segment of American businessmen would probably be pleased. But growing federal power means increased discretion vested in appointive officials whose behavior can neither be anticipated nor controlled. The behavior of state and local bureaucrats, by contrast, can often be anticipated *because* it can be controlled by businessmen and others.

Knowing this, liberals have always resolved most questions in favor of enhancing federal power. The "hacks" running local administrative agencies were too often, in liberal eyes, the agents of local political and economic forces—businessmen, party bosses, organized professions, and the like. A federal bureaucrat, because he was responsible to a national power center and to a single President elected by a nationwide constituency, could not so easily be bought off by local vested interests; in addition, he would take his policy guidance from a President elected by a process that gave heavy weight to the votes of urban, labor, and minority groups. The New Deal bureaucrats, especially those appointed to the new, "emergency" agencies, were expected by liberals to be free to chart a radically new program and to be competent to direct its implementation.

It was an understandable illusion. It frequently appears in history in the hopes of otherwise intelligent and far-sighted men. Henry II thought his clerks and scribes would help him subdue England's feudal barons; how was he to know that in time they would become the agents of parliamentary authority

Reprinted by permission of the author and the publisher from James Q. Wilson, "The Bureaucracy Problem," *The Public Interest*, No. 6 (Winter 1967), pp. 3–9. © National Affairs, Inc. 1967.

directed at stripping the king of his prerogatives? And how were parliament and its cabinet ministers, in turn, to know that eventually these permanent undersecretaries would become an almost self-governing class whose day-to-day behavior would become virtually immune to scrutiny or control? Marxists thought that Soviet bureaucrats would work for the people, despite the fact that Max Weber had pointed out why one could be almost certain they would work mostly for themselves. It is ironic that among today's members of the "New Left," the "Leninist problem"—i.e., the problem of over-organization and of self-perpetuating administrative power—should become a major preoccupation.

This apparent agreement among polemicists of the Right and Left that there is a bureaucracy problem accounts, one suspects, for the fact that nonbureaucratic solutions to contemporary problems seem to command support from both groups. The negative income tax as a strategy for dealing with poverty is endorsed by economists of such different persuasions as Milton Friedman and James Tobin, and has received favorable consideration among members of both the Goldwater brain trust and the Students for Democratic Society. Though the interests of the two groups are somewhat divergent, one common element is a desire to scuttle the social workers and the public welfare bureaucracy, who are usually portrayed as prying busybodies with pursed lips and steel-rimmed glasses ordering midnight bedchecks in public housing projects. (Police officers who complain that television makes them look like fools in the eyes of their children will know just what the social workers are going through.)

Now that everybody seems to agree that we ought to do something about the problem of bureaucracy, one might suppose that something would get done. Perhaps a grand reorganization, accompanied by lots of "systems analysis," "citizen participation," "creative federalism," and "interdepartmental coordination." Merely to state this prospect is to deny it.

There is not one bureaucracy problem, there are several, and the solution to each is in some degree incompatible with the solution to every other. First, there is the problem of accountability or control—getting the bureaucracy to serve agreed-on national goals. Second is the problem of equity—getting bureaucrats to treat like cases alike and on the basis of clear rules, known in advance. Third is the problem of efficiency—maximizing output for a given expenditure, or minimizing expenditures for a given output. Fourth is the problem of responsiveness—inducing bureaucrats to meet, with alacrity and compassion, those cases which can never be brought under a single national rule and which, by common human standards of justice or benevolence, seem to require that an exception be made or a rule stretched. Fifth is the problem of fiscal integrity—properly spending and accounting for public money.

Each of these problems mobilizes a somewhat different segment of the public. The problem of power is the unending preoccupation of the President and his staff, especially during the first years of an administration. Equity concerns the lawyers and the courts, though increasingly the Supreme Court seems to act as if it thinks its job is to help set national goals as a kind of auxiliary White House. Efficiency has traditionally been the concern of businessmen who thought, mistakenly, that an efficient government was one that didn't spend very much money. (Of late, efficiency has come to have a broader and more accurate meaning as an optimal relationship between objectives and resources. Robert McNamara has shown that an "efficient" Department of Defense costs a lot more money than an "inefficient" one; his disciples are now carrying the message to all parts of a skeptical federal establishment.) Responsiveness has been the concern of individual citizens and of their political representatives, usually out of wholly proper motives, but sometimes out of corrupt ones. Congress, especially, has tried to retain some power over the bureaucracy by intervening on behalf of tens of thousands of immigrants, widows, businessmen, and mothers-of-soldiers, hoping that the collective effect of many individual interventions would be a bureaucracy that, on large matters as well as small, would do Congress's will. (Since Congress only occasionally has a clear will, this strategy only works occasionally.) Finally, fiscal integrity—especially its absence—is the concern of the political "outs" who want to get in and thus it becomes the concern of "ins" who want to keep them out.

Obviously the more a bureaucracy is responsive to its clients—whether those clients are organized by radicals into Mothers for Adequate Welfare or represented by Congressmen anxious to please constituents—the less it can be accountable to presidential directives. Similarly, the more equity, the less responsiveness. And a preoccupation with fiscal integrity can make the kind of program budgeting required by enthusiasts of efficiency difficult, if not impossible.

Indeed, of all the groups interested in bureaucracy, those concerned with fiscal integrity usually play the winning hand. To be efficient, one must have clearly stated goals, but goals are often hard to state at all, much less clearly. To be responsive, one must be willing to run risks, and the career civil service is not ordinarily attractive to people with a taste for risk. Equity is an abstraction, of concern for the most part only to people who haven't been given any. Accountability is "politics," and the bureaucracy itself is the first to resist that (unless, of course, it is the kind of politics that produces pay raises and greater job security). But an absence of fiscal integrity is welfare chiseling, sweetheart deals, windfall profits, conflict of interest, malfeasance in high places—in short, corruption. Everybody recognizes *that* when he sees it, and none but a few misguided academics have anything good to say about it. As a result, fiscal scandal typically becomes the standard by which a bureaucracy is judged (the FBI is good because it hasn't had any, the Internal Revenue Service is bad because it has) and thus the all-consuming fear of responsible executives.

If it is this hard to make up one's mind about how one wants the bureaucracy to behave, one might be forgiven if one threw up one's hands and let nature take its course. Though it may come to that in the end, it is possible—and important—to begin with a resolution to face the issue squarely and try to think through the choices. Facing the issue means admitting what, in our zeal for new programs, we usually ignore: *There are inherent limits to what can be accomplished by large hierarchical organizations.*

The opposite view is more often in vogue. If enough people don't like something, it becomes a problem; if the intellectuals agree with them, it becomes a crisis; any crisis must be solved; if it must be solved, then it can be solved—and creating a new organization is the way to do it. If the organization fails to solve the problem (and when the problem is a fundamental one, it will almost surely fail), then the reason is "politics," or "mismanagement," or "incompetent people," or "meddling," or "socialism," or "inertia."

Some problems cannot be solved and some government functions cannot, in principle, be done well. Notwithstanding, the effort must often be made. The rule of reason should be to try to do as few undoable things as possible. It is regrettable, for example, that any country must have a foreign office, since none can have a good one. The reason is simple: it is literally impossible to have a "policy" with respect to *all* relevant matters concerning *all* foreign countries, much less a consistent and reasonable policy. And the difficulty increases with the square of the number of countries, and probably with the cube of the speed of communications. The problem long ago became insoluble and any sensible Secretary of State will cease trying to solve it. He will divide his time instead between *ad hoc* responses to the crisis of the moment and appearances on Meet the Press.

The answer is not, it must be emphasized, one of simply finding good people, though it is at least that. Most professors don't think much of the State Department, but it is by no means clear that a department made up only of professors would be any better, and some reason to believe that it would be worse. One reason is that bringing in "good outsiders," especially good outsiders from universities, means bringing in men with little experience in dealing with the substantive problem but many large ideas about how to approach problems "in general." General ideas, no matter how soundly based in history or social science, rarely tell one what to do tomorrow about the visit from the foreign trade mission from Ruritania or the questions from the congressional appropriations subcommittee.

Another reason is that good people are in very short supply, even assuming we knew how to recognize them. Some things literally cannot be done—or cannot be done well—because there is no one available to do them who knows how. *The supply of able, experienced executives is not increasing nearly as fast as the number of problems being addressed by public policy.* All the fellowships, internships, and "mid-career training programs" in the world aren't likely to increase that supply very much, simply because the essential qualities for an executive—judgment about men and events, a facility for making good

guesses, a sensitivity to political realities, and an ability to motivate others—
are things which, if they can be taught at all, cannot be taught systematically or
to more than a handful of apprentices at one time.

This constraint deserves emphasis, for it is rarely recognized as a constraint
at all. Anyone who opposed a bold new program on the grounds that there was
nobody around able to run it would be accused of being a pettifogger at best
and a reactionary do-nothing at worst. Everywhere except in government, it
seems, the scarcity of talent is accepted as a fact of life. Nobody (or almost
nobody) thinks seriously of setting up a great new university overnight, because anybody familiar with the university business knows that, for almost
any professorship one would want to fill, there are rarely more than five (if
that) really top-flight people in the country, and they are all quite happy—
and certainly well-paid—right where they are. Lots of new business ideas don't
become profit-making realities because good business executives are both hard
to find and expensive to hire. The government—at least publicly—seems to
act as if the supply of able political executives were infinitely elastic, though
people setting up new agencies will often admit privately that they are so
frustrated and appalled by the shortage of talent that the only wonder is why
disaster is so long in coming. Much would be gained if this constraint were
mentioned to Congress *before* the bill is passed and the hopes aroused, instead
of being mentioned afterward as an excuse for failure or as a reason why
higher pay scales for public servants are an urgent necessity. "Talent Is
Scarcer Than Money" should be the motto of the Budget Bureau.

If administrative feasibility is such a critical issue, what can be done about
it? Not a great deal. If the bureaucracy problem is a major reason why so
many programs are in trouble, it is also a reason why the problem itself cannot be "solved." But it can be mitigated—though not usually through the kinds
of expedients we are fond of trying: Hoover Commissions, management
studies, expensive consultants, coordinating committees, "czars," and the like.
The only point at which very much leverage can be gained on the problem *is*
when we decide what it is we are trying to accomplish. When we define our
goals, we are implicitly deciding how much, or how little, of a bureaucracy
problem we are going to have. A program with clear objectives, clearly stated,
is a program with a fighting chance of coping with each of the many aspects
of the bureaucracy problem. Controlling an agency is easier when you know
what you want. Equity is more likely to be assured when over-all objectives
can be stated, at least in part, in general rules to which people in and out of
the agency are asked to conform. Efficiency is made possible when you know
what you are buying with your money. Responsiveness is never easy or wholly
desirable; if every person were treated in accordance with his special needs,
there would be no program at all. (The only system that meets the responsiveness problem squarely is the free market.) But at least with clear objectives

we would know what we are giving up in those cases when responsiveness seems necessary, and thus we would be able to decide how much we are willing to tolerate. And fiscal integrity is just as easy to insure in a system with clear objectives as in one with fuzzy ones; in the former case, moreover, we are less likely to judge success simply in terms of avoiding scandal. We might even be willing to accept a little looseness if we knew what we were getting for it.

The rejoinder to this argument is that there are many government functions which, by their nature, can never have clear objectives. I hope I have made it obvious by now that I am aware of that. We can't stop dealing with foreign nations just because we don't know what we want; after all, they may know what *they* want, and we had better find out. My argument is advanced, not as a panacea—there is no way to avoid the problem of administration—but as a guide to choice in those cases where choice is open to us, and as a criterion by which to evaluate proposals for coping with the bureaucracy problem.

Dealing with poverty—at least in part—by giving people money seems like an obvious strategy. Governments are very good at taking money from one person and giving it to another; the goals are not particularly difficult to state; measures are available to evaluate how well we are doing in achieving a predetermined income distribution. There may be many things wrong with this approach, but administrative difficulty is not one of them. And yet, paradoxically, it is the last approach we will probably try. We will try everything else first—case work, counseling, remedial education, community action, federally-financed mass protests to end "alienation," etc. And whatever else might be said in their favor, the likelihood of smooth administration and ample talent can hardly be included.

Both the White House and the Congress seem eager to do something about the bureaucracy problem. All too often, however, the problem is described in terms of "digesting" the "glut" of new federal programs—as if solving administrative difficulties had something in common with treating heartburn. Perhaps those seriously concerned with this issue will put themselves on notice that they ought not to begin with the pain and reach for some administrative bicarbonate of soda; they ought instead to begin with what was swallowed and ask whether an emetic is necessary. *Coping with the bureaucracy problem is inseparable from rethinking the objectives of the programs in question.* Administrative reshuffling, budgetary cuts (or budgetary increases), and congressional investigation of lower-level boondoggling will not suffice and are likely, unless there are some happy accidents, to make matters worse. Thinking clearly about goals is a tough assignment for a political system that has been held together in great part by compromise, ambiguity, and contradiction. And if a choice must be made, any reasonable person would, I think, prefer the system to the clarity. But now that we have decided to intervene in such a wide range of human affairs, perhaps we ought to reassess that particular trade-off.

J. Edgar Hoover: The Compleat Bureaucrat

JOSEPH KRAFT

Roosevelt's first Attorney General, Homer Cummings, once showed up for work on a Sunday without a pass. He was stopped at the gate of the Justice Department by a guard, and there ensued the usual conversation with the usual result: the guard had the last word. "I don't care if you are the Attorney General," he said. "Nobody gets in without a pass. You couldn't get in without a pass even if you were J. Edgar Hoover."

This little episode tells a lot about the importance of Mr. Hoover and the FBI. It has been—in season and out, by friend and foe, from the agency's beginnings down to the latest squabbles with Martin Luther King and the Warren Commission—consistently exaggerated. To critics, Mr. Hoover is the advance guard of the police state. To boosters, he is the modern knight errant. For better or worse, he is made to cast a shadow larger than life.

Scratch a stereotype, however, and you find a model. The stereotype of Hoover as good guy is based on the model of how Russia became the Soviet Union. The stereotype of Hoover as bad guy depends on a model of how Germany passed under the rule of the truncheon. But if anything can be said to be alien to anything else, those experiences are alien to America. Set in his native habitat, Mr. Hoover emerges as a figure of far more ordinary dimensions —less a mover and shaker than a medium; less a source of action than a means. And what is his native habitat? It is the vast, sprawling apparatus of the federal bureaucracy with its untidy lines to the seats of political power in the White House and the Congress. Hoover is in the most literal sense the "G-Man"—the Government Man par excellence. He is the supreme example of the successful civil servant—the compleat bureaucrat.

Hoover's whole life has been spent in the atmosphere of the civil service. His father was a minor government employee. His mother came from a family of Swiss *fonctionnaires*. His elder brother worked in the Steamboat Inspection Service of the Department of Commerce. He grew up, and for many years lived, in the Seward Park section of Washington—a kind of civil service colony. He was educated at the alma mater of the federal bureaucracy—George Wash-

Reprinted from Joseph Kraft, "J. Edgar Hoover: The Compleat Bureaucrat," *Commentary*, February 1965, pp. 59–62, by permission. Copyright © 1965 by the American Jewish Committee.

ington Law School. His first job was in that mammoth filing cabinet, the Library of Congress. And the only other place in which he has ever been employed is the Justice Department. One of the very few persons who has worked closely with him, and who was both naive and candid enough to write an unvarnished account, was struck most of all by the civil service imprint. Former Attorney General Francis Biddle, in the second volume of his autobiography, speaks of Hoover as "A career man in the truest sense . . . he cares for power and more power; but unlike many men, it is power bent to the purpose of his life's work —the sucess of the FBI."

Before it became the FBI, and before Hoover's advent as chief in 1924, the Government Investigating Division was a private hole-in-the-corner goon squad for the Attorney General. Its arts were the arts of snooping, bribery, and blackmail. It acted independently of the rest of the government and without reference to other law enforcement agencies. Its agents were political hacks and con men. One of these, for example, was the notorious Gaston B. Means, an accused (though not convicted) murderer and forger who played some kind of role in most of the sordid scandals of the Harding Administration, including the cover-up of the President's illegitimate daughter by Nan Britton.

Hoover, by professionalizing it, drove this shameful organization out of existence—an accomplishment that virtually everyone acknowledges and honors. At the heart of almost everything the Bureau now does is that monument to bureaucratic endeavor—a central fingerprint file. Through the central files, and the courses of the Police Academy, the FBI maintains the closest relations with other law-enforcement agencies across the country. The agents are well-trained, upstanding men with unmistakable pride in their work, and a record of never having been stained by corruption. Though it has inspired snobbish smiles, their uniform (dark suit, handkerchief in pocket, snap brim fedora) is a badge of respectability. "When a man becomes part of this bureau," Hoover once said, "he must conduct himself, both officially and unofficially, as to eliminate the slightest possibility of criticism as to his conduct or actions." Perhaps alone among the law-enforcement agencies of the nation, the FBI never wantonly or ignorantly tramples on the traditional safeguards against search and seizure, unwarranted arrest, and forced confession. Its one transgression —wiretapping—is at least docketed in the best bureaucratic fashion. Mr. Hoover can cite authority for the wiretapping he does (in a memorandum from President Roosevelt), describe the procedure (approval of the Attorney General), and indicate the number of taps (about 75) in progress at any one moment. Finally, given the general, and sometimes idolatrous, popularity of the FBI, it is especially illuminating to compare the agents with the astronauts in the matter of vulgar commercialization. Hoover has simply not allowed it to happen. Indeed, manufacturers who sell products to the FBI are specifically forbidden by contract from advertising the fact.

Not that the Director of the FBI is averse to publicity. As his critics have pointed out ad nauseam, Hoover plays vigorously and with great flair the widely misunderstood (and often wrongly impugned) Washington game of coloring, slanting, leaking, and managing the news. It is typical that the day after the Warren Commission Report was released with its criticisms of the FBI's relations to the Secret Service, a section of Hoover's testimony to the Commission (in which he criticized the State Department) was leaked to the press. There seems to be little doubt that Hoover regularly exaggerates both the exploits of the Bureau, and the dangers posed by those it opposes. Whatever the individual malignity of Dillinger, "Baby Face" Nelson, or Ma Baker, it is hard to believe that, in the days of fifteen million unemployed at home and Adolf Hitler abroad, any of these hillbilly criminals was really Public Enemy Number One. Hyperbole, to put it mildly, also marked the Bureau's attitude toward the menace of left-wing subversion after the two world wars. Can anyone seriously agree with Hoover that the protest demonstrations that took place against the House Un-American Activities Committee in San Francisco in May 1960 constituted a "successful Communist coup"?

But the real point is not that Hoover sometimes exaggerates; it is that every other bureau in Washington does the same thing. For years, for example, the military services contributed to a very large overestimation of the Soviet forces in Eastern Europe. Secretary McNamara has an annual field day in disposing of Air Force claims as to what manned bombers can do, and Secretary Rusk could probably perform a similar job on the Peace Corps' evaluation of its impact abroad. Has anyone recently found the Reclamation Bureau balancing its accomplishments against the point that the food surplus perhaps discourages the opening up of new land? How reasonable, in retrospect, were the claims of the FCC as to what ultra-high-frequency stations could do to improve the quality of television? In other words, far from acting in a singular manner in puffing his bureau and building up its services, Hoover simply follows the bureaucratic norm.

In this connection it is worth recalling the evacuation of more than 100,000 Nisei from the West Coast by the U.S. Army in the days following Pearl Harbor. That project has been called, by the American Civil Liberties Union, "the worst single wholesale violation of civil rights of American citizens in our history." But at the time it was endorsed by many men notable for their sensitivity to the cause of civil liberties, Earl Warren and Walter Lippmann among them. And who was against it? Perhaps most vigorously of all, J. Edgar Hoover. He denied the existence of subversive activities among the Japanese and, according to Biddle, who was Attorney General then, submitted a memorandum arguing that the demand for evacuation was "based primarily upon public and political pressure rather than upon factual data." No doubt, Hoover's position was influenced by the fact that the evacuation was conducted by another agency —the army—with the implication that the FBI was not capable of keeping tabs on subversive tendencies among the Nisei. But the point is that with a bureaucratic interest at stake, Hoover behaved in a way completely at odds with the image of scare-monger so dear to his liberal critics. On the contrary, in defense of his bureaucratic position, he was a model of zeal for civil liberties.

Similarly with two lacunae in the FBI record that have recently been much remarked upon. There is abundant evidence that the Bureau has not thrown itself heart and soul either into the fight against organized crime or into the fight for civil rights. In dealing with the former problem, the last two administrations have felt the need to set up, outside the Bureau, special investigatory units. "The FBI," one member of these special units has asserted, "is not set up to do battle with the criminal syndicate. . . ." Fred Cook, in his recent book on the Bureau,[1] points out that the FBI has played no part either in bringing to book, or directing attention to, the "names of Costello, Adonis, Luciano, Anastasia, Accarde and Genovese."

The reason for this reluctance to cope with organized crime is obscure. But one good possibility lies in the requirements for such work. It would demand the infiltration of agents into million-dollar criminal rings skilled in the ways of buying influence, and with temptations to burn. It would expose the agents, in other words, to the nearly certain danger of corruption. This is not a prospect attractive to a man whose life work has been the building of an incorruptible force. And it is again worth noting that in defending his bureaucratic interests, Mr. Hoover has fallen back on the purest democratic ethos. "Nothing," he told a meeting of police chiefs in 1960, "could be more dangerous to our democratic ideals than the establishment of an all-powerful police agency on the federal scene."

Equally abundant evidence suggests that until recently the Bureau has been less than keen to become involved in civil rights matters. Martin Luther King and others have been complaining about FBI inactivity for years. The Justice Department, when trouble loomed in Mississippi last spring, dispatched a special investigating unit—from outside the FBI. Even after the trouble came to a head in the Philadelphia murders, Hoover was counseling the President to send to Mississippi U.S. marshals, or marines, or troops, or sailors—anyone, in short, but the FBI.

The reason for Hoover's reluctance to enter the civil rights field is not so obscure as the reason for his reluctance to enter the fight against organized crime. For one thing, civil rights action has tended to bring the FBI into conflict with local forces of law and order throughout the South. More important still, zeal in matters of civil rights has not, at least until recently, been a way to win favor either in the White House or in the power fastnesses of the Congress.

And there lies the true crux of the whole issue. For Hoover, like any good bureaucrat, is extremely sensitive to the wishes of the political powers. Dozens of chairman of important congressional committees can probably endorse the view once expressed by Parnell Thomas of the House Un-American Activities

Committee that "the closest relationship exists between Mr. Hoover and this committee." For like all the great bureaucratic corps within departments— like the armed services in the Defense Department, like the Public Health Service in HEW, like the Reclamation Bureau in Interior, and the Forest Service in Agriculture—the FBI in Justice has formed independent alliances with major congressional figures who preside over its appropriations.

At the same time, Hoover has always tried to cultivate the closest relations with the White House. That explains the flowers sent to Walter Jenkins when he first entered the hospital; and it explains why Hoover immediately began going around Attorney General Kennedy and directly to President Johnson after the assassination in Dallas. The true use to which Hoover puts the great gossipy knowledge that he has of the doings of public officials is described by Francis Biddle:

> I sought to invite his confidence; and before long, lunching alone with me in a room adjoining my office, he began to reciprocate by sharing some of his extraordinary broad knowledge of the intimate details of what my associates in the Cabinet did and said, of their likes and dislikes, their weaknesses and their associations. It was as if he were saying to me that he trusted me enough to know that I would not repeat information which, except to his Chief, it would have been highly indiscreet of him to communicate, and would have been embarrassing had his revelation been communicated to the V.I.P. whom it concerned. Edgar was not above relishing a story derogatory to an occupant of one of the seats of the mighty, particularly if the little great man was pompous or stuffy. And I confess that, within limits, I enjoyed hearing it. His reading of human nature was shrewd, if perhaps colored with the eye of an observer to whom the less admirable aspects of behavior were being constantly revealed.
>
> He knew how to flatter his superior, and had the means of making him comfortable. The Attorney General, when he was traveling, could count on an agent to meet him at the station, to settle him on his plane with an armful of newspapers, to take him in an FBI car wherever he wished to go. But he also showed a friendly thoughtfulness on more than one occasion when it was not called for, and made me feel that our relationship was not without cordiality on both sides.

Occasionally, very occasionally, there are high public officials suspicious and ornery enough by nature to resist such blandishments. The prime case in point is President Johnson. If he has not been looking for a new FBI chief, as *Newsweek* claimed, he has certainly shown a disposition to keep a tight rein on the FBI's activities. He denied Hoover authority over the investigation of the Kennedy assassination. He has kept protection of the President in the hands of the Secret Service. He personally intervened with Hoover to push the FBI into the civil rights field, and to have the Bureau open an office in Mississippi.

Undoubtedly other Presidents, and even Attorney Generals, could have done what President Johnson is doing. But for most of them, resisting the assiduous services of the FBI has seemed not worth the trouble. In fact, almost all of what look like independent acts by the Bureau have been things done for the pleasure of the political leadership. Attorney General Mitchell Palmer wanted the anti-anarchist raids of 1919–1920. Homer Cummings deliberately boosted Hoover as a "gangbuster." Can anyone say that Herbert Brownell or Dwight Eisenhower was unhappy when Hoover testified to the effect that the Democrats had ignored his advice in promoting Harry Dexter White to a position of great influence? It was none other than Franklin Roosevelt who gave Hoover the mandate under which he continues to tap wires. And here is Biddle's account of what happened on another occasion when the FBI had been found to be wiretapping, and Hoover went to explain the incident to Roosevelt:

> FDR was delighted; and with one of his great grins, intent on every word, slapped Hoover on the back when he had finished. "By God, Edgar, that's the first time you've been caught with your pants down!" The two men liked and understood each other.

That is the usual attitude of men in power. It is fatuous, in these circumstances, to heap praise and blame on Hoover. One does not become either angry or exultant with the queen because it takes the jack. It is the players who count, not the cards.

The Bureaucracy in Pressure Politics

J. LEIPER FREEMAN

It is not a novel statement that we live in a society of "organization men," but we have yet to comprehend adequately the implications of this fact. Today's bureaucratic world is a reality within which the vast majority of Americans are enmeshed. Large, complex, specialized, hierarchical organizations are means of achieving the mass production, communications, services, regulation, and destruction possible in modern society. These bureaucracies are both public and private, large and small, demanding and lenient; but in any case they are the dominating form of social organization in America today.

Although bureaucracies are primarily regarded as organizations which exe-

Reprinted by permission of the author and the publisher from J. Leiper Freeman, "The Bureaucracy in Pressure Politics," *The Annals of the American Academy of Political and Social Science,* Vol. 319 (September 1958), pp. 11–19.

cute policies assigned to them by society, they must also be reckoned with as sources of influence upon social policies. The nature of this influence is basically twofold. First, members of bureaucracies can give shape to stated policies through the exercise of choice and judgment in administering them. Second, in attempting to affect the objectives and working conditions which society will authorize for their organizations, members of bureaucracies necessarily engage in pressure politics.

It is with this second aspect of bureaucratic behavior that this article is chiefly concerned. Furthermore, it is confined to pressure politics engaged in by governmental, as opposed to private, bureaucracies and to pressure politics aimed at influencing official governmental policies.

Public bureaucracies—national, state, and local—today employ about one-eighth of the labor force of the United States. About 3 million of these members of public bureaucracies are in the armed forces; slightly more than 2.2 million are civilian employees of the federal government; more than 1.1 million are classroom teachers in the public schools; about 3.5 million are otherwise employed by the state and local governments. If these bureaucrats, numbering between 9 and 10 million, formed one large group sharing a common identity, they would constitute a force in pressure politics to defy the imagination. But public bureaucrats are divided into many bureaucracies by levels of government, by special functions, by special technologies, by differing clienteles, and by territories. The result is a patchwork of official organizations devoted to limited, specialized interests.

Bureaucracies as Pressure Groups

Since a public bureaucracy is concerned with special and limited aspects of public policy, to a degree it resembles the ordinary private pressure group. It is a congregating place for individuals concerned with the same subjects. Some of these interested individuals become members of the administrative agency while others join groups which look to that organization as a rallying point, and the agency takes a leading part in representing their interests. In this representative process perhaps the bureaucracy's most important function is to promote the idea that its special area of concern is important—be it education, air power, or mental health. The bureaucracy also promotes special solutions to policy problems in its area. Finally, it promotes objectives which are of particular interest to its members *as bureaucrats*. These are matters such as their working conditions, status, and compensation, as well as the maintenance and survival of their organization.

A public bureaucracy, as part of the official government, is subject to some controls over its pressure politics which do not apply to private groups. There are laws at the federal level to restrict the public relations and legislative activities of bureaucrats. Federal agencies are forbidden by an act passed in

1913 to use public funds to compensate "any publicity expert unless explicitly appropriated for that purpose."² Another act, passed in 1919, provides that appropriations shall not be used, unless explicitly authorized by Congress, "directly or indirectly to pay for any personal service, advertisement, telegram, telephone, letter, printed or written matter, or other device, intended or designed to influence in any manner a Member of Congress, to favor or oppose, by vote or otherwise, any legislation or appropriation by Congress, whether before or after the introduction of any bill or resolution proposing such legislation or appropriation. . . ."³

These general restrictions, however, have served mainly as policy statements to be used as threats against agency officials rather than as bases for actual cases. "Publicity experts" have not been hired, but "information," "education," and "publication" officers have been employed in good quantity.⁴ Although these publicists have often been flayed in the halls of Congress, no cases have arisen in which they have been held as violators of the law. Furthermore, despite the prohibitions against spending public funds to influence a member of Congress, there has remained a great latitude for legislative activity by public administrators. The expectations of Congressmen in this regard were well summarized by Representative Frank Buchanan in his committee's investigation of bureaucratic lobbying in 1950:

> . . . It is equally necessary for the executive branch of Government to be able to make its views known to Congress on all matters in which it has responsibilities, duties, and opinions. The executive agencies have a definite requirement to express views to Congress, to make suggestions, to request needed legislation, to draft proposed bills or amendments, and so on. And there is, of course, the power centered in the executive branch to overrule by veto any action of Congress which is not supported by a clear two-thirds majority of both Houses.⁵

Chief Executive Controls

It is safe to conclude that such statutory restrictions are not important limitations upon administrative propagandizing and lobbying in the federal government, and they are even less so in state and local governments where laws governing political activities of bureaucrats are generally less numerous and less stringent. Instead, more meaningful controls over bureaucratic pressure politics are to be found in the powers of the chief executive.

At all levels of government today there is a tendency toward giving the chief executive more effective authority over finance, organization, and personnel to help him control the actions of administrative agencies. These sanctions do not necessarily remove bureaucrats from the arena of pressure politics, but they tend to channel their activities along lines amenable to the chief executive. The stronger these sanctions are—in the case of the city manager or strong

mayor form of municipal executive, or the strong Governorship, or the Presidency—the smaller the relative autonomy allowed bureaucrats in legislative
and public relations.

In the federal government, the Bureau of the Budget and the provisions of
the Budgeting and Accounting Act of 1921 aid the President in establishing
central control over tendencies toward agency autonomy in seeking appropriations. Executive departments and bureaus are prohibited from seeking amounts
larger than those requested for them in the President's budget when they appear
before appropriations committees of Congress. Nevertheless, there have been
instances in which questioning by committee members has brought into the
record a bureau's original requests which perhaps the Budget Bureau had
eliminated or curtailed. This device for circumventing the prescribed budget
procedure is probably welcomed by an administrator, with friendly committee
members and sympathetic interest groups doing the prodding. Yet, on the
whole, the executive budget is a significant means of coordinating administrative requests for funds.

In proposals for legislation, the Bureau of the Budget is also of some help to
the President since it has the power to require that agencies' legislative requests
should be submitted to it to determine whether they are "in accord with the
program of the President." This does not prevent an agency from submitting
proposals to Congress which are not "in accord," but it is supposed to enable
Congress to know whether measures are consonant with the President's program when it takes action on them. There is no clear agreement among persons
who have studied the effectiveness of this procedure, but the most recent evaluation indicates that in recent years it has become somewhat more effective in
curbing autonomous action by the various agencies.[6]

The organizational status of a bureaucracy in the executive hierarchy deter-
mines to some degree the autonomy its members will have in their public and
legislative relations. The more independently an agency is located in the structure of executive authority, the less formal power the chief executive can exercise over its political activities as well as on its administration of the laws. Thus,
independent commissions and government corporations may enjoy some
measure of independence from central direction of their political entrepreneur-
ship which is not available to regular departments.

PERSONNEL AND SCHEDULE C

Under the kind of government most often found in the United States, with
a popularly elected chief executive having constitutional authority separate
from the legislative branch, the President needs and usually has a coterie of
political appointees. They serve both as political directors of the agencies and
as leaders of the bureaucracies in their attempts to promote policies in their
special spheres of interest.

The federal government under the Eisenhower administration enlarged the number of offices in this category by creating the so-called Schedule C positions for policy-making personnel in order to give the Republicans a larger crew of high-echelon officials. The major rationale for this enlargement was that the huge bureaucracies inherited from the previous administration, largely protected by civil service status, would otherwise be so intractable that the new administration would not be able to curb their autonomous tendencies. The results of this measure are not yet clear, although it has led to the removal of certain posts at the bureau-chief level from merit system status and to the creation of a number of new assistant secretaries and administrative assistants, who are patronage appointees. They compose an enlarged group of party representatives engaged in legislative liaison, public relations, and policy development at higher levels of the administration. They may have also reduced the political leeway of officials at lower levels.[7]

Bureaucratic Autonomy

Despite the restrictions which may be placed upon bureaucracies because they are part of the government, they still have considerable autonomy within the executive structure to engage in pressure politics. They enjoy certain advantages by being in the official family which help to offset the restrictions placed upon them. One advantage is the fact that they are expected by legislators to make recommendations to the legislative body on a continuing, legitimate basis. Furthermore, they may have the blessings of the Chief Executive in their legislative operations and consequently can speak with considerable force as the administration's specialists.

When Representative Buchanan voiced the thought that bureaucrats should "make their views known" to Congress, he was speaking with restraint. Virtually no piece of legislation of any consequence reaches any advanced stage of the legislative process without at least one administrative agency making some statement concerning it. On many bills, the chances are great that the proposal originated in an executive agency. Furthermore, in the highly decisive stage of the legislative process—committee hearings—officials from the administration are invariably among the most regular and most crucial witnesses. Legislators at all levels of government, despite their defensiveness toward bureaucracy, like to hear from the bureaucrats most intimately concerned when making up their minds about proposed legislation, and the bureaucrats oblige them energetically.

The various bureaucracies are also expected by the Chief Executive and the leaders of the administration to carry a good deal of the burden of legislative leadership for the executive branch in their own special areas. This aspect of lobbying by administrative agencies is sometimes overlooked or unduly subordinated by students of the subject because of a preoccupation with the desirability of integrated executive leadership. In reality the Chief Executive cannot personally get involved in every legislative skirmish without tending to reduce his effectiveness and dissipating his resources for political leadership. On lesser matters and indeed on many that are of considerable importance, the bureaucracies are depended upon by the top level of the executive branch to work out the proposals, to secure their introduction, to mobilize support from the public and elsewhere, and to negotiate with the committees and the leaders of the legislative branch to secure favorable action.[8]

General Legislative Liaison

Administrative agencies do not wait until a specific proposal is to be urged upon the legislature to cultivate harmonious relations with legislators. A continuous process of legislative liaison is maintained. This may be found at all levels of government and at all tiers of administration within these levels, although it is most marked at the higher echelons of federal administration. In the federal government, the growth of this process is reflected in recent institutional developments in which the major agencies have appointed high ranking officials with sizeable staffs to spend their full time on it. Every bureau is also equipped to consider requests from Congressmen and to furnish them information speedily. In the field offices, major headquarters follow the same pattern.

Accommodating legislative requests and inquiries where legitimately possible serves to keep agencies in the good graces of legislators and opens the way for suggestions and requests from administrators in return. Field officials usually work with Representatives and Senators from their own area. In Washington, where the liaison machinery is more elaborate and more concerned with agency-wide problems, particular attention is focused upon congressional leaders and members of key committees.

While a good part of this activity is precautionary in that it is intended to keep legislators from becoming annoyed with an agency, it is also part of the agency's attempt to "cast bread upon the waters," to maintain a reservoir of good will, and to keep the solons aware of the important work the agency is doing.

At the state and local levels, legislative liaison has not become as highly organized and institutionalized as it has at the national level, but the essential ingredients are the same.

Strategy With Committees

Because so much of the meaningful work of legislative bodies is done in committees rather than in the full assemblies, the relations of spokesmen for the bureaucracies with committee members specializing in given policy areas are crucial aspects of administrative pressure politics. Committee members and agency officials who work together on common problems can build up the kind of understanding which maximizes the effect of agency opinions upon committee decisions. Committee recommendations in turn have a primary effect upon the content of laws passed by the parent body. Committee hearings, therefore, are not merely means by which legislative groups exert control over bureaucracies, they are also critical opportunities for bureaucrats to influence legislation.

In general, committee members need information on policy questions, and administrative officials are in a position to have a vast store of it to present. This information, derived from the elaborate network of a bureaucracy, is a source of power. By presenting it strategically, leaders from the bureaucracy can use hearings to good advantage. Since hearings are usually covered by the press, the information presented may not only make a direct impression upon the committee members but also furnish ammunition to the agency's friends among the public.

USING HIGHER-ECHELON SUPPORT

Leaders of a bureaucracy who appear before legislators to advocate any new laws or changes in policy which their agency desires usually try to enlist the support of others. In many instances one of the most helpful sources of support is the chief executive or others in the higher echelons of the administration. Many things that an agency desires are not regarded as being of vital importance to the top leaders of the administration, even though the chief executive and his advisors may have nothing against their passage. If, however, the bureau chief and department officials seeking the legislation can secure from the chief executive a statement to the legislative committee, or a comment to the press, or a paragraph in a speech favorable to their proposal, they may very well enhance its possibilities of adoption.

The effectiveness of this action is, of course, related to the state of the chief executive's popularity and prestige with the legislators. If the bureaucrats decide that the chief executive would in a given instance be more of an albatross than a guardian angel, they will naturally hope that he will not associate himself with their legislative project in any way.

The use of higher-echelon support is also available to bureaucrats as a defense against unwanted legislation. Their advice is given much weight in questions regarding the use of the chief executive's veto power on legislation falling within their special spheres of competence.

MOBILIZING EMPLOYEE SUPPORT

One of the great reservoirs of political strength available to agency leaders in certain kinds of legislative activities lies in their organization's employees. This is naturally more true of the larger organizations since elected officals tend to be impressed by numbers. In the federal government, the Post Office

Department (with over 500,000 employees) is a good example of an agency which tends to profit appreciably from employee support.

There is no particular evidence, however, that employees are necessarily helpful to their agency leaders on *all* legislative matters. Detailed studies of municipal department heads' legislative strategies show that they are not inclined to view their employees as important sources of support in dealing with the city council except on matters such as salaries, job conditions, and the like.[9] The reason is that public employee organizations tend to concentrate their efforts on their interests as bureaucrats, often relegating larger-policy questions to a secondary position. For this reason, agency leaders are often faced with the problem of tying employee benefits to other policy objectives and thereby evoking a maximum effort by the mass of the bureaucrats in their organizations to influence the legislative body.

At the federal level, a recent example of the linking of employee interests with broader policy objectives was seen in the fight waged by the Post Office Department to secure a modernization of the postal service and the most comprehensive revision of postage rates in over twenty years. Within the postal service, postmasters and postal employees were convinced that new buildings and equipment and increases in salaries were not to be obtained without the revision, and they contributed to the effort to obtain it. Legislative representatives from state and national organizations of postmasters conferred with the legislators. Organizations of postal employees lobbied and propagandized for it heavily.

The employees of the Brooklyn Post Office paid for a full-page advertisement in the New York *Times* to reprint an article by Senator Olin D. Johnston, Chairman of the Senate Committee on Post Office and Civil Service, which in general advocated modernization of the service and increasing the postage rates. Readers were urged to clip the article and mail it to their Senators.[10]

MOBILIZING CLIENTELE SUPPORT

Employees are, after all, not always the most appropriate pleaders in behalf of a bureaucracy in the legislative arena. Legislators are inclined to regard employees as pleading their own cases and therefore may discount their contentions. Consequently, administrative leaders seek to have their proposals endorsed by private groups who carry weight with legislators.

The easiest groups of this type for most agencies to mobilize are the so-called clientele groups. In many instances they are highly organized and easily identified. The Veterans Administration counts heavily on the American Legion and to a lesser extent on other veterans organizations to support its recommendations to Congress. In fact, it seldom tends to make a recommendation to Congress that is not reasonably acceptable to these organizations, so strong is their partnership in all pressure politics dealing with veterans affairs.

The pattern is similar with many other agencies and their clienteles such as the Commerce Department and business organizations; the Labor Department and the unions; and the Agriculture Department and the Farm Bureau, the Grange, and other farmer organizations. These other groups do not, however, always show the same degree of collaboration as that evinced by the Veterans Administration and its customers.

In fact, many of the difficulties attending Secretary Ezra Benson's efforts [1958] to convince Congress that his department's recommendations are the answer to the farm problems of the United States are related to an estrangement between the present leadership of the Department of Agriculture and significant portions of its clientele. Agency leaders who fail to maintain the confidence of their patrons are apt to lose the most crucial element of their support in legislative relations. Groups that are not in the clientele of an agency are more difficult to encourage to take as much interest and exert as much effort in the agency's behalf.

OTHER GROUP SUPPORT

Bureaucracies welcome and at times aid the organization of groups to serve as their sponsors. These groups are not necessarily composed of steady customers of an agency, but they are made up of people who for various reasons are interested in its aims and its existence. Some of these groups are completely unofficial in nature; but many are given some official recognition in the agency's operations, rendering them quasi-public in character. By elaborating their administrative structure, public bureaucracies at all levels of American government have enlisted the participation of interested and often influential citizens in their business to give them advice and sometimes even to help them set and administer policies. In turn, the bureaucracies expect and usually receive support for their legislative objectives.

Among the many groups of this type to be found at the federal level are, for example, the various reserve officer associations of the military branches, or the very exclusive advisory committee of the Commerce Department, or any of the many other advisory committees in other units. Over the years the Agriculture Department has built up one of the most complex systems of citizen participation in administration at the local level that could be imagined. Some of its major programs are handled at the county level by committees elected by farmers and working in conjunction with full-time paid employees of the Department. In this way, for example, the Agricultural Stabilization and Conservation Service enlists sponsors composed of local farm leaders in county after county across the nation.[11]

In local governments, outstanding examples of sponsor groups are to be found in Parent-Teacher Associations or in "Friends of the Library." And at a more official and formal level they may be found in the plethora of boards and commissions which are officially charged with setting policies for various municipal agencies.

The way in which board sponsorship works to an administrator's advantage was observed a few years ago in a New England city.[12] The head of the library board was the woman with the most prestige in town, and the librarian was regarded as her protegee. These two ladies got the board chairman's husband to agree to buy a bookmobile for the public library if the city would agree to maintain it. Then the city council was presented with this proposition at a meeting in which the library board was well represented and virtually able to make the matter one in which the council would appear cheap if it refused. The council, seeing that it had little choice, voted the funds to maintain the bookmobile and, of course, to furnish a driver.

PRESSURE BY ADMINISTRATIVE DECISION

Bureaucrats can often generate pressure upon legislators through the exercise of their legitimate discretion in the course of conducting the public's business. One of the most recent and most widely argued examples was furnished by Postmaster General Arthur Summerfield. He gave orders to curtail mail deliveries one day a week last year [1957] when Congress was showing reluctance to appropriate some funds which Mr. Summerfield said were necessary to prevent deficiencies in his agency. Despite outraged cries, Congress gave Mr. Summerfield the money. After all, people wanted their mail on Saturdays.

Looking again at the municipal level, the water commissioner of a New England city used his administrative powers to help arouse public support and pressure upon the council for a bond issue to expand the water supply—a measure which certain industries in the city favored. Although it was a hot and dry summer, the commissioner helped the drought along for some people by diverting water to the country club from a main which served many residences in a high part of the city. When the residents on this main could not draw bath water, not knowing that their water was being siphoned off to the golfers' showers, they were even more emphatic than the Water Commissioner and his industrialist supporters that the water supply needed expansion. Eventually the Council voted the bonds.[13]

General Publicity Activities

The ultimate aim of bureaucratic publicity is in large measure to create a climate of opinion which will be favorable to its objectives. Some of an agency's publicity is necessary to the administrative process of making more acceptable to the public the things it has already been assigned to do. But the cultivation of favorable public images also may serve to build up support for legislation which the agency desires but does not have, and it is difficult to separate one function of bureaucratic publicity from the other.

The many books and articles written about the exploits of the Federal Bureau of Investigation agents, the continuous, favorable publicity accorded to Mr. J. Edgar Hoover, and the speeches and writings of Mr. Hoover all help to make the jobs which are assigned to the FBI easier to accomplish. Yet this publicity also makes the agency more successful in its relations with Congress, for Congressmen are sensitive to the image maintained among the public at large.

Of course, the FBI is unusually fortunate in comparison with other federal bureaus in the nature and extent of its publicity, but many administrative units get a good deal of coverage on a fairly steady basis. There are abundant opportunities for members of the higher echelons of the bureaucracy not only to release news through regular channels and to talk to reporters, but also to make addresses, write articles, and in other ways create publicity for their organizations. Furthermore, in the field offices, regional press coverage is generally well maintained, especially for the larger agencies, and this substantially supplements the publicity emanating from Washington. Since nine-tenths of federal employees are not in Washington, there is immense opportunity for publicity to be generated at local levels, where it can often affect the constituents of Congressmen most directly.

There is also usually a network of friendly media especially interested in the subjects dealt with by an agency and willing to help carry the propaganda battle. Some of these are "trade" publications, which, combined with official publications and reports, give bureaucracies ample outlets to reach the most interested audiences. Due to the limited nature of general public interest in most public problems, it is frequently more important to reach the highly concerned portion of the public than to try to publicize in general.

Bureaucrats can become victims of their own overzealous publicity tactics. Legislators are capable of being very sensitive to what they regard as improper administrative propagandizing, especially if it encroaches on their domains. It does not help administrative leaders and the agencies they represent to become branded as propagandists. The kinds of retribution they suffer in such instances vary from oratorical chastisement in the legislative halls to denial of the very objects which they seek to have the legislators bestow—funds and authority.

The Courts

Observers of the American scene have always been bewildered by the role of law and the courts in our society. Because of the compact theory of government, the written Constitution, the complexities of the federal system, and the reluctance to give discretionary power to government officials, the United States has become a highly legalistic nation in which the judiciary makes political decisions that in other countries are made by legislative or executive branches.

Though commonplace, such judicial participation in American political decision-making is seldom perceived by the citizens. Most people have faith in the courts because they believe that courts make legal rather than political decisions and that ours is a "government of laws and not of men." Thus, much of the criticism directed against the U.S. Supreme Court is based on the mistaken belief that the Court is deviating from its proper judicial role to become a policy-making body.

Dahl, however, in "The Supreme Court as a National Policy-Maker," finds that the policy-making role is not new. In fact, the Court's policy decisions are usually closely attuned to the policies of the President and the Congress, and only during short, transitional periods (as in the last two decades) is the Court out of step with these major decision-makers.

Much of the recent criticism of the Court stems from the inability of the average newspaper reader to understand how the nine justices on the Court can split 5 to 4 on the proper interpretation of the law. In "5-to-4: Are the Justices

Really Objective?" Freund suggests that the misunderstanding is, in fact, caused by the Constitution itself. Disagreement about the meaning of the Constitution is inevitable, given that document's broad phraseology and the Court's task of reconciling vague language with specific situations.

In "Civil Disobedience: The Law Is Never Blind," Sax suggests that, contrary to what most laymen think, *all law*—not just the Constitution—is vague and susceptible to different interpretations. In fact, he argues, because there is so much room for maneuver within the constraints placed on prosecutors and trial judges, the decision can frequently be interpreted either way—and for equally cogent reasons. He states that, for example, "the southern oligarchs were not indicted for criminal conspiracy when they produced their massive resistance campaign against the school integration decision . . . , while . . . war resisters were readily brought to trial under the umbrella of the vague and amorphous conspiracy doctrine."

Often the government tries to use criminal prosecution to limit dissent and force conformity on its citizens, and it is in these cases that the courts have become deeply involved in protecting civil rights. An illustrative case is *United States v. O'Brien,* which came about when David O'Brien burned his draft card to protest the Vietnam war and was arrested and convicted on a 1965 congressional amendment to the 1948 Universal Military Training and Service Act prohibiting the destruction of draft cards. O'Brien argued that his action was a form of symbolic speech and therefore protected by the First Amendment. The U.S. Court of Appeals agreed and voided his conviction as an abridgment of free speech—but at the same time it upheld his conviction under the 1948 law requiring him to be in possession of the draft card. Since neither O'Brien nor the government was happy with this decision, both appealed to the Supreme Court. The Court rejected O'Brien's contention, deciding that the United States had a vested interest in requiring him to carry the card. More importantly, the Court stated: "We cannot accept the view that an apparently limitless variety of conduct can be labeled speech. . . ."

Enforcing criminal laws against dissenters may not only restrict freedom of speech; it also raises fundamental questions about the limits of police action. Certainly nearly everyone would be against police torture of suspects and would allow an accused to have an attorney at his trial—but what other rights does the accused have? When, for example, does the right to have an attorney begin? The Supreme Court entered this particular controversy when, in 1964, it held that a suspect in police custody could not be denied his right to consult an attorney. For this decision, the Court was bitterly attacked—but instead of retreating, in *Miranda v. Arizona* it went even further. This case—actually four cases, combined for argument and decision—came about when Miranda was convicted of kidnapping and rape on the basis of a confession he gave after police held him in custody for two hours without telling him of his right to have an attorney. In New York, Vignera, another figure in the *Miranda* case, had been convicted (for robbery) under similar circumstances. So had Stewart in California, although the supreme court of that state had reversed the conviction because of the absence of an attorney. Westover, another *Miranda* defendant, had been warned of his rights by the FBI—but only after he had already been questioned by local police for fourteen hours without being informed of his right to an attorney. For all these cases the Supreme Court ruled that police must inform a suspect in their custody—before any questioning begins—of his right to remain silent and of his right to have an attorney present at any point in the proceedings. Because police had failed to provide adequate safeguards, the Court ruled the confessions invalid and overturned the convictions of the four defendants.

Any distraught citizen can challenge the government, in a civil suit, when he feels his constitutional rights have been violated. And this is what happened when the State of New York wrote a prayer for school children supposedly to improve the moral climate of the community. The parents of ten pupils went to court to have the law declared unconstitutional on the grounds that the state was establishing a religion, and in *Engel et al. v. Vitale et al.* the Supreme Court agreed by a vote of 6 to 1.

This last decision is examined by Beaney and Beiser in "Prayer and Politics: The Impact of *Engel* and *Schempp* on the Political Process." The article emphasizes that, like American politics in general, which is a web of interaction of culture, politics, and governmental institutions, judicial decisions are not separate from the rest of society—they are affected by and in turn affect it.

Decision-Making in a Democracy: The Supreme Court as a National Policy-Maker

ROBERT A. DAHL

To consider the Supreme Court of the United States strictly as a legal institution is to underestimate its significance in the American political system. For it is also a political institution, an institution, that is to say, for arriving at decisions on controversial questions of national policy. As a political institution, the Court is highly unusual, not least because Americans are not quite willing to accept the fact that it *is* a political institution and not quite capable of denying it; so that frequently we take both positions at once. This is confusing to foreigners, amusing to logicians, and rewarding to ordinary Americans who thus manage to retain the best of both worlds.

I

A policy decision might be defined as an effective choice among alternatives about which there is, at least initially, some uncertainty. This uncertainty may arise because of inadequate information as to: (a) the alternatives that are thought to be "open"; (b) the consequences that will probably ensue from choosing a given alternative; (c) the level of probability that these consequences will actually ensue; and (d) the relative value of the different alternatives, that is, an ordering of the alternatives from most preferable to least preferable, given the expected consequences and the expected probability of the consequences actually occurring. An *effective* choice is a selection of the most preferable alternative accompanied by measures to insure that the alternative selected will be acted upon.

No one, I imagine, will quarrel with the proposition that the Supreme Court, or indeed any court, must make and does make policy decisions in this sense. But such a proposition is not really useful to the question before us. What is critical is the extent to which a court can and does make policy decisions by

Reprinted by permission of the author and the publisher from Robert A. Dahl, "Decision-Making in a Democracy: The Supreme Court as a National Policy-Maker," *Journal of Public Law*, Vol. 6, No. 2 (1957), pp. 279–295.

going outside established "legal" criteria found in precedent, statute, and Constitution. Now in this respect the Supreme Court occupies a most peculiar position, for it is an essential characteristic of the institution that from time to time its members decide cases where legal criteria are not in any realistic sense adequate to the task. A distinguished associate justice of the present Court has recently described the business of the Supreme Court in these words:

> It is essentially accurate to say that the Court's preoccupation today is with the application of rather fundamental aspirations and what Judge Learned Hand calls "moods," embodied in provisions like the due process clauses, which were designed not to be precise and positive directions for rules of action. The judicial process in applying them involves a judgment . . . . that is, on the views of the direct representatives of the people in meeting the needs of society, on the views of Presidents and Governors, and by their construction of the will of legislatures the Court breathes life, feeble or strong, into the inert pages of the Constitution and the statute books.[1]

Very often, then, the cases before the Court involve alternatives about which there is severe disagreement in the society, as in the case of segregation or economic regulation; that is, the setting of the case is "political." Moreover, they are usually cases where competent students of constitutional law, including the learned justices of the Supreme Court themselves, disagree; where the words of the Constitution are general, vague, ambiguous, or not clearly applicable; where precedent may be found on both sides; and where experts differ in predicting the consequences of the various alternatives or the degree of probability that the possible consequences will actually ensue. Typically, in other words, although there may be considerable agreement as to the alternatives thought to be open [(a)], there is very serious disagreement as to questions of fact bearing on consequences and probabilities [(b) and (c)], and as to questions of value, or the way in which different alternatives are to be ordered according to criteria establishing relative preferability [(d)].

If the Court were assumed to be a "political" institution, no particular problems would arise, for it would be taken for granted that the members of the Court would resolve questions of fact and value by introducing assumptions derived from their own predispositions or those of influential clienteles and constituents. But, since much of the legitimacy of the Court's decisions rests upon the fiction that it is not a political institution but exclusively a legal one, to accept the Court as a political institution would solve one set of problems at the price of creating another. Nonetheless, if it is true that the nature of the cases arriving before the Court is sometimes of the kind I have described, then the Court cannot act strictly as a legal institution. It must, that is to say, choose among controversial alternatives of public policy by appealing to at least some criteria of acceptability on questions of fact and value that cannot be found in or deduced from precedent, statute, and Constitution. It is in this sense that the Court is a national policy-maker, and it is this role that gives rise to the problem of the Court's existence in a political system ordinarily held to be democratic.

Now I take it that except for differences in emphasis and presentation, what I have said so far is today widely accepted by almost all American political scientists and by most lawyers. To anyone who believes that the Court is not, in at least some of its activities, a policy-making institution, the discussion that follows may seem irrelevant. But to anyone who holds that at least one role of the Court is as a policy-making institution in cases where strictly legal criteria are inadequate, then a serious and much debated question arises, to wit: Who gets what and why? Or in less elegant language: What groups are benefited or handicapped by the Court and how does the allocation by the Court of these rewards and penalties fit into our presumably democratic political system?

II

In determining and appraising the role of the Court, two different and conflicting criteria are sometimes employed. These are the majority criterion and the criterion of Right or Justice.

Every policy dispute can be tested, at least in principle, by the majority criterion, because (again: in principle) the dispute can be analyzed according to the numbers of people for and against the various alternatives at issue, and therefore according to the proportions of the citizens or eligible members who are for and against the alternatives. Logically speaking, except for a trivial case, every conflict within a given society must be a dispute between a majority of those eligible to participate and a minority or minorities; or else it must be a dispute between or among minorities only.[2] Within certain limits, both possibilities are independent of the number of policy alternatives at issue, and since the argument is not significantly affected by the number of alternatives, it is convenient to assume that each policy dispute represents only two alternatives.[3]

If everyone prefers one of two alternatives, then no significant problem arises. But a case will hardly come before the Supreme Court unless at least one person prefers an alternative that is opposed by another person. Strictly speaking, then, no matter how the Court acts in determining the legality or constitutionality of one alternative or the other, the outcome of the Court's decision must either (1) accord with the preferences of a minority of citizens and run counter to the preferences of a majority; (2) accord with the preferences of a majority and run counter to the preferences of a minority; or (3) accord with the preferences of one minority and run counter to the preferences of another minority, the rest being indifferent.

In a democratic system with a more or less representative legislature, it is unnecessary to maintain a special court to secure the second class of outcomes.

A case might be made out that the Court protects the rights of national majorities against local interests in federal questions, but so far as I am aware, the role of the Court as a policy-maker is not usually defended in this fashion; in what follows, therefore, I propose to pass over the ticklish question of federalism and deal only with "national" majorities and minorities. The third kind of outcome, although relevant according to other criteria, is hardly relevant to the majority criterion, and may also be passed over for the moment.

One influential view of the Court, however, is that it stands in some special way as a protection of minorities against tyranny by majorities. In the course of its 167 years, in seventy-eight cases, the Court has struck down eighty-six different provisions of federal law as unconstitutional,[4] and by interpretation it has modified a good many more. It might be argued, then, that in all or in a very large number of these cases the Court was, in fact, defending the rights of some minority against a "tyrannical" majority. There are, however, some exceedingly serious difficulties with this interpretation of the Court's activities.

III

One problem, which is essentially ideological in character, is the difficulty of reconciling such an interpretation with the existence of a democratic polity, for it is not at all difficult to show by appeals to authorities as various and imposing as Aristotle, Locke, Rousseau, Jefferson, and Lincoln that the term democracy means, among other things, that the power to rule resides in popular majorities and their representatives. Moreover, from entirely reasonable and traditional definitions of popular sovereignty and political equality, the principle of majority rule can be shown to follow by logical necessity.[5] Thus to affirm that the Court supports minority preferences against majorities is to deny that popular sovereignty and political equality, at least in the traditional sense, exist in the United States; and to affirm that the Court *ought* to act in this way is to deny that popular sovereignty and political equality *ought* to prevail in this country. In a country that glories in its democratic tradition, this is not a happy state of affairs for the Court's defenders; and it is no wonder that a great deal of effort has gone into the enterprise of proving that, even if the Court consistently defends minorities against majorities, nonetheless it is a thoroughly "democratic" institution. But no amount of tampering with democratic theory can conceal the fact that a system in which the policy preferences of minorities prevail over majorities is at odds with the traditional criteria for distinguishing a democracy from other political systems.[6]

Fortunately, however, we do not need to traverse this well-worn ground; for the view of the Court as a protector of the liberties of minorities against the tyranny of majorities is beset with other difficulties that are not so much ideological as matters of fact and logic. If one wishes to be at all rigorous about the question, it is probably impossible to demonstrate that any particular Court decisions have or have not been at odds with the preferences of a "national majority." It is clear that unless one makes *some* assumptions as to the kind of evidence one will require for the existence of a set of minority and majority preferences in the general population, the view under consideration is incapable of being proved at all. In any strict sense, no adequate evidence exists, for scientific opinion polls are of relatively recent origin, and national elections are little more than an indication of the first preferences of a number of citizens—in the United States the number ranges between about 40 and 60 percent of the adult population—for certain candidates for public office. I do not mean to say that there is no relation between preferences among candidates and preferences among alternative public policies, but the connection is a highly tenuous one, and on the basis of an election it is almost never possible to adduce whether a majority does or does not support one of two or more policy alternatives about which members of the political elite are divided. For the greater part of the Court's history, then, there is simply no way of establishing with any high degree of confidence whether a given alternative was or was not supported by a majority or a minority of adults or even of voters.

In the absence of relatively direct information, we are thrown back on indirect tests. The eighty-six provisions of federal law that have been declared unconstitutional were, of course, initially passed by majorities of those voting in the Senate and in the House. They also had the President's formal approval. We could, therefore, speak of a majority of those voting in the House and Senate, together with the President, as a "lawmaking majority." It is not easy to determine whether any such constellation of forces within the political elites actually coincides with the preferences of a majority of American adults or even with the preferences of a majority of that half of the adult population which, on the average, votes in congressional elections. Such evidence as we have from opinion polls suggests that Congress is not markedly out of line with public opinion, or at any rate with such public opinion as there is after one discards the answers of people who fall into the category, often large, labelled "no response" or "don't know." If we may, on these somewhat uncertain grounds, take a "lawmaking majority" as equivalent to a "national majority," then it is possible to test the hypothesis that the Supreme Court is shield and buckler for minorities against national majorities.

Under any reasonable assumptions about the nature of the political process, it would appear to be somewhat naive to assume that the Supreme Court either would or could play the role of Galahad. Over the whole history of the Court, on the average one new justice has been appointed every twenty-two months. Thus a President can expect to appoint about two new justices during one term of office; and if this were not enough to tip the balance on a normally divided Court, he is almost certain to succeed in two terms. Thus, Hoover had three appointments; Roosevelt, nine; Truman, four; and Eisenhower, so far, has had four. Presidents are not famous for appointing justices hostile to their own views on public policy nor could they expect to secure confirmation of a man whose stance on key questions was flagrantly at odds with that of the dominant majority in the Senate. Justices are typically men who, prior to appointment, have engaged in public life and have committed themselves publicly on the great questions of the day. As Mr. Justice Frankfurther has recently reminded us, a surprisingly large proportion of the justices, particularly of the great justices who have left their stamp upon the decisions of the Court, have had little or no prior judicial experience.[7] Nor have the justices—certainly not the great justices—been timid men with a passion for anonymity. Indeed, it is not too much to say that if justices were appointed primarily for their "judicial" qualities without regard to their basic attitudes on fundamental questions of public policy, the Court could not play the influential role in the American political system that it does in reality play.

The fact is, then, that the policy views dominant on the Court are never for long out of line with the policy views dominant among the lawmaking majorities of the United States. Consequently it would be most unrealistic to suppose that the Court would, for more than a few years at most, stand against any major alternatives sought by a lawmaking majority. The judicial agonies of the New Deal will, of course, quickly come to mind; but Mr. Roosevelt's difficulties with the Court were truly exceptional. Generalizing

TABLE 9-1

The Interval Between Appointments to the Supreme Court

INTERVAL IN YEARS	PERCENT OF TOTAL APPOINTMENTS	CUMULATIVE PERCENT
Less than 1	21	21
1	34	55
2	18	73
3	9	82
4	8	90
5	7	97
6	2	99
–	–	–
12	1	100
Total	100	100

NOTE: The table excludes the six appointments made in 1789. Except for the four most recent appointments, it is based on data in the Encyclopedia of American History, pp. 461–462 (Morris ed., 1953). It may be slightly inaccurate because the source shows only the year of appointment, not the month. The twelve-year interval was from 1811 to 1823.

over the whole history of the Court, the chances are about one out of five that a President will make one appointment to the Court in less than a year, better than one out of two that he will make one within two years, and three out of four that he will make one within three years. Mr. Roosevelt had unusually bad luck: he had to wait four years for his first apointment; the odds against this long an interval are four to one. With average luck, the battle with the Court would never have occurred; even as it was, although the "court-packing" proposal did formally fail, by the end of his second term Mr. Roosevelt had appointed five new justices and by 1941 Mr. Justice Roberts was the only remaining holdover from the Hoover era.

It is to be expected, then, that the Court is least likely to be successful in blocking a determined and persistent lawmaking majority on a major policy and most likely to succeed against a "weak" majority; e.g., a dead one, a transient one, a fragile one, or one weakly united upon a policy of subordinate importance.

IV

An examination of the cases in which the Court has held federal legislation unconstitutional confirms, on the whole, our expectations. Over the whole history of the Court, about half the decisions have been rendered more than four years after the legislation was passed.

TABLE 9-2

Percentage of Cases Held Unconstitutional, Arranged by Time Intervals Between Legislation and Decision

NUMBER OF YEARS	NEW DEAL LEGISLATION %	OTHER %	ALL LEGISLATION %
2 or Less	92	19	30
3–4	8	19	18
5–8	0	28	24
9–12	0	13	11
13–16	0	8	6
17–20	0	1	1
21 or More	0	12	10
Total	100	100	100

Of the twenty-four laws held unconstitutional within two years, eleven were measures enacted in the early years of the New Deal. Indeed, New Deal measures comprise nearly a third of all the legislation that has ever been declared unconstitutional within four years after enactment.

TABLE 9-3

Cases Holding Legislation Unconstitutional Within Four Years After Enactment

INTERVAL IN YEARS	NEW DEAL		OTHER		TOTAL	
	No.	%	*No.*	%	*No.*	%
2 or Less	11	29	13	34	24	63
3–4	1	3	13	34	14	37
Total	12	32	26	68	38	100

It is illuminating to examine the cases where the Court has acted on legislation within four years after enactment—where the presumption is, that is to say, that the lawmaking majority is not necessarily a dead one. Of the twelve New Deal cases, two were, from a policy point of view, trivial; and two, although perhaps not trivial, were of minor importance to the New Deal program.[8] A fifth[9] involved the NRA, which was to expire within three weeks of the decision. Insofar as the unconstitutional provisions allowed "codes of fair competition" to be established by industrial groups, it is fair to say that President Roosevelt and his advisers were relieved by the Court's decision on a policy they had come to find increasingly embarrassing. In view of the tenacity with which Mr. Roosevelt held to his major program, there can hardly be any doubt that had he wanted to pursue the major policy objective involved in the NRA codes, as he did, for example, with the labor provisions, he would not have been stopped by the Court's special theory of the Constitution. As to the seven other cases,[10] it is entirely correct to say, I think, that whatever some of the eminent justices might have thought during their fleeting moments of glory, they did not succeed in interposing a barrier to the achievement of the objectives of the legislation; and in a few years most of the constitutional interpretation on which the decisions rested had been unceremoniously swept under the rug.

The remainder of the thirty-eight cases where the Court has declared legislation unconstitutional within four years of enactment tend to fall into two rather distinct groups: those involving legislation that could reasonably be regarded as important *from the point of view of the lawmaking majority* and those involving minor legislation. Although the one category merges into the other, so that some legislation must be classified rather arbitrarily, probably there will be little disagreement with classifying the specific legislative provisions involved in eleven cases as essentially minor from the point of view of the lawmaking majority (however important they may have been as constitutional interpretations).[11] The specific legislative provisions involved in the remaining fifteen cases are by no means of uniform importance, but with one or two possible exceptions it seems reasonable to classify them as

TABLE 9-4

Number of Cases Involving Legislative Policy Other Than Those Arising Under New Deal Legislation Holding Legislation Unconstitutional Within Four Years After Enactment

INTERVAL IN YEARS	MAJOR POLICY	MINOR POLICY	TOTAL
2 or Less	11	2	13
3–4	4	9	13
Total	15	11	26

major policy issues from the point of view of the lawmaking majority.[12] We would expect that cases involving major legislative policy would be propelled to the Court much more rapidly than cases involving minor policy, and, as the table below shows, this is in fact what happens.

Thus, a lawmaking majority with major policy objectives in mind usually has an opportunity to seek for ways of overcoming the Court's veto. It is an interesting and highly significant fact that Congress and the President do generally succeed in overcoming a hostile Court on major policy issues.

TABLE 9-5

Type of Congressional Action Following Supreme Court Decisions Holding Legislation Unconstitutional Within Four Years After Enactment (Other Than New Deal Legislation)

CONGRESSIONAL ACTION	MAJOR POLICY	MINOR POLICY	TOTAL
Reverses Court's Policy	10[13a]	2[13d]	12
Changes Own Policy	2[13b]	0	2
None	0	8[13e]	8
Unclear	3[13c]	1[13f]	4
Total	15	11	26

NOTE: For the cases in each category, see note 13.

It is particularly instructive to examine the cases involving major policy. In two cases involving punitive legislation enacted by Radical Republican Congresses against supporters of the Confederacy during the Civil War, the Court faced a rapidly crumbling majority whose death knell as an effective national force was sounded with the election of 1876.[14] Three cases are difficult to classify and I have labelled them "unclear." Of these, two were decisions made in 1921 involving a 1919 amendment to the Lever Act to control prices.[15] The legislation was important, and the provision in question was clearly struck down, but the Lever Act terminated three days after the decision and Congress did not return to the subject of price control until World War II, when it experienced no constitutional difficulties arising from these cases (which were primarily concerned with the lack of an ascertainable standard of guilt). The third case in this category successfully eliminated stock dividends from the scope of the Sixteenth Amendment, although a year later Congress enacted legislation taxing the actual income from such stock.[16]

The remaining ten cases were ultimately followed by a reversal of the actual policy results of the Court's action, although not necessarily of the specific constitutional interpretation. In four cases,[17] the policy consequences of the Court's decision were overcome in less than a year. The other six required a long struggle. Workmen's compensation for longshoremen and harbor workers was invalidated by the Court in 1920;[18] in 1922 Congress passed a new law which was, in its turn, knocked down by the Court in 1924;[19] in 1927 Congress passed a third law, which was finally upheld in 1932.[20] The notorious income tax cases[21] of 1895 were first somewhat narrowed by the Court itself;[22] the Sixteenth Amendment was recommended by President Taft in 1909 and was ratified in 1913, some eighteen years after the Court's decisions. The two child labor cases represent the most effective battle ever waged by the Court against legislative policy-makers. The original legislation outlawing child labor, based on the commerce clause, was passed in 1916 as a part of Wilson's New Freedom. Like Roosevelt later, Wilson was somewhat unlucky in his Supreme Court appointments; he made only three appointments during his eight years, and one of these was wasted, from a policy point of view, on McReynolds. Had McReynolds voted "right," the subsequent struggle over the problem of child labor need not have occurred, for the decision in 1918 was by a Court divided five to four, McReynolds voting with the majority.[23] Congress moved at once to circumvent the decision by means of the tax power, but in 1922 the Court blocked that approach.[24] In 1924 Congress returned to the engagement with a constitutional amendment that was rapidly endorsed by a number of state legislatures before it began to meet so much resistance in the states remaining that the enterprise miscarried. In 1938, under a second reformist President, new legislation was passed, twenty-two years after the first; this a chastened Court accepted in 1941,[25] and thereby brought to an end a battle that had lasted a full quarter-century.

The entire record of the duel between the Court and the lawmaking majority, in cases where the Court has held legislation unconstitutional within four years after enactment, is summarized in Table 9-6.

Thus the application of the majority criterion seems to show the following: First, if the Court did in fact uphold minorities against national majorities, as both its supporters and critics often seem to believe, it would be an extremely anomalous institution from a democratic point of view. Second, the elaborate "democratic" rationalizations of the Court's defenders and the hostility of

TABLE 9-6

Type of Congressional Action After Supreme Court Decisions Holding Legislation Unconstitutional Within Four Years After Enactment (Including New Deal Legislation)

CONGRESSIONAL ACTION	MAJOR POLICY	MINOR POLICY	TOTAL
Reverses Court's Policy	17	2	19
None	0	12	12
Other	6*	1	7
Total	23	15	38

*In addition to the actions in Table 9-5 under "Changes Own Policy" and "Unclear," this figure includes the NRA legislation affected by the *Schechter Poultry* case.

its "democratic" critics are largely irrelevant, for lawmaking majorities generally have had their way. Third, although the Court seems never to have succeeded in holding out indefinitely, in a very small number of important cases it has delayed the application of policy up to as much as twenty-five years.

V

How can we appraise decisions of the third kind just mentioned? Earlier I referred to the criterion of Right or Justice as a norm sometimes invoked to describe the role of the Court. In accordance with this norm, it might be argued that the most important policy function of the Court is to protect rights that are in some sense basic or fundamental. Thus (the argument might run) in a country where basic rights are, on the whole, respected, one should not expect more than a small number of cases where the Court has had to plant itself firmly aganist a lawmaking majority. But majorities may, on rare occasions, become "tyrannical"; and when they do, the Court intervenes; and although the constitutional issue may, strictly speaking, be technically open, the Constitution assumes an underlying fundamental body of rights and liberties which the Court guarantees by its decisions.

Here again, however, even without examining the actual cases, it would appear, on political grounds, somewhat unrealistic to suppose that a Court whose members are recruited in the fashion of Supreme Court justices would long hold to norms of Right or Justice substantially at odds with the rest of the political elite. Moreover, in an earlier day it was perhaps easier to believe that certain rights are so natural and self-evident that their fundamental validity is as much a matter of definite knowledge, at least to all reasonable creatures, as the color of a ripe apple. To say that this view is unlikely to find many articulate defenders today is, of course, not to disprove it; it is rather to suggest that we do not need to elaborate the case against it in this essay.

In any event the best rebuttal to the view of the Court suggested above will be found in the record of the Court's decisions. Surely the six cases referred to a moment ago, where the policy consequences of the Court's decisions were overcome only after long battles, will not appeal to many contemporary minds as evidence for the proposition under examination. A natural right to employ child labor in mills and mines? To be free of income taxes by the federal government? To employ longshoremen and harbor workers without the protection of workmen's compensation? The Court itself did not rely upon such arguments in these cases, and it would be no credit to their opinions to reconstruct them along such lines.

So far, however, our evidence has been drawn from cases in which the Court has held legislation unconstitutional within four years after enactment. What of the other forty cases? Do we have evidence in these that the Court has protected fundamental or natural rights and liberties against the dead hand of some past tyranny by the lawmakers? The evidence is not impressive. In the entire history of the Court there is not one case arising under the First Amendment in which the Court has held federal legislation unconstitutional. If we turn from these fundamental liberties of religion, speech, press, and assembly, we do find a handful of cases—sometimes less than ten—arising under Amendments Four to Seven in which the Court has declared acts unconstitutional that might properly be regarded as involving rather basic liberties.[26] An inspection of these cases leaves the impression that, in all of them, the lawmakers and the Court were not very far apart; moreover, it is doubtful that the fundamental conditions of liberty in this country have been altered by more than a hair's breadth as a result of these decisions. However, let us give the Court its due; it is little enough.

Over against these decisions we must put the fifteen or so cases in which the Court used the protections of the Fifth, Thirteenth, Fourteenth, and Fifteenth Amendments to preserve the rights and liberties of a relatively privileged group at the expense of the rights and liberties of a submerged group: chiefly slaveholders at the expense of slaves,[27] white people at the expense of colored people,[28] and property holders at the expense of wage earners and other groups.[29] These cases, unlike the relatively innocuous ones of the preceding set, all involved liberties of genuinely fundamental importance, where an opposite policy would have meant thoroughly basic shifts in the distribution of rights, liberties, and opportunities in the United States—where, moreover, the policies sustained by the Court's action have since been repudiated in every civilized nation of the Western world, including our own. Yet, if our earlier argument is correct, it is futile—precisely because the basic distribution of privilege *was* at issue—to suppose that the Court could have possibly acted much differently in these areas of policy from the way in which it did in fact act.

VI

Thus the role of the Court as a policy-making institution is not simple; and it is an error to suppose that its functions can be either described or appraised by means of simple concepts drawn from democratic or moral theory. It is possible, nonetheless, to derive a few general conclusions about the Court's role as a policy-making institution.

National politics in the United States, as in other stable democracies, is dominated by relatively cohesive alliances that endure for long periods of time. One recalls the Jeffersonian alliance, the Jacksonian, the extraordinarily long-lived Republican dominance of the post-Civil War years, and the New Deal alliance shaped by Franklin Roosevelt. Each is marked by a break with past policies, a period of intense struggle, followed by consolidation, and finally decay and disintegration of the alliance.

Except for short-lived transitional periods when the old alliance is disintegrating and the new one is struggling to take control of political institutions, the Supreme Court is inevitably a part of the dominant national alliance. As an element in the political leadership of the dominant alliance, the Court of course supports the major policies of the alliance. By itself, the Court is almost powerless to affect the course of national policy. In the absence of substantial agreement within the alliance, an attempt by the Court to make national policy is likely to lead to disaster, as the *Dred Scott* decision and the early New Deal cases demonstrate. Conceivably, the cases of the last three decades involving the freedom of Negroes, culminating in the now famous decision on school integration, are exceptions to this generalization; I shall have more to say about them in a moment.

The Supreme Court is not, however, simply an *agent* of the alliance. It is an essential part of the political leadership and possesses some bases of power of its own, the most important of which is the unique legitimacy attributed to its interpretations of the Constitution. This legitimacy the Court jeopardizes if it flagrantly opposes the major policies of the dominant alliance; such a course of action, as we have seen, is one in which the Court will not normally be tempted to engage.

It follows that within the somewhat narrow limits set by the basic policy goals of the dominant alliance, the Court *can* make national policy. Its discretion, then, is not unlike that of a powerful committee chairman in Congress who cannot, generally speaking, nullify the basic policies substantially agreed on by the rest of the dominant leadership, but who can, within these limits, often determine important questions of timing, effectiveness, and subordinate policy. Thus the Court is least effective against a current lawmaking majority—and evidently least inclined to act. It is most effective when it sets the bounds of policy for officials, agencies, state governments or even regions, a task that has come to occupy a very large part of the Court's business.[30]

Few of the Court's policy decisions can be interpreted sensibly in terms of a "majority" versus a "minority." In this respect the Court is no different from the rest of the political leadership. Generally speaking, policy at the national level is the outcome of conflict, bargaining, and agreement among minorities; the process is neither minority rule nor majority rule but what might better be called *minorities* rules, where one aggregation of minorities achieves policies opposed by another aggregation.

The main objective of Presidential leadership is to build a stable and dominant aggregation of minorities with a high probability of winning the Presidency and one or both houses of Congress. The main task of the Court is to confer legitimacy on the fundamental policies of the successful coalition. There are times when the coalition is unstable with respect to certain key policies; at very great risk to its legitimacy powers, the Court can intervene in such cases and may even succeed in establishing policy. Probably in such cases it can succeed only if its action conforms to and reinforces a widespread set of explicit or implicit norms held by the political leadership; norms which are not strong enough or are not distributed in such a way as to insure the existence of an effective lawmaking majority but are, nonetheless, sufficiently powerful to prevent any successful attack on the legitimacy powers of the Court. This is probably the explanation for the relatively successful work of the Court in enlarging the freedom of Negroes to vote during the past three decades and in its famous school integration decisions.[31]

Yet the Court is more than this. Considered as a political system, democracy is a set of basic procedures for arriving at decisions. The operation of these procedures presupposes the existence of certain rights, obligations, liberties and restraints; in short, certain patterns of behavior. The existence of these patterns of behavior in turn presupposes widespread agreement (particularly among the politically active and influential segments of the population) on the validity and propriety of the behavior. Although its record is by no means lacking in serious blemishes, at its best the Court operates to confer legitimacy, not simply on the particular and parochial policies of the dominant political alliance, but upon the basic patterns of behavior required for the operation of a democracy.

5-to-4: Are the Justices Really Objective?

PAUL FREUND

The recurrence of 5-to-4 decisions of the Supreme Court raises once again the question whether the judicial process is really objective in resolving important issues of constitutional law.

Given a constitutional text written in plain and, for the most part, non-technical English, how are we to explain the sharp divergence of views in applying the Constitution to an undisputed set of facts? Is there no explanation except that the judges are free to impose their personal social beliefs on the country in the name of the Constitution?

The first thing to observe is that constitutional guarantees like due process of law; freedom of speech, press and assembly, and equal protection of the laws do not supply ready-made answers to concrete, changing and unforeseen problems as those problems arise in life. Moreover, various constitutional guarantees may point in opposite directions. Criminal trials are to be fair, and the press to be free; how then do we decide whether the news media may or may not publish distorted and sensational accounts of a criminal suspect or a trial in progress?

Agreement a Wonder

Working with mandates so deliberately spacious and sometimes ambiguous as these, the wonder may well be that there is as much agreement as we actually find among the judges in their resolution of the controversies before them. For the dramatic dissents that capture public attention should not obscure the very substantial measure of common ground among the judges. One of the recent 5-to-4 decisions that captured public attention was the case of the civil rights demonstrators who were convicted for refusing to leave the courtyard of a jail. Justice Black's majority opinion was widely regarded as a significant retreat by the Court from its previous positions. Actually, all the members of the Court would clearly have agreed that a demonstration in the gallery of a legislative hall could be punished without any infringement of freedom of speech or assembly. By the same token, there would have been agreement

Reprinted by permission of the author and the publisher from Paul Freund, "5-to-4: Are the Justices Really Objective?", *The Boston Globe.* The article was reprinted in *Harvard Today,* Spring 1967.

that a peaceful demonstration in the public park would have been immune from prosecution. Thus the precise and narrow issue is not to be found in the constitutional text.

Granted that the cleavages may not be as wide or as deep as the rhetoric of the opinions might suggest, the question still remains: How are we to account for the differences that do exist, except in terms of willful and unconstrained predilection? When Justice Cardozo had to describe the judicial process, he referred to several ingredients that enter into a decision; the most important, in his view, were logic, history, and social utility. The real problem is how they shall be mixed in order to reach a satisfying conclusion. When this kind of question was put to Justice Frankfurter, he was fond of quoting the reply of Velasquez to a lady who asked him how he mixed his paints. "Madame," he said, "I mix them with taste."

"Mix With Judgment"

Two recent examples will illustrate how judges have to mix their ingredients with judgment as artists mix theirs with taste.

The Supreme Court ruled in another 5-to-4 decision that Georgia might elect its governor by vote of the legislature after a popular election produced no majority for any candidate. The dissenters argued that this result was repugnant to the principle of reapportionment cases, the equality of weight to each person's vote, since the legislature might select for governor a candidate who would not prevail in a run-off.

On the other hand, Justice Black for the majority reasoned that Georgia could regard the popular vote as having exhausted itself and a new kind of election as having been substituted in which each legislator was free to vote his own choice. Both opinions were perfectly logical; they simply differed in the premises from which they started. The dissent regarded the whole selection process as a unit, while the majority looked on it as two separate processes. In choosing between these premises, the dissent would have extended the majoritarian philosophy of the reapportionment cases. Speaking for the court, Justice Black gave controlling weight to the long history of the legislative role in the election of a governor in Georgia, a role dating back to the state constitution of 1824. Both positions were rationally defensible. What would be indefensible is a judicial decision motivated by a personal preference for candidate Maddox or candidate Callaway.

The other illustration involves the validity of a poll tax as a condition of voting in state elections. Here the court ruled the condition on the suffrage to be a violation of equal protection of the laws. Justice Black, dissenting, relied heavily on the long history of the poll tax in relation to voting rights, reflecting a tolerable judgment that the privilege of voting might be made to rest on a financial stake of the voter in his government.

But the majority were not persuaded by the weight of this history, in view of marked changes in the sharing of tax burdens and in our general outlook on the relevance of poverty to the rights of citizenship. There is no suggestion that Justice Black is personally more enamored of the poll tax than are his colleagues.

The upshot is that judges are constrained but not wholly so, and are free but by no means completely at large. This ought not to be so surprising when we recall that even scientists, who are thought to be engaged in an exact discipline, differ sharply when they reach frontier questions. On the same evidence and with the same principles of reasoning one astronomer will maintain the "big-band" view of the cosmos and another the "steady-state" theory. So, also, will one philosopher maintain a theory of freedom of the will and another of determinism.

The judges, like the scientists and the philosophers, may see the same phenomenon in different lights, with different predictions of what will in time satisfy thoughtful minds. The pursuit of justice, after all, is not necessarily easier than the pursuit of truth.

Civil Disobedience: The Law Is Never Blind

JOSEPH L. SAX

Nobody is opposed to civil disobedience; people simply want the laws that they deem important to be vigorously enforced and those they consider unfair to be ignored. Most motorists consider the idea of a speed trap outrageous, but rarely complain when policemen conceal themselves in public washrooms to ferret out homosexuals. The annual antics of American Legion conventioneers are viewed as harmless enough fun, but let political protestors go out in the streets and all the rigors of the law relating to trespass, obstruction of traffic, and disturbing the peace are suddenly remembered, whereupon we are solemnly told that acquiescence in illegality is the first step on the road to anarchy.

Reprinted by permission of the author and the publisher from Joseph L. Sax, "Civil Disobedience: The Law Is Never Blind," *Saturday Review,* September 28, 1968, pp. 22–25, 56. Copyright 1968 Saturday Review, Inc.

Through the miracle of prosecutorial discretion—a device central to the operation of the legal system, but widely ignored in discussions of civil disobedience—criminality can be, and is, produced or ignored virtually at will by law enforcement officials. Businessmen know that if the building and fire laws were fully implemented they could be in court virtually every day, a fact which is allegedly brought home to them when they are so unwise as to refrain from buying tickets to the annual policemen's ball.

Justice Jackson once said that "a prosecutor has more control over life, liberty, and reputation than any other person in America . . . he can choose his defendant . . . a prosecutor stands a fair chance of finding at least a technical violation of some act on the part of almost anyone." No more profound statement was ever made about the legal system.

The law is so vast in its technical coverage and so open-ended in its possibilities for interpretation by police officers, prosecutors, and judges that it becomes almost meaningless to talk about civil disobedience as if there were conduct which "the law"—as some external force—declared illegal.

In fact, no society could operate if it did not tolerate a great deal of technically or arguably illegal conduct on the ground that certain laws were obsolescent and others unwise as written or as applied to particular situations. A few weeks ago, newspapers carried the story of a man who had lured several boys to a mountain cabin, bound and then sexually abused them. One of the boys worked himself free, seized a rifle, and killed his abductor. The local prosecutor announced that no proceedings against the boy were contemplated, a result undoubtedly approved by every reader. Because the law of self-defense is so restrictive in permitting the use of deadly force, a technical case of murder might have been made out against the boy; the circumstances, however, made clear that it would have been unjust to prosecute. It is not strict obedience to the law, but the sense of justice, which we require in the administration of the legal system.

The same breadth of discretion which produced justice in the case of the abducted boy can be turned toward less attractive ends, depending on the inclinations of those who are charged with administering the law. To be sure, such discretion is not generally exercised arbitrarily. It is used to "fill the interstices," as lawyers sometimes put it—that is, to act in accordance with what it is thought the legislature would have done if it had considered the particular circumstances of the pending case. It is only a special class of cases which ordinarily raise the danger of unjust manipulation—those where political considerations make prosecution indiscreet, or, conversely, where there are special political incentives to go forward.

In the former category are cases where the rich and the powerful find themselves able to "settle" potential criminal prosecutions. Thus, the southern oligarchs were not indicted for criminal conspiracy when they produced their massive resistance campaign against the school integration decision, or led the fight to stand in the schoolhouse door, while Dr. Spock and other war resisters were readily brought to trial under the umbrella of the vague and amorphous conspiracy doctrine.

No one who sat through the four weeks of trial in which Benjamin Spock, William Sloane Coffin, Mitchell Goodman, and Michael Ferber were convicted of conspiracy to abet violation of the draft law could have doubted that Judge Francis Ford was persuaded of the rightness of the government's case against them, or that the trial reflected his persuasion. The fact that one of the five defendants was ultimately acquitted is not a tribute to the fairness of the trial, but is, rather, a measure of the sloppiness with which the government put its case together.

The possibilities for judicial management were most clearly illuminated by the way in which Judge Ford handled the question of the Vietnam War. A principal issue which the defense wished to raise was that the conduct of the Vietnam war violated international treaties governing such questions as the treatment of civilians and devastation of cities and towns. If the conduct of the war was illegal, the defendants argued, then to advocate refusal to participate in the war would be lawful, for it is not a crime to counsel one to refuse to do an illegal act. Moreover, even if the defendants were wrong about the legality of the war, they might have been found to have had a reasonable and good-faith belief in its illegality. Such a belief might itself have been sufficient to produce an acquittal under the legal precedents governing their case.

For each of these reasons it was tactically essential to the defendants that they be permitted to introduce evidence about the conduct of the war; not only would such evidence lend support to the foregoing claims, but it would have converted the trial from a turgid reiteration of the defendants' speeches to a dramatic inquiry into the justification for the radical political posture in which they found themselves.

Had the judge permitted such evidence to be introduced, and had the jury been told that they might have acquitted upon finding the defendants' beliefs to be reasonable and held in good faith, the chances for acquittal would obviously have been vastly increased. A sympathetic, or less hostile, judge might very well, and rationally, have taken such a course. And had there been an acquittal, the case would have been at an end; Dr. Spock and his co-defendants would walk the streets today as fully free men, and there would be no issue of civil disobedience to talk about in their case.

To anyone who appreciated the freedom of choice available to Judge Ford during the trial, and his ample use of it, it was particularly ironic to hear the prosecuting attorney's closing argument on civil disobedience:

> They feel something is wrong or right. They feel it and they act on that feeling on their conscience.

> Is this country going to be tied to a string that is tied to Mr. Coffin's conscience? Is it going to be tied to a string, even to the conscience of a man as sincere and as dedicated and as great as Dr. Spock?
>
> It can't be.

The prosecutor failed to remind the jury of the extent to which their decision had been tied to a string that was tied to Francis Ford's inclinations, or that they wouldn't have been there at all had not some prosecutor decided that these five people, out of the thousands who had acted similarily, ought to be tried.

There is no answer to the question of whether Dr. Spock and his co-defendants violated "the law." It is not that law imposes no constraints upon a judge; it is simply that there is so much room for maneuver within those constraints that either of two conflicting results can frequently be produced. Francis Ford presided over their conviction; another judge could have found a dozen cogent reasons, all supported by precedent and good legal logic, to have dismissed the indictment before the trial ever began. Nor is the opportunity for appeal necessarily any solution, for the process of choice continues right up the judicial ladder. A dozen wrong men—all part of the same legalistic tradition—produce as little justice as one.

Since the law could have been used either to acquit or convict, the only truly relevant question is whether it was just that the law be used to convict. It is no easy task to make lawyers peek out from behind that supposedly value-free facade, "the law," and begin to talk about unjust laws and unjust administration of the law; but out they must come and face the reality of prosecutorial and judicial discretion.

There are a series of quite concrete considerations which can be applied to resolve the issue of the Spock-Coffin case and other similar prosecutions. Of course, they have no scientific certainty, and many may disagree as to the answers. But such uncertainty is the essence of the problem, and one deceives himself if he thinks he can avoid such individualization by recourse to the law —he is only tying himself to a string which is tied to some Francis Ford.

The first question is what social good is to be achieved by incarcerating men like Spock, Coffin, Goodman, and Ferber. They do not present the immediate danger to others of those who commit violent acts. Indeed, by advocating a form of passive resistance to governmental fiat, they operate at one of the least abrasive levels of conduct respecting an impact on the rights or property of others.

Moreover, the nature of their resistance is such that a layer of governmental decision is always imposed between their action and the prospect of harm to others. For example, it is clearly less intrusive for one opposed to school integration to boycott the schools than it is to stand in the doorway and prevent others from entering. And the boycott is very far removed from the acts of those who express their dissent by throwing a stone or a bomb. This is not to suggest that passive resistance should always be insulated from legal sanctions, but merely that the society's willingness to tolerate such conduct should be much greater than for direct action.

Another conventional rationale for incarceration is the desire to deter others similarly inclined. Where dissenting political activity is involved, history strongly suggests the inefficacy of such a response. One is hard-pressed to cite a political movement which has been suppressed through the jailing of its leaders. While it was said in the Spock-Coffin case that the prosecution was not directed at ideology, but rather at particular conduct, the record suggests the dubiousness of the distinction made by the government between thought and action.

The defendants were charged only with talking and publishing, collecting and returning some draft cards, and engaging in peaceful demonstrations. Even the government did not urge that any of this conduct in itself put a significant burden on the prosecution of its policies. The essence of the government's case was that the defendants' persuasiveness and prestige were an incitement to young men to resist the draft—not that their touching of draft cards, or any such formal acts, were at the heart of the danger which they supposedly posed to the state. Yet it was the formal act of participating in a draft card return which made the government's technical legal case against them. Upon such sands is the difference between criminality and innocence built in "the law." A common-sense inquiry into the justice of their prosecution makes it easy to see that it was their respectability, ideology and forcefulness which were really at stake. Those elements are not likely to be amenable to incarceration.

It is also important to ask whether the society is likely to be affirmatively benefited by the defendants' acts. Here two considerations apply. Are they raising an important issue which ought to be confronted by the public, and are they raising it in as minimally abrasive a way as circumstances and the limitations of legal institutions permit? Certainly the former question can be answered affirmatively; the attempt to promote an investigation of the conduct of the Vietnam war in light of American treaty obligations is decidedly a matter of great public importance. And the inability to get that issue raised in any conventional proceeding, such as the formal committee of inquiry which defendant Marcus Raskin had been urging, invites some degree of tolerance for their unconventional conduct. This element of a constructive goal in their acts ought to weigh heavily in vindication of their conduct and distinguish it from activity which is limited to active obstruction of a matter adequately settled through some political or legal institution.

As one turns away from legalistic thinking about the problems of protest, it becomes apparent that no large, general formulae are going to resolve the infinitely varied issues which arise. In the common situation where a group of housewives block a bulldozer's path to protest the destruction of a park, for example, there are at least two good reasons to refrain from prosecution at the outset, though technically a conviction might easily be obtained for trespassing or the obstruction of traffic. Often such a maneuver is designed to inform the general public of an unknown situation and to promote more serious consideration by the appropriate public officials.

Certainly these are acceptable goals, and as a practical matter only newspaper publicity is likely to be an effective prod. Considering the tendency of the papers to ignore less dramatic moves and the generally minimal adverse impact on the project by a few days' obstruction, the ladies' tactic would seem an appropriate and tolerable means of promoting the political process. We ought not to balk at taking into account the reality that a neighborhood group is unlikely to be very effective in going through the more conventional channels used by established lobbies or that they are unlikely to have the means to produce a substantial paid advertising campaign.

Once having achieved appropriate attention, however, the social benefit of their protest is generally exhausted; having been prodded, the political process in an area such as this tends to be viable, and the public need not accommodate itself to perpetual obstruction. In fact, this is precisely the way such matters are usually resolved; prosecutorial discretion is exercised to refrain from initiating a criminal prosecution at the early publicity stage of protest. We accommodate to a degree of civil disobedience whose social usefulness outweighs its detriments, and hang "the law" which says obstructing traffic is a crime.

Refusal to pay income taxes for reasons of political protest presents another variant of the problem. The device is a useful one, for the refusal to pay taxes is a serious act and the degree to which it is adopted on a particular issue can be a significant measure of the breadth and depth of public feeling on that issue. While a government cannot be expected simply to ignore the nonpayment of taxes, it has at its command an intermediate device whereby it can accommodate to both the positive and negative aspects of such refusals.

Where political protest is involved in the refusal, the government can refrain from criminal prosecution, while going forward to recover the money due by attaching other assets of the taxpayer. This process involves some cost and inconvenience to the taxpayer, as it does to the government; yet from the point of view of both, the price thus paid is small considering the benefits of promoting vigorous interchange between them. Again, this is a device which the government seems to use with many tax protests; and again the rigors of the civil disobedience dilemma are resolved at the low visibility level of a discretionary decision.

As one moves on toward more overt direct action, such as the recent situation in which the Reverend Philip Berrigan poured blood over some draft board records in protest against the Vietnam war, the problem obviously becomes more difficult. Nonetheless, certain guidelines can be used to ask how accommodating we ought to be. Certainly it is relevant to weigh the symbolic content of the act against its adverse impact on the state.

Where only a few records are defaced, and they are easily replaced or duplicated, and where the protest involves an issue as imminent in its impact on human life as war, it is reasonable to ask for a substantial degree of tolerance. Whatever the statute relating to the destruction of government records might say, or however the free speech provision might be read by lawyers, it is the essence of a justly administered system that it be able to distinguish between an act with so little destructive impact and one in which whole sets of files were systematically destroyed. And even in such a case, consideration ought at least to be given to the moral differential between property destruction and the effort to preserve life from the ravages of war.

It is precisely these distinctions which the formal legal system seems to be so unwilling to consider, as evidenced by the Supreme Court decision this year upholding the conviction of a draft-card burner; that, surely, was an act overwhelmingly of protest content, with only the most trivial justification of need for possession of selective service documents by individual registrants.

Both the draft-card burning case and that of Father Berrigan—in which sentences of six years were imposed—are illustrative of another element in the formal legal system produced by its unwillingness to recognize a certain tolerant flexibility as an essential of justice. This is the general refusal to review sentences.

It is fruitless to argue abstractly, as the debates over civil disobedience usually do, about whether Father Berrigan should have been convicted. The real issue is whether we ought to be willing in substantial measure to accommodate ourselves to such protests as his in recognition of their social value. There would be little to debate if Berrigan had been sentenced to a symbolic thirty days in jail; the injustice of his case is the extraordinarily vindictive nature of sentence, by which he is classed with those who commit the most vicious crimes against the personal liberty of others.

Similarly irrelevant is the fear that every man will become a law unto himself. That is not the issue at all; no one in his right mind would suggest that a man should be exculpated from criminal responsibility simply because he thinks he ought to be. Rather, the issue is whether the public will be willing to tolerate some conduct that policemen, prosecutors, and judges think ought not to be tolerated.

The principal weapon available to implement a counterforce to such officials is an independent public unwilling to abdicate consideration of the justice with which the law is enforced. Where the criminal law is employed against political opponents of government, such independence is most urgently needed, lest self-interest affect the usual restraint through which justice and the law are harmonized. A public less bedazzled by the mystique of "the law" and more willing to look through to the question of justness will inevitably be strengthened in its ability to impose upon public officials pressure to be less (or, as the case may be, more) vigorous in seeking to attribute criminality to particular kinds of conduct.

A substantial outcry by the press and general public against the Spock trial would have gone far to stifle the prospect of other such prosecutions; instead, we got the widespread response that "the law" left the government little choice but to proceed as it did. Sometimes more direct action may be required. Jurors may simply have to refuse to convict, or grand jurors to indict. An independent citizenry has ways.

Finally, it should be noted that at no point is it suggested that weight ought to be given to the fact that the actor is sincerely and conscientiously committed to his point of view. That issue is one of the typical red herrings thrust into ordinary civil disobedience debates. As is often and correctly pointed out, one can be as sincere and conscientious about exterminating the Jews as about ending the war in Vietnam. It is not sincerity that counts, but the justness of one's goals and the appropriateness of the means employed to reach them. The greatest danger of all is that an excessive focusing upon the legality of situations tends to blind one to the obligation to make humane judgments, a responsibility that cannot be obscured by the observation that no scientific consensus can be reached. A society which cares about itself requires a citizenry that is ready to see a moral difference between one who protests against the killing in a place such as Vietnam and one who protests to prevent black children from getting a decent education. To abdicate that responsibility is only to begin the march in law-abiding lockstep toward moral oblivion.

United States v. O'Brien

319 U. S. 367

Mr. Chief Justice Warren delivered the opinion of the Court, saying in part:

On the morning of March 31, 1966, David Paul O'Brien and three companions burned their Selective Service registration certificates on the steps of the South Boston Courthouse. A sizable crowd, including several agents of the Federal Bureau of Investigation, witnessed the event.[32] Immediately after the burning, members of the crowd began attacking O'Brien and his companions. An FBI agent ushered O'Brien to safety inside the courthouse. After he was advised of his right to counsel and to silence, O'Brien stated to FBI agents that he had burned his registration certificate because of his beliefs, knowing that he was violating federal law. He produced the charred remains of the certificate, which, with his consent, were photographed.

For this act, O'Brien was indicted, tried, convicted, and sentenced in the United States District Court for the District of Massachusetts.[33] He did not contest the fact that he had burned the certificate. He stated in argument to the jury that he burned the certificate publicly to influence others to adopt his antiwar beliefs, as he put it, "so that other people would reevaluate their positions with Selective Service, with the armed forces, and reevaluate their place in the culture of today, to hopefully consider my position."

The indictment upon which he was tried charged that he "willfully and knowingly did mutilate, destroy, and change by burning . . . [his] Registration Certificate (Selective Service System Form No. 2); in violation of Title 50, App., United States Code, Section 462(b)." Section 462(b) is part of the Universal Military Training and Service Act of 1948. Section 462(b)(3), one of six numbered subdivisions of § 462(b), was amended by Congress in 1965, 79 Stat. 586 (adding the words italicized below), so that at the time O'Brien burned his certificate an offense was commited by any person,

> "who forges, alters, *knowingly destroys, knowingly mutilates,* or in any manner changes any such certificate . . . ." [Italics supplied.]

In the District Court, O'Brien argued that the 1965 Amendment prohibiting the knowing destruction or mutilation of certificates was unconstitutional because it was enacted to abridge free speech and because it served no legitimate legislative purpose.[34] The District Court rejected these arguments holding that the statute on its face did not abridge First Amendment rights, that the court was not competent to inquire into the motives of Congress in enacting the 1965 amendment, and that the Amendment was a reasonable exercise of the power of Congress to raise armies.

On appeal, the Court of Appeals for the First Circuit held the 1965 Amendment unconstitutional as a law abridging freedom of speech. At the time the Amendment was enacted, a regulation of the Selective Service System required registrants to keep their registration certificates in their "personal possession at all times." 32 CFR § 1617.1 (1962). Wilful violations of regulations promulgated pursuant to the Universal Military Training and Service Act were made criminal by statute. 50 U. S. C. App. § 462 (b) (6). The Court of Appeals, therefore, was of the opinion that conduct punishable under the 1965 Amendment was already punishable under the nonpossession regulation, and consequently that the Amendment served no valid purpose; further, that in light of the prior regulation, the Amendment must have been "directed at public as distinguished from private destruction." On this basis, the court concluded that the 1965 Amendment ran afoul of the First Amendment by singling out persons engaged in protests for special treatment. The court ruled, however, that O'Brien's conviction should be affirmed under the statutory provision, 50 U. S. C. App. § 462 (b) (6), which in its view made violation of the nonpossession regulation a crime, because it regarded such violation to be a lesser included offense of the crime defined by the 1965 Amendment. . . .

*   *   *   *   *

O'Brien first argues that the 1965 Amendment is unconstitutional as applied to him because his act of burning his registration certificate was protected "symbolic speech" within the First Amendment. His argument is that the freedom of expression which the First Amendment guarantees includes all modes of "communication of ideas by conduct," and that his conduct is within this definition because he did it in "demonstration against the war and against the draft."

We cannot accept the view that an apparently limitless variety of conduct can be labeled "speech" whenever the person engaging in the conduct intends thereby to express an idea. However, even on the assumption that the alleged communicative element in O'Brien's conduct is sufficient to bring into play the First Amendment, it does not necessarily follow that the destruction of a registration certificate is constitutionally protected activity. This Court has held that when "speech" and "nonspeech" elements are combined in the same course of conduct, a sufficiently important governmental interest in regulating the nonspeech element can justify incidental limitations on First Amendment freedoms. To characterize the quality of the governmental interest which must appear, the Court has employed a variety of descriptive terms: compelling; substantial; subordinating; paramount; cogent; strong. Whatever imprecision inheres in these terms, we think it clear that a government regulation is sufficiently justified if it is within the constitutional power of the Government; if it furthers an important or substantial governmental interest; if the governmental interest is unrelated to the suppression of free expression; and if the incidental restriction on alleged First Amendment freedoms is no greater than is essential to the furtherance of that interest. We find that the 1965 Amendment to § 12 (b) (3) of the Universal Military Training and Service Act meets all of these requirements, and consequently that O'Brien can be constitutionally convicted for violating it.

The constitutional power of Congress to raise and support armies and to make all laws necessary and proper to that end is broad and sweeping [*Lichter* v. *United States*, 334 U. S. 742 (1948)]. The power of Congress to classify and conscript manpower for military service is "beyond question" [*Lichter* v. *United States*]. Pursuant to this power, Congress may establish a system of registration for individuals liable for training and service, and may require such individuals within reason to cooperate in the registration system. The issuance of certificates indicating the registration and eligibilty classification of individuals is a legitimate and substantial administrative aid in the functioning of this system. And legislation to insure the continuing availability of issued certificates serves a legitimate and substantial purpose in the system's administration. . . .

In conclusion, we find that because of the Government's substantial interest in assuring the continuing availability of issued Selective Service certificates, because amended § 462 (b) is an appropriately narrow means of protecting this interest and condemns only the independent noncommunicative impact of conduct within its reach, and because the noncommunicative impact of O'Brien's act of burning his registration certificate frustrated the Government's interest, a sufficient governmental interest has been shown to justify O'Brien's conviction.

* * * * *

O'Brien finally argues that the 1965 Amendment is unconstitutional as enacted because what he calls the "purpose" of Congress was "to suppress freedom of speech." We reject this argument because under settled principles the purposes of Congress, as O'Brien uses that term, is not a basis for declaring this legislation unconstitutional.

It is a familiar principle of constitutional law that this Court will not strike down an otherwise constitutional statute on the basis of an alleged illicit legislative motive. As the Court long ago stated:

> "The decisions of this court from the beginning lend no support whatever to the assumption that the judiciary may restrain the exercise of lawful power on the assumption that a wrongful purpose or motive has caused the power to be exerted." [*McCray* v. *United States*, 195 U. S. 27, 56 (1904).]

This fundamental principle of constitutional adjudication was reaffirmed and the many cases were collected by Mr. Justice Brandeis for the Court in *Arizona* v. *California*, 283 U. S. 423, 455 (1931).

Inquiries into congressional motives or purposes are a hazardous matter. When the issue is simply the interpretation of legislation, the Court will look to statements by legislators for guidance as to the purpose of the legislature, because the benefit to sound decision-making in this circumstance is thought sufficient to risk the possibility of misreading Congress' purpose. It is entirely a different matter when we are asked to void a statute that is, under well-settled criteria, constitutional on its face, on the basis of what fewer than a handful of Congressmen said about it. What motivates one legislator to make a speech about a statute is not necessarily what motivates scores of others to enact it, and the stakes are sufficiently high for us to eschew guesswork. We decline to void essentially on the ground that it is unwise legislation which Congress had the undoubted power to enact and which could be reenacted in its exact form if the same or another legislator made a "wiser" speech about it. . . .

Miranda v. Arizona

384 U. S. 436

Mr. Chief Justice Warren delivered the opinion of the Court, saying in part:

The cases before us raise questions which go to the roots of our concepts of American criminal jurisprudence; the restraints society must observe consistent with the Federal Constitution in prosecuting individuals for crime. More specifically, we deal with the admissibility of statements obtained from an individual who is subjected to custodial police interrogation and the necessity for procedures which assure that the individual is accorded his privilege under the Fifth Amendment to the Constitution not to be compelled to incriminate himself. . . .

We start here, as we did in *Escobedo* [v. *Illinois*, 1964], with the premise that our holding is not an innovation in our jurisprudence, but is an application of principles long recognized and applied in other settings. We have undertaken a thorough re-examination of the Escobedo decision and the principles it announced, and we reaffirm it. That case was but an explication of basic rights that are enshrined in our Constitution—that "No person . . . shall be compelled in any criminal case to be a witness against himself," and that "the accused shall . . . have the Assistance of Counsel"—rights which were put in jeopardy in that case through official overbearing. These precious rights were fixed in our Constitution only after centuries of persecution and struggle. And in the words of Chief Justice Marshall, they were secured "for ages to come and . . . designed to approach immortality as nearly as human institutions can approach it" [*Cohens* v. *Virginia* (1821)]. . . .

Our holding will be spelled out with some specificity in the pages which follow but briefly stated it is this: the prosecution may not use statements, whether exculpatory or inculpatory, stemming from custodial interrogation of the defendant unless it demonstrates the use of procedural safeguards effective to secure the privilege against self-incrimination. By custodial interrogation, we mean questioning initiated by law enforcement officers after a person has been taken into custody or otherwise deprived of his freedom of action in any significant way. As for the procedural safeguards to be employed, unless other fully effective means are devised to inform accused persons of their right of silence and to assure a continuous opportunity to exercise it, the following measures are required. Prior to any questioning, the person must be warned that he has a right to remain silent, that any statement he does make may be used as evidence against him, and that he has a right to the presence of an attorney, either retained or appointed. The defendant may waive effectuation of these rights, provided the waiver is made voluntarily, knowingly and intelligently. If, however, he indicates in any manner and at any stage of the process that he wishes to consult with an attorney before speaking there can be no questioning. Likewise, if the individual is alone and indicates in any manner that he does not wish to be interrogated, the police may not question him. The mere fact that he may have answered some questions or volunteered some statements on his own does not deprive him of the right to refrain from answering any further inquiries until he has consulted with an attorney and thereafter consents to be questioned.

*   *   *   *   *

The constitutional issue we decide in each of these cases is the admissibility of statements obtained from a defendant questioned while in custody or otherwise deprived of his freedom of action in any significant way. In each, the defendant was questioned by police officers, detectives, or a prosecuting attorney in a room in which he was cut off from the outside world. In none of these cases was the defendant given a full and effective warning of his rights at the outset of the interrogation process. In all the cases, the questioning elicited oral admissions, and in three of them, signed statements as well which were admitted at their trials. They all thus share salient features—incommunicado interrogation of individuals in a police-dominated atmosphere, resulting in self-incriminating statements without full warnings of constitutional rights.

An understanding of the nature and setting of this in-custody interrogation is essential to our decisions today. The difficulty in depicting what transpires at such interrogations stems from the fact that in this country they have largely taken place incommunicado. From extensive factual studies undertaken in the early 1930s, including the famous Wickersham Report to Congress by a Presidential Commission, it is clear that police violence and the "third degree" flourished at that time. In a series of cases decided by this Court long after these studies, the police resorted to physical brutality—beatings, hanging, whipping —and to sustained and protracted questioning incommunicado in order to extort confessions. The Commission on Civil Rights in 1961 found much evidence to indicate that "some policemen still resort to physical force to obtain confessions." . . . The use of physical brutality and violence is not, unfortunately, relegated to the past or to any part of the country. Only recently in Kings County, New York, the police brutally beat, kicked and placed lighted cigarette butts on the back of a potential witness under interrogation for the purpose of securing a statement incriminating a third party [*People* v. *Portelli*, 15 N. Y. 2d 235 (1965)].

The examples given above are undoubtedly the exception now, but they are sufficiently widespread to be the object of concern. Unless a proper limitation upon custodial interrogation is achieved—such as these decisions will

advance—there can be no asurance that practices of this nature will be eradi-
cated in the foreseeable future. . . .

Again we stress that the modern practice of in-custody interrogation is
psychologically rather than physically oriented. As we have stated before,
"Since *Chambers* v. *Florida* [1940] this Court has recognized that coercion
can be mental as well as physical, and that the blood of the accused is not the
only hallmark of an unconstitutional inquisition." [*Blackburn* v. *Alabama*
(1960).] Interrogation still takes place in privacy. Privacy results in secrecy
and this in turn results in a gap in our knowledge as to what in fact goes on in
the interrogation rooms. A valuable source of information about present police
practices, however, may be found in various police manuals and texts which
document procedures employed with success in the past, and which recommend various other effective tactics. These texts are used by law enforcement
agencies themselves as guides. It should be noted that these texts professedly
present the most enlightened and effective means presently used to obtain statements through custodial interrogation. By considering these texts and other
data, it is possible to describe procedures observed and noted around the country. . . . [The Court here quotes at length from a number of books on criminal
investigation.]

From these representative samples of interrogation techniques, the setting
prescribed by the manuals and observed in practice becomes clear. In essence,
it is this: To be alone with the subject is essential to prevent distraction and to
deprive him of any outside support. The aura of confidence in his guilt under-
mines his will to resist. He merely confirms the preconceived story the police
seek to have him describe. Patience and persistence, at times relentless questioning are employed. To obtain a confession, the interrogator must "patiently
maneuver himself or his quarry into a position from which the desired objective
may be obtained." When normal procedures fail to produce the needed result,
the police may resort to deceptive stratagems such as giving false legal advice.
It is important to keep the subject off balance, for example, by trading on his
insecurity about himself or his surroundings. The police then persuade, trick,
or cajole him out of exercising his constitutional rights.

Even without employing brutality, the "third degree" or the specific stratagems described above, the very fact of custodial interrogation exacts a heavy
toll on the individual liberty and trades on the weakness of individuals. This
fact may be illustrated simply by referring to three confession cases decided by
this Court in the Term immediately preceding our *Escobedo* decision. In
Townsend v. *Sain* (1963), the defendant was a 19-year-old heroin addict,
described as a "near mental defective," id., at 307–310. The defendant in
Lynumn v. *Illinois* (1963) was a woman who confessed to the arresting
officer after being importuned to "cooperate" in order to prevent her children
from being taken by relief authorities. This Court as in those cases reversed
the conviction of a defendant in *Haynes* v. *Washington* (1963), whose persist-

ent request during his interrogation was to phone his wife or attorney. In other settings, these individuals might have exercised their constitutional rights. In the incommunicado police-dominated atmosphere, they succumbed.

In the cases before us today, given this background, we concern ourselves primarily with this interrogation atmosphere and the evils it can bring. In No. 759, *Miranda v. Arizona*, the police arrested the defendant and took him to a special interrogation room where they secured a confession. In No. 760, *Vignera v. New York*, the defendant made oral admissions to the police after interrogation in the afternoon, and then signed an inculpatory statement upon being questioned by an assistant district attorney later the same evening. In No. 761, *Westover v. United States*, the defendant was handed over to the Federal Bureau of Investigation by local authorities after they had detained and interrogated him for a lengthy period, both at night and the following morning. After some two hours of questioning, the federal officers had obtained signed statements from the defendant. Lastly, in No. 584, *California v. Stewart*, the local police held the defendant five days in the station and interrogated him on nine separate occasions before they secured his inculpatory statement.

In these cases, we might not find the defendants' statements to have been involuntary in traditional terms. Our concern for adequate safeguards to protect precious Fifth Amendments rights is, of course, not lessened in the slightest. In each of the cases, the defendant was thrust into an unfamiliar atmosphere and run through menacing police interrogation procedures. The potentiality for compulsion is forcefully apparent, for example, in *Miranda*, where the indigent Mexican defendant was a seriously disturbed individual with pronounced sexual fantasies, and in *Stewart*, in which the defendant was an indigent Los Angeles Negro who had dropped out of school in the sixth grade. To be sure, the records do not evince overt physical coercion or patent psychological ploys. The fact remains that in none of these cases did the officers undertake to afford appropriate safeguards at the outset of the interrogation to insure that the statements were truly the product of free choice.

It is obvious that such an interrogation environment is created for no purpose other than to subjugate the individual to the will of his examiner. This atmosphere carries its own badge of intimidation. To be sure, this is not physical intimidation, but it is equally destructive of human dignity. The current practice of incommunicado interrogation is at odds with one of our Nation's most cherished principles—that the individual may not be compelled to incriminate himself. Unless adequate protective devices are employed to dispel the compulsion inherent in custodial surroundings, no statement obtained from the defendant can truly be the product of his free choice. . . .

Engel et al. v. Vitale et al.

370 U. S. 421

Mr. Justice Black delivered the opinion of the Court.

The respondent Board of Education of Union Free School District No. 9, New Hyde Park, New York, acting in its official capacity under state law, directed the School District's principal to cause the following prayer to be said aloud by each class in the presence of a teacher at the beginning of each school day:

> "Almighty God, we acknowledge our dependence upon Thee, and we beg Thy blessings upon us, our parents, our teachers and our Country."

This daily procedure was adopted on the recommendation of the State Board of Regents, a governmental agency created by the State Constitution to which the New York Legislature has granted broad supervisory, executive, and legislative powers over the State's public school system. These state officials composed the prayer which they recommended and published as a part of their "Statement on Moral and Spiritual Training in the Schools," saying: "We believe that this Statement will be subscribed to by all men and women of good will, and we call upon all of them to aid in giving life to our program."

Shortly after the practice of reciting the Regents' prayer was adopted by the School District, the parents of ten pupils brought this action in a New York State Court insisting that use of this official prayer in the public schools was contrary to the beliefs, religions, or religious practices of both themselves and their children. Among other things, these parents challenged the constitutionality of both the state law authorizing the School District to direct the use of prayer in public schools and the School District's regulation ordering the recitation of this particular prayer on the ground that these actions of official governmental agencies violate that part of the First Amendment of the Federal Constitution which commands that "Congress shall make no law respecting an establishment of religion"—a command which was "made applicable to the State of New York by the Fourteenth Amendment of the said Constitution." The New York Court of Appeals, over the dissents of Judges Dye and Fuld, sustained an order of the lower state courts which had upheld the power of New York to use the Regents' prayer as a part of the daily procedures of its public schools so long as the schools did not compel any pupil to join in the prayer over his or his parents' objection. We granted certiorari to review this important decision involving rights protected by the First and Fourteenth Amendments.

We think that by using its public school system to encourage recitation of the Regents' prayer, the State of New York has adopted a practice wholly inconsistent with the Establishment Clause. There can, of course, be no doubt that New York's program of daily classroom invocation of God's blessings as prescribed in the Regents' prayer is a religious activity. It is a solemn avowal of divine faith and supplication for the blessings of the Almighty. The nature of such a prayer has always been religious, none of the respondents has denied this, and the trial court expressly so found:

> "The religious nature of prayer was recognized by Jefferson and has been concurred in by theological writers, the United States Supreme Court and State courts and administrative officials, including New York's Commissioner of Education. A committee of the New York Legislature has agreed.
> "The Board of Regents as *amicus curiae*, the respondents and intervenors all concede the religious nature of prayer, but seek to distinguish this prayer because it is based on our spiritual heritage. . . ."

The petitioners contend among other things that the state laws requiring or permitting use of the Regents' prayer must be struck down as a violation of the Establishment Clause because that prayer was composed by governmental officials as a part of a governmental program to further religious beliefs. For this reason, petitioners argue, the State's use of the Regents' prayer in its public school system breaches the constitutional wall of separation between Church and State. We agree with that contention since we think that the constitutional prohibition against laws respecting an establishment of religion must at least mean that in this country it is no part of the business of government to compose official prayers for any group of the American people to recite as a part of a religious program carried on by government.

It is a matter of history that this very practice of establishing governmentally composed prayers for religious services was one of the reasons which caused many of our early colonists to leave England and seek religious freedom in America. The Book of Common Prayer, which was created under governmental direction and which was approved by Acts of Parliament in 1548 and 1549, set out in minute detail the accepted form and content of prayer and other religious ceremonies to be used in the established, tax-supported Church of England. The controversies over the Book and what should be its content repeatedly threatened to disrupt the peace of that country as the accepted forms of prayer in the established church changed with the views of the particular ruler that happened to be in control at the time. Powerful groups representing some of the varying religious views of the people struggled among themselves to impress their particular views upon the Government and obtain amendments of the Book more suitable to their respective notions of how religious services should be conducted in order that the official religious establishment would advance their particular religious beliefs. Other groups, lacking the necessary political power to influence the Government on the matter, decided to leave England and its established church and seek freedom in America from England's governmentally ordained and supported religion.

It is an unfortunate fact of history that when some of the very groups which had most strenuously opposed the established Church of England found themselves sufficiently in control of colonial governments in this country to write their own prayers into law, they passed laws making their own religion the official religion of their respective colonies. Indeed, as late as the time of the Revolutionary War, there were established churches in at least eight of the thirteen former colonies and established religions in at least four of the other five. But the successful Revolution against English political domination was shortly followed by intense opposition to the practice of establishing religion by law. This opposition crystallized rapidly into an effective political force in Virginia where the minority religious groups such as Presbyterians, Lutherans, Quakers and Baptists had gained such strength that the adherents to the established Episcopal Church were actually a minority themselves. In 1785–1786, those opposed to the established Church, led by James Madison and Thomas Jefferson, who, though themselves not members of any of these dissenting religious groups, opposed all religious establishments by law on grounds of principle, obtained the enactment of the famous "Virginia Bill for Religious Liberty" by which all religious groups were placed on an equal footing so far as the State was concerned. Similar though less far-reaching legislation was being considered and passed in other States. . . .

There can be no doubt that New York's state prayer program officially establishes the religious beliefs embodied in the Regents' prayer. The respondents' argument to the contrary, which is largely based upon the contention that the Regents' prayer is "non-denominational" and the fact that the program, as modified and approved by state courts, does not require all pupils to recite the prayer but permits those who wish to do so to remain silent or be excused from the room, ignores the essential nature of the program's constitutional defects. Neither the fact that the prayer may be denominationally neutral nor the fact that its observance on the part of the students is voluntary can serve to free it from the limitations of the Establishment Clause, as it might from the Free Exercise Clause, of the First Amendment, both of which are operative against the States by virtue of the Fourteenth Amendment. Although these two clauses may in certain instances overlap, they forbid two quite different kinds of governmental encroachment upon religious freedom. The Establishment Clause, unlike the Free Exercise Clause, does not depend upon any showing of direct governmental compulsion and is violated by the enactment of laws which establish an official religion whether those laws operate directly to coerce nonobserving individuals or not. This is not to say, of course, that laws officially prescribing a particular form of religious worship do not involve coercion of such individuals. When the power, prestige, and financial support of government is placed behind a particular religious belief, the indirect coercive pressure upon religious minorities to conform to the prevailing officially approved religion is plain. But the purposes underlying the Establishment Clause go much further than that. Its first and most immediate purpose rested on the belief that a union of government and religion tends to destroy government and to degrade religion. The history of governmentally established religion, both in England and in this country, showed that whenever government had allied itself with one particular form of religion, the inevitable result had been that it had incurred the hatred, disrespect, and even contempt of those who held contrary beliefs. That same history showed that many people had lost their respect for any religion that had relied upon the support of government to spread its faith. The Establishment Clause thus stands as an expression of principle on the part of the Founders of our Constitution that religion is too personal, too sacred, too holy, to permit its "unhallowed perversion" by a civil magistrate. Another purpose of the Establishment Clause rested upon an awareness of the historical fact that governmentally established religions and religious persecutions go hand in hand. The Founders knew that only a few years after the Book of Common Prayer became the only accepted form of religious services in the established Church of England, an Act of Uniformity was passed to compel all Englishmen to attend those services and to make it a criminal offense to conduct or attend religious gatherings of any other kind— a law which was consistently flouted by dissenting religious groups in England and which contributed to widespread persecutions of people like John Bunyan who persisted in holding "unlawful [religious] meetings . . . to the great disturbance and distraction of the good subjects of this kingdom . . . ." And they knew that similar persecutions had received the sanction of law in several of the colonies in this country soon after the establishment of official religions in those colonies. It was in large part to get completely away from this sort of systematic religious persecution that the Founders brought into being our Nation, our Constitution, and our Bill of Rights with its prohibition against any governmental establishment of religion. The New York laws officially prescribing the Regents' prayer are inconsistent both with the purposes of the Establishment Clause and with the Establishment Clause itself.

It has been argued that to apply the Constitution in such a way as to prohibit state laws respecting an establishment of religious services in public schools is to indicate a hostility toward religion or toward prayer. Nothing, of course, could be more wrong. The history of man is inseparable from the history of religion. And perhaps it is not too much to say that since the beginning of that history many people have devoutly believed that "More things are wrought by prayer than this world dreams of." It was doubtless largely due to men who believed this that there grew up a sentiment that caused men to leave the cross-currents of officially established state religions and religious persecution in Europe and come to this country filled with the hope that they could find a place in which they could pray when they pleased to the God of their faith in the language they chose. And there were men of this same faith in the power of prayer who led the fight for adoption of our Constitution and also for our Bill of Rights with the very guarantees of religious freedom that forbid the sort of governmental activity which New York has attempted here. These men knew that the First Amendment, which tried to put an end to governmental control of religion and of prayer, was not written to destroy either. They knew rather that it was written to quiet well-justified fears which nearly all of them felt arising out of an awareness that governments of the past had shackled men's tongues to make them speak only the religious thoughts that government wanted them to speak and to pray only to the God that government wanted them to pray to. It is neither sacrilegious nor antireligious to say that each separate government in this country should stay out of the business of writing or sanctioning official prayers and leave that purely religious function to the people themselves and to those the people choose to look to for religious guidance.

It is true that New York's establishment of its Regents' prayer as an officially approved religious doctrine of that State does not amount to a total establishment of one particular religious sect to the exclusion of all others— that, indeed, the governmental endorsement of that prayer seems relatively insignificant when compared to the governmental encroachments upon religion which were commonplace 200 years ago. To those who may subscribe to the view that because the Regents' official prayer is so brief and general there can be no danger to religious freedom in its governmental establishment, however, it may be appropriate to say in the words of James Madison, the author of the First Amendment:

> "[I]t is proper to take alarm at the first experiment on our liberties. . . . Who does not see that the same authority which can establish Christianity, in exclusion of all other Religions, may establish with the same ease any particular sect of Christians, in exclusion of all other Sects? That the same authority which can force a citizen to contribute three pence only of his property for the support of any one establishment, may force him to conform to any other establishment in all cases whatsoever?"

The judgment of the Court of Appeals of New York is reversed and the cause remanded for further proceedings not inconsistent with this opinion.

Reversed and remanded.

Prayer and Politics:
The Impact of Engel *and* Schempp
on the Political Process

WILLIAM M. BEANEY, EDWARD N. BEISER

To many Americans the outright refusal of some state and local authorities to accept the constitutional rules set forth in the 1954 school segregation case[35] was shocking and unprecedented. Students of American public law, however, have long recognized that the pronouncements of any court, high or low, may prove in practice to have far less significance because of the conscious resistance of officials whose duties include the administration of the newly announced law. A quite different explanation of non-enforcement occasionally arises from the ignorance of officeholders as to the actual law applicable to a situation confronting them, but non-enforcement resulting from official ignorance has far less negative impact on social values than do inaction and opposition originating in avowed resistance to court-declared norms of behavior. While the openness and pervasiveness of resistance after 1954 seemed novel, Americans of every generation since the founding of the Republic have chosen at times to disregard unpopular laws, or to temper their application so that they remain formally alive, but become meaningless in practice.

Students of constitutional law have, on the whole, been disinclined to examine the impact of Supreme Court decisions.[36] They have preferred to trace the development of doctrine in successive Court decisions with the tacit assumption that the law is obeyed except in those relatively rare instances where state or lower federal courts have refused to follow the mandate of the highest court. Just as lower courts presumably accept the highest court's decisions, all officials presumably feel bound to obey the law. The reasons for this attitude are not hard to find. Despite a long history of resistance to certain laws, our political system, which has been remarkably viable, is based on the principle of the rule of law and all that is implied by that principle. The fair and even application of law is part of the official doctrine. The status of the Constitution as fundamental law raises Supreme Court decisions interpreting that document to the highest position in the hierarchy of law.

Reprinted by permission of the authors and the publisher from William M. Beaney and Edward N. Beiser, "Prayer and Politics: The Impact of *Engel* and *Schempp* on the Political Process," *Journal of Political Law,* Vol. 13, No. 2 (1964), pp. 475–503.

If our official doctrine tends to prevent recognition of reality, the practical difficulty of tracing a pattern of non- or partial observance is an equally substantial reason for eschewing such studies. In such a vast nation it is impossible to take more than a sampling of the many thousands of communities which refuse to accept, or fail to comply with, a Supreme Court decision. An explicit act or statement signifying outright opposition to, or announced refusal to adhere to, a decision by responsible officials permits obvious conclusions to be drawn, but how is one to discern the more subtle forms of resistance—the averting of official eyes from local practices, the whispered suggestion that officials or citizens are free to do as they have been accustomed to doing, or the *subrosa* encouragement to do what has not previously been done? Even if these and other patterns of circumvention are discovered, documentation may be all but impossible.

Yet, it seems obvious that students of our legal system should not be satisfied with an acceptance of the official theory that court decisions, and particularly Supreme Court decisions that affect important public policy issues, are universally accepted as the law. It is grossly misleading and dangerous to treat law as a significant form of social control by concentrating on the rules handed down by courts. The realist persuasion in legal philosophy, if it has done nothing else, has warned us against ignoring the ways in which law affects or may leave untouched the daily lives of those to whom it ostensibly applies.

When a court decision impinges on an activity of only a few persons, the tracing of impact is a simple and obvious process. A steel seizure case,[37] for example, poses a single question with respect to consequences: Did the United States relinquish control of the seized mills to their private corporate owners? But seldom will the question and the answer be so simple. Some decisions, may have few consequences beyond resolving the specific dispute because of the varying contexts in which official action curtailing speech takes place. The impact of decisions affecting behavior of law enforcement officials are difficult to trace because of the difficulty of observing post-decision conduct. If any conclusions are to be reached they must inevitably be based on the judgment of a few well-placed observers, or on the frequency of future cases where a breach of the rule of the earlier decision can be documented.

These preliminary remarks are intended to serve as qualifications of the present brief study of some of the principal political and governmental responses to *Engel v. Vitale*[38] in June 1962, outlawing the use of a Regents' prescribed prayer in New York public schools, and the decision of *School Dist. v. Schempp*[39]—*Murray v. Curlett*[40] in June 1963, prohibiting the reading of Bible passages or saying of prayers as religious exercises in public schools throughout the nation, a decision which is analyzed at length in another part of this symposium. A careful state-by-state study of what has occurred since these Court pronouncements has not been undertaken because of limitations of time and resources. What follows is based on data available in newspaper and other printed accounts, supplemented by interviews with those possessing first-hand knowledge of various facets of this subject.

The New York Prayer Case

The reaction to the Court's decision declaring unconstitutional the use in public schools of a prayer prepared by the New York Regents was not long in forthcoming. And, at least in Congress, it was as one-sided as it was violent. Senator Talmadge (D., Ga.) denounced the decision as "unconscionable . . . an outrageous edict. . . ."[41] Congressman Williams (D., Miss.) insisted that the decision constituted "a deliberately and carefully planned conspiracy to substitute materialism for spiritual values and thus to communize America."[42] Congressman Sikes' (D., Fla.) description of the Court's action as infamous was probably closer to the mood of Congress than Senator Sparkman's (D., Ala.) milder comment: "a tragic mistake."[43] And Congressman Becker (R., N.Y.), who was to become the leader of the opposition to the Court on this issue, informed his colleagues that *Engel* was "the most tragic decision in the history of the United States."[44]

The immediate congressional reaction stressed what was to become one of the major themes of opponents of the Court's decisions: any opposition to religious activities in the public schools was an attack upon religion and upon God Himself. For Senator Robertson (D., Va.) this was the most extreme ruling the Supreme Court had ever made in favor of atheists and agnostics.[45] And Congressman Abernathy (D., Miss.) insisted that it would be "most pleasing to a few atheists and world Communism."[46] Representative Rivers (D., S.C.) denounced the Court for having "now officially stated its disbelief in God Almighty," while Senator Ervin (D., N.C.), widely regarded as an authority on constitutional law, insisted that "the Supreme Court has made God unconstitutional."[47] Nor was this reaction limited to Southerners. Senator McCarthy (D., Minn.) denounced the decision as leading to "not only a secularized government but a secularized society."[48]

Congressman Andrews of Alabama managed to criticize the Court on two counts in one pithy utterance: "They put the Negroes into the schools and now they have driven God out of them."[49] The extent and one-sidedness of congressional reaction is indicated by the fact that the Court's usual friends by and large did not attempt to defend the *Engel* decision, but restricted their activities to attempts at minimizing the scope of the decision. Senator Javits (R., N.Y.), for example, insisted that *Engel* did not prohibit prayer *per se*, but only governmentally prescribed prayer.[50] Except for Congressman Celler's (D., N.Y.) statement that he would oppose attempts to overturn *Engel* by amending the Constitution, the lone voice heard in support of the decision in the face of this onslaught was that of Congressman Lindsay (R.) of New York.[51]

Congressional reaction was expressed in several other forms as well. Congressman Haley (D., Fla.) offered an amendment to a judiciary appropriations bill to earmark out of the Supreme Court's appropriations funds to purchase "for the personal use of each Justice a copy of the Holy Bible," but his resolution was rejected 47–66.[52] And on September 27, the House voted unanimously to place the motto "In God We Trust" behind the Speaker's desk. Lest the motivation behind this sudden religious impulse escape anyone, Congressman Randall (D., Mo.) pointed out that "we have given perhaps not directly but yet in a not so subtle way" our answer to the Supreme Court's decision.[53]

The type of congressional action which posed the most serious threat to the Court's holding, and with which this article will be primarily concerned, was the introduction of proposed amendments to the Constitution to allow public schools to conduct religious exercises. Congressman Frank Becker (R., N.Y.) introduced his amendment the day after *Engel* was decided. His language is typical of this type of proposal: "Prayers may be offered in the course of any program in any public school or other public place in the United States."[54]

Twenty-two senators and fifty-three representatives introduced amendments in response to *Engel*, as indicated in the following table:[55]

TABLE 9-7

*Members of Congress Introducing Anti-*Engel *Amendments (87th Congress, 2d Session)*

PARTY AFFILIATION	HOUSE	SENATE
Republicans	26	12
Southern Democrats	19	8
Non-Southern Democrats	8	2
Total	53	22

Congressional hostility toward the Court's decision was further demonstrated at hearings conducted by Senator Eastland's Judiciary Committee, just one month after *Engel* was decided. Testimony by various senators shows that they were acutely aware that the Court was soon to consider the constitutionality of Bible reading and the recitation of the Lord's Prayer in public schools, and that it was fully expected that both practices would be prohibited. Thus one of the joint resolutions before the committee anticipated the Court's action in *Schempp*, by proposing to amend the Constitution to allow prayer and Bible reading in public schools. It is interesting to note that in their general frame of reference as well as in their specific resolutions, the senators were significantly affected not only by what the Court had done—but by what it might be expected to do in the future.

One who reads the hearings cannot help but be impressed by the tremendous impact of Mr. Justice Douglas' concurring opinion in *Engel*.[56] Again and again witnesses pointed to it as an example of what the Court would do in the future. Critics of the Court's action, especially California's Episcopal Bishop James A. Pike and Senator Stennis (D., Miss.), relied heavily on statements in his opinion. The fact that Mr. Justice Douglas had already taken an extreme position which the critics charged that the Court as a whole might assume in the future greatly strengthened their position, since Douglas' opinion made concrete what might otherwise have been dismissed as idle speculation.

The short Senate Judiciary Committee hearings, with Senator Eastland, the chairman, absent, provided a field day for opponents of the Court. While the critical statements of such organizations as the American Legion and Young Americans for Freedom were countered by statements submitted by such groups as the American Civil Liberties Union, Anti-Defamation League, the Baptist Joint Committee on Public Affairs, and others, the oral testimony of the witnesses was unanimous in opposing the Court's action. The principal theme of the several witnesses—as had been the case in the initial congressional reaction—was that the decision represented a concerted attack on God and on religion in American life. Bishop Pike, for example, insisted that the result of the decision was "secularism, whether by intent or by default. I am not implying for a moment that the proponents or supporters of the decision of the Supreme Court intentionally wish an atheistic result. Nevertheless, when it is by default we simply *cut off the whole spiritual dimension of life*, and without even a reference to it. What we have left is actually a secularist view of life."[57]

The Eastland Committee hearings also provided a platform for those who had other bones to pick with the Court. There were repeated references in the testimony to persistent abuses by the Supreme Court of its judicial function. It is hardly coincidental that the overwhelming majority of congressmen and senators who participated in these hearings were southerners. Table 9-7 indicated that more than half of the amendments to the Constitution introduced to reverse *Engel* were introduced by representatives of the 11 states of the former Confederacy. And Bishop Pike—the one noncongressional witness at the hearings—began his testimony with a strong states' rights argument.[58] Apart from allowing opponents of the Court and of the *Regents' Prayer* decision to vent their spleen, the hearings accomplished nothing. No final report was issued, nor was any legislation proposed.

The reaction of the late President Kennedy differed significantly. In response to a question at his regular news conference, he said:

> The Supreme Court has made its judgment. Some will disagree and others will agree. In the efforts we're making to maintain our constitutional principles, we will have to abide by what the Supreme Court says. We have a very easy remedy here, and that is to pray ourselves. We can pray a good deal more at home and attend our churches with fidelity and em-

phasize the true meaning of prayer in the lives of our children. I hope, as a result of that decision, all Americans will give prayer a greater emphasis.[59]

The late President Hoover, however, voiced a strong dissent:

The interpretation of the Constitution is a disintegration of one of the most sacred of American heritages. The Congress should at once submit an amendment to the Constitution which establishes the right to religious devotion in all government agencies—national, state, or local.[60]

If the two former Presidents divided evenly, the Governors did not. At a meeting at Hershey, Pennsylvania, on July 3, the Governors' Conference resolved that:

Whereas the recent majority opinion of the United States Supreme Court in the New York *School Prayer* case has created far reaching misunderstanding as to the nation's faith and dependence in God; and
Whereas the Governors assembled . . . acknowledge their dependence upon God and the power of prayer to Him; . . .
Resolved, that the Governors' Conference urge upon the Congress of the United States to propose an amendment to the Constitution of the United States that will make clear and beyond challenge the acknowledgment by our nation and people of their faith in God and permit the free and voluntary participation in prayer in our public schools.[61]

The resolution passed unanimously, with only Governor Rockefeller of New York abstaining.[62]

The reaction of the nation's press was mixed. As might have been expected, the Court was defended by such newspapers as the New York *Times*, New York *Herald Tribune*, New York *Post*, St. Louis *Post-Dispatch*, Washington *Post*, Milwaukee *Journal*, and Chicago *Sun-Times*, among others. Critics of the Court included the Hearst newspapers, the New York *News*, Baltimore *Sun*, Boston *Globe*, Chicago *Tribune*, and Los Angeles *Times*.[63] The moderate New York *Herald Tribune* was amazed at "the sight of so many otherwise responsible newspapers getting completely swept off their feet by the tide of emotionalism."[64] Twenty-seven of the sixty-three newspapers examined by one writer were found to have published editorials opposed to the *School Prayer* decision; sixteen favored the decision in editorials; and eleven were more or less neutral. "The strongest opposition came from papers in the northern Midwest. Contrary to common newspaper reports, more southern papers were neutral or favorable to the opinion than opposed. . . . Twenty papers published critical cartoons; twelve published favorable cartoons."[65]

Of particular interest and no little surprise, was the reaction of the Negro community. Dr. Martin Luther King, actively engaged in the Albany, Georgia, kneel-in controversy, called the Court's action "a sound and good decision reaffirming something that is basic in our Constitution, namely, separation of church and state."[66] Such leading Negro newspapers as the *Amsterdam News*, Chicago *Defender*, and Pittsburgh *Courier* expressed their support of the decision.[67] And the NAACP, which rarely takes public positions on issues that do not directly affect Negroes, and which had never done so in the area of church-state relations, unanimously passed a resolution supporting the *Engel* decision at its national convention in Atlanta on July 2–8. In addition, it submitted a strong pro-decision statement to the Eastland Committee.[68]

This reaction seemed to indicate a realization on the part of the Negro community that the attack on the Court which followed the *Engel* decision was in fact directed at the Court for its civil rights decisions as well as its stand on the Regents' prayer, and that if the Court were slapped down in this area, it might be more cautious in cases which directly affect the Negro community.

The leadership of the religious community tended to divide on denominational lines. Roman Catholic spokesmen were extremely critical of the Court. Cardinal Spellman, for example, was "shocked and frightened that the Supreme Court had declared unconstitutional a simple and voluntary declaration of belief in God by public school children. The decision strikes at the very heart of the Godly tradition in which America's children have for so long been raised."[69] Cardinal Spellman's representative at the Senate hearings supported an amendment to the Constitution to reverse *Engel*, denouncing the decision as "a grave error in judicial judgment, a decision out of line with the conscience and religious heritage of the American people and one which foreshadows an ominous tendency to undermine cherished traditions of this Nation."[70] "Preposterous" was the term used by the Brooklyn *Tablet* to describe the decision, while the Jesuit weekly *America* used the adjectives "asinine," "stupid," "doctrinaire," and "unrealistic."[71]

Jewish religious and organizational leaders, on the other hand, were almost unanimous in their support of the Court's action. The New York Board of Rabbis, the Rabbinical Assembly of America, and the Commission of Social Action of Reform Judaism were among the many organizations expressing their support.[72]

Protestant leadership was divided. Episcopal Bishop James A. Pike announced that "the Supreme Court has just deconsecrated the nation." The Reverend Dr. Billy Graham and Dr. Reinhold Niebuhr reacted critically, Graham in the following words: "God pity our country when we can no longer appeal to God for help."[73] And, as noted above, Bishop Pike appeared in person before the Eastland Committee to urge strongly the modification of the First Amendment to prohibit not the "establishment of religion," but rather "the recognition as an established church of any denomination, sect, or organized religious association."[74] Dr. Leo Pfeffer notes with some amusement that if this amendment were achieved, "use of tax-raised funds for parochial schools would become constitutional—a development which Bishop Pike along with practically all other Protestant leaders strongly opposes."[75]

Equally strong statements supporting the Court's decision were issued by other elements within the Protestant camp. The Joint Baptist Committee on Public Affairs, with a constituency of more than 17,000,000 members, reacted very favorably to *Engel*.[76] *Christian Century*, widely regarded as the leading Protestant publication in America, endorsed the decision, as did a group of Protestant theologians, including the Dean of the Harvard Divinity School.[77]

The Response to the Lord's Prayer and Bible Reading Decisions[78]

When the decision in *Schempp* was handed down on June 17, 1963, the immediate reaction was less violent than those who had experienced the stormy reaction to *Engel* had anticipated. A careful observer concluded that "the reaction in the total American community to the ruling was markedly more positive than it had been to the Court's decision in the *Regents' Prayer* case one year earlier."[79] *Time* magazine called the reaction "relatively mild" and "nothing compared to that of 1962."[80] The Attorney General's office reported that it had received many fewer letters reacting against *Schempp* than it had in response to *Engel*, and a Court aide reported that the volume of critical mail was well below that of the previous decision.[81] A study of 185 editorials in newspapers published in 35 states and the District of Columbia found that 61 percent approved the Court's decision, a marked shift from earlier editorial stands, especially in the Northeast and Midwest.[82] It appears that there was also a decrease in the number of hostile "Letters to the Editor" in these same papers, although a majority opposed the decision. The reactions expressed in readers' letters to periodicals also were milder in tone when contrasted with the bitter outpouring which had followed the earlier decision.[83]

But there is little doubt that an overwhelming majority of the public disapproved of the Court's position. The Gallup Poll posed the following question: "The U.S. Supreme Court has ruled that no state or local government may require the reading of the Lord's Prayer or Bible verses in public schools. What are your views on this?" Results released on August 30, 1963, showed that 70 percent of those polled opposed the decisions, only 24 percent approved, while 6 percent had no opinion.

The greater restraint shown by editors and readers was matched by a more moderate tone in the responsive statements of religious leaders. The most significant shifts occurred in the ranks of Protestant and Catholic spokesmen, with the dominant note a plea for respect for the Court's decision coupled with assertions that the banning of Bible reading and required prayers in public schools did not represent a new judicial attitude of hostility toward religion. In many instances spokesmen seemed intent on calming public fears arising from the attention paid by the press and other news media to Mr. Justice Douglas' concurring opinion in *Engel*, which was widely accepted as a threat by the Court to sweep away every recognition of religion in American public life.

Some of the positive points enunciated by Protestant spokesmen were: the church and home had responsibility for developing proper religious attitudes in the young; perfunctory religious observances, which was the proper character- ization of many school ceremonies, were a waste of time at least and perhaps bred improper views of religious doctrine; the church now had a duty to im- prove its own program of religious instruction; and finally, the decisions did not prevent public schools from initiating programs of effective teaching about the past and present roles of religion in society.[84]

Whereas expressions of opinion by Catholic leaders after *Engel* had been almost uniformly critical, several Catholic Bishops and Archbishops now is- sued statements calling for restraint.[85] The distinguished Catholic legal scholar, Father Robert F. Drinan, S.J., Dean of the School of Law at Boston College, said "formal religion rightfully belongs in the home, in churches, and syna- gogues, and in their respective schools. . . ." Cardinal Ritter joined the St. Louis Church Federation and the Rabbinical Association in a statement pledg- ing cooperation and respect for the decision "as the law of the land" regardless of the merits, or lack thereof, of the decision itself.[86] Part of the Catholic press, including *America*, opposed the ruling, a position probably shared by their leaders. And, it seems clear that the majority of people of both the Catholic and Protestant faiths opposed the banning of prayers and Bible reading from the public schools, despite the statements of church leaders supporting the Court or counseling acceptance of its mandate.

As had been the case a year earlier, the reaction of Jewish groups was almost uniformly favorable. Among the organizations which issued statements sup- porting the Court's action were the American Jewish Committee, the American Jewish Congress, the Anti-Defamation League, the Rabbinical Council of America, and the Synagogue Council of America.[87] Since the Gallup Poll cited above did not classify respondents according to religion, it is impossible to know the extent to which the unanimous position of the Jewish organizations reflected the attitudes of the Jewish community.

The failure of the 1963 decision to touch off public and press outcries com- parable to those engendered by the *Regents' Prayer* case, while at first glance surprising, seems readily explainable. The shock value of the first decision was great—both the public and press seem to have been caught unawares—so that much of the bitter first commentary was uninformed, and frequently was based on sentences ripped out of the context of the Court's opinion, or to be found only in the concurring opinion of Mr. Justice Douglas. The 1963 de- cision, on the other hand, was anticipated, although some defenders of the Court had given the misleading impression that the *Regents'* case represented the judicial response to an officially prescribed prayer and had no wider ap- plication. It had also become evident that many of the severest critics of the Court's 1962 decision were staunch opponents of the Court's desegregation stand, a fact which gave pause to religious spokesmen who were unwilling to help weaken the Court's moral authority in the crucial area of race relations. It appears also that some of the more perceptive Catholic leaders believed other church-state issues to be of greater importance, particularly the question of federal financial assistance to education and thus did not choose to become involved in the present controversy. In any event, the generally milder initial reaction to the 1963 decision was to prove illusory to those who thought that this portended widespread acceptance of the Court's ruling. Both in the affected states and in Congress, unmistakable evidence of resistance and opposition in various forms soon appeared and battle was joined.

The State Response to Schempp

The *Regents' Prayer* case affected only an estimated 10 percent of the public school districts in a single state—New York. But the *Schempp* decision was directly applicable to a very substantial portion of the nation's school systems. In mid-1963 when these cases were decided, thirty-seven states and the District of Columbia permitted religious exercises in the public schools.[88] Thirteen of these *required* Bible reading by law,[89] and twelve others specifically permitted Bible reading by law or judicial decision.[90] It was reported that the Bible was read in 76 percent of the southern schools, 67 percent of eastern schools, 18 percent of midwestern schools, and 11 percent of the western schools. Overall, the Court's 1963 decisions affected almost 42 percent of the nation's public schools.

As one might expect, state reaction to the *Schempp* decision ranged from forthright declarations that a state or a specific school's system would not be bound, to equally strong statements advocating and insisting upon full compliance. In between these clearly defined attitudes were various official stances in which spokesmen suggested either that the Court's decisions were not applicable, or that each local system was to be permitted to decide its own policy, or, as was common, said nothing to acknowledge that a new rule was in effect, which left to local school officials the decision to continue or terminate religious ceremonies.

Most of the instances of outright defiance occurred in the South where, since 1954, opposition by public officials to any of the Court's controversial rulings can be anticipated almost as a reflex action. The Alabama State Board of Education denounced the Court for issuing a decision that was "a calculated effort to take God out of the public affairs of the nation."[91] Governor Wallace was even more explicit: "I would like for the people of Alabama to be in defiance of such a ruling. . . . I want the Supreme Court to know we are not going to conform to any such decision. I want the State Board of Education to tell the whole world we are not going to abide by it."[92]

And several days later, perhaps copying a tactic from the civil rights movement he has so bitterly opposed, the Governor told newsmen that he was prepared to stage a pray-in. The Governor stated that if the Court rules "that we cannot read the Bible in some school, I'm going to that school and read it myself."[93] Having stood in the doorway of a schoolhouse to thwart the federal courts, Wallace was apparently prepared to pray in a classroom to accomplish much the same end. Showing an appreciation of legal niceties, the Alabama State Board of Education ordered daily Bible reading as a part of a "prescribed course of study," which on its face placed the state practice within a category permitted by the decisions.[94] Wallace's Mississippi colleague, Ross Barnett, announced that he was "going to tell every teacher in Mississippi to conduct prayers and Bible reading despite what the Supreme Court says."[95] And Mississippi's chief law enforcement officer, Attorney General Joe Patterson, advised "all principals to continue to recognize the supremacy and many blessings of a great and just God as we have always done in our public schools."[96] South Carolina's State Superintendent of Education, Jesse Anderson, obviously felt that the decision did not apply in his state, for he announced that "South Carolina will continue to feel free to do in each school or classroom the normal thing which the teacher feels should be done."[97]

Outright defiance was not confined to the deep South. The Kentucky State Superintendent of Public Instruction, Wendell Butler, instructed local school districts to "continue to read and pray until somebody stops you. I don't want to make anybody stop."[98] The Kentucky State Board of Education opened its June 26 meeting with the customary Bible reading, sermon, and prayer, one board member saying, "If the procedure is illegal, I move to violate the Constitution."[99] And Rhode Island State Commissioner of Education Robinson declared that he did "not now or in the future intend to prostitute the office of Commissioner of Education of Rhode Island to further the cause of the irreligious, the atheistic, the unreligious, or the agnostic."[100]

Many who did not openly defy the Court sought to evade the impact of the decisions by employing one or more of the following devices: attempting to distinguish the case; limiting the scope of the case by interpretation (usually by misinterpretation); reading a patriotic song such as "America" or the fourth stanza of the Star Spangled Banner ("In God is our trust"); using hymns, prayers, etc., as part of "music appreciation"; using the Bible as "literature" with no intention of conducting literary study, or, as noted above in the case of Alabama, making Bible reading part of a "course of study." The first of these tactics was employed by the Attorney General of Delaware, David Buckson, who insisted that his state's statute had not been considered by the Court:

> Despite the expressed opinion that this particular [Bible reading] law may be unconstitutional and may be unenforceable if challenged, the fact remains that the Delaware statute is still the law of Delaware and will remain so until repealed or modified by the General Assembly or declared

by a court of competent jurisdiction to be violative of the State or Federal Constitution.[101]

Similar arguments were used by the defiant residents of Hawthorne, New Jersey, when they refused to comply with the state Commissioner of Education's orders to terminate religious practices on the ground that the New Jersey statutes had not been tested in court.[102]

The most prevalent misinterpretation of *Schempp* was the insistence that prayers and Bible readings were permissible as long as state compulsion did not enter the picture. Governor Sanford of North Carolina announced that:

> We will go on having Bible reading and prayer in the schools of this state just as we always have. . . . We do not require the Bible reading and prayer, but we do these things because we want to. . . . As I read the decision, this kind of thing is not forbidden by the Court, and indeed, it should not be.[103]

Much the same views were expressed by U.S. District Judge Johnson J. Hayes, at the First Baptist Church of Statesville, N. C., when he said that the ruling prohibited the government from requiring religious observances, but did not preclude a teacher from leading students in the Lord's Prayer on a voluntary basis.[104] Arkansas Attorney General Bennett told state school officials that the Arkansas Bible reading law was *not* struck down because children were not compelled to participate.[105] Perhaps the most interesting "interpretation" of the decisions was that of the Superintendent of Schools of Little Rock, Arkansas: "We understand the Supreme Court ruling was not mandatory. . . ."[106]

The device most widely used to permit the continuation of religious practices in the schools, however, was to avoid establishing any official policy. Oklahoma State Superintendent of Public Instruction Hodge felt that since the state had no law requiring Bible reading, the decision as to whether religious practices could continue was a matter for the individual teacher to decide. Ohio State Superintendent Holt insisted that the State Board of Education take no position, and leave all interpretations to local school systems.[107] The Manchester *Union Leader* quoted New Hampshire State Board of Education chairman John C. Driscoll as saying that "it is up to each local school board to determine for itself, consistent with the Constitution as interpreted by the Supreme Court . . . , what it is going to permit for practices within the format of regular school exercises."

And, lest any of its readers fail to realize the significance of this "local option" policy, the *Union Leader's* editorial continued by adding that "there is nothing to prevent school teachers or the students themselves from conducting their own noncompulsory prayer exercises within the classroom. . . ."[108] In Iowa, Superintendent Johnston felt that since this was a local matter, "custom in their own community ought to determine what they should do."[109] There is little doubt that in each of the states in which the authorities chose to rely on "local custom" rather than on the Court's decisions, they had an accurate idea of what "local custom" would dictate.[110]

The picture was not completely one sided, however. There are states in which the Court's decisions are apparently being enforced. Silent meditation is allowed in some. In Maryland, for example, State Superintendent of Schools Thomas C. Pullen, Jr. informed all school superintendents that "any attempt to circumvent the decision of the Supreme Court by indirection or chicanery would be improper and not in the spirit of the administration of the public schools in Maryland."[111] In New Jersey, the Hughes administration insisted on strict compliance. State Commissioner of Education Raubinger informed local school boards that "there can be no option or discretionary choice in the matter."[112] The State Board of Education threatened to cut off state aid, and in one case obtained a state supreme court injunction, in order to force compliance by a defiant school district.[113] In Massachusetts, Attorney General Edward W. Brooke issued a twenty-two page directive urging compliance without resort to sophistry of any sort. "No official of government of whatever station can, in good conscience, disobey the mandate of the Supreme Court. . . ."[114] As in New Jersey, some Massachusetts towns resisted the state's attempt to bring about compliance; Brooke was forced to go into court to compel the town of North Brookfield to comply.[115] Similarly, in Pennsylvania, the state authorities were faced with open defiance at one time of as many as twenty-two school districts.[116]

It should be noted that in some sections of the country the Court's decision would have little impact, for Bible reading and prayer were not widely practiced. Eleven states—mostly western—specifically barred such activities.[117]

Of course, the official reactions of state and local officials do not give us anything like a complete picture of what is actually going on in classrooms throughout the country; and the available data are at best fragmentary. A careful survey, which probably tends to understate the situation, reported that at the time school opened in 1963, prayer or Bible reading took place in the public schools of 10 states, and that in three—Arkansas, Alabama, and Delaware—Bible reading or the Lord's Prayer were *required* by law.[118] In addition, it was estimated that in some seven other states the official "hands off" policy allows religious practices to continue on a local basis. Spot checks indicate that the Court's decisions are being violated in many other areas. The *Religious News Service* reported, for example, that as of September 27, 1963, less than 20 of Connecticut's 169 towns had acted to implement in some way the Court's decision.[119] The Des Moines *Sunday Register* observed that "as Iowa's public schools prepare to begin another year the impact of the U.S. Supreme Court's latest ruling against school prayer is *almost unnoticeable.* . . . Most schools will make no change from past policy."[120] The Atlanta *Journal* reported that most Georgia school boards are unofficially encouraging continuation of religious exercises, including chapel.[121] A major study of policy and practice in Indiana, published in April, 1964, showed that the reading of the Bible at the opening of the school day was permitted or practiced in approximately one-third of the responding school corporations and that nearly one-half permitted or practiced the reciting of the Lord's Prayer, while 60 percent allowed a pupil or teacher to lead the saying of a prayer, commonly in conjunction with the noon meal. Less than 6 percent of the respondents reported a change in school board policy as a result of the 1963 Court decision.[122] These figures, it should be noted, are based on replies of school board superintendents, who might be expected to *minimize* the extent to which illegal practices are going on in their schools.

How are we to understand this apparently widespread defiance of a Supreme Court ruling? A comment in the Indianapolis *Star* probably answers this question. "No Supreme Court decision handed down to us because of a disgruntled [*sic*] atheist mother who doesn't want her child to know there is a God should influence our School Board."[123]

Reports from many other states that could not be accused of having an anti-Court bias tend to support the conclusion that forthright compliance with the Court's mandate has been the exception rather than the rule in many parts of the nation, and that a tremendous number of suits will be necessary to convert many state and local officials to a policy that conforms to the rulings of the supposed "final arbiter" of constitutional question.[124] Whether or not President Jackson ever said "John Marshall has made his decision, now let him enforce it," his sentiment aptly describes the response of many of the nation's school districts to the Court's decisions in *Schempp* and *Murray*.[125]

The Becker Amendment

In light of popular support for the continuation of Bible reading and prayers in the public schools, and the obvious reluctance of many states to abandon practices which have been in effect for several decades, it was hardly to be expected that Congress would stay out of the controversy engendered by the 1963 decision. The initial congressional reaction, though largely reflecting opposition, was more restrained than that of a year earlier when the *Regents' Prayer* decision was handed down. There was some of the damning language which followed the earlier decision. Congressman O'Konski (R., Wis.), for example, suggested mental tests for the Justices, and Senator Ellender (D., La.), continuing a long-standing quarrel with the Court, referred to the "eight silly old men."[126] Senator Thurmond (D., S.C.) called it "another major triumph of secularism and atheism which are bent on throwing God completely out of our national life," while his colleague Senator Robertson (D., Va.) insisted that "we will become as Godless a nation as is the Soviet Union."[127] Striking a more positive note, Senator Johnston (D., S.C.) urged teachers to defy the decisions, and Congressman Ashmore (D., S.C.) moved that "In God We Trust" be placed in the Supreme Court building in much the same spirit that had led the House to place that motto behind the Speaker's desk a year earlier.[128] By and large, however, the violent outburst which had followed *Engel* was missing.

But whatever personal views members of Congress may have held, those of their constituents were made increasingly clear by a barrage of letters and petitions heavily weighted against the prayer and Bible reading decisions. And this unusually heavy flood of mail was soon followed by congressional action in the form of numerous bills proposing amendments to the Constitution intended to reverse the *Schempp* decision. A comparison of Tables 9-7 and 9-8 indicates that almost twice as many members of Congress felt impelled to introduce such amendments as had been the case after *Engel*. In all, 146 amendments were introduced as of March 24, 1964. We are thus faced with an interesting paradox: popular reaction to *Engel* was much greater than the outcry after *Schempp;* yet at the same time positive political action was much more significant after *Schempp* than it had been a year earlier. Several factors may help us to understand this situation. First, as indicated above, the 1963 decisions directly affected a much wider segment of the American public than had the *Regents' Prayer* case. Thus while the immediate outcry from public figures may have been greater after *Engel,* the *Schempp* decision was much more likely to stir up a widespread wave of opposition. Second, while it was not likely that congressional action in response to *Engel* could have been taken in time to affect the 1962 congressional elections, the elections of 1964 were constantly in the minds of congressmen as Congress convened after the summer 1963 recess. And finally, we must interject into the 1963/64 situation the effects of the untiring efforts of Congressman Frank Becker (R., N.Y.).

Although the Senate had chosen to act following *Engel,* through its Judi-

TABLE 9-8

Party Affiliation of Authors of Constitutional Amendments to Reverse Schempp
(88th Congress, 2d Session)

PARTY AFFILIATION	HOUSE	SENATE
Republicans	64	15
Southern Democrats*	30	8
Non-Southern Democrats	19	4
Total	113	27

*"Southern Democrats" represent the 11 states of the former Confederacy. The table is based on the *Congressional Record*, 88th Congress, both sessions. One might have expected many southerners would have introduced such resolutions. It is important to realize that the pattern of behavior among southern Congressmen was far from uniform. As indicated in Table 9-9, there were southern states in which resentment against the Court would be expected to be high, in which the congressmen did not feel called upon to introduce such amendments.

TABLE 9-9

Number of Congressmen Introducing Amendments to Reverse Schempp
(88th Congress, 1st and 2d Sessions)

STATE	DEMOCRATS	REPUBLICANS
Alabama	3 out of 8	———
Arkansas	0 out of 4	———
Florida	5 out of 10	1 out of 2
Georgia	3 out of 10	———
Louisiana	1 out of 8	———
Mississippi	5 out of 5	———
North Carolina	7 out of 7	2 out of 2
South Carolina	4 out of 6	———
Tennessee	0 out of 3	3 out of 3
Texas	2 out of 19	0 out of 2
Virginia	0 out of 6	2 out of 2
Total	30 out of 86	8 out of 11

Note that almost all southern Republicans introduced "anti-Court" amendments. But compare the behavior of congressmen from Mississippi and North Carolina with that of Democrats from Virginia and Arkansas. The authors attempted to correlate the above indicated pattern with such factors as V. O. Key's "Black Belt" thesis; income distribution; presence of an opposition party; and religious affiliation of both congressmen and population, without success. Whatever caused this interesting pattern, it warns us to avoid the danger of viewing the South monolithically in this matter.

ciary Committee, the House was to be the center of the fight between supporters and opponents of amendments following *Schempp.* And the battle focused increasingly on the efforts of Representative Becker to push through such an amendment, and those of Representative Emmanuel Celler (D., N.Y.), powerful chairman of the House Judiciary Committee, to forestall any attack on the Court's ruling. Becker had proposed an amendment after *Engel,* and on the day after the 1963 decision was handed down, he introduced another. Firmly convinced that the Court had struck a serious blow against the religious training of the nation's youth, Becker devoted all his personal efforts to a crusade to convince the public and his colleagues that the great majority of Americans favored and were entitled to the continuation of religious ceremonies in the public schools. A devout Catholic, Congressman Becker had been educated in public schools, as had his children, and he regarded as wholly salutary the modest practices by which the public schools recognized the roles of God and of religion. Becker's zeal was reinforced by his conception of the opponents he was combatting: "I certainly believe that the atheists intend to bury religion. . . ."[129] Since he did not intend to seek reelection in 1964, Becker was prepared to devote virtually his entire energies to the task at hand. He made numerous public addresses, carried on a heavy correspondence, and made himself available as a leader in the fight to get an amendment through both Houses of Congress. Recognizing that the chairman of the Judiciary Committee was unalterably opposed to any such amendment and would not let such a bill out of his committee unless compelled to do so, Becker sought to unite those who agreed with him on one form of amendment, and, by introducing a discharge petition, either to force the holding of hearings, or to get his amendment out of Celler's committee and to the floor, where he anticipated favorable action by the required two-thirds of the House. With the unprecedented number of almost 115 fellow amendment seekers, he thought his chances of success were high, since only 218 signatures were necessary to discharge the bill from the committee. Becker faced two major difficulties from the start: one was the ingrained reluctance of many members to sign a discharge petition on any subject, particularly where the powerful Judiciary Committee was involved; the other was the coincidence of this issue and the Civil Rights Bill, eventually enacted in 1964, which tended to divide supporters of a prayer amendment.[130]

The bill which was to become identified in the public's mind as the "Becker Amendment" was not the bill introduced originally by the Representative, but was the product of a drafting effort by six members of Congress designated to perform this task following a meeting of amendment supporters in late August, 1963.[131] The amendment proposed in House Joint Resolution 693, introduced on September 10, 1963, provided that:

> Sec. 1. Nothing in this Constitution shall be deemed to prohibit the offering, reading from, or listening to prayers or Biblical scriptures, if participation therein is on a voluntary basis, in any governmental or public school, institution, or place.
>
> Sec. 2. Nothing in this Constitution shall be deemed to prohibit making reference to, belief in, reliance upon, or invoking the aid of God or a Supreme Being in any governmental or public document, proceeding, activity, ceremony, school, institution, or place, or upon any coinage, currency, or obligation of the United States.
>
> Sec. 3. Nothing in this article shall constitute an establishment of religion.

Ratification by three-fourths of the state legislatures within seven years was required by the last section of the proposed amendment.

During this period petitions and letters continued to pile up in congressional offices, and especially in those of members of the House Judiciary Committee. The campaign on behalf of an amendment to overcome the Court's decisions now had a clearer focus. From now on the battle was to be waged exclusively in terms of the Becker Amendment.

Although the volume of mail favoring the Becker Amendment continued to mount and members of the House continued to sign Becker's discharge petition, supporters of the decision did not view the matter seriously. The natural congressional opposition to discharge petitions under any circumstances and the feeling that the Judiciary Committee and especially its chairman could not be stampeded, along with the relative mildness of the initial reactions to the 1963 decision, led usually well-informed observers to believe that the Becker

Amendment would peacefully die in committee. But support for the amendment from constituents of all types continued to mount, largely as a result of the activities of Congressman Becker and of organizations supporting his position. The New York *Times* reported that "largely through his efforts, it is conceded widely in Congress that congressional mail on this issue has grown to flood proportions, exceeding the mail of the civil rights controversy."[132] Congressman Lionel Van Deerlin (D., Cal.) wrote that his colleagues "are being inundated with constituent mail, the great bulk of which favors such an amendment."[133] A form letter used by Congressman R. G. Stephens (D., Ga.) to reply to constituents apologized for the fact that a printed reply was being used, but said that it was necessitated by the fact that he had had over one thousand letters on the subject. On February 18, the House Republican Policy Committee voted to support the Becker Amendment.[134] Congressman Alec G. Olson (D., Minn.) informed a constituent that he believed "this is a result of the large volume of mail running in favor of this amendment. In any case, I have received correspondence which is at least 200 to 1 in favor of such an amendment. . . ."[135] Gradually the number of signatures on the discharge petition rose so that eventually it contained almost 170 names.[136] And, the *Wall Street Journal* reported, "it is no secret that many more members, including some hostile to the proposal and others adverse to the irregular procedure, have warned Mr. Celler that pressure from home would force them to sign unless he made some move."[137]

How is it that the members of Congress—who were surely well aware that much of the mail they were receiving was "inspired"—were sensitive to public sentiment to the extent that the *Wall Street Journal* pointed out that "for the most part, even lawmakers adamant in their opposition have kept silent in public"?[138] The answer is probably to be found in the way the issue was phrased by Becker and his suporters. In an election year, no congressman wanted to be placed in a position of appearing to vote against God, which was exactly the role into which supporters of the Court were being forced. One powerful southern committee chairman, who had recently tied the house up in knots by the exercise of his individual power, wrote to a clergyman in his district that, despite his personal opposition to the Becker Amendment, "I have been somewhat silent on the subject matter, waiting for the hysteria to subside."[139] Congressman Neil Staebler (D., Mich.) felt constrained to begin a form letter: "Thank you for your recent letter concerning the question of religious practices in the schools. *As you know, we use prayers regularly in Congress.*" And Congressman Holifield's (D., Cal.) form letter opposing Becker began by stressing the fact that it was as "a believer in true freedom of religious choice . . . as a believer in a Supreme Being . . . [and] as a believer in the efficacy of sincere prayer" that he could not support Becker's proposal.[140] The bind in which Congressman Charles Wilson (D., Cal.) found himself is illustrated by a letter in which he urged opponents of the bill to obtain support for their position from the ministers of religion. "Any help you can give in this regard will be much appreciated."[141] Congressman Becker put additional pressure on his colleagues by threatening to come into the district of every congressman who failed to support his amendment and actively campaign against him in the forthcoming election.

Early in 1964 it became apparent that Congressman Celler would have to schedule hearings, in order to avoid having the bill taken out of his committee. And indeed, by the middle of February he reacted to the Republican Policy Committee's demand for hearings by dryly remarking that a staff study was in progress, and that hearings would be scheduled when it was completed.[142] Opponents of the Becker Amendment who had previously been relatively inactive suddenly realized that if they did not stop Becker's juggernaut at the committee hearings, their worst fears would be fulfilled. Meeting in New York on St. Patrick's Day, 1964, an *ad hoc* committee consisting of representatives of numerous Protestant, Jewish, and civil liberties groups opposed to the amendment decided that at that time the Becker Amendment had an excellent chance of receiving the approval of a majority of the Judiciary Committee, that if reported out favorably it was likely to pass easily in the House, and that while the Senate might delay passage of the bill, it would eventually pass there as well, an estimate concurred in by close students of the situation not present at the meeting.

Faced with this prospect, the members of the *ad hoc* group decided to coordinate their organizational efforts. It was agreed that probably the most important function the group could play would be to mobilize leaders of the religious community to oppose the Becker Amendment, in order to make it "respectable" and "safe" for congressmen to oppose the Becker proposal. Similar attempts would be made to get law school deans and teachers to voice their opposition. And a drive to "inspire" a countervailing flood of mail would be undertaken. In order to maximize the support which they could hope to mobilize, it was decided to pitch the anti-Becker campaign in terms of protecting the sanctity of the First Amendment. It was hoped that this tactic might be particularly useful in obtaining the support of liberal Catholic elements.

Two days after the *ad hoc* committee met, Chairman Celler announced that hearings would begin on April 22. He indicated that he was in no hurry to report out an amendment, and that the nature and importance of the subject matter required mature and deliberate consideration of the best thinking on both sides of the question.[143] Congressman Becker was "amazed" that Celler had scheduled the hearings for the end of April, having expected them to begin on April 1. He denounced him for employing delaying tactics, and threatened to continue to push his discharge petition, which, he claimed, contained over 160 signatures.[144] Accusing Celler of "total and unalterable opposition" to his proposal, he insisted that it was only after "insurmountable pressure"—largely from the discharge petition—that the chairman had acted. He further accused

Celler of having deliberately scheduled the hearings to begin on the first day of the New York World's Fair, so as to minimize the amount of public attention they would receive. The chairman replied: "I never dreamed of the World's Fair."[145]

As the hearings commenced, the *ad hoc* committee of organizations opposing the Becker Amendment, and their coordinator—Rev. Dean M. Kelley of the National Council of Churches[146]—believed that a majority of the Judiciary Committee members were in favor of the amendment. Their immediate goal, therefore, was to attempt through personal visits with the uncommitted and, hopefully, changeable members of the committee to reverse this balance. In addition, they made plans to present an imposing group of witnesses against the amendment, paying particular attention to religious leaders and legal scholars.

The anti-Becker campaign received some assistance from the Judiciary Committee's staff study, published on March 24, 1964, which pointed out in considerable detail the various difficulties presented by proposed amendments, including that of Congressman Becker. Though, in true staff style, it avoided taking an overt position on the merits, it raised so many questions and doubts concerning the form and substance of the several proposals that several members of the committee strongly objected to its release.

The *ad hoc* committee representatives quickly discovered that one of the major factors weakening the opponents of the Becker Amendment was their lack of communication on this matter. Congressmen contacted by Rev. Kelley were amazed to find out that certain of their colleagues shared their views.[147] As indicated above, the anti-religion charge raised by Becker's side had silenced many opponents. And in their silence they assumed that they were alone.

We have here an interesting insight into the legislative process, particularly with respect to the role of political parties in that process. One of the benefits a busy congressman derives from his party affiliation is information. He can quickly determine how most of his colleagues stand on a given issue. But the Becker Amendment fight had not become a partisan issue, and thus the party whips were not performing their usual function of consolidating support for, or opposition to, this piece of legislation. Congressman Becker's monumental efforts on behalf of his cause had taken the place of the party machinery for supporters of the bill, but opponents of the amendment were left in virtual legislative isolation. Kelley and the interest groups he represented quickly moved into this gap, making every effort to bring members opposed to the amendment together and providing them with "ammunition" for use during the hearings.

As the result of the efforts of the *ad hoc* committee, a substantial volume of anti-amendment mail began to arrive in congressional offices and that of the committee as the hearings began on April 22, a flow that continued until their termination. While it never equaled the volume of pro-amendment mail, it was sufficient to justify some Congressmen in concluding that public sentiment was hardly as one-sided as they had suspected.

The hearings themselves were originally planned to last two weeks, or so Becker thought.[148] But once Chairman Celler decided to hold the hearings with the entire committee present, previous plans had to be abandoned. The hearings ran from April 22 through June 3, 1964, giving both sides an ample opportunity to parade their forces. The three volumes and 2774 pages of testimony by 197 witnesses, with numerous prepared statements, letters, and other data, are evidence that the opportunity was seized by both sides, but particularly by Becker's opponents. It may well be that, realizing that the Becker forces were in a position of advantage as the hearings opened, the chairman felt that delay would give opponents a chance to catch up. It is extremely likely that Representative Celler was aware that by June Congress would be rushing toward adjournment in time for the Republican Presidential Convention in San Francisco. In any event, efforts made from time to time by pro-Becker committee members to limit the prolonged questioning of witnesses came to naught.[149] In addition, the chairman, who is generally regarded as a very effective presiding officer, used his position to blunt the effectiveness of pro-amendment witnesses, helped the critics over rough spots, and clearly sought to shape arguments that might appeal to the uncommitted members. It is a gross understatement to say that had Celler favored the proposed amendment, the anti-Becker forces would have had a much more difficult time.

Although any effort to summarize briefly or evaluate the testimony of the contending forces is inevitably highly subjective, a few observations reflecting the authors' impressions may be of some value. The arguments of the Becker supporters followed the pattern previously established: the people favor such practices; the Court's decisions are an attack on God and on religion; this country was founded on a belief in God, and cannot exist without it; majorities have rights, and they need not always bow to the will of an "atheistic" minority.

Without question, the most significant testimony in opposition to the proposal was that of the religious leaders organized by Rev. Kelley and his associates. The unanimous opposition of such distinguished theologians as Dr. Eugene Carson Blake, chief officer of the United Presbyterian Church, and former president of the National Council of Churches; Methodist Bishop John Wesley Lord of Washington, D.C.; Dr. Edwin Tuller, General Secretary of the American Baptist Convention; Dr. Fredrik Schiotz, President of the American Lutheran Church; Presiding Protestant Episcopal Bishop Arthur Lichtenberger; and many others, made it difficult for Becker supporters to insist that only the Godless opposed them, and made it considerably "safer" for election-conscious congressmen to oppose the Becker Amendment.[150] While it is quite probable that the virtual unanimity of these spokesmen did not correspond fully to the actual views of all their religious constituents—and indeed, the

Becker forces strove valiantly to establish this point—they placed the prestige of organized religion against the attempt to tamper with the First Amendment. Important, too, was the union in opposition of leading Protestant, Jewish, and Catholic spokesmen (especially those from Catholic law schools) so that an appearance of trans-denominational solidarity was maintained. It is likely that the impact which the testimony of the religious leaders had on the members of the committee, the membership of Congress as a whole, and on the general public was the major factor which tipped the balance against the Becker forces.

Equally impressive, and perhaps almost as significant, was the testimony of legal scholars who attacked the amendment. Such distinguished professors as Paul A. Freund of Harvard, Philip B. Kurland of Chicago, and Paul E. Kauper of Michigan bolstered the position of the opponents.[151] Particularly striking was a statement of opposition signed by 223 of the nation's best known law school deans and teachers, drawn up by Professors Freund; Wilbur G. Katz of Wisconsin; Robert P. Drinan, S.J., Dean of Boston College Law School; and Leo Pfeffer, General Counsel of the American Jewish Congress, as the hearings came to their close.[152]

The testimony of the opponents of the amendment was intended to sway the opinion of wavering congressmen. Which version of the Bible would be used? Would the Koran qualify under the amendment? Who would decide which prayers to say? Could the "Ave Maria" be employed? And again and again they returned to the basic theme: "Thou shalt not touch the Bill of Rights."

The Becker Amendment movement, while endorsed widely, was essentially a one-man crusade. Although various organizations lent their support, and vigorous statements were made by several witnesses, the strategy used and the calibre of the witnesses did not match the efforts of the anti-amendment forces.[153] To one who tries to read the pro-Becker testimony objectively, it seems that in the minds of many witnesses popular support for continuance of school prayers and Bible reading was regarded as the decisive factor. With notable exceptions, such as Charles Wesley Lowry,[154] many pro-Becker witnesses seemed to have adopted the simple equation—the people want prayers in schools; the Court took them away; we, on behalf of the people, must restore them. When the chairman or other committee members attempted to draw them out as to the effects of the various provisions of the amendment, they were often unable to follow the subtleties of the questioner. They frequently seemed annoyed by the complexities of issues framed by opponents.

Press coverage of the hearings was relatively full, and though the public was unable to gain a very coherent notion of the trend of the debates, it appears that the testimony of the anti-Becker church leaders and that of the legal authorities opposing the measure dominated the reports, especially in the later sessions. This may help to explain the increase in the anti-Becker mail, and a number of editorials throughout the nation urging that the amendment not pass.[155]

The real test of the effectiveness of the opposition lay in the impact on members of the Judiciary Committee. Although any judgment must be made with considerable reservation, it would seem that the direction of change of views of committee members was almost exclusively in one direction—against the amendment. At the beginning of the hearings, as noted above, the *ad hoc* committee had estimated that the Becker amendment would easily win a majority in the committee; by the end of May, they expected that the Becker Amendment would probably be opposed by as many as 20 of the 35 members. By that time it was doubtful that any amendment then in prospect could attract a majority of the committee. It was apparent that the drive for a discharge petition had passed its crest; not only could it not gain the necessary 218 signatures, but members who had signed the petition were prepared to remove their names should the total approach 210. And even if a bill were discharged, it was doubtful that it could obtain a majority in the House, much less the required two-thirds majority. The *Wall Street Journal* doubted that as many as 8 members of the committee still supported an amendment.[156]

The use of public hearings as a means of shaping the thinking of committee members has been increasingly discounted by political analysts in recent years. They have tended to view them as a show with little relevance to the actual struggle over important public issues. The Becker Amendment hearings would appear to cast serious doubt as to the validity of these conclusions, for, as we have seen, the hearings had a significant impact *both* on congressional opinion and on public opinion. The Becker hearings point to many aspects of the legislative process which students of future contests would do well to keep in mind. A combination of factors: expert, if belated, planning by opponents; their ability to gain the support of heavier "guns" at the hearings; and the natural advantage that our political system provides those opposing legislative action, was all too much for the Becker cause, regardless of its popular support. Also, the skillful operation of an experienced committee chairman and ally was of inestimable value to the anti-amendment forces.

One might be tempted to conclude as Congressman Becker did that the final outcome—the failure of the committee to report the Becker bill and of the drive to gain enough signatures to discharge the committee—represented a defeat for the democratic process. But it is probably correct to say that this is precisely a situation envisaged by and acceptable to the framers of the Constitution. The great danger, according to Madison in *Federalist No. 10,* lay in factions representing a majority. To prevent these majorities from riding roughly over minorities our elaborate system of separated powers and checks and balances was established. The nature of the committee system of the Congress is clearly consistent with the spirit of the legislative "filter" of which Madison spoke.

Although Congressman Becker has continued his efforts to win acceptance for the constitutional recognition of prayers and Bible reading, and promises to continue the work after his retirement from Congress, the momentum of the pro-amendment forces is gone. "Unleashing Frank Becker at this point is about like unleashing Chiang Kai-Shek," commented one member of the Judiciary Committee in the middle of June.[157] It had been widely assumed that the committee would report out a resolution expressing the "sense of Congress" that the Court reverse or restrict its decisions as a face-saving device to get many Congressmen "off the hook." However, this suggestion dropped out of sight, and Congress adjourned without considering such a proposal.

Congressman Becker took his battle to the Republican National Convention, where the Chairman of the Platform Committee commented on the large amount of mail he had received on the subject.[158] The Convention approved a plank in the platform pledging support for a constitutional amendment:

> . . . permitting those individuals and groups who choose to do so to exercise their religion freely in public places, provided religious exercises are not prepared or *prescribed* by the state or political subdivision thereof and no person's participation therein is coerced, thus preserving the traditional separation of church and state.[159]

But little was made of the prayer issue in the presidential campaign save as a small part of a broadside attack on the Supreme Court. In American politics a succession of major issues emerge and disappear too swiftly to provide many second chances for any one. It is unlikely that the Becker Amendment will prove an exception to that rule.

The New Politics

American democracy is based on a permanent tension between governmental power and individual liberties, between majority rule and minority rights. The right to dissent, the right to say "no," is an essential part of democracy. Yet, as Handlin, in "Dissent and Democracy," states:

> The conditions of protest change when it is launched not against authority or tradition, but against decisions made in the name of a popular majority. Dissent, then, runs counter to another fundamental principle of American society—that government operates through the consent of the governed expressed in the rule of the majority.

Free discussion is essential to keep the government responsive to the will of the people and to provide means for creating change; yet, as Handlin observes:

> . . . the very existence of that freedom imposes peculiar obligations on the dissenter. On the one hand, he has the duty to obey even when he disagrees, since the decision is not the act of a despot but of the citizenry of which he is a part. On the other hand, every participant in a democracy shares the responsibility for the measures taken in its name; and the man who believes some such measure wrong has the duty to say so.

But can a dissident minority go beyond verbal protest without undermining the orderly processes that, in the long run, are its strongest protection? Handlin, at least, is willing to acknowledge the right of a Thoreau to refuse to pay his taxes in protest and go to jail as a result. He further argues that:

> To differentiate himself from the lawless, the conscientious dissenter who goes beyond verbal protest must persuade others of his integrity. He must be prepared to accept the consequences of his dissent, acknowledge the right of the state to punish him as evidence of the depth of his convictions.

The civil rights movements in the early 1960s, described in Zangrando's "From Civil Rights to Black Liberation: The Unsettled 1960's," meet these criteria. The tactic of civil disobedience, which was used to force recognition of Negro rights, was seized upon by other dissident groups to announce their dissatisfaction with American society and politics. Many, both black radicals and white student radicals, went beyond the early stages of civil disobedience to advocate and practice a politics of confrontation. Protest appears to have become an American way of life. It is against this background, therefore, that the different perspectives of John Cogley, Sidney Hook, Paul Goodman, and Bayard Rustin should be viewed.

Where do we go from here? Many protesters argue that the American political system has failed and must be drastically overhauled, and some observers feel the country may be in for a very long seige of confrontation politics as young people, Negroes, and other minority groups struggle for power. In "The Old Politics, the New Politics, the *New,* New Politics," Kristol agrees:

> We are headed for a time of trouble, in which our political authorities are going to have to cope with an unreasonable revolution of rising material expectations on the part of the majority, an equally unreasonable revolution of utopian spiritual expectations on the part of a significant minority, and with a general breakdown of individual and social discipline.

Yet Kristol also believes the old political order has not failed, contending that during the past decades, we have created "pretty much the kind of economic, social and political order that was intended." At the same time, he maintains, "we have created a moral and cultural order that is dismissive of—more than that: contemptuous of—these very intentions. The Old Politics didn't fail, it succeeded, and that is precisely what is held against it."

Whatever the truth of this pessimistic view, it represents one way in which the nature of the society shapes the operations and products of the political system.

Dissent and Democracy

OSCAR HANDLIN

The unprecedented issues of the 1960s have focused attention upon the inter-relationships in our society of dissent, democracy and foreign policy. Americans have long recognized the right of citizens to disagree with the established policy of the government; and restraints upon that right have been less burdensome in the past decade than ever before in history. As a result, dissenters have been able to speak out vigorously against policies established by popular majorities through democratic procedures.

The resultant tensions have been especially severe when they arose from disagreements in the field of foreign policy, for the issues involved affected not only the security of the United States but also the interests of the large part of the world which looked to America for leadership.

The problem of reconciling dissent with diplomacy is peculiar to democracy. Authoritarian regimes have their own mechanisms for suppressing discordant voices; a free government must be prepared to deal with dissenters without emulating such methods of internal control. And the problem is particularly urgent in the 1960s when the stakes have a grave and momentous character. The elected leaders of government have it in their power to destroy the whole world; and their decisions involve considerations which sometimes are not readily communicated to a wide public.

As a result, it is impossible to speak of absolutes in this area. Dissenters have the right of speaking out and making their views known. The majority has the right to set the limits within which decisions are made. Yet there are points at which these rights conflict and are qualified by offsetting obligations, for the course of diplomacy is tortuous and burdensome. Can the majority act but still be cognizant of the privileges of dissenters? Can dissenters speak out without impeding the right of the majority to decide? Can our chosen leaders make decisions yet remain responsive to the views of both the majorities and the minorities they represent?

It is therefore necessary to scrutinize closely each of the elements that maintain the delicate balance a soundly functioning society must preserve. Whence does the minority derive the right to dissent? Why does the majority have the

Excerpted from Oscar Handlin *et al*, "Dissent, Democracy and Foreign Policy—a Symposium," *Headline Series* No. 190, pp. 3–12. New York, Foreign Policy Association, August 1968.

right to set policy and within what limits? And to what extent do foreign relations differ from the other problems of policy in a democracy?

The Freedom to Say No

The ability to dissent is one of the cherished rights of American society. It is enshrined in the First Amendment, which forbids the Congress to make any law abridging the freedom of speech, or of the press or of the right of assembly—a prohibition which was extended to the states by the Fourteenth Amendment. But recognition of the value of dissent antedated the formal constitutional statements which safeguarded it. It had deep roots in the social institutions and the national character of the Americans. Despite occasional infringements under the pressure of presumed or actual emergencies, the privilege of saying No without thereby becoming subject to punishment has been an important ingredient of the freedom of the nation throughout its history.

The right to dissent acquired strength from the circumstance that it was both a tactic and a principle. For a long time it proved a useful device among those who lacked power but wished to assert points of view different from those of their rulers. But in time, dissent also acquired intrinsic value as a posture with a moral character of its own.

For hundreds of years dissent was a tactic in the hands of people who challenged the force of authority. As late as the 18th century, the most important social rules and controls were imposed and enforced by governments which claimed the backing of authority. That authority could be regarded as the divine right of a monarch, as the sole custody of truth by an established church, as the binding force of custom in a village or as the restraints of legal precedent. Men who had new ideas which did not conform to those validated by church, state or society or men who wished to take novel courses had to claim the right to dissent from the established views. Usually this was a tactic. The Puritans who came to Massachusetts Bay, for instance, asserted their own right to dissent from the church established in England, but were by no means ready to concede a similar right to the antinomians, Baptists, Quakers and other opponents in the New World.

Yet, gradually, experience taught that dissent was a matter of principle as well as a tactic. There was a value inherent in the right and not merely a circumstance of its utility as an instrument to serve a particular purpose. To secure recognition of the principle of free expression called for a slow transformation of conventional habits of thought. As long as men believed that truth could be established by some authoritative external source, they were reluctant to tolerate error. Only as they surrendered faith in authority and began to conceive that the truth emerged from the examination of diverse perceptions of it, did they understand the value of dissent.

The principle was first asserted with reference to religion. In America,

Roger Williams maintained, as did the Baptists later, that no human church could be truly certain of its own holiness or of its conformity with the divine percepts. Therefore it was best to allow each individual to follow the guidance of his own conscience and to worship in his own way.

The more generalized view rested on a similar foundation. From the 18th-century Enlightenment onward, a growing confidence in the power to reason to uncover the truth had as a concomitant the willingness to concede that there could be no certainty of the correctness of any proposition, no matter how authoritative or how determined were those who maintained it. No prince or potentate could use his power to impose his views on others. Nor, for that matter, could a scientist or expert use his knowledge to coerce others into accepting his opinions. Truth would triumph over error only through the open exposure of all points of view. "Who ever knew Truth put to the worse in a free and open encounter?" asked John Milton. To give light was the task of the leader, the people could find their own way.

The liberal creed which safeguarded the right to dissent gained increasing acceptance in the 19th century. Freedom of expression came to be regarded as an essential element of human dignity. Not only did it assure the evocation of a multitude of viewpoints, it also guaranteed respect for the conscience of every single human being. Furthermore, the acceptance of dissent amounted to an affirmation of the worth of novelty against authority and custom and was thus progressive. As a result, it had a special relationship to the American tendency to cherish the rugged individual and to value the principle of non-conformity.

Therefore dissent, whether as a tactic or a principle, became part of a continuing tradition. Americans sometimes exaggerated the extent of their commitment to that tradition and tended to close their eyes to departures from it. A direct line seemed to extend from the Puritans, who were portrayed as proponents of the freedom of conscience, to the patriots of the Revolutionary era, who fought for the rights of self-expression, to the abolitionists, who wished to free the slaves, to the multitude of 19th-century reformers, and on to the anti-imperialists and pacifists. A common willingness to dissent from accepted standards made heroes of all these critics and crusaders.

The Voice of the People

The problem assumed a more difficult form when dissent ceased to be directed against an absolute monarch or an authoritarian church and found its mark in developing democratic institutions. In this respect dissent is like revolution; one must understand not only the act of protest but also the object at which it is launched. Certainly its character changes when dissent is expressed not against authority, but against the will of the majority.

Not all dissenters after all have found places in the pantheon of American heroes. For instance, the Tories during the Revolution and the Copperheads during the Civil War were no doubt dissenters. The former wished to maintain the connection with Britain, the latter were sympathetic either to the cause of the South or to slavery. Both claimed the right of dissent; yet neither was particularly interested in liberty. They therefore posed to the dominant majority the question of the extent to which the right to dissent was due to those who would not themselves respect it if they held power. If dissent were merely a tactic, these people did not deserve it. But if dissent were a principle, then even they had a right to it.

Once the right of dissent is recognized as a principle, it becomes available to every member of society in a democracy. It may be asserted not only against the rule of the majority but also against the very procedures of law and order. The Ku Klux Klan of the Reconstruction period acted against measures which furthered racial equality in the South, and the White Citizens' Councils of the 1950s dissented from the Supreme Court's doctrine of desegregation. Some college students have occupied buildings to express their disagreement with the war in Vietnam just as others attempted to exclude James Meredith, a Negro, from the University of Mississippi. A society which refuses to define heresy cannot objectively draw a clear line in terms of the target of the protest. It must concede the right to all. Dissenters have objected not only to the dominant views of sexual morality and to restrictions on the use of drugs but also to the use of fluorine in the water supply and to the theory of evolution.

Democracy thus complicates the concept of dissent. The conditions of protest change when it is launched not against authority or tradition, but against decisions made in the name of a popular majority. Dissent, then, runs counter to another fundamental principle of American society—that government operates through the consent of the governed expressed in the rule of the majority.

It does not follow from that principle that any given majority is always correct or just or capable of making the choices appropriate to any particular crisis. The deficiencies of democracy are well known. More than a century ago a conservative British statesman warned that popular governments were reluctant to face the truth, were prone to increase expenditures without providing the means, entered into wars from passion and not from reason and were likely ignominiously to seek a peace that might endanger their independence. Moreover, the tyranny of a multitude can threaten liberty as much as the tyranny of a monarch.

Nevertheless, despite its shortcomings, majority rule furnishes a moral basis for political action. The fact that it proceeds from the wishes of the people validates the use of power by a democracy. The law enacted by consent is not simply a brutal use of force but an expression of the community's sense of order.

Open discussion in a free marketplace of ideas is essential to keep the government responsive to the will of the people and to provide lawful means for effecting change. Yet the very existence of that freedom imposes peculiar obligations on the dissenter. On the one hand, he has the duty to obey even when he disagrees, since the decision is not the act of a despot but of the citizenry of which he is a part. On the other hand, every participant in a democracy shares the responsibility for the measures taken in its name; and the man who believes some such measure wrong has the duty to say so.

A consciousness of the shortcomings, actual and potential, of majority rule has placed various procedural and substantive safeguards in the American system to prevent the abuse of the rights of the minority. The majority cannot act except through the processes of law; and some privileges, like those set forth in the Bill of Rights, are altogether beyond its reach. John C. Calhoun, who early perceived the nature of the problem, proposed to give the minority of Southern slaveholders a veto over the possible emancipation by the free-state majority. The underlying argument, which has occasionally been repeated in other contexts, is that the intensity of commitment of the minority deserves special recognition as against the more diffuse commitment or apathy of the majority. But Americans rejected his solution at the time and since. The will of the majority was to prevail, although in ways that would infringe as little as possible upon the rights of the minority.

The tension between the right of the majority to act and the right of the minority to disagree is least dangerous when the protest is verbal. The government which has the support of its people need place few limitations upon the freedom of speech. The arguments of the coffee-house anarchists or the village atheist will only sharpen the loyalty of the citizen and strengthen the faith of the churchgoer. The freedom of the dissenting minority to speak out is a useful corrective to complacency in a democracy.

The problem is altogether different when dissent takes the form of refusal to act in accordance with the law or indeed when it takes the form of a determination to impede the execution of the law. The minority under those circumstances must take heed lest it undermine the orderly procedures which in the long run are its own best safeguards.

The justification of the dissenter who goes beyond speech to direct action rests upon an appeal to conscience. There are occasions, he insists, when a higher law than that of the state must prevail even though the latter is validated by the majority. "In the forum of conscience," Chief Justice Charles Evans Hughes explained, "duty to a moral power higher than the state has always been maintained." Men of good conscience, outraged by the fugitive slave laws in the 1850s or by segregation in the 1950s, deliberately violated government-set rules out of a conviction that those measures were so unjust that they could not be obeyed.

The claim of conscience was easiest to recognize when it was set within a clear religious context. God spoke to those who heard his voice and commanded them not to obey the dictates of Caesar. Without a theistic basis, however, it is more difficult to appeal to conscience. The dissenter who does so labors under the necessity of demonstrating the authenticity of his convictions. He must show that his refusal to obey is not merely a matter of convenience or interest and is more than a stubborn insistence upon setting his personal judgment against that of the majority; it is an absolutely compelling imperative. Otherwise the desire of each man to follow his own preference would "overturn all polities, and instead of government and order, leave nothing but anarchy and confusion." The government, Justice Robert H. Jackson pointed out, "cannot let any group ride roughshod over others simply because their 'consciences' tell them to do so."

The dissenters in a democracy have an uncommon stake in the preservation of respect for the law. Rousseau long ago noted that "As soon as it is possible to disobey with impunity, disobedience is legitimate; and, the strongest being always in the right, the only thing that matters is to act so as to become the strongest." The conscientious minority has most to lose when great issues are left to the rule of force.

The principle is as valid now as it was in the 18th century. The National Advisory Commission on Civil Disorders pointed out in 1968 that defiance of the legal authorities by those convinced that they alone understood the truth created a climate "that tends toward the approval and encouragement of violence as a form of protest. . . ." It found that "a general erosion of respect for authority in American society and the reduced effectiveness of social standards and community restraints" reinforced the impulse to "go beyond constitutionally protected rights of petition and free assembly and resort to violence to attempt to compel alteration of laws and policies. . . ." And violence bred counterviolence.

To differentiate himself from the lawless, the conscientious dissenter who goes beyond verbal protest must persuade others of his integrity. He must be prepared to accept the consequences of his dissent, acknowledge the right of the state to punish him as evidence of the depths of his conviction. This was the classical argument of Socrates, who rejected Crito's invitation to escape an unjust punishment and preferred to die "in innocence, a sufferer and not a doer of evil; a victim, not of the laws, but of men." When dissenters claim the rights of conscience and then resort to legal quibbling to evade the consequences, they weaken the moral basis of their position and put themselves on a plane with people who seek loopholes to evade their tax obligations or those who drive through red lights when no policeman is watching.

The effectiveness of dissent depends not only on the justice of the cause and on the fervor of those who participate but also on the way in which they conduct themselves. The contrast between the orderly, decent behavior of the Negroes who sat in at the lunch counters or boycotted Jim Crow buses and the mobs who jeered at them lent force to those protests. By contrast, the outrageous conduct of the people who objected to the court order to desegregate the Little Rock schools exposed the poverty of their dissent.

Moreover, those who take a stand against the majority must be totally honest and consistent. That is their only moral justification. Since they claim to be bound by conscience, they must follow wherever the rule leads them without seeking special exemptions. Pacifists like the late A. J. Muste who muted their criticism of Hitler in order to justify American neutrality in 1941 or those Quakers who attack the role of the United States in Vietnam but defend the violence of the Maoist Red Guards put themselves into an anomalous position. By the same token, when the blood poured over the records of a draft office turned out to be that of animals, it eroded the moral strength of the protestors who had originally asserted that it was their own.

In any case, the claim of conscience in a democracy can only extend so far as to exempt the individual from involvement. It cannot justify the imposition of his views on others. Thoreau refused to pay a poll tax that would support an unjust war and went to prison as a result; he did not try to prevent others from paying theirs. At the very beginning of our history, Roger Williams stated the whole issue concisely. Denying that he had ever argued for "an infinite liberty of conscience," he compared society to "a ship to sea, with many hundred souls" aboard, of whom some were Catholics and Protestants, others Jews and Turks. ". . . . All the liberty of conscience that ever I pleaded for turns upon these two hinges—that none of the Papists, Protestants, Jews or Turks be forced to come to the ship's prayers or worship" nor prevented from conducting their own if they wished. Notwithstanding this liberty, it was the duty of the captain to "command the ship's course, yea, and also command that justice, peace and sobriety be kept and practiced. . . ." If any seamen or passengers refused to "help, in person or purse, toward the common charges or defence; if any refused to obey the common laws and orders"; if any mutinied or "preached or . . . wrote that there ought to be no commanders or officers . . . no laws nor orders, nor corrections nor punishments . . . in such cases . . . the commander or commanders may judge . . . and punish such transgressors. . . ."

Three centuries after Williams wrote this, the need for order aboard ship is greater than ever. The millions of interdependent individuals in our complex society cannot all have their own way. They can sustain their common enterprises in freedom only within agreed-upon rules. The speed and graphic character of modern communications, with their bewildering succession of sensational images, are less conducive to reflection and calm debate than were the pamphlets and sermons that moved our ancestors. Mercurial changes of mood can alter popular attitudes in a matter of months; and the fashions that sweep through society can affect ideas as well as clothes. Under these conditions, rational discussion is essential and its conduct demands both the freedom to dissent and the willingness to restrain dissent within the limits of law. Democracy provides the mechanism. The question is, Will men have the patience to use it?

From Civil Rights to Black Liberation: The Unsettled 1960s

ROBERT L. ZANGRANDO

During the past decade, the nature of relations between black and white Americans has changed with a decisive swiftness that many whites have refused to recognize and few have begun to comprehend. Established patterns of protest—such as the NAACP's efforts for legal and judicial redress—remain important and will be continued, but they no longer predominate. Today's attempts to achieve freedom for black people are varied and fluid. They form a mosaic of diverse groups, multiple leaderships, competing ideologies and innovative tactics, which to most whites (and even to some Negroes) seems a troublesome cacophony of disparate voices. However, this diversity carries a very different meaning if viewed in positive terms as a composite of forces that exhibit a universal reality: the resolve of black people to structure their own lives and futures unhindered by the once-familiar tendency of white reformers to play leadership roles in decision-making processes.

In the early years of this decade, the Southern Christian Leadership Conference, the Congress of Racial Equality and the Student Nonviolent Coordinating Committee startled the nation from its apathy on racial issues by carrying out a series of imaginative activities that included sit-ins, picketing, demonstrations, freedom rides, voter registration drives and community organization projects. These tactics emphasized the willingness of those who believed in civil rights to "put their bodies on the line," and they were implemented by the ready participation of local residents acting (at times) under the coordination of outside field workers. Dr. Martin Luther King, Jr., became the inspirational leader of this nonviolent movement and functioned as a mediator among the several civil rights organizations and between the black community and white America. In the fall of 1962, national attention was riveted on James Meredith's attempt to enroll at the University of Mississippi; his admission was effected by President John F. Kennedy's use of federal troops. Thus, by the beginning of 1963, the centennial year of the Emancipation Proclamation, an entirely new set of forces had been mobilized on behalf of minority group rights: joint initiative by field workers and local residents, participatory, direct

Reprinted from Robert L. Zangrando, "From Civil Rights to Black Liberation: The Unsettled 1960s," *Current History*, Vol. 57, No. 339 (November 1969), pp. 281–286, 289.

action by black and white people, and some degree of federal involvement. These forces revolutionized the civil rights movement in the South and permanently altered the thrust and style of Negro protest throughout the nation. They seemed to herald a new day for American democracy.

However, a combination of political expediencies, white racism (exhibited in hesitation, indifference and outright oppositon) and the diversion of energies to the war in Vietnam eroded the prospects for interracial justice. As quickly as it had emerged, the integrationist "We Shall Overcome" comradery dissolved, and the years since 1965 have been marked by growing mistrust across race lines.

The major test of the civil rights movement had occurred in mid-1964. Building on the nationwide reaction against Southern white violence, and on the unprecedented display of interracial rapport during the 1963 March on Washington, the movement prepared to challenge racism in a systematic fashion through its Mississippi Summer Project. It was the high moment of unity. After months of debate, Congress had passed the Civil Rights Act of 1964; at the same time, the main protest organizations agreed to coordinate their efforts in Mississippi through the Council of Federated Organizations. The COFO program had three interrelated components: Freedom Schools, community service projects and an extensive voter registration drive on behalf of the Mississippi Freedom Democratic party. M.F.D.P. was an integrated party designed to rally the disfranchised in the state and to seek recognition at the Democratic National Convention as the party of loyal Mississippi Democrats ready to support Lyndon Johnson and a liberal national platform. The Summer Project was thoughtfully conceived and courageously executed to bring out-of-state assistance to people who wanted to help themselves, and to do it with at least the tacit support of an attentive nationwide audience. However, its success was only partial; the odds against it were too great.

After some hesitation, the Democratic National Convention refused to recognize the 68-member M.F.D.P. delegation. Instead, it offered two at-large seats. Many political observers—some close friends of the civil rights movement among them—urged the M.F.D.P. to accept. To the M.F.D.P. delegates who had worked so hard and risked so much this compromise was out of the question. Moreover, the very suggestion convinced them that those who had not been close to the Summer Project on a daily basis could not comprehend the nature of racist oppression or the spiritual vigor of the freedom movement as it had taken shape in Mississippi. The congressional challenge through which the M.F.D.P. later tried to prevent the seating of the five white Mississippi Representatives at the opening of the 89th Congress proved to be only an emphatic coda to the integrationist symphony of the Summer Project. Even the subsequent agonies at Alabama's Selma Bridge, President Lyndon Johnson's Howard University commencement speech in June, 1965 (in which he talked of economic and social freedoms beyond political rights alone), and the enactments of the Economic Opportunity Act and the Voting Rights Act seem, in retrospect, dramatic vestiges of a once widespread campaign for interracial justice. The main thrust of the campaign had been turned aside by the movement's most highly-placed liberal friends—Negro and white—at the 1964 Democratic Convention.

The refusal to seat the M.F.D.P. convinced S.N.C.C. militants—who had been the most important field-leadership element during the Summer Project —that there was no longer any reason to adhere to the integrationist, non-violent, direct-action tactics that had carried them through their most difficult days in the lonely, hazardous backwaters of the rural South. Now the Establishment was exposed for the corrupt and corrupting force many of them had suspected it might show itself to be, and the time had come to formulate new goals, new ideologies and new methods. During the fall of 1964, S.N.C.C. held a series of week-long institutes for its field workers drawn from across the South. Angry, bitter men and women turned their attentions inward to the black community to devise ways in which it could be organized for action. As early as November, 1963, some black S.N.C.C. workers had urged a diminished role for whites in the movement; after the frustrations of mid-1964, it was easier for them to sweep away the reservations held by their black colleagues. S.N.C.C. did allow some 300 whites to participate in its 1965 summer projects, but this was the last time the group would rely so extensively on white volunteers. The transition in the composition of its teams was not black racism, as some alarmed commentators chose to call it, but a frank recognition of the reality of race in America: black people, the victims of racial oppression, must depend upon themselves and their own judgments. Once that realization became prevalent among Afro-Americans, the black liberation movement was born.

Liberation Movement

Early in 1965, Stokely Carmichael of S.N.C.C. entered Lowndes County, Alabama, to help organize the Black Panther party. S.N.C.C. teams and black area residents assumed great personal risks in an attempt to transform a county where, in 1964, not a single Negro citizen was registered to vote, despite a black numerical majority of four to one. Partly because of white intimidation, the Black Panthers lost their 1966 election bid to gain control of the courthouse in Alabama, but the party had become a new symbol of black militancy to be hailed and copied at other points across the nation. The Panthers represented an effort to work within—but thereby to change—the broader confines of the political system. In that sense they had much in common with the objectives of S.N.C.C., CORE, S.C.L.C., and even the NAACP. However, a number of competing spokesmen and philosophies sought to lead Afro-Americans away from that system.

Active in the mid-1930s, and nationally prominent since the late 1950s, the native-born black American Elijah Muhammad (Elijah Poole) and the "Nation of Islam" had long been in the vanguard of those who advocated complete black separation from white America. Muhammad urged black people to renounce everything that smacked of white dominance: the Christian religion, surnames that derived from a European heritage, economic and political affiliation with white "devils," and the United States itself as a source of national identity. The self-help and strict, puritanical code of ethics that Muslims preached held wide appeal for certain quarters of black America, for they symbolized a renewed version of community with self-determination that had by the 1960s proved psychically and functionally rewarding to its adherents.

Elijah Muhammad's best known disciple was Malcolm X (Malcolm Little), an angry and disciplined black leader whose forceful logic and frank rhetoric about black liberation won thousands of supporters for the Nation of Islam. In 1964, Malcolm broke with Elijah Muhammad and set himself upon a course that was continually evolving until his assassination by Muslim rivals in February, 1965. Malcolm had consistently denounced white oppression, but after his visit to the Near East and Africa in 1964 he no longer based his philosophy on hatred of whites alone. Rather, he chose to stress the beauty of black culture, its historic contributions, the joy of black brotherhood and community, and the wisdom of working with whites whenever it would be useful for black people to do so—provided that the power to decide policy and action alternatives lay in black hands.

Malcolm articulated for a national audience what others had verbalized for smaller groups. He justified self-defense and the wisdom of striking back with force when others chose to employ violence against black people. Robert Williams, deposed NAACP leader of Monroe, North Carolina, had also upheld the right of black people to invoke force for defensive purposes, and his 1962 book on self-defense had made him a hero to black militants tired of turning the other cheek to aggression. In 1966, the Deacons for Defense and Justice, operating in Louisiana, announced their determination to use arms for defensive purposes. Similarly, local units of the Black Panthers in California have stocked weapons and, in the spring of 1969, black students at Cornell University introduced a new dimension to Northern campus activism when they took up arms with the claim that it was their last resort in an alien and embattled environment. Negroes, often the victims of Southern white violence, have long kept weapons close at hand, but since the mid-1960s black people throughout the nation have bluntly asserted their right of armed protection against white aggressors—be they civilians or public authorities.

While COFO field workers were employing nonviolent, direct action against white racism in Mississippi, riots were erupting in Northern metropolitan areas, in what would become annual outbreaks of open rebellion among the nation's black ghetto residents. Though unrelated to the mainstream of the civil rights movement, the riots offered somber evidence of discontent and bitterness throughout black America. Fed by conditions of discrimination, economic deprivation and political powerlessness, the riots were often precipitated by (and frequently aggravated and prolonged by) public authorities whose actions indicated they had no understanding whatever of the smoldering hatred to which they had contributed. The rioters seized upon instances of abuse—a "routine" arrest, the shooting of a civilian by a policeman or some similar incident enacted once too often—to vent their anger against the two most visible elements of white society within the ghetto: the policeman and the white store owner. Though white liberals and Negro moderates condemned forms of violence they considered irrational and counterproductive, ghetto residents generally displayed effective restraint in not attacking the property of "soul brothers." Their conduct exhibited a buoyant sense of comradery and community that might, under other circumstances, be channeled toward more concerted and far-reaching action alternatives against white society than the simple, short-run destruction of shops.

Moreover, by mid-1966 it was increasingly apparent that unrest and anger could coalesce around a positive ideological focus within black America. In a search for protection and liberation, for self-development and self-determination, the black community seized upon the concept of Black Power—a concept whose origins sprang from the unsettled domestic and international conditions of the decade. The phrase "Black Power" was employed in June, 1966, to rally militant participants during the completion of James Meredith's March for Freedom from Memphis, Tennessee, to Jackson, Mississippi. Stokely Carmichael—along with CORE's Floyd McKissick—gave it voice. The phrase signaled an open breach between moderates and militants within the civil rights movement.

Arguing that black people must deal with the white majority from positions of political and economic strength, advocates of Black Power stressed—as had Malcolm—the beauty and joys of being black in a white, alien culture, and the necessity for structured group action to develop political, economic and cultural resources. Moderates, Roy Wilkins of the NAACP and Whitney Young of the National Urban League among them, warned against the possible excesses of Black Power and echoed the fear of white liberals that the slogan might prove in fact to be merely a cover for a new wave of racism—this time black racism. Its adherents denied that this was its design or its necessary consequence. They likened Black Power to examples in the American past of ethnic and minority group action, practiced by those with European backgrounds who had come together for coordinated efforts on their own behalf.

In part, at least, Black Power reflected the worldwide thrust of non-whites against the backwash of colonial domination and of European and United States interference in African, Asian and Latin American affairs. Concern over and identification with the newly independent African states afforded black Americans contemporary models of peoples who had won their national freedoms. The African experiences of the mid-twentieth century also produced two concepts adapted to American needs. One was the cultural and racial sense of Negritude, popularized in the United States by the American Society of African Culture; the other was the politico-activist theory of Frantz Fanon, who described the manner in which violence must be utilized by colonial victims against oppressor nations. Testifying to the impoverished state of interracial rapport within the United States, black militants seized upon these two ideas to construct various formulations about the reciprocity of black identity and revolution in the service of black liberation. Furthermore, militants increasingly urged black people to dissociate themselves from the decay of white society. While most Americans angrily, but incorrectly, labeled this black separatism and segregation in reverse, it should be viewed as a positive expression of black nationalism, voluntarily pursued and thus decidedly different from the traditional variants of white-imposed segregation. Furthermore, the implementation of black nationalism need not close off avenues of access and mobility for those who wish to move back and forth at will between white society and the black community.

The movement for black liberation took place in a setting of domestic unrest characterized by growing frustration over and distrust of traditional values, established authority and customary patterns of decision making. Dissatisfaction with the war in Vietnam, with the failures of Congress and of local and state governments to prosecute the war on poverty with vigor, and with the summary reception accorded the Poor People's Campaign in Washington, D. C., in the summer of 1968 sharpened the belief among black, radical and student dissenters that national priorities had been ill conceived and foolishly pursued, both at home and abroad, in the face of glaring injustices and widespread, unattended human misery.

New Forms of Protest

Today, black protest is strikingly different, in tone and composition, from its counterpart of 1960. While many of the same spokesmen and organizations endure and represent positions not dissimilar from those in the earlier period, there is now a wider range of groups urging more numerous action alternatives and protest ideologies upon the black community. Though frequently criticized by militants, the NAACP and the Urban League remain the principal vehicles for joint efforts by Negro moderates and white liberals. In like fashion, Bayard Rustin of the A. Philip Randolph Institute continues to call for a coalition of black leaders with labor and liberal reform spokesmen in pursuit of federally funded programs for employment and urban renewal.

Campaigns to bring more black voters to the polls have begun to yield results in the election of new black Congressmen from outside the South and the installation of several dozen elected black officials in local and county governments within the South. Julian Bond's seating in the Georgia state legislature represents a powerful new trend in Southern politics. On another, related front, the recently-activist National Welfare Rights Organization continues to mobilize America's disadvantaged across racial lines. Heavily committed to multiracial efforts for a quarter of a century, CORE has shifted its emphasis to black militancy; and while S.C.L.C. retains its endorsement of nonviolence, it has deliberately shifted to programs concerned more directly with labor organizing, and economic, educational and political activities at the community level, rather than the initiation of massive demonstrations intended to influence Congress and the general public.

At the extremes, there are a number of exceedingly vocal, active and militant groups. At the far left are those that view the race problem as a factor of class, as much as caste, disabilities. The Progressive Labor Movement, for example, has assumed a Marxist-Leninist-Maoist position. Like the more traditionalistic Marxists of the Communist Party-U.S.A., the P.L.M. must devise ways to train a generation of black militants to think ideologically in terms of the class struggle. While the problems of racist discrimination and the deprivations suffered by workers are not incompatible, the increasing enthusiasm for Black Power and black identity may make difficult, if not impossible, the task of orienting protest around dialectical materialism, however defined and modified.

Among the Black Power groups, there are important differences regarding strategies and tactics, although these differences would melt in any open crisis or confrontation with white society as a whole. For the most part, Eldridge Cleaver and the Black Panthers have agreed to work purposefully with white radical forces for common political and economic objectives, provided that such cooperation does not sacrifice the interests of the black community. The 1968 Presidential campaign of the Peace and Freedom party and joint efforts with the Students for a Democratic Society are examples of this collaboration. At the same time, some Black Power leaders feel that Afro-Americans must fashion their own plans and conduct their own programs apart from any involvement with white radicals. Ron Karenga and his militant organization, US, represent this approach. During the summer of 1969, Stokely Carmichael announced from Africa that he had resigned from the Black Panthers because of their work with white radicals; Carmichael asserted that the only path to liberation lay in effecting a united front of black people in Africa and in the United States.

In positive terms, however, the factors that unite rather than divide Black Power advocates are the more important. Whatever their positions on tactics and potential allies, all Black Power leaders agree on the need for black people to cultivate a sense of community and group esprit, an identity grounded in the affirmative recognition of their blackness and common heritage, and an orientation that perceives mutual interests and cultural ties with each other and with Africa. The energetic work of black theater groups, such as LeRoi Jones' Newark ensemble, The Spirit House Movers and Players, and the Mafundi Institute in Los Angeles, has generated a broadened awareness of black culture, black community and black unity against white oppression in either its latent or manifest forms.

The insistence upon community control of neighborhood schools is meant to provide another instrument for training oneself and one's children to "think black." Black cultural identity forms the cement that will hold the community together, not merely for survival—however courageously practiced in the past —but also for the more positive political and economic action programs that will make black liberation meaningful. At the national level, the annual Black Power conferences, the first of which met after the Newark riot of 1967, are to provide periodic opportunities for interchange and policy formulation on a front far broader than can be offered by intensive, day-to-day community development.

Given the current racial situation in the United States, it seems clear that we have entered a revolutionary era. Diffuse ghetto rebelliousness and coordinated black militancy indicate this. So, too, do the refusals of noted black leaders to lend their time and energies to meetings that appear to them and their followers to be cordial but ineffectual gatherings to search for "moderate" procedural solutions without substantive meaning. Contrasted with the concern for a "federal presence" and with the eagerness to work with the federal government during the early part of the decade, the ease with which black militants dissociated themselves from Lyndon Johnson's White House conference in June, 1966, and the unwillingness of CORE director Floyd McKissick to meet with the President shortly after the assassination of Dr. King (because no black militants were present) reveal the extent of black disenchantment with white society and its authority figures.

Afro-Americans will increasingly look inward to the black community. Coordinating organizations such as Newark's United Brothers, the Black Consortium in Chicago, the Self-Determination Federation of Detroit, the United Black Front in the District of Columbia, and the Black Congress of Los Angeles will be on the cutting edge of this process, mobilizing otherwise disparate elements in the work of black liberation. Groups will shift, dissolve and re-form in response to new challenges and opportunities, external and internal, but the recognition of black identity will sustain the action within black America. Simultaneously, established organizations, the NAACP and the Urban League among them, and newer groups and activities such as the Black Economic Development Conference and S.C.L.C.'s Operation Breadbasket will keep open the lines to various resources and forms of ad hoc co-operation with white society.

For the most part, white America neither understands nor trusts the new thrust for black liberation. Having little inclination for and almost no practice in "thinking black," the white society tends to ignore or denounce ideologies and action patterns it does not share. In the period from 1960 to 1965, the nation showed a willingness to accede to a number of reforms sought by the civil rights movement. Cold war tensions had lessened and the national economy was enjoying a new and sustained buoyancy. Because the majority of middle class whites and those who aspired to that status felt they could relax their fears about familiar international and domestic crises, they were able to respond positively to civil rights appeals. Accordingly, some progress was made; some hopes were generated. But by 1969, the war in Vietnam and the diversion of American resources to new rounds of military spending had combined with the uncertainties of the domestic economy, the spiral of inflation, and the pressures of rising taxes and interest rates to create another series of foreign and domestic crises. Feeling themselves increasingly pinched and harassed, middle class whites will not risk a renewed investment of their tangible resources and psychic energies in working with the black quest for freedom. However, that quest is now too far advanced and too fully sustained by vibrant ideologies centering around black identity to be reversed.

What the United States needs is not a refurbished brand of "tolerance," as the white liberals of the 1940s knew the term, but a bold acceptance and deliberate, sustained endorsement of diversity. The American nation needs a "creative pluralism"; it must lend its weight and its resources to movements and philosophies it cannot directly and fully share nor immediately understand. In the long run, such creative pluralism can help the entire society to evolve imaginative and unique instruments for freedom and human dignity. The changes in the United States will be abrupt and painful. Whether white America has the flexibility to respond in broadly creative and mature ways has yet to be determined.

Dissent Is Not Enough

JOHN COGLEY

The logic of those opposed to civil disobedience lock, stock and barrel is the best case I know *for* it. That logic at its crudest, and perhaps most forthright, holds "My country right or wrong, but right or wrong my country." The final value, then, is obedience to the law of the land, just or unjust; obedience takes precedence over religion, morality, and personal conscience.

For the believing Jew or Christian, such a view is nothing short of idolatry. It puts the law, or the democratic process if you will, above everything else, on earth or in heaven. Yaweh's commandment, the first, was: "You shall have no other gods before me." Peter, the leader of Jesus's apostles, said without reservation: "We must obey God rather than men."

But civil disobedience is not only a problem for the religious-minded. The atheist and agnostic have claims on their conscience no less demanding. Obeying God rather than men, or putting conscience above consensus, is not merely a matter of dissent, or of protesting by legal means when one is actually involved in doing evil. For many, it is a matter of simply refusing to be implicated, of drawing the line and saying: "Hereon I stand . . . I can do no other."

In practice, this may mean refusing military service, whether or not the refusal falls within the legal limits of conscientious objection. It may mean illegally encouraging and abetting others to resist the draft. It may mean withholding the taxes that buy instruments of human destruction. It may mean refusing to observe civil defense regulations. It may take any number of forms, all of them requiring that man-made laws be broken in order that a higher law be upheld.

Some Germans, a pitiful few, practiced civil disobedience during the Nazi period. Today we honor their memory. Two decades ago, at Nuremberg, we established the principle that under some circumstances such disobedience is a moral duty. During the war-crimes trials some were sentenced to death for not practicing it and others were given prison terms. We took these drastic steps not because the prisoners were patriotic Germans but because they obeyed inhumane, immoral, and reprehensible orders.

In their own defense a number of Germans argued that their obedience was

Reprinted from John Cogley, "Dissent Is Not Enough," *The New York Times Magazine,* November 26, 1967. © 1967 by The New York Times Company. Reprinted by permission.

unwilling. They had dissented as much as they could, they claimed, until the final showdown, when it was obey or else. But we knew then how to distinguish between dissent and disobedience. Dissent, we decided, was not enough. Is it enough in the U.S. today for the growing number who feel that the nation is embarked on an immoral course in Vietnam?

More and more Americans are becoming convinced it is not. They feel an obligation to go beyond the "good Germans" of a quarter century ago who went along with whatever the Nazis did.

When, for example, these Americans learn that *both* sides in Vietnam have tortured prisoners, they do not want to be implicated in the excesses of "our side." When they learn that our forces are killing civilians, turning villages into a wasteland, and destroying crops, they want no part of the brutal business. They are as horrified by the scorched-earth policy in 1967 as they were in 1942. When they read in *The Saturday Evening Post* that one million children have been injured in Vietnam and a quarter of a million youngsters have been killed, they feel the time has come to withdraw all support, military, political, and financial, whatever the law demands.

The Nuremberg judiciary determined what constitutes a war crime: "ill-treatment of civilian populations, murder or ill-treatment of prisoners of war, wanton destruction of cities, towns, or villages, inhuman acts committed against any civilian population."

Dissent, it has been made painfully clear, is not enough to put an end to such outrages; as the dissent has escalated so has the war. The man who takes religion, morality, and conscience seriously has no choice then, it seems to many, but to respond with a resounding, unequivocal, unqualified Luther-like "No" whenever he is either asked for his support or it is legally demanded from him.

There are, to be sure, limits on justifiable civil disobedience. Those opposed to the Vietnam war have no right to destroy law and order at home or to practice sedition or sabotage. To say they did would be to turn the case for civil disobedience into a charter of anarchism. Their moral, not legal, right to disobey extends only as far as their moral duty: to resist evil, to refuse to cooperate with evil-doing, to do all in their power to persuade others that the evil they see *is* evil, and to encourage others to have no part in it.

We asked this much of the Germans caught in an infinitely more restrictive straitjacket than we find ourselves in. We can ask no less of ourselves, whatever the cost.

The Resisters Support
U.S. Traditions and Interests

PAUL GOODMAN

The great majority of resisters do not consider themselves as lawless, whether they impede the draft, refuse war taxes, or try to bar recruiters and war contracts from the campuses. We hold that it is the Vietnam policy that is illegitimate. It has been created by a hidden government of military-industrial lobbyists and the CIA; the Executive has gone beyond his mandate; there has been no genuine debate and voting in Congress; the public has been lied to and brainwashed. The government is a usurper, so sovereignty reverts to the people more directly. It is the resisters who support American traditions and interests, and our behavior is itself traditional, not unlike the civil rights movement, the labor movement, populism, abolitionism (and nullification), and the American Revolution itself. As in the previous cases, most action has been nonviolent though often disobedient to authorities, and there has also been sporadic violence, usually started by authorities.

Rather than "defying" the law, most resisters welcome a test of legitimacy in the courts, believing that, when everything is duly aired, we will be found lawful, just as recently the civil rights trespassers were found (or became) lawful. In American tradition, the meaning of law is always emerging. The government has been loath to accept the challenge, choosing instead to pick off individuals, hoping to deter. Now, however, the draft card burners are being subpoenaed and there may be a massive showdown.

The aim of testing the law and nonviolent confrontation, trying to persuade by putting oneself on the line, is to get the Americans to make up their minds and change their minds; it is not to frighten or compel. Unfortunately, since the populace has been sluggish and complacent, occasional violence seems to be advantageous to wake people up; certainly it is mainly violent incidents that the TV and press want to notice. And naturally, resisters are frustrated by their powerlessness when, even now as I write this, our government is killing those people. Yet I cannot accept the *putschist* use of violence, for instance, to "take over" a draft board or burn it down by a physical power play. This is unacceptable not because it is a fantasy—in a complex technology a few

Reprinted from Paul Goodman, "The Resisters Support U.S. Traditions and Interests," *The New York Times Magazine,* November 26, 1967. © 1967 by The New York Times Company. Reprinted by permission.

clever people can make a shambles—but because out of the shambles can come only the same bad world.

Nonviolent confrontation asks, "What is your real will, when you confront our resistance and have to think, feel, and decide? Do you mean, in order to continue your routine, to jail so many, beat so many, investigate so many, bring police on the campus, pass panicky unconstitutional laws, invoke martial law, poison the community further?" By and large, except as an awakener, violence prevents confrontation. Attacked physically, a policeman or soldier responds routinely as a professional, with tear gas or bayonet, but the aim is to get him to think and feel as man and citizen. Confronted, he may respond routinely anyway, but hopefully he cannot continue to do so.

It is possible that the Americans do really intend the Vietnam war or don't care at all. They may be truly complacent with their standard of living, arrogant about American power, indifferent to the lapse of democracy and the militarizing of society, deaf to world outrage, callous about gooks. If this were so, we resisters would have to think in other terms, of exile or "underground." But there is evidence that we are succeeding, that we represent the general will of the body politic.

I here lay all my stress on the legitimacy of resistance. It does not follow, however, that our movement is not radical or even revolutionary, perhaps beyond what many moral resisters think. The Vietnam war is not something isolated that can just be written off. Really to get out of it—and especially the young want really to get out of it and will continue to fight for that—will require a major reconstruction of the American economy, the use of technology, the system of education, foreign relations, the structure of authority, and the whole quality of American life. This year the military budget is $84 billion. More significantly, 86 percent of the money for research and development is for military purposes. Is that the future we intend?

A Right Way to Remedy a Wrong, a Wrong Way to Secure a Right

SIDNEY HOOK

The right of dissent is integral to a free society; otherwise it lapses into tyranny. But there must be limits to dissent when it takes the form of action; otherwise the result is anarchy.

Actions are civilly disobedient when they openly defy on grounds of conscience laws that have been sustained by the supreme legal authorities. To a democrat, resort to civil disobedience is never politically legitimate where methods of due process are available to remedy evils. If these remedies are unavailing and the issue appears of transcendent importance, a democrat may on moral or religious grounds resort to civil disobedience in the hope that he will open the minds of his fellow citizens to second thoughts. In that case he must willingly accept his punishment. Otherwise he has abandoned his faith in democracy, and in effect acts as if he were at war against the democratic community. In that event the community has the duty to protect itself against him, and to constrain him if he resorts to warlike actions instead of argument.

The limits of civil disobedience in a democracy begin when it becomes uncivil, when resistance to law, passive or active, takes the form of violence or has consequences leading to social chaos. This is the aim of those critics of American Vietnam policy who urge "resistance" rather than "dissent." They often rationalize their resistance by denying that we live in a democratic society. Having failed to influence national policy by rational means within the law, they seek to coerce the community by obstructive techniques outside the law. They scoff at majority rule which is a necessary but not a sufficient condition of our Bill of Rights democracy.

A free society can recognize and respect the scruples of a conscientious objector to war who civilly disobeys the law and accepts his punishment. But if he forcibly tries to prevent others from fulfilling their duty to their country he is neither a genuine pacifist nor a democrat.

Some who have already gone beyond dissent to "resistance" have shown by their actions that they no longer believe in the democratic process. Wherever they have the power to do so, they deny to those who disagree with them the right to be heard, they disrupt meetings, threaten bodily harm to speakers, trespass and take over public places, and act more like Storm Troopers or the Communist squads that used to break up Socialist meetings.

The law is not always wrong and the voice of conscience is not always right—especially when consciences conflict. If the dictate of a man's conscience cannot withstand rational analysis and criticism by those who disagree with him, this is presumptive evidence of the unwisdom of acting on it.

I do not believe that civil disobedience with respect to American Vietnam policy, if one is opposed to it, is justified. The issues are not black and white, but large and complex, about which intelligent men of goodwill and character may differ. There are no easy solutions. All-out escalation or scuttle-and-run are not the only alternatives to present policy.

Those who practice resistance are encouraging the Hanoi regime to persist in its intransigent refusal to negotiate the issues. This is not the only factor, but it may be crucial in certain situations.

The practice of "resistance" is self-defeating and therefore politically unintelligent. Public revulsion at its excesses will strengthen the hawks and build up popular support for them. It will also harden the resolution of present policy-makers.

Resort to resistance creates a precedent which will have a pernicious effect on the quality of future public debate. The appeal to the streets and violent mass action will take the place of the appeal to evidence, good sense, and common interest, on which a healthy democracy depends.

By inspiring a backlash of reaction, resistance will make dissent more difficult, and tempt those who are sickened by civil disorder to support extreme measures of repression. Democracy in the long run is not viable unless its citizens recognize that there is a right way to remedy a wrong and a wrong way to secure a right.

The Political Response Must Be Weighed

BAYARD RUSTIN

Since the dawn of civilization there has been an ongoing conflict between man and organized society; in modern times, between man and state. Antigone, Socrates, and the early Christians accepted death rather than submit to laws they considered morally wrong. Thoreau was jailed for refusing to pay taxes because he opposed both slavery and the "unjust war with Mexico." And the abolitionist faced slander, brutality, loss of property, and imprisonment in defiance of the Fugitive Slave Law and the Dred Scott decision.

In all these cases, those who broke the law felt not only a personal moral imperative but also what George Fox called "the secure faith" that their open and nonviolent opposition would ultimately bring others to see the truth and thus help improve society. Traditionally, two compelling ideas underlay the disobedient's secure faith. First, he had affection for, and faith in, his country, and sought by his action to improve or change a particular law or condition which he sincerely believed injurious to himself, to others, and to the state itself.

During his trial, Socrates sought to clarify this point when he calmly turned to his accuser, Anytus, and said, "Men of Athens, I honor and love you . . . but I shall never cease from the practice and teaching of philosophy, exhorting anyone whom I meet and saying to him . . . from virtue comes every other good, *public* and private. This is my teaching."

In other words, Socrates argued that his teaching, far from corrupting Athens or its youth, would improve both.

Secondly, practitioners of civil disobedience have defended their action not as "a right" but rather as "a duty" to themselves, to others, and ultimately to their society. Their allegiance has been to a "higher law" which they felt the state ignored to its detriment.

In the apology, Socrates also made this point when he told the court, "I shall never alter my ways, not even if I have to die many times. . . . for I will obey God rather than you . . . and so I bid you farewell."

In addition to these two principles, most resisters have seriously struggled with the following questions:

(1) Have I exhausted the available constitutional methods of bringing about the desired change?

(2) Do the people I urge to join me sincerely seek to improve the society or do they wish to excite passions that would destroy society itself?

(3) What is likely to be the effect of the resistance on me, on others, and in the community?

(4) Are my own motives and objectives clear to myself and to others; is my aim genuine social change or mere self-gratification?

(5) Given that I oppose specific laws, am I prepared, out of my deep respect for law itself, to suffer the consequences of my disobedience?

Adherence to the standards embodied in these questions can result in morally defensible acts of disobedience. But morally defensible acts are not always or necessarily relevant in political terms. And it is precisely in political terms that peace in Vietnam, like civil rights at home, finally will be determined.

No eternal algebraic formula can guarantee that a given act of disobedience will stimulate the necessary political response. What disturbs me, however, about much of the recent antiwar resistance is that it does not seek a political response at all; it therefore becomes self-corrupting.

Today we are not faced, like Antigone, Socrates, or the early Christians, with surrender or death. Political alternatives remain open. They must, therefore, be considered along with moral concern if progress is to be achieved.

The Old Politics, the New Politics, the New, New Politics

IRVING KRISTOL

Many people, these past months, have been talking about a New Politics; but so far as I can see, no one seemed to have a clear idea as to what this New Politics meant. In the light of the election returns, there will now be a tendency to surmise that it never meant anything at all. This, I think, would be a mistake. I have a feeling that, in the course of the nineteen-sixties, American politics has indeed been in the process of moving, not simply and familiarly from left to right or from right to left, but on to a new political spectrum altogether. Which is to say: There may well be a new politics emerging—but this new politics is only too likely to be poles apart from what the advocates of the New Politics have in mind.

Reprinted from Irving Kristol, "The Old Politics, the New Politics, the *New*, New Politics," *The New York Times Magazine,* November 24, 1968. © 1968 by The New York Times Company. Reprinted by permission.

As enunciated by such spokesmen as the late Robert Kennedy, Eugene McCarthy, and—at least during the latter part of his campaign—by Nelson Rockefeller, the New Politics seemed to signify an especially keen sensitiveness to the political mood of young people on the campuses and black militants in the ghettos. The mood of both these groups is certainly turbulent, often to the point of rebelliousness, and it would be exceedingly difficult not to pay attention to it, even if one wanted not to. (A great many Americans obviously want not to.) On the other hand, there is this to be said about the mood: (1) it is not easy to tell what the purpose and intent of this turbulence is; and (2) it is the mood of two minority groups—and not especially influential minorities at that.

It is the second point about which many people still have a great number of illusions. Any man who thinks that he can stake out a political career by appealing to young students or black militants has failed to do his political arithmetic. There aren't enough of either. Though, as a result of the postwar baby boom, the median age of the American population has been lowered, it has not been lowered by all *that* much. It is now about 26 years, and as a consequence of the decline in the birth rate that set in a decade ago, it is not likely to get much beneath this figure in your lifetime or mine.

The United States is certainly a somewhat younger country than it was in 1950, when the median age was 30. But the change has not been of such an order as to permit one to say that some kind of deep and far-reaching demographic transformation has occurred. After all, the median age of the American *electorate* in 1968 was 45 years. Even if the vote were given to the 18-year-olds by 1972, that would only reduce the median age of the electorate to 42 years. So, if the young are to inherit the earth, someone else will have to vote them the legacy.

Moreover, not all young people are on campuses—a majority of those between the ages of 18 and 22 still work for a living. And of those who are on campuses, the polls show that only a minority—perhaps 20 percent—are sufficiently dissatisfied with the political and social arrangements now existing to be attracted to a left-of-center New Politics. In addition, there is the fact that among young workers, resistance to this kind of New Politics is especially strong. At one point in this recent campaign, close to a third of the young workers in the 21–29 age group said they would vote for George Wallace. It is nice to know that not all that many actually did. But it would nevertheless appear beyond doubt that there are all sorts of ways of making a particular appeal to young people.

A not too dissimilar kind of conclusion emerges when one examines the question of black militancy. A majority of American blacks—65 percent—are not poor (though they are certainly poorer than their white counterparts). The majority of American blacks do not live in central-city slums—unless one automatically defines a slum as a place where Negroes live. (As Nathan Glazer has pointed out, the proportion of nonwhites now living in substandard housing is about 30 percent.) And, as opinion polls indicate, the majority of American blacks, while intensely dissatisfied with their present condition and desirous of a faster movement toward equality, do not think that revolutionary changes are necessary for them to achieve this accelerated rate of progress. The black militants certainly have their constituency, but despite the best efforts of the mass media—which have a fondness for militancy because it comes across so well on film and makes for more dramatic headlines—this constituency is of minor significance in our political system.

Indeed, one often is tempted to conclude that the cry for a New Politics really has amounted to little more than a demand from certain groups that the political process concede to them greater power and influence than they are entitled to under our traditional democratic formulas. The young students have all sorts of thoughts about how to make this a better country to live in, and they see no reason why they should have to persuade the majority of the validity of ideas which seem to them self-evident. Similarly, the black militants feel that a redress of the all-too-real injustices the Negroes have suffered in the past, or still suffer, should entitle them to something more than one man, one vote.

Was there more than this in the cry for a New Politics? As a matter of fact, I think there was, and is. I do believe that there may well be a new politics emerging in the United States—emerging slowly, incoherently, amid vast confusion. Of only one thing I am absolutely certain: The new politics that is in fact emerging will, in the event, have little connection with what people who now talk so much about "the New Politics" have in mind. For the *real* new politics will emerge from the condition of the *majority* of Americans, and will reflect their strong but contradictory sentiments about this condition. More important, it will have to do something about resolving this contradiction which afflicts the American mood.

This contradiction has many aspects, but let us begin with the simplest and plainest: The American people today have a far greater degree of material prosperity than ever before, but somehow seem to be enjoying it less. How is this to be explained?

Most of our liberal social critics, wedded to a quite vulgar, materialistic notion of politics, can only reply that the dissatisfaction arises from needs that are still unfulfilled. This won't wash, however, as is evidenced by the fact that these same critics have a terribly difficult time in defining these needs—or, when they think they have, arousing any great popular interest in them. I cannot, in my lifetime, remember a moment when liberal reformers were so barren of legislative proposals. Medicare was their last great popular cause. They won that handsomely, and have been searching for new issues ever since, without much success. American liberalism, during these past four decades, was able to immobilize a political majority in order to have the Federal Government pass laws that would obviously, instantly and tangibly benefit this majority.

It no longer seems able to mobilize a majority in this way and for this purpose. And this is a fact of the greatest importance, marking as it does the end of a political era in American history.

To be sure, there are a great many *minorities* within the American population that clearly need help. But what liberal reformers have discovered in these past eight years is that their habitual response—passing a law which funds a program—is inadequate. It is inadequate for two reasons:

First, it is not so easy to get majority support for such a program. It is not merely that a majority is inevitably somewhat callous and inattentive toward minority problems—though, human nature being what it is, this is sadly true. But what is also true is that this majority, though affluent by historical standards, isn't all *that* affluent. (Probably no more mischievous phrase has been invented in our time than "the affluent society.") The median family income in this country is about $8,000—and it just isn't easy to persuade a family with such an income that its tax burden should be increased substantially for the benefit of those who earn $4,000 a year or so—or who even, as in New York City, receive that sum annually in welfare benefits.

And this increase in taxes would have to happen for any significant income redistribution in favor of the poor to take place. You can't finance what we now call an anti-poverty program merely by taxing the rich. There just aren't enough of them. As a matter of fact, there never were enough of them. The social expenditures of the New Deal, Fair Deal, New Frontier and Great Society did not to any important extent represent a redistribution of wealth from rich to poor. Mainly, the money came from putting the idle resources of the economy to work—it was *new* money, created by the new economics.

Once that has been done, however, and the economy is fairly efficiently using its available resources, as is now the case, such social expenditures have to come from general taxation—i.e., from the average taxpayer. And the average taxpayer resists, because he is probably in debt and is persuaded he needs the money as much as anyone else. In country after country—in England, France, Germany, Sweden, and now in the United States—the proliferation of welfare programs is running head-on into a stonewall of taxpayers' resistance. In any kind of political system short of a police state, that stonewall will prevail.

Secondly, we have discovered in these past years that it just doesn't suffice to pass a law in order to solve minorities' problems. Precisely because they are minorities, the laws run into immense administrative problems. It is far easier, in a democracy, to help everyone over 65 than it is, say, to help poor blacks over 65 who live in central-city ghettos. These "special purpose" programs have a way of not quite hitting the mark. Somehow, the money never seems to reach the people for whom it is intended—or, if it does, it never has the effect it was supposed to have.

The widespread disillusionment with our welfare system is a case in point.

And the disillusionment is well-earned. After all, we in New York City have abolished poverty—we really have—in the sense that the dole for a family of four now puts this family above the Administration's poverty line. Somehow, this statistical abolition of poverty in New York City has changed hardly anything at all, and the poor seem not even aware that it has happened. No wonder that, within the ranks of liberal reformers themselves, there has been an increasing skepticism about all such government programs.

So this, then, is the dilemma of American liberalism today. It cannot come up with legislative programs that appeal to the majority, and it has not been able to create viable programs for the various minorities that need help. And it would seem fair to conclude that the future of American politics in the decades immediately ahead will be shaped along lines quite different from those familiar liberal ones we have all grown accustomed to.

This does not mean, however, that it will be shaped along familiar conservative ones. Indeed, it is quite certain that it will not be.

The conservatives in the United States today do have some real opportunities, and it is not altogether inconceivable that the Republican Administration will be able to take advantage of some of them during the next four years. Above all, they might undertake an overhaul of the welfare state. Such an overhaul would aim at having the Government provide money (or its equivalent—i.e., vouchers) with which the individual citizens could purchase social welfare in the open market, instead of having the Government try to provide, directly and institutionally, such services as education, housing, medical care, etc. There is now considerable dissatisfaction among all levels of the population at the bumbling and ineffectual way Government bureaucrats go ahead providing such things. There has also arisen, during the past 10 years, an eminently respectable and increasingly influential body of economic analysis—emanating largely from the University of Chicago—which persuasively argues the desirability of so redefining the idea of "the welfare state" as to have the Government act as a kind of financial guarantor against "ill-fare" without the Government attempting to estimate, provide, and distribute differential benefits to each individual. (Prof. Milton Friedman's "negative income tax," as a substitute for our divers welfare programs—aimed, as the case may be, at the old, the sick, the blind, the abandoned, the unemployed, the underemployed, etc.—is the most notable example of this approach.) It is possible, therefore, that action along these lines will be taken by a Republican Administration, and I, for one, would be interested to see if it could work.

Aside from such a possible overhaul of the welfare state, however, conservatives in this country today do not have much of a program. They have no particular views on what to do about the universities, for instance—an area which is obviously becoming more of a mess every day. They do not even have any kind of consensus on what to do about trade unions, though the present state of trade unions continually affronts conservative opinion. In both cases, American conservatives have simply failed *intellectually*. They have not been able to come up with—have not really tried very hard to come up with—any kind of thoughtful analysis that could lead to workable reforms.

Conservatives in America have always been more than a little weak-minded, and sometimes positively anti-intellectual in their bias. This attitude has been extremely costly. It means that when a conservative administration does take office, it pursues no coherent program but merely takes satisfaction in not doing the things that the liberals may be clamoring for. This, in effect, is what happened during the two terms of President Eisenhower—eight relatively placid years, in retrospect, but also years that permitted various problems to build up in an explosive way, and ensured that this period would, in the end, amount to little more than an interregnum.

Not only are conservatives lacking a program that an administration in Washington can refer to. They also share with liberals—indeed, with all modern political creeds—a basic orientation that is inherently self-defeating for conservatives. This orientation affirms that we are living through a "revolution of rising expectations," that this revolution is a good thing, and that the prime function of government is to satisfy the demands generated by this revolution.

That we are in fact living through a revolution of rising expectations is indisputable. This revolution arises partly out of economic growth itself—the knowledge that one's condition will be better in the future makes all present limitations and restraints particularly irksome. (People have far more patience with the inevitable than they do with the temporary.) It also arises out of the very nature of contemporary society, which can only achieve growth through the constant creation and expansion of demand. So it is not a revolution anyone has much control over. And yet left to run its own course, it is ultimately frustrating to its presumed beneficiaries.

It is frustrating for two reasons:

(1) Even when economic growth is rapid, people are still disappointed with the results. This is not simply explained by the fact that the human appetite is an unruly and insatiable force. It also derives from the fact that economic growth never provides people with the goods and benefits that they anticipate. As Bertrand de Jouvenel has pointed out, the future always disappoints us because it is so unimaginably different. A woman living in the year 1900, and being told of the economic growth that was in store for her society in the decades ahead, would have expected perhaps to be able to hire a maid or two. Instead, she was given the vacuum cleaner and washing machine. Similarly, we today automatically assume that economic growth will give us, for example, more commodious living space. But it will almost certainly not give us any such thing. Instead, we may have the opportunity to visit the moon. This whole process is very unsettling; the psychological costs of economic growth are real even if they aren't measurable.

(2) It is fantastic to believe that we can just project current rates of economic growth indefinitely. The current rate in the United States is at about double the historic rate that prevailed for the century and a half before World War II. Were this current rate to continue, and to compound itself uninterruptedly, all Americans would be enormously rich 50 years from now. The median income of the American family would be something like $35,000 (in constant dollars).

That just isn't going to happen; history is not a fairy tale and the more extravagant a long mathematical projection appears, the more ridiculous it is to take it seriously. Something will go wrong—inflation will get out of hand, we'll stumble into an expensive little war or even a big one, etc.; this projection will be interrupted; and the social and political order will stand indicted for breach of promise. I still recall vividly the assurance of one of President Kennedy's staff, five years ago, that the big problem looming up was how to spend the "surplus" $6-billion a year that the economy was "automatically" generating.

Now, this revolution of rising expectations is a problem for all political creeds, as I have said. But it is an especially acute problem for conservatism. The political ethos of conservatism is more naturally inclined to revere the past and appreciate the present than it is to exult in the future. It has no natural claim, therefore, to be the manager of a revolution of rising expectations. One can even put it more strongly: There is a kind of self-betrayal and self-contradiction in conservatism pretending to be capable of "superior performance" in this task of management.

If conservatism means anything, it means that existing institutions and social arrangements derive their legitimacy, not from superior performance as measured by some abstract standard, but from the presumption that they embody a kind of accumulated wisdom—accumulated over generations, incrementally and organically—that is beyond the contrivance of any set of living politicians, no matter how clever. Though many people usually think of liberalism as "idealistic" and conservatism as "materialistic," the reverse is more nearly true. Conservatism cannot take honest root in a situation where the criteria of success or failure are ruthlessly materialistic.

What this comes down to, in political terms, is that conservatism can take advantage of the inevitable failures of liberal administrations to achieve a temporary power. But it cannot, in our terms, offer a viable alternative. It is always *faute de mieux*.

In view of the difficulties besetting liberalism and conservatism, radicalism would seem to have an awful lot going for it. And so it does—except that this awful lot just doesn't go very far. Ours is an age that breeds radicals with an almost awesome ease. But it is also an age that breeds disillusioned radicals with an equal degree of fertility.

The basic trouble with modern radicalism is that it can never become radical enough without at the same time becoming irrelevant. Thus, sooner or later every radical movement confronts the fact that, if it wishes to capitalize on the revolution of rising expectations, if it aims to increase the material welfare of the people, it must come to terms with the structure and functioning of modern society—and this society, whatever its ostensible political creed, does not permit too many liberties to be taken with it before it balks and malfunctions.

I am not suggesting that it is impossible for the modern industrial system to support different kinds of political regimes. It clearly is possible, and the differences are by no means negligible. What I am suggesting is that any regime which tries to impose a priori radical goals or revolutionary ideals on a modern industrial system will find that this imposition can only be maintained by political violence and political repression—not a single, modern radical movement has been able to create a society in which, over the longer term, people are freer, or feel freer, than they were before. And this would seem to imply (what I believe to be the case) that the relationship between modern radicalism and modern industrial society is inherently perverse.

An instance of this perversity is represented by the demand of the New Left that our representative democracy be transformed into a "participatory democracy." Now, as it happens, we know quite a great deal about what we now call "participatory democracy." It is precisely what most political theorists, prior to the American and French Revolutions, meant by "democracy" when they used that term. It is the kind of democracy that prevailed in classical Athens, in some of the theocratic city-states of the Reformation period, in some of our own early colonial settlements, on the Israeli kibbutzim. It is the kind of democracy that works only in small communities, ethnically homogeneous communities, ideologically homogeneous communities, and economically homogeneous communities.

Our Founding Fathers discussed this whole matter very acutely in "The Federalist Papers." They decided that this kind of democracy, in so large and varied a nation as the United States, could only lead to incessant civil conflict, chaos and eventually tyranny. So they opted for a *democratic republic,* constructed around the principle of representation. Such a republic allows for ideological and economic diversity, and also for a high degree of civil concord. Representatives are able to bargain, to compromise, to coexist with one another in a way that active participating masses of citizens cannot.

It is no accident that those who begin by demanding "participatory democracy" almost invariably end up by celebrating the virtues of a one-party dictatorship which mystically incarnates the "participatory" people. It is also no accident that such a one-party dictatorship, when it tries to manage a modern, modernized economy, ends up in a blind alley—for such an economy naturally moves toward innovation and differentiation, which in turn threatens the stability of the regime.

I would say that the only really radical group in American society today are the hippies and their associated sects. They are truly radical because they are dropouts from the revolution of rising expectations and reject the materialistic ethos that is the basis of the modern social order. Unfortunately, their kind of radicalism is also tainted at the source: Though they are not materialists, they are certainly hedonists, and hedonism cannot of itself generate the kind of self-discipline and self-denial that would make a radical alternative viable. If you want to reject the bourgeois, acquisitive, affluent society, you need people who are oriented toward the production of transcendental values, not the consumption of temporal goods. And the hippies, alas, are as consumption-oriented as the rest of us, even if they prefer to consume sex and drugs rather than, say, detergents and automobiles.

I seem to have landed this analysis in a dead end, in that I have outlined a very troubled situation to which the liberal, conservative and radical responses are all desperately inadequate. But, in political analysis as in mathematics, an impasse can tell us something about the way we have been looking at a problem. And in this case, what I think it tells us is the following: Our problem is not really political at all. It is cultural, in the largest sense of that term. It is not the case that our institutions are functioning badly; by all the familiar "objective" indices—increasing wealth, increasing education, increasing leisure—they are working quite well. What is happening to our institutions is that they are being inexorably drained of their legitimacy.

One can put it this way: We have, over these past decades, created pretty much the kind of economic, social and political order that was intended. Any social critic of the year 1900 who could observe America today would have to concede that truly remarkable progress has been made. As a matter of fact, if you go back only to the nineteen-thirties and forties, and read the radical social criticism of that time, you will discover that most of the economic promises which were made in the name of a radically reconstructed social order have in fact been more than fulfilled by our unreconstructed but evolving one. (You don't have to be very old to recall the derision that greeted Henry Wallace's promise of 60 million jobs. Yet we surpassed that figure long ago.) *But,* at the same time, we have created a moral and cultural order which is dismissive of—more than that: contemptuous of—these very intentions. The Old Politics didn't fail, it succeeded, and that is precisely what is held against it.

This reality is obscured by the fact that so many critics of the Old Politics have failed to come up with a new, adequate vocabulary and habitually speak in the older, familiar jargon of socio-economic criticism. They talk stridently of the problem of poverty and the problem of the Negroes, both of which are indeed problems, but neither of which in itself is a crisis beyond our management. Even if we don't do much better than we have these past 10 years— and I believe we can—it is still demonstrable by simple arithmetic that in 15 years' time the proportion of poor people in this country will have sharply decreased and that the blacks will be much, much closer to economic equality. (The poverty population is shrinking at a rate of about 3 to 4 percent a year, even as the total population grows. As for the Negroes, some 30 percent of Negro families now earn more than $7,000 a year, as against less than half that percentage only eight years ago.)

In any kind of reasonable historical perspective, these are not critical or intractable challenges to the present system. But a reasonable historical perspective is of the least possible appeal to the advocates of the New Politics. They don't really mean to criticize the established order because it has not successfully coped with this or that particular problem. Rather, they seize upon the problem because they have lost all belief in the legitimacy of the established order.

The real clue to what is going on is the revolt on the campus. Here, too, the students bewilder us by talking of new things in an old way—they insist that their "rights" are unrecognized, that they are "underprivileged" when it comes to the distribution of power. But these students aren't 19th-century farmers or 20th-century factory workers in avant-garde costume. They are largely from the upper-middle classes and the heart of their complaint is spiritual, not material. They feel that American life and American society are devoid of both moral authority and moral significance. And what they really mean by a New Politics is one that would give moral direction and moral purpose to American life.

Now, this sounds innocuous enough, even rather uplifting. But it is a truly radical, a profoundly radical demand—more radical, even, than the overwhelming majority of students realize. For if there is any single cardinal principle around which the American polity is constructed, it is that it is *not* the function of government to define the moral purpose of American life—or to provide the social discipline necessary to achieve this moral purpose.

I am not saying that the American republic is a morally neutral institution, or a morally indifferent one. Rather, I am pointing to the fact that the American political tradition explicitly leaves the governance of moral life to our nonpolitical institutions—to the family, the churches, the schools. Ours is a *limited* government of a *free* society, and it is rooted in the assumption that it is the task of government to reconcile conflicting interests in a reasonable way. But this assumption, in turn, is only valid if our nongovernmental institutions see to it that the American people, no matter how diverse, all do behave in a reasonable way—i.e., a self-disciplined way. And this kind of discipline is learned in the home, in church, in school. If you want a polity with an overriding moral purpose, then you want a government that *rules,* that *forms* the young citizen according to some preconceived political end, and that (subtly or crudely) *represses* all deviations from its orthodoxy.

It is a truism of political philosophy that no social order can have an enduring stability which is not based on some kind of consensus among its citizens as to (1) what is good or bad, and (2) what are the proper actions to take to settle the inevitable differences of opinion over what is good or bad. In the American political tradition, the purpose of government is confined to the second part of that proposition; it is left to free, nonpolitical institutions to cope with the first part.

Yet it is obvious that, in the course of recent decades, our nonpolitical institutions have been coping ever more ineffectually with the obligations that the American political tradition imposes upon them. Young people are emerging in our society who find themselves deprived of any sense of personal moral purpose—who see the institutions of their society as mere incarnations of power and prejudice, who have been thoroughly instructed in their rights as Americans but hardly at all in their obligations as Americans, and who in the end can find moral purpose only in a wild explosion of moral outrage. Nor is it any surprise that they then begin to cast longing eyes on other political regimes—Castro's Cuba, or Mao's China—where the Government mobilizes the people for purported moral ends. People, especially young people, fear a meaningless life more than they do an unfree one.

I do not need to recount how we came to reach our present condition. The broad outlines are familiar enough, since this is something that anyone over 40 has seen with his own eyes in his own lifetime. Suffice it to say that we reached our present condition as the result of making progress. We have progressively diminished the moral authority of all existing institutions and have successfully instructed our children to take a skeptical, critical, "creative" attitude toward them. So far as concerns religion and the family, this has been going on for a long time, but its consequences were muted by the fact that, more and more, the traditional functions of family and church in transmitting values were taken over by our schools.

Now, that last bastion is beginning to crumble. Our schools no longer transmit values for the most part; they regard it as their job to question values. One can hardly blame the schools, though many are tempted to do so. Why should they, and they alone, be the sustainers of traditional authority? If parents can't and won't do it, and if clergymen can't and won't do it, how can one reasonably ask educators and teachers to do it? They, too, want a part of the cultural action. They, too, want to be "progressive," just like everyone else. And so they are.

Thus we have a void, created by the progressive diminution of traditional authorities. And into this void spills a debased version of avant-garde culture —an antibourgeois culture, an "adversary culture," in Lionel Trilling's phrase —which was originally limited to a handful of bold artists and thinkers, but which is now being diffused through the popular arts and the educational system. This avant-garde culture used to be a "highbrow" culture, and set itself up in opposition to "lowbrow" or "middlebrow" culture. One hears very little of such opposition these days, since it has in truth ceased to exist. Twenty years ago, avant-garde intellectuals would have scorned Playboy magazine as an opiate for the masses. Now they write regularly for it, are well paid for their contributions—and at the same time are more often than not respected professors in our universities.

It is not easy to say who has taken over whom. There has been a merger, based on money (which the organs of mass culture always had) and an arty pornography and a vague antibourgeois radicalism, both of which used to be the property of the avant-garde. And out of this merger there has been born a new cultural mode, a mass culture that is, compared with the mass cultures of the past, of fairly high artistic quality, but which is also filled to overflowing with an instructive animus to, and rejection of, all traditional authorities, all traditional moral values, and most especially of the bourgeois order, in its moral, political and socio-economic aspects. It is this culture, moreover, which is more and more becoming the substance of the educational curriculum in our colleges and even our high schools.

Where all this will end, I haven't the faintest idea. But I do know it does have a crucial connection with the New Politics. Up to now, the New Politics signified a process of accommodation to this trend—it speaks for all those alienated youngsters and self-denigrating, upper-middle-class parents who think "The Graduate" is an absolutely wonderful and utterly truthful movie. But I believe the election of 1968 revealed that this is only a passing and temporary phenomenon. Most Americans do not despise themselves, do not think they are unfit to be parents, do not think their way of life is irremediably nasty or corrupt. And we have seen evidence, especially in the unexpected national appeal of George Wallace, that they, too, will be moving toward their own version of a New Politics—one that will be considerably less liberal, considerably less tolerant, and perhaps even downright repressive.

I see the future of American politics as being considerably less liberal than it has been in past decades, while being in no true sense of the term conservative. We are headed for a time of trouble, in which our political authorities are going to have to cope with an unreasonable revolution of rising material expectations on the part of the majority, an equally unreasonable revolution of utopian spiritual expectations on the part of a significant minority, and with a general breakdown of individual and social discipline. Not since the Civil War has this republic faced so fundamental a challenge. Whether the American Republic can cope with it remains to be seen. But I fear that, in attempting to cope with it, this republic will find itself involved with a *new* New Politics that will not be very congenial to those of us who rather liked the Old Politics, for all its deficiencies—or to those who set great store on yesterday's New Politics.

Notes

CHAPTER ONE. CONTEXT OF
AMERICAN POLITICS

Fundamental Principles of Democracy

[1]That the awareness is so consistently forgotten attests to the need of uniting research
in political theory with research in public
opinion.

[2]We are not arguing, of course, that these
propositions are incorrrect in any absolute
sense. Good arguments can no doubt be advanced in support of each of the positions
we label as "incorrect." Our point is simply
that they are incorrect *in the sense* of being
undemocratic, i.e., inconsistent with general
principles of democracy.

[3]See Angus Campbell and Homer C.
Cooper, *Group Differences in Attitudes and
Votes* (Ann Arbor, 1956).

[4]Those statements with particular salience
for one of the regional subcultures (southern
anti-Negro sentiment) constitute an exception.

[5]For a discussion of this approach to con-
trolled qualitative data, see Herbert Hyman,
Survey Design and Analysis (Glencoe, 1955),
Chap. 7.

[6]The lack of extended consensus cannot,
however, be attributed to the possibility that
the responses classified as "correct" are
actually "incorrect," for we found consensus
neither in acceptance nor in rejection of the
statements.

[7]The latter approach is, of course, a fruitful type of investigation, but it is not called
for by our problem. For a functional analysis of opinions, see M. Brewster Smith,
Jerome S. Bruner, and Robert W. White,
Opinions and Personality (New York, 1956).

[8]*Op. cit.*, p. 123.

[9]*Op. cit.*, p. 132.

[10]*The New Belief in the Common Man*
(Boston, 1942).

*How American Democracy Really
Works*

[11]James Madison, "Vices of the Political
System of the United States," April 1787, in
The Writings of James Madison, Gaillard
Hunt (ed.) (New York: G. P. Putnam's
Sons, 1901), vol. 2, p. 336.

[12]A. A. Ekirch, Jr., *The Decline of American Liberalism* (New York: Longmans,
Green & Co., 1955), p. 220.

[13]A. Lawrence Lowell, *Public Opinion and Popular Government* (New York: Longmans, Green & Co., 1913), pp. 2–3.

[14]Harold D. Lasswell, *Politics: Who Gets What When and How* (Gloucester, Mass.: Peter Smith Publisher, 1950), p. 235.

[15]John C. Livingston and Robert G. Thompson, *The Consent of the Governed* (New York: The Macmillan Company, 1963), p. 36.

[16]Lester Milbrath, "The Political Party Activity of Washington Lobbyists," *The Journal of Politics*, 20 (May, 1958), 339.

[17]Lewis A. Froman, Jr., *People and Politics: An Analysis of the American Political System* (Englewood Cliffs, N.J.: Prentice-Hall, 1962), pp. 83–84.

[18]*Ibid.*, p. 84.

[19]Princeton, N.J.: Princeton University Press, 1951.

[20]E. E. Schattschneider, *The Semisovereign People: A Realist's View of Democracy in America* (New York: Holt, Rinehart and Winston, 1960), pp. 132–133.

[21]John C. Wahlke, William Buchanan, Heinz Eulau, and LeRoy Ferguson, "Toward Pressure Groups," in S. Sidney Ulmer (ed.), *Introductory Readings in Political Behavior* (Chicago: Rand McNally & Company, 1961), p. 390.

[22]Schattschneider, p. 102.

[23]Edward Hollett Carr, *The New Society* (Boston: Beacon Press, 1951), p. 61.

[24]Robert A. Dahl, *Modern Political Analysis* (Englewood Cliffs, N.J.: Prentice-Hall, 1963), pp. 56–57.

[25]John Fischer, "Unwritten Rules of American Politics," *Harper's Magazine* (November, 1948), 36.

[26]Robert A. Dahl, *Who Governs? Democracy and Power in an American City* (New Haven: Yale University Press, 1961), p. 17.

[27]Aristotle, *On the Constitution of Athens* [Appendix IV, in Barker ed., 379–383], quoted in Dahl, *Modern Political Analysis*, pp. 56–57.

[28]Dahl, *Modern Political Analysis*, p. 63.

[29]John Vance Cheney (ed.), *Inaugural Addresses of the Presidents of the United States from Washington to Lincoln* (Chicago: The Lakeside Press, Christmas, 1906), p. 34.

[30]*Ibid.*

[31]Livingston and Thompson, pp. 48–49.

[32]John Wise, *A Vindication of the Government of New England Churches* (1717), reprinted in Alpheus Thomas Mason, *Free Government in the Making* (Fair Lawn, N.J.: Oxford University Press, 1956), p. 69.

[33]Thrasymachus, Hobbes, Jeremy Bentham, and Marx all interpreted the search for power as rational and conscious pursuit of self-interest. But Freud showed that the desires, terrible in their untamed lawlessness, of which Socrates spoke, did more than drive human beings into conflict with one another as Hobbes argued. They also drive human beings into conflict with themselves. These inner conflicts, according to Freud, are fierce gales that often blow out the flickering light of reason.

Robert A. Dahl and Charles E. Lindbloom, *Politics, Economics and Welfare* (New York: Harper & Row, 1953), p. 67.

[34]Livingston and Thompson, pp. 43–44.

[35]*Ibid.*, p. 57.

[36]Herman C. Pritchett, *The American Constitutional System* (New York: McGraw-Hill, 1963), p. 3.

[37]*Ibid.*

[38]Andrew Hacker, *The Study of Politics: The Western Tradition and American Origins* (New York: McGraw-Hill, 1963), p. 87.

[39]The historical changes in the key doctrines of restraint on government are summarized by Edward S. Corwin in "Introduction," *The Constitution of the United States of America: Analysis and Interpretation* (Washington: Government Printing Office, 1953).

[40]"The Constitution provided for a national government largely independent of the federated government. It contemplated, of course, that the people of the states would control the national government. But it contemplated also that the control would be direct not through the agency of state governments . . . it did arrange things in such a way that state officials had to use the political party, not state government, to make their influence felt in Washington."—William H. Riker, "The Senate and American Federalism," *American Political Science Review*, 49 (June, 1955), 454.

[41]Morton Grodzins, "Centralization and Decentralization in the American Federal System," in Robert A. Goldwin (ed.), *A Nation of States: Essays on the American Federal System* (Chicago: Rand McNally & Company, 1963), p. 7.

[42]*Myers v. United States*, 272 U.S. 52 (1926), 293.

[43]Hacker, p. 84.

[44]J. K. Galbraith, *American Capitalism*,

the Concept of Countervailing Power (Boston: Houghton Mifflin Company, 1952), p. 1.

[45]*Ibid.*, p. 4.

[46]*Ibid.*, p. 11.

[47]D. George Stigler, "The Economist Plays with Blocs," *American Economic Review*, 44 (May, 1954), 10.

[48]Max M. Kampelman, "The Legislative Bureaucracy: Its Response to Political Change," *The Journal of Politics*, 16 (August, 1954), 539.

[49]See, for example, Robert A. Dahl, *A Preface to Democratic Theory* (Chicago: University of Chicago Press, 1956), p. 132.

[50]Dahl and Lindbloom, *Politics, Economics and Welfare*, p. 44.

[51]Livingston and Thompson, p. 37.

[52]Alan T. Peacock, *Income Redistribution and Social Policy* (London: Johnathan Cape, Ltd., 1954), pp. 185–186.

[53]Robert J. Lampman, *The Share of Top Wealth Holders in National Wealth: 1922–1956* (Princeton, N.J.: Princeton University Press, 1962), p. 24.

[54]Gabriel Kolko, *Wealth and Power in America: An Analysis of Social Class and Income Distribution* (New York: Frederick A. Praeger, 1962), p. 15.

[55]Peacock, p. 198.

[56]This analysis concludes that there is only a 2 percent variation between the lowest and highest percentage of income which goes into all United States taxes from income groups up to $15,000. The range is from 20.4 to 21.6 percent for 1958. The percentage of income paid in taxes for those earning $15,000 and above, however, was 34.4 percent. If Social Security taxes were included, the percentages of income going to taxes varied from 23.9 for the $8,000 to $9,999 income class to 28.3 for the under $2,000 class. The $15,000 and over group averages 35.9 percent of income going to all taxes. Tax Foundation, Inc., *Allocation of the Tax Burden by Income Class* (New York: Tax Foundation, Inc., 1960).

[57]Jacob Cohen and Morton Grodzins, "How Much Economic Sharing in American Federalism?" *American Political Science Review*, 57 (March, 1963), 16–19.

[58]Fischer, 27–36, 30 particularly.

[59]J. William Fulbright, *The Elite and the Electorate* (New York: The Fund for the Republic, 1963), p. 4.

[60]It should be kept in mind that there are exceptions to this tendency. These exceptions, such as the relocation into a type of concentration camp of American citizens of Japanese descent early in World War II, usually take place when emotional waves roll through the country silencing most opponents of the groups instigating drastic action. See Morton Grodzins, *Americans Betrayed: Politics and the Japanese Evacuation* (Chicago: University of Chicago Press, 1949).

[61]Peter H. Odegard, "A Group Basis of Politics: A New Name for an Ancient Myth," *Western Political Quarterly* (September, 1958), 699.

How American Democracy Really Works: A Radical View

[62]It is true that many of the Negroes in combat in Vietnam are formally volunteers. But when they can escape from the black belt of the South or the ghettoes of the North only by enlisting in the Army, then we have compulsion. As one VISTA worker in Alabama told me recently, many young Negroes he encountered were happy to be accepted by the armed forces. But their motive was escape, not patriotism.

[63]Harvey Swados, "The UAW and Walter Reuther," *Dissent*, Autumn 1963.

CHAPTER TWO. THE MAKING OF THE CONSTITUTION

The Founding Fathers

[1]The view that the right to vote in the states was severely circumscribed by property qualifications has been thoroughly discredited in recent years. See Chilton Williamson, *American Suffrage from Property to Democracy, 1760–1860* (Princeton, 1960). The contemporary position is that John Dickinson actually knew what he was talking about when he argued that there would be little opposition to vesting the right of suffrage in freeholders since "The great mass of our Citizens is composed at this time of freeholders, and will be pleased with it." Max Farrand, *Records of the Federal Convention*, vol. 2, p. 202 (New Haven, 1911). (Henceforth cited as *Farrand*.)

[2]The classic statement of the *coup d'etat* theory is, of course, Charles A. Beard, *An Economic Interpretation of the Constitution of the United States* (New York, 1913), and

this theme was echoed by Vernon L. Parrington, Merrill Jensen, and others in "populist" historiographical tradition. For a sharp critique of this thesis see Robert E. Brown, *Charles Beard and the Constitution* (Princeton, 1956). See also Forrest McDonald, *We the People* (Chicago, 1958); the trail-blazing work in this genre was Douglas Adair, "The Tenth Federalist Revisited," *William and Mary Quarterly*, Third Series, vol. VIII (1951), pp. 48–67.

[3]A basic volume, which, like other works by Warren, provides evidence with which one can evaluate the author's own opinions, is Charles Warren, *The Making of the Constitution* (Boston, 1928). The best brief summary of the forces behind the movement for centralization is chap. 1 of *Warren* (as it will be cited hereafter).

[4]On Pennsylvania see Robert L. Brunhouse, *Counter-Revolution in Pennsylvania* (Harrisburg, 1942) and Charles P. Smith, *James Wilson* (Chapel Hill, 1956), chap. 15; for New York, which needs the same sort of microanalysis Pennsylvania has received, the best study is E. Wilder Spaulding, *New York in the Critical Period, 1783-1789* (New York, 1932).

[5]Stanley Elkins and Eric McKitrick, "The Founding Fathers: Young Men of the Revolution," *Political Science Quarterly*, vol. 76, p. 181 (1961).

[6]*Warren*, p. 55.

[7]In *La Republique des Camarades* (Paris, 1914).

[8]See Frank Monaghan, *John Jay* (New York, 1935), chap. 13.

[9]"[T]he situation of the general government, if it can be called a government, is shaken to its foundation, and liable to be overturned by every blast. In a word, it is at an end; and, unless a remedy is soon applied, anarchy and confusion will inevitably ensure." Washington to Jefferson, May 30, 1787, *Farrand*, III, 31. See also Irving Brant, *James Madison, The Nationalist* (New York, 1948), chap. 25.

[10]Merrill Jensen, *The New Nation* (New York, 1950). Interestingly enough, Prof. Jensen virtually ignores international relations in his laudatory treatment of the government under the Articles of Confederation.

[11]The story of James Madison's cultivation of Washington is told by Brant, *op. cit.*, pp. 394–397.

[12]The "message center" being the Congress; nineteen members of Congress were simultaneously delegates to the Convention. One gets a sense of this coordination of effort from Broadus Mitchell, *Alexander Hamilton, Youth to Maturity* (New York, 1957), chap. 22.

[13]See Sir Lewis Namier, *The Structure of Politics at the Accession of George III*, 2nd ed. (New York, 1957); *England in the Age of the American Revolution* (London, 1930).

[14]The Annapolis Convention, called for the previous year, turned into a shambles: only five states sent commissioners, only three states were legally represented, and the instructions to delegates named varied quite widely from state to state. Clinton and others of his persuasion may have thought this disaster would put an end to the drive for reform. See Mitchell, *op. cit.*, pp. 362–367; Brant, *op. cit.*, pp. 375–387.

[15]See Hamilton M. Bishop, *Why Rhode Island Opposed the Federal Constitution* (Providence, 1950) for a careful analysis of the labyrinthine political course of Rhode Island. For background see David S. Lovejoy, *Rhode Island Politics and the American Revolution* (Providence, 1958).

[16]The terms "radical" and "conservative" have been bandied about a good deal in connection with the Constitution. This usage is nonsense if it is employed to distinguish between two economic "classes"—e.g., radical debtors versus conservative creditors, radical farmers versus conservative capitalists, etc.—because there was no polarization along this line of division; the same types of people turned up on both sides. And many were hard to place in these terms: does one treat Robert Morris as a debtor or a creditor? or James Wilson? See Brown, *op. cit.*, *passim*. The one line of division that holds up is between those deeply attached to states' rights and those who felt that the Confederation was bankrupt. Thus, curiously, some of the most narrow-minded, parochial spokesmen of the time have earned the designation "radical" while those most willing to experiment and alter the *status quo* have been dubbed "conservative"! See Cecelia Kenyon, "Men of Little Faith," *William and Mary Quarterly*, vol. 12, p. 3 (1955).

[17]Yet, there was little objection to this crucial modification from any quarter—there almost seems to have been a gentlemen's agreement that Rhode Island's *liberum veto* had to be destroyed.

[18]See Mason's letter to his son, May 27, 1787, in which he endorsed secrecy as "a

proper precaution to prevent mistakes and misrepresentation until the business shall have been completed, when the whole may have a very different complexion from that in which the several crude and indigested parts might in their first shape appear if submitted to the public eye." *Farrand*, III, 28.

[19]See Madison to Jefferson, June 6, 1787, *Farrand*, III, 35.

[20]Cited in *Warren*, p. 138.

[21]See, e.g., Gottfried Dietze, *The Federalist, A Classic on Federalism and Free Government* (Baltimore, 1960); Richard Hofstadter, *The American Political Tradition* (New York, 1948); and John P. Roche, "American Liberty" in M. Konvitz and C. Rossiter, eds., *Aspects of Liberty* (Ithaca, 1958).

[22]"I hold it for a fundamental point, that an individual independence of the states is utterly irreconcilable with the idea of an aggregate sovereignty," Madison to Randolph, cited in Brant, *op. cit.*, p. 416.

[23]The Randolph Plan was presented on May 29, see *Farrand*, I, 18–23; the state legislatures retained only the power to *nominate* candidates for the upper chamber. Madison's view of the appropriate position of the states emerged even more strikingly in Yates' record of his speech on June 29: "Some contend that states are sovereign when in fact they are only political societies. There is a graduation of power in all societies, from the lowest corporation to the highest sovereign. The states never possessed the essential rights of sovereignty. . . . The states, at present, are only great corporations, having the power of making by-laws, and these are effectual only if they are not contradictory to the general confederation. The states ought to be placed under the control of the general government—at least as much so as they formerly were under the king and British parliament." *Farrand*, I, 471. Forty-six years later, after Yates' "Notes" had been published, Madison tried to explain this statement away as a misinterpretation: he did not flatly deny the authenticity of Yates' record, but attempted a defense that was half justification and half evasion. Madison to W. C. Rives, Oct. 21, 1833. *Farrand*, III, 521–524.

[24]Resolution 6 gave the National Legislature this power subject to review by the Council of Revision proposed in Resolution 8.

[25]Resolution 6.

[26]*Ibid.*

[27]See the discussions on May 30 and 31. "Mr. Charles Pinkney wished to know of Mr. Randolph whether he meant to abolish the State Governts. altogether . . . Mr. Butler said he had not made up his mind on the subject and was open to the light which discussion might throw on it . . . Genl. Pinkney expressed a doubt . . . Mr. Gerry seemed to entertain the same doubt." *Farrand*, I, 33–34. There were no denunciations—though it should perhaps be added that Luther Martin had not yet arrived.

[28]*Farrand*, I, 54. (Italics added.)

[29]*Ibid.*, p. 242. Delaware's delegates had been instructed by their general assembly to maintain in any new system the voting equality of the states. *Farrand*, III, 574.

[30]*Ibid.*, p. 240.

[31]*Ibid.*, p. 250.

[32]*Ibid.*, p. 258.

[33]*Ibid.*, p. 178.

[34]*Ibid.*, p. 274.

[35]*Ibid.*, pp. 275–276.

[36]"But it is said that this national government is to act on individuals and not on states; and cannot a federal government be so framed as to operate in the same way? It surely may." *Ibid.*, pp. 182–183; also *ibid.* at p. 276.

[37]*Farrand*, III, 613.

[38]*Farrand*, I, 177.

[39]*Ibid.*, p. 182.

[40]*Ibid.*, p. 255.

[41]J. C. Hamilton, cited *ibid.*, p. 293.

[42]See, e.g., Mitchell, *op. cit.*, p. 381.

[43]Hamilton to Washington, July 3, 1787, *Farrand*, III, 53.

[44]A reconstruction of the Hamilton Plan is found in *Farrand*, III, 617–630.

[45]Said William Samuel Johnson on June 21: "A gentleman from New-York, with boldness and decision, proposed a system totally different from both [Virginia and New Jersey]; and though he has been praised by every body, he has been supported by none." *Farrand*, I, 363.

[46]See his letter to Washington cited *supra* note 43.

[47]*Farrand*, III, 338.

[48]*Farrand*, I, 321.

[49]Maryland's politics in this period were only a bit less intricate than Rhode Island's: the rural gentry, in much the same fashion that Namier described in England, divided up among families—Chases, Carrolls, Pacas, Lloyds, Tilghmans, etc.—and engaged in

what seemed, to the outsider, elaborate political Morris dances. See Philip A. Crowl, *Maryland During and After the Revolution* (Baltimore, 1943). The Maryland General Assembly named five delegates to the Convention and provided that "the said Deputies or such of them as shall attend . . . shall have full Power to represent this State." *Farrand*, III, 586. The interesting circumstance was that three of the delegates were Constitutionalists (Carroll, McHenry and Jenifer), while two were opposed (Martin and Mercer); and this led to an *ad hoc* determination of where Maryland would stand when votes were taken. The vote on equality of representation, to be described *infra*, was an important instance of this eccentricity.

[50]This formulation was voted into the Randolph Plan on May 30, 1787, by a vote of six states to none, with one divided. *Farrand*, I, 30.

[51]*Farrand*, I, 335–336. In agreeing, Randolph stipulated his disagreement with Ellsworth's rationale, but said he did not object to merely changing an "expression." Those who subject the Constitution to minute semantic analysis might do well to keep this instance in mind; if Randolph could so concede the deletion of "national," one may wonder if any word changes can be given much weight.

[52]According to Luther Martin, he was alone on the floor and cast Maryland's vote for equality of representation. Shortly thereafter, Jenifer came on the floor and "Mr. King from Massachusetts, valuing himself on Mr. Jenifer to divide the State of Maryland on this question . . . requested of the President that the question might be put again; however, the motion was too extraordinary in its nature to meet with success." Cited from "The Genuine Information, . . ." *Farrand*, III, 188.

[53]Namely Baldwin's vote *for* equality of representation which divided Georgia—with Few absent and Pierce in New York fighting a duel, Houston voted against equality and Baldwin shifted to tie the state. Baldwin was originally from Connecticut and attended and tutored at Yale, facts which have led to much speculation about the pressures the Connecticut delegation may have brought on him to save the day (Georgia was the last state to vote) and open the way to compromise. To employ a good Russian phrase, it was certainly not an accident that Baldwin voted the way he did. See *Warren*, p. 262.

[54]For various contemporary comments, see *Warren*, pp. 814–818. On Adams' technique, see Zoltan Haraszti, "The Composition of Adams' *Defense*," in *John Adams and the Prophets of Progress* (Cambridge, 1952), chap. 9. In this connection it is interesting to check the Convention discussions for references to the authority of Locke, Montesquieu, and Harrington, the theorists who have been assigned various degrees of paternal responsibility. There are no explicit references to James Harrington; one to John Locke (Luther Martin cited him on the state of nature, *Farrand*, I, 437); and seven to Montesquieu, only one of which related to the "separation of powers" (Madison in an odd speech, which he explained in a footnote was given to help a friend rather than advance his own views, cited Montesquieu on the separation of the executive and legislative branches, *Farrand*, II, 34). This, of course, does not prove that Locke and Co. were without influence; it shifts the burden of proof, however, to those who assert ideological causality. See Benjamin F. Wright, "The Origins of the Separation of Powers in America," *Economica*, vol. 13 (1933), p. 184.

[55]I share Willmoore Kendall's interpretation of Locke as a supporter of parliamentary supremacy and majoritarianism; see Kendall, *John Locke and the Doctrine of Majority Rule* (Urbana, 1941). Kendall's general position has recently received strong support in the definitive edition and commentary of Peter Laslett, *Locke's Two Treatises of Government* (Cambridge, 1960).

[56]The American Locke is best delineated in Carl Becker, *The Declaration of Independence* (New York, 1948).

[57]See John P. Roche, "The Electoral College: A Note on American Political Mythology," *Dissent* (Spring, 1961), pp. 197–199. The relevant debates took place July 19–26, 1787, *Farrand*, II, 50–128, and September 5–6, 1787, *ibid.*, pp. 505–531.

[58]See the discussion on August 22, 1787, *Farrand*, II, 366–375; King seems to have expressed the sense of the Convention when he said, "the subject should be considered in a political light only." *Ibid.* at 373.

[59]*Farrand*, II, 374. Randolph echoed his sentiment in different words.

[60]Mason to Jefferson, cited in *Warren*, p. 584.

[61]August 29, 1787, *Farrand*, II, 449–450.

[62]*Ibid.*, p. 451. The plainest statement of

the matter was put by the three North Carolina delegates (Blount, Spaight, and Williamson) in their report to Governor Caswell, September 18, 1787. After noting that "no exertions have been wanting on our part to guard and promote the particular interest of North Carolina," they went on to explain the basis of the negotiations in cold-blooded fashion: "While we were taking so much care to guard ourselves against being over reached and to form rules of Taxation that might operate in our favour, it is not to be supposed that our Northern Brethren were Inattentive to their particular Interest. A navigation Act or the power to regulate Commerce in the Hands of the National Government . . . is what the Southern States have given in Exchange for the advantages we Mentioned." They concluded by explaining that while the Constitution did deal with other matters besides taxes—"there are other Considerations of great Magnitude involved in the system"— they would not take up valuable time with boring details! *Farrand*, III, 83–84.

⁶³See John C. Calhoun, *A Disquisition on Government* (New York, 1943), pp. 21–25, 38. Calhoun differed from Mason, and others in the Convention who urged the two-thirds requirement, by advocating a functional or interest veto rather than some sort of special majority, i.e., he abandoned the search for quantitative checks in favor of a qualitative solution.

⁶⁴The Committee on Detail altered the general grant of legislative power envisioned by the Virginia Plan into a series of specific grants; these were examined closely between August 16 and August 23. One day only was devoted to the Judicial Article, August 27, and since no one raised the question of judicial review of *Federal* statutes, no light was cast on the matter. A number of random comments on the power of the judiciary were scattered throughout the discussions, but there was another variable which deprives them of much probative value: the proposed Council of Revision which would have joined the executive with the judges in *legislative* review. Madison and Wilson, for example, favored this technique—which had nothing in common with what we think of as judicial review except that judges were involved in the task.

⁶⁵For what it may be worth, I think that judicial review of congressional acts was logically on all fours with review of state enactments and that it was certainly consistent with the view that the Constitution could not be amended by the Congress and President, or by a two-thirds vote of Congress (overriding a veto), without the agreement of three-quarters of the states. *External* evidence from that time supports this view, see Charles Warren, *Congress, the Constitution, and the Supreme Court* (Boston, 1925), pp. 41–128, but the debates *in* the Convention prove nothing.

⁶⁶Or so Madison stated, *Farrand*, II, 643. Wilson too may have contributed; he was close to Franklin and delivered the frail old gentleman's speeches for him.

⁶⁷See a very interesting letter, from an unknown source in Philadelphia, to Jefferson, October 11, 1787: "Randolph wishes it well, & it is thought would have signed it, but he wanted to be on a footing with a popular rival." *Farrand*, III, 104. Madison, writing Jefferson a full account on October 24, 1787, put the matter more delicately—he was working hard on Randolph to win him for ratification: "[Randolph] was not inveterate in his opposition, and grounded his refusal to subscribe pretty much on his unwillingness to commit himself, so as not to be at liberty to be governed by further lights on the subject." *Ibid.*, p. 135.

⁶⁸See Edward P. Smith, "The Movement Towards a Second Constitutional Convention in 1788," in J. F. Jameson, ed., *Essays in the Constitutional History of the United States* (Boston, 1889), pp. 46–115.

⁶⁹See Bishop, *op. cit., passim*.

⁷⁰See *Elliot's Debates on the Federal Constitution* (Washington, 1836), vol. 3, pp. 436–438.

⁷¹This should be quoted to give the full flavor: "Without vanity, I may say I have had different experience of [militia] service from that of [Henry]. It was my fortune to be a soldier of my country. . . . I saw what the honorable gentleman did not see—our men fighting. . . ." *Ibid.*, p. 178.

⁷²*Ibid.*, p. 329.

⁷³Washington offered him the Chief Justiceship in 1796, but he declined; Charles Warren, *The Supreme Court in United States History* (Boston, 1947), vol. 1, p. 139.

⁷⁴He was a zealous prosecutor of seditions in the period 1798–1800; with Justice Samuel Chase, like himself an alleged "radical" at the time of the Constitutional Convention, Martin hunted down Jeffersonian heretics. See James M. Smith, *Free-*

dom's Fetters (Ithaca, 1956), pp. 342–343.

75Crosskey in his sprawling *Politics and the Constitution* (Chicago, 1953), two vols., has developed with almost unbelievable zeal and intricacy the thesis that the Constitution *was* designed to establish a centralized unitary state, but that the political leadership of the Republic in its formative years betrayed this ideal and sold the pass to states' rights. While he has unearthed some interesting newspaper articles and other material, it is impossible for me to accept his central proposition. Madison and the other delegates, with the exceptions discussed in the text *supra*, did *want* to diminish the power of the states and create a vigorous national government. But they were not fools, and were, I submit, under no illusions when they departed from Philadelphia that this end had been accomplished. The crux of my argument is that *political realities* forced them to water down their objectives and they settled, like the good politicians they were, for half a loaf. The basic difficulty with Crosskey's thesis is that he knows *too* much —he assumes that the Framers had a perfectly clear idea of the road they were taking; with a semantic machete he cuts blandly through all the confusion on the floor of the meeting to the *real* meanings. Thus, despite all his ornate research apparatus, there is a fundamentally nonempirical quality about Crosskey's work: at crucial points in the argument he falls back on a type of divination which can only be described as Kabbalistic. He may be right, for example, in stating (without any proof) that Richard Henry Lee did *not* write the "Letters from a Federal Farmer," but in this country, spectral evidence has not been admissible since the seventeenth Century.

Madison's "New System"

76Gaillard Hunt (ed.), *The Writings of James Madison* (New York: G. P. Putnam's Sons, 1900–1910), II, pp. 337–338.

77*Ibid.*, p. 338.

78William C. Rives and Philip R. Fendall (eds.), *Letters and Other Writings of James Madison* (published by order of Congress; Philadelphia, 1865), I, p. 171; hereafter referred to as Congress Ed.

79*Ibid.*, p. 285.

80Hunt, *op. cit.*, II, p. 338.

81*Ibid.*, pp. 338–339.

82*Ibid.*, p. 346.

83*Ibid.*, pp. 346–347.

84*Ibid.*, p. 348.

85*Ibid.*

86Congress Ed., *op. cit.*, I, p. 285.

87Hunt, *op. cit.*, II, p. 340.

88*Ibid.*, p. 337.

89*Ibid.*, p. 339.

90Julian P. Boyd (ed.), *The Papers of Thomas Jefferson* (Princeton, N.J.: Princeton University Press, 1951), XII, p. 103.

91*Ibid.*

92Hunt, *op. cit.*, V, p. 19.

Our Federal Union Reconsidered

93Max Farrand, ed., *The Records of the Federal Convention*, June 26, vol. I, p. 423.

94*Ibid.*, p. 449.

95"The plan of government now proposed," Richard Henry Lee complained, "is evidently calculated totally to change, in time, our condition as a people. Instead of being thirteen republics, under a federal head, it is clearly designed to make us one consolidated government." "Whether such a change can ever be effected, in any manner," Lee added ominously, "whether it can be effected without convulsions and civil wars; whether such a change will not totally destroy the liberties of this country—time only can determine." *Letters from the Federal Farmer to the Republican*, October 8, 1787, collected in P. L. Ford, ed., *Pamphlets on the Constitution of the United States*, pp. 282–283.

For a summary of the various interpretations of "consolidated system," see James Wilson's speech in Jonathan Elliot, *The Debates in the Several State Conventions on the Adoption of the Federal Constitution* (2nd ed.), vol. II, pp. 466–467.

For opponents of ratification, "consolidation" went even beyond that envisaged by Alexander Hamilton. See his interpretation in *Federalist* No. 32. See also James Wilson's speech, in Elliot, *op. cit.*, vol. II, pp. 401–402.

96T. J. Randolph, ed., *The Writings of Thomas Jefferson*, vol. II, p. 274.

97The approach made herein is at variance with the view recently propounded by scholars, such as J. G. Randall—that the Civil War was a "tragic mistake," being motivated primarily by economic consideration, and used to foist "exploitive capitalism" on the United States. See, in this connection, Louis Hacker's provocative review, *Fortune*, July, 1947, vol. XXXIV, No. I, pp. 6–9.

[98]For a discussion of these divisive efforts prior to 1839, see John Quincy Adams, *The Jubilee of the Constitution:* A discourse delivered April 30, 1839, at the request of the New York Historical Society (New York, 1839), pp. 67–69.

[99]Lincoln's words of August 22, 1862, in answer to Horace Greeley's demand for emancipation, in J. G. Nicolay and J. Hay, eds., *Abraham Lincoln, Complete Works* (Gettysburg ed.), vol. VIII, p. 15. The same thought was expressed in his Peoria speech, October 16, 1854, *ibid.*, vol. II, p. 140.

[100]The quoted words are those of Alexander Hamilton in *Federalist* No. 22.

[101]Language of James Wilson. Elliot, *op. cit.*, vol. II, p. 408.

[102]H. Niles, *Principles and Acts of the Revolution* (Baltimore, 1822), pp. 27, 30.

[103]Edmund C. Burnett, *Letters of Members of the Continental Congress* (Washington, 1921), vol. I, pp. 14–15.

[104]Mary A. Benjamin, ed., *The Collector*, New York, February, 1947, vol. LX, No. 21.

[105]J. D. Richardson, ed., *Messages and Papers of the Presidents*, vol. VI, p. 5.

[106]"There was . . . no congeniality of principle between the Declaration of Independence and the Articles of Confederation. The foundation of the former was a superintending Providence—the rights of man, and the constituent revolutionary power of the people. That of the latter was the sovereignty of organized power, and the independence of the separate or dis-united States. The fabric of Declaration and that of the Confederation, were each consistent with its own foundation, but they could not form one consistent symmetrical edifice. . . . The corner stone of the one was *right*—that of the other was *power*.

"The work of the founders of our Independence was thus but half done. . . . For these United States, they had formed no *Constitution*. Instead of resorting to the source of all constituted power, they had wasted their time, their talents, and their persevering, untiring toils, in erecting and roofing and buttressing a frail and temporary shed to shelter the nation from the storm, or rather a mere baseless scaffolding on which to stand, when they should raise the marble palace of the people, to stand

the test of time." Adams, *op. cit.*, pp. 17–18, *passim.*

[107]John Quincy Adams, *An Eulogy on the Life and Character of James Madison*, delivered September 27, 1836, at the request of the Mayor, Aldermen, and common council of the City of Boston (Boston, 1836), p. 12.

[108]Farrand, ed., *op. cit.*, vol. II, p. 469.

[109]"America now exhibits to the world," James Wilson observed in the Pennsylvania ratifying convention, "a gentle, a peaceful, a voluntary, and a deliberate transition from one constitution of government to another. In other parts of the world, the idea of revolution in government is, by a mournful and an indissoluble association, connected with the idea of wars and all the calamities attendant on wars. But happy experience teaches us to view such revolutions in a very different light—to consider them only as progressive steps in improving the knowledge of government, and increasing the happiness of society and mankind." Elliot, *op. cit.*, vol. II, p. 406. See also Dr. Benjamin Rush, *infra*, note 19.

[110]"The whole people," John Quincy Adams explained in 1839, "declared the Colonies *in their united condition*, of RIGHT, free and independent States. . . . But there still remained the last and crowning act, which the People of the Union alone were competent to perform—the institution of civil government, for that compound nation, the United States of America" (Adams' emphasis). Adams, *The Jubilee of the Constitution*, pp. 15, 16, 40.

[111]Niles, *op. cit.*, p. 402. The same position is taken by Joel Barlow in an oration delivered at the North Church, Hartford, Conn., July 4, 1787, *ibid.*, p. 386.

[112]Adams, *An Eulogy*, pp. 23–24.

[113]*Ibid.*, p. 26.

[114]Farrand, ed., *op. cit.*, June 8, vol. I, p. 166.

[115]*Ibid.*, pp. 340–341, 437.

[116]*Ibid.*, pp. 324, 329.

[117]Elliot, *op. cit.*, vol. II, pp. 403, 429.

[118]*Federalist* No. 22.

[119]Elliot, *op. cit.*, vol. II, pp. 461, 466.

[120]"Genuine Information," etc., delivered to the Legislature of the State of Maryland, November 29, 1787. Reprinted in Farrand, ed., *op. cit.*, vol. III, p. 193. Martin's emphasis.

[121]See his *Letters from a Federal Farmer*,

supra, note 112, and Elliot, *op. cit.*, vol. III, pp. 70–71, 184–192.

¹²²Elliot, *op. cit.*, vol. III, pp. 54, 72. Joseph Taylor and Samuel Spencer took the same stand in the North Carolina ratifying convention. See Elliot, *op. cit.*, vol. IV, pp. 33, 80. " 'We the People?' I ask why not," John Randolph said in reply. "The government is for the people, and the misfortune was, that the people had no agency in the government before." *Ibid.*, p. 59.

¹²³H. A. Cushing, ed., *The Writings of Samuel Adams* (New York, 1908), vol. IV, p. 324.

¹²⁴Elliot, *op. cit.*, vol. III, p. 59.

¹²⁵Hamilton in *Federalist* Nos. 22 and 15.

¹²⁶In the Virginia ratifying convention, Madison dealt with the same question: "Who are the parties to it? The people— but not the people as composing one great body; but the people as composing thirteen sovereignties: were it, as the gentleman asserts, a consolidated government, the assent of a majority of the people would be sufficient for its establishment . . . but, Sir, no State is bound by it, as it is, without its own consent." Elliot, *op. cit.*, vol. III, pp. 114–115.

Chief Justice John Marshall cast Madison's refinements brusquely aside in 1819, saying: "It is true, they assembled in their several states (for purposes of ratifying the Constitution)—and where else could they have assembled? No political dreamer was ever wild enough to think of breaking down the lines which separate the states, and of compounding the American people into one common mass. Of consequence, when they act, they act in their States. But the measures they adopt do not, on that account cease to be the measures of the people themselves, or become the measures of the State governments." *McCulloch v. Md.*, 4 Wheaton 316, p. 402.

Marshall points up his meanings even more sharply: "It has been said, that the people had already surrendered their powers to the State sovereignties and had nothing more to give. But surely, the question whether they may resume and modify the powers granted to government does not remain to be settled in this country. Much more might the legitimacy of the General Government be doubted, had it been created by the States. The powers delegated to the State sovereignties were to be exercised by

themselves, not by a distinct and independent sovereignty, created by themselves. . . . The government of the Union, then, . . . is, emphatically, and truly, a government of the people. In form and substance it emanates from them." *Ibid.*, pp. 403–404.

¹²⁷Hamilton conceded (*Federalist* No. 32) that "the plan of the Convention aims only at a partial union or consolidation," but he undermined the concession by adding that "the State governments would clearly retain all the rights of sovereignty which they before had, and which *were not, by that act* [the Constitution] *exclusively delegated to the United States.*" Except for the word "exclusively," the emphasis is mine.

The supremacy or "sovereignty" of the central government *vis-à-vis* the states in foreign affairs had been recognized and enforced under the Articles of Confederation. See John Jay's argument of October, 1786, *Secret Journals of the Acts and Proceedings of Congress*, vol. IV, pp. 203–204, 209–210. James Wilson went further, claiming sovereignty for the central government, under certain circumstances, even in domestic affairs.

In his argument upholding the 1781 Act of Congress incorporating the Bank of North America, Wilson appears not to have been embarrassed for want of an express or implied grant of such powers. "To many purposes," he argued, "the United States are to be considered as one undivided, independent nation; and as possessed of all the rights, and powers, and properties by the laws of nations incident to such. Whenever an object occurs to the direction of which no particular state is competent, the management of it must, of necessity, belong to the United States in congress assembled." J. D, Andrews, ed., *Works of James Wilson* (1896), vol. I, p. 558.

Article VI, Paragraph 2, of the Constitution removes all doubts as to national dominance by providing specifically for the supremacy of the national government generally. And since the national government acts directly on individuals, that supremacy is enforceable in the Federal courts. Nor does the Tenth Amendment impair this supremacy. Therein "the powers *not delegated* to the United States . . . are reserved to the States respectively, or to the people." The Tenth Amendment, far from qualifying or limiting national power, in effect repeats the words of Article VI, Paragraph 2: "This Constitution, and the Laws of the United States which shall be made in Pursuance thereof; and all Treaties made, or which shall be made, under the Authority of the United States, shall be the supreme Law of the Land; and the Judges in every State shall be bound thereby, any Thing in the Constitution or Laws of any State to the Contrary notwithstanding."

[128]*Federalist* No. 23.

[129]*Federalist* No. 9.

[130]*Federalist* No. 31.

[131]*Federalist* No. 23.

[132]Douglass Adair, "The Authorship of the Disputed Federalist Papers," *William and Mary Quarterly*, April and July, 1944.

[133]In *Federalist* No. 45, Madison said: ". . . if . . . the Union be essential to the happiness of the people of America, is it not preposterous, to urge as an objection to a government, without which the objects of the Union cannot be attained, that such a government may derogate from the importance of the governments of the individual States? Was, then, the American Revolution effected, was the American Confederacy formed, was the precious blood of thousands spilt, and the hard-earned substance of millions lavished, not that the people of America should enjoy peace, liberty, and safety, but that the government of the individual States, that particular municipal establishments, might enjoy a certain extent of power, and be arrayed with certain dignities and attributes to sovereignty? We have heard of the impious doctrine in the Old World, that the people were made for kings, not kings for the people. Is the same doctrine to be revived in the New, in another shape—that the solid happiness of the people is to be sacrificed to the views of political institutions of a different form?..."

Madison continued this nationalistic theme in *Federalist* No. 46: "The federal and State governments are in fact but different agents and trustees of the people, constituted with different powers, and designed for different purposes. The adversaries of the Constitution seem to have lost sight of the people altogether in their reasoning on this subject; and to have viewed these different establishments, not only as mutual rivals and enemies, but as uncontrolled by any common Superior in their efforts to usurp the authorities of each other. These gentlemen must be reminded of their error.

They must be told that the ultimate authority wherever the derivative may be found, resides in the people alone."

Madison has stated his nationalistic position quite bluntly in the Philadelphia Convention: "There is a gradation of power in all societies, from lowest corporation to the highest sovereign. The states never possessed the essential rights of sovereignty. These were always vested in Congress (even under the Articles of Confederation)." Farrand, ed., *op. cit.*, vol. I, p. 471. Here Madison seemed to consider the states, as did Dr. Johnson (*ibid.*, p. 461), "as districts of people composing one political Society."

At certain points, Madison also endorsed Hamilton's broad conception of the powers granted the national government, saying in *Federalist* No. 44 that "No axiom is more clearly established in law, or in reason, than that whenever the end is required, the means are authorized; wherever a general power to do a thing is given, every particular power necessary for doing it is included."

[134]Supporters of the states-compact theory of the Union have made much of the fact that until September 12 the Preamble read: "We the people of the States of New Hampshire, Massachusetts," etc. It was then changed by the Committee on Style to "We, the people of the United States," proving (it was argued) that the Constitution emanates from the people of the states, rather than the people of the United States. But, as we have seen, this distinction was unimportant in 1787, the states being regarded "as districts of people forming one political society." Note that the Preamble, in its original form, did not read, "We the States."

[135]See Edward S. Corwin's "'We, the People'," published in the *Doctrine of Judicial Review* (Princeton, 1914), pp. 81–108, 98.

[136]G. Hunt, ed., *Writings of James Madison*, vol. VI, p. 326.

[137]P. L. Ford, ed., *Writings of Thomas Jefferson*, vol. VII, p. 287.

[138]John C. Taylor, *Construction Construed and Constitutions Vindicated* (Richmond, 1820), pp. 59, 97, 132–133, 155–156, 200, *passim*.

[139]John C. Taylor, *New Views of the Constitution of the United States* (Washington, 1823).

[140]For a detailed discussion of Madison's contribution to the doctrine of Nullification and Secession, see Edward S. Corwin,

"National Power and State Interposition, 1787–1861," *Michigan Law Review*, May 1912, vol. X, pp. 535–551.

[141]Letter to James Duane, September 3, 1780. H. C. Lodge, ed., *The Works of Alexander Hamilton* (New York, 1904), vol. I, p. 213.

[142]Richardson, ed., *Messages and Papers of the Presidents*, vol. VI, p. 5.

[143]Chief Justice Salmon P. Chase in *Texas v. White*, 7 Wallace (1869), p. 700.

[144]*Missouri v. Holland*, 252 U. S. 416 (1920), p. 433.

[145]This is not to imply that the Madisonian theory of the Union and of national power has since been devoid of usefulness. Following the Civil War the doctrine of "dual sovereignty" was freely invoked in leading Supreme Court cases as a limitation on national power to regulate our economy. Here constitutional theory was brought to the service of the *laissez-faire* dogma. See in this connection Edward S. Corwin, *Twilight of the Supreme Court* (New Haven, 1934); and my article, "The Conservative World of Mr. Justice Sutherland, 1833–1910," *American Political Science Review*, vol. XXXII, No. 30, June 1938.

[146]Language of John Quincy Adams, *The Jubilee of the Constitution*, p. 55.

CHAPTER THREE. FEDERALISM

The States and the Nation

[1]Carey C. Thompson in *Public Affairs Comment*, Institute of Public Affairs, University of Texas, September 1959. Others have echoed this statement in recent years, particularly as the evidence from studies of American federalism has come in. One of the most authoritative recent statements to this effect was that of (the then) Senator Hubert Humphrey in his speech before the National Association of County Officials, July, 1964.

[2]The very word "decentralization" implies the legal investment of power in a central government which may or may not choose to devolve those powers of local governments, as it wills. The desires and interests of the local governments can be made effective only insofar as they can be effectively expressed by local representatives in the councils of the central government. In any unitary system, even a decentralized

one, the ultimate power—including the power to alter or abolish all subnational governments—rests with the central government. The American system can be more appropriately termed "noncentralized" because there is no central government with absolute authority over the states in a unitary sense, but, instead, a strong national government coupled with strong state governments in which authority and power are shared, legally and practically.

[3]For further discussion of these distinctions, see the articles on "Decentralization," "Federalism," and "Federation" in *Encyclopedia of the Social Sciences* (New York and London: Macmillan Co., 1931).

[4]This summary paraphrases the words of Chief Justice Salmon P. Chase in *Texas vs. White*, 7 Wallace 700 (1869), whose description of the constitutional position of the states remains classic.

[5]For some examples of state action of this sort before the turn of the century, see Gilbert T. Stephenson, *Race Distinctions in American Law* (New York and London: D. Appleton and Co., 1910).

[6]William Anderson discusses this at length in *The Nation and the States, Rivals or Partners?* (Minneapolis: University of Minnesota Press, 1955).

[7]For a good history of the reformers' activities at the state and national level in this period, see Arthur Schlesinger, Jr.'s trilogy, "The Age of Roosevelt," particularly volumes I and II, *The Crisis of the Old Order* (Boston: Houghton Mifflin Co., 1957) and *The Coming of the New Deal* (Boston: Houghton Mifflin Co., 1959).

[8]Morton Grodzins describes this procedure in "American Political Parties and the American System," *Western Political Quarterly XIII* (December, 1960).

[9]See Daniel J. Elazar, *The American Partnership* (Chicago: University of Chicago Press, 1962), Part II.

[10]See Grodzins.

[11]For a description of the involved nature of intergovernmental collaboration, see Morton Grodzins, "The Federal System," in *Goals for Americans* (Englewood Cliffs, N.J.: Prentice-Hall, 1960), chap. 12.

[12]*Ibid.*

[13]See Carl B. Swisher, *The Growth of Constitutional Power in the United States* (rev. ed.; Chicago: University of Chicago Press, 1963).

[14]The tidelands oil case is particularly in-

teresting as it generated a tremendous amount of controversy, with states lining up on both sides. For a history of the case, see Ernest R. Bartley, *The Tidelands Oil Controversy: A Legal and Historical Analysis* (Austin: University of Texas Press, 1953).

[15]A description of this relationship is available in the report on *Twenty-Five Grant-in-Aid Programs* submitted to the Commission on Intergovernmental Relations (Washington: U.S. Government Printing Office, 1955).

[16]This incident is described in Nelson A. Rockefeller, *The Future of Federalism* (Cambridge: Harvard University Press, 1962).

[17]This is true in the twenty-five states studied in Governmental Affairs Institute, *A Survey Report on the Impact of Federal Governments*, submitted to the Commission on Intergovernmental Relations (Washington: U.S. Government Printing Office, 1956). The writer has confirmed the statement in three additional states (Georgia, Minnesota, and Wisconsin) through field research.

[18]Field research, Davenport and Des Moines, Iowa, 1960, and *General Laws of Iowa*, 1961.

[19]The writer has evidence of extensive use of federal personnel stationed locally to lobby for community development projects requiring federal aid in Arkansas, Georgia, Illinois, and Colorado from his field work in those states in 1958, 1960, 1961, and 1962. Evidence of this in other states is available in the files of the Workshop in American Federalism (formerly of the University of Chicago).

[20]Tax Foundation, *Facts and Figures on Government Finances*, 1962–1963 (Englewood Cliffs, N.J.: Prentice-Hall, 1963).

[21]Interview with Lewis Dexter (formerly affiliated with Governor Furcolo on this project), September 9, 1957.

[22]See Elazar, Part II.

[23]See Jack W. Peltason, *Federal Courts in the Political Process* (New York: Random House, 1955); and John R. Schmidhauser, *The Supreme Court: Its Politics, Personalities, and Procedures* (New York: Holt, Rinehart & Winston, 1960).

[24]To say the courts are least influenced by politics is not to say that they are uninfluenced. On the contrary, the standard pattern of recruiting judges from among active politicians has helped make the courts more sensitive to the nuances of the political process than might otherwise be thought to be the case. Indeed, at the lower court levels, the sensitivity of judges often works in the states' favor, neutralizing less sensitive high court decisions.

[25]See V. O. Key, Jr., *Politics, Parties, and Pressure Groups* (4th ed.; New York: Thomas Y. Crowell Co., 1958), chap. 22.

[26]See J. Leiper Freeman, *The Political Process: Executive-Legislative Relations* (New York: Random House, 1955) for further discussion of the role of the committee system.

[27]Kenneth E. Gray has made a thorough study of "case-work" which is summarized in "Congressional Interference in Administration," a paper presented at the 1962 Annual Meeting of the American Political Science Association, Washington, D.C. This section draws heavily on his work.

[28]*The Impact of Federal Grants.*

[29]Briefly, most Northerners had always held the views that the national government emerged at the same time as the state governments—during the Revolution; that the Union was permanent unless all parties agreed to its dissolution; and that, under the Constitution, the national government was supreme. By the same token, most Southerners had always believed that the states antedated the national government, which they had created; that the Union was held together by a compact, dissolvable by any of the parties to it; and that sovereignty ultimately resided in the states. Both theories are of equal age and status in the history of American political thought. See Ralph H. Gabriel, *The Course of American Democratic Thought* (2nd ed.; New York: Ronald Press Co., 1956).

[30]For a study of the Court's changing role, see John R. Schmidhauser, *The Supreme Court as Final Arbiter in Federal-State Relations*, 1789–1957 (Chapel Hill: University of North Carolina Press, 1958).

[31]Grodzins refers to the extent of these satisfactions in "The Federal System."

Creative Tensions

[32]James MacGregor Burns, *The Deadlock of Democracy* (Englewood Cliffs, New Jersey: Prentice-Hall, 1963).

[33]Michael V. DiSalle, *The Power of Life or*

Death (New York: Random House, 1965), p. 9.

The Relationship of Federal to Local Authorities

[34]*A Congressional Quarterly*, August 26, 1966, p. 1,860.

[35]Charles E. Lindblom, "The Rediscovery of the Market," *The Public Interest* (Summer, 1966), p. 100.

CHAPTER FOUR. POLITICAL PARTIES AND ELECTORAL SYSTEM

Quest for Party Government

[1]Austin Ranney, *The Doctrine of Responsible Party Government* (Urbana: University of Illinois Press).

[2]Committee on Political Parties of the American Political Science Association, *Toward a More Responsible Two-Party System* (New York: Rinehart, 1950).

[3]A word of semantic distinction may be helpful here. "Party government" refers to leadership by a majority political party in the important decision-making processes of government; the "responsible" party is one able to organize majorities and officials behind party programs and thus be responsible to its voters for the conduct of office. It is not, therefore, a gross oversimplification to say that the "responsible" party is one capable of "party government."

[4]See Ranney, *The Doctrine of Responsible Party Government*, chaps. 1 and 2, for an analysis of what party government presumes about democracy.

[5]I am using "liberal" in the sense it is used in contemporary American politics; the liberal position favors popular, participatory democracy and positive government. Conservatism, on the other hand, generally connotes a preference for limited government and for the wisdom of political leaders and elites.

[6]E. E. Schattschneider, *Party Government* (New York: Rinehart, 1942), p. 208.

[7]*Toward a More Responsible Two-Party System*, p. 15.

[8]The bibliography critical of the concept of party responsibility is a very long one. Pendleton Herring's *The Politics of Democ-*

racy (New York: Rinehart, 1940) early presented a view contra the reformers.

[9]See Leon D. Epstein, "A Comparative Study of Canadian Parties," *American Political Science Review*, LVIII (1964), pp. 46–59.

[10]A highly centralized party such as the Indian Congress Party can maintain control over nomination and renomination of candidates to the national parliament and thus exercise a potent sanction upon those parliamentarians of the party who break party discipline. In 1957, for example, the national Parliamentary Board of the party, the agency of the party which selects and approves the candidates for local constituencies, declined to renominate almost one-third of the party's incumbent members of parliament.

[11]This is substantially the point V. O. Key makes in *The Responsible Electorate* (Cambridge: Harvard University Press, 1966). On the failure of the American voter to make the perceptions and decisions the goals of party responsibility would demand, see Donald E. Stokes and Warren E. Miller, "Party Government and the Saliency of Congress," in Angus Campbell, *et al.*, *Elections and the Political Order* (New York: Wiley, 1966), pp. 194–211.

[12]Donald E. Stokes, "Spatial Models of Party Competition," *ibid.*, pp. 161–179, develops this and related points.

[13]All of the quotations following are from the report of the Committee, *Toward a More Responsible Two-Party System* (New York: Rinehart, 1950). The italics in the original have been eliminated.

[14]See James MacGregor Burns, *The Deadlock of Democracy* (Englewood Cliffs, N.J.: Prentice-Hall, 1963), especially chap. 14. Note also that Burns is dealing with the parties in terms of his own, somewhat different, frame of reference, most especially the distinction between the presidential and the congressional parties. See also Stephen K. Bailey, *The Condition of Our National Political Parties* (New York: Fund for the Republic, 1959).

Candidate Selection

[15]The Wisconsin failures are noted in Leon D. Epstein, *Politics in Wisconsin* (Madison: University of Wisconsin Press, 1958), pp. 94–95. In California, there was a

conspicuous failure in the Democratic senatorial primary of 1964.

[16]V. O. Key, Jr., *American State Politics: An Introduction* (New York: Alfred A. Knopf, 1956), p. 271.

[17]David B. Truman, *The Governmental Process* (New York: Alfred A. Knopf, 1951), p. 291.

[18]Frank J. Sorauf, *Party and Representation* (New York: Atherton Press, 1963), pp. 53, 55, 148. Comparable data have been reported for Indiana in Thomas Watts, "Informal Party Leadership and Its Role in Candidate Selection" (unpublished paper, 1963).

[19]Jesse Unruh, Speaker of the California Assembly, cited by James Q. Wilson, *The Amateur Democrat* (Chicago: University of Chicago Press, 1962), p. 296.

[20]V. O. Key, Jr., *Politics, Parties, and Pressure Groups* (New York: Crowell-Collier, 1964), p. 453.

[21]E. E. Schattschneider, *The Struggle for Party Government* (College Park: University of Maryland Press, 1948), p. 36.

[22]Avery Leiserson, "National Party Organizations and Congressional Districts," *Western Political Quarterly*, XVI (September, 1963), 639.

[23]*Ibid.*, p. 641.

[24]David B. Truman, "Federalism and the Party System," in Arthur MacMahon (ed.), *Federalism Mature and Emergent* (New York: Columbia University Press, 1955), pp. 115–136.

[25]Key, *Politics, Parties, and Pressure Groups*, p. 342.

[26]Key, *American State Politics*, p. 169.

[27]*Ibid.*, p. 167.

[28]Julius Turner, "Primary Elections as the Alternative to Party Competition in Safe Districts," *Journal of Politics*, XV (May, 1953), 197–210.

[29]Key, *American State Politics*, p. 179.

[30]Epstein, *op. cit.*, p. 134.

[31]Sorauf, *op. cit.*, p. 114.

[32]The question is especially relevant to open primaries, but it was also relevant to California's former provision for cross-filing by candidates in closed primaries—that is, permitting candidates to run and sometimes win both the Republican and Democratic primaries. The effect of this is described by Winston Crouch *et. al.*, *California Government and Politics* (Englewood Cliffs, N.J.: Prentice-Hall, 1964), pp. 63–64.

[33]Henry Pelling, *The Origins of the Labour Party* (London: MacMillan, 1954), p. 68.

[34]The usefulness of primaries in absorbing rising strata of American society into existing parties is suggested in the well-known study of New Haven politics by Robert A. Dahl, *Who Governs?* (New Haven: Yale University Press, 1961), p. 114.

CHAPTER FIVE. INTEREST GROUPS

Lobbying as Protest: The NAACP

[1]Although the writer bears full responsibility for the views expressed, this project was supported in part by a grant from Morgan State College.

[2]Donald R. Matthews, *U. S. Senators and Their World* (Chapel Hill: University of North Carolina Press, 1960), pp. 178–180.

[3]James Weldon Johnson, *Along This Way: The Autobiography of James Weldon Johnson* (New York: The Viking Press, 1933), p. 361.

[4]David B. Truman, *The Governmental Process: Political Interests and Public Opinion* (New York: Alfred A. Knopf, 1951), pp. 336, 339.

[5]Johnson, *op. cit.*, pp. 363–372.

[6]U. S. Congress, Senate Subcommittee of the Committee on the Judiciary, *Hearings, To Prevent and Punish the Crime of Lynching*, 69th Cong., 1st Sess., 1926, pp. 6–37; U. S. Congress, Senate Subcommittee of the Committee on the Judiciary, *Hearings, Punishment for the Crime of Lynching*, 73rd Cong., 2nd Sess., 1934, pp. 9–37, 168–169.

[7]NAACP Annual Report (1932), p. 22; (1934), pp. 23–24.

[8]U. S. Congress, Senate Subcommittee of the Committee on the Judiciary, *Hearings, Punishment for the Crime of Lynching*, 74th Cong., 1st Sess., 1935, pp. 32–59; NAACP Annual Report (1935), pp. 20–21; (1936), pp. 4–6; (1937), p. 6; (1938), pp. 4–5; (1945), pp. 11–12; U. S. Congress, Senate Subcommittee of the Committee on the Judiciary, *Hearings, Crime of Lynching*, 76th Cong., 3rd Sess., 1940, pp. 51–84.

[9]Walter F. Murphy and C. Herman Pritchett, *Courts, Judges and Politics* (New York: Random House, 1961), p. 279.

[10]Walter White, *A Man Called White: The Autobiography of Walter White* (New York: The Viking Press, 1948), pp. 104–105.

White succeeded Johnson as NAACP executive secretary.

[11]*Ibid.*, pp. 105–107.

[12]Matthews, *op. cit.*, pp. 194–196.

[13]White, *op. cit.*, pp. 106–110.

[14]PM, May 7, 1941, p. 18; cited by Herbert Garfinkel, *When Negroes March: The March on Washington Movement in the Organizational Politics for FEPC* (Glencoe: The Free Press, 1959), p. 17.

[15]"A. Philip Randolph," editorial in the *Chicago Defender*, Feb. 6, 1941; cited in *ibid.*, p. 37. On discrimination in the armed forces, see Lee Nichols, *Breakthrough on the Color Front* (New York: Random House, 1954).

[16]Garfinkel, *op. cit.*, pp. 104–105; White, *op. cit.*, pp. 189–194; *NAACP Annual Report* (1942), pp. 4–6.

[17]White, *op. cit.*, p. 194.

[18]Louis C. Kesselman, *The Social Politics of FEPC: A Study in Reform Pressure Movements* (Chapel Hill: University of North Carolina Press, 1948), pp. 38–39; Garfinkel, *op. cit.*, pp. 158–162.

[19]*NAACP Annual Report* (1934), pp. 5–8; (1935), p. 5; (1938), p. 14; (1949), pp. 14–15.

[20]Kesselman, *op. cit.*, p. 92; Garfinkel, *op. cit.*, p. 158. For more on the Mobilization, see *The Crisis*, LVII (1950), *passim*.

[21]Cited in Paul Lewinson, *Race, Class and Party: A History of Negro Suffrage and White Politics in the South* (New York: Oxford University Press, 1932), pp. 84–85.

[22]V. O. Key, Jr., *Southern Politics in State and Nation* (New York: Alfred A. Knopf, 1949), pp. 599–602.

[23]Will Maslow and Joseph B. Robison, "Civil Rights and the Fight for Equality, 1862–1952," *University of Chicago Law Review*, XX, No. 3 (Spring, 1953), pp. 377–378.

[24]Other legal triumphs notwithstanding, civil rights forces have failed to win court nullification of the poll tax. Jack Greenberg, *Race Relations and American Law* (New York: Cornell University Press, 1959), p. 145.

[25]U. S. Congress, Senate Subcommittee of the committee on the Judiciary, *Hearings, Poll Taxes*, 77th Cong., 2nd Sess., 1942, pp. 335–337.

[26]NAACP *Annual Report* (1943), pp. 14–15; J. E. Christensen, "The Constitutionality of National Anti-Poll-Tax Bills," *Minnesota Law Review*, XXXIII, No. 3 (Feb., 1949), p. 220.

[27]U. S. Congress, House, Subcommittee on Elections of the Committee on House Administration, *Hearings, Anti-Poll-Tax Legislation*, 80th Cong., 1st Sess., 1947, p. 126.

[28]NAACP *Annual Report* (1948), pp. 46–47.

[29]*The Washington Post*, March 5, 1917; quoted by Bertram M. Gross, *The Legislative Struggle: A Study in Social Combat* (New York: McGraw-Hill), 1953, p. 378.

[30]U. S. Congress, Senate Committee on Rules and Administration, *Hearings, Limitation on Debate in the Senate*, 82nd Cong., Ist Sess., 1951, pp. 37–39.

[31]*Background Memorandum Concerning Majority Rule in the Senate of the United States*, n.d. (from the office of Senator Paul H. Douglas).

[32]Austin Ranney and Wilmoore Kendall, *Democracy and the American Party System* (New York: Harcourt, Brace and Co., 1956), p. 176.

[33]Maslow and Robison, *op. cit.*, pp. 400–401.

[34]NAACP *Annual Report* (1959), p. 42.

[35]Johnson, *op. cit.*, p. 373.

[36]Roy Wilkins, *Forty Years of the NAACP* (NAACP pamphlet, 1949), p. 6; cited by Warren D. St. James, *The National Association for the Advancement of Colored People: A Case Study in Pressure Groups* (New York: Exposition Press, 1958), p. 45.

[37]Harry Eckstein, *Pressure Group Politics: The Case of the British Medical Association* (Stanford: Stanford University Press, 1960), pp. 162–163.

Why Poor People's Campaign Failed

[38]Michael Harrington has adequately dealt with Newfield in the *Voice*, but it is surely time to inquire, if only in an aside, exactly what is the craft of the Newfields of this world. Are they intellectual leaders of a movement? But they have inspired no movement; nobody follows them. Are they journalists? No one—Left, Right, or Center—would accept without further verification the "facts" they offer. Are they, then, astute political commentators whose analyses of events we find useful for informed judgments? I do not know a single soul, literally, who would anchor his political views in the

subjective, extremely personal, and forever shifting sands of their prejudices. What, then, is the art they practice? They play a dual role. With regard to the radical activists, they are sponges which drink in the movement's gossip; their ears prick up at the slightest sound of a split, a sellout, a heretical tactic. In the process, they convince themselves of their own instinctively correct radicalism and at the same time constitute themselves as a credentials committee for the American Left, such as it is. They keep out impurities, these righteous arbiters of radicalism, and in so doing evade scrutiny of their own specific contributions. The second aspect of their role—what makes it professionally feasible, since the activist Left will not pay for their services—is the ideological entertainment they provide for a growing section of the swinging middle class. Political beachcombers like Newfield provide such people with a running commentary on who's "in" and who's "out" in the radical world, thus allowing them to feel engaged without budging too much. For this product his consumers reward him with a wage and some little renown.

39About two days before the "Call" went to the printer, I read its text to Rev. Young, with Rustin on the line. Young had some criticisms, and the document was modified accordingly. One of his suggestions—that the reference to integration be deleted— Rustin opposed as a pull-back from the fourteen points. Rustin proposed a conference call with Abernathy for midnight, and Young agreed to arrange it. When, by 4 a.m., Abernathy had not called, Rustin wired him, complaining of the breakdown in communications and stating that the "Call" had to be at the printer by noon the following day. Some twenty-four hours after the deadline, Abernathy called to say he couldn't understand what the fuss was about as he had full confidence in Rustin and knew the "Call" would be O.K.

40I am not here using the precise Marxian definition of *lumpenproletariat*—i.e., bohemians, petty racketeers, fly-by-night people, the debris of other classes. But I am stressing that the life of the poor, like that of the Marxian *lumpenproletariat*, is characterized by a lack of cohesion and structure. The proletariat can be poor but it is disciplined by its conditions of work; the *lumpenproletariat* is both poor and shady, up for grabs.

CHAPTER SIX. THE CONGRESS

Theories of Congress

1U. S. Congress, Joint Committee on the Organization of the Congress, *Hearings*, Part 3 (Washington: Government Printing Office, 1945), pp. 670–671.

2Two useful examples are Aaron Wildavsky, *The Politics of the Budgetary Process* (Boston: Little, Brown & Co., 1964); and Samuel Huntington, *The Common Defense* (New York: Columbia University Press, 1961), esp. pp. 123–146.

3Ralph K. Huitt, "What Can We Do About Congress?" *Milwaukee Journal*, Part 5 (December 13, 1964), p. 1.

4See Ralph K. Huitt, "Congressional Reorganization: The Next Chapter," (a paper presented at the annual meeting of the American Political Science Association, Chicago, September 8–12, 1964).

5Ernest S. Griffith, *Congress: Its Contemporary Role* (New York: New York University Press, 1951), p. 7.

6James Burnham, *Congress and the American Tradition* (Chicago: Henry Regnery, 1959), p. 276.

7Burnham, pp. 277–278.

8Wilmoore Kendall, *The Conservative Affirmation* (Chicago: Henry Regnery, 1963), pp. 15, 30–31, 85.

9Maj. Gen. Thomas A. Lane (USA, Ret.), in U. S. Congress, Joint Committee on the Organization of the Congress, *Hearings*, Part 7 (Washington: Government Printing Office, 1965), p. 1090. Referred to hereafter as *Joint Committee Hearings* (1965).

10Lane, *Joint Committee Hearings* (1965).

11*Saturday Evening Post* (March 21, 1964), p. 10. See also the remarks of Senator Clark in *Joint Committee Hearings*, Part 1 (1965), pp. 18–19.

12Burnham, p. 349.

13Griffith, p. 3. See also Kendall, pp. 41ff.

14Ralph K. Huitt, "Congressional Organization in the Field of Money and Credit" in Commission on Money and Credit, *Fiscal and Debt Management Policies* (Englewood Cliffs, N. J.: Prentice-Hall, 1963), p. 494. For a discussion of the "defensive advantages" that minorities exercise in the congressional system, see David B. Truman, *The Governmental Process* (New York: Alfred A. Knopf, 1951), chaps. 11 and 12.

15See the discussion of numerical and concurrent majorities in Burnham, chaps. 24–25.

[16]In [one] analysis, John S. Saloma distinguishes between "Presidential-Constitutionalists" and "Whigs," the latter of whom advocate strong congressional leadership and weak executives. See his "Congressional Performance: Evaluation and Implications for Reform." For an analysis that is vintage Whiggism, see Alfred de Grazia's *Republic in Crisis* (New York: Federal Legal Press, 1965).

[17]Burnham, p. 350.

[18]*Wesberry v. Sanders*, 376 U. S. 1 (1964). In the wake of this decision, House Judiciary Committee Chairman Emmanuel Celler (D-N.Y.) sponsored a bill (H.R. 5505) during the 89th Congress that would require congressional districts to deviate no more than 15 percent (greater or less) from the average size in a given state. The bill also specifies that districts be of "contiguous territory, in as compact form as practicable." The House passed the measure; but, as of this writing, the Senate had not acted upon it.

[19]See Andrew Hacker, "The Voice of 90 Million Americans," *New York Times Magazine* (March 4, 1962).

[20]See Martin Shapiro, *Law and Politics on the Supreme Court* (New York: Free Press of Glencoe, 1964), pp. 50–75.

[21]Some ideologues (from both right and left) have urged a polarization of our two parties into a Liberal and a Conservative Party. Such a development would most probably be dysfunctional for conservatives favoring the literary theory of Congress since polarization would reduce the legislative "braking" function of dispersed, decentralized parties.

[22]A dessenter here is Samuel P. Huntington, who argues that centralized congressional leadership would revivify Congress. For reasons that will become apparent in the following sections, this development might actually have the opposite effect. See Huntington, "Congressional Responses to the Twentieth Century," in *The Congress and America's Future*, ed. David B. Truman.

[23]*Federalist*, 70.

[24]Leonard D. White, *The Federalists* (New York: Macmillan, 1956), p. 510. "Statist" methods and democratic objectives find their convergence in Herbert Croly, *The Promise of American Life*, ed. Arthur M. Schlesinger, Jr. (Cambridge: Harvard University Press, 1965).

[25]Richard Bolling, *House Out of Order* (New York: E. P. Dutton & Co., 1965), p. 27. On the Jeffersonian strategy, see James M. Burns, *The Deadlock of Democracy* (Englewood Cliffs, N. J.: Prentice-Hall, 1963), chap. 2. A thorough historical review is provided in Wilfred Binkley, *The President and Congress* (New York: Alfred A. Knopf, 1947).

[26]Edward S. Corwin, *The President, Office and Powers*, 4th ed. (New York: New York University Press, 1957), p. 272.

[27]Clinton Rossiter, *The American Presidency* (New York: New American Library, 1956), p. 151.

[28]"Strength to Govern Well," *Washington Post* (July 4, 1963), p. A19.

[29]Walter Lippmann, *The Public Philosophy* (Boston: Little, Brown & Co., 1954), pp. 54–57.

[30]The case is put in two of Burns' books, *Congress on Trial* (New York: Harper & Row, 1949), and *Deadlock of Democracy* (Englewood Cliffs, N. J.: Prentice-Hall, 1963).

[31]December 17, 1962. Reprinted in *Congressional Quarterly Weekly Report* (December 21, 1962), p. 2278.

[32]Burns, *Deadlock*, p. 337. For a remarkably similar analysis, see Burnham, p. 327.

[33]Woodrow Wilson, *Constitutional Government in the United States* (New York: Columbia University Press, 1908), p. 68. See also Corwin, chap. 1.

[34]Burns, *Congress on Trial*, p. 59.

[35]Joseph S. Clark, *Congress: The Sapless Branch* (New York: Harper & Row, 1964), p. 30.

[36]Clark, p. 235.

[37]Lippmann, p. 30.

[38]Chet Holifield (D-Calif.) in *Joint Committee Hearings*, Part 2 (1965), p. 185.

[39]Lippmann, p. 30. For a description of these congressional roles in military policy making, see Huntington, *The Common Defense*, pp. 123–146.

[40]Joseph P. Harris, *Congressional Control of Administration* (Washington: Brookings Institution, 1964), p. 295. Also, see Walter Lippmann in *Newsweek* (January 20, 1964), pp. 18–19.

[41]See, for example, Robert Dahl, *Congress and Foreign Policy* (New York: Harcourt, Brace & World, 1950), p. 143.

[42]Clark, p. 109. See also Holifield in *Joint Committee Hearings* (1965).

[43]For an exposition of the Fulbright view-

point, see James A. Robinson, *Congress and Foreign Policy-Making* (Homewood, Ill.: Dorsey Press, 1962), pp. 13 and 212–214.

[44]American Political Science Association, Committee on Political Parties, *Toward a More Responsible Two-Party System* (New York: Rinehart & Co., 1950), p. 1.

[45]Burns, *Congress on Trial*, pp. 142–143.

[46]A discussion of theories of the political party is found in Samuel Eldersveld, *Political Parties: A Behavioral Analysis* (Chicago: Rand-McNally & Co., 1964).

[47]*Toward a More Responsible Two-Party System*, pp. 15ff.

[48]Burns, *Congress on Trial*, p. 110.

[49]*Toward a More Responsible Two-Party System*, p. 57 (italics in the original).

[50]Bolling, p. 242.

[51]*Toward a More Responsible Two-Party System*, pp. 88–89.

[52]*Toward a More Responsible Two-Party System*, pp. 57–64. See also Burns, *Deadlock*, pp. 327–332; and Bolling, pp. 239ff.

[53]We would place the strength of the "hard-core" party-government advocates in the House during the 88th Congress at about 15 percent of the membership. This 15 percent is the proportion of our random sample that gave an unambiguous pro-party-government response on all four of the propositions.

Folkways of the Senate

[54]The most significant recent exceptions are R. K. Huitt, "The Morse Committee Assignment Controversy: A Study in Senate Norms," *American Political Science Review*, vol. 51 (June, 1957), pp. 313–329; C. Melnik and N. Leites, *The House Without Windows* (Evanston: Row, Peterson, 1958); C. E. Gilbert, *Problems of a Senator: A Study of Legislative Behavior*, unpublished Ph.D. thesis, Northwestern University, 1955.

[55]The best of these is W. S. White, *Citadel: The Story of the U. S. Senate* (New York, 1957) but see also the same author's *The Taft Story* (New York, 1954); Jerry Voorhis, *Confessions of a Congressman* (Garden City, 1947); John F. Kennedy, *Profiles in Courage* (New York, 1956), chap. 1; G. W. Pepper, *In the Senate* (Philadelphia: University of Pennsylvania Press, 1930).

[56]Most of the interviews were conducted in Washington between January and Sep-

tember, 1956. A few follow-up interviews were held during 1958. While the senators, staff members, lobbyists and journalists interviewed were in no sense "samples" of these groups, a strenuous and generally successful effort was made to interview rough cross sections of each. On the whole, however, high rapport was deemed more desirable, given the exploratory nature of the study, than a highly "representative" but uncommunicative group of respondents.

The interviews were of the "focused" type. No formal interview schedule was used, but standardized topics were raised in each interview as time allowed. The interviews varied in length from about 15 minutes to several hours. Notes were not taken during the course of the interview but were written up immediately thereafter as nearly verbatim as possible. All quotations not otherwise cited are from these interviews; when not otherwise indicated in the text the quotations are from an interview with a past or present member of the Senate. All respondents were assured that their remarks would not be attributed to them.

Readers . . . need not be told that these interviewing procedures are far from ideal. But even if feasible on Capitol Hill, systematic surveys, using highly structured interviews and a representative sample of respondents, are most fruitful when variables are well identified and when all types of respondents are likely to be equally cooperative. Neither condition held in this case. This suggested that greater pay-offs might be achieved by the less rigorous interviewing methods used.

[57]*Washington Post and Times Herald*, February 19, 1956.

[58]Cf. Harry S Truman's comments: "I learned [upon entering the Senate] . . . that the estimates of the various members which I formed in advance were not always accurate. I soon found that, among my ninety-five colleagues, the real business of the Senate was carried on by unassuming and conscientious men, not by those who managed to get the most publicity." *New York Times*, October 3, 1955.

[59]*Providence* (R.I.) *Evening Journal*, February 8, 1956.

[60]See George Goodwin, Jr., "The Seniority System in Congress," *American Political Science Review*, vol. 53 (June, 1959), pp. 412–436.

[61]*Congressional Record*, April 24, 1956, p. 6148. References here and herein are to the daily edition.

[62]*Ibid.*, June 13, 1956, pp. 9147–9148.

[63]*Cf. ibid.*, June 11, 1956, p. 8990: Mr. HILL. Mr. President, although I greatly love the Senator from Illinois, and although he has been very generous toward me in his remarks on the bill— Mr. DOUGLASS. I had hoped I would soften up the Senator from Alabama. (Laughter).

[64]Alben W. Barkley, *That Reminds Me* (Garden City, 1954), p. 255.

[65]Ralph E. Flanders, "What Ails the Senate?" *The New York Times Magazine*, May 9, 1954, p. 62.

[66]*Congressional Record*, February 16, 1956, pp. 2300–2301.

[67]*Ibid.*, June 13, 1956, p. 9153.

[68]William Benton, "For Distinguished Service in Congress," *The New York Times Magazine*, July 24, 1955, p. 38; Ralph E. Flanders, *op. cit.*, p. 13.

[69]This "institutional patriotism" extends down to the staff level. For example, one staff member said in the course of an interview: "I'm an apologist for the Senate and Senators. When I came here I thought just like the normal academic 'liberal' that the Senate was bumbling and incompetent, that Senators were strictly from Kokomo and that if you wanted something done you had to go to the executive branch. Well, all that is a lot of stuff. It's just not true."

[70]That is, the folkways contribute to the survival of the system without change. For a brilliant analysis of the promise and pitfalls of functional analysis see R. K. Merton, *Social Theory and Social Structure* (Glencoe: The Free Press, 1949), chap. 1.

[71]Tom Connally (as told to Alfred Steinberg), *My Name is Tom Connally* (New York, 1954), p. 88.

[72]*Providence Evening Journal*, February 8, 1956.

[73]The number of speeches made by each senator was determined by referring to the Index of the *Congressional Record* for the 83rd and 84th Congresses. The number of speeches given by senators serving during the entire four-year period ranged from 28 to 1,953. All senators who gave more than 500 speeches were ranked as high in floor speaking; those who gave from 250 to 499 speeches were ranked as medium; those who gave less than 250 speeches were ranked as low. (Cutting points of 200 and 400 were used to distinguish between the low, medium and high floor speakers in individual Congresses.)

The index of specialization was computed from data in the *Congressional Quarterly Almanac* by determining the proportion of all public bills and resolutions introduced by each senator during the 83rd and 84th Congresses that were referred to the two committees receiving the largest number of his bills and resolutions. (The "two highest" rule was adopted after experimenting with an index based on the proportion of public bills and resolutions referred to committees on which the senator served. This measure had the unfortunate characteristic of discriminating against members of the Appropriations Committee and was therefore abandoned.) Co-sponsors were ignored, except in the case of bills and resolutions introduced by two senators. The index numbers so obtained ranged from .295 to .95 for the members of the Senate serving during the entire 83rd and 84th Congresses. Senators with scores below .50 were considered to have low indices of specialization; those from .50 to .69, medium; and those above .70, high.

Both measures have distinct limitations. The first entirely ignores the length of Senate speeches, while the second is based on the arguable assumption that the bills and resolutions introduced by a senator adequately reflect the breadth of his legislative interests. Moreover, the jurisdictions of Senate committees are sufficiently broad and overlapping so that two bills on different subjects may be referred to the same committee while two bills with similar subjects may be referred to different committees. By assigning equal weights to all speeches and bills, both indices also disregard the fact that some speeches and some bills are more "important" than others. Despite these crudities, both measures seem to be as adequate as can be constructed from published data without a prohibitively high expenditure of time and effort.

[74]The larger study upon which this article draws includes a full scale analysis of the social backgrounds and career lines of post-World War II senators. For a preliminary report on this analysis and a brief discussion of sources utilized see my "United States Senators and the Class Structure," in H.

Eulau, S. J. Eldersveld and M. Janowitz (eds.), *Political Behavior: A Reader in Theory and Research* (Glencoe: The Free Press, 1956), pp. 184–193.

[75]This conclusion must be treated with more than the usual scholarly caution. Only a longitudinal study or one using far more elaborate cross tabulation than is possible here can adequately isolate the effects of seniority on conformity to the folkways.

[76]Douglass Cater, "Estes Kefauver, Most Willing of the Willing," *The Reporter*, November 3, 1955, p. 16.

[77]The typology of state party systems is from A. Ranney and W. Kendall, "The American Party System," *The American Political Science Review*, vol. 48 (June 1954), pp. 477–485.

[78]William S. White, "Realistic Reformer from Tennessee," *The New York Times Magazine*, March 4, 1956, p. 32. On the same point, *cf.* Jerry Voorhis, *op. cit.*, esp. at p. 62.

[79]An index of Conservatism-Liberalism was constructed in the following manner. The roll-call voting ratings of the *New Republic*, October 15, 1956, were obtained and the total number of "liberal" votes cast by each senator on *domestic policy* issues was divided by the total number of votes cast on the eight domestic issues listed. (Senators who cast less than six votes were omitted.) This operation yields a Conservatism-Liberalism score which can, and did, vary from .00 to 1.00. All senators with scores above .67 were classified as liberals; those with scores ranging from .34 to .66, moderates; and those with scores below .33, conservaties.

An index of this sort generally tends to be multi-dimensional, *cf.* D. McRae, Jr., "Some Underlying Variables in Legislative Roll Call Votes," *Public Opionion Quarterly*, vol. 18 (Summer, 1954), pp. 191–196, although the omission of foreign policy votes may have mitigated this common failing to some degree. The labor involved in constructing a more adequate measure of roll-call voting through Guttman scaling seemed excessive for the purpose of this analysis.

[80]As was the case for the index of specialization, the data for this index were obtained from the *Congressional Quarterly Almanac*. Private bills were ignored, as were co-sponsorships (except in cases in which bills and resolutions were introduced jointly by two Senators). The index numbers ob-tained by dividing the number of bills and resolutions passed by the number introduced ranged from .00 to .49 for the senators who served during the entire period of the 83rd and 84th Congresses. All senators with scores below .15 were considered low in effectiveness; those with scores from .15 to .34, medium; and those with scores of .35 and above were rated as high.

This measure is, of course, based on the assumption that a senator's bill-sponsoring "batting average" is a fair index of his overall "effectiveness" in the Senate. This assumption might be disputed on a number of grounds. First, a senator might be highly "effective" in, say, his committee work but still unsuccessful in shepherding his own bills through the legislative machinery. It is the author's impression that this is a fairly rare occurrence. Second, by weighing all bills and resolutions equally, the measure gives disproportionate importance to minor legislation. It is precisely on minor matters, however, that a sponsor's standing with his colleagues is important in getting legislative results. Third, the measure ignores the fact that many bills and resolutions are not intended to pass by their sponsors. But senators who habitually introduce bills with no intention of their passing are very different kinds of senators than those who introduce bills only when they intend to see them through. The first type is concerned with the *propaganda* consequences of his actions *outside the Senate*, while the latter is concerned with direct *legislative* pay-offs. This narrowly legislative conception of the senator's role is exactly the role definition the folkways demand.

At my suggestion Warren H. Hollinshead, *A Study of Influence Within the United States Senate* (unpublished AB thesis, Amherst College, 1957), checked this index of legislative effectiveness against "influence" rankings obtained through interviews with a panel of Senate legislative assistants. The correlation between the two measures was very high.

[81]"Should the new legislator wish to be heard," George Washington advised his favorite nephew upon his election to the Virginia House of Delegates in 1787, "the way to command attention of the House is to speak seldom, but to important subjects, except such as relate to your constituents and, in the former case, make yourself perfectly master of the subject. Never exceed a

decent warmth, and submit your sentiments with diffidence. A dictatorial style, though it may carry conviction, is always accompanied with disgust." J. A. Carroll and M. W. Ashworth [continuing D. S. Freeman's biography], *George Washington* (New York, 1957), vol. VII, p. 591.

Inside Capitol Hill

[82]Old heads often quiz young ones on the issues or tactics that brought the newcomer campaign victory—but only to learn for themselves what democratic pitfalls elder statesmen should avoid back home where things may be changing.

[83]Exception: Representative Richard Bolling (Missouri) is a gadfly hot for major House reforms; when he came to Rules, however, he was a favored protege of then-Speaker Rayburn. Only after revealing his reformer instincts and a stubborn independence did Bolling fall from favor. He plunged to brimstone depths last year by publicly suggesting that Speaker McCormack should step down for reasons of advancing age and decreasing skills.

CHAPTER SEVEN. THE PRESIDENCY

Presidents of Action and Restraint

[1]This model is drawn from Henry Murray's theory of needs, Henry A. Murray, *Explorations in Personality* (New York: Oxford University Press, 1938), and from the concept of the ego as an integrating mechanism in M. Brewster Smith, Jerome S. Bruner, and Robert W. White, *Opinions and Personality* (New York: John Wiley and Sons, 1956).

[2]Richard E. Neustadt, *Presidential Power* (New York: John Wiley and Sons, 1960).

Three Models Reconsidered

[3]William Howard Taft, *Our Chief Magistrate and His Powers* (New York: Columbia University Press, 1916), p. 78.

[4]*Ibid.*, p. 138.

[5]For further development of the Madisonian and Jeffersonian concepts and practices see Robert A. Dahl, *A Preface to Democratic Theory* (Chicago: The University of Chicago Press, 1956), esp. chap. 1, "Madisonian Democracy"; and James M. Burns, *The Deadlock of Democracy* (Englewood Cliffs, N.J.: Prentice-Hall, Inc., 1963), esp. chaps. 1 and 2.

[6]Arthur S. Link, *Woodrow Wilson and the Progressive Era* (New York: Harper & Row, 1954), p. 225.

[7]Samuel I. Rosenman, *Working with Roosevelt* (New York: Harper & Row, 1952), chap. 24.

Presidential Power

[8]The reader will want to keep in mind the distinction between two senses in which the word *power* is employed. When I have used the word (or its plural) to refer to formal constitutional, statutory, or customary authority, it is either qualified by the adjective "formal" or placed in quotation marks as "power(s)." Where I have used it in the sense of effective influence upon the conduct of others, it appears without quotation marks (and always in the singular). Where clarity and convenience permit, *authority* is substituted for "power" in the first sense and *influence* for power in the second sense.

[9]See, for example, his press conference of July 22, 1959, as reported in the *New York Times* for July 23, 1959.

[10]See Douglass Cater, *The Fourth Branch of Government*, Boston: Houghton-Mifflin, 1959.

[11]With the exception of the Vice-Presidency, of course.

[12]See David B. Truman's illuminating study of party relationships in the 81st Congress, *The Congressional Party*, New York: Wiley, 1959, especially chaps. 4, 6, and 8.

[13]As Secretary of the Interior in 1939, Harold Ickes refused to approve the sale of helium to Germany despite the insistence of the State Department and the urging of President Roosevelt. Without the Secretary's approval, such sales were forbidden by statute. See *The Secret Diaries of Harold L. Ickes*, New York: Simon and Schuster, 1954, vol. 2, esp. pp. 391–393, 396–399. See also Michael J. Reagan, "The Helium Controversy," in the case book on civil-military relations prepared for the Twentieth Century Fund under the editorial direction of Harold Stein.

In this instance the statutory authority ran to the Secretary as a matter of *his* discretion. A President is unlikely to fire Cabinet officers for the conscientious exercise of such authority. If the President did so, their successors might well be embarrassed both publicly and at the Capitol were they to reverse decisions previously taken. As for a President's authority to set aside discretionary determinations of this sort, it rests, if it exists at all, on shaky legal ground not likely to be trod save in the gravest of situations.

[14]Truman's *Memoirs* indicate that having tried and failed to make Stevenson an avowed candidate in the spring of 1952, the President decided to support the candidacy of Vice President Barkley. But Barkley withdrew early in the convention for lack of key northern support. Though Truman is silent on the matter, Barkley's active candidacy nearly was revived during the balloting, but the forces then aligning to revive it were led by opponents of Truman's Fair Deal, principally Southerners. As a practical matter, the President could not have lent his weight to *their* endeavors and could back no one but Stevenson to counter them. The latter's strength could not be shifted, then, to Harriman or Kefauver. Instead the other Northerners had to be withdrawn. Truman helped withdraw them. But he had no other option. See Memoirs by Harry S. Truman, vol. 2, *Years of Trial and Hope*, Garden City; Doubleday, 1956, copr. 1956 Time Inc., pp. 495–496.

[15]The reference is to Stassen's public statement of July 23, 1956, calling for Nixon's replacement on the Republican ticket by Governor Herter of Massachusetts, the later Secretary of State. Stassen's statement was issued after a conference with the President. Eisenhower's public statements on the vice-presidential nomination, both before and after Stassen's call, permit of alternative inferences: either that the President would have preferred another candidate, provided this could be arranged without a showing of White House dictation, or that he wanted Nixon on condition that the latter could show popular appeal. In the event, neither result was achieved. Eisenhower's own remarks lent strength to rapid party moves which smothered Stassen's effort. Nixon's nomination thus was guaranteed too quickly to appear the consequence of popular demand. For the public record on this matter see reported statements by Eisenhower, Nixon, Stassen, Herter, and Leonard Hall (the National Republican Chairman) in the *New York Times* for March 1, 8, 15, 16; April 27; July 15, 16, 25–31; August 3, 4, 17, 23, 1956. See also the account from private sources by Earl Mazo in *Richard Nixon: A Personal and Political Portrait*, New York: Harper, 1959, pp. 158–187.

[16]Stenographic transcript of presidential press conference, October 19, 1950, on file in the Truman Library at Independence, Missouri.

[17]Jonathan Daniels, *Frontier on the Potomac*, New York: Macmillan, 1946, pp. 31–32.

[18]Transcript of presidential press conference, June 18, 1958, in *Public Papers of the Presidents: Dwight D. Eisenhower, 1958*, Washington: The National Archives, 1959, p. 479. In the summer of 1958, a congressional investigation into the affairs of a New England textile manufacturer, Bernard Goldfine, revealed that Sherman Adams had accepted various gifts and favors from him (the most notoriety attached to a vicuna coat). Adams also had made inquiries about the status of a Federal Communications Commission proceeding in which Goldfine was involved. In September 1958, Adams was allowed to resign. The episode was highly publicized and much discussed in that year's congressional campaigns.

[19]As reported in Marriner S. Eccles, *Beckoning Frontiers*, New York: Knopf, 1951, p. 336.

CHAPTER EIGHT. THE BUREAUCRACY

J. Edgar Hoover

[1]Fred J. Cook, *The FBI Nobody Knows*, Macmillan, 423 pp., $5.95.

Bureaucracy in Pressure Politics

[2]38 Stat. L. 212.

[3]41 Stat. L. 68.

[4]James L. McCamy, *Government Publicity* (Chicago: University of Chicago Press, 1939), p. 7; V. O. Key, Jr., *Politics, Parties, and Pressure Groups* (New York: Thomas Y. Crowell Company, 1952), pp. 731–732.

[5]United States Congress, House, Select

Committee on Lobbying Activities, *Legislative Activities of Executive Agencies*, Hearings, 81st Congress, 2nd Session, Part 10 (Washington, 1950).

[6]Richard E. Neustadt, "Presidency and Legislation: The Growth of Central Clearance," *American Political Science Review*, vol. 48 (September 1954), pp. 641ff. For a different point of view, see Arthur A. Maass, "In Accord with the Program of the President?" in Carl J. Friedrich and J. K. Galbraith (Eds.), *Public Policy* (Cambridge, Mass: Graduate School of Public Administration, Harvard University, 1953), pp. 77–93.

[7]Herman Miles Somers, "The President, the Congress, and the Federal Government Service" in *The Federal Government Service* (New York: The American Assembly, Columbia University, 1954), p. 71.

[8]In connection with the above and some of the following points, see J. Leiper Freeman *The Political Process: Executive Bureau-Legislative Committee Relations* (New York: Doubleday and Company, 1955), chaps 3–5.

[9]Based on interviews and observations in the "Bay City" project, conducted at the Harvard Graduate School of Education under a grant from the W. K. Kellogg Foundation. "Bay City" is a pseudonym for a Massachusetts city of nearly 50,000 population where a series of related research inquiries were conducted on local decision-making during the period 1952–55 by a professional staff consisting chiefly of Peter H. Rossi, Alice S. Rossi, James M. Shipton, and the present writer.

[10]New York *Times*, Tuesday, February 18, 1958, p. 13.

[11]Reed L. Frischknecht, "The Democratization of Administration: The Farmer Committee System," *American Political Science Review*, vol. 47 (September 1953), pp. 704ff.

[12]See note 9, *supra*.

[13]*Ibid.*

CHAPTER NINE. THE COURTS

Decision-Making in a Democracy

[1]Frankfurter, The Supreme Court in the Mirror of Justices, 105 U. of Pa. L. Rev. 781, 793 (1957).

[2]Provided that the total membership of the society is an even number, it is technically possible for a dispute to occur that divides the membership into two equal parts, neither of which can be said to be either a majority or minority of the total membership. But even in the instances where the number of members is even (which should occur on the average only half the time), the probability of an exactly even split, in any group of more than a few thousand people, is so small that it may be ignored.

[3]Suppose the number of citizens, or members eligible to participate in collective decisions, is n. Let each member indicate his "most preferred alternative." Then it is obvious that the maximum number of most preferred alternatives is n. It is equally obvious that if the number of most preferred alternatives is more than or equal to $n/2$, then no majority is possible. But for all practical purposes those formal limitations can be ignored, for we are dealing with a large society where the number of alternatives at issue before the Supreme Court is invariably quite small. If the number of alternatives is greater than two, it is theoretically possible for preferences to be distributed so that no outcome is consistent with the majority criterion, even where all members can rank all the alternatives and where there is perfect information as to their preferences; but this difficulty does not bear on the subsequent discussion, and it is disregarded. For an examination of this problem, consult Arrow, Social Choice and Individual Values (1951).

[4]Actually, the matter is somewhat ambiguous. There appear to have been seventy-eight cases in which the Court has held provisions of federal law unconstitutional. Sixty-four different acts in the technical sense have been construed, and eighty-six different provisions in law have been in some respects invalidated. I rely here on the figures and the table given in Library of Congress, Legislative Reference Service, Provisions of Federal Law Held Unconstitutional By the Supreme Court of the United States 95, 141–147 (1936), to which I have added United States v. Lovett, 328 U.S. 303 (1946), and United States ex rel. Toth v. Quarles, 350 U.S. 11 (1955). There are some minor discrepancies in totals (not attributable to the differences in publication dates) between this volume and Acts of Congress Held Unconstitutional in Whole or in Part by the

Supreme Court of the United States, in Library of Congress, Legislative Reference Service, The Constitution of the United States of America, Analysis and Interpretation (Corwin ed., 1953). The difference is a result of classification. The latter document lists seventy-three acts held unconstitutional (to which Toth v. Quarles, supra, should be added) but different sections of the same act are sometimes counted separately.

[5]Dahl, A Preface to Democratic Theory, chap. 2 (1956).

[6]Compare Commager, Majority Rule and Minority Rights (1943).

[7]Frankfurter, op. cit., supra note 1, at 782–784.

[8]Booth v. United States, 291 U.S. 339 (1934), involved a reduction in the pay of retired judges. Lynch v. United States, 292 U.S. 571 (1934), repealed laws granting to veterans rights to yearly renewable term insurance; there were only twenty-nine policies outstanding in 1932. Hopkins Federal Savings & Loan Ass'n v. Cleary, 296 U.S. 315 (1935), granted permission to state building and loan associations to convert to federal ones on a vote of 51 percent or more of votes cast at a legal meeting. Ashton v. Cameron County Water Improvement District, 298 U.S. 513 (1936), permitted municipalities to petition federal courts for bankruptcy proceedings.

[9]Schechter Poultry Corp. v. United States, 295 U.S. 495 (1935).

[10]United States v. Butler, 297 U.S. 1 (1936); Perry v. United States, 294 U.S. 330 (1935); Panama Refining Co. v. Ryan, 293 U.S. 388 (1935); Railroad Retirement Board v. Alton R. Co., 295 U.S. 330 (1935); Louisville Joint Stock Land Bank v. Radford, 295 U.S. 555 (1935); Rickert Rice Mills v. Fontenot, 297 U.S. 110 (1936); Carter v. Carter Coal Co., 298 U.S. 238 (1936).

[11]United States v. Dewitt, 9 Wall. (U.S.) 41 (1870); Gordon v. United States, 2 Wall. (U.S.) 561 (1865); Monongahela Navigation Co. v. United States, 148 U.S. 312 (1893); Wong Wing v. United States, 163 U.S. 228 (1896); Fairbank v. United States, 181 U.S. 283 (1901); Rassmussen v. United States, 197 U.S. 516 (1905); Muskrat v. United States, 219 U.S. 346 (1911); Choate v. Trapp, 224 U.S. 665 (1912); Evans v. Gore, 253 U.S. 245 (1920); Untermyer v. Anderson, 276 U.S. 440 (1928); United States v.

Lovett, 328 U.S. 303 (1946). Note that although the specific legislative provisions held unconstitutional may have been minor, the basic legislation may have been of major policy importance.

[12]Ex parte Garland, 4 Wall. (U.S.) 333 (1867); United States v. Klein, 13 Wall. (U.S.) 128 (1872); Pollock v. Farmers' Loan & Trust Co., 157 U.S. 429 (1895), rehearing granted 158 U.S. 601 (1895); Employers' Liability Cases, 207 U.S. 463 (1908); Keller v. United States, 213 U.S. 138 (1909); Hammer v. Dagenhart, 247 U.S. 251 (1918); Eisner v. Macomber, 252 U.S. 189 (1920); Knickerbocker Ice Co. v. Stewart, 253 U.S. 149 (1920); United States v. Cohen Grocery Co., 255 U.S. 81 (1921); Weeds, Inc. v. United States, 255 U.S. 109 (1921); Bailey v. Drexel Furniture Co., 259 U.S. 20 (1922); Hill v. Wallace, 259 U.S. 44 (1922); Washington v. Dawson & Co., 264 U.S. 219 (1924); Trusler v. Crooks, 269 U.S. 475 (1926).

[13]a Pollock v. Farmers' Loan & Trust Co., 157 U.S. 429 (1895); Employers' Liability Cases, 207 U.S. 463 (1908); Keller v. United States, 213 U.S. 138 (1909); Hammer v. Dagenhart, 247 U.S. 251 (1918); Bailey v. Drexel Furniture Co., 259 U.S. 20 (1922); Trusler v. Crooks, 269 U.S. 475 (1926); Hill v. Wallace, 259 U.S. 44 (1922); Knickerbocker Ice Co. v. Stewart, 253 U.S. 149 (1920); Washington v. Dawson & Co., 264 U.S. 219 (1924).

b Ex parte Garland, 4 Wall. (U.S.) 333 (1867); United States v. Klein, 13 Wall. (U.S.) 128 (1872).

c United States v. Cohen Grocery Co., 255 U.S. 81 (1921); Weeds, Inc. v. United States, 255 U.S. 109 (1921) Eisner v. Macomber, 252 U.S. 189 (1920).

d Gordon v. United States, 2 Wall. (U.S.) 561 (1865); Evans v. Gore, 253 U.S. 245 (1920).

e United States v. Dewitt, 9 Wall. (U.S.) 41 (1870); Monongahela Navigation Co. v. United States, 148 U.S. 312 (1893); Wong Wing v. United States, 163 U.S. 228 (1896); Fairbank v. United States, 181 U.S. 283 (1901); Rassmussen v. United States, 197 U.S. 516 (1905); Muskrat v. United States, 219 U.S. 346 (1911); Choate v. Trapp, 224 U.S. 665 (1912); United States v. Lovett, 328 U.S. 303 (1946).

f Untermyer v. Anderson, 276 U.S. 440 (1928).

14Ex parte Garland, 4 Wall. (U.S.) 333 (1867); United States v. Klein, 13 Wall. (U.S.) 128 (1872).

15United States v. Cohen Grocery Co., 255 U.S. 81 (1921); Weeds, Inc. v. United States, 255 U.S. 109 (1921).

16Eisner v. Macomber, 252 U.S. 189 (1920).

17Employers' Liability Cases, 207 U.S. 463 (1908); Keller v. United States, 213 U.S. 138 (1909); Trusler v. Crooks, 269 U.S. 475 (1926); Hill v. Wallace, 259 U.S. 44 (1922).

18Knickerbocker Ice Co. v. Stewart, 253 U.S. 149 (1920).

19Washington v. Dawson & Co., 264 U.S. 219 (1924).

20Crowell v. Benson, 285 U.S. 22 (1932).

21Pollock v. Farmers' Loan & Trust Co., 157 U.S. 429 (1895).

22Nicol v. Ames, 173 U.S. 509 (1899); Knowlton v. Moore, 178 U.S. 41 (1900); Patton v. Brady, 184 U.S. 608 (1902); Flint v. Stone Tracy Co., 220 U.S. 107 (1911).

23Hammer v. Dagenhart, 247 U.S. 251 (1918).

24Bailey v. Drexel Furniture Co., 259 U.S. 20 (1922).

25United States v. Darby, 312 U.S. 100 (1941).

26The candidates for this category would appear to be Boyd v. United States, 116 U.S. 616 (1886); Rassmussen v. United States, 197 U.S. 516 (1905); Wong Wing v. United States, 163 U.S. 228 (1896); United States v. Moreland, 258 U.S. 433 (1922); Kirby v. United States, 174 U.S. 47 (1899); United States v. Cohen Grocery Co., 255 U.S. 81 (1921); Weeds, Inc. v. United States, 255 U.S. 109 (1921); Justices of the Supreme Court v. United States ex rel. Murray, 9 Wall. (U.S.) 274 (1870); United States ex rel. Toth v. Quarles, 350 U.S. 11 (1955).

27Dred Scott v. Sandford, 19 How. (U.S.) 393 (1857).

28United States v. Reese, 92 U.S. 214 (1876); United States v. Harris, 106 U.S. 629 (1883); United States v. Stanley (Civil Rights Cases), 109 U.S. 3 (1883); Baldwin v. Franks, 120 U.S. 678 (1887); James v. Bowman, 190 U.S. 127 (1903); Hodges v. United States, 203 U.S. 1 (1906); Butts v. Merchants & Miners Transportation Co., 230 U.S. 126 (1913).

29Monongahela Navigation Co. v. United States, 148 U.S. 312 (1893); Adair v. United States, 208 U.S. 161 (1908); Adkins v.

Children's Hospital, 261 U.S. 525 (1923); Nichols v. Coolidge, 274 U.S. 531 (1927); Untermyer v. Anderson, 276 U.S. 440 (1928); Heiner v. Donnan, 285 U.S. 312 (1932); Louisville Joint Stock Land Bank v. Radford, 295 U.S. 555 (1935).

30"Constitutional law and cases with constitutional undertones are of course still very important, with almost one-fourth of the cases in which written opinions were filed [in the two most recent terms] involving such questions. Review of administrative action . . . constitutes the largest category of the Court's work, comprising one-third of the total cases decided on the merits. The remaining . . . categories of litigation . . . all involve largely public law questions." Frankfurter, op. cit. note 1, at 793.

31Rice v. Elmore, 165 F.2d 387 (C.A. 4th, 1947), cert. denied 333 U.S. 875 (1948); United States v. Classic, 313 U.S. 299 (1941); Smith v. Allwright, 321 U.S. 649 (1944); Grovey v. Townsend, 295 U.S. 45 (1935); Brown v. Board of Education, 347 U.S. 483 (1954); Bolling v. Sharpe, 347 U.S. 497 (1954).

United States v. O'Brien

32At the time of the burning, the agents knew only that O'Brien and his three companions had burned small white cards. They later discovered that the card O'Brien burned was his registration certificate, and the disputed assumption is that the same is true of his companions.

33He was sentenced under the Youth Corrections Act, 18 U.S.C. §5010 (b), to the custody of the Attorney General for a maximum period of six years for supervision and treatment.

34The issue of the 1965 Amendment was raised by counsel representing O'Brien in a pretrial motion to dismiss the indictment. At trial and upon sentencing, O'Brien chose to represent himself. He was represented by counsel on his appeal to the Court of Appeals.

Prayer and Politics

35Brown v. Board of Educ., 347 U.S. 483 (1954).

[36]Some exceptions include Patric, "The Impact of a Court Decision: Aftermath of the McCollum Case," 6 J. Pub. L. 455 (1957); Patric & Sorauf, "Zorach v. Clauson: The Impact of a Supreme Court Decision," 53 *Am. Pol. Sci. Rev.* 777 (1959). A notable study of the impact of Supreme Court decisions on Congress is Murphy, *Congress and the Court* (1962). There are numerous studies examining various aspects of efforts to implement the desegregation rulings. See, for example, Peltason, *Fifty-Eight Lonely Men* (1961).

[37]Youngstown Sheet & Tube Co. v. Sawyer, 343 U.S. 579 (1952).

[38]370 U.S. 421 (1962).

[39]374 U.S. 203 (1963).

[40]*Ibid.*

[41]108 Cong. Rec. 11675 (1962).

[42]*Id.* at 11734.

[43]*Id.* at 11775, 11844.

[44]*Id.* at 11719.

[45]*Id.* at 11708.

[46]*Id.* at 11718.

[47]Dr. Leo Pfeffer, *Information Bulletin No. 6*, Commission on Law and Social Action of the American Jewish Congress, p. 2, August 15, 1962 [hereinafter cited as *CLSA Bull.* 1].

[48]108 *Cong. Rec.* 11844 (1962).

[49]Quoted by Kurland, "The Regents' Prayer Case: Full of Sound and Fury, Signifying . . ." *Supreme Court Rev.* 3 (Kurland ed. 1962).

[50]For Sen. Javits' comments, and similar remarks by Sen. Wiley and Congressmen Van Zant and James W. Davis, see *Congressional Record* of June 29, 1962, *passim*.

[51]As of June 27, 1962. *Congressional Record Digest*, Anti-Defamation League of B'nai Brith.

[52]108 *Cong. Rec.* 14360 (1962).

[53]*Id.* at 21102.

[54]Quoted in *Hearings on Prayer in Public Schools and Other Matters Before the Senate Committee on the Judiciary*, 87th Cong., 2nd Sess. 71 (1962) [hereinafter cited as *1962 Senate Hearings*].

[55]"Southern Democrats" includes representatives of the eleven states of the old Confederate States of America. This is the usage of V. O. Key in *Southern Politics* (1949).

[56]370 U.S. at 437.

[57]*1962 Senate Hearings* 56. (Emphasis added.)

[58]*Id.* at 51. Bishop Pike misstated the text of the Tenth Amendment in his comment that the amendment "makes clear that those things not *specifically* given to the federal government by authority, are reserved to the states and the people." (Emphasis added.)

[59]*CLSA Bull.* 3.

[60]*Ibid.*

[61]*1962 Senate Hearings* 210.

[62]*CLSA Bull.* 3.

[63]*Supreme Court Rev.*, *op. cit. supra* note 15, at 2 *n.*7.

[64]*Ibid.*

[65]Newland, *Press Coverage of the U.S. Supreme Court*, 17 *Western Political Q.* 15, 30, (1964).

[66]*CLSA Bull.* 1. We rely heavily on Dr. Pfeffer's analysis at this point.

[67]*Ibid.*

[68]*1962 Senate Hearings* 149. The statement refers to the NAACP Convention's action.

[69]Kurland *op. cit. supra* note 49, at 2 n.5.

[70]*1962 Senate Hearings* 140.

[71]*Supreme Court Rev.*, *op. cit. supra* note 49, at 2 n.5.

[72]*Ibid.* See also *CLSA Bull.* 4.

[73]*Supreme Court Rev.*, *op. cit. supra* note 49, at 2 n.5.

[74]*1962 Senate Hearings* 55.

[75]*CLSA Bull.* 4.

[76]*Ibid.*

[77]*Ibid.*

[78]*School Dist. v. Schempp*, 374 U.S. 203 (1963).

[79]Arnold Forster (Director of civil liberties division, ADL), *Memorandum to All ADL Regional Offices*, July 11, 1963, p. 1 [hereinafter cited as Forster].

[80]*Time*, June 28, 1963, p. 13.

[81]Chicago *American*, June 30, 1963.

[82]Forster, *supra* note 79, at 1. The survey included 169 papers in 115 cities.

[83]*Id.* at 2.

[84]*Id.* at 4.

[85]*Id.* at 3. A survey of Roman Catholic diocesan papers by the weekly *Ave Maria* revealed that 35 had gone on record opposing any congressional action to overturn the court decision, while only eight favored it. After *Engel*, a large majority of the same papers had attacked the Court's decision. *Time*, June 19, 1964, p. 62.

[86]Forster, *supra* note 79, at 3.

[87]*Id.* at 5.

[88]N. Y. *Times*, June 18, 1963, p. 27, col. 5, quoting a study by R. H. Diernfield, for the Public Affairs Press.

[89]*Ibid.* The states were Alabama, Arkansas, Delaware, Florida, Georgia, Idaho, Kentucky, Maine, Massachusetts, New Jersey, Pennsylvania, Tennessee, and the District of Columbia.

[90]*Ibid.* The states were Colorado, Iowa, Indiana, Kansas, Michigan, Minnesota, Mississippi, Nebraska, North Dakota, Ohio, Oklahoma, and Texas.

[91]Religious News Service (Domestic), Aug. 6, 1963 (hereinafter cited as RNS).

[92]*Ibid.*

[93]N. Y. *Times*, Aug. 6, 1963, p. 17, col. 3.

[94]American Jewish Committee, Jewish Information Service, *Bible Reading After the Schempp-Murray Decision*, December, 1963, at 43 (prepared by Mrs. S. Dawidowicz) [hereinafter cited as Dawidowicz].

[95]New Orleans *Times Picayune*, June 20, 1963, p. 6.

[96]Jackson *Clarion Ledger*, June 18, 1963, p. 1.

[97]RNS, June 18, 1963.

[98]Louisville *Courier Journal*, June 27, 1963. (The following September, the Kentucky Attorney General reversed this decision. RNS, Sept. 11, 1963.)

[99]*Ibid.*

[100]Providence *Evening Bulletin*, Oct. 8, 1963.

[101]Wilmington *Morning News*, Aug. 16, 1963, p. 24.

[102]For further details, see the N. Y. *Herald Tribune*, Sept. 5, 1963, p. 3, col. 2.

[103]RNS, Sept. 16, 1963.

[104]Dawidowicz, *supra* note 61, at 43–44.

[105]*Id.* at 43.

[106]RNS, Sept. 9, 1963.

[107]ADL, *Report on Reactions in Public School Systems Throughout the Country to the Supreme Court's Decisions on Bible Reading and Prayer*, Fall, 1963, p. 9 (unpublished).

[108]Manchester *Union Leader*, October 30, 1963, editorial.

[109]Des Moines *Sunday Register*, Aug. 25, 1963.

[110]Other "local option" states were Florida, Georgia, and Virginia.

[111]Dawidowicz, *supra* n. 94, at 44.

[112]Newark *Star Ledger*, Sept. 5, 1963, p. 1.

[113]5 N.J. 435 (1950). The major battle took place in Hawthorne, New Jersey, site of *Doremus v. Board of Education*, 342 U.S. 429 (1952), in which the state courts had sustained Bible reading in the public schools. The issue was avoided by the Supreme Court on jurisdictional grounds. See the Newark *Evening News*, Sept. 12, 1963, for details surrounding the issuing of the injunction.

[114]Directive from Attorney General's office, Aug. 20, 1963, at 21.

[115]See the Boston *Herald*, Oct. 14, 1963, p. 1.

[116]RNS, Sept. 26, 1963.

[117]Diernfield study, *supra* note 88.

[118]ADL report, *supra* note 107.

[119]RNS, Sept. 27, 1963.

[120]Des Moines *Sunday Register*, Aug. 25, 1963. (Emphasis added.)

[121]Quoted in a memo in the ADL files from its Atlanta office, dated Oct. 1963.

[122]John C. Hill, *Religion and the Public Schools: Policy and Practice in Indiana*, Research Bulletin No. 14, School of Education, Indiana University, April, 1964. Summary and conclusions. (No pagination.)

[123]Indianapolis *Star*, Nov. 25, 1963.

[124]Delaware provides an example of the difficulties which may be involved in bringing such suits. Mrs. Mary DeYoung of Middletown, Delaware, brought suit in August, 1963, to enjoin the practice of prayer in the public schools. Mrs. DeYoung was both a parent and a teacher in the Middletown Public School. The court found in favor of the plantiffs. However, before the decision was handed down, Mrs. DeYoung was informed that her contract as a teacher in the Middletown school would not be renewed. She did not have tenure, and was thus not entitled to receive specific reasons for her "discharge." Mrs DeYoung, it should be noted, had an excellent teaching record, and had received an "A" rating for her work during the school year 1962/63. The Board of Education claimed that her participation in the Bible case had caused administrative problems, especially because parents requested that their children be taken out of her class, a contention disputed by her attorney. If the Court's decisions are to be implemented in the absence of vigorous enforcement by state officials, local citizens must be prepared to bring suit, and to subject themselves to the kinds of pressures illustrated by Mrs. DeYoung's experience. We are grateful to Irvin Morris,

Esq., for details of the DeYoung case. Letter to the authors, July 17, 1964.

[125]On May 20, 1964, Mr. Hugh L. Elsbree, Director of the Legislative Reference Service of the Library of Congress, sent a telegram to the Attorneys General of the fifty states, asking them to report any actions taken in response to the 1963 decisions, and to indicate the policies and practices then in existence. While many of the replies were not fully responsive, it is clear that at least the following states were *admittedly* not in compliance with the Court's pronouncements: Alabama, Arkansas, Florida, Idaho, Mississippi, North Carolina, North Dakota, and Oklahoma. The tone of numerous other state responses indicated a "hands off" policy by state officials.

We noted above the action taken by New Jersey state officials to insure compliance with the Court's action. Yet despite these sincere and vigorous efforts, the authors are aware of at least one case in which the Lord's Prayer was used in a New Jersey public school as recently as the spring of 1964, and suspect that this was not an isolated incident.

[126]Forster, *supra* note 79, at 6.

[127]*Ibid.*

[128]*Ibid.*

[129]*Hearings on School Prayers Before the House Committee on the Judiciary*, 88th Cong., 2nd Sess. 2008 (1964) [hereinafter cited as *1964 House Hearings*].

[130]Note that the battle over Becker's discharge petition probably hurt the attempt to discharge the Civil Rights Bill from the House Rules Committee at about the same time. Many Congressmen who were afraid to "fight God" but who opposed Becker refused to sign his petition on the grounds that as a matter of principle they never signed discharge petitions. This prevented some from signing the civil rights discharge petition.

[131]RNS, Aug. 26, 1963. The six were Becker, W. Baring (D., Nev.), W. Cramer (R., Fla.), D. Fuqua (D., Fla.), H. R. Kornegay (D., N.C.), and D. Latta (R., Ohio).

[132]N. Y. *Times*, April 23, 1964, p. 14, col. 5.

[133]Personal letter to Mr. Dore Schary, in the ADL files.

[134]N. Y. *Times*, Feb. 19, 1964, p. 21, col. 3.

[135]Letter to Mr. Merrill Keller, St. Paul, Minn., March 13, 1964, in ADL files.

[136]It is impossible to know exactly how many signatures appear on a discharge petition at a given moment, as this figure is never officially released, and members can withdraw their names at any time. The *Wall Street Journal* reported that 166 signatures were said to have been obtained. This appears to square with other published reports, and with Becker's claims. *Wall Street Journal*, April 22, 1964, p. 1, col. 4.

[137]*Id.* at 1.

[138]*Ibid.*

[139]Letter on file at the ADL.

[140]These form letters are on file at the ADL. (Emphasis added.)

[141]Letter to Mr. Dore Schary on file at the ADL.

[142]N. Y. *Times*, Feb. 19, 1964, p. 21, col. 5.

[143]N. Y. *Times*, March 20, 1964, p. 17, col. 1.

[144]*Cong. Rec.* 5696 (1964).

[145]N. Y. *World Telegram and Sun*, March 24, 1964.

[146]It is likely that one of the reasons that Rev. Kelley was chosen to represent the *ad hoc* group—in addition to his experience in such matters—was the desire of the Jewish groups involved to minimize their role in the fight against the Becker Amendment. They were very sensitive to the charge that the Court's decision had been brought about by a minority of "Jews, atheists, and Communists."

[147]Interview with Rev. Dean Kelley, July 20, 1964.

[148]See his letter to Chairman Celler, published in the Committee Report, *1964 House Hearings*, 1058.

[149]See, e.g., *1964 House Hearings*, 690–691.

[150]Among the many religious leaders who opposed the Becker Amendment at the hearings were: Father George Bacopoulos, Chancellor, Greek Orthodox Archdiocese North and South America; Rabbi Irwin Blank, Synagogue Council of America; Dr. E. Carlson, Baptist Joint Committee on Public Affairs; Rt. Rev. Wm. Creighton, Protestant Episcopal Bishop of Washington; Rabbi M. Eisendrath, Union of American Hebrew Congregation; Mr. Moses Feuerstein, Union of Orthodox Jewish Congregations; and Rabbi Harry Halpern, United Synagogues of America.

[151]Other law school professors who testified against the Becker Amendment were: C. J. Antieau (Georgetown); Dean J. B.

Fordham (U. of Penn.); W. G. Katz (Wisconsin); W. G. Keneally, S.J. (Boston College); and J. C. Kirby (Vanderbilt).

[152]*1964 House Hearings* 2483–2485.

[153]Among the organizations which supported Becker were: Committee for the Preservation of Prayer and Bible Reading in Public Schools; Constitutional Prayer Foundation; Massachusetts Citizens for Public Prayer; Project Prayer; Foundation for Religious Action in the Social Order (FRASCO); International Council of Christian Churches; International Christian Youth in the U.S.A.; and the American Legion.

In addition, the legislatures of the following states petitioned Congress to approve a Becker-type amendment: Kentucky, Massachusetts, Michigan, New Jersey, Pennsylvania (senate), and South Carolina.

It is interesting to speculate about the extent and significance of right-wing support for the Becker Amendment. Rowland Evans and Robert Novak, writing in the New York *Herald Tribune* of May 12, 1964, p. 12, col. 1, stated that "although members of the House Judiciary Committee do not know it, the 'Citizens Congressional Committee' now flooding Capitol Hill with mail backing the prayer amendment is operated, financed, and directed by Gerald L. K. Smith, notorious promoter of extreme Right Wing causes. Smith's backstage maneuvering is the best evidence to date that neo-Fascist hate groups have infiltrated the high pressure campaign to change the Bill of Rights. . . ." They pointed to the May, 1964, issue of Smith's *The Cross and the Flag*, which said: "The bill has been held up by the Jew, Emmanuel Celler, who is chairman of the Judiciary Committee."

Of all the groups supporting Becker, perhaps the most active was Dr. Carl McIntire's International Christian Youth, and its "Project America." They presented petitions alleged to contain 1,000,000 signatures to the committee. McIntire threw the full weight of his many organizations—and his radio broadcasts on over 500 stations—behind Becker. In its November 21, 1963 article headed "Fighting the Bible," McIntire's *Christian Beacon* spoke of Congressman Cellar—"A Jew" who was blocking hearings on this amendment. *Id.* at 8. And, it went on: "It is going to be up to the great rank and file of the Christian people of the United States to stand against this coalition of modernists, Jews, infidels, Unitarians and atheists in their determination to keep the Bible out of the schools."

It is often unfair to blame the leaders of a movement for the kind of extremist support they may inadvertently attract. But in the case at hand this does not appear to have been unwelcomed support. McIntire's *Christian Beacon* of March 26, 1964, quoted Becker in a front-page story as encouraged by International Christian Youth's "Project America" petition drive. And the Rev. Billy James Hargis' magazine *Christian Crusade*, of August, 1964, printed abstracts of a letter it received from Congressman Becker thanking it "sincerely for the work the *Christian Crusade* has been doing in behalf of the 'Prayer Amendment' to the Constitution. Your great ability to reach the people throughout the United States has helped immeasurably in rallying their support for this truly vital Cause. . . ." *Id.* at 13. Note that the capital "C" appeared in the original! It is interesting to note further that several pro-Becker witnesses who appeared before the Celler Committee—including representatives of the American Legion's Americanism Committee and Victor Jory's "Project Prayer"—felt compelled to disclaim any connection with the extreme Right's attacks on the Court.

[154]*1964 House Hearings*, 1125.

[155]See, e.g., N. Y. *Herald Tribune*, May 10, 1964, p. 22, col. 1, editorial entitled "It's not a vote against God."

[156]*Wall Street Journal*, June 16, 1964, p. 3, col. 2.

[157]*Ibid.*

[158]N. Y. *Times*, July 5, 1964, p. 32, col. 3.

[159]N. Y. *Times*, July 13, 1964, p. 16, col. 1.

70 71 72 73   12 11 10 9 8 7 6 5 4 3 2 1